Praise for David E. Hoffman's

THE DEAD HAND

"A stunning feat of research and narrative. Terrifying." —John le Carré

"*The Dead Hand* is a brilliant work of history, a richly detailed, gripping tale that takes us inside the Cold War arms race as no other book has. Drawing upon extensive interviews and secret documents, David Hoffman reveals never-before-reported aspects of the Soviet biological and nuclear programs. It's a story so riveting and scary that you feel like you are reading a fictional thriller."

—Rajiv Chandrasekaran, author of
Imperial Life in the Emerald City: Inside Iraq's Green Zone

"*The Dead Hand* is deadly serious, but this story can verge on pitch-black comedy—*Dr. Strangelove* as updated by the Coen Brothers."

—*The New York Times*

"In *The Dead Hand*, David Hoffman has uncovered some of the Cold War's most persistent and consequential secrets—plans and systems designed to wage war with weapons of mass destruction, and even to place the prospective end of civilization on a kind of automatic pilot. The book's revelations are shocking; its narrative is intelligent and gripping. This is a tour de force of investigative history."

—Steve Coll, author of *Ghost Wars* and *The Bin Ladens*

"[A] taut, crisply written book. . . . *The Dead Hand* puts human faces on the bureaucracy of mutual assured destruction, even as it underscores the institutional inertia that drove this monster forward. . . . A fine book indeed."

—T. J. Stiles, *Minneapolis Star Tribune*

"An extraordinary and compelling story, beautifully researched, elegantly told, and full of revelations about the superpower arms race in the dying days of the Cold War. *The Dead Hand* is riveting."

—Rick Atkinson, Pulitzer Prize–winning
author of *An Army At Dawn*

"No one is better qualified than David Hoffman to tell the definitive story of the ruinous Cold War arms race. He has interviewed the principal protagonists, unearthed previously undiscovered archives, and tramped across the military-industrial wasteland of the former Soviet Union. He brings his characters to life in a thrilling narrative that contains many lessons for modern-day policy makers struggling to stop the proliferation of weapons of mass destruction. An extraordinary achievement."

—Michael Dobbs, author of *One Minute to Midnight: Kennedy, Khrushchev, and Castro on the Brink of Nuclear War*

DAVID E. HOFFMAN

THE
DEAD
HAND

David E. Hoffman served for 27 years as a reporter and editor at the *Washington Post*. He covered the White House during the presidencies of Ronald Reagan and George H.W. Bush, and was subsequently diplomatic correspondent and Jerusalem correspondent. From 1995 to 2001, he was Moscow bureau chief, and later foreign editor and assistant managing editor for foreign news.

www.thedeadhandbook.com

Also by David E. Hoffman

The Oligarchs: Wealth and Power
in the New Russia

THE
DEAD HAND

REAGAN, GORBACHEV
AND THE UNTOLD STORY OF
THE COLD WAR ARMS RACE

DAVID E. HOFFMAN

ICON BOOKS

To My Parents

Howard and Beverly Hoffman

Previously published in the USA in 2009 by Doubleday,
a division of Random House, Inc., New York,
and in Canada by Random House of Canada Limited, Toronto

This edition published in the UK in 2011 by
Icon Books Ltd, Omnibus Business Centre,
39–41 North Road, London N7 9DP
email: info@iconbooks.co.uk
www.iconbooks.co.uk

Sold in the UK, Europe, South Africa and Asia
by Faber & Faber Ltd, Bloomsbury House,
74–77 Great Russell Street,
London WC1B 3DA or their agents

Distributed in the UK, Europe, South Africa and Asia
by TBS Ltd, TBS Distribution Centre, Colchester Road,
Frating Green, Colchester CO7 7DW

This edition published in Australia in 2011
by Allen & Unwin Pty Ltd,
PO Box 8500, 83 Alexander Street,
Crows Nest, NSW 2065

ISBN: 978-184831-230-2 (hardback)
ISBN: 978-184831-253-1 (paperback)

Book design by Michael Collica
Map designed by Gene Thorp

Printed and bound in the UK
by CPI Mackays, Chatham, Kent ME5 8TD

CONTENTS

"Science has brought us to a point at which we might look forward with confidence to the conquest of disease and even to a true understanding of the life that animates us. And now we have cracked the atom and released such energies as hitherto only the sun and the stars could generate. But we have used the atom's energies to kill, and now we are fashioning weapons out of our knowledge of disease."

—Theodor Rosebury, *Peace or Pestilence: Biological Warfare and How to Avoid It*, 1949

Key Sites in *The Dead Hand*

ATLANTIC
OCEAN

BRITAIN

*North
Sea*

NETH.

WEST
GERMANY

EAST
GERMANY

DEN.

NORWAY

SWEDEN

FINLAND

Helsinki

Baltic Sea

CZECH.

POLAND

ROM.

Chernobyl

Kiev

UKRAINE

*Dnieper
R.*

*Black
Sea*

Crimea
Yalta

Foros
*Gorbachev held here
during 1991 coup*

Privolnoye

Stavropol

TURKEY

SYRIA

IRAQ

*Caspian
Sea*

SAUDI
ARABIA

IRAN

AFGHANISTAN

PAKISTAN

*Mathias
Rust flight,
1987*

*Lake
Ladoga*

*Lake
Onega*

Leningrad

Obolensk

Moscow

Serpukhov-15

Arzamas-16

Kirov

Volga R.

Perm

Grot

• Nizhny Tagil

Sverdlovsk
Scene of 1979 anthrax outbreak

Chelyabinsk-70

Chelyabinsk

Kapustin Yar

Volga R.

Ural R.

Perimeter test launch, 1984

KAZAKHSTAN

Stepnogorsk

Pavlodar

Semipalatinsk

Ust-Kamenogorsk

*Aral
Sea*

Tyuratam

**Vozrozhdeniye
Island**

Syr Darya

Sary Shagan

*Lake
Balkhash*

Alma-Alta

*Barents
Sea*

A R C T

*Nuclear reactor
waste dumping
(approximate)*

*Kara
Sea*

U R A L M T N S.

Ob R.

U N I O N   O F   S O V I

Novosibirsk

Irtysh R.

THE DEAD HAND

PROLOGUE

I. Epidemic of Mystery

"Are any of your patients dying?" asked Yakov Klipnitzer when he called Margarita Ilyenko on Wednesday, April 4, 1979. She was chief physician at No. 24, a medium-sized, one-hundred-bed hospital in Sverdlovsk, a Soviet industrial metropolis in the Ural Mountains. Her hospital often referred patients to a larger facility, No. 20, where Klipnitzer was chief doctor. Klipnitzer saw two unusual deaths from what looked like severe pneumonia. The patients, he told Ilyenko, were "two of yours." No, Ilyenko told him, she did not know of any deaths. The next day he called again. Klipnitzer was more persistent. "You still don't have any patients dying?" he asked. Klipnitzer had new deaths with pneumonia-like symptoms. "Who is dying from pneumonia today?" Ilyenko replied, incredulous. "It is very rare."

Soon, patients began to die at Ilyenko's hospital, too. They were brought in ambulances and cars, suffering from high fevers, headaches, coughs, vomiting, chills and chest pains. They were stumbling in the hallways and lying on gurneys. The head of admissions at Hospital No. 20, Roza Gaziyeva, was on duty overnight between April 5 and 6. "Some of them who felt better after first aid tried to go home. They were later found on the streets—the people had lost consciousness," she recalled. She tried to give mouth-to-mouth resuscitation to one ill patient, who died. "During the night, we had four people die. I could hardly wait until morning. I was frightened."

On the morning of April 6, Ilyenko raced to the hospital, threw her bag into her office, put on her white gown and headed for the ward. One patient looked up at her, eyes open, and then died. "There are dead bodies, people still alive, lying together. I thought, this is a nightmare. Something is very, very wrong."

Death came quickly to victims. Ilyenko reported to the district public health board that she had an emergency. Instructions came back to her that another hospital, No. 40, was being set up to receive all the patients in an infectious disease ward. The word spread—*infection!*—and with it, fear. Some staff refused to report for work, and others already at work refused to go home so as not to expose their families. Then, disinfection workers arrived at hospital No. 20, wearing hazardous materials suits. They spread chlorine everywhere, which was a standard disinfectant, but the scene was terrifying, Ilyenko recalled. "There was panic when people saw them."[1]

Sverdlovsk, population 1.2 million, was the tenth-largest city in the Soviet Union and the heartland of its military-industrial complex. Guns, steel, industry and some of the best mechanical engineering schools in the Soviet Union were Sverdlovsk's legacy from Stalin's rush to modernize during World War II and after. Since 1976, the region had been run by a young, ambitious party secretary, Boris Yeltsin.

Hospitals No. 20 and 24 were in the southern end of the city, which slopes downward from the center. Streets lined with small wooden cottages and high fences were broken up by stark five-story apartment buildings, shops and schools. The Chkalovsky district, where Ilyenko's hospital was located, included a ceramics factory where hundreds of men worked in shifts in a cavernous building with large, high windows.

Less than a mile away, to the north-northwest, was Compound 32, an army base for two tank divisions, largely residences, and, adjacent to it, a closed military microbiology facility. Compound 19, which comprised a laboratory, development and testing center for deadly pathogens, including anthrax, was run by the 15th Main Directorate of the Ministry of Defense. On Monday April 2, 1979, from morning until early evening, the wind was blowing down from Compound 19 toward the ceramics factory.[2]

Inside Compound 19, three shifts operated around the clock, experimenting with anthrax and making it in batches. Anthrax bacteria were grown in fermentation vessels, separated from the liquid growth medium and dried before they were ground up into a fine powder for use in aerosol form. Workers at the compound were regularly given vaccinations. The work was high risk.

Anthrax is an often-fatal infection that occurs when spores of the bacteria *Bacillus anthracis* enter the body, either through the skin, ingestion or inhalation. The bacteria germinate and release toxins that can quickly bring on death if untreated. In Russia, the disease was known as *Sibirskaya yazva*, or Siberian ulcer, because of the black sores that form when it is contracted through cuts in the skin. In nature, the disease most commonly spreads through contact with infected animals, usually grazing animals such as cows, goats and sheep, which ingest the spores from the soil. The inhalation variety is dangerous to humans. Breathing the spores into the lungs can kill those infected if not treated. A single gram of anthrax contains around a trillion spores. Odorless and colorless, the spores are extremely stable, and can remain dormant for as long as fifty years or more. For these reasons, anthrax was well suited for a biological weapon. According to one estimate, 112 pounds of anthrax spores released along a 1.2-mile line upwind of a city of 500,000 residents would result in 125,000 infections—and kill 95,000 people.[3]

What exactly happened at Compound 19 is still unknown. By one account, a filter was removed and not properly replaced, and anthrax spores were released into the air.[4]

To the south, sheep and cattle in villages began to die. Anthrax had been present in rural areas in the past, although it was not common. At the same time, people started getting sick. The first records of those admitted to hospitals came on Wednesday, April 4, when Ilyenko got Klipnitzer's phone call. "What was strange for us, it was mainly men dying, not many women, and not a single child," she said.[5] Ilyenko began keeping records of names, ages, addresses and possible reasons for the deaths, but she didn't know what was happening, or why.

On April 10, as the crisis deepened, Faina Abramova, a retired pathologist who had been a lecturer at the Sverdlovsk Medical Institute, was summoned to Hospital No. 40 and asked to autopsy a thirty-seven-year-old man who died over the weekend. He had been at Compound 32, the army base with the tank divisions, for reserve duty, gone home to a nearby village and, for no apparent reason, became suddenly ill. Abramova, a spirited professional, was puzzled by the case. The man did not show classic signs of influenza and pneumonia. But the autopsy showed infection of the lymph nodes and the lungs. Abramova had also noticed the man suffered from cerebral bleeding, a distinctive red ring around the brain known as "cardinal's cap."[6]

"We started thinking what other diseases may cause this pathology," she recalled. "We looked up the books, and we went through them all together, and it looked like anthrax."

That evening, Abramova attended a reception, which was also attended by Lev Grinberg, her protégé, a young pathologist with thick glasses, black hair and a beard. As they danced at the reception, Abramova whispered to him that she had autopsied the man earlier that day, and diagnosed his death as anthrax. Grinberg was stunned. "I asked, where in our godforsaken Sverdlovsk can we have anthrax?" he recalled.

The next day, Grinberg saw the evidence for himself. He was instructed to go to Ilyenko's hospital. "I saw a horrible picture," he recalled. "It was three women, they had identical changes, sharp hemorrhagic changes in their lungs, in the lymph nodes, and the tissue of lymph nodes was hemorrhaging." Abramova took samples and materials from the autopsies.

Word of the outbreak reached Moscow. Late on April 11, Vladimir Nikiforov, a chief of the infectious diseases department at the Central Postgraduate Institute, located within the Botkin Hospital in Moscow, arrived in Sverdlovsk. Also arriving in the city was Pyotr Burgasov, the Soviet deputy minister of health, who had once worked at Compound 19, in the 1950s. On April 12, at 2 P.M., Nikiforov assembled all the doctors who had been involved and asked for their observations and the autopsies. Abramova was last to speak. She told him: anthrax.

Nikiforov, an eminent, courtly scientist who had studied anthrax

throughout his career, announced that he agreed with her. He reassured
the doctors it could not spread from human to human. But from where
had it come? Burgasov declared the source was contaminated meat from
a village located 9.3 miles from the city. No one spoke up. No one knew
for sure; the uncertainty was frightening.

In Chkalovsky's neighborhoods, residents were told to watch out for
contaminated meat. A widespread vaccination program began; according to Ilyenko's notes, 42,065 people were vaccinated in the days that followed. Broadsheet leaflets dated April 18 were distributed warning
people not to buy meat outside the stores, to watch out for anthrax symptoms such as headaches, fever, cold and cough followed by abdominal
pains and high temperatures, and not to slaughter animals without permission.[7] Buildings and trees were washed by local fire brigades, stray
dogs shot by police and unpaved streets covered with fresh asphalt.

Ilyenko wrote in her notes on April 20, "358 got sick. 45 died. 214 in
Hospital 40." She was not asked to relinquish her notes, and kept them at
home. The 45 who died at her hospital were only part of the story; the
total number of deaths from anthrax was more than 60 people.

Carried by the steady wind, the spores floated through the ceramics
factory, south of Compound 19. Vladlen Krayev, chief engineer, was
present when the outbreak began among his 2,180 employees. He
recalled that the factory had a ventilator that sucked air from outside,
pumping it into furnaces, and provided ventilation for the workers. In
the first weeks, about eighteen factory workers died. The crisis stretched
on for seven weeks, much longer than might be expected, given the two-
to-seven-day incubation period for anthrax described in textbooks at the
time.[8]

Grinberg recalled that Nikiforov made an unusual decision, ordering
that all the dead be autopsied even though government regulations prohibited autopsy for anthrax victims because the spores can spread. As
Grinberg and Abramova worked through the long days, the two pathologists began to take notes out of sight. They wrote these notes on cards,
and sometimes they wrote the official reports on carbon paper and kept
the copies. "No one checked," Abramova recalled. The head of the
regional health department came and told them "not to talk too much
about it, and don't discuss it on the phone."

They conducted forty-two autopsies. They saw anthrax had damaged the lungs and lymph nodes. Grinberg said he suspected inhalation anthrax but didn't know for sure. "Perhaps we didn't know definitely, but we were not talking about it much. Honestly speaking, we were very tired, it was hard work, we had a feeling, myself for example, as if we were working under war conditions. They were feeding us, bringing us meals, to the center at No. 40. There was a huge amount of chlorine. Disinfection was done every day. And we were going home on the trams after the working shift, and people were rushing away because we smelled of chlorine. The way I remember it, on the 10th day, about the end of the second week, we were thinking about keeping this material, that it should be preserved and studied."

Although it was prohibited, Grinberg persuaded a friend who was a photographer to secretly take color photographs of the autopsies using East German slide film. Abramova also preserved tissue samples.

In May, as the crisis eased, Nikiforov assembled all those who had participated in the hospital work and told them: the anthrax had come from tainted meat. But quietly, he told Abramova to keep investigating. He played a double game. In public, he was an official of the state, and loyal to the official story. But he also gave the pathologists a private signal to hide and protect their evidence. Nikiforov later died of a heart attack. "We are certain that he knew the truth," Grinberg said.[9]

But the people of the Soviet Union and the outside world did not.

II. Night Watch for Nuclear War

The shift change began at 7 P.M. on September 26, 1983. Stanislav Petrov, a lieutenant colonel, arrived at Serpukhov-15, south of Moscow, a top-secret missile attack early-warning station, which received signals from satellites. Petrov changed from street clothes into the soft uniform of the military space troops of the Soviet Union. Over the next hour, he and a dozen other specialists asked questions of the outgoing officers. Then his men lined up two rows deep and reported for duty to Petrov. Their twelve-hour shift had begun.[10]

Petrov settled into a comfortable swivel chair with arms. His command post overlooked the main floor of the early-warning station through a window. In front of him were telephones to connect to head-quarters and electronic monitors. Out on the floor, beyond the specialists and their consoles, a large map covered the far wall. At the center of the map was the North Pole. Above the pole and beyond it—as it might be seen from space—were Canada and the United States, inverted. Below the pole stretched the vast lands of the Soviet Union. This was the path that nuclear missiles would take if ever launched. The map showed the location of Minuteman missile bases in the United States. Petrov knew those bases held one thousand intercontinental ballistic missiles carrying nuclear warheads that could cross the Arctic and reach the Soviet Union in thirty-five minutes. On the main floor, a dozen men monitored electronic consoles with a singular mission: using satellites to spot a launch and give the leaders of the Soviet Union an added margin of ten minutes' warning, or maybe twelve minutes, to decide what to do.

Petrov, forty-four, had served in the military for twenty-six years, rising to deputy chief of the department for combat algorithms. He was more of an engineer than a soldier. He liked the logic of writing formulas, often using English-based computer languages. On most days, he was not in the commander's chair but at a desk in a nearby building, working as an analyst, responding to glitches, fine-tuning the software. But twice a month, he took an operations shift in order to keep on top of the system.

When Petrov first arrived eleven years earlier, the station was new, with equipment still in crates and the rooms empty. Now, it had grown into a bristling electronic nerve center. Seven satellites orbiting above the earth were positioned to monitor the American missile fields, usually for a period of six hours. Each satellite was a cylinder six feet long and five feet around, and sent streams of data to the command center.[11] The brain of the center was the M-10, the best supercomputer that existed in the Soviet Union, which analyzed the data and searched for signs of a missile attack.

The satellite system was known as Oko, or "Eye," but the individual spacecraft were known to Petrov by simple numbers, one through nine. On this night, No. 5 was reaching the highest point of its orbit, about 19,883 miles above the Earth. From space, it scanned the very edge of the Earth, using infrared sensors to detect a missile launch. The satellite could spot the heat given off by a rocket engine against the black background of space, a delicate trick requiring the satellite to be in the right position, steady and aimed at the distant point where the Earth met the darkness of the cosmos. Of the whole fleet, No. 5 had the highest sensitivity, but its task was complicated by the time of day. The satellite was aimed at missile fields that were passing from daylight to twilight during Petrov's shift. Dusk was often a blurry, milky zone that confused the satellites and computers. The operators knew of the challenge, and watched closely.

Usually, each satellite picked up fifteen or twenty objects of interest, and the computers at Serpukhov-15 examined the data on each, checking against the known characteristics of a rocket flare. If it did not look like a missile, the objects would be discarded by the computer and a new target grabbed for examination. The computer ran continuous checks against the data streaming in from space. The satellites also carried an optical telescope, with a view of the Earth. This was a backup, allowing the ground controllers to visually spot a missile attack, but the images were dim—in fact, special operators had to sit in a darkened room for two hours so they could see through the telescopes.

On this night, satellite No. 5 was bringing in more data than usual. Instead of fifteen to twenty targets, it was feeding the computer more than thirty. Petrov figured the elevated levels were due to the satellite's heightened sensitivity. They watched it closely as it approached the apogee of its orbit, when it would be positioned to monitor the American missile fields. At 10 P.M., Petrov paused for tea.

Petrov and his men had watched many test launches from Vandenberg Air Force Base in California and from Cape Canaveral in Florida, as well as Soviet test launches from Plesetsk in northern Russia. With the satellites, they could rapidly detect the rocket's bright flare moments after it rose into the sky; they had seen a few tests fail, too.

For all the years Petrov worked at the early-warning center, they had been rushed. The satellite system was put into service in late 1982, even though it was not ready. Petrov and his men were told: it was an important project for the country, don't worry about the shortcomings. They will be fixed later, you can compensate for the problems, look the other way for now. Petrov knew why they were in such a hurry. The United States and the Soviet Union threatened each other with missiles on hair-trigger alert. The two superpowers had between them about 18,400 nuclear warheads poised to be launched from missiles in silos, on submarines hidden under the seas and from bombers. And there were many smaller, or tactical, nuclear weapons arrayed along the front lines of the Cold War confrontation in Europe. In the event of a nuclear attack, a decision whether to retaliate would have to be made in minutes, and enormous efforts were made by each superpower to gain precious time for warning. With ground-based radar alone, which could not see beyond the curvature of the Earth, the incoming missiles might not be detected until the final seven to ten minutes of their flight. But with the early-warning satellites, a launch could be spotted sooner. The Americans already had stationed their satellites to watch over the Soviet missile fields. The Soviet Union was in a hurry to catch up. They rushed to build Serpukhov-15 and launch their own satellites.

A fear haunted the old men who ruled the Soviet Union, led by General Secretary Yuri Andropov, a frail and paranoid former KGB chief who in the autumn of 1983 was suffering from kidney failure. The fear was a sudden attack that might destroy the entire leadership in Moscow before they could leave the Kremlin. If they could be decapitated, wiped out without warning by a surprise attack, their threat to retaliate was simply not credible. That is why Petrov's mission was so important. The satellites, the antennas, the computers, the telescopes, the map and the operations center—they were the night watch for nuclear war.

Petrov heard the rhetoric, but he didn't believe the superpowers would come to blows; the consequences were just too devastating. Petrov thought the Soviet leaders were pompous and self-serving, and—in private—he was disdainful of the party bosses. He did not take seriously their bombast about America as the enemy. Yet the furor in recent months had been hard to ignore. President Ronald Reagan had called the Soviet Union an "evil empire" in March, and only a few weeks before Petrov's night at the operations center, Soviet Air Defense Forces had shot down a Korean airliner in the Far East, killing 269 people.

Petrov saw himself as a professional, a technician, and took pride in overcoming long odds. He understood the enormity of the task, that in early warning there could be no room for false alarms. His team had been driven hard to eliminate the chance for error. While they had tried strenuously to make the early-warning system work properly, the apparatus was still troubled. A system to make decisions about the fate of the Earth was plagued by malfunctions. Of the first thirteen satellites launched in the test phase from 1972 to 1979, only seven worked for more than one hundred days.[12] The satellites had to be launched constantly in order to keep enough of them aloft to monitor the American missile fields. They often just stopped sending data back to Earth.

At 12:15 A.M., Petrov was startled. Across the top of the room was a thin, silent panel. Most of the time no one even noticed it. But suddenly it lit up, in red letters: LAUNCH.

A siren wailed. On the big map with the North Pole, a light at one of the American missile bases was illuminated. Everyone was riveted to the map. The electronic panels showed a missile launch. The board said "high reliability." This had never happened before. The operators at the consoles on the main floor jumped up, out of their chairs. They turned and looked up at Petrov, behind the glass. He was the commander on duty. He stood, too, so they could see him. He started to give orders. He wasn't sure what was happening. He ordered them to sit down and start checking the system. He had to know whether this was real, or a glitch. The full check would take ten minutes, but if this was a real missile attack, they could not wait ten minutes to find out. Was the satellite holding steady? Was the computer functioning properly?

As they scrambled, Petrov scrutinized the monitors in front of him. They included data from the optical telescope. If there was a missile, sooner or later they would see it through the telescope. Where was it headed? What trajectory? There was no sign of it. The specialists who sat in the darkened room, also watching the telescope, spotted nothing. The computer specialists had to check a set of numbers spewing out of the hard-copy printer. Petrov scrutinized the data on his monitor, too. Could it be a technical error?

If not, Petrov ran through the possibilities. If just one missile, could it be an accidental or unauthorized launch? He concluded it was not likely. He knew of all the locks and precautions—and just one person could not launch a missile. Even the idea of two officers conspiring to launch a missile seemed impossible. And if one missile was launched, he thought, what did that mean? This was not the way to start a nuclear war. For many years, he had been trained that a nuclear war would start only with a massive strike. He said it again, to himself: this is not the way to start a nuclear war.

He had a microphone in one hand, part of the intercom system to the main floor. With the other hand, he picked up the telephone to call his commanders, who oversaw the whole early-warning system, including the separate radars. Petrov had to quickly reach his own conclusion; the supervisors would want to know what was happening. He had not completed his own checks, but he could not wait. He told the duty officer, in a clipped tone: "I am reporting to you: this is a false alarm."

He didn't know for sure. He only had a gut instinct.

"Got it," the officer replied. Petrov was relieved; the officer did not ask him why.

The phone was still in his hand, the duty officer still on the line, when Petrov was jolted again, two minutes later.

The panel flashed: another missile launched! Then a third, a fourth and a fifth. Now, the system had gone into overdrive. The additional signals had triggered a new warning. The red letters on the panel began to flash MISSILE ATTACK, and an electronic blip was sent automatically to the higher levels of the military. Petrov was frightened. His legs felt paralyzed. He had to think fast.

Petrov knew the key decision-makers in a missile attack would be the General Staff. In theory, if the alarm were validated, the retaliation would be directed from there. Soviet missiles would be readied, targets fed in and silo hatches opened. The Soviet political leadership would be alerted. There would be only minutes in which to make a decision.

The siren wailed. The red sign flashed.

Petrov made a decision. He knew the system had glitches in the past; there was no visual sighting of a missile through the telescope; the satellites were in the correct position. There was nothing from the radar stations to verify an incoming missile, although it was probably too early for the radars to see anything.

He told the duty officer again: this is a false alarm.

The message went up the chain.

INTRODUCTION

This book is the story of people—presidents, scientists, engineers, diplomats, soldiers, spies, scholars, politicians and others—who sought to brake the speeding locomotive of the arms race. They recoiled from the balance of terror out of personal experience as designers and stewards of the weapons, or because of their own fears of the consequences of war, or because of the burdens that the arsenals placed on their peoples.

At the center of the drama are two key figures, both of them romantics and revolutionaries, who sensed the rising danger and challenged the established order. Mikhail Gorbachev, the last leader of the Soviet Union, abhorred the use of force and championed openness and "new thinking" in hopes of saving his troubled country. Ronald Reagan, fortieth president of the United States, was a master communicator and beacon of ideals who had an unwavering faith in the triumph of capitalism and American ingenuity. He dreamed of making nuclear weapons obsolete, once and for all.

They were not alone. Many others with imagination, determination, guile and conscience sought to rein in the danger. The goal of the book is to tell the story of how the Cold War arms race came to an end, and of its legacy of peril—and to tell it from both sides. Too often in the past, the history has been obscured by American triumphalism, which reflected only one side, or by secrecy and disinformation in Moscow, which masked what really happened inside the Soviet Union and why. With fresh evidence, it is now possible to see more clearly the deliberations that unfolded behind closed doors in the Kremlin during Gorbachev's tumultuous rule. It was there, in arguments, meetings, documents and phone calls, that Gorbachev, deftly maneuvering and cajoling, faced off against the entrenched and powerful forces of the military-industrial complex and began a radical change in direction. It was there Gorbachev decided to abandon whole missile systems; turn the Soviet Union away from global confrontation; cut military spending and troops in Europe; and take the blueprint for a colossal Soviet "Star Wars" missile defense system, which designers and engineers had laid on his desk, and bury it in his bottom drawer. It is also possible with the new evidence, especially diaries and contemporaneous documents, to see more clearly how Gorbachev and Reagan viewed each other, how their perceptions fed into actions and how they wrestled with their own internal conflicts, ideology and an enormous stockpile of mistrust to lead the world, haltingly, out of the years of confrontation.

While nuclear weapons were the overwhelming threat of the epoch, another frightening weapon of mass casualty was being grown in flasks and fermenters. From 1975 to 1991, the Soviet Union covertly built the largest biological weapons program in the world. Soviet scientists experimented with genetic engineering to create pathogens that could cause unstoppable diseases. If the orders came, Soviet factory directors were ready to produce bacteria by the ton that could sicken and kill millions of people. The book explores the origins and expansion of this illicit, sprawling endeavor, for which Russia has yet to give a full accounting.

Much of the writing about the end of the Cold War stops at the moment the Berlin Wall fell in November 1989, or when the Soviet flag was lowered on the Kremlin in December 1991. This book attempts to go further. It begins with the peak of tensions in the early 1980s, leads us through the remarkable events of the Reagan and Gorbachev years and then shows how the Soviet collapse gave way to a race against time, an urgent search for the nuclear and biological hazards that were left behind.

The book will begin with the "war scare" of 1983, a period of confrontation, anger and danger. But to understand it, we must first see the gathering storm in the decades that preceded it, a great contest of wills, a duel of deterrence. The atomic bomb was never used in combat in the Cold War between the United States and the Soviet Union, 1947–1991. Rather, the two sides held each other in a balance of terror by deploying thousands of nuclear weapons on missiles, submarines and strategic bombers. Over decades, the danger intensified as the weapons were invented and reinvented to carry enormous destructive power, enhanced by ever-faster delivery, superaccuracy and invulnerability.

In the words of one of the early nuclear strategists, Bernard Brodie, the atomic bomb was the "absolute weapon" that would change warfare forever.[1] The bomb greatly increased the chance that it would be regular people who would die at the start. As a group of six Harvard professors put it in a study in 1983: "For the first time in history, nuclear weapons offer the possibility of destroying a country before one has defeated or destroyed its armed forces." And nuclear war would certainly come faster than any war in history. It might be over in a matter of hours. It might start before leaders could rethink their decisions or change their minds. It could lead to the death of millions of people even before a false alarm was discovered to be false.[2]

At the outset of the Cold War, the United States threatened the Soviet Union with a single, devastating blow aimed at cities and industry. The first American nuclear weapons each weighed thousands of pounds, and were to be carried by lumbering strategic bombers that would take hours to reach their targets. By contrast, a half century later, the warhead on a missile could be delivered across oceans in thirty minutes. Rear Admiral G. P. Nanos, director of Strategic Systems Programs in the U.S. Navy, said in 1997 that if one drew a circle with a radius the length of the Trident submarine—560 feet—the warheads on a Trident II D5 missile could be accurately targeted into that circle from a distance of four thousand nautical miles.[3]

But this achievement in power and deadly accuracy inspired a profound dread among those who might one day have to press the button launching those missiles.

In the United States, a master plan for carrying out a nuclear war was first drafted in 1960, at the end of President Dwight Eisenhower's term.

The scope of the Single Integrated Operational Plan was awesome. Given adequate warning time, the United States and allies would launch their entire strategic force of about 3,500 nuclear weapons against the Soviet Union, China and satellite states. Eisenhower dispatched his science adviser, George B. Kistiakowsky, to the headquarters of the Strategic Air Command in Offutt, Nebraska, on November 3–5, 1960, to study the newly drafted plan. Kistiakowsky reported back that the plan would "lead to unnecessary and undesirable overkill." Eisenhower confided to Captain E. P. "Pete" Aurand, his naval aide, that the estimates—the sheer number of targets, the redundant bombs for each—"frighten the devil out of me."[4]

President John F. Kennedy was no less unsettled. Briefed on the war plan on September 14, 1961, he commented afterward to Secretary of State Dean Rusk, "And we call ourselves the human race."[5]

Kennedy and his defense secretary, Robert S. McNamara, were uneasy with the Eisenhower-era idea of massive retaliation. They felt the threat of a single, enormous nuclear strike did not fit the more fragmented and complex competition they faced with the Soviet Union as tensions flared first over Berlin and then over Cuba. When the war plan was revised in the spring and summer of 1962, the new plan gave the president more flexibility and choices in waging a possible nuclear attack, including the ability to hold back forces in reserve, to avoid population centers and industry and to leave out some countries as targets. A key feature of the new plan, put into effect just before the Cuban missile crisis of October 1962, was to aim largely at Soviet weapons, and not at cities and industry, an idea known as *counterforce*. If one thinks of cocked pistols aimed at each other, counterforce was an effort to shoot the gun out of the hand of the enemy.[6] It seemed to be more humane to aim at missiles rather than cities, but counterforce also raised deeply disturbing questions. Could it make the use of nuclear weapons more tempting, since it implied a limited nuclear strike was possible? And to be successful, would the counterforce option have to be carried out first—to shoot before you were shot, to preempt an attack? This was the haunting fear of many decades to come, the idea of a disarming, bolt-from-the-blue first strike.

While Kennedy wanted to spare the cities, McNamara realized over time that it was impossible to aim at every Soviet weapon without unleashing an expensive new round of the arms race, an escalation with no end in sight. As a result, McNamara shifted to a strategy that he called "assured destruction," which required building the number of weapons needed to destroy 20 to 25 percent of the Soviet population and 50 percent of the industrial base. McNamara capped the number of Minuteman missiles to be built at one thousand. His analysts concluded, "The main reason for stopping at 1,000 Minuteman missiles, 41 Polaris submarines and some 500 strategic bombers is that having more would not be worth the cost." McNamara hoped that the Soviets would also reach a plateau—and stop building.[7] A critic of McNamara proposed adding "mutual" to "assured destruction" and the idea of Mutual Assured Destruction, known pointedly as MAD, was born. For many Americans, this idea of equal vulnerability and mutual deterrence came to define the Cold War.[8]

Locked in global confrontation, the United States and the Soviet Union were each rooted in centuries of radically different history, geography, culture and experience. Peering through a veil of suspicion, the superpowers often wrongly judged each other's intentions and actions. They engaged in deceptions that only deepened the dangers. As the Harvard professors observed in 1983, "The United States cannot predict Soviet behavior because it has too little information about what goes on inside the Soviet Union; the Soviets cannot predict American behavior because they have too much information."

An early but telling example was the so-called missile gap. The Soviet Union announced on August 26, 1957, the first test of an intercontinental ballistic missile at full range, and successfully launched the world's first artificial satellite, Sputnik, into orbit on October 4. For the next four years, Premier Nikita Khrushchev misled the West with claims that the Soviet Union was turning out missiles "like sausages," that super-missiles were in "serial production" and "mass production." John F. Kennedy raised alarms about the "missile gap" in his 1960 campaign, but found out that it didn't exist.[9] Khrushchev had concealed weakness—by bluffing.

A disaster was narrowly averted in the Cuban crisis of October 1962, when Khrushchev took an enormous gamble by stationing nuclear weapons and missiles on the island. The brinksmanship ended as both Kennedy and Khrushchev exercised restraint. But long after Khrushchev

withdrew the weapons, and after his ouster in 1964, the Cuban crisis lingered in the minds of Soviet leaders, who feared inferiority to the United
States. Starting in the mid-1960s, Soviet missile production zoomed
upward; hundreds were rolled out every year.

The Soviet Union, looking through an entirely different prism than
the United States, saw nuclear weapons as a blunt instrument for deterrence. If attacked, they would respond with crushing punishment. By
many accounts, in the early decades they did not adopt the limited
nuclear options that were embraced in the United States; they thought
that the use of even one atomic bomb would trigger escalation, so they
prepared for all-out war.[10] They did not put much stock in the American
idea that mutual vulnerability could lead to stability. They feared both
powers would be constantly striving to get ahead, and they threw their
resources into the quest. When the Soviet Union finally reached approximate parity with the United States in the early 1970s, the thinking began
to change. Instead of threatening a preemptive first strike, as in the earlier
years, they moved toward a posture of preparing for assured retaliation, a
second strike. At this time they also began the first strategic arms control
negotiations with the United States, and détente blossomed.[11]

The Soviet buildup was driven by a powerful and hidden force, the
defense industrialists. Leonid Brezhnev ruled by consensus over a dys-
functional group of aging sycophants, and by the mid-1970s, Brezhnev
was in such ill health that he largely ceased to lead. The industrialists
filled the vacuum. They had great influence over what weapons would be
produced, by some accounts even more than the military. A striking
example was the climax of an intense internal conflict over the next generation of intercontinental ballistic missile. In July 1969, at a vacation
lodge near Yalta, a vexed Brezhnev assembled his top military leaders
and missile designers. The competition pitted two of the most storied
designers, Mikhail Yangel and Vladimir Chelomei, against each other.
Yangel proposed a four-warhead missile, the SS-17, designed to fit in
newly constructed, hardened silos, best to ensure retaliation if the Soviet
Union were attacked, but expensive. Chelomei had initially proposed to
upgrade his older SS-11 missile in existing silos, which were not hardened, but offered the military more warheads more cheaply, perfect for
threatening a preemptive first strike at the enemy. At the time of the
Yalta meeting, Chelomei shifted gears and proposed a new missile, the

SS-19, with six warheads, which would also require new, expensive hardened silos. Mstislav Keldysh, president of the Academy of Sciences, who had Brezhnev's confidence, was appointed to head a commission to resolve the dispute. At Yalta he took the floor and lamented that in all the rush to build missiles, the country had not even decided on a strategic doctrine: whether the purpose was to threaten a first strike, or to preserve the force for retaliation. But Keldysh could not settle the rivalry. In the end, all three missile options were approved at great cost, the kind of decision that would eventually bankrupt the Soviet Union.[12]

In the 1970s, the United States began to deploy a Minuteman III missile that could carry up to three warheads instead of just one. The new device was called a Multiple Independently-targetable Re-Entry Vehicle, or MIRV, and it would allow each of the three warheads to aim at separate targets, leading to a new surge in the size of the arsenals. The Soviets matched and surpassed this technology, and in the mid-1970s began the deployment of a new generation of land-based missiles. One of them, the SS-18, could carry a payload seven to eight times as large as the American missile. In fact, there were plans at one point to put as many as thirty-eight warheads atop each giant SS-18.

As the arsenals grew, so did the complexity of the U.S. war plan. On January 27, 1969, a week after taking office, President Richard Nixon went to the Pentagon for a briefing on the Single Integrated Operation Plan (SIOP). "It didn't fill him with enthusiasm," recalled Henry Kissinger, then Nixon's national security adviser and later secretary of state. In the event of nuclear war, Nixon was told, he would have three functional tasks: Alpha, for strikes on the most urgent military targets; Bravo, for secondary military targets; and Charlie, for industrial and urban targets. If the president ordered an attack of Alpha and Bravo, urban areas would be spared. All three would mean total war. But the choices Nixon would face in an emergency were mind-numbingly complex. There were five attack options constructed from the three main tasks, and as many as ninety lesser variations.[13] On May 11, 1969, Nixon flew on the National Emergency Airborne Command Post, a Boeing 707 filled with communications gear, and participated in a nuclear war exercise. His chief of staff, H. R. Haldeman, wrote in his diary, "Pretty scary. They went through the whole intelligence and operational briefings—with interruptions, etc. to make it realistic." Haldeman added that Nixon "asked a lot of questions about our nuclear capability and kill results. Obviously worries about the lightly tossed-about millions of deaths."[14]

The same fears troubled Soviet leaders. In 1972, the General Staff presented to the leadership results of a study of a possible nuclear war after a first strike by the United States. They reported: the military had been reduced to one-thousandth of its strength; 80 million citizens were dead; 85 percent of Soviet industry was in ruins. Brezhnev and Prime Minister Alexei Kosygin were visibly terrified by what they heard, according to Adrian Danilevich, a general who took part. Next, three launches of intercontinental ballistic missiles with dummy warheads were planned. Brezhnev was provided a button in the exercise and he was to push it at the proper moment. Defense Minister Andrei Grechko was standing next to Brezhnev, and Danilevich next to Grechko. "When the time came to push the button," Danilevich recalled, "Brezhnev was visibly shaken and pale and his hand trembled and he asked Grechko several times for assurances that the action would not have any real world consequences." Brezhnev turned to Grechko and asked, "'Are you sure this is just an exercise?'"[15]

Recognizing the overwhelming destructive power of nuclear weapons, Nixon decided in 1969 that the United States would renounce biological weapons. In 1972, more than seventy nations, including the Soviet Union and the United States, signed the Biological and Toxin Weapons Convention, a four-page international agreement banning the development and production of biological weapons, and the means of delivering them. The treaty entered into force in 1975. But the Soviet Union promptly betrayed its signature on the treaty. Brezhnev approved a secret plan to covertly expand Soviet germ warfare efforts under the cover of a civilian enterprise. The Soviet program grew and grew into a dark underside of the arms race.

The biological weapons treaty came at the peak of détente, Nixon's policy to wrap the Soviet Union in a web of new international agreements and understandings that would make the Cold War manageable and less threatening. A centerpiece of détente was the signing of the SALT I agreement in Moscow on May 26, 1972, by Nixon and Brezhnev. The most significant part of this agreement was the Anti-Ballistic Missile Treaty, which effectively ended the prospect of an expensive arms race in missile defenses.[16] But on offensive arms, the long-range missiles that were growing in size and destructive capacity, the SALT I agreement was basically just a stopgap measure. It froze fixed *launchers* for land-based and submarine-based missiles on each side, but included no precise numbers of missiles or warheads to be frozen. The core argument for the SALT I treaty and détente was that equal levels of missiles and launchers were not as important as the overall strategic balance, and in that the two sides were roughly equal. If the United States stopped the cycle of building new missiles, the reasoning went, it was likely the Soviets would too. Kissinger said, "And one of the questions which we have to ask ourselves as a country is what in the name of God is strategic superiority? What is the significance of it, politically, militarily, operationally, at these levels of numbers? What do you do with it?"[17]

Détente foundered in the late 1970s, in part on fears in the West that the Soviet Union was reaching for strategic superiority. A small band of defense policy conservatives and hawkish strategists in the United States raised alarms about Soviet intentions and actions. Albert Wohlstetter of the University of Chicago published a series of influential articles questioning whether the U.S. intelligence community had underestimated Soviet military spending and weapons modernization. Paul Nitze, who for a generation had been one of the "wise men" of the U.S. government, an arms control negotiator on SALT I and former secretary of the navy, wrote an article in *Foreign Affairs* in January 1976 that warned the Soviets were not satisfied with parity or essential equivalence in nuclear weapons, but "will continue to pursue a nuclear superiority that is not merely quantitative but designed to produce a theoretical war-winning capability."[18]

These claims—that the Soviet Union was seeking superiority over the United States and preparing to fight and win a nuclear war—could not be proven, but they gained a foothold in the United States at a time of deep uncertainty in the aftermath of the Vietnam War and the Watergate scandal. In 1976, the Central Intelligence Agency carried out an extraordinary competition to examine Soviet intentions. It set up two separate teams to assess the available intelligence, pitting the agency's own analysts against a team of outsiders. Both teams were given the same raw material. The CIA insiders were Team A, and the outsiders Team B. The outsiders were led by Richard Pipes, professor of history at Harvard, long a fierce critic of Soviet communism; the others on Team B were also drawn from critics of détente who had been warning of a Soviet quest for military superiority. When finished in November, the Team B report on Soviet intentions was unequivocal that Moscow was on a dangerous drive for supremacy, and that the CIA had badly underestimated it. Soviet leaders "think not in terms of nuclear stability, mutual assured destruction or strategic sufficiency, but of an effective nuclear war-fighting capability," they wrote.[19]

On the other side of the exercise, Team A did not share the shrill sense of alarm. They said the Soviets might want to achieve nuclear war-fighting capability and superiority, but that it wasn't a realistic, practical goal. When completed, the overall yearly intelligence estimate hewed to Team A's view that the Soviets "cannot be certain about future U.S. behavior or about their own future strategic capabilities relative to those of the U.S." The State Department's top intelligence official was even more cautious. Soviet leaders, he said, "do not entertain, as a practical objective in the foreseeable future, the achievement of what could reasonably be characterized as a 'war winning' or 'war survival' posture."[20]

In later years, many of the findings of Team B were found to have been overstated. Soviet missile accuracy and the pace of weapons modernization were exaggerated. But at the time, the conclusions seemed ominous, hammering another nail into the coffin of détente. In July 1977, Pipes wrote an article in the journal *Commentary* titled "Why the Soviet Union Thinks It Could Fight and Win a Nuclear War." Soon after work was finished on Team B, Nitze, Pipes and others helped to found an advocacy group, the Committee on the Present Danger, to raise public alarm about the Soviet military buildup. The committee's board included Ronald Reagan, the former California governor, who had presidential ambitions and a base of support among social, economic and defense conservatives. The committee campaigned from 1977 to 1979 against a SALT II treaty, then under negotiation, distributing maps showing the American cities that could be destroyed by a single Soviet SS-18 missile.[21]

The Soviet leadership, with Brezhnev ailing, blundered in this period, deploying the SS-20 Pioneer, a new generation of medium-range missiles in Europe, apparently not anticipating that this would lead to apprehension in the United States and among its allies. NATO responded with a proposal to negotiate, but also to deploy Pershing II and ground-launched cruise missiles in Europe as a counterweight. A new arms race was getting underway. The leaders in Moscow stumbled again with the invasion of Afghanistan in December 1979. President Jimmy Carter, who had signed the SALT II treaty with Brezhnev, pulled back the treaty from the Senate, and détente was dead.

In the summer of 1980, Carter was facing a reelection challenge from Reagan and deepening tensions with Moscow. He approved two secret directives on nuclear war. Presidential Directive 58, signed June 30, called for a multibillion-dollar program to protect the president and other government leaders from a nuclear attack. Presidential Directive 59, signed July 25, put into effect a revised and expanded list of targeting choices a president would have at his disposal in the event of nuclear war. The new plan focused on attacking the Soviet political leadership, as well as military targets and war-supporting industry, and it envisioned limited nuclear strikes as well as a protracted conflict. Carter ordered upgrades for communications and improved satellites that would allow a president to choose military targets in real time after a nuclear exchange had begun. According to a senior Pentagon official, Presidential Directive 59 was developed in part to let the Soviet leadership know something very specific and frightening: they had been personally placed in the American nuclear crosshairs.[22]

By 1982, the combined strategic arsenals of the superpowers held the explosive power of approximately 1 million Hiroshimas. Even with their huge arsenal, Soviet leaders feared they could perish in a decapitating missile attack before they had a chance to respond. They drew up plans for a system to guarantee a retaliatory strike. They envisioned a fully automatic system, known as the Dead Hand, in which a computer alone would issue the order to launch. But they had second thoughts, and instead created a modified system in which the decision to launch all the

land-based missiles would be made by a small crew of duty officers surviving deep underground in a globe-shaped concrete bunker. The system
was fully tested in November 1984 and placed on duty a few months later.
At the climax of mistrust between the superpowers, one of them had built
a Doomsday Machine.

The book is based on interviews, memoirs, diaries, news accounts and
archival materials. An invaluable source was a collection of internal documents from the Defense Department of the Central Committee of the
Communist Party of the Soviet Union. Revealed here for the first time,
these papers shed new light on the decisions and thinking of key Soviet
participants in the Gorbachev years. They show how Gorbachev stood up
to the generals and the powerful military-industrial complex, and also
how the Soviet Union concealed the germ warfare program. The papers
were collected by Vitaly Katayev, an aviation and rocket designer by
training. In 1974, Katayev was transferred from the missile complex in
Dnepropetrovsk, Ukraine, to become a staff man on the Central Committee, in the heart of the Kremlin decision making, where he remained
for almost two decades, often writing meticulous entries in his journals
and preserving sheaves of original documents. Katayev knew the missiles, the designers and the political leaders. Like many others in this
story, he came to realize, from his own experience, that the arms race had
become a competition of colossal excess.

After the Soviet collapse in 1991, new and unexpected threats surfaced
almost immediately. Rickety trains hauled nuclear warheads back from
Eastern Europe and Central Asia into Russia; tons of highly enriched
uranium and plutonium lay unguarded in warehouses; microbiologists
and nuclear bomb designers were in desperate straits. This book traces
the struggle of individuals to seize the moment and contain the danger.
They were only partly successful. Today, the weapons to destroy civilization, the legacy of the Cold War, are still with us. They are the Dead
Hand of our time, a lethal machine that haunts the globe long after the
demise of the men who created it.

PART

ONE

---— 1 ——

AT THE PRECIPICE

On July 31, 1979, Ronald Reagan walked through a pair of twenty-five-ton blast doors at Cheyenne Mountain, Colorado, headquarters of the North American Air Defense Command. Behind the doors were four and a half acres of chambers and tunnels surrounded by granite two thousand feet thick to shield it from an atomic bomb. Constructed of carbon steel plates, the fifteen buildings inside rested on 1,319 giant springs, each weighing approximately one thousand pounds, to cushion against shock. Built in the early 1960s, the complex was the nerve center of a system of satellites and radar for monitoring against a nuclear attack.[1]

Reagan, who sought the Republican nomination in 1976 but lost to Gerald Ford, was preparing to run for president again. He had flown from Los Angeles for briefings about nuclear weapons. Martin Anderson, a policy adviser to the campaign, accompanied Reagan that day, along with Douglas Morrow, a screenwriter and producer who had known Reagan in his Hollywood days and suggested that Reagan see the facility.[2] From the outside of the mountain, at the North Portal, entering a one-third-mile-long tunnel, Anderson recalled they didn't think the complex looked very impressive. But once deep inside the mountain, standing in front of the huge blast doors, they began to sense the enormous scope. They were given briefings on the relative nuclear capabilities of the United States and the Soviet Union, and shown the command center, a room with a giant electronic map of North America. Anderson asked Air Force General James Hill, the commander, what would happen if a Soviet SS-18 missile were to hit within a few hundred yards of the command center. The Soviets had already deployed the SS-18 and an upgraded version was in flight tests. "It would blow us away," Hill replied. When he heard this, "a look of disbelief came over Reagan's face," Anderson recalled. "The discussion continued, and we pressed the issue of what would really happen if the Soviets were to fire just one nuclear missile at a U.S. city."

Hill replied that "we would pick it up right after it was launched, but by the time the officials of the city could be alerted that a nuclear bomb would hit them, there would be only ten or fifteen minutes left. That's all we can do. We can't stop it."

On the flight back to Los Angeles, Reagan was deeply concerned. "He couldn't believe the United States had no defense against Soviet missiles," Anderson recalled. Reagan slowly shook his head and said, "We have spent all that money and have all that equipment, and there is nothing we can do to prevent a nuclear missile from hitting us." At the end of the flight, Reagan reflected on the dilemma that might confront a U.S. president if faced with a nuclear attack. "The only options he would have," Reagan said, "would be to press the button or do nothing. They're both bad. We should have some way of defending ourselves against nuclear missiles."[3]

Reagan was a staunch anti-Communist and defense hard-liner. In the summer of 1979 he was speaking out in his syndicated radio address against the new SALT II treaty, saying it favored the Soviet Union.[4] But on the threshold of a new campaign, his advisers felt there was a real chance that Reagan would frighten voters if he spoke openly about nuclear weapons and war. This risk was acknowledged in a memorandum that Anderson wrote in early August, a few weeks after Cheyenne Mountain. At this point, Reagan's campaign had several part-time defense and foreign policy experts, but the only permanent policy adviser was Anderson, a conservative economist on leave from the Hoover Institution at Stanford University. Anderson had earlier written memos on the economy and energy. In the ten-page Policy Memorandum No. 3, "Foreign Policy and National Security," he grappled with a way for Reagan to talk about nuclear strategy without alarming voters.

Anderson acknowledged that Reagan's strong views on national defense were regarded as a political liability, that people worried he was somewhat inexperienced and might plunge the country into "Vietnam-like wars" abroad. But, Anderson added, "The situation has now changed significantly." The reason was that growing Soviet military power "has been increasingly perceived as a clear and present danger to the national security of the United States." Anderson cautioned that Reagan could not tackle this theme directly. He had to find a way to take advantage of the mood without frightening voters with an "overly aggressive stance that would be counterproductive."

Under the heading "National Defense," Anderson sketched out three options for the campaign. One would be to continue the course the United States was on, relying on SALT II, and "try to appease and ingratiate ourselves with the Soviets." Anderson dismissed this as "dangerous folly." Another option would be for Reagan to argue the United States must "match the Soviet buildup," sharply increasing defense spending. But this has "serious problems," he acknowledged, because it could alienate voters. "Substantial increases in the attack missile capability of the United States would be a powerful, emotional issue to deal with politically—especially by Reagan," he cautioned. Then Anderson offered a third way, suggesting Reagan propose development of what he called a "Protective Missile System." Anderson acknowledged missile defenses were outlawed by the 1972 Anti-Ballistic Missile Treaty, but "perhaps it is now time to reconsider the concept." Anderson argued that missile defense would be "far more appealing to the American people" than just nuclear retaliation and revenge.[5]

Despite the recommendation of Policy Memorandum No. 3, in the campaign that unfolded in the next fifteen months, Reagan did not talk about missile defense. The subject was just too delicate. A statement on the topic was put into the Republican Party platform, but it was not part of Reagan's campaign stump speech nor did it figure in his major campaign addresses on foreign policy.

Nonetheless, Reagan held radical notions about nuclear weapons: he dreamed of abolishing them. Personally, he recoiled from the concept of mutual assured destruction, or MAD.[6] Reagan also intensely disliked the idea that he, as president, would have to make decisions about nuclear weapons in the event of a sudden crisis. He worried that a nuclear explosion would lead to the end of the Earth and expressed belief in the biblical story of Armageddon. "I swear I believe Armageddon is near," he wrote in his diary on the day Israel bombed an Iraqi nuclear reactor in 1981.[7] In his desk drawer, Reagan kept a collection of 3 × 5 cards. One carried a quotation from President Eisenhower's "Atoms for Peace" address to the United Nations in 1953, in which Eisenhower pledged the United States would help solve "the fearful atomic dilemma—to devote its entire heart and mind to find the way by which the miraculous inventiveness of man shall not be dedicated to his death, but consecrated to his life."[8]

Alongside these views, other powerful convictions and experiences guided Reagan's thinking. In his 1940 movie *Murder in the Air*, he starred as Secret Service agent Brass Bancroft, who stops a spy and saves a top-secret death-ray invention that can shoot down airplanes.[9] It was fantasy, but Reagan put great faith in the power of American technology to solve problems, going back to his many years selling General Electric with the slogan "Progress is our most important product." Reagan also distrusted treaties with the Soviet Union, influenced by a book written by a friend, Laurence W. Beilenson, a lawyer and founder of the Screen Actors Guild. The book argued that nations follow treaties only as long as it is in their interest to do so.[10] From his experience in the Screen Actors Guild, Reagan was confident in his personal skills as a negotiator—a belief that if he could appeal to the human side of Soviet leaders, he could persuade them.

All these ideas lived in peaceful coexistence in Reagan's mind. He had a remarkable ability to hold many differing notions at the same time, deploying them as needed and concealing them if required. The stereotype of Reagan as a rigid ideologue does not explain these twists and turns, this untroubled shifting of gears, so central to his character. In 1980, he waged a campaign for the presidency on the grounds that the nation needed a large military expansion, including modernization of missiles, bombers and submarines that carried nuclear weapons. But he kept silent about his own notions that nuclear weapons should be abolished. The Great Communicator did not communicate his dreams about a world without the atomic bomb. His campaign advisers weren't sure what to make of it when Reagan talked privately about abolishing nuclear weapons. "Nobody on the campaign staff raised any serious objections to his idea of reducing the stockpiles of nuclear weapons," Anderson recalled, "but on the other hand, and it's difficult as a former campaign staffer to admit this, nobody believed there was the slightest possibility it could ever happen. And when Reagan began to talk privately of a dream he had when someday we might live in a world free of all nuclear missiles, well, we just smiled."

For reasons of political tactics, Reagan in 1980 kept his focus on two topics that could be raised in campaign speeches without as much political risk: opposing the SALT II treaty and warning that the Soviets were driving toward military superiority.[11] He voiced the alarms of Nitze, Wohlstetter, Pipes and others that the Soviets were posing a "window of vulnerability" for the United States. In a foreign policy address to the Veterans of Foreign Wars convention on August 18, 1980, in Chicago, Reagan quoted approvingly Nitze's remark that Kremlin leaders "do not want war; they want the world." Reagan added, "For that reason, they have put much of their military effort into strategic nuclear programs. Here the balance has been moving against us and will continue to do so if we follow the course set by this administration. The Soviets want peace and victory. We must understand this and what it means to us. They seek a superiority in military strength that, in the event of a confrontation, would leave us with an unacceptable choice between submission or conflict."[12]

With his silky voice, slightly cocked head, crinkly smile, old-fashioned suits and gauzy nostalgia for an era of American leadership in the 1950s, Reagan projected a sense of purpose and unbridled optimism, and he conveyed it at a time of troubling doubts for Americans. On November 4, 1979, nine days before Reagan formally announced his candidacy for president, Iranian students seized the U.S. Embassy in Tehran and took Americans hostage. In December, the Soviet Union invaded Afghanistan. Voters were fatigued from Vietnam, Watergate, high inflation and energy shortages. From President Carter they had heard about the need for sacrifice and discipline; Reagan, by contrast, offered them a sky-is-the-limit vision that days of plenty could be returned to American life.[13]

This optimism also ran through Reagan's ambitions for competition with the Soviet Union. He believed that communism and socialism would ultimately give way to a victory of the American way. While others saw the Soviet Union as an unfortunate yet permanent bastion of global power, Reagan envisioned relentless competition aimed at overturning the status quo. "The great dynamic success of capitalism had given us a powerful weapon in our battle against Communism—*money,*" Reagan later recalled. "The Russians could never win the arms race; we could outspend them forever."[14] He declared in his 1980 campaign speech that he wanted to "show by example the greatness of our system and the strength of American ideals." He added,

> The truth is we would like nothing better than to see the Russian people living in freedom and dignity instead of being trapped in a backwash of history as they are. The greatest fallacy of the Lenin-Marxist philosophy is that it is the "wave of the future." Everything about it is primitive: compulsion in place of free initiative; coercion in place of law; militarism in place of trade; and empire-building in place of self-determination; and luxury for a chosen few at the expense of the many. We have seen nothing like it since the Age of Feudalism.

Reagan's description of the Soviet system as backward and restrictive was a penetrating insight. But there was also a hidden contradiction in this argument. How could the Soviet Union be threatening militarily while also "primitive" and rotting from within? How could it sustain a global arms race abroad while people stood in lines at home? The answer offered by many at the time was that the Soviet military had first claim on the country's resources, and therefore the defense sector could fatten itself while the rest of the country suffered. This was true; hypermilitarization of the Soviet state did siphon off a huge portion of the country's resources. But it was also true that, in many instances, the internal rot sapped military power. The Soviet defense machine was undermined by the very weaknesses Reagan spotted elsewhere in the system. A reckoning was coming for the Soviet Union. And even if he did not see every detail clearly, Reagan seemed to understand the big picture very well: the system as a whole was tottering and vulnerable.

———

Soviet leaders had not trusted Carter, but they reacted with anger and paranoia to Reagan. At his first press conference as president, Reagan was asked if the Kremlin was still "bent on world domination that might lead to a continuation of the Cold War" or whether "under other circumstances détente is possible." Reagan responded that détente had been a "one way street that the Soviet Union has used to pursue its own aims," and added that Soviet leaders "have openly and publicly declared that the only morality they recognize is what will further their cause, meaning they reserve unto themselves the right to commit any crime, to lie, to cheat, in order to attain that, and that is moral, not immoral, and we operate on a different set of standards. I think when you do business with them, even at a détente, you keep that in mind."

In Moscow, the aging leadership wanted most of all to preserve the strategic parity they felt they had achieved in the late 1970s, recalled Anatoly Dobrynin, former ambassador to Washington. "For all their revolutionary rhetoric," he said, "they hated change. . . ." They wanted some kind of military détente, even if political cooperation was out of the question, but the era of détente was over. Reagan didn't believe in it. "In retrospect, I realize that it had been quite impossible for me at that moment to imagine anything much worse than Carter," Dobrynin said. "But it soon became clear that in ideology and propaganda Reagan turned out to be far worse and far more threatening."[15]

Nonetheless, the Soviet Union was not at the top of Reagan's agenda in his first year, which was devoted to driving Congress to approve lower taxes, budget cuts and defense rearmament. Reagan believed that before serious attention could be given to dealing with the Soviets, the United States had to first embark on a demonstrable military buildup. Reagan resumed building the B-1 bomber Carter had canceled, pushed ahead with a new basing mode for a new land-based missile, the MX, and with construction of a new Trident II D-5 submarine-launched ballistic missile with more accuracy and range. Reagan also secretly approved more aggressive U.S. naval and air maneuvers aimed at the Soviet Union. His CIA director, William Casey, expanded covert actions around the globe aimed at hemming in the Soviets. But Reagan did not rush to advance superpower diplomacy. He did not meet or talk to Soviet leaders.

After surviving an assassination attempt on March 30, 1981, when he was shot by John Hinckley Jr. outside the Washington Hilton Hotel, Reagan began to think about what he could do to end the arms race.

"Perhaps having come so close to death made me feel I should do whatever I could in the years God had given me to reduce the threat of nuclear war; perhaps there was a reason I had been spared," he recalled later. In the first week after leaving the hospital, he took out a yellow legal pad and wrote a personal letter to Brezhnev, by hand. Still in his bathrobe and pajamas, Reagan passed it around to aides at a meeting April 13. The State Department didn't like it and rewrote it into a stiff message. Reagan didn't like the rewrite, and in the end, Brezhnev got two letters, one formal and one in Reagan's hand.[16] James A. Baker III, who was Reagan's chief of staff, recalled that the letter was "Reagan 101: a sermon that basically said the Soviets had it wrong on economics, politics, and international relations, and that the United States had it right. It's as if the president thought maybe Brezhnev didn't know this stuff and that if he just heard it, he'd come to his senses."[17] Brezhnev replied in "the standard polemical form, stressing their differences," without any effort to be personal, recalled Dobrynin. Reagan remembered "an icy reply from Brezhnev."[18]

At a private moment at an economic summit in Ottawa on July 19, 1981, French President François Mitterrand gave Reagan some stunning news. The French had recruited a defector in place in Moscow, whom the French had code-named "Farewell," and he had provided a huge treasure trove of intelligence. Colonel Vladimir Vetrov was an engineer whose job was to evaluate the intelligence collected by the KGB's technology directorate—Directorate T—responsible for finding and stealing the latest in Western high technology. A special arm of the KGB, known as Line X, carried out the thefts. Motivated to help the West, Vetrov had secretly photographed four thousand KGB documents on the program. After Mitterrand spoke to Reagan, the materials were passed to Vice President George H. W. Bush, and then to the CIA in August.

The dossier "immediately caused a storm," recalled Thomas C. Reed, a former Pentagon official who later worked on the National Security Council staff under Reagan. "The files were incredibly explicit. They set forth the extent of Soviet penetration into U.S. and other Western laboratories, factories and government agencies."[19]

Vetrov revealed the names of more than two hundred Line X officers in ten KGB stations in the West. "Reading the material caused my worst nightmares to come true," said Gus Weiss, a White House official. "Since 1970, Line X had obtained thousands of documents and sample products in such quantity that it appeared the Soviet military and civilian sectors were in large measure running their research on that of the West, particularly the United States. Our science was supporting their national defense."[20]

Rather than roll up the Line X officers and expel them, Reagan approved a secret plan to exploit the Farewell dossier for economic warfare against the Soviet Union. The plan was to secretly feed the Line X officers with technology rigged to self-destruct after a certain interval. The idea came from Weiss, who approached Casey, who took it to Reagan. The CIA worked with American industry to alter products to be slipped to the KGB, matching the KGB's shopping list. "Contrived computer chips found their way into Soviet military equipment, flawed turbines were installed on a gas pipeline, and defective plans disturbed the output of chemical plants and a tractor factory," Weiss said. "The Pentagon introduced misleading information pertinent to stealth aircraft, space defense, and tactical aircraft."

Oil and gas equipment was at the top of the Soviet wish list, and the Soviets needed sophisticated control systems to automate the valves, compressors and storage facilities for a huge new pipeline to Europe. When the pipeline technology could not be purchased in the United States, the KGB shopped it from a Canadian firm. However, tipped by Vetrov, the CIA rigged the software sold from Canada to go haywire after a while, to reset pump speeds and valve settings to create pressures far beyond those acceptable to the pipeline joints and welds. One day, the system exploded. "The result was the most monumental non-nuclear explosion and fire ever seen from space," Reed recalled. The blast was starting to trigger worried looks in the U.S. government that day, he recalled, when, at the National Security Council, "Gus Weiss came down the hall to tell his fellow NSC staffers not to worry." The explosion had been one of the first fruits of the Reagan confrontation.

Soviet leaders were jittery. Sometime in 1981 they realized that the United States had been tapping one of their most secret military cables linking naval bases with commanders in the Far East. The tap in the Sea of Okhotsk had been placed by U.S. submarines in an operation code-named Ivy Bells. The Soviets may have been alerted when the U.S.S. *Seawolf,* a reconnaissance submarine, set down by accident right atop the Soviet cable. Also, in 1980, Ronald Pelton, who had worked at the National Security Agency, began selling information about Ivy Bells to the Soviets for money.[21] On learning of the tap, the Soviets sent a scavenger ship and found the super-secret device, pulling it up from the ocean floor. There was no mistaking what it was: one part inside said "Property of the United States Government."[22]

In May 1981, Brezhnev denounced Reagan's policies in a secret address to a major KGB conference in Moscow. An even more dramatic speech was given by Yuri Andropov, chairman of the KGB, who declared that the new U.S. administration was actively preparing for nuclear war. He said there was now the possibility of a nuclear first strike by the United States, and the overriding priority of Soviet spying should be to collect intelligence on the nuclear threat from the United States and NATO. Andropov announced that the KGB and the GRU, Soviet military intelligence, were launching a new program to collect intelligence around the world. It was code-named RYAN, the acronym of *Raketno-Yadernoe Napadenie*—nuclear missile attack. The GRU was responsible for monitoring any Western military preparations for a first strike on the Soviet Union, while the KGB's task was to look for advance warning of an attack decision by the United States and its NATO allies. The first instructions went out to KGB residencies in November 1981.[23]

When he was president, Reagan carried no wallet, no money, no driver's license, "no keys in my pockets—only secret codes that were capable of bringing about the annihilation of much of the world as we knew it," he said in his memoir. He carried a small, plastic-coated card in his coat which "listed the codes I would issue to the Pentagon confirming that it was actually the president of the United States who was ordering the unleashing of our nuclear weapons." In an emergency, Reagan would have to choose options for responding to nuclear attack. "But everything would happen so fast that I wondered how much planning or reason could be applied in such a crisis," he said. "The Russians sometimes kept submarines off our East Coast with nuclear missiles that could turn the White House into a pile of radioactive rubble within six or eight minutes. *Six minutes* to decide how to respond to a blip on a radar scope and decide whether to release Armageddon! How could anyone apply reason at a time like that?"

In early 1982, Reagan got a closer and more disturbing look at the options. His national security adviser in the first year, Richard Allen, had resigned, and Reagan turned to a trusted friend, William P. Clark, who had been his executive secretary in Sacramento and later a California Supreme Court justice. Reagan and Clark shared a love of horseback riding through the California hills. At the White House, Clark cut an imposing figure, in dark suits and expensive, hand-tooled black cowboy boots. Clark had served as deputy secretary of state in 1981, but otherwise had little national security experience. Most importantly, he enjoyed Reagan's confidence and shared the president's political and social conservatism, and his strong anti-communism.

When he became national security adviser, Clark brought Thomas C. Reed into the White House with him. Reed once designed nuclear weapons at the Lawrence Livermore National Laboratory in California. He served in Reagan's gubernatorial offices during the first term in Sacramento, and ran Reagan's 1970 reelection campaign. Reed also had experience in Washington; in 1973, he was the Pentagon director of telecommunications and command and control systems, where he worked on modernizing the nuclear communications systems. Later, he served as secretary of the air force under President Gerald Ford. He knew well the workings of global military communications linking NORAD and other military bases to the Pentagon war room.

Reed saw a worrisome disconnect when he got to the White House. The network of communications with the president was a jumble of telephones, radios and hideouts dating from Eisenhower. When he examined the system to evacuate the president in the event of a nuclear attack, Reed was further alarmed; nuclear missiles could arrive before the president even got out of the White House in a helicopter. Carter's directives in 1980 called for upgrades to the system of presidential command and control, and the creation of a steering group. Reed became chairman of the group, but found the Carter directive was mired in the bureaucracy, and the Defense Department was balking at taking any action.[24] Reed said, "The system as I found it would have been headless within minutes of an attack."

This fear of decapitation of the leadership was just one sign of the immense tensions building at the time between Moscow and Washington. With rapid advances in weapons technology, a lightning strike could wipe out either party within minutes. The Americans worried about Soviet submarines carrying nuclear missiles off the East Coast, or surfacing in the Arctic. The Soviets were fearful of American missiles in Europe reaching the Kremlin. In the early summer of 1982, the Pentagon circulated a 125-page, five-year defense plan that called on U.S. forces to be ready to fight a protracted nuclear war, and to decapitate the Soviet leadership. The document asserted that American forces must be able to "render ineffective the total Soviet (and Soviet-allied) military and political power structure."[25]

The Soviets were especially worried about the Pershing II medium-range missiles that the North Atlantic alliance was preparing to deploy in West Germany in 1983. The Kremlin feared these missiles had the range to reach Moscow, although the United States said they could not go that far.

In February 1982, Reed learned that a regular high-level nuclear weapons exercise was planned for the coming weeks. The purpose was to test the ability of the National Military Command Center, the war room at the Pentagon that would receive first word from Cheyenne Mountain of a nuclear attack, to support the president and secretary of defense in a crisis. Reed seized on the exercise as a chance to get Reagan involved, and to force an overhaul of the antiquated system. On February 27, Reed, Clark and a few other White House staffers explained the basics to Reagan—how he would get information in a crisis, how he would be protected personally and how he would send messages out to the forces. "We described the ways in which the start of nuclear hostilities might appear," Reed recalled, "the times available for response, and the forces at his disposal."

The formal exercise, code-named Ivy League, began on Monday March 1, 1982, in the White House Situation Room.[26] Former Secretary of State William P. Rogers played the role of president. The reason for a stand-in was to make sure the real president didn't tip his hand, revealing how he might react in an actual crisis. The exercise started with a threat briefing. Reed recalled, "An intelligence officer laid out the Soviet order of battle, then the warning systems began to report simulated missile launches and impact predictions. The minutes flew by until a screen in that cramped basement room began to show red dots on a map of the U.S.-simulated impacts. The first ones annihilated Washington, so this briefing was assumed to be taking place in some airborne command post over the central plains."

"Before the President could sip his coffee, the map was a sea of red," Reed said. "All the urban centers and military installations in the U.S. were gone. And then, while he looked on in stunned disbelief, he learned that the Soviet air force and the second round of missile launches were on their way in. For the next half hour more red dots wiped out the survivors and filled in the few holes in the sea of red."

Rogers sat at the head of the table, and Reagan sat next to him. Rogers went through the plan, asking questions about how to respond, what options were available and how much time. Reagan was gripping his coffee mug, surprised at the suddenness of the destruction.[27] "In less than an hour President Reagan had seen the United States of America disappear," Reed recalled, adding: "I have no doubt that on that Monday in March, Ronald Reagan came to understand exactly what a Soviet nuclear attack on the U.S. would be like."

That evening, Reagan and his advisers and several senior Pentagon officials gathered once again in the Situation Room. This time, there was no stand-in president. Reagan was given a full and careful briefing on the Single Integrated Operational Plan, the secret nuclear war plan. The briefing was about the precise steps Reagan would have to take. According to Reed, Reagan didn't know much about it, although he was first briefed on it after the 1980 election. "The SIOP briefing was as scary as the earlier presentation on the Soviet attack," Reed said. "It made clear to Reagan that with but a nod of his head all the glories of imperial Russia, all the hopes and dreams of the peasants in Ukraine, and all the pioneering settlements in Kazakhstan would vanish. Tens of millions of women and children who had done nothing to harm American citizens would be burned to a crisp."

At a third meeting, attended only by Clark and Reed, the president rehearsed the procedures by which he would select options from the war plan and insert the authenticator code from the card in his pocket. Then the exercise ended. But, Reed said, "I have no doubt that in Reagan's mind it was not over at all." The exercise "was something that really had happened to him. It focused his mind on the need for protection from those red dots."

In early 1982, Reagan embarked on a radical plan to confront the Soviet Union from within. In the years of Cold War containment, no administration before had tried to exploit the Soviet Union's internal tensions with a hope of toppling the regime or forcing it into dramatic change.[28] On February 5 Reagan ordered a study of U.S. national security objectives and the Cold War, the first of his presidency. Reed, who oversaw the interagency work that went into the study, said Reagan had decided to go beyond the assumptions of the past. Words like *détente*, *containment* and *mutual assured destruction* were "out," he said, and "the Cold War was no longer to be viewed as some permanent condition, to be accepted with the inevitability of the sun's rising and setting."[29] At the time, this was an audacious idea. John Lewis Gaddis, the Yale professor and Cold War historian, recalled that when Reagan took office, the Soviet Union seemed an unyielding presence. "It was not at all clear then that the Soviet economy was approaching bankruptcy, that Afghanistan would become Moscow's Vietnam, that the appearance of a Polish labor union called Solidarity portended the end of Communism in Eastern Europe, or that the U.S.S.R. would disappear in just over a decade," he said.[30]

The study led to a top-secret order, National Security Decision Directive 32, which Reed drafted. Titled "U.S. National Security Strategy," the directive incorporated the long-standing Cold War policy of containment. But the Reagan directive also went further, and raised a new, more ambitious goal: to force the Soviet Union "to bear the brunt of its economic shortcomings, and to encourage long-term liberalizing and nationalist tendencies within the Soviet Union and allied countries." Reagan wrote in his diary after a briefing on the Soviet economy, "They are in very bad shape and if we can cut off their credit they'll have to yell 'Uncle' or starve."[31]

The extreme delicacy of Reagan's directive was evident in the way Clark handled the paperwork. Reagan took the draft directive home with him to review on the evening of May 4, 1982. On May 5, at 9:30 A.M., in the presence of Reed and Clark, he signed it. But it was so explosive that Clark did not put it into the White House filing and distribution system until May 20. Clark apparently feared there would be interference from others in the cabinet.[32]

Reagan had struck a confrontational approach to the Soviet Union from the outset of his presidency, from his first words about lying and cheating, to his rearmament program, and with the CIA's covert actions in Afghanistan and Central America. The new directive accelerated this drive and made it the official policy of the United States.

On May 9, Reagan turned to nuclear arms control in a commencement address at his alma mater, Eureka College, marking the fiftieth anniversary of his own graduation. In one eloquent passage, Reagan talked about the horror of nuclear war and vowed to "ensure that the ultimate nightmare never occurs." He also used the address to make his first major proposal since taking office for controlling long-range nuclear weapons— including the ballistic missiles that were so fearsome and fast. He called for both the United States and Soviet Union to reduce their ballistic missile warheads to "equal levels, equal ceilings at least a third below the current levels," and then specified that "no more than half of those warheads be land-based." These words sounded equitable, but they were not. The Soviets had a much larger share of their warheads on land-based missiles, while the U.S. weapons were predominantly at sea and in the air. Reagan was often ignorant of such details, and nearly a year later, he confessed that he did not realize that the Soviet strategic force was heavily concentrated in land-based missiles. The Eureka speech underscored his passive management style, often more focused on performing than the details of governing.[33]

Brezhnev wrote back to Reagan that the Eureka College proposal "cannot but cause apprehension and even doubts as to the seriousness of the intentions of the U.S. side."

While reading Brezhnev's letter, Reagan jotted down in the margin, "He has to be kidding."

When Brezhnev complained that Reagan's proposals were one-sided, cutting deeper into Soviet weapons than American ones, Reagan wrote, "Because they have the most."

At the bottom of the letter, Reagan added, "He's a barrel of laughs."[34]

———

Across the United States, the nuclear freeze movement gained ground in 1982, inspired by antinuclear protests in Western Europe. Churches, universities and city councils in the United States were organizing to protest the nuclear arms race. A march from the United Nations to New York's Central Park on June 12 drew three-quarters of a million people. Jonathan Schell published *The Fate of the Earth*, a best seller which declared that nuclear weapons threatened human existence and called for their elimination. The American Catholic bishops drafted a Pastoral Letter on War and Peace expressing fear of the nuclear arms race. Reagan went to Europe in early June concerned that he was being depicted "as a shoot from the hip cowboy aching to pull out my nuclear six-shooter and bring on doomsday." Reagan recalled later that "I wanted to demonstrate that I wasn't flirting with doomsday." But he also used the trip to advance his confrontation with Moscow. A few days before departure, he wrote in his diary that he was fed up with those who advised him to go easy on the Soviets, so as not to upset the allies. "I finally said to h--l with it. It's time to tell them this is our chance to bring the Soviets into the real world and for them to take a stand with us—shut off credit, etc."[35]

One of the most secret but daring thrusts by Reagan came on June 7. He met Pope John Paul II for fifty minutes in the Vatican library. Both had survived assassination attempts the previous year. Their talk centered on Poland, the pope's birthplace, where the Soviet-backed regime had imposed martial law and outlawed the Solidarity movement. The journalist Carl Bernstein reported in 1992 that Reagan and the pope agreed on a plan to support Solidarity underground, smuggling in tons of equipment, including fax machines, printing presses, transmitters, telephones, shortwave radios, video cameras, photocopiers, telex machines, computers and word processors. The goal was to destabilize General Wojciech Jaruzelski, a pointed and direct challenge to the Kremlin.[36] The pope's authorized biographer, George Weigel, recalled that both Reagan and John Paul "believed that Communism was a moral evil, not simply wrongheaded economics. They were both confident of the capacity of free people to meet the Communist challenge. Both were convinced that, in the contest with communism, victory, not mere accommodation, was possible." Weigel recalled the pope later said the Vatican had maintained a distance from the U.S. covert campaign in Poland, but he confirms the close coordination on intelligence. Weigel quotes the pope saying that while Reagan decided the policy, "My position was that of a pastor, the Bishop of Rome, of one with responsibility for the Gospel, which certainly contains principles of the moral and social order and human rights . . . The Holy See's position, even in regard to my homeland, was guided by moral principle."[37]

On the day after seeing the pope, Reagan traveled to London for an open declaration of his policy, delivered to the British Parliament. He spoke in the Royal Gallery of the House of Lords, calling for a "crusade for freedom." His speech overflowed with optimism about the demise of totalitarianism and the triumph of individual endeavor over collectivism, and described anew his abhorrence of nuclear war. There was not much applause for these statements at the time. Britain was still fighting in the Falklands, which dominated the headlines, and the speech did not get the attention it deserved as one of the most important Reagan ever delivered.

The boldest part of the address was Reagan's assertion that Soviet communism would expire. "It may not be easy to see," Reagan declared, "but I believe we now live at a turning point.

> In an ironic sense, Karl Marx was right. We are witnessing today a great revolutionary crisis—a crisis where the demands of the economic order are colliding directly with those of the political order. But the crisis is happening not in the free, non-Marxist West, but in the home of Marxism-Leninism, the Soviet Union.
>
> It is the Soviet Union which runs against the tide of history by denying freedom and human dignity to its citizens. It is also in deep economic difficulty. The rate of growth in the Soviet gross national product has been steadily declining since the '50s and is less than half of what it was then. The dimensions of this failure are astounding: a country which employs one fifth of its population in agriculture is unable to feed its own people . . . Overcentralized, with little or no incentives, year after year, the Soviet system pours its best resource into the making of instruments of destruction.

Reagan closed the address with a prediction that the "march of freedom and democracy" would "leave Marxism-Leninism on the ash-heap of history as it has left other tyrannies which stifle the freedom and muzzle the self-expression of the people."

On a quick visit to Berlin two days later, Reagan drove to Checkpoint Charlie, the drab opening in the Berlin Wall. He stepped out of his limousine, surveying the thirteen-foot-high wall, stretching out in both directions, gray and pockmarked, East German guards looking back at him from their guardhouses. Of the wall, he said, "It's as ugly as the idea behind it."[38]

On June 25, Reagan recruited George Shultz, the chairman of Bechtel, to be his new secretary of state, replacing Al Haig. Shultz had been in Europe and recalled thinking about the state of the world as he flew home for his first meeting with Reagan.

"Relations between the superpowers were not simply bad," he recalled, "they were virtually non-existent."[39]

At the same time, Reed, the National Security Council official, was growing more worried about the lack of a serious plan for the president's command and control in the event of a nuclear alert. No one wanted to advertise it, but while the United States was spending billions to modernize strategic weapons, the means to command these forces was, in the words of one official, "the weakest link in the chain."[40] Furthermore, Reagan did not want to fly away in a helicopter if America was threatened with nuclear war. "I want to sit here in the office," he told Reed. Referring to Vice President Bush, the president added, "Getting into the helicopter is George's job."

On June 19, 1982, Reed got Reagan's approval for a new effort.[41] The result was a plan that, in the event of attack, would preserve the presidency as an institution, instead of the president himself. On September 14, Reagan signed a top-secret directive, titled "Enduring National Leadership."[42] Instead of running for the helicopter, the president would remain in the Oval Office, ready to make decisions, order retaliation or negotiate, while his potential successors would vanish to distant and safe locations. The overall effort was called "Continuity of Government," and it became a massive secret government program. Reed said the plan was to give a designated successor "the world's biggest laptop" from which he could continue to govern if the real president were killed. "You basically say, hmmm, things are getting dicey—vanish. The guy doesn't go into the basement, he vanishes with a communications set, and a linkage to all the other arms of government so that he can be the president." As Reed put it, "Our contribution was to survive the presidency, not the president."

After World War II, large underground installations were built outside of the capital. One was Mount Weather in Virginia's Blue Ridge Mountains, seventy miles from Washington, and another was at Raven Rock Mountain, six miles north of Camp David on the Pennsylvania-Maryland border. Both could serve as military command posts in the event of war. But the Reagan planners realized that a president might not make it to these bunkers in time. They devised a plan to dispatch three teams from Washington to separate, secure locations around the United States. Each team had to be prepared to proclaim a new American "president" and assume command of the country, according to author James Mann. If the Soviet Union was able to hit one team with a nuclear weapon, the next one would be ready. "This was not some abstract textbook plan, but was practiced in concrete, thorough and elaborate detail," Mann said. Each time a team left Washington, usually for several days of exercises, it brought one member of Reagan's cabinet who would serve as the successor "president." The entire program—intended to be carried out swiftly, under extreme stress and amid the potential chaos of impending nuclear war—was extra-legal and extra-constitutional. It established a process of presidential succession, Mann pointed out, that is nowhere in the Constitution or federal law. A secret agency, the National Program Office, spent hundreds of millions of dollars a year to keep the continuity-of-government program ready.[43]

On November 11, 1982, Reagan was awakened at 3:30 A.M. with word of Brezhnev's death in Moscow. Two days later, he visited the Soviet

Embassy to pay his respects, and wrote in the book of condolences, "I express my condolences to the family of President Brezhnev and the people of the Soviet Union. May both our peoples live jointly in peace on this planet. Ronald Reagan." In Moscow, Yuri Andropov was elevated to be Brezhnev's successor. His first comments reflected the dark mood of the Soviet leadership. "We know very well," Andropov said, "that peace cannot be obtained from the imperialists by begging for it. It can be upheld only by relying on the invincible might of the Soviet armed forces."[44]

When Reagan had warned of a "window of vulnerability" in 1980, the most worrisome threat came from Soviet land-based missiles, especially the new generation, the SS-17, SS-18 and SS-19. By 1982, the Soviet missile force had grown to fourteen hundred launchers carrying over five thousand warheads. The U.S. missile force had 1,047 launchers and about 2,150 warheads.[45] The fear was that in a first strike, just a portion of the Soviet force could wipe out nearly all the American missiles still sitting in their silos. Reagan struggled—as had Presidents Ford and Carter—to respond to the Soviet buildup with the development of a new-generation American super weapon, the MX, or Missile Experimental. The 100-ton MX would be three times more accurate than the Minuteman III, and carry ten warheads, each independently targetable. Under the original plan to deploy two hundred MX missiles, the Soviets would face the prospect of two thousand warheads raining down on their silos. That would begin to ease concerns about the window of vulnerability.

But the MX ran into political opposition, especially over complex schemes to base the missile so it would not be vulnerable to a Soviet first strike. Reagan scrapped Carter's idea of a vast racetrack. Reagan's administration tried three different ideas, and in 1982 came up with "Dense Pack," to base 100 MX missiles in super-hardened silos in a strip fourteen miles long and 1.5 miles wide in southwestern Wyoming. The thinking behind Dense Pack was that incoming Soviet missiles would commit "fratricide," exploding so close to each other as to neutralize the impact and leaving much of the MX force intact. In an effort to build political support, Reagan delivered a nationally televised appeal for the MX missile on November 22, 1982, renaming it "Peacekeeper." He acknowledged that people had become more fearful that the arms race was out of control. "Americans have become frightened and, let me say, fear of the unknown is entirely understandable," he said. Despite his appeal, on December 7, the House voted to reject funding for the MX, and the next day the chairman of the Joint Chiefs of Staff, Army General John W. Vessey Jr., revealed in Senate testimony that three of the five joint chiefs opposed the Dense Pack basing plan. The MX was in deep trouble, and the political deadlock worried U.S. military leaders.[46] The MX was their answer to preserving the land-based leg of the strategic triad, the land-sea-air combination at the backbone of deterrence. That summer, Admiral James D. Watkins, chief of naval operations, had concluded the United States was heading into a dangerous dead end, what he called a "strategic valley of death."[47] Robert Sims, a retired navy captain who was then a spokesman for the National Security Council, said the joint chiefs had concluded "this is probably the last missile this Congress is ever going to go for. They were frustrated. They weren't certain they would get the MX and they knew they couldn't get anything after MX. So they said, 'We've got to look beyond MX.' "[48]

It was in this environment of political deadlock that Reagan began to look over the horizon. What happened next was a blend of old imaginings and fresh pragmatism, animated by Reagan's faith in American high technology and a touch of science fiction. In the final months of 1982 and then early 1983, Reagan embraced a grand dream: to build a massive globe-straddling shield that would protect populations against ballistic missiles and make nuclear weapons "impotent and obsolete." The missile defense was never constructed. It was nothing more than a ghost invention. But the concept preoccupied and puzzled the Soviet Union for years to come. To understand Reagan, it is important to understand the origins of the dream.

As a boy, Reagan read fiction voraciously, including the science fiction of Edgar Rice Burroughs, among them *Princess of Mars*, a story with visions of polished domes over cities and impregnable walls. By the time he reached young adulthood, Reagan abhorred warfare. At twenty years old, he wrote a wrenching sketch of combat while at Eureka College in 1931. The piece was titled "Killed in Action" and described a

World War I trench battle scene.[49] Reagan was appalled at the power of the nuclear bombs on Hiroshima and Nagasaki. Appearing before a leftist audience in 1945, he gave a dramatic reading of a poem, "Set Your Clock at U235," by Norman Corwin, which referred ominously to "skies aboil with interlocking fury."[50]

To these ideas, Reagan added a philosophy of anti-communism, which he polished on the speaking circuit in the 1950s and 1960s. In one notable address, he outlined a strategy of pushing the Soviet economic system to collapse. It was the early 1960s, when Khrushchev and Kennedy were in power. Reagan fumed that Kennedy and the "liberal establishment of both parties" have been pursuing "a policy of accommodation with the Soviet Union."

"The theory goes something like this," Reagan said. "As time goes on the men in the Kremlin will come to realize that dogmatic communism is wrong. The Russian people will want a chicken in every pot, and decide some features of decadent capitalism make for more plentiful poultry, while their system hasn't even provided a pot. By a strange paradox us decadent capitalists will have discovered in the meantime that we can do without a few freedoms in order to enjoy government by an intellectual elite which obviously knows what is best for us. Then on some future happy day Ivan looks at Joe Yank, Joe looks at Ivan, we make bridge lamps out of all those old rockets, and discover the cold war just up and went away . . ."

Reagan said disdainfully: "Our foreign policy today is motivated by fear of the bomb, and is based on pure conjecture that maybe communism will mellow and recognize that our way is better." He wanted permanent competition with the Soviets, not "appeasement" and "accommodation."

"If we truly believe that our way of life is best aren't the Russians more likely to recognize that fact and modify their stand if we let their economy come unhinged so that contrast is apparent?" Reagan said. "Inhuman though it may sound, shouldn't we throw the whole burden of feeding the satellites on their slave masters who are having trouble feeding themselves?"[51]

Reagan often tore out articles from *Human Events*, a far right-wing newspaper, and other sources, stuffing them into his pockets for later use in speeches. He frequently got facts wrong, as journalists liked to point out. But aside from his carelessness with details, there was a method. Reagan borrowed disparate ideas, radical as well as mainstream, and fastened them together.

So it was with his vision of missile defense. The visit to NORAD in 1979 had rekindled the idea. Another prompt came from Daniel O. Graham, a retired army lieutenant general, a hawkish former head of the Defense Intelligence Agency, who was a member of the Committee on the Present Danger. Graham created a study group known as High Frontier, chaired by Karl R. Bendetsen, a former undersecretary of the army and retired chief executive of Champion International Corporation, a forest products company. Several of Reagan's wealthy kitchen cabinet friends backed the effort and provided money to carry out the study. Reagan met at the White House for nineteen minutes with Bendetsen and two other members on January 8, 1982. Bendetsen handed the president a memo claiming the Soviets had already surpassed the United States in military offensive power, and urging Reagan to start a crash effort to research strategic defenses.[52]

Yet another prompt came from Edward Teller, the theoretical physicist who founded the Lawrence Livermore Laboratory and played a key role in the development of the hydrogen bomb. As California governor, Reagan had visited Livermore for a two-hour briefing on missile defense in November 1967. Teller, a Hungarian who fled fascism in the 1930s, had long dreamed of a weapon that could shoot down ballistic missiles in flight. At the time Reagan visited Livermore, the Johnson administration had announced plans to build a very limited missile-defense system, Sentinel. Later, Nixon redirected it to a larger system called Safeguard, a two-layered defense built to protect 150 Minuteman missiles in North Dakota. Safeguard was taken down in 1976, having become essentially useless against a Soviet missile force carrying MIRVs, which enlarged the potential number of incoming warheads beyond the ability of Safeguard.

Nonetheless, Teller continued to nurse his dream of a weapon that could shoot down missiles. He claimed that nuclear weapons were about to make the leap to a "third generation," the first generation being atomic bombs and the second the hydrogen bomb. The third generation, he said, would be nuclear-pumped X-ray lasers in space that could destroy ballistic missiles.

Teller met with Reagan in the Oval Office for a half hour on September 14, 1982. Teller, then seventy-four years old, shook hands with Reagan. "Mr. President," he said. "Third generation, third generation." Reagan looked momentarily confused, as if Teller were preparing to talk about his relatives.[53] Then Teller explained his vision of an X-ray laser that he called Excalibur. An effective missile defense would turn mutual assured destruction on its head, Teller said—and lead to "assured survival" instead. Reagan asked him if an American antimissile system could really be made to work. "We have good evidence that it would," Teller replied. In his memoirs, Teller recalled feeling afterward that the meeting was not very successful; a National Security Council staffer "injected so many questions and caveats that I felt discouraged about the conference."[54] But Reagan had been listening. "He's pushing an exciting idea," Reagan wrote in his diary that night, "that nuclear weapons can be used in connection with Lasers to be non-destructive except as used to intercept and destroy enemy missiles far above the earth." Reagan may not have fully grasped that Teller was talking about setting off nuclear explosions in outer space.[55]

The MX political impasse weighed heavily on the Joint Chiefs of Staff when they filed into the White House Cabinet Room at 11 A.M. on December 22, 1982, to meet Reagan. At one point near the end of the meeting, Anderson said, Reagan asked the military leaders, "What if we began to move away from our total reliance on offense to deter a nuclear attack and moved toward a relatively greater reliance on defense?" After the chiefs went back to the Pentagon, Anderson said, one of them telephoned Clark, the national security adviser, and asked, "Did we just get instructions to take a hard look at missile defense?"

"Yes," Clark said, according to Anderson.[56]

Soon after, on January 3, 1983, the president announced creation of a bipartisan commission to review the entire strategic weapons program and to recommend alternative basing modes for the land-based missiles. This was an attempt to break the political stalemate.[57]

In the same weeks, Admiral James D. Watkins, the chief of naval operations, the top officer of the navy, accelerated his own search for answers. Watkins had no concrete suggestions for revising the structure of U.S. strategic forces, nor was he prepared to suggest a replacement for offensive nuclear deterrence, according to historian Donald R. Baucom.[58] But Watkins and the other chiefs were notified they would meet with Reagan again soon. The joint chiefs were also looking for a way out of the political deadlock.

On January 20, 1983, Watkins had lunch with a group of high-level advisers that included Teller, who described his hopes for the nuclear-pumped X-ray laser. Watkins found Teller intensely excited about the idea, predicting it could be ready in the next twenty years. Watkins did not favor the nuclear explosions in space, but he directed his staff to help him come up with a short, five-minute presentation he could make "which would offer a vision of strategic defense as a way out of the MX debate." On February 5, Watkins presented it to the other chiefs in Vessey's office and was surprised: the other chiefs went along, weary of the gridlock with Congress. They agreed the chairman, Vessey, would present it to the president.

The day of the meeting with Reagan, February 11, was cold and snowy; road conditions were so bad that the joint chiefs had to take four-wheel-drive vehicles to the White House. The five military men sat on one side of the table and Reagan on the other, flanked by Defense Secretary Caspar Weinberger and the White House deputy national security adviser, Robert C. McFarlane. The son of a Democratic congressman, McFarlane was a career marine officer who had worked in the White House in the Nixon-Ford years, and was extremely sensitive to the intermingling of military affairs and national politics. McFarlane recalled that he was brooding in these months about what seemed like a political dead end. The nuclear freeze movement was popular, the MX was in trouble in Congress and the Soviets were building land-based missiles while the United States was stalled. McFarlane began to think they needed a technological way out of the impasse, such as missile defense. In January, he privately lunched with Watkins.[59]

Weinberger did not share the enthusiasm of the chiefs for missile defense, and as he introduced the military leaders at the meeting, he told Reagan, "I don't agree with the chiefs, but you should hear them out."

Then Vessey, the chairman, gave a presentation about the problems of the land-sea-air triad caused by the congressional votes. But in the last part of his talk, Vessey suggested that it was time to take another look at strategic defenses. "We move the battle from our shores and skies," said the briefing paper from which Vessey read. "Thus, we are kept from the dangerous extremes of (a) threatening a preemptive strike, or (b) passively absorbing a Soviet first strike—we have found the middle ground." This was "more moral and therefore far more palatable to the America people . . ." Watkins then spoke and strongly supported Vessey.

McFarlane intervened to drive home the point: "Mr. President, this is very, very important." He added, "For 37 years we have relied on offensive deterrence based on the threat of nuclear counter-attack with surviving forces because there has been no alternative. But now for the first time in history what we are hearing here is that there might be another way which would enable you to defeat an attack by defending against it and over time relying less on nuclear weapons."

"Do you all feel that way?" Reagan asked. One by one, the president questioned the chiefs, and they responded affirmatively. The chiefs had not proposed a crash program to build missile defense; they had only proposed taking a harder look at it, given the political obstacles they had all confronted in Congress. But Watkins asked a rhetorical question that captured all Reagan had been thinking. "Would it not be better if we could develop a system that would protect, rather than avenge, our people?"

"Exactly," Reagan said, seizing a slogan. "Don't lose those words."

That evening, in his diary, Reagan wrote of the meeting with enthusiasm. He said that out of the session had come "a super idea. So far the only policy worldwide on nuclear weapons is to have a deterrent. What if we tell the world we want to protect our people, not avenge them; that we're going to embark on a program of research to come up with a defensive weapon that could make nuclear weapons obsolete? I would call upon the scientific community to volunteer in bringing such a thing about."[60]

The next day, Saturday, February 12, 1983, the capital was buried in one of the heaviest snowfalls of the century. The Reagans invited Shultz and his wife, O'Bie, to an informal dinner at the White House. Talkative and relaxed, Reagan offered Shultz a look at his "real feelings, his beliefs and desires," Shultz recalled. Reagan told Shultz of his abhorrence of mutual assured destruction. The Friday meeting with the joint chiefs was still on his mind. "How much better it would be, safer, more humane, the president felt, if we could defend ourselves against nuclear weapons," Shultz said. "Maybe there was a way, and if so, we should try to find it." What Shultz didn't grasp was that Reagan was going to do something about it—soon.

Reagan was also eager to test his own negotiating skills. Arms control talks with Moscow were deadlocked. In his diary, Reagan wrote, "Found I wish *I* could do the negotiating with the Soviets . . ." Shultz said Reagan "had never had a lengthy session with an important leader of a Communist country, and I could sense he would relish such an opportunity." Shultz, seeking a thaw in negotiations, offered to bring Dobrynin to the White House for a meeting the following Tuesday. Despite objections from aides, Reagan agreed.

When Dobrynin showed up at the State Department for a routine scheduled appointment with Shultz at 5 P.M., the secretary said he had a surprise: a meeting with the president. They left from the State Department basement garage, so as not to be noticed, and arrived at the East Gate of the White House, not usually used for official visitors, then went to Reagan's living quarters. They talked intensively over coffee for nearly two hours. "Sometimes we got pretty nose to nose," Reagan wrote.[61] They ranged over many topics, including Reagan's insistence that the Soviets sought world conquest, and Dobrynin's rebuttal that "we are not proclaiming a world crusade against capitalism." Reagan pressed Dobrynin to grant permission to emigrate for a group of Pentecostals who had taken refuge in the American Embassy almost five years earlier. Reagan promised not to embarrass the Kremlin or "crow" if the request was met. Dobrynin passed it on. "For the Soviet leadership, Reagan's request looked distinctly odd, even suspicious," Dobrynin recalled. "After almost three years in office and at his first meeting with the Soviet ambassador, the president actually raised only one concrete issue—the Pentecostals—as if it were the most important issue between us." But Jack F. Matlock Jr., who was then Soviet specialist on the National Security Council, reflected later that the Pentecostals were "a testing point in Reagan's mind."

"Ronald Reagan was intensely interested in the fate of individuals in trouble," Matlock said. "He wanted to do everything in his power to help them. His harsh judgment of the Soviet leaders was based, more than any other single factor, not on the ideology he talked about so much, but on his perception of the way they treated their own people."[62]

In early 1983, at the lunch hour in London, a man often drove his car to an underground garage at a British intelligence safe house on Connaught Street, pulled a plastic cover over it to conceal the diplomatic license tags and went upstairs. The man was Oleg Gordievsky, and he was the KGB's second-ranking official in the London office. He was also secretly an agent for the British and had been working with them for many years. Their relationship had begun in the 1970s, when Gordievsky was posted by the KGB to Denmark. Emotional, determined and realistic about the failures of the Soviet system, Gordievsky grew disillusioned with communism and fell in love with the West. "My feelings were immensely strong," he recalled, "because I was living and working on the frontier between the totalitarian world and the West, seeing both sides, and constantly angered by the contrast between the two.

"The totalitarian world was blinded by prejudice, poisoned by hatred, riddled by lies. It was ugly, yet pretending to be beautiful; it was stupid, without vision, and yet claiming to be fit to lead the way and pioneer a path to the future for the rest of mankind. Anything I could do to damage this monster, I gladly would."

When transferred back to Moscow from 1978 to 1982, he suspended his cooperation with the British, but resumed when he was posted to London in 1982. Gordievsky's handler there was a man named Jack, and a woman, Joan. Originally they planned to meet once a month, but Gordievsky had so much to tell them, the frequency intensified to once a week. At first they spread out a big lunch for him, but later, with time so short, Gordievsky suggested just sandwiches and a can of beer. Gordievsky was known by a cover name, Felix.[63]

Gordievsky said the British questioned him hard on political matters. He told them that by early 1983, the Soviet leaders were in a "a state of acute apprehension" about Reagan. The British generally didn't show emotion in response to his comments, Gordievsky recalled. They sat still, writing in their notepads. They asked simple questions. But one day they were alarmed. Gordievsky had told them something stunning: the First Chief Directorate of the KGB in Moscow had sent instructions to the London station to watch for signs of preparation for nuclear war. This was RYAN—the global intelligence effort started by Andropov in 1981 to collect intelligence on a possible nuclear first strike—which was intensifying in early 1983.

The British "were all under the impression of the prevailing American theory about the balance of the nuclear powers, and the balance will guarantee the peace," Gordievsky recalled. They were dumbfounded that "the Soviet machine, the Politburo, the Central Committee, the Ministry of Defense," were worried about "a sudden nuclear attack outside the context of a conflict. It was against all American theories, and also British."

In the face of these doubts, Gordievsky promised: "I will take a risk. I will put the documents in my pocket and come to the meeting, and you will make photocopies." Soon, he brought them thirteen pages plus a cover memorandum detailing how the intelligence collection was to be carried out. Gordievsky recalled later that his chief handler, Jack, "was astonished and could scarcely believe" the papers, "so crass were the Center's demands and so out of touch with the real world."

On February 17, a document marked *sovershenno sekretno,* or top secret, had arrived in London for the top KGB official, known as the resident. Arkady Guk was a boastful but ineffective resident who drank heavily. The importance of the document was indicated by the fact it was addressed to each resident by name, marked "strictly personal," and ordered to be kept in his special file. The title of the document was ominous: "Permanent operational assignment to uncover NATO preparations for a nuclear missile attack on the USSR."

"The February directive for Guk contained unintentional passages of deep black comedy, which revealed terrifying gaps in the Center's understanding of Western society in general and of Britain in particular," Gordievsky recalled. For example, Guk was told that an "important sign" of British preparations for nuclear war would probably be "increased purchases of blood and a rise in the price paid for it" at blood-donor centers. He was ordered to report immediately any changes in blood prices. The KGB failed to realize that British blood donors are unpaid. Likewise, the KGB headquarters had a "bizarre, conspiratorial image of the clerical and capitalist elements in the establishment, which, it believed, dominated British society," so Guk was ordered to watch for signs that the church and bankers had been given advance warning of nuclear war.

The February instructions contained a staggering workload, page after page of demands. The London residency was supposed to watch the number of cars and lighted windows at government and military installations, and report any changes. It had to identify routes, destinations and methods of evacuation of government officials and their families, and devise plans to monitor preparations for their departure.[64]

While the Soviets watched for signs of war preparation, Reagan decided to speak bluntly about his views of the Soviet system, as he had done in the British Parliament. He was worried about the expanding nuclear freeze movement. In early March 1983, he wrote in his diary, "I'm going to take our case to the people, only this time we are declassifying some of our reports on the Soviets and can tell the people a few frightening facts: We are still dangerously behind the Soviets and getting farther behind." In his memoirs, he noted that Nancy Reagan tried to persuade him to "lower the temperature of my rhetoric." He said he refused.[65]

On March 8, Reagan flew to Orlando, Florida, for a speech to a group of evangelical Christian ministers. In the address, Reagan described the Soviet Union as "the focus of evil in the modern world" and urged the ministers to reject the nuclear freeze. "So in your discussions of the nuclear freeze proposals," he said, "I urge you to beware the temptation of pride—the temptation of blithely declaring yourself above it all and label both sides equally at fault, to ignore the facts of history and the aggressive impulses of an evil empire, to simply call the arms race a giant misunderstanding and thereby remove yourself from the struggle between right and wrong and good and evil."

The words "evil empire" came to embody Reagan's view of the Soviet Union. He later recalled that he did it on purpose. "I made the 'Evil

Empire' speech and others like it with malice aforethought; I wanted to remind the Soviets we knew what they were up to."[66]

Enthusiastic about what he heard from the joint chiefs about missile defenses in February, Reagan decided to announce his idea. The commission he had appointed on the MX was due to report in April, but Reagan pushed his staff to come up with an announcement on missile defense even before the commission was finished. The president was to deliver a nationally televised address about the defense budget on March 23. Although McFarlane had reservations about moving so quickly, he began to draft an insert for the address that would launch a research effort toward strategic defense. McFarlane typed the first draft March 19. It was a major change from decades of American reliance on offensive forces. The president did not consult Congress, the allies, or even the cabinet until the last minute. Nor did he consult the commission on strategic forces, which was still hard at work. McFarlane said it was Reagan's idea to keep it under wraps to keep his potential opponents off-guard.[67]

The idea had materialized largely outside the official policy-making channels. Just weeks before, Reagan signed a new directive on overall strategy toward the Soviet Union in the wake of Brezhnev's death. The nine-page document covered all the key military, political and economic questions. Yet this key document, a foundation of American policy, included not a single word about missile defense.[68] Likewise, by this point, Reagan had submitted four separate defense budget requests to Congress; none made a priority of missile defense.[69] The joint chiefs were surprised; they had no idea that Reagan was going to act so quickly.[70] Shultz heard of the proposal only two days before Reagan went on national television, and had grave doubts about it.[71] Weinberger was opposed, and learned of it at the last minute, while traveling in Europe. Some of Reagan's aides learned only on the day of the speech. Reagan's diary shows that after Shultz objected on March 21, he rewrote the section on strategic defense; the next day he rewrote more of the speech— "much of it was to change bureaucratic into people talk."[72] Reagan said he was working on it "right down to deadline" on March 23. Among others, Teller had been invited as a guest to witness the broadcast, sitting on a folding chair in the East Room of the White House while Reagan spoke from the Oval Office.

In the address, Reagan described yet again the window of vulnerability. The Soviets, he said, "have enough accurate and powerful nuclear weapons to destroy virtually all of our missiles on the ground." Reagan said deterrence had worked—so far. He promised to keep negotiating with Moscow. But then Reagan said he wanted to offer another way.

In words he had written by hand into the text, and which echoed what Watkins had said in their meeting, Reagan declared, "Wouldn't it be better to save lives than to avenge them?" Reagan said that in recent months, he and his advisers and the Joint Chiefs of Staff "have underscored the necessity to break out of a future that relies solely on offensive retaliation for our security." Reagan added, "Over the course of these discussions, I have become more and more deeply convinced that the human spirit must be capable of rising above dealing with other nations and human beings by threatening their existence."[73]

"Let me share with you a vision of the future which offers hope. It is that we embark on a program to counter the awesome Soviet missile threat with measures that are defensive. Let us turn to the very strengths in technology that spawned our great industrial base, and that have given us the quality of life we enjoy today."

Reagan then asked: "What if free people could live secure in the knowledge that their security did not rest upon the threat of instant U.S. retaliation to deter a Soviet attack, that we could intercept and destroy strategic ballistic missiles before they reached our own soil or that of our allies?" He summoned "the scientific community in our country, those who gave us nuclear weapons, to turn their great talents now to the cause of mankind and world peace, to give us the means of rendering these nuclear weapons impotent and obsolete."

The president then announced that, as "an important first step," he was ordering up "a comprehensive and intensive effort to define a long-term research and development program to begin to achieve our ultimate goal of eliminating the threat posed by strategic nuclear missiles." He closed by saying, "My fellow Americans, tonight we're launching an effort which holds the promise of changing the course of human history. There will be risks, and results take time. But I believe we can do it. As we cross this threshold, I ask for your prayers and your support. Thank you. Good night. And God bless you."

Reagan's invention, his vision, was no more than these words. He had spent only twenty-nine minutes on television. Nothing he described about missile defense was in existence, no one in his government had formally proposed it, and whether anything so ambitious could be built was in serious doubt. But he had performed. "I made no optimistic forecasts—said it might take 20 yrs. or more but we had to do it," Reagan wrote in his diary after the address. "I felt good."

WAR GAMES

Four days after Reagan's speech, Andropov lashed out. He accused the United States of preparing a first-strike attack on the Soviet Union, and asserted that Reagan was "inventing new plans on how to unleash a nuclear war in the best way, with the hope of winning it." But Reagan's hazy vision was not Andropov's deepest fear. Rather, it was the looming deployment of the Pershing II missile in Europe, which the Kremlin thought could reach Moscow in six minutes. The Soviets felt events were turning against them.

Starting in the late 1970s, under Brezhnev, the Soviet Union had deployed the Pioneer missile, known in the West as the SS-20, with 243 missiles aimed at Western Europe and 108 targeted on Asia. The Pioneer had a maximum range of 3,100 miles, more than enough to hit Paris and London, but it was classified as medium or intermediate range, less than the big intercontinental ballistic missiles. The Russian historian Dmitri Volkogonov said "astronomical amounts of money were spent" on the Pioneer. But, he added, "The short-sighted Soviet strategists had handed the Americans a knife with which to cut the Soviet throat."[1] In response to the Pioneer deployments, NATO decided in 1979 to station 108 single-warhead Pershing II and 464 ground-launched cruise missiles in Europe, in range of the Soviet Union, as a counterweight while seeking to negotiate. Reagan had proposed in 1981 to eliminate this entire class of medium-range missiles, but the Soviets refused and negotiations went nowhere.[2]

By 1983, Andropov was consumed with the threat of the approaching Pershing II missile deployment, expected in West Germany in December. The Pershing II was feared for its accuracy and speed—the missile could fly at nearly Mach 8, greater than six thousand miles per hour, and carried high-precision guidance systems. The ground-launched cruise missile could fly under radars. These were the weapons that the Soviet leaders feared could lead to decapitation. The Pershing IIs were so worrisome that builders of the Moscow antiballistic missile system were urged to alter it to detect and intercept them.[3]

Andropov and the Politburo met on May 31, the day after Reagan and leaders of the Western industrial democracies had concluded a summit in Williamsburg, Virginia. Although they quarreled privately over the missiles, the Western leaders issued a statement calling on the Soviet Union to "contribute constructively" to the arms control talks.

The statement triggered irritation in the Politburo. According to minutes of the meeting, the aging Soviet leaders wrestled with how to stop the Pershing IIs and ground-launched cruise missiles. Not one word was spoken in the meeting specifically about Reagan's antimissile speech or his grand dream. The Politburo members sounded uncertain, without new ideas. Defense Minister Dmitri Ustinov insisted, "Everything that we are doing in relation to defense we should continue doing. All of the missiles that we've planned should be delivered, all of the airplanes put in those places where we've designated."[4]

Andropov's fear of the Pershing II missiles ran through his instructions to the KGB to keep watch for signs of a nuclear attack. The February document that Gordievsky had leaked to the British described, in an attachment, how advance knowledge of a possible attack would give the Kremlin precious minutes to ready retaliation. The instructions said, "For instance, noting the launching of strategic missiles from the continental part of the USA and taking into account the time required for determining the direction of their flight in fact leaves roughly 20 minutes reaction time. This period will be considerably curtailed after deployment of the 'Pershing 2' missile in the FRG [Federal Republic of Germany], for which the flying time to reach long-range targets in the Soviet Union is calculated at 4–6 minutes." The instructions added, "It is thus fully evident that the problem of uncovering the threat of RYAN must be dealt with without delay."[5]

Gordievsky said the KGB agents in London were constantly being urged by Moscow to spread propaganda against the Pershing II missiles. "We discussed it quite a lot in the meetings in the morning with the military attaché," he recalled. "He said, 'They fly from Britain to Moscow in eight minutes! And they penetrate underground bunkers.' Apart from that, there were a number of telegrams. *Develop a campaign! Develop a campaign! Use all your contacts in order to develop a propaganda campaign against the Pershings and the cruise missiles as well!* They were very worried." The Kremlin leaders "knew they would be the first to die, and didn't want to die."[6]

The Soviet quest for intelligence about a possible attack also extended to East Germany. The KGB assigned a major role in the operation to East German intelligence under Markus Wolf. By the early 1980s, Wolf said in his memoirs, "with the U.S. rearmament program and the advent of the aggressive Reagan administration, our Soviet partners had become obsessed with the danger of a nuclear missile attack . . ." His intelligence service "was ordered to uncover any Western plans for such a surprise attack, and we formed a special staff and situation center, as well as emergency command centers, to do this. The personnel had to undergo military training and participate in alarm drills. Like most intelligence people, I found these war games a burdensome waste of time, but these orders were no more open to discussion than other orders from above." In 1983, the East Germans completed five years of construction on project 17/5001, an underground bunker near the village of Prenden, outside of Berlin, to house the leadership in the event of nuclear war. The bunker was a sealed mini-town that would have protected four hundred people for two weeks after a nuclear attack.[7]

Of Andropov's fifteen months in power, half his time was spent in the hospital. During a working holiday in February 1983, Andropov's health suffered a sharp decline. "He had had kidney trouble all his life, and now it seemed his kidneys had given up altogether," wrote Volkogonov.[8] The Kremlin doctor, Yevgeny Chazov, recalled that Andropov's kidneys failed completely. Andropov's doctors decided to put him on an artificial kidney. A special ward was set up for treatment twice a week at a Moscow hospital.[9] Andropov started to have trouble walking. That summer, Andropov's colleagues had an elevator installed in the Lenin Mausoleum so he would not have to endure the stress of walking eleven and a half feet up the steps.

At the May 31 Politburo meeting, Andropov called for tougher propaganda against Reagan and the West. "We need to show more vividly and broadly the militaristic activities of the Reagan administration and countries of Western Europe supporting it," he said. Andropov also suggested that such propaganda would "mobilize the Soviet people" on the economic front. But at the same time, there was a downside.

"Certainly," he said, "we shouldn't frighten our people of war."

Ever since the previous autumn, as Andropov's paranoia deepened about a possible nuclear missile attack from Western Europe, there had also been ominous new threats on the Pacific horizon. The United States carried out extensive war games, realistic and provocative, off the Soviet coast in the Far East. In late September 1982, two U.S. aircraft carriers, the U.S.S. *Enterprise* and the U.S.S. *Midway*, sailed within three hundred miles of the Soviet Union's major Pacific Fleet base at Petropavlovsk-Kamchatsky. This was the only Soviet base in the Far East with direct access to the open ocean and home to the Delta-class ballistic missile–carrying submarines. The base was at the end of the sparsely populated Kamchatka Peninsula. After brushing by the peninsula, the American ships sailed south along the Kuril Islands, including four islands held by the Soviets since World War II but claimed by Japan, before entering the Sea of Japan on October 3. During the exercise, the *Enterprise* was the subject of extensive Soviet air, surface and underwater surveillance, according to the records of the commanding officer, R. J. Kelly.[10] Later in the autumn, while in the Indian Ocean, the *Enterprise* happened upon a Soviet aircraft carrier, the *Kiev*. The commander decided to use the ship to carry out "a practice long-range strike against the surface force." The *Enterprise* sent several aircraft on a mock attack against the Soviet ship. A navy intelligence official said the planes flew "seven hundred nautical miles toward the *Kiev*, made contact, visual contact, with the *Kiev* and then came back."[11]

In these war games, the *Enterprise*, a nuclear-powered supercarrier,

1,123 feet long, was the center of Battle Group Foxtrot, made up of a dozen ships, accompanied by bombers and refueling tankers in the skies and submarines below. They were secretly collecting electronic intelligence, watching how the Soviet forces responded, monitoring their communications and radar. The exercises reflected the "forward strategy" of the navy secretary, John Lehman, to confront the Soviets in waters close to home. Lehman said his "forward strategy" meant always "keeping the Soviets concerned with threats all around their periphery." Lehman sought to build a six-hundred-ship navy, including fifteen carrier battle groups, and the navy had been a major beneficiary of Reagan's rearmament program.[12]

Reagan had also secretly approved psychological operations against the Soviets. The point was to show the United States could deploy aircraft carrier battle groups close to sensitive Soviet military and industrial sites, apparently without being detected or challenged early on. In the Pacific, the U.S. forces charged toward Soviet bastions to see how they would react. As one intelligence official put it, they wanted to go up Ivan's nose.[13]

In the weeks after Reagan's speech on strategic defense, the United States ratcheted up the pressure. In April and May 1983, the U.S. Pacific Fleet conducted its largest exercises since World War II in the North Pacific, off the Kamchatka Peninsula. Forty ships, including three aircraft carrier battle groups, participated in a massive exercise code-named FLEETEX 83-1. The *Enterprise* left Japan on March 26 and was joined by the *Midway* four days later. They sailed north through the Sea of Japan and out the Tsugaru Strait together, meeting the U.S.S. *Coral Sea* on April 9. For about two weeks, all three carriers conducted a counterclockwise sweep of the northwestern Pacific Ocean. The exercise involved twenty-four-hour flight operations off the *Enterprise*, attempting to force the Soviets to react by turning on radars and scrambling aircraft to meet intruders. The exercise was explicitly aimed at rehearsal for antiaircraft and antisubmarine warfare, showing how the three-carrier battle group would support other forces in the event of all-out conflict. Watkins, chief of naval operations, later told Congress that such exercises were designed to show the Soviets that the United States would not be intimidated. "Our feeling is that an aggressive defense, if you will, characterized by forward movement, early deployment of forces, aggressiveness on the part of our ships, is the greatest deterrent we can have," he told the Senate Armed Services Committee in 1984. "And the Soviets really understand that. We can get their attention with that concept . . . We can make a difference. Kamchatka is a difficult peninsula. They have no railroads to it. They have to resupply it by air. It is a very important spot for them, and they are as naked as a jaybird there, and they know it."[14]

On April 4, the Americans flew up Ivan's nose. According to author Seymour M. Hersh, the *Midway* slipped away from the other carriers after shutting off all electronic equipment that could be monitored by the Soviets. The *Midway* steamed south toward the Kurils and the Soviets did not track it. A group of at least six navy planes from the *Midway* and the *Enterprise* violated Soviet borders by flying over the island of Zelyony in the Kuril archipelago, which stretches between Kamchatka and Japan. Hersh described it as "a flagrant and almost inevitable error, triggered by the aggressive fleet exercise and the demand of senior officers for secret maneuvers and surprise activities." The navy subsequently told the State Department the flyover was an accident. But the larger, more aggressive maneuvers were clearly a part of Lehman's deliberate strategy. The Soviets protested in a formal message to the American Embassy in Moscow on April 6.[15]

At the time of the flyover, Gennady Osipovich, an experienced pilot, was stationed at an air base, Sokol, on Sakhalin Island, a long, thin volcanic peninsula that stretches north-south along the other side of the Sea of Okhotsk from Kamchatka. Osipovich, a stolid man with thick black hair streaked gray, was deputy commander of a regiment. For thirteen years he had been flying the Su-15 interceptor, a fast but fuel-guzzling, twin-engine fighter designed in the 1960s to stop enemy bombers in an attack. The interceptors could reach twice the speed of sound but not remain aloft for long; they had limited auxiliary fuel tanks. Moreover, once airborne, pilots had to follow precise orders for their every move from the ground controllers. The job of the interceptors was to scramble fast and stop the intruder. There was little individual discretion or initiative.[16]

In the spring of 1983, Soviet pilots were haggard from the war of

nerves with the Americans. They were constantly chasing and responding to spy planes that buzzed the Soviet borders. Osipovich had flown
more than one thousand missions to intercept them. Unfortunately, the
navy F-14 flyover of Zelyony Island in April caught them by surprise.
According to Osipovich, the American planes zoomed in for fifteen minutes during a period when fog shrouded the island. The violation of the
Soviet border brought trouble for the pilots; an investigating commission
was established to probe how they failed. "After that incident," Osipovich
recalled, "a commission flew out to the regiment and gave us a dressing-
down. They really berated us." When the commission left, the commander told the pilots that if there was ever air combat over the Kurils,
they would not have enough fuel to get back home and would have to
eject from their planes somewhere over land to save their own lives. The
stress was enormous. "For several weeks we kept our guns at the ready
and waited," Osipovich said. The tension only abated some in the months
that followed. He was so stressed out, he said, that he was urged to take a
vacation.

After the three-carrier battle group exercise at the end of April, the
Enterprise steamed for San Francisco Bay. The carrier had been away
from a port for thirty days, the longest single stretch of the year. When
the navy studied the Soviet reactions to the exercise, they were puzzled.
While the Soviet air monitoring was heavy, the surface surveillance was
"nearly non-existent," Kelly noted in one report. Another commander
recalled that despite the unique nature of the exercise—the only one
using three carriers in decades—"the Soviet reaction was mild." The
Soviets sent their standard Bear and Badger aircraft by every other day.
"The primary adversary for all considered was the weather," the commander said, which included fog, low temperatures, high winds and low
visibility.

After the exercise, however, the Soviets learned much more about
what the Americans were doing. The ship had sent 57,000 messages and
received more than 243,000 during the year; encrypted electronic communications were the backbone of the navy's system of command. In the
communications room, some of the sensitive paper messages were quietly

spirited away by Jerry Whitworth, forty-four, the senior chief radioman, a lanky, bearded sailor who had served more than twenty years. He hid the messages in his locker. Whitworth had been spying for the Soviet Union since 1976 as part of a ring led by another navy veteran, John Walker. Whitworth met Walker between two and four times a year, giving him twenty-five to fifty rolls of undeveloped film from a small Minox camera carrying some of the most ultra-secret information of the Cold War, including the cryptographic keys that unlocked the navy's electronic communications around the world. Thus, for years, the Soviets had been reading the navy's mail.[17]

On this cruise, undetected, Whitworth stole paper copies of the messages about the fleet exercise. He also made tape recordings of his observations. "We've been playing a lot of games with the Russians while we were in the I.O.," or Indian Ocean, he dictated one night. "There was a Russian carrier, Kiev . . . It was down there and we played a lot of games with her. And now we're up in Japan and Korean area and we've been surveiled every day by the Russians. Every day. Flashed messages all over the place. They've been disrupting our flight operations too. Which pisses off the air devils. It kind of makes me laugh to tell you the truth . . ."[18] When the *Enterprise* returned to its home port in Alameda, California, on April 28, 1983, Whitworth possessed nearly the entire playbook of the exercise, including messages about the F-14 flyover. Whitworth had decided to end his espionage, but he had one more load of documents to share with Walker. Whitworth photographed about one-third of the messages he had taken from the ship with the Minox camera, but he deliberately put the lens out of focus so the film would be useless; he was holding back, perhaps as an insurance policy to get more money in the future. However, wanting to give Walker something valuable, he included the actual documents about the F-14 intrusion into Soviet airspace. They met June 3, 1983, and Whitworth gave Walker a large envelope filled with films and documents. Walker scribbled notes on the back of the envelope as Whitworth briefed him. "All messages . . . secret and one top secret," Walker wrote. He delivered the film and documents to the KGB wrapped in a plastic garbage bag at a dead drop on June 12, 1983.

At a time of profound worry about nuclear war, the Kremlin had been given an original, firsthand look at U.S. war games. Vitaly Yurchenko, a top KGB official who defected to the United States in 1985, told U.S. officials that the Walker spy ring was "the most important operation in the KGB's history," and had led the Soviets to decipher more than one million encrypted messages. Whitworth provided the Soviets with a full year of operational message traffic from the U.S.S. *Enterprise*, some of it top secret, and compromised the operations order for FLEETEX 83-1, a navy damage assessment later discovered.[19] Among other things, Whitworth compromised the plans for "primary, secondary and emergency communications" to be used by the president to link up with military forces. The damage assessment found the information given the Soviets by the Walker spy ring would "give the Soviets an ability to make almost real-time tactical decisions because they knew the true strength of our forces, their plans for combat, the details of our logistic support and the tactical doctrine under which our forces operated."[20]

Four days after Walker's drop of the plastic garbage bag of secrets to the KGB, Andropov told the Central Committee that there had been an "unprecedented sharpening of the struggle" between East and West. And Moscow KGB headquarters sent an alarmist telegram to residencies in the United States and other European capitals, stressing the high priority of the RYAN intelligence-gathering operation, and claiming the Reagan administration was continuing preparations for nuclear war.[21]

Reagan was buffeted by one crisis after another in the spring and summer of 1983. On April 18, the U.S. Embassy in Beirut was destroyed by a massive explosion, which killed seventeen U.S. citizens, including the senior CIA analyst for the Middle East, and forty others. When the caskets came home on Saturday, April 23, it was a traumatic moment for Reagan. "I was too choked up to speak," he recalled. Shultz was pushing for greater engagement with Moscow while Clark was resisting. At one point Clark proposed to Reagan that he take over the Soviet account. Shultz threatened to resign. Reagan was "visibly shaken," Shultz recalled, and asked him to stay on.

In early July, Reagan decided to write a personal letter to Andropov, perhaps another test of whether he could reach out on a human level to a Soviet leader. Reagan drafted his letter in longhand. He wrote,

Let me assure you the govt & the people of the United States are
dedicated to the cause of peace & the elimination of the nuclear
threat. It goes without saying that we seek relations with all
nations based on "mutual benefit and equality." Our record since
we were allies in W. W. II confirms that.

Mr. Sec General don't we have the means to achieve these goals
in the meetings we are presently holding in Geneva? If we can
agree on mutual, verifiable reductions in the number of nuclear
weapons we both hold could this not be a first step toward the
elimination of all such weapons? What a blessing this would be
for the people we both represent. You and I have the ability to
bring this about through our negotiations in the arms control
talks.

Scratched out by Reagan, after the last words of his longhand draft,
was another mention of his goal, "reduction talks that could lead to the
total elimination of all such weap." Had he sent the letter he wrote, it
would have been an extraordinary document, the first time any president
ever tabled such a sweeping proposal to eliminate all nuclear weapons.
But the letter never left the White House. The next morning, Reagan
gave the draft to Clark, who consulted experts on the White House staff.
They were astonished that Reagan would suggest wiping out all nuclear
weapons. On July 9, Clark wrote to Reagan suggesting that references to
nuclear weapons be taken out of the letter, so the Soviets wouldn't be
tempted to raise the ante at the stalled Geneva arms negotiations. Reagan
agreed, and sent a formulaic letter to Andropov on July 11.[22] Andropov
and Reagan exchanged two more letters that summer, but nothing came
of them. Andropov told a group of visiting U.S. senators that the Soviet
Union would ban anti-satellite weapons if the United States would do the
same, but the offer was brushed off by the Reagan administration. Reagan headed for his 688-acre ranch in the Santa Ynez mountains. After
August 12 he wrote nothing in his diary for the rest of the month. For
two weeks, he concentrated on building a wood fence at the ranch. It was
finished August 30, 1983.[23]

Kremlin fears of a nuclear missile attack were growing ever more intense. On August 4 in Moscow, Andropov insisted at a Politburo meeting that "maximum obstructions" be put in the way of the deployment of American missiles in Europe. "We must not waste time," he said.[24] On August 12, new instructions from Moscow landed at the London residency. These instructions, marked "top secret" and signed by KGB chairman Vladimir Kryuchkov, were an attempt to figure out if the intelligence services of the West were somehow helping prepare for a nuclear attack.

The sixteen-point checklist was largely a mirror image of the Soviet contingency plans for war with the West. The KGB agents in Bonn, Brussels, Copenhagen, London, Oslo, Paris, Rome and Lisbon were told to watch out for such things as "a sharp increase in the activity of all forms of intelligence," especially on the readiness of Warsaw Pact forces; possible positioning of agents to awaken sleeper cells in the East to "operate in wartime conditions"; closer coordination between the CIA and Western spy agencies; an "increase in the number of disinformation operations" against the Soviet Union and its allies; "secret infiltration of sabotage teams with nuclear, bacteriological and chemical weapons into the countries of the Warsaw Pact"; and expanding the network of sabotage-training schools and émigrés and setting up sabotage teams with them. The instructions strongly reflect the police state mentality of the KGB. They were looking for signs of what *they* would do in the event of war, such as imposing military censorship and postal censorship, or restricting people from using the telephone and telegraph.[25]

When Gordievsky returned to London on August 18, 1983, after a long break in Moscow, he resumed meeting his British handlers. Gordievsky said he immediately passed to the British the latest KGB instructions on nuclear missile attack.[26]

Gordievsky had once taken part in meetings at KGB headquarters about the RYAN operation, but he regarded the whole thing as foolish. "My reaction was very simple," he said. "I said it was just another folly." He found his KGB colleagues also took the demands from Moscow with skepticism. "They were not seriously worried about the risk of nuclear war," he recalled, "yet none wanted to lose face and credit at the Centre by contradicting the First Chief Directorate's assessment. The result was that RYAN created a vicious spiral of intelligence-gathering and evaluation, with foreign stations feeling obliged to report alarming information even if they did not believe it." Gordievsky and others fed the vicious spiral: they clipped newspapers and passed the clippings along as intelligence.

But when Gordievsky brought the cables from Moscow to the British, they took them quite seriously. They worried about the deep paranoia. They copied the documents and sent them to the CIA.

The elements were now in place for a superpower miscalculation. Andropov had urgently raised the prospect of a nuclear attack in the telegrams about the RYAN intelligence-gathering operation. Reagan had escalated the rhetoric with his "evil empire" speech and announced his futuristic Strategic Defense Initiative in March. Documents from the U.S.S. *Enterprise* about the navy's F-14 flyover and the provocative naval exercises off the Soviet coast in April were now in Soviet hands. The threatening Pershing II missiles were nearing deployment in Germany. The interceptor pilots on Sakhalin Island had already been burned once, and were warned not to let it happen again.

Into this maelstrom of suspicions and fears flew a large, stray bird.

3

WAR SCARE

When Korean Air Lines flight 007 left Anchorage at 4 A.M. local time on August 31, the crew was well familiar with the planned route across the Pacific, which came close to the airspace of the Soviet Union before crossing Japan and heading to Seoul. The pilot of the Boeing 747 was Captain Chun Byung-in, forty-five years old, a veteran of the Korean Air Force who had logged 6,619 hours flying jumbo jets, including eighty-three flights across the northern Pacific in the previous decade. His copilot, Son Dong-Hwin, forty-seven, had made the crossing fifty-two times. And the navigator, Kim Eui Dong, thirty-two, had made forty-four flights across the ocean. In addition to the flight crew, there were twenty cabin attendants, six Korean Air Lines employees transferring back to Seoul, and two hundred forty passengers, among them sixty-two Americans, including Representative Larry McDonald, an extreme right-wing Democrat from Georgia who was chairman of the John Birch Society.[1]

The flight plan was to take R20, the northernmost of five passenger airline routes across the ocean. These highways in the sky were fifty nautical miles wide and one thousand feet high. Route R20 was nearest the Soviet Union. The flight's departure from Anchorage was delayed to account for headwinds, and to bring the plane into Seoul's Kimpo International Airport at precisely 6 A.M. on September 1.

Soon after takeoff, an error was made. The autopilot was improperly set and the crew did not notice. Instead of picking up the Inertial Navigation System, which would have steered the plane on the proper route, the autopilot was instead set at a constant magnetic heading. This may have been caused by the failure to twist a knob one further position to the right.

The flight began to drift northward of Route R20. About 50 minutes into the flight, the crew of KAL 007 reported crossing Bethel, the first waypoint, at 31,000 feet. They didn't know it, but the plane was already 13.8 miles north of Bethel and outside the air route.

As they crossed the ocean, Chun and his crew saw nothing amiss, according to their communications with air traffic controllers. After Bethel, at the next waypoint, they reported all was well, but they were sixty-nine miles north of their route. At the next spot, they were 115 miles off course. After five hours in the air, they reported passing another waypoint, when in fact they were 184 miles north, heading directly toward the Kamchatka Peninsula of the Soviet Union. At one point the flight crew exchanged messages with another passenger plane that reported dramatically different winds—this should have alerted them they were off course. But it did not. The voices in the cockpit showed no alarm. They talked about mundane matters. One of the crew remarked, "Having a dull time . . ."

"I have heard there is currency exchange at our airport," one said.

"What kind of money?" answered another.

"Dollar to Korean money," came the response.

"Captain, sir, would you like to have a meal?" asked a cabin attendant. "What?"

"Meal, is it already time to eat?"

"Let's eat later."

Another plane flew in the sky that night, circling close to the Soviet Union, an RC-135 four-engine jet used for intelligence missions by the U.S. air force. The RC-135, a converted Boeing 707, was a familiar spy plane, known to the Soviets. Osipovich, the interceptor pilot, recalled he had chased it many times. The RC-135 flights were monitoring Soviet ballistic missile tests on an intelligence mission known as Cobra Ball. The plane was crammed with cameras and special windows down one side to photograph a Soviet missile warhead as it neared its target. The upper surface of the wing on the side of the cameras was painted black to avoid reflection. The RC-135s were based on Shemya Island, a remote rocky outcropping in Alaska's Aleutian Islands.

Soviet missile tests often aimed at the Kamchatka Peninsula. How the missiles landed could help the United States monitor arms control treaties and look for violations. The pictures could show how many MIRVs came from a missile and the final trajectory. The RC-135 planes flew in circular or figure-eight orbits with camera lenses aimed at the Soviet coastline, in anticipation of a test.

On the night of August 31, a missile test was expected and the RC-135 loitered in the sky, waiting. The RC-135 had a wingspan of 130 feet, compared to the 747, which stretched 195 feet and 10 inches across. Both had four engines, located under the wings. The 747 featured a prominent hump on the front of the fuselage for the upper passenger deck. As the RC-135 circled, at about 1 A.M., the larger 747 flew by, seventy-five miles south.

This was a critical moment of confusion for the Soviets. They had been tracking the RC-135 by radar. When the missile test didn't happen, the RC-135 headed back to its base on Shemya Island, but Soviet radar didn't see it turn and go home. On the way home, the RC-135 crossed the flight path of the 747 at one point. The Soviet radar somehow lost the RC-135 and picked up the 747, now unexpectedly heading directly for Kamchatka. The plane was given a number, 6065, and the track was annotated with an "81," which meant one unidentified aircraft.[2] It was the off-course Korean Air Lines flight, but the Soviet ground controllers thought it might be an RC-135. The radar tracked the plane as it approached Kamchatka, but not constantly. Radar contact was lost, and picked up again while the plane was about halfway over the peninsula.

When the airliner approached Kamchatka, Soviet air defense forces were slow to react. Controllers were groggy, commanders had to be awakened, and there were radar gaps. Transcripts of ground control conversations show they spotted the plane just as it flew over the air defense forces base at Yelizovo. They scrambled four interceptors. These planes zigzagged in the air for twenty minutes but could not find the jet, which was actually north of them, and they were forced to return to base. The plane flew on, straight out over the Sea of Okhotsk and toward Sakhalin Island, about seven hundred miles away. Radar contact was lost at 1:28 A.M.

The plane appeared again on Sakhalin Island radars at 2:36 A.M. Once again it was given the track number 6065. However, this time the annotation was changed to "91," which meant one military aircraft.

The command post duty officer at the Su-15 regiment at Sokol tried that night to use a long-distance phone operator to reach a radar station, Burevestnik. Located on Iturup Island in the Kurils, Burevestnik had sent a message saying that a target was approaching Sakhalin.[3]

"Good morning," the duty officer said to the long-distance operator, giving his secret code word, Oblako 535, and asking her to put through an urgent call to Burevestnik.

"Yes, high priority, urgent," he insisted when she asked for the code again.

"Very well, wait," she told him.

She asked for his phone number, then for his name. He gave it, and she didn't understand. He gave it again.

He impatiently clicked on the receiver.

Four minutes passed. "There is no answer," she replied.

"No answer?"

"No."

"But why?"

"I don't know why, there is no answer."

"Did Burevestnik not answer?"

"There was no answer at the number at Burevestnik."

"That cannot be . . ."

The operator asked, "What is that? What kind of organization is that?"

"It's a military organization," the duty officer said. "I need it now, operator, whatever it takes, but I must call there. It's a matter of national importance. I'm not joking."

"Just a minute. Just a minute."

Five minutes after he started making the call, with the airliner flying eight miles a minute toward Sakhalin, the command post duty officer asked, "Well, what [is happening], eh?"

"Calling, no answer."

Osipovich was napping at Sokol when the airliner approached Sakhalin. He was on duty, having taken the night shift so he could have the next day free; it was the first day of school and he was supposed to speak at his daughter's class on the theme of "peace." He ate and then dozed off watching television, and then awoke to check the guard.

Unexpectedly, the phone rang as he was getting dressed. He was ordered to rush out to the Su-15 and prepare for takeoff. The weather was poor as a frontal system rolled into Sakhalin. At 2:42 A.M. Osipovich ran to the plane and took off, flying toward the ocean, climbing to 26,000 feet. His call sign was "805." Soon another Su-15 was in the air, and then a MiG 23 from the Smirnykh air base, also on Sakhalin. Osipovich had no idea what was going on; perhaps it was an elaborate training mission?

Soviet radar had resumed tracking the airliner and given it the same number as before, 6065. The conversations among ground controllers show they thought it might be an RC-135, although some had doubts. Not once in all the ground conversations nor in the transmissions to the pilots did anyone mention a Boeing 747. They directed Osipovich minute by minute toward the target, and told him: "The target is military, upon violation of State border destroy the target. Arm the weapons."

Osipovich at first could only see the target as a dot, two or three centimeters. He had studied the RC-135s and knew the various Soviet civilian airliners, but he later recalled he had never studied the shape of foreign aircraft such as the Boeing 747.

A ground controller speculated, "If there are four jet trails, then it is an RC-135." The 747 also had four engines.

"805, can you determine the type?" Osipovich was asked by the ground controller.

"Unclear," he said.

Confusion reigned on the ground. No one wanted to be responsible for allowing another intrusion like the one on April 4. The Sokol command post duty officer, speaking to a superior, was asked if the incident was serious. "Yes, it looks serious, like on the fourth, but a bit worse," he replied.

At 3:09 A.M. an order was given to destroy the plane, but then rescinded. The Sokol command post duty officer wondered if the Americans would really fly a spy plane directly into Soviet airspace. They usually circled outside territorial waters. "Somehow this all looks very suspicious to me," he said. "I don't think the enemy is stupid, so . . . Can it be one of ours?"

He called another command center at Makarov, on the eastern tip of the island, to see what they knew about the plane's flight. "It hasn't bombed us yet," was the reply.

As he closed on the 747, about fifteen miles behind it, Osipovich saw his missile lock-on light illuminate. *Yolki palki!* he said, meaning "What the hell!" He turned off the missile lock-on and flew closer.

At 3:14 A.M., the commander of the Far East Military District was given a report. He was told Osipovich was ready to fire, but "he cannot identify it visually because it is still dark."

"We must find out, maybe it is some civilian craft or God knows who," said the commander.

"The pilot sees only a shadow," said another ground controller.

"He cannot determine the type?"

"No way . . . it is dark, dark."

Osipovich was now getting closer, 7.4 miles behind the airliner, which crossed Sakhalin. "It is flying with flashing lights," he reported. Shortly after 3:12, Osipovich tried to contact the airliner by the Soviet friend-or-foe electronic identification system, but there was no response because the plane was civilian and did not carry a compatible military responder.

The Soviet ground controllers asked Osipovich six times whether the airliner was showing navigation lights, on the assumption that a plane without them might be on a spy mission. At 3:18, Osipovich reported, "The air navigation light is on, the flashing light is on."

The Sokol ground controller told Osipovich to flash his lights briefly as a warning, and he did. Then, at 3:20, he was ordered to shoot a warning

burst from his cannons. He did. There was no response. Then, unexpectedly, the airliner seemed to slow.

Unbeknownst to the Soviets, at 3:20, air traffic controllers in Tokyo
had given Captain Chun permission to climb from 33,000 to 35,000 feet,
and this caused the airliner to slow. Cockpit voice recordings show Chun
and his crew never knew what was happening around them. Investigators later concluded that the change in altitude was seen by the Soviets as
an evasive action and reinforced the suspicion that it was an RC-135 spy
plane.

"805, open fire on the target," ground control instructed Osipovich.
But at that moment, Osipovich said he couldn't because he had almost
overtaken the airliner. "Well, it should have been earlier, where do I go
now, I am already abeam of the target?" This statement that he was
"abeam," or alongside the airliner, suggested, to some, in retrospect, that
Osipovich should have seen the 747's distinctive hump. But investigators
said radar tracks show that Osipovich was consistently behind the 747,
and to the right. Osipovich also recalled later that his own plane "began to
rock" at this point; he did not say why.[4]

In the next radio transmission, Osipovich said, "Now, I have fallen
back from the target." He added the airliner was at 33,000 feet and on his
left. He does not indicate his own altitude—above or below the 747. If he
was below the 747, it would have been harder to see the plane's hump.

At 3:24, Osipovich's radio crackled with orders: "805, approach target
and destroy target!" The airliner was just slipping away from the
Sakhalin coast. Osipovich recalled later it was at this point he had finally
gotten a look at the plane, and he realized suddenly it was larger than an
RC-135.

"Soon I could see it with my own eyes," he recalled. "It was a big plane,
and I thought it was a military-cargo plane because it had a flickering
flash-light. There were no passenger plane routes, and there had been no
occasions of any passenger planes losing their way . . . I could see it was a
large plane. It wasn't a fighter plane, but either a reconnaissance plane or
a cargo plane."[5]

He fired. At 3:25, two R98 air-to-air missiles streaked ahead, one a
heat-seeker that locked onto a source of infrared radiation such as the
engine exhaust, the other guided by a radar. They each carried forty-four
pounds of high explosive designed to produce fourteen hundred steel

fragments. The heat-seeking missile was fired first and took thirty seconds to reach the airliner. Osipovich saw an explosion.

"The target is destroyed," he reported.

He broke away to the right. He was low on fuel, and landed back on the island.

The explosion tore a hole in the plane five feet wide and the cabin pressure plunged. "What's happened?" asked a surprised cockpit crew member at the blast. The missile had sliced through the control cables and the Boeing pitched up, pressing people into their seats. The engines remained on, but the speed brakes—the flaps that usually try to stop the plane on the runway—extended from the wing, the landing gear came down and passengers were told to put out cigarettes and prepare for an emergency descent. "Put the mask over your nose and mouth and adjust the headband," the passengers were told on the public address system. The first officer radioed to Tokyo, barely able to speak through his mask. "Rapid compressions descend to one zero thousand."

At 33,850 feet, the plane leveled off and rolled, falling toward the sea at five thousand feet per minute. All were lost.

Reagan was awakened in the middle of the night at Rancho del Cielo by a phone call from Clark about the missing plane. Nancy Reagan recalled her husband's first reaction was, "My God, have they gone mad?" and "What the hell are they thinking of?"[6]

Like punch-drunk fighters, the United States and Soviet Union began swinging wildly at each other in a melee of anger, indignation and error.

An ultra-secret Japanese-U.S. listening post had monitored some of the radio transmissions from Osipovich to his ground controller. A portion of these intercepts were sent to Washington, translated and transcribed. The initial transcript showed Osipovich was guided to the intruder and included his declaration "the target is destroyed." In Washington, these words seemed to shout from the page. They showed the Soviets were guilty of wanton murder. But the transcript was only a piece of raw intelligence, far from the whole story. It did not reflect the intense confusion among the Soviet ground controllers, nor the presence of the RC-135. All through the event, the Soviet military had never made a careful effort at identification, inflamed as they were by their fears of another flyover like the one in April. This climate of chaos and misjudgment on the ground was not reflected in the printed transcript of the radio intercept. The catastrophe was a window into the weaknesses of the Soviet military system, an example of how imprecise judgments and poor equipment could go terribly awry, but that was not what Reagan and his men saw in the transcript.

In Washington, according to Seymour Hersh, a small group of analysts with air force intelligence realized within hours that the Soviets did not deliberately shoot down the airliner. These analysts prepared a secret presentation, using color slides, showing how the Cobra Ball mission may have led to the confusion. But in the heat of the moment, the presentation got little attention. The presentation made it to the White House twenty-three hours later, and even then made no impact amid the emotions of the day. As Hersh put it, the presentation "crash-landed."[7]

Shultz seized on the transcript of Osipovich to make a point. He wanted to go public with it. Shultz recalled in his memoir that, after an intense debate, he persuaded the CIA to let him use the transcript, even though it had come from ultra-secret intelligence gathering in Japan. For reasons that are unknown, Shultz did not wait until more complete information or transcripts could be examined. He apparently did not see the air force presentation.

On September 1, at 10:45 A.M., Shultz appeared before reporters at the State Department. In remarks delivered in a cold fury, he declared, "The United States reacts with revulsion to this attack. Loss of life appears to be heavy. We can see no excuse whatsoever for this appalling act." Shultz claimed the Soviets had tracked the airliner for two and a half hours, when in fact they had difficulty following it and lost track. He claimed unambiguously that the pilot was in position "with a visual contact with the aircraft, so that with the eye you could inspect the aircraft and see what it was you were looking at." With the press conference, Shultz launched what became a major U.S. rhetorical offensive against the Soviets, accusing them of deliberately killing the people on the airliner.

Reagan cut short his vacation and returned to Washington. He invited congressional leaders to the White House on Sunday for what became a dramatic, closed-door meeting. Reagan played an eight-minute tape, a fragment of the intercept in which Osipovich said "the target is destroyed." Senator Strom Thurmond, the South Carolina Republican, said Reagan should seek revenge by expelling 269 KGB agents from the United States.

The briefing also led to the first public acknowledgment of the presence of the RC-135. The House Majority leader, Jim Wright, D-Texas, told reporters after the briefing that he heard the spy plane mentioned on the tape. White House officials rushed to say Wright was wrong, but they acknowledged, in the process of the denials, that there had been an RC-135 in the skies the day of the shoot down, which made for front-page stories the next day in the *Washington Post* and the *New York Times*. On Monday morning, September 5, Shultz asked for a full intelligence briefing about the spy plane, which he got at 8 A.M. Later that day, the State Department sent a four-page background paper to all American embassies that claimed the RC-135 could not have caused the shoot down. "The Soviets traced the Korean aircraft and the U.S. aircraft separately and knew there were two aircraft in the area, so we do not believe this was a case of mistaken identity," the background paper said. It was wrong, like so much else said about the incident.[8]

Reagan recalled he wanted to spend the day by the White House pool. Instead, he sat in his damp trunks on a towel in his study rewriting a speech on a legal pad. The Osipovich tape had become a powerful propaganda bludgeon. Reagan said he rewrote the speech to "give my unvarnished opinion of the barbarous act." During the address that evening, Reagan played part of the tape. "The 747 has a unique silhouette unlike any other plane in the world," Reagan said. "There is no way a pilot could mistake this for anything other than a civilian airliner." Reagan acknowledged there was an RC-135 in the air that night, but dismissed the possibility of confusion over it, saying it was back on the ground "for an hour when the murderous attack took place . . ."

Reagan added, "And make no mistake about it—this attack was not just against ourselves or the Republic of Korea. This was the Soviet Union against the world and the moral precepts which guide human relations among people everywhere. It was an act of barbarism, born of a society which wantonly disregards individual rights and the value of human life and seeks constantly to expand and dominate other nations."

While Reagan and Shultz were shaking their fists at Soviet brutality, within two days U.S. intelligence agencies had concluded the whole thing was probably an accident. At the CIA, Douglas MacEachin, deputy director of the operations center, had been on vacation in Boston, and rushed back to headquarters. Using large maps, he and others spent hours charting every known fact about the stray airliner, including the radio intercepts. Within a few hours, MacEachin recalled, they decided the Soviets had made a mistake, the same conclusion air force intelligence had also reached.[9] In fact, the Soviets had not been sure what the airliner was, and had probably confused it with the American RC-135.[10]

The deputy CIA director, Robert M. Gates, later disclosed that this conclusion had been mentioned in the President's Daily Brief—his morning intelligence report—on September 2. But some officials, he said, "just got carried away."[11]

Andropov learned of the shoot down early on the morning of September 1, while he was still at home on the outskirts of Moscow. He was told that a U.S. warplane had been downed over Sakhalin. He knew the rules: if a foreign plane was detected in Soviet airspace, the intruder must be given a visual or radio signal ordering it to land on Soviet territory, and if ignored, the nearest border command post could order the plane destroyed. It had happened before. According to Dmitri Volkogonov, the historian, the practice was always to deny a shoot down: "It came down by itself."[12]

At the Kremlin later in the day, just before a Politburo meeting, Defense Minister Dmitri Ustinov approached Andropov and told him, "A plane's been shot down. It turned out not to be American, but South Korean, and a civil aircraft, at that. We'll find out more and report in greater detail." Volkogonov said Andropov clearly had other sources of information, and replied, "Fine. But I was told there'd been a spy plane above Kamchatka. I'm flying to the Crimea later today after the meeting. I must have a rest and get some treatment. As for the plane, you sort it out."

Dobrynin recalled seeing Andropov that day. Looking haggard and worried, Andropov ordered Dobrynin to rush back to Washington to deal with the crisis, saying, "Our military made a gross blunder by shooting down the airliner and it probably will take us a long time to get out of this mess." Andropov called the generals "blockheads" who didn't understand the implications of what they had done. Dobrynin said Andropov "sincerely believed," along with the military, that the plane had made an intrusion into Soviet airspace as part of an intelligence mission to check Soviet radars. But even that, Andropov said, was no excuse for shooting it down instead of forcing it to land.[13]

After the three-hour Politburo meeting, Andropov went on holiday to Simferopol, where he stayed at one of several luxury villas reserved for the Soviet leadership. Accompanying him was not only his usual staff, but an entire medical facility. At this point, Konstantin Chernenko, long a weak acolyte of Brezhnev, took over running the Politburo meetings. Andropov never returned to the table.

Dobrynin said Andropov "was actually ready to admit the mistake publicly" but was talked out of it by Ustinov. The Soviet reaction was to lie about the events and cover up. The first bulletin from TASS on September 1 did not even mention the plane being shot down:

> An unidentified plane entered the air space of the Soviet Union over the Kamchatka peninsula from the direction of the Pacific Ocean and then for the second time violated the air space of the USSR over Sakhalin Island on the night from August 31 to September 1. The plane did not have navigation lights, did not respond to queries and did not enter into contact with the dispatcher service.
>
> Fighters of the anti-aircraft defense, which were sent aloft toward the intruder plane, tried to give it assistance in directing it to the nearest airfield. But the intruder plane did not react to the signals and warnings from the Soviet fighters and continued its flight in the direction of the Sea of Japan.[14]

The Politburo met again September 2, with Chernenko presiding. The Soviet rulers circled the wagons, and worried about whether to even admit the plane had been shot down. Foreign Minister Andrei Gromyko said he favored admitting that shots were fired but to insist "that we acted legally." Defense Minister Ustinov then told the group, "I can assure the Politburo that our pilots acted in complete conformity with the requirements of their military duty, and everything stated in the submitted memorandum is the honest truth. Our actions were absolutely correct, insofar as the American-built South Korean aircraft flew 500 kilometers into our territory. It is extremely difficult to distinguish this aircraft by its shape from a reconnaissance aircraft. Soviet military pilots are prohibited from firing on passenger aircraft. But in this situation their actions were perfectly justified because in accordance with international regulations the aircraft was issued with several notices to land at our airfield."

Mikhail Gorbachev, a younger, rising star among the aging Politburo members, said, "The aircraft remained above our territory for a long time. If it went off track, the Americans could have notified us, but they didn't."

Ustinov claimed the Korean aircraft had no lights. After firing warning shots, he said, the Soviet pilot "informed the ground that the aircraft was a combat one and had to be taken down."

Gromyko: "We cannot deny that our plane opened fire."

Viktor Grishin, then the Moscow party first secretary, asked, "And what was the South Korean pilot saying?"

Ustinov: "We didn't hear anything."

The KGB chief, Viktor Chebrikov, described the sea search, in waters up to 328 feet deep; Soviet ships and Japanese fishing vessels were in the area. "This means they can raise the plane's black box, and we can too," said Gromyko. The others worried aloud that evidence of a deliberate shoot down would come out. Gorbachev asked whether the Americans had detected the actual firing of the Soviet interceptor.

Chebrikov: "No, they haven't. But I want to re-emphasize that our actions were entirely legitimate."

Nikolai Tikhonov, a Brezhnev man and chairman of the Council of Ministers, said, "If we acted correctly, legitimately, then we have to say straight out that we shot this plane down."

Gromyko: "We have to say that shots were fired. This should be said straightforwardly, to prevent our adversary from accusing us of deception."

Grishin: "First of all, I'd like to underline that we should declare openly that the plane was shot down." But he wanted the information dribbled out: first announce an investigation, and only later admit "the plane was fired at."

Gorbachev: "First of all, I want to say that I'm convinced that our actions were lawful. Given that the aircraft remained above the Soviet territory for about two hours, it is difficult to presume that this was not a pre-planned action. We must show precisely in our statements that this was a crude violation of international conventions. We must not wait it out silently at the moment, we must take up an offensive position. While confirming the existing version, we must develop it further, by saying that we are seriously investigating the current situation."[15]

In fact, the "existing version" was a lie. Gorbachev, said Volkogonov, "was concerned only about finding a way to extricate the leadership from an unseemly affair, and to shift the blame onto the other side." The Politburo session reveals "a shocking lack of remorse—or even the expression of remorse—for the 269 victims of the crash," Volkogonov added. "The tragic case of the South Korean Boeing became a pathetic symbol of Andropov's rule."[16]

Moscow did not acknowledge the shoot down until September 6 and delayed an official explanation for three more days. The obfuscation only deepened suspicions in the West. By silence and untruths, the Soviets seemed to be behaving exactly as Reagan said, like an evil empire. They claimed the plane was carrying out a CIA mission, deliberately flying into sovereign Soviet airspace as a trick. Then, with disclosure of the RC-135 in Washington, the Soviet propaganda machine went into overdrive. On September 5, *Pravda*, the party newspaper, said Reagan's statements were "permeated with frenzied hatred and malice towards the Soviet state and socialism . . ."[17] On September 9, at a two-hour press conference, Marshal Nikolai Ogarkov asserted that the regional air defense unit had identified the intruding plane as an RC-135. He insisted that the plane was on an intelligence mission.

"The way this incident was dealt with throws light on the mentality of the Soviet leadership," Volkogonov wrote later. "Andropov himself was silent on the issue for more than a month . . . The plane's 'black box' had been found and brought to the surface. It was decided to say nothing of this, either to the world's press or to Seoul, and Soviet ships were kept in the area for another two weeks to give the impression that the fruitless search was still going on."

Reagan's speeches bristled with outrage and revulsion, but in actions, he did not ratchet up confrontation. He rejected Thurmond's demand to expel the KGB agents.[18] Shultz won Reagan's approval to go ahead with a scheduled meeting in Madrid with Foreign Minister Andrei Gromyko. Reagan did not want to close off nuclear arms control talks over the shoot down. "If anything," Reagan recalled in his memoirs, "the KAL incident demonstrated how close the world had come to the precipice and how much we needed nuclear arms control: If, as some people speculated, the Soviet pilots simply mistook the airliner for a military plane, what kind of imagination did it take to think of a Soviet military man with his finger close to a nuclear push button making an even more tragic mistake?"

In Madrid, Shultz raised the airliner in his private, first meeting with Gromyko. "The atmosphere was tense," he recalled. "He was totally unresponsive." A larger meeting that followed was "brutally confrontational," Shultz recalled. "At one point, Gromyko stood up and picked up his papers as though to leave. I think he half-expected me to urge him to sit down. On the contrary, I got up to escort him out of the room. He then sat down, and I sat down." Gromyko said it was the most tense meeting he had ever conducted in dealing with fourteen secretaries of state. Shultz said "the meeting became so outrageous and pointless that we just ended it."

The United States had attempted to embarrass Soviet officials and challenge their lies. The Soviet leaders saw the episode as a provocation, a deliberate attempt to trip them up.

On September 27 in Washington, Gates, the deputy CIA director, delivered to Shultz an intelligence assessment that said relations between the United States and the Soviet Union were as "pervasively bleak" as at any time since Stalin's death in 1953. Gates said the Soviet leaders feared Reagan's administration more than any in history.[19]

On September 28, Andropov issued one of the harshest condemnations ever of the United States, published in both *Pravda* and *Izvestia* and read on the evening television news broadcast. The Reagan administration, Andropov said, is on "a militarist course that represents a serious threat to peace . . . if anyone had any illusion about the possibility of an evolution for the better in the policy of the present administration, recent events had dispelled them completely." According to Dobrynin, the word "completely" was emphasized. "The Soviet leadership had collectively arrived at the conclusion that any agreement with Reagan was impossible," Dobrynin said.

A few days later, in the Crimea, Andropov went for a short walk in the park; lightly dressed, he became tired, and took a breather on a granite bench in the shade. His body became thoroughly chilled, and he soon began shivering uncontrollably. Volkogonov quotes Chazov, who treated Andropov for several years, as saying that when he examined Andropov in the morning, he found widespread inflammation, requiring surgery. "The operation was successful, but his body was so drained of strength that the post-operative wound would not heal . . . His condition gradually worsened, his weakness increased, he again stopped trying to walk, but still the wound would not heal . . . Andropov began to realize that he was not going to get any better."[20] Chazov wrote in his memoir, "On Sept. 30, 1983 the final countdown on Andropov's health began."[21]

In London, three "flash" telegrams from Moscow arrived in quick succession on Oleg Gordievsky's desk on September 4. The first claimed that the shoot down was being used by the United States to whip up anti-Soviet hysteria. The second and third suggested that the airliner was on an intelligence mission. This story was later embroidered with bogus reports that the captain of the plane had boasted of his spying and shown friends the intelligence gear on the plane. None of the telegrams actually acknowledged that a Soviet interceptor had shot down the airliner. Two more telegrams followed a few days later urging KGB agents to plant stories that the Americans and Japanese were in full radio contact with the plane. At one point, it was falsely claimed, the pilot had radioed, "We're going over Kamchatka."[22] Gordievsky recalled, "So manifestly absurd was this lie that many of my colleagues in the Residency were dismayed by the damage done to the Soviet Union's international reputation."[23]

Guk, the KGB chief in London, had been in Moscow during the shoot down, and he later took Gordievsky aside and told him that eight of the eleven Soviet air defense radar stations on Kamchatka and Sakhalin were not functioning properly.[24] Dobrynin heard a similar account from Ustinov in Moscow.[25]

The telegrams from Moscow were passed to the British. Geoffrey Howe, then foreign secretary, recalled that one "very powerful impression quite quickly built up in my mind: the Soviet leadership really did believe the bulk of their own propaganda. They did have a genuine fear that 'the West' was plotting their overthrow—and might, just might, go to any lengths to achieve it."[26] Prime Minister Margaret Thatcher, who also knew of the reports, visited Washington and met with Reagan on September 29. She found him worried that "the Russians seemed paranoid about their own security" and asking, "did they really feel threatened by the West or were they merely trying to keep the offensive edge?"[27]

"We had entered a dangerous phase," Thatcher recalled years later. "Both Ronald Reagan and I were aware of it." Her reaction was to reach out to specialists. "What we in the West had to do was to learn as much as we could about the people and the system which confronted us," she wrote in her memoirs, "and then to have as much contact with those living under that system as was compatible with our continued security." In the days after the shoot down, Thatcher arranged a seminar at her country home, Chequers, with Soviet experts. A list of possible participants came to her from the Foreign Office. "This is NOT the way I want it," she wrote on the list, demanding "some people who have really studied Russia—the Russian mind—and who have had some experience of living there."[28]

Eight scholars were invited, including Professor Archie Brown of St. Antony's College, Oxford University. Brown submitted a paper on the Soviet political system and power structure. At the seminar, Brown identified Gorbachev, the youngest member of the Politburo, as a likely future general secretary, saying he was "the best-educated member of the Politburo and probably the most open-minded," and "the most hopeful choice from the point of view both of Soviet citizens and the outside world."[29]

Thatcher was listening.

In the autumn, a wave of fear about nuclear war—a war scare—gripped both the Soviet Union and the United States. Soviet attacks on Reagan reached a fever pitch. According to Elizabeth Teague, a Soviet domestic affairs analyst at Radio Liberty, Soviet media in the years before 1983 had refrained from making personally abusive remarks about Western leaders. But after the Korean airliner was shot down, Soviet press portrayals of Reagan reached an unusually bitter level. "Reagan was described as dangerous, lying, unscrupulous, hypocritical, even criminal," Teague recalled, "as a man who 'scraped his fortune together' by speculating in real estate while governor of California, defrauding the Internal Revenue Service, collaborating with the Mafia, and switching his political allegiances whenever it served his personal advantage."

"In short," she added, "he was portrayed as a man who could not be trusted and with whom it was impossible to do business."[30]

The Soviet media repeated over and over again that the danger of nuclear war was higher than at any time since World War II. This may have been an outgrowth of Andropov's demand in the spring for tougher propaganda to oppose the looming Pershing II deployments, and to rally the Soviet people for still more sacrifice at home. A documentary film shown on national television portrayed the United States as a dangerous "militaristic" power bent on world domination. The forty-five-minute film contrasted scenes of U.S. nuclear explosions and various U.S. missiles with scenes of war victims, Soviet war memorials and declarations of Moscow's peaceful intentions. An internal letter to Communist Party members warned of a deterioration of relations with the United States over the next several years.[31] Svetlana Savranskaya, a university student in Moscow that autumn, recalled the war scare was very real, especially for older people. They were taken into shelters once a week for civil defense lessons. They were told they would have only eleven minutes to find shelter before the bombs would arrive from

Europe. "I remember going home and looking up at a map and asking, how long would it take the missiles to hit from the United States?" she said.[32]

At Camp David for Columbus Day weekend, Reagan watched the videotape of a forthcoming made-for-television movie, *The Day After,* about a fictional nuclear attack on a typical American city, Lawrence, Kansas. The film, starring Jason Robards, was scheduled for nationwide broadcast in November. It portrayed a bucolic and happy Midwestern town, the home of the University of Kansas, with boys playing football in the late-afternoon sun, a farm family preparing for a wedding, games of horseshoes in the backyard—the America that Reagan had long idealized. Then, in the background, news reports carry word of a crisis in Europe that blossoms into a full-scale nuclear alert. "We are not talking Hiroshima here," says one character in the film. "Hiroshima was peanuts." The crisis quickly spins out of control and European cities are hit with tactical nuclear weapons. Then, all eyes of Lawrence, Kansas, are cast skyward as America's Minuteman missiles are fired at the Soviet Union from nearby military bases. The B-52s take off. Within thirty minutes, the Soviet missiles arrive and hit Lawrence, setting off the blast, heat and fallout of nuclear explosions. In the second half of the film, Robards, who plays a hospital surgeon, roams through a devastated landscape. He turns pale and his hair falls out from the radiation. He sees sickness, disease and lawlessness. When Robards urges a pregnant woman who survived the blast to have hope, she retorts, "Hope for what? We knew the score, we knew all about bombs and fallout, we knew this could happen for forty years and no one was interested! Tell me about hope!"

The film highlighted many of the fears of the day about nuclear war. It called attention to nuclear winter—that after a nuclear blast, the climate would change and snow would fall in summer.

In his diary, Reagan wrote:

Columbus Day. In the morning at Camp D. I ran the tape of the movie ABC is running on the air November 20. It's called "The Day After." It has Lawrence, Kansas wiped out in a nuclear war with Russia. It is powerfully done, all $7 mil. worth. It's very effective & left me greatly depressed. So far they haven't sold any of the 25 spot ads scheduled & I can see why . . . My own reaction was one of our having to do all we can to have a deterrent & to see there is never a nuclear war.[33]

Edmund Morris, Reagan's official biographer, said the film left Reagan "dazed" and produced the only admission he could find in Reagan's papers that he was "greatly depressed." Four days later, he said, Reagan was "still fighting off the depression caused by *The Day After*."[34]

The next day, October 11, Jack F. Matlock Jr., the top Soviet specialist on the National Security Council, met a Soviet journalist he had known in earlier tours in Moscow. Sergei Vishnevsky, fifty-three, was a veteran columnist from *Pravda*. Matlock assumed he was bringing a message of some kind—Vishnevsky had good party connections and perhaps KGB connections too. "His trade is propaganda and his specialty the U.S.," Matlock wrote in a memo afterward. They met at a cafeteria across the street from the Old Executive Office Building.

Vishnevsky was direct, so intent on making his points that he did not stop to debate Matlock on anything. His message: "The state of U.S.-Soviet relations has deteriorated to a dangerous point. Many in the Soviet public are asking if war is imminent." Vishnevsky told Matlock he was worried that Andropov's September 28 statement "was virtually unprecedented and is a reflection of the leadership's current frustration . . ." While the point of the Andropov warning was, in part, to prepare the Soviet people for belt-tightening, Vishnevsky said "the leadership is convinced that the Reagan administration is out to bring their system down and will give no quarter; therefore they have no choice but to hunker down and fight back."[35]

Vishnevsky said the Soviet economy was "a total mess, and getting worse," and the leadership needed to lessen tensions to concentrate on economic matters. Moreover, he said, the Soviet leadership saw Reagan as increasingly successful, with the American economy improving and Reagan likely to run for reelection in 1984. The Soviets now realized they could not stop the Pershing II missile deployments, due in two months. Nor did they know what to do about these events; they were locked into their positions by their own truculence. Reagan's reaction to the Korean airliner incident left Soviet leaders "wallowing in the mud."

In October, Reagan was given a fresh briefing on the ultra-secret SIOP, the Single Integrated Operational Plan, the procedures for nuclear war. This was the sixth generation of the war plan, known as SIOP-6, which took effect on October 1, 1983. The new plan reflected the desire to give the president options to fight a protracted nuclear war.[36] Reagan wrote in his diary: "A most sobering experience with Cap W and Gen. Vessey in the Situation room, a briefing on our complete plan in the event of a nuclear attack."[37]

Reflecting later in his memoirs, Reagan recalled, "In several ways, the sequence of events described in the briefings paralleled those in the ABC movie. Yet there were still some people at the Pentagon who claimed a nuclear war was 'winnable.' I thought they were crazy. Worse, it appeared there were also Soviet generals who thought in terms of winning a nuclear war."[38]

Shultz told Reagan in mid-October all the recent arms control proposals had gone nowhere. "If things get hotter and hotter, and arms control remains an issue," Reagan told Shultz, "maybe I should go see Andropov and propose eliminating all nuclear weapons." Shultz reminded him that it wasn't likely Andropov would give up nuclear weapons. "Without an arsenal of nuclear weapons, the Soviets are not a superpower."

Very suddenly, Reagan was swept into one of the most chaotic and uncertain periods of his presidency. Clark resigned as his national security adviser, to become secretary of the interior. Reagan promoted Clark's deputy, Robert C. McFarlane, who had spent most of his time in previous months negotiating the Lebanon crisis. Across Western Europe, antinuclear rallies brought 2 million people into the streets to protest against the plan to deploy the Pershing II missiles.

On October 23, at 6 A.M., a lone driver steered a yellow Mercedes truck through the parking lot at the U.S. marine encampment at the Beirut International Airport in Lebanon. The truck, laden with the equivalent of over twelve thousand pounds of TNT, blew up and killed 241 U.S. military personnel and injured one hundred others, the most severe military death toll in Reagan's presidency.[39] When McFarlane woke him in the middle of the night with the news, Reagan's face turned ashen. McFarlane recalled "he looked like a man, a 72-year-old man, who had just received a blow to the chest. All the air seemed to go out of him. 'How could this happen?' he asked disbelievingly. 'How bad is it? Who did it?' " Then, on October 25, Reagan ordered U.S. forces to invade the tiny Caribbean island of Grenada, on grounds that American students on the island were imperiled by instability following a coup.[40] On October 27, Reagan led the memorial service at Camp Lejeune, North Carolina, for the Marines lost in Beirut. He was, McFarlane recalled, "clearly heart-broken."

In the middle of it all, a secret written analysis from the CIA was brought to Reagan. It contained Gordievsky's reports about RYAN, the KGB intelligence-gathering operation for signs of a nuclear attack. McFarlane recalled it reached Reagan in October, amid the Grenada and Lebanon crises, although the precise date is not known.[41] Thatcher knew of the Gordievsky information as well, and may have told Reagan about it on her visit a few weeks earlier.

McFarlane was at first unsure whether the Soviets were as paranoid as it seemed in the Gordievsky materials. "It raised questions in my mind about whether this apparent paranoia was real, or a propaganda scheme being fed to Western Europe to drive a wedge between us and the allies," McFarlane said. The presence of Foreign Minister Gromyko in the Polit-buro, he felt, was reassuring—with four decades' experience in dealing with the United States, surely Gromyko knew that the United States would not launch nuclear war. But McFarlane said he grew more worried when separate intelligence reporting from Prague and Budapest showed that people were "genuinely alarmed about this." McFarlane said on reading the material "I thought it was plausible that it was the real deal."[42]

On October 28, Matlock sent a short, worried note to McFarlane. The American ambassador in Moscow, Arthur Hartman, had reported on an unsettling meeting with Gromyko. "The major thrust of Gromyko's comment," Matlock said, "was that the Soviet leaders are convinced that the Reagan administration does not accept their legitimacy, and that therefore it is not prepared to negotiate seriously with the USSR, but is actually dedicated to bringing down the system." While Matlock noted there may be a "large self-serving element" in this argument, "I believe it is an argument used in policy debates among the Soviet leadership."[43]

Driven by fears of a nuclear attack, in November 1983, construction crews were furiously excavating a deep underground bunker in the Ural Mountains for a new top-secret command center for the Strategic Rocket Forces. When complete, from this sheltered burrow the commanders could manage a nuclear war. Twice a day, explosions echoed through the mountains as construction crews burrowed deeper and deeper into the granite. Tunnels already reached thousands of feet into the rock, but the project was far from complete. Water filled the dim passageways. The first electronic gear was being brought into the depths of the cavity for tests. The code name for the bunker was *Grot*, or grotto in Russian. The excavation at Grot, and the extensive underground bunkers for the leadership in Moscow, provoked worry and puzzlement among the American intelligence analysts. They wondered, what were the Soviets thinking? That they could survive and fight a nuclear war?

Soviet paranoia reached a zenith at the time of a planned NATO exercise in Europe scheduled for November 2–11. The exercise, Able Archer '83, was designed to practice the procedures for a full-scale simulated release of nuclear weapons in a European conflict. The Soviets had long feared that training exercises could be used as a disguise for a real attack; their own war plans envisioned the same deception. According to Gordievsky, two features of Able Archer '83 caused particular alarm in Moscow. First, the procedures and message formats for the shift from conventional to nuclear war were quite different from those on previous exercises. Second, this time, imaginary NATO forces were to be moved through all the alert phases, from normal readiness to general alert. The exercise may have been misinterpreted by the KGB as a real alert.[44]

In the original scenario of the Able Archer exercise, high-level officials were to play a role, including the secretary of defense and chairman of the Joint Chiefs of Staff, with cameo appearances by Reagan and Bush. If the

Soviets knew this, it may have contributed to their anxiety. McFarlane recalled that on learning in general of Soviet worry about the exercise, he asked the president to pull out, and Reagan agreed. "It wasn't a hard sell," McFarlane recalled. Reagan felt puzzlement and anxiety.[45]

On November 5, Moscow sent to the KGB residency in London a detailed checklist of possible preparations for a surprise nuclear attack. By this time, the KGB had established a "Strategic Section" in the Moscow headquarters for evaluating intelligence from RYAN.[46] The telegram from Moscow warned that once a decision for a surprise nuclear attack had been made, there would only be seven to ten days before it was carried out, and that a close eye should be kept on British government officials and their workplaces for hints that something was underway.

On the night of November 8 or 9, flash telegrams were sent from Moscow to Soviet intelligence agents across Western Europe, mistakenly reporting an alert at U.S. bases. The telegrams gave two possible reasons for the U.S. alert. One was concern for the security of U.S. bases in the wake of the Beirut bombing. That might be normal and understandable. The other reason, Gordievsky said, was that it marked the start of preparations for a nuclear first strike. The Soviet intelligence agents were to report urgently on the reasons for the American "alert" and other indicators of war planning.[47]

During the Able Archer exercise, Gates recalled, there was considerable activity by Soviet and other Warsaw Pact military forces. Soviet military weather broadcasts were taken off the air during the exercise. Units of the Soviet Fourth Air Army had gone to increased readiness, and all combat flight operations were suspended from November 4 to 10, he added. Tensions eased slightly at the end of the exercise on November 11.

The superpowers did not trip a wire into war, but Reagan crossed a bridge of his own. For the first time, uncharacteristically introspective, he acknowledged that the Soviet leaders may have harbored true fears of attack. He wrote in his diary November 18: "I feel the Soviets are so defense minded, so paranoid about being attacked that without being in any way soft on them, we ought to tell them no one here has any intention of doing anything like that. What the h--l have they got that anyone would want. George is going on ABC right after its nuclear bomb film Sunday night. It shows why we must keep on doing what we're doing."

When ABC broadcast the film *The Day After* on November 20, it drew 100 million viewers, then the second-largest audience in history for a single television program. The first Pershing II missiles were deployed in Germany three days later, on November 23. The Soviets then walked out of the arms control talks in Geneva.

Reagan later recalled in his memoir, "Three years had taught me something surprising about the Russians: Many people at the top of the Soviet hierarchy were genuinely afraid of America and Americans. Perhaps this shouldn't have surprised me, but it did. In fact, I had difficulty accepting my own conclusion at first." He said he felt "it must be clear to anyone" that Americans were a moral people who, since the founding of the nation, "had always used our power only as a force for good in the world." After World War II, the United States rebuilt the economies of its former enemies, he noted.

"During my first years in Washington," Reagan said, "I think many of us in the administration took it for granted that the Russians, like ourselves, considered it unthinkable that the United States would launch a first strike against them. But the more experience I had with the Soviet leaders and other heads of state who knew them, the more I began to realize that many Soviet officials feared us not only as adversaries but as potential aggressors who might hurl nuclear weapons at them in a first strike; because of this, and perhaps because of a sense of insecurity and paranoia with roots reaching back to the invasions of Russia by Napoleon and Hitler, they had aimed a huge arsenal of nuclear weapons at us."

In December, Reagan was thinking anew about his dream of eliminating all nuclear weapons. "This is his instinct and his belief," Shultz told his aides at the State Department. "The president has noticed that no one pays any attention to him in spite of the fact that he speaks about this idea publicly and privately."[48] Shultz promised Reagan to study the idea. Reagan told Shultz on December 17 that he wanted to make a major speech about his desire to get rid of nuclear weapons. Reagan drafted a letter to

Andropov on December 19 saying "we do not seek to challenge the security of the Soviet Union and its people."[49]

When Reagan spoke on January 16, 1984, many journalists assumed that it was the opening salvo of his reelection campaign. Reagan felt rejuvenated by his success with the Pershing II missiles, and he had decided to run for a second term. But this was not the only motivation. Reagan had read the top-secret reports from Gordievsky about Soviet war fears; he had personally rehearsed the nuclear war plan, the SIOP; and he had experienced a real crisis with the Soviets over the KAL shoot down. His own desire to eliminate nuclear weapons burned even more intensely than before. "Something has happened to the man," a White House official said of Reagan.[50]

In the address, which was broadcast also to Europe, Reagan did not refer once to an "evil empire" nor to communism falling into the dustbin of history. He did not talk about changing the Soviet system from within. Rather, he declared, "We do not threaten the Soviet Union." He stressed "dialogue," "constructive cooperation" and "peaceful competition." And he declared, "My dream is to see the day when nuclear weapons will be banished from the face of the Earth."

Then Reagan delivered the ending he had written himself:

Just suppose with me for a moment that an Ivan and an Anya could find themselves, oh, say, in a waiting room or sharing a shelter from the rain or a storm with a Jim and Sally. And there was no language barrier to keep them from getting acquainted.

Would they then debate the differences between their respective governments? Or would they find themselves comparing notes about their children and what each other did for a living? Before they parted company, they would probably have touched on ambitions and hobbies and what they wanted for the children and problems of making ends meet.

And as they went their separate ways, maybe Anya would be saying to Ivan: "Wasn't she nice. She also teaches music." And Jim would be telling Sally what Ivan did or didn't like about his boss. They might even have decided they were all going to get together for dinner some evening soon.

Above all they would have proven that people don't make wars.

People want to raise their children in a world without fear and
without war. They want to have some of the good things over and
above bare subsistence that make life worth living. They want to
work at some craft, trade or profession that gives them satisfaction
and a sense of worth. Their common interests cross all borders.

If the Soviet Government wants peace, then there will be peace.
Together we can strengthen peace, reduce the level of arms and
know in doing so that we have helped fulfill the hopes and dreams
of those we represent and, indeed, of people everywhere. Let us
begin now.

Reagan had turned a corner. He was ready for the next act in the great
drama.

Two days after Reagan's speech, Gordievsky got another telegram from
Moscow on the RYAN intelligence-gathering operation. The spymasters
were still searching for signs of nuclear war. The KGB believed that clues
to a possible nuclear first strike could be found by looking at banks, post
offices and slaughterhouses. The KGB urged its agents to check out
"mass slaughter of cattle and putting meat into long cold storage."

On January 2, 1984, Fritz W. Ermarth became the national intelligence
officer for the Soviet Union, taking up a key position attempting to synthesize intelligence from many different sources to guide policy makers.
Ermarth had previously worked on Soviet issues at the CIA and the
White House National Security Council. Almost immediately, the
deputy director for intelligence, Gates, gave him an urgent assignment: to
write a Special National Intelligence Estimate on the tense situation with
the Soviet Union. "The issue was terribly important," Gates recalled.
"Had the United States come close to a nuclear crisis the preceding fall
and not even known it? Was the Soviet leadership so out of touch that
they really believed a preemptive attack was a real possibility? Had there
nearly been a terrible miscalculation?"

Ermarth's report was finished May 18, 1984. He concluded that the war scare did *not* lead the Soviets to fear nuclear attack. Ermarth said "we knew a lot about Soviet and Warsaw Pact war plans. In effect, we had many of their military cook books."[51] Thus, he said, the United States could easily compare what the Soviets were doing with the real war plans. "This permitted us to judge confidently the difference between when they might be brewing up for a real military confrontation or, as one wag put it, just rattling their pots and pans." He concluded they were just rattling the pots and pans.

Ermarth's report declared at the outset: "We believe strongly that Soviet actions are not inspired by, and Soviet leaders do not perceive, a genuine danger of imminent conflict or confrontation with the United States."[52] Ermarth said that there were plenty of other explanations for Soviet behavior, including a propaganda campaign. The Kremlin may have been seeking ways to raise anxiety about the deployment of the Pershing II missiles and encourage the antinuclear movement in Western Europe. Ermarth took note of the heightened Soviet alerts during Able Archer, but he didn't think much of them. His conclusion was: "Although the Soviet reaction was somewhat greater than usual, by confining heightened readiness to selected air units, Moscow clearly revealed that it did not in fact think there was a possibility at this time of a NATO attack."[53]

Ermarth knew about Gordievsky's materials and RYAN. But there were a few important secrets that Ermarth did not know. When he wrote the estimate, he did not know the full extent of the provocative, top-secret U.S. naval exercises in the Pacific Ocean during the spring of 1983. The navy had not told him.[54] "I tried to find out more about it but was unsuccessful," he said. "I think some sort of junior people in the office of naval intelligence just said, 'You've got to understand, we've got some stuff going on here we can't talk about.'" Among other things, Ermarth said he didn't know about the F-14 flyover.[55]

Gates concluded that, in retrospect, the CIA had missed an important turning point. "After going through the experience at the time, then through the post-mortems, and now through the documents, I don't think the Soviets were crying wolf," he wrote in his memoirs. He added of the Soviets, "They may not have believed a NATO attack was imminent in November 1983, but they did seem to believe that the situation was very dangerous. And U.S. intelligence had failed to grasp the true extent of their anxiety."[56] Although it remains classified, a review of the CIA's performance on the war scare came to a similar conclusion in 1990.[57]

The war scare was real.

THE GERM NIGHTMARE

In the years after World War II, the United States built an offensive biological weapons program, but it was abandoned by President Nixon in 1969. Three years later, the Biological and Toxin Weapons Convention was signed, prohibiting the development and production of germs for warfare. The Soviet Union joined, and became one of the three nations to serve as a depository, or custodian, of the agreement. Then, in an audacious turn, Soviet leaders secretly broke their obligations and expanded research on offensive biological weapons through a vast and concealed complex of laboratories and institutes disguised as civilian facilities. Codes were created to keep track of all the pathogens and branches of the program. Bacteria were identified by the prefix "L." Plague was L1, tularemia L2, brucellosis L3 and anthrax L4. Viruses were "N." Smallpox was N1, Ebola was N2, Marburg N3 and so on. One part of the effort was called "Project Factor," which was shortened from "virulence factor," or "pathogenic factor." Virulence is the relative ability of a pathogen to cause death. Boosting the virulence of bacteria and viruses made them more lethal. In parallel to Factor, other projects included "Bonfire," a quest to create a new generation of germs that would resist antibiotics, while "Flute" attempted to fashion mind-altering compounds—a weapon that might cause a whole army to go crazy.[1] "Ferment" was the name given to a drive for genetic engineering. Chemical weapons were "Foliant." Separately, Soviet scientists were also working on germs to wither crops and devastate livestock. This was called "Ecology."[2]

In 1984, Sergei Popov was among the scientists at the forefront of Project Factor. He was thirty-four years old then, a bright young researcher, tall with a genial manner and a slightly reedy, pleasant voice. Popov worked in a scientific institute at Koltsovo, a small town amid the forests in western Siberia, twenty miles southeast of a much larger city, Novosibirsk. In the long Siberian winters, he rose when it was still dark and cold to get his young daughter ready for school. He described himself as a disciplined person, not strongly against authority, vaguely hopeful in the future of socialism, but aware of its deficiencies. He and his wife, Taissia, were both dedicated scientists, drawn to Koltsovo in 1976 by the promise of greater opportunity for research. Around him, the institute was growing quickly. Dozens of new buildings were being constructed, and modern equipment installed. The formal name was the Institute of Molecular Biology, and it later became known as Vector. In microbiology, "vector" refers to a vehicle for transferring fragments of DNA from one cell to another.[3]

Popov had grown up nearby, in Novosibirsk, and earned his university degrees there. Just south of the city was Akademgorodok, or Academic Town, which included the Novosibirsk State University and dozens of prestigious institutes for research into physics, mathematics, geology, chemistry and social sciences. With wide boulevards lined with pine, birch, spruce and cedar, and a large concentration of scientists, Akademgorodok was known for relatively free thinking in contrast to the stifling, ideological atmosphere of Moscow. The son of railway engineers, Popov was attracted to mathematics as a youth. His parents recognized his talent and sent him to a special school with an advanced program in mathematics. As a teenager, he was interested in chemistry. When he was sixteen years old, he decided to design his own rocket fuel. He succeeded, but it exploded in his face and eyes; a piece of glass got stuck in his eyelid, and acid burned him from head to toe. His scars eventually healed.

In 1984, at Vector, Popov was head of the chemistry department. He was facing a new challenge, the dawn of an ambitious quest to penetrate the secrets of the smallpox virus. Four years earlier, the World Health Organization had triumphantly announced that smallpox had been eradicated from the face of the Earth. Millions of lives had been spared. But what the outside world didn't know was that smallpox was an object of experimentation for the scientists at Vector.

The virus, which had killed more people than all the wars of the twentieth century combined, was itself to be made into a weapon of war.

When he started at Koltsovo, Popov was dreaming only about science. He and his wife were lured by the promises of Lev Sandakhchiev, a compact, intense, chain-smoking scientist of Armenian descent who was assistant scientific director of Vector, and became director in 1979. Sandakhchiev was known to many as a restless hustler for his fledgling institution. He offered them salaries that were 50 percent higher than elsewhere. He had plentiful job vacancies, which meant they could expect career advancement; he persuaded the authorities to allocate foreign currency to him for purchasing reagents and equipment; and he could offer them a good apartment, which was scarce elsewhere. Popov knew the location well, and as he rode his bicycle around, he marveled at the construction, including a new nine-story apartment building. Something big was happening here. Sandakhchiev told them they would be engaged in applied science, taking academic discoveries and creating useful products. Sergei and Taissia arrived with high hopes. "It was very attractive, and we knew nothing about biological weapons at that time," Popov said. "Nobody even said a single word about it. It's not like we were invited to do some kind of biological weapons research. No, no. Not at all. So we were completely naïve and we did not understand what was going on. And we were invited to join a new institution, and that was it."

Sandakhchiev was in a hurry. He wanted to push the frontiers of genetic engineering in biological weapons. The sprawling facility included special departments for every step: to develop and produce culture media; to grow cells for the production of viruses; to grow the viruses; to isolate and manipulate DNA; to isolate the necessary enzymes; to test the results on animals, and more. His institute did achieve some gains in civilian research, but at the core, it was a laboratory to discover new methods of using viruses to kill people on a massive scale.

After earning his doctorate at Novosibirsk State University in 1976,

Popov became a junior scientist in the chemistry department at Vector. Chemistry was vital to unwrapping the secrets of genes. In the first year or two, he recalled, the scientists were given basic training in microbiology. They practiced growing viruses using harmless species variants, known as bacterial phages. In 1978, Popov was promoted to head of the chemistry department, and he began to learn the true goals Sandakhchiev had in mind. He got his clearance for access to top-secret information. "And at that point I became irreversibly involved in the biological weapons program."

"So it was quite innocent," he recalled. "They said, you are in the position of a department head, and you need to understand that in addition to academic research, we need to develop some military projects to defend our country." Popov was prohibited from travel abroad without special permission. They asked him to sign a statement promising to keep the deepest secrets. "That was the beginning," he said, "a very critical step. I committed myself. I signed the papers because there was no choice. Everybody was polite and nobody insisted, but I know very few people in my position who refused to cooperate. The refusal would be a kind of suicide, meaning the KGB would be after you for the rest of your life, and you would never get a decent job. I admire those people who had the courage to say 'no.' They were more mature than I was."

Popov said he also had doubts about whether germs would ever be used in war, even as he became more deeply involved. "I never believed those weapons could ever be used. I always believed they would never be used, because it was so absurd, everything was so absurd and so self-destructive." He said it would be "ridiculous" to use germs on a battlefield, the impact being so unpredictable. He added, "The only justification for me to be involved in this absurdity was that I was pushed . . . There was a popular saying that if they fire you, there will be just one place to find a job. It will be the Western Siberia Hat Company." That was a metaphor for a humiliating dead end. At Koltsovo, by contrast, promising research challenges, facilities, and opportunity beckoned.

The KGB had a large presence at the institute, supervising documents, watching management, keeping an eye out for spies. Each employee went through a meticulous background check. Links to the outside world were forbidden, and contacts with foreigners rare. "And there was great, great suspicion regarding somebody who came from abroad,"

Popov recalled. "The KGB instructed us how to deal with the visitor, the KGB assigned a special person to follow every step of that visitor, and everybody who contacted that visitor fell under the KGB's suspicion, so it was a lot of trouble to even talk to the foreigner." Some scientific articles from overseas journals were distributed, but general Western literature was prohibited. Suspicion was rife. Once, the scientific secretary of the institute was accused of reading literature about yoga, Popov recalled. "And also he had been noticed standing on his head. Head down, and legs up, and that was clearly unacceptable for a person in his position. Although he did it purely at his leisure at home, his abnormal behavior raised the suspicion that if he was capable of doing something like this, he could not be trusted. He was dismissed."

The true purpose of Koltsovo was concealed with a "legend," or cover story. "The so-called open legend provided to everybody was that the purpose of the institute was to push the development of industrial microbiology. And we wanted to know how to modify microbes, how to make them producers of different kinds of biological substances. It was a legitimate goal, which covered up the biological weapons program, because its purpose sounded exactly like the peaceful program. There was only one exception—those modified microbes had, ultimately, to be killers."

Amid all the secrecy, Popov recognized a fault in the cover story. A normal institute of this size would be a source of dozens or hundreds of scientific papers in the professional journals. But Popov said scientists were severely restricted in what they could publish. Any paper had to say nothing about their real work, and fit the cover story. "It had to be a confusing, or misleading, or irrelevant story," he said. The dearth of serious papers from a facility with thousands of research workers would be suspicious. If not making discoveries for science, what were they doing? But Popov was told by high-level officials that the United States had a hidden biological weapons program too, and he believed it. There was hardly any discussion of the 1972 treaty. "You know, the overall perception was that we were quite undeveloped, which was mainly true," Popov said, reflecting on his thinking in those times. "We thought about ourselves as a country that needed to develop its own capability in terms of biological weapons. We feared being without them, and nobody essentially ever doubted that the Americans had the best biological weapons. And think about the predominant social mentality of the Soviets at that time. Who ever doubted that Americans were always cheating on us? Nobody did, simply because we always did—and expected others would be stupid not to behave in the same way."

Viruses are extraordinarily small, submicroscopic particles, hundreds of times smaller than a grain of sand, that infect a biological organism and cause disease. They were first discovered by Dmitri Ivanovsky, a Russian microbiologist, in 1892, and six years later by Martinus Beijerinck, a Dutch microbiologist and botanist. Ivanovsky was trying to understand why tobacco mosaic disease, in the sap of tobacco plants, could not be captured by a porcelain filter that trapped bacteria. He realized that the disease particle was so small that it was passing through the filter. Viruses are barely life-forms, consisting of nothing more than a protein shell and bits of genetic material and sometimes a membrane. But they can be destroyers, carrying incredibly high virulence and contagiousness. They have caused smallpox and influenza epidemics. They work by infecting a host cell, then directing the cell to replicate and produce more viruses. Unlike bacteria, they cannot be treated with antibiotics.

Sandakhchiev's dream was to build viral demons the world had never known—viruses that would attack troops or populations. But there were formidable hurdles to be overcome in this still-backward realm of Soviet science. The researchers had to learn to walk before they could run, and one of the early challenges was to synthesize genetic material, to make artificial DNA. At the time, methods were known in the West for creating simple genes, but the Soviet Union was still far behind. In the first six months of 1980, Sandakhchiev sent Popov on an extraordinary mission. Popov went to the University of Cambridge, England, to the famous Laboratory of Molecular Biology, a center of many of the world's advances in microbiology, to absorb and copy the technology for DNA synthesis and bring it back. Travel abroad by a participant in the Soviet bioweapons program was highly unusual, and Popov's trip had to be approved by the Central Committee of the Communist Party in Moscow. Popov went alone, without his family, posing as a civilian researcher for six months, studying intensively, and returned to Koltsovo with the know-how. He also had been given a glimpse of life in the West—something he never forgot.[4]

When he returned to Koltsovo, laborious and time-consuming synthesis of DNA got underway. The fragments of genetic material had to be fabricated from nucleotides, the fundamental units of nucleic acids, one by one. For a small gene, this might be feasible. For example, somatostatin, a growth regulatory hormone, is a tiny protein, only fourteen amino acids long. Scientists could synthesize it by making a DNA chain forty-two nucleotides long. But more complex genes could require hundreds or thousands of nucleotides. In his laboratory, Popov recalled, he often had more than fifty scientists with doctorate training engaged in this arduous work. "The labs were filled up with flasks, bottles of solvents and reagents, people standing in front of numerous fume hoods, doing that tedious, step-by-step chemical procedure."

Yet the restless Sandakhchiev pushed him hard to synthesize enough genetic material to make artificial viruses. "From the beginning it seemed like a crazy idea," Popov said, "but Sandakhchiev was a master of ambitious projects who set high goals. While we were struggling with making DNA fragments of 15 to 20 units long, he dreamed about thousands. We understood that in order to really speed things up we had to do the synthesis automatically. Sandakhchiev came up with the idea to build a huge warehouse or factory with automatic robots assembling DNA of different viruses. One virus a month, that would be an ideal productivity. And you could assemble biological weapons one after another."

The World Health Organization campaign against smallpox had taken more than a decade to complete. Now Sandakhchiev was proposing to create a new virus every month.

"There was a green light given to Sandakhchiev's idea," Popov recalled. "What if the Soviet Union would be able to produce disease agents one after another? Agents with unbelievable efficacy, and without a means of protection against them? That was his brilliant idea." Popov was told to study how to construct a "synthesizer," an assembly line—what would it take? Sandakhchiev was interested in making SV40, a virus that causes cancer in monkeys, since the genetic sequence was the only one already known. It was more than five thousand nucleotides long. Popov told him it would require two or three years. Sandakhchiev was disappointed; he still wanted a new virus every month. "To me it sounded like extreme stupidity," Popov said, but "Sandakhchiev clearly understood the rules of the game with the Soviet military lobby. He stunned the generals with crazy, crazy, crazy ideas, well ahead of others."

In the early 1980s, Popov and others at Vector, in conjunction with another institute in Moscow, genetically engineered an agent to create artificial interferon, an antiviral substance produced in the body.[5] Popov was decorated with a high state award for his work on interferon. Interferon was a valuable civilian invention, and part of Vector's cover story. Meanwhile, behind the curtain, Vector began to study smallpox, hoping to give it new life as a biological weapon.

The smallpox virus is called *Variola*. The most severe and common is *Variola major*. Over the course of human history, *Variola major* claimed hundreds of millions of lives, and caused the most feared of deadly scourges. Historically, *Variola major* had an overall fatality rate of about 30 percent.[6] Those who contracted smallpox suffered terribly. Jonathan Tucker, who has written extensively on smallpox, described it this way: "After a two-week incubation period, smallpox racked the body with high fever, headache, backache, and nausea, and then peppered the face, trunk, limbs, mouth and throat with hideous, pus-filled boils. Patients with the infection were in agony—their skin felt as if it was being consumed by fire, and although they were tormented by thirst, lesions in the mouth and throat made it excruciating to swallow." For those who survived, the disease ran its course in two or three weeks. But it was highly transmissible, spread in the air by talking or sneezing, and remained contagious in clothing and bed linens. As recently as 1967, the disease sickened between 10 and 15 million people each year in forty-three countries and caused an estimated 2 million deaths.[7]

A long campaign to eradicate smallpox ended with the World Health Organization (WHO) declaration of success May 8, 1980. The WHO recommended the end of vaccinations worldwide. "The conquest of smallpox," Tucker said, "the first—and so far, only—infectious disease to have been eradicated from nature by human effort, was among the greatest medical achievements of the twentieth century."

Now, at Vector, Popov urged Sandakhchiev to consider smallpox for reengineering in Project Factor, instead of re-creating SV40 or making artificial viruses. Why not invent something new out of smallpox? Smallpox was simple to grow, easily aerosolized, caused a disease with a high mortality and was stable in storage.

Popov did not at this point work directly on the dangerous smallpox virus, but used models with related viruses, such as *vaccinia* or *ectromelia*, mousepox. The models acted like a stand-in for the real thing. Popov recalled the institute was also coming under pressure from Moscow to produce results. It had been established almost ten years earlier and Sandakhchiev was being criticized for not producing more dramatic breakthroughs. "We were pushed very hard by the Central Committee to accelerate," Popov recalled. "There were promises and big investments in the program, but no output. And that's when Factor became a focus of my research."

As he began trying to manipulate some microbes, Popov faced a serious difficulty. It was hard to get organisms to increase the amount of toxin they discharged. They could emit a small amount, but if he tried to make them more productive, there was an unexpected side effect: the microbe became less poisonous. The virulence of the organism would decline, instead of increasing. "If we made them good producers," he said, "we often ended up with poor killers." Through years of work, Popov searched for a solution.

His work eventually took him in a slightly different direction. Working with others, he found a way to set off a biological trigger, or switch, to deceive the body's immune system. Normally, when there's a disease, the body attacks it. But in this new concept, if the microbe is made to appear similar to the human body, the immune system would be triggered not only against the invader, but to attack the healthy person, to turn on itself. This made the genetically engineered organism a powerful killer—without having to produce more of the poison.

"The idea was to subvert the natural regulation of the human body and direct it against itself," Popov explained to me. "All this would require only a biological switch, or signal, which the body is expected to follow."

The body's immune system could be fooled to attack the body itself.

There were different possible targets considered in the research, Popov said, but a decision was made to have the immune system turn against the body's nervous system. Thus, if developed into a real weapon, it would cause victims to suffer in two waves. The first might be small-pox. But then, perhaps after a period of recovery, the body would turn on its own nervous system, and the victims would be paralyzed and die. The second wave would be unexpected; no vaccine could stop the process. "As a weapon, the thing would be absolutely untreatable," he said. "Abso-lutely untreatable, because first of all it may come as a surprise after the initial disease has gone away, the person may recover completely. And then the new wave of disease would be the death response . . ."

In 1985, Popov built what is known as the "construct" of his idea, a piece of DNA that would be inserted somewhere into a genome. It was only the start, but it was significant enough that Sandakhchiev no longer needed the earlier proposal to manufacture large quantities of artificial DNA. They could make the deadly agents with just small bits of genetic material. And it became clear that a whole new generation of agents for potential use in weapons was beckoning.

At Koltsovo, scientists like Popov broke through barriers of knowl-edge, but building actual weapons was the job of the military, which maintained its own separate laboratories. Vector was a research facility. The "customer" was the 15th Main Directorate of the Ministry of Defense. Periodically, the customer came to visit Vector, to check on progress. And there was finally something to tell them.

Secluded in the forests outside of Moscow, another scientist was fighting his own battle. While Vector sought to alter viruses, Igor Domaradsky attempted to reengineer the genetic makeup of bacteria into an unstop-pable warrior. Domaradsky walked with a slight limp; he had suffered polio as a child, and tuberculosis and malaria as an adult. He had a repu-tation for being irritable, hard to contain, and he later called himself a troublemaker, an inconvenient man. He was always restless. He yearned for the rewards of scientific discovery but worked in service of weapons of death.[8]

In 1984, he was fifty-nine years old. During the week, he lived alone in Protvino, a small town one hundred miles south of Moscow. He drove through the mixed forests of birch and bogs each day to start work at a secret laboratory. The location was called Obolensk, after ancient princes who once ruled the forests. He was fond of the drive, and often, in winter, came face-to-face with roaming elk. He remembered when Obolensk was carved out of the woods. At first, there were temporary "huts," long, crude one-story barracks for researchers. By the early 1980s, the modern Korpus No. 1 rose out of the forest. Outwardly, it appeared to be another eight-story, boxy Soviet office building. But inside it was 400,417 square feet dedicated to the study and manipulation of dangerous pathogens. The third floor was devoted to especially hazardous materials. Massive airlocks and seals guarded against leaks.[9] Obolensk itself was dark and marshy, and Domaradsky considered it a privilege to have his apartment ten miles to the south in Protvino, in the fresh air near the banks of the Oka River.

The laboratory at Obolensk was known as Post Office Box V-8724, one of dozens of closed Soviet cities and laboratories devoted to Cold War military work.[10] Domaradsky worked in the laboratory during the week, living in his Protvino apartment, and drove two hours back to Moscow to see his family on weekends, sometimes lingering in the city on Monday. His wife, Svetlana Skvortsova, was a talented actress and teacher who thrived in Moscow's rich cultural life. Domaradsky worked in lonesome isolation.

The enforced solitude caused him to ponder all that he had done. In the apartment, he began collecting papers and hiding notes of his life's work, making illicit photocopies so the evidence of his achievements would not be destroyed by the secret services that watched over him.

On weekday mornings, Domaradsky switched on the radio in his apartment to listen to Radio Free Europe, the BBC and Deutsche Welle, the German broadcaster, which were easier to receive in the countryside than in the big cities. "Nobody bothered me, and I luxuriated in my freedom to listen to foreign radio, learning a great deal of news about the USSR and the world that was not available in Moscow." He would then put on a record of his favorite music. Sometimes he went skiing, in the mornings or evenings after work, through a park and forest. Food shortages were common, but Domaradsky was permitted to shop at the small elite "Ryabinka" grocery store for directors of a nearby physics institute. While Soviet citizens were in lines for the basics, the store carried such rare commodities as instant coffee and caviar, delivering them to his door and taking his order for the next delivery. He felt well off, but his science was difficult, and its goals, he knew, were dreadful.

Tularemia, commonly known as "rabbit fever," is caused by a bacterium that is highly infectious. It is formally known as *Francisella tularensis* and is found in animals, especially rodents, rabbits and hares. In the early 1980s, the microbe became the object of Domaradsky's research. He yearned to work on several other pathogens at the same time, but the Soviet bosses wanted results from tularemia. He was searching for a way to make tularemia into an agent that would infect people while resisting both antibiotics and vaccines. He was searching for an unstoppable supergerm.

In general, the Soviet military preferred to use contagious pathogens like the smallpox virus and plague because they could cause epidemics. The military would simply light the spark, and the disease would spread like wildfire on its own. Tularemia is not contagious, and thus cannot be passed from human to human. Yet the military retained interest in tularemia because it required as few as ten microorganisms inhaled or ingested to infect someone.[11] Tularemia is also stable and easy to aerosolize; the microorganism can survive for weeks at low temperatures.

Unlike viruses, which are nothing more than a few genes and protein, with perhaps a membrane, bacteria live inside rigid outer walls. The wall is critical to the cell's survival, giving it structure and support. Without it, the cell dies. In the 1930s and 1940s, antibiotics were developed that could attack bacteria; the first was penicillin. These drugs could slow or even kill the bacteria in several ways: weaken the cell wall, inhibit its growth or stop its replication. Antibiotics helped defeat infections that have threatened man through the centuries. Diseases such as rheumatic fever, syphilis and bacterial pneumonia became easily treatable. These miracle medicines held promise that some diseases could be wiped out. By the 1940s, there were dozens of antibiotics, but then came another twist: bacteria acquired resistance to them. Within a few years, many of the powerful wonder drugs were losing their efficacy. The remaining bacteria were no longer vulnerable to antibiotics, as a result of natural selection—those which were genetically able to resist the drugs had survived. Over time only the resistant bacteria remained, and the drugs lost their effectiveness.[12]

The goal of Domaradsky's research was to build a new microbe that would be resistant to many antibiotics. As an instrument of war, it would slice through helpless populations or armies like a scythe. According to Ken Alibek, who rose to become deputy director of the Soviet bio-weapons program in the late 1980s, Domaradsky had once proposed to develop a strain of tularemia that would stand up against a whole spectrum of antibiotics, overcome vaccines and at the same time not lose its virulence. "The Soviet army wasn't satisfied with weapons resistant to one type of antibiotic," Alibek said. "The only worthwhile genetically altered weapon, for military strategists, was one that could resist all possible treatments."[13] The generals wanted a strain that could resist up to ten different antibiotics at once, Alibek recalled. The proposal was audacious, complex and difficult to fulfill.

Domaradsky had little to work with. Knowledge in the Soviet Union about the tularemia microbe was scant. "We had no data on its biochemistry or its genetics," he said. Domaradsky persuaded the Moscow authorities to let him recruit the best researchers in the country for his project.

By his own account, Domaradsky's long struggle was complicated by constant pressure from the Soviet leadership, which wanted results delivered on a rigid schedule of five-year plans. The biological weapons program was under the purview of a powerful agency, the Military Industrial Commission, which set down deadlines that Domaradsky found infuriating. By 1984, he had been working on the tularemia idea for nearly eight years. Every month, the bosses arrived from Moscow in official cars, driving up to Obolensk with sirens wailing and lights flashing. The visitors, impatient, wanted to know how the project was going, and turned to Domaradsky. His research was slow and painstaking. "That microbe does not recognize genetic information, nor does it possess the right genes for antibiotic resistance on its own," he said of tularemia. While Domaradsky reported making progress toward conquering resistance to antibiotics, he said, "we were nowhere near" the second goal of creating a germ that could also overcome vaccines.

Once, Domaradsky bitterly fought with his bosses when they suggested changing the outward appearance of the germ by attaching another organism, staphylococcus, to the tularemia bacteria. "This amounted to trying to stick a piece of the staphylococcus germ directly onto the surface of the tularemia cells, which could not possibly have worked," he recalled. The creation would never replicate. "It's a little like sticking the wings of a crow onto a cat and hoping the cat will produce flying kittens," Domaradsky scolded.

Domaradsky had been appointed scientific director of Obolensk in 1978. Four years later, a new general director was appointed, Major General Nikolai Urakov, who had come from a military laboratory in Kirov. Urakov was tall, his hair always combed in a swoop back from his forehead, a man of military style and bearing. He loved expressions such as "master the situation!" and "burn with a white-hot iron!," which meant to utterly destroy something.

While Domaradsky treasured his independence, and was eager to follow his curiosity into different subjects, Urakov tried to force progress on the tularemia project, and refused to let Domaradsky work on other pathogens. He made Domaradsky's life miserable, sometimes calling meetings about tularemia on Saturday so the scientist could not visit his family in Moscow. "Being a soldier to the marrow of his bones, Urakov respected only force and brooked no arguments," Domaradsky complained years later in his memoir. "For me and my colleagues, however, the most difficult aspect of Urakov's regime was the complete neglect of fundamental science. Everyone who has ever dealt with the genetics of bacteria knows how complicated it is to produce a new strain, indeed to create a new species! In order to make Urakov realize this, we reported to him every detail of our work: how we obtained different variants, and the methods we used." But Domaradsky said the director would not listen.

"I don't need your strains! I need just one strain!" Urakov declared. "We are not playing here, we are making a weapon!"

In the laboratory, Domaradsky faced a huge obstacle: if a bacterium acquired some new characteristic, it could lose others. This happened to tularemia. "Having become resistant to several antibiotics, the strain lost its virulence, which was unacceptable to the military," he said. If the virulence fell, or if a test animal managed to survive a day longer, the military regarded it as a serious setback. "The desired bioweapons strain had to be fully virulent and deliverable in aerosol form. One germ cell had to be enough to start a lethal infection in a monkey," Domaradsky said. "Furthermore, the infection had to be *incurable*."

Domaradsky came up with a fresh approach. He suggested taking two strains, both of which had lost virulence because of genetic engineering, but both having gained resistance to different antibiotics, and combining them into one super-germ. The pair, working together, might compensate for what each had lost in the genetic engineering. Domaradsky called this the "binary" approach, and had high hopes for it. The result might be "a rapidly growing, extremely virulent, and essentially untreatable disease, which would bring about the same result as if we had managed to produce a single super strain with its virulence and other properties intact." He estimated the pair might be resistant to six or eight antibiotics at once. "This would make countering a biological weapons attack all but impossible," he said, "especially on a large scale."

But Urakov stubbornly rejected his plan.

As a young man, Domaradsky experienced the hardships and horrors of the early decades of the Soviet Union. Born in Moscow in 1925, he grew up in Saratov, along the Volga River, where his father had been sent after arrest and imprisonment during Stalin's Great Terror. A grandfather was also arrested. Domaradsky never forgot the persecution of his relatives, the cruelty and violence of the system and the hunger of those early years. In late 1942, Domaradsky's family fled to safety in Kazakhstan. In 1943, at seventeen years old, Domaradsky was summoned by the military for duty, but he was rejected because of the polio limp. He decided to study medicine and returned to Saratov after the war. By 1950, he had graduated from university and was assigned a research job at the All Union Anti-Plague Institute in Saratov, known informally as Mikrob.

Plague, the Black Death of the Middle Ages, has long been feared in Russia, and epidemics swept southern parts of the country in the nineteenth and early twentieth centuries. As a result, the Soviet Union established a network of specialized institutes to prevent and control plague outbreaks, and the Mikrob institute became the nerve center for the whole country, organizing investigations of the steppes and the deserts. Rodents such as marmots, gerbils and prairie dogs carried plague and it sometimes flared into epizootic outbreaks, an epidemic among animals that could spill over into human populations. The agent, *Yersinia pestis*, is transmitted from sick rodents to humans through fleas. In the field,

Soviet plague-control researchers had to be microbiologists, epidemiologists, zoologists, parasitologists and sometimes general practitioners.

The biochemistry of the plague microbe had not been studied in the Soviet Union. For his doctorate, Domaradsky decided to examine the organism's protein metabolism. He successfully defended his doctorate in 1956. Within a year, at thirty-one years old, he was appointed director of the anti-plague institute at Irkutsk in Siberia, which handled plague control and research for the entire Far East. In 1964, he was transferred to the anti-plague institute in Rostov-on-Don. It was a time of turmoil. The focus of the institute was being shifted from routine work on plague control to devising new ways to defend against biological weapons. This was Domaradsky's first, tentative step into the world of germ warfare. The search for defenses against biological attack was known as "Problem No. 5."[14]

In the Cold War years of the 1950s and 1960s, both superpowers built arsenals of biological weapons from existing, known pathogens. Domaradsky viewed his work as a contribution to civil defense, a prudent measure to protect the population in the event of attack, just as underground bunkers would protect citizens from nuclear bomb fallout. The move to Rostov gave Domaradsky a rich opportunity to research the plague microbe just at the moment when microbiology was resurfacing in the Soviet Union.

Genetics expanded rapidly in the West with the discovery of the structure of DNA by James Watson, Francis Crick and Maurice Wilkins in 1953. In the decades that followed, scientists found ways to manipulate DNA in the laboratory. But in the Soviet Union, this was known only to a few Soviet scientists through smuggled journals and reports.

The field was paralyzed for a generation, starting in the 1930s, because of the influence of Trofim Lysenko, an agronomist who claimed that the acquired characteristics of plants and animals could be altered by tailoring their environment, and then passed from one generation to the next. Lysenko denied the fundamentals of genetics. He became a member of the Academy of Sciences, and his critics were persecuted and sent to the prison camps, including the great botanist and geneticist Nikolai Vavilov. By the 1950s, genetics disappeared as a discipline in the Soviet Union. Lysenko's downfall came only a year after the ouster of Nikita Khrushchev as Soviet leader in October 1964.[15]

Lysenko had left few scientists untouched. Domaradsky recalled that he had to insert some "rubbish" into his own doctorate dissertation to conform with Lysenko. But with Lysenko's influence fading in the early 1960s, Domaradsky could push more deeply into the genetics of plague. At the Rostov laboratories, Domaradsky and his researchers made a major advance in understanding the nature of plasmids, strands of genetic material found in bacteria that carry the codes for such things as virulence and antibiotic resistance. Plasmids are used in genetic engineering because they can replicate without harming the organisms they come from and can be transferred into another bacterium, even of a different bacterial species. Domaradsky considered one of his triumphs the development of an antibiotic-resistant strain of plague that could be used for vaccines. It was developed for civil defense, he told himself; the Rostov institute had never been working directly on weapons. "On the other hand, there was a dark side to that research," Domaradsky later acknowledged, "though I did not realize it at the time." The dark side was that his discovery could just as easily be applied to *Yersinia pestis* to create a new, killer plague.

For centuries, humans have sought to use toxins and toxic agents in war. The very terms "toxic" and "toxin" are derived from the ancient Greek *toxikon pharmakon* (arrow poison). The first biowarfare was conducted with what are called fomites—the crude use of filth, animal carcasses and contagion as weapons. These have been used to contaminate wells, reservoirs and other water sources of armies and civilian populations under attack since antiquity, through the Napoleonic era and into the twentieth century.[16]

In World War I, advances in science and military technology gave rise to widespread use of chemical weapons. The use of German chlorine gas at Ypres on April 22, 1915, opened an epoch of horror. Over the next three years, 113,000 tons of chemical weapons agents were used in battle, killing more than 91,000 and wounding 1.2 million.[17] In the aftermath, 128 nations signed an international agreement, the Geneva Protocol, on June 17, 1925, pledging never to use chemical or biological agents in war. The United States, despite being the country that championed the treaty, did not ratify the agreement at the time, and many nations signed but said they would reserve the right to retaliate with chemical weapons as a deterrent.[18]

The Geneva Protocol was little more than a no-first-use agreement. It did not stop basic research, production or possession of chemical and biological weapons, and there were no provisions for inspection.

Chemical weapons consist of inert substances, such as arsenic, while biological weapons are made from living things, such as bacteria and viruses. A third category are toxins, which are isolated from living organisms, but unlike bacteria or viruses, they can't replicate.

In the years that followed the Geneva Protocol, the race to discover biological weapons did not stop.

Japan's quest was horrific. After reading of the Geneva accord in 1927, a Japanese military scientist, Lieutenant General Shiro Ishii, traveled the globe, and concluded Japan should arm itself with the weapon others were forsaking. The Japanese biological weapons program included four biological warfare units in China between 1936 and 1945. The largest of them during World War II was known as Unit 731, at Ping Fan in occupied Manchuria. Japan cultivated deadly bacteria and carried out large-scale, open-air testing of live pathogens, including anthrax as bacterial slurry in bombs. Japan also tested pathogens on prisoners of war. The precise death toll is not known but was in the thousands, and perhaps more if various epidemics are included. Japanese aircraft also dropped ceramic bombs containing plague-infested fleas, and grain to attract rats, in a series of field tests of aerial biological bombs on eleven Chinese cities in 1940. In the end, the military effectiveness of the Japanese weapons remains unclear. But the toll in death and suffering overall was large.[19]

For Russian troops in the wars at the turn of the twentieth century—the Russo-Japanese war, World War I and the civil war of 1918–1921—infectious diseases transmitted naturally caused far greater casualties than battlefield wounds. Typhus was feared the most; an epidemic during the civil war made a deep impression on the military commanders—disease had been more deadly than bullets. The Red Army looked for methods to defend against disease, but also experimented with biological weapons.[20] A British spy, in a secret intelligence report sent to London, described open-air tests of a crude aerial bomb in October 1926 on Kulali Island in the Caspian Sea. The bomb contained ampoules of tetanus bacilli in a steel cylinder, with blades that would cause it to rotate as it fell. At the right moment, the bomb exploded and the germs were broadcast out—the tests showed they were spread up to five hundred meters away and did not lose their virulence.[21]

In 1928, a full-scale biowarfare program was ordered by the Soviet Union's Revolutionary Military Council. The decree ordered the transformation of typhus into a battlefield weapon. The main biowarfare laboratory was located in Leningrad. One hundred miles north, at a prison camp on Solovetsky Island in the White Sea, additional tests were made in the 1930s with typhus, Q fever, glanders and melioidosis.

At the start of World War II, with the German advance, all the Soviet germ warfare facilities were hurriedly evacuated eastward by rail to the city of Kirov, where the whole effort was reassembled in the regional hospital.

At war's end, the Soviet Union had acquired and weaponized a group of biological warfare agents they referred to as the golden triangle: plague, anthrax and cholera. Soviet troops had overrun the Japanese biological weapons headquarters in Manchuria in 1945. They found buildings destroyed by the retreating Japanese, but they seized prisoners and documents. In 1949, the Soviets tried a dozen Japanese prisoners who testified about germ warfare experiments. Details of the Japanese biological weapons program were sent to Moscow, including "blueprints for biological warfare assembly plants, far larger and more complex than our own." Stalin ordered the Japanese plans to be used to build a military research facility in Sverdlovsk. Yet another laboratory run by the military was opened in the city of Zagorsk, north of Moscow, in 1953 for the study of viruses. And a remote base for germ warfare testing, which had been used in 1937–1938, was reactivated in the Aral Sea in the early 1950s.[22]

Through the 1950s and 1960s, American intelligence agencies struggled to learn more about Soviet biological weapons, but without much success. There was a tantalizing hint about the island in the Aral Sea. It was first identified as a potential bioweapons testing site by Walter Hirsch, a captured German chemical warfare expert who mentioned the site in a 1951 report he wrote for the United States.[23] The American intelligence community then examined everything they could find about the Aral Sea, but came up with nothing. A 1954 CIA intelligence estimate declared:

The USSR has the technical knowledge, trained personnel, and
facilities necessary for a program of research and development in
biological warfare, and we believe that such a program is almost
certainly in progress. Firm evidence on the subject is, however,
exceedingly scanty, and is likely to remain so because of the ease
with which such a program can be concealed. Our estimates must
be almost exclusively of what the USSR is capable of
accomplishing in this field, rather than of what it has in fact
accomplished.[24]

In 1957, high-altitude photography of the island in the Aral Sea by
U-2 spy planes showed more than 150 buildings, grouped into two settlements about two and a half miles apart. Still, intelligence analysts found
the photos inconclusive. Another U-2 photo run was made in 1959. The
photos offered no more clues; the U.S. analysts still had doubts. They said
the facilities seemed too crude for testing of biological weapons. In 1965,
the Soviet program still remained a mystery. A CIA study that year concluded: "Despite a considerable expenditure of time and resources, the
pursuit of intelligence on biological warfare activities in the USSR has
been unrewarding. There is no firm evidence of the existence of an offensive Soviet BW program." The CIA analysts were puzzled because they
expected to find a Soviet germ warfare program, but had not. They titled
their report "The Enigma of Soviet BW."[25]

The United States entered the search for biological weapons early in
World War II, following Great Britain, which feared the Axis powers
would use the weapons. In October 1941, Secretary of War Henry
Stimson asked the National Academy of Science for advice about the
dangers. The response in February 1942 was that biological warfare was
feasible.[26] In May, a small civilian agency was set up, the War Reserve
Service, under George W. Merck, chairman of Merck & Company, the
pharmaceutical company, to begin developing a biological weapons program. In December, the army's Chemical Warfare Service took over and
prepared a large-scale research and development program. By April
1943, ground was broken for a research facility at Camp Detrick, Mary-

land, a small air national guard training site forty-five miles north of Washington. In December 1943, the Office of Strategic Services had received "inconclusive" intelligence that Germany might use biological weapons, perhaps putting anthrax or Botulinum toxin in their cross-channel rockets.[27] The U.S. program was expanded, and more fully integrated into the War Department. Alarm about a possible German biological weapon led British Prime Minister Winston Churchill to ask the United States for 500,000 anthrax munitions. The army refitted a plant at Vigo, Indiana, in 1944 for the production of anthrax spore slurry. The Vigo plant was equipped with twelve 20,000-gallon fermenters, capable of producing fill for 240 four-pound anthrax bombs an hour. The plant underwent safety tests, but the war ended before production began.[28] The Germans never weaponized biological agents; it turned out the Japanese program was much more active. During the war, the American biological weapons program was conducted with the secrecy equivalent of the Manhattan Project, and details were unveiled only in January 1946 by Merck. One aspect that remained hidden until later was the United States grant of immunity from prosecution to the leaders of Japan's notorious Unit 731 in exchange for details about their research.[29]

During the Korean War, extensive propaganda from the Soviet Union and China accused the United States of using biological weapons in Korea. Documents declassified in recent years show that although the United States attempted to accelerate and acquire biological weapons during the war, the effort to create a viable weapons program was unsuccessful.[30] After the war, the program expanded with the Cold War and competition with the Soviet Union. A facility built at Pine Bluff, Arkansas, for large-scale fermentation, concentration, storage and weaponization of microorganisms began production in 1954. Human experimentation using military and civilian volunteers started in 1955. Biological bombs were detonated inside a one-million-liter hollow metallic spherical aerosolization chamber at Fort Detrick, Maryland, known as "the 8 ball."[31] An open-air testing site was built at Dugway Proving Ground in Utah. In May 1962, the army created a biological and chemical warfare coordinating organization, the Deseret Test Center, located at Fort Douglas, Salt Lake City, Utah. This center served as the headquarters for the biological warfare test operation. The United States carried out as many as 239 open-air trials between 1949 and 1969. Among them,

American cities were unknowingly used as laboratories to test aerosols and dispersal methods; the test sites included tunnels on the Pennsylvania Turnpike.[32] These field tests were carried out with harmless microbes that simulated the behavior of biological warfare. In the 1950s, an American program known as St. Jo developed and tested bombs and delivery methods for possible wartime use of anthrax weapons against Soviet cities. One hundred seventy-three test releases were made of noninfectious aerosols in Minneapolis, St. Louis and Winnipeg, Canada, cities chosen to have approximately the same climate, urban and industrial development and topography as Soviet cities. The weapon to be used was a cluster bomb holding 536 biological bomblets, each containing thirty-five milliliters of anthrax spore slurry and a small explosive charge.[33] Much more ambitious tests with live agents were used in sea trials carried out in 1965 and 1968 against monkeys as targets on ships and islands in the Pacific Ocean. The 1968 test showed that a single airborne dissemination tank could disperse a virulent infectious agent over nearly a thousand square miles.[34] British trials using simulants between 1963 and 1969 also showed that if released by a ship or airplane along a hundred-mile-long line, significant concentrations of bacterial aerosol had passed more than fifty miles inland after a few hours. The trials confirmed that aerosolized bacteria could remain viable for several hours in the open, with 80 percent of the population infected up to forty miles, and half the population infected between forty and eighty miles inland.[35]

There was growing concern among scientists about the use of chemical and biological weapons in war. On February 14, 1967, some five thousand scientists, including seventeen Nobel Prize winners and 129 members of the U.S. National Academy of Sciences, asked President Lyndon Johnson in a petition to "re-establish and categorically declare the intention of the United States to refrain from initiating the use of chemical and biological weapons." Among those who organized the effort were Matthew Meselson, professor of molecular biology at Harvard University. The petition prompted a White House effort to draft a statement saying the United States would not be the first to use biological weapons in the future, but the military objected, and Johnson never issued the statement.[36]

Then came an accident. It involved a chemical weapons test but had much broader repercussions. At 5:30 P.M. on Wednesday, March 13, 1968, an air force jet roared over a circular target grid laid out at Dugway Proving Grounds on the Utah desert floor and sprayed 320 gallons of the lethal nerve gas VX. As the plane zoomed up, a valve failed to close. The deadly VX continued to pour from the plane, was picked up by wind gusts and spread as far as forty-five miles away. Within three days, thousands of sheep in the Skull and Rush valleys were sickened or died.[37] The incident came to light only a year later when revealed in a television newsmagazine broadcast.[38] Representative Richard McCarthy, a Democrat of Buffalo, New York, who saw the broadcast, began to challenge the army, angered by the secrecy surrounding chemical and biological weapons. "The rule seemed to be: tell as little as possible, and if you get caught in a mistake, fabricate your way out of it," McCarthy said. Although some scientific research results from the U.S. program were openly published, there were also secret parts, including the Pacific Ocean field tests.

Nixon had just taken office. His new defense secretary, Melvin Laird, a former eight-term congressman from Wisconsin, aware of the congressional mood, wrote to National Security Adviser Henry Kissinger that "it is clear the administration is going to be under increasing fire" from Congress. Laird urged a full-scale review of American germ warfare policy.[39]

Nixon faced huge protests at the time over Vietnam. The United States had used herbicides such as Agent Orange to defoliate forests and destroy rice crops, and tear gas to force out North Vietnamese fighters from bunkers, drawing international condemnation. Also, that summer the United Nations issued a startling report by fourteen scientists emphasizing the powerful impact of biological weapons, which, if used, could transform a society and its environment. The scientists said that in an attack, biological weapons would infect a wide area. The use of ten tons of agent might cover 38,610 square miles, slightly larger than the state of Indiana. The notion of using biological weapons in war "generates a sense of horror," the scientists said. "Mass disease, following an attack, especially of civilian populations, could be expected not only because of the lack of timely warning of the danger but because effective measures of protection or treatment simply do not exist or cannot be provided on an adequate scale."[40] The World Health Organization, providing the scientific and medical details for the UN panel, estimated that 110 pounds of dry anthrax, if used by a single bomber against a target city in a suitable aerosol form, would affect an area far in excess of 7.7 square miles, "with tens to hundreds of thousands of deaths."[41]

On November 25, 1969, Nixon announced the United States would unilaterally stop all offensive biological weapons research and destroy the stocks, while maintaining a program of defensive research. He also pledged no first use of chemical weapons, but said the United States would retain them. He vowed to finally send the 1925 Geneva Protocol to the Senate for ratification and he endorsed a British proposal for a follow-up treaty to limit biological weapons. It was the first time in the Cold War that an entire class of weapons was discarded unilaterally.[42]

Why did Nixon do it? He appears to have acted, at least in part, out of a personal desire to show that he was a more effective leader than his predecessors had been, especially Kennedy and Johnson. Nixon asserted to Kissinger the decision "wouldn't have been possible without Nixon trust. And . . . Eisenhower didn't even suggest these things."[43] According to diaries kept by his chief of staff, H. R. Haldeman, Nixon called Haldeman the night of the announcement and wanted to talk politics, urging Haldeman to convene a staff meeting for the next day so Kissinger could emphasize at the meeting that President Johnson could not have attained all Nixon had done—including the biological weapons decision—because Johnson "didn't have the confidence of the people or the world leaders."[44]

Nixon also adopted the view that nuclear weapons were the supreme deterrent and made biological weapons unnecessary. In his briefing for members of Congress, Kissinger's written talking points said, "We do not need BW for deterrence when we have nuclears." After Kissinger's press briefing, Nixon asked Kissinger in their phone conversation "if he was able to get across the point on deterrent, and K said he had." White House speechwriter William Safire, who drafted Nixon's renunciation, asked the president whether a few biological weapons should be retained as a deterrent. "We'll never use the damn germs, so what good is biological warfare as a deterrent?" Nixon replied. "If somebody uses germs on us, we'll nuke 'em."[45]

Nixon was also urged by scientists to give up biological weapons. Meselson, who knew Kissinger from Harvard, submitted a memorandum to him in September 1969, saying the United States should ratify the Geneva Protocols, outlawing the use of chemical and biological weapons in war. Meselson wrote, "Very small quantities of disease germs would be sufficient to cover large areas: a light aircraft can deliver enough to kill populations over several thousand square miles." Medical defenses can be "rendered ineffective" against germ warfare, he said, and "reliable early warning systems have not yet been devised." As a deterrent to attack, he added, the United States already had nuclear weapons. Thus, "we have no need to rely on lethal germ weapons and would lose nothing by giving up the option to use them first." Meselson added, "Our major interest is to keep other nations from acquiring them."[46]

Separately, scientists on a panel of the President's Science Advisory Committee finished a report in August urging Nixon to scrap offensive biological weapons research and destroy the stockpiles.[47]

Nixon announced his decision in the Roosevelt Room of the White House after informing congressional leaders. In his talking points for the press and members of Congress, Kissinger said, "Control and effectiveness of BW agents is questionable."[48] Nixon adopted this argument in his announcement: "Biological weapons have massive, unpredictable, and potentially uncontrollable consequences. They may produce global epidemics and impair the health of future generations."[49] In fact, the American and British trials had shown biological weapons could be well-controlled strategic weapons. Nixon had omitted the related category of toxins from his first statement, but on February 14, 1970, renounced them as well.

A few months after the toxins announcement, Laird sent an inventory of the U.S. biological weapons arsenal to the White House. It included 220 pounds of anthrax dried agent. According to Laird's list, the U.S. also had 804 pounds of dried tularemia bacteria and 334 pounds of the incapacitating agent Venezuelan equine encephalomyelitis virus, dried, with another 4,991 gallons in liquid suspension. Also in liquid suspension were 5,098 gallons of Q fever. The list said the United States had filled 97,554 munitions with toxins, biological agents or simulants.[50] The United States also stockpiled 158,684 pounds of wheat rust and 1,865 pounds of rice blast, both to be used as anti-crop weapons. No missiles were armed with biological warheads, although a bomblet-containing warhead for the short-range surface-to-surface Sergeant missile had been designed. There were eight aircraft sprayers.[51] General Earle Wheeler, chairman of the Joint Chiefs of Staff, had told Nixon at the National Security Council meeting that the Pine Bluff facility could go into production on thirty days' notice.[52] The military arsenal was destroyed by 1973, although the CIA was admonished during a congressional hearing two years later for illegal retention of extremely small amounts of toxin samples.

In his original declaration, Nixon expressed hope that other nations would follow the U.S. example. The Soviet Union did not.[53]

THE ANTHRAX FACTORY

Ground zero for testing smallpox and other biological weapons in the Soviet Union was a hot, arid and sandy island, isolated and remote. It was named Vozrozhdeniye, or Rebirth Island, and located in the middle of the Aral Sea, once the fourth-largest inland sea in the world. In the early 1970s, the sea was drying up. Rivers that fed the sea had been diverted for cotton irrigation by Soviet planners. The shoreline receded and water deteriorated, while pesticide runoff increased, threatening birds, fish and small mammals with extinction.

In mid-July 1971, a Soviet civilian research ship, the *Lev Berg*, named after a famous Russian biologist and geologist, set sail from Aralsk, a city of fifty thousand then at the northern tip of the sea. On those summer days, the mission of the *Lev Berg* was to sample the ecological damage. The ship left July 15 and made a long circle around the shoreline. Winds across the water always drifted in a southerly direction. On July 31, the *Lev Berg* was south of Vozrozhdeniye Island. The ship then returned to home port August 11. A twenty-four-year-old woman who had worked on the deck of the ship, hauling nets and archiving samples, went home and became very ill. In the weeks that followed, she came down with smallpox, then spread it to nine other people in Aralsk. Three died, including two infants under one year old.[1]

No direct evidence exists that a smallpox test was the reason for the outbreak, but a senior Soviet official, Pyotr Burgasov, said years later that a test had been conducted there. At the time of the smallpox outbreak, Burgasov was Soviet deputy minister of health.[2] He recalled: "A highly potent smallpox formula was being tested on Vozrozhdeniye Island in the Aral Sea . . .

> Suddenly I got a report saying that deaths from unknown causes had been registered in the town of Aralsk. Here is what happened: A research vessel from the Aralsk Shipping Company came within 15 kilometers of the island (it was forbidden to approach closer than 40 kilometers) and a lab assistant went out on deck twice a day, taking plankton samples. Smallpox pathogen—a mere 400 grams of the formula had been exploded on the island—"got" her; she contracted smallpox, and when she returned home to Aralsk, she infected several more people, some of them children. There were no survivors. When I had pieced together the facts, I called the chief of the USSR General Staff, asking him to forbid Alma-Ata–Moscow trains to stop in Aralsk. Thus a nation-wide epidemic was prevented. I called Andropov, KGB head at the time, and told him about the exceptionally potent smallpox formula developed on Vozrozhdeniye Island. He ordered me to keep mum. This is what real bacteriological weapons are like! Minimum effective range: 15 kilometers. You can easily imagine what would have happened had there been not just one lab assistant, but 100 or 200 people around at the time.[3]

The smallpox outbreak was hushed up by the Soviet authorities and never reported to the World Health Organization.

In 1971, the same year as the Aralsk outbreak, a renewed diplomatic effort was made to strengthen international control over germ warfare. The 1925 Geneva Protocol had covered both chemical and biological weapons. The British proposed at the Conference on Disarmament in Geneva to separate germ warfare from chemical weapons, and to tackle biological weapons first. The idea was that it would be easier to ban germ warfare before moving on to chemical weapons.[4] Nixon's decision to close down the American biological weapons program had given a new impetus to negotiations.

The Soviet Union had long insisted on an "immediate and simultaneous ban" on both biological and chemical weapons. But in March 1971, they suddenly agreed to split the two issues. The Soviet Union and the United States approved a new treaty prohibiting biological weapons, which was sent to the United Nations in August and approved unanimously by the General Assembly in December. The Biological and Toxin Weapons Convention was signed in London, Washington and Moscow on April 10, 1972. The four-page agreement banned the development and production of biological weapons, and the means of delivering them. Specifically, Article 1 declared:

> Each state party to this Convention undertakes never in any
> circumstances to develop, produce, stockpile or otherwise acquire
> or retain: (1) Microbial or other biological agents, or toxins
> whatever their origin or method of production, of types and in
> quantities that have no justification for prophylactic, protective or
> other peaceful purposes; (2) Weapons, equipment or means of
> delivery designed to use such agents or toxins for hostile purposes
> or in armed conflict.

But just as the Geneva Protocol a half century earlier had been weak, so was the new biological weapons treaty. It lacked on-site inspection mechanisms, because the Soviets had refused to accept any. It did not prohibit research if carried out for defensive purposes. At the time, Western diplomats reasoned it was better to get the treaty signed without verification than to have no agreement at all. The treaty simply left it up to each country to police itself. There were no penalties for cheating. There was no organization to monitor compliance.

Nixon had little faith in the new treaty. He was reluctant to even attend the signing ceremony. On the day he signed it, Nixon privately told Kissinger it was a "silly biological warfare thing which doesn't mean anything," and the next day, speaking to Treasury Secretary John Connally, he called it "that jackass treaty on biological warfare."[5]

The Biological Weapons Convention, which took effect on March 26,

1975, was the first post–World War II disarmament treaty in which an entire class of weapons was to be done away with. But the hopes for it were in vain.

In the winter months of 1972, Igor Domaradsky was recuperating from tuberculosis at a rest home outside of Moscow. One day, an official car arrived unexpectedly to pick him up. Domaradsky was driven to the Soviet health ministry in Moscow, and then to the Kremlin. High-ranking officials told him that he was being officially transferred from Rostov to Moscow to work for an organization involving microbiology. They were vague about what Domaradsky would do. That summer, in preparation, he defended a new doctorate dissertation in biology. "Had I known what was in store for me I would not have wanted to do it," he recalled later of the move to Moscow, "and I would certainly have refused."[6] He was assigned to work at a government agency, Glavmikro-bioprom, which was a shortened name for the main directorate of the microbiological industry. Originally, the agency was created to help improve agriculture and medicine, such as creating artificial sweeteners and proteins. When Domaradsky got a small office there, he recalled, he wasn't sure why.

In the West, genetics and molecular biology were accelerating. The experiments of cutting, pasting and copying DNA fragments by Herb Boyer and Stanley Cohen in California were pushing the science of molecular biology to new levels. Many of the advances came just as Domaradsky was transferred to Moscow. The 1973 experiments of Cohen and Boyer marked the dawn of genetic engineering.[7]

Soviet leaders made a momentous decision. Up to this point, their germ warfare program had been a military one. They had signed the new biological weapons treaty. But in deepest secrecy, they decided to violate the agreement, and to expand their pursuit of offensive biological weapons to exploit the new advances in genetic engineering. In the past they had used natural pathogens for weapons. Now they rushed to modify nature and create dangerous new agents. Domaradsky was recruited to be at the center of the program.

The germ warfare effort was far different from the nuclear arms race.

Both superpowers formally negotiated on nuclear weapons. Nuclear weapons were legal by the rules of the day. The countries made treaties, set limits and went to great lengths to regulate the competition by arms control negotiations, which they discussed in the open. To protect against cheating, they created verification regimes. But when the Soviet leaders expanded their biological weapons program in the early 1970s, they moved into a dark underside of the arms race. The Soviet program was illegal by the terms of a treaty that Soviet leaders had signed. They broke their own promises, and there was no regulation, verification or enforcement. Their actions give the lie to decades of Soviet propaganda about seeking disarmament. Almost every participant in the Soviet program has said they assumed the United States was also cheating. But in fact the U.S. program had stopped.

At the time, Brezhnev was influenced by a leading molecular biologist, Yuri Ovchinnikov, vice president of the Soviet Academy of Sciences. He and several colleagues persuaded Brezhnev to harness the new gene-splicing technology for offensive military purposes. According to Ken Alibek, who became deputy director of the Soviet biological weapons program, Ovchinnikov "understood the significance of what he had read in Western scientific journals, and he knew that there were no Soviet laboratories, and few Soviet scientists, equipped to match that level of work." When it came to convincing the military of the value of this new quest, Alibek said, "Ovchinnikov was persuasive. The most skeptical military commander would have to agree that it was dangerous, if not outrageous, to be behind the West in anything. Ovchinnikov found an influential ally in Leonid Brezhnev. The onetime metallurgical engineer who led the Soviet Union for eighteen years until his death in 1982 regarded the magisterial *akademiks* of the Soviet scientific establishment with a respect bordering on awe. Ovchinnikov was soon giving private lectures on genetics to Brezhnev and his aides. Slowly the message sank in."[8]

The message was: they had to catch up. As part of the effort, Domaradsky recalled that several prominent Soviet scientists scoured the West for literature on molecular biology and genetics. Among them was Victor Zhdanov, a noted virologist who had initially proposed the global campaign to eradicate smallpox in 1958. Zhdanov won the high regard of Western scientists, and was often permitted to travel abroad. Domaradsky described Zhdanov as sophisticated and worldly. But Zhdanov was also aware of the terrible secrets—plans for a new generation of Soviet biological weapons.

In microbiology, a fine line exists between research that offers the promise of improved human life—better vaccines, drugs and agricultural products—and research that could be used to exploit human vulnerability to toxins and infectious disease. In the early phases, the same laboratory can be used for either purpose. Joshua Lederberg, the Nobel laureate, wrote that in biological weapons, the "underlying science is unalterably dual-use." This allowed the Soviet leaders to hide their weapons program.[9]

In 1973, soon after the treaty was signed but before it took effect, Brezhnev established a new organization, Biopreparat. The cover story would be that Biopreparat was making medicines and vaccines. But the truth was that Biopreparat was the dual-use mechanism for a recharged and ambitious Soviet effort to discover new offensive biological weapons. Under the cover of civilian pharmaceuticals, Biopreparat would be researching the most dangerous pathogens known to man. To guide it, Brezhnev ordered the creation of a secret, inner council. Brezhnev put the respected virologist Zhdanov in charge of the council, and Domaradsky was named deputy director.

Within the council, Domaradsky was also put in charge of a "special department" for planning biological weapons development. He had frequent contact with the military bioweapons laboratories, government ministries, Academy of Sciences, and security services. He was now at the "brain center" of the germ warfare research program. The code word for the new offensive weapons drive was "Ferment." Eventually, it grew to employ tens of thousands of workers and received the equivalent of hundreds of millions of dollars in funding.[10]

In 1974, the Soviet government issued another decree, this one public, seeking to accelerate Soviet work in microbiology. "The meaning of this order was clear," Domaradsky said, "to let the nation and the world know that we had at last awakened and resolved to overcome our backwardness in this field."[11] But once again, the open decree was intended to conceal the truth. The Biopreparat-run laboratories were secretly intended for weapons work and were being erected at Koltsovo and Obolensk. By Alibek's account, it was the most ambitious Soviet arms program since development of the hydrogen bomb.[12]

In his new assignment, Domaradsky was to work in the shadows. All documents concerning Ferment were transported with armed escort in special vehicles. Meetings of the council were held in a specially sound-proofed hall, which was checked for bugs by the security services before every meeting. Domaradsky's subscriptions to scientific literature had to be screened in advance by the security service. He was prohibited to travel outside the Soviet bloc, and often not even there. "I knew too much," he acknowledged. The travel restrictions, often imposed on those with access to top-secret materials, nonetheless caused him embarrassment. "I had to think up some reason for turning down pressing and very tempting invitations from my foreign colleagues." He would say he had broken his leg, or come down with an illness, or he had "family problems." Once, he was on the verge of leaving for an international conference on microbiology in Munich. At the very last minute, the KGB man accompanying the delegation stopped Domaradsky in the street, told him he could not go and demanded his ticket and travel money back.

Domaradsky and his researchers held ten "inventor's certificates," for introducing genetic material into plague, but these papers were classified. Keeping such papers secret was common procedure. Domaradsky was given only a number and date of registration. To see his own certificates he had to enter a special security room and could not take any documents out.

Domaradsky was deeply conflicted. He desired to explore science, yet was aware he was contributing to instruments of death. The pathogens he developed would eventually be turned into weapons, although he did not deal with the actual bombs, just the germs. "I found the science of Problem Ferment intriguing indeed," he said. "The attraction of that science seemed more important to me than what was to be done with its results." He added, "Compromising with my conscience seemed, at the time, like a small price to pay." Domaradsky said his family's long struggle with persecution had taught him to be ready to bend. "To survive, I had to hide my true attitude toward the Soviet regime from childhood; I learned quite early to adapt myself to this regime."

Moreover, Domaradsky felt a "vaulting pride" at being in the heart of the Soviet effort. He had a secure Kremlin phone, car and good salary.

"We saw ourselves engaged in patriotic work," he said, "advancing the study of molecular biology, immunology, and genetics in the Soviet Union, where these fields had been allowed to languish." He knew of the treaty prohibiting biological weapons, but assumed Americans were also cheating.

At the core of the entire bioweapons effort, Domaradsky was in position to see the paperwork, talk to the military and visit the laboratories. As Biopreparat took shape, Domaradsky drafted a plan, approved in 1975, to expand the drive for genetically engineered germ weapons in five major directions, including resistance to antibiotics. This was a key turning point. Programs got underway to transfer the genes from various deadly agents into the cells of bacteria, or into the DNA of viruses, to boost the pathogenetic factors. Domaradsky wanted to inject the genetic material directly into plague. These programs were called "Bonfire" and "Factor." While Domaradsky worked as deputy director of the council in Moscow, the council also set up a parallel program to use genetically altered viruses and germ weapons to devastate crops and livestock, Project "Ecology."

As a young man, Domaradsky had admired the heroic workers of the anti-plague institutes, who protected the public from scourge. Now, the same institutes were quietly dragged into the search for agents of killing. According to Domaradsky, the "Problem No. 5" for civil defense became a cover story for weapons work. The institutes were asked to gather dangerous pathogens they found on the steppe, and to study what made them virulent, so they could be fed into the Biopreparat flasks.

The Biological Weapons Convention entered into force on March 26, 1975. That June, Alexei A. Roshchin, the Soviet ambassador to the disarmament committee in Geneva, declared: "At the present time, the Soviet Union does not have in its possession any bacteriological (biological) agents or toxins, weapons, equipment or means of delivery specified in Article 1 of the Convention."[13]

Whether Roshchin was aware of the reality is unknown, but Domaradsky certainly knew the truth. "I knew that I was part of a system that was out of control, but I could not think of an alternative way to live my life," Domaradsky reflected later. "Like my colleagues, I faced a terrible choice: remain with a corrupt and non-functioning system, doing work of (at best) a certain moral ambiguity, or sacrifice my entire scientific career."

Soon after the biological weapons treaty was ratified, U.S. intelligence satellites picked up signs of unusual new factories being built in the Soviet Union. William Beecher, the military correspondent of the *Boston Globe*, reported that satellites detected six potential biological warfare facilities. The plants "feature extremely high smokestacks and refrigerated storage bunkers associated with germ warfare production," Beecher wrote.[14]

Then in April 1979 came the Sverdlovsk anthrax epidemic. Fragmentary reports began to reach the West. The intelligence community had long suspected a secret Soviet biological weapons program existed. Now perhaps there was evidence.

The first reports began filtering into the U.S. Central Intelligence Agency through Soviet émigrés. A top-secret CIA intelligence report on October 15, 1979, cited an unnamed Soviet émigré as saying that three close friends had told him in May "of an accident at a biological warfare (BW) institute in Sverdlovsk which resulted in 40 to 60 deaths. Other sources have also heard rumors of such an accident." The report was vague, but noted there was "a suspect BW installation in Sverdlovsk" and that "two reports of the accident suggested a disease that also affects cattle, and one source identified the bacterial agent anthrax as a possible cause."[15]

In December, Soviet forces invaded Afghanistan. The SALT II treaty was endangered. If the Soviets were found to have violated the five-year-old biological weapons treaty, it would be yet another serious setback to ratification of the nuclear arms agreement.

Unexpectedly, fresh intelligence arrived in Washington about Sverdlovsk. A secret CIA report on January 28, 1980, said: "Recent intelligence strengthens allegations that an accident at a BW installation caused civilian casualties in southern Sverdlovsk during April 1979." This report added the claim of a possible explosion at the plant that caused the release. The report said that "pathogenic bacteria allegedly escaped into the air and spread over industrial and residential areas of southern Sverdlovsk." The report also took note that, "An announcement about an anthrax epidemic in a public health context appears to have been designed to prevent a possible panic among Sverdlovsk's

million-plus population. The magnitude of the epidemic and the caus-
ative organism remain conjecture."

In January and February 1980, a practicing surgeon from a
Sverdlovsk hospital gave U.S. intelligence agencies a new and more
detailed account, which the Defense Intelligence Agency described in a
top-secret report March 3. Although some details were vague, the surgeon was correct about many specifics. He said the accident occurred
inside a military installation where "dispersible biological weapons"
were produced. He said that in April 1979 there had been a "loud explosion which was attributed to a jet aircraft"—this later turned out to be an
error—and he noted that within four days, victims had been arriving at
Hospital No. 20.

He also recounted the symptoms of the victims, the deaths of workers
at the ceramics factory, the decision to send patients to hospital No. 40
and the announcement that tainted meat caused the outbreak. He added,
"This explanation was not accepted by the doctors in attendance because
the fatalities were caused by the pulmonary type of anthrax as opposed to
the gastric or skin anthrax which would be more likely if one had eaten
or handled contaminated beef." The intelligence agency concluded in the
report that the information "presents a very strong circumstantial case for
biological weapons activity" at the facility.

In Moscow on Monday, March 17, 1980, the U.S. ambassador, Thomas
Watson, raised the Sverdlovsk anthrax epidemic in a quiet inquiry with
the Soviet Foreign Ministry.[16] The ministry did not respond right away.
In Washington on Tuesday, March 18, a State Department spokesman,
responding to questions from journalists, read out a public statement saying there were "disturbing indications" that "a lethal biological agent"
might have hit Sverdlovsk in 1979 and this had raised questions "about
whether such material was present in quantities consistent with" the biological weapons treaty. The Soviets were surprised by the State Department's public announcement, which they hadn't expected.[17] The Soviet
response came on Thursday, March 20, that the outbreak was caused by
contaminated meat.[18] The issue was extremely sensitive because that
same week in Geneva, diplomats from fifty-three countries were winding up the first five-year review conference of the Biological Weapons
Convention. They were on the verge of approving a final declaration.
The U.S. ambassador to the talks, Charles Flowerree, told his Soviet

counterpart, Victor Israelyan, about the message of concern over Sverdlovsk delivered in Moscow.

The Soviets decided to keep stonewalling. On Friday, March 21, acting on instructions from Moscow, Israelyan made a public statement to the conference. He reassured the conference there was nothing to worry about. "There are no grounds whatsoever" for the questions raised by the United States, he said. "In March–April 1979 in the area of Sverdlovsk there did in fact occur an ordinary outbreak of anthrax among animals, which arose from natural causes, and there were cases where people contracted an intestinal form of this infection as a result of eating meat from cattle which was sold against the regulations established by the veterinary inspectorate."[19]

The same day, after this statement, the conference approved a final declaration on the Biological Weapons Convention. The treaty was working, the member states declared. No one had filed any complaints about violations. Indeed, the word "violation" did not even appear in the final declaration. All the nations that signed the treaty reaffirmed their "strong determination for the sake of all mankind" to avoid biological weapons.[20]

A week later, the United States passed a secret message back to Moscow, saying that "reports available to us indicate a prolonged outbreak of pulmonary anthrax in Sverdlovsk, involving a large number of fatalities. Based on our experience, we would expect an outbreak of anthrax resulting from contaminated meat to have been of relatively short duration and to have resulted in only a small number of fatalities."[21]

In Washington, the Central Intelligence Agency turned to experts, including Matthew Meselson, the Harvard molecular biologist who had earlier urged Nixon to outlaw biological weapons. Meselson got a call from Julian Hoptman, the CIA's longtime analyst of biological weapons. For a week, Meselson stayed at Hoptman's home, and, with secret clearances, worked at Hoptman's office at CIA headquarters. They pored over the raw intelligence reports, but the evidence was ambiguous. Hoptman had located the practicing surgeon from Sverdlovsk mentioned in the DIA report, who had emigrated to Israel, and interviewed him. But other sources traveling through Sverdlovsk heard nothing about an epidemic. It turned out the report of an explosion was not correct, but there were many unanswered questions,

especially about the diagnosis. In notes he made from that week, Meselson wrote, "The main technical question in my mind at this point
concerns the diagnosis of respiratory anthrax." Was the anthrax inhaled
by the victims, which might point to biological weapons dispersed in
an aerosol, or was it ingested by them, which could be explained by distribution of bad meat? Or was it some other respiratory disease altogether?

A related puzzle was why the cases continued for seven weeks. The
textbooks Meselson consulted had suggested the incubation period for
anthrax was a few days. If there was a single cloud of spores, there should
have been a rapid fall-off of new cases. Instead, people kept getting sick
for quite some time. In his work in Hoptman's office, Meselson concluded that they needed to know much, much more before they could
reach a conclusion. Where did the victims work when they were
exposed? Where did they live? Which direction were the winds blowing? What would they learn if they plotted all the victims on a map, and
then drew an ellipse from Compound 19—how many would be inside
that ellipse? And what was going on at Compound 19? Did the local
authorities respond with drug therapy, and if they did, was it effective?
Why were there so many fatalities if they had drugs readily available? At
this early stage, Meselson was cautious, and probing. Meselson also
learned that a Northwestern University physicist, Donald Ellis, had been
on an academic exchange program with his family in Sverdlovsk at the
time. He tracked down Ellis, who recalled he heard nothing about the
epidemic. This added to Meselson's sense of caution.[22]

Biological weapons were the ultimate challenge for spies, soldiers and
scientists. From space, satellites could photograph intercontinental ballistic missile silos, and they could be counted. But germs were another matter. A satellite might spot an unusual building compound, like the one in
Sverdlovsk, but seeing flasks in laboratories proved nearly impossible.
That is why understanding Sverdlovsk was so important. It was a tantalizing bit of genuine evidence. With Sverdlovsk, the enormity of the
Soviet germ warfare program had been glimpsed, but was still not
proven.

———

After the Sverdlovsk accident, Soviet officials shipped a large supply of anthrax bacteria out of the city to a distant storage facility at Zima, near Irkutsk in Siberia. They wanted to get anthrax production running again, but they needed a new location. They knew Compound 19 would be suspect. Compound 19 was a military facility; now the Soviet officials wanted to hide the anthrax production more carefully. The best cover was Biopreparat, the supposedly civilian pharmaceutical enterprise. In 1981, Brezhnev approved relocating the Sverdlovsk facility. The destination was a remote desert town, Stepnogorsk, in northern Kazakhstan. This was a Biopreparat operation, and Ken Alibek was chosen to run it.[23]

Alibek was an ethnic Kazakh. After graduation from the Tomsk Medical Institute as a military doctor, he was assigned to a biopesticide factory at Omutninsk in western Russia, a training ground for those who would work on biological weapons.[24] From the start, he recalled, "there were no orientation lectures or seminars, but if we had any doubts as to the real purpose of our assignment, they were quickly dispelled." They were asked to sign a pledge of secrecy, then called in one by one to meet their KGB instructors.

"You are aware that this isn't normal work," the officer told Alibek as he sat down, more a declaration than a question.

"Yes," Alibek replied.

"I have to inform you that there exists an international treaty on biological warfare, which the Soviet Union has signed," the officer said. "According to that treaty no one is allowed to make biological weapons. But the United States signed it too, and we believe the Americans are lying."

"I told him, earnestly, that I believed it too," Alibek recalled. "We had been taught as schoolchildren and it was drummed into us as young military officers that the capitalist world was united in only one aim: to destroy the Soviet Union. It was not difficult for me to believe that the United States would use any conceivable weapon against us, and that our own survival depended on matching their duplicity."

The officer nodded at Alibek's comment. He was satisfied. "You can go now," he said. "And good luck."

Many years later, Alibek remembered those five minutes as the first and last time any official brought up a question of ethics for the rest of his career.[25]

———

Alibek was sent to Stepnogorsk in 1983. The new germ warfare plant was attached to a civilian facility, the Progress Scientific and Production Association, which made pesticides and fertilizer and provided a cover story. Within a few weeks of his assignment, Alibek was summoned to Moscow for briefings. Biopreparat had moved to a headquarters at No. 4a Samokatnaya Street, an elegant building with tall, arched windows, once the home of the nineteenth-century vodka merchant Pyotr Smirnoff. Inside, Alibek was shown a secret decree Brezhnev had signed in 1982. "An intelligence officer pulled the decree from a red folder tied with a string, placed it gravely on a desk, and stood behind me while I read," he recalled. "I already knew the gist of the order: we were to transform our sleepy facility in northern Kazakhstan into a munitions place that would eventually replace Sverdlovsk."

The weapon was to be the "battle strain," known as Anthrax 836. "Once I'd worked out the technique for its cultivation, concentration, and preparation, I was to develop the infrastructure to reproduce it on a massive scale—a goal that had eluded our military scientists for years. This meant assembling batteries of fermenters, drying and milling machines, and centrifuges, as well as the equipment required for preparing and filling hundreds of bombs."[26]

"My job in Stepnogorsk was, in effect, to create the world's most efficient assembly line for the mass production of weaponized anthrax."

Officially, Alibek was deputy director of Progress, the civilian enterprise, but he had a secret title as "war commander" of the entire installation. "I was expected to take control of the factory during what the army called 'special periods' of rising tensions between the superpowers. Upon receipt of a coded message from Moscow, I was to transform Progress into a munitions plant. Strains of virulent bacteria would be pulled from our vaults and seeded in our reactors and fermenters. Anthrax was our main agent at Stepnogorsk, but we also worked with glanders and were prepared to weaponize tularemia and plague." The pathogens would be poured into bomblets and spray tanks and loaded onto trucks for shipment to a railroad station or airfield. "I was to maintain production until I received an order from Moscow to stop, or until our plant was destroyed."

Alibek said he took seriously the prospect of a Cold War confrontation with the United States. Reagan's election and military buildup were alarming. "Our soldiers were dying in Afghanistan at the hands of U.S.-backed guerrillas, and Washington was about to deploy a new generation of cruise missiles in Western Europe, capable of reaching Soviet soil in minutes. Intelligence reports claimed that Americans envisioned the death of at least sixty million Soviet citizens in the case of a nuclear war.

"We didn't need hawkish intelligence briefings to persuade us of the danger," he added. "Our newspapers chafed over Reagan's description of our country as an evil empire, and the angry rhetoric of our leaders undermined the sense of security most of us had grown up with during the détente of the 1970s. Although we joked among ourselves about the senile old men in the Kremlin, it was easy to believe that the West would seize upon our moment of weakness to destroy us."

On a plain nine miles from Stepnogorsk, an old uranium-mining town, the Progress enterprise was lined with high gray walls and an electric-wire fence. The surrounding land had been stripped of all vegetation, partly as a safeguard in the event of a leak. The barren space served as a security zone to stop intruders. Motion sensors were everywhere. Inside, dozens of buildings were arranged on a grid of narrow streets. New buildings rose off the desert floor. Building 221 was the main production facility; building 231 for the drying and milling of agents. Building 600 was the research center and housed the largest indoor testing facility built in the Soviet Union up to that time.[27] It had two giant stainless steel testing chambers hidden inside. One was to test the decay rate and dissemination capacities of aerosol mixtures contained in Soviet germ bombs. The second one was for testing animals.

"Bioweapons are not rocket launchers," Alibek explained in his memoir. "They cannot be loaded and fired. The most virulent culture in a test tube is useless as an offensive weapon until it has been put through a process that gives it stability and predictability. The manufacturing technique is, in a sense, the real weapon, and it is harder to develop than individual agents."

To weaponize anthrax, Alibek and his workers began with freeze-dried spores in stoppered vials, stored in metal trays in a refrigerated vault, each positioned over a soft towel soaked in disinfectant, labeled with its own tag identifying the strain. No one was allowed into the vault alone; at least two people, a lab technician and a scientist, had to be present when a vial was taken down from the shelf, checked against a list and wheeled on a metal cart into the laboratory. There, the scientist put nutri-ent media into the vial, and then drew the mixture out and transferred it to larger bottles, which were left in heated boxes to incubate for one or two days. The liquid culture was then siphoned off into large flasks, which were connected to air-bubbling machines, turning it into a light froth. The oxygen allowed the bacteria to grow more efficiently. At this stage, it looked translucent and light brown, like Coca-Cola, Alibek said. "Each new generation of bacteria is transferred into progressively larger vessels, until there is enough anthrax to pipe under vacuum pressure into a room containing several fermenters," he recalled. The giant fermenters incubated the substance for one or two days longer, and the bacteria con-tinued to multiply before being put into centrifuges and concentrated. In the end, after mixing with stabilizing substances, the mixture would be loaded into munitions. The grounds were dotted with underground bunkers for storage and filling the bombs, and laced by rail lines to haul them away. If the order were given, Stepnogorsk was to make 300 tons of anthrax a year.[28]

THE DEAD HAND

In the final weeks of his life, Andropov had few visitors. One of them was Mikhail Gorbachev, the youngest member of the Politburo, who had been Andropov's protégé. They met for the last time in December 1983. "When I entered his room he was sitting in an armchair and made a weak attempt to smile," Gorbachev recalled. "We greeted each other and embraced. The change since my last meeting with him was striking. I saw a totally different person in front of me. He was puffy-faced and haggard; his skin was sallow. His eyes were dim, he barely looked up, and sitting was obviously difficult. I exerted every effort to glance away, to somehow disguise my shock."[1]

Within days of this meeting, Andropov prepared remarks he was scheduled to give to a Central Committee plenum. The text was typed up as usual, but Andropov was too ill to appear in person. He wrote an additional note of six paragraphs in his own hand. He called one of his top assistants, Arkady Volsky, to his bedside December 24 and gave him the note. Andropov had written in the last paragraph: "For reasons which you will understand, I will not be able to chair meetings of the Politburo and Secretariat in the near future. I would therefore request members of the Central Committee to examine the question of entrusting the leadership of the Politburo and Secretariat to Mikhail Sergeyevich Gorbachev." Volsky was stunned. He consulted two other aides, and they, too, were taken aback. Until then, Konstantin Chernenko had been considered the number two leader in the party. Andropov was proposing to skip Chernenko and go right to Gorbachev to lead the country. The aides took the precaution of photocopying Andropov's note, and then submitted it to the Central Committee apparat to be typed and included with Andropov's other remarks for distribution before the meeting.

Two days later, at the plenum, Volsky opened the red-leather-covered portfolio and discovered the last paragraph written by Andropov was missing. When he protested, he was told to keep quiet. The aging dinosaurs at the helm of the Soviet Union—Chernenko, Defense Minister Dmitri Ustinov, and Chairman of the Council of Ministers Nikolai Tikhonov—had quietly blocked Andropov's attempt to name Gorbachev his successor. The old guard had kept their grip on power.[2]

Andropov died February 9, 1984, and the ailing Chernenko was chosen as his successor. British Prime Minister Margaret Thatcher flew to Moscow for the funeral, arriving on February 13 in the bitter cold. On the day of the funeral, she met Chernenko for a short, private meeting. He read rapidly from a text, stumbling over his words from time to time. Thatcher recalled that she had been urged to wear fur-lined boots; at the Andropov funeral, guests had to stand for a long period in the cold. The boots had been expensive, she said. "But when I met Mr. Chernenko, the thought crossed my mind that they would probably come in useful again soon."[3]

At seventy-two years old, Chernenko had never been more than a shadow of Brezhnev as his chief of staff and a party apparatchik. Suffering from an advanced stage of emphysema, Chernenko faltered during his televised inaugural speech from a podium atop Lenin's tomb, running out of breath in the middle of sentences. He was unable to hold a salute to the military parade as it passed before him in Red Square. At one point during Andropov's funeral, Gromyko turned to Chernenko and instructed him in a whisper—loud enough to be picked up by microphones—"Don't take off your hat."[4] Two weeks later, in another televised address, Chernenko stumbled, lost his breath, paused for half a minute and, when he resumed, skipped an entire page of his text. Chernenko was a transitional figure, and his colleagues sensed it. "Whom did we acquire in the post of General Secretary?" asked Gorbachev. "Not merely a seriously sick and physically weak person but, in fact, an invalid.

It was common knowledge, and immediately visible with the naked eye. It was impossible to disguise his infirmity and the shortness of breath caused by emphysema."[5]

Anatoly Chernyaev, who was then deputy director of the International Department in the Central Committee, recalled that when Chernenko was to meet the king of Spain, aides wrote out his main points on small cards, with no long sentences, so that Chernenko would seem to be talking and not reading. "That was in the beginning," Chernyaev said. "Later, Chernenko couldn't even read the notes anymore, but just stumbled through them with no idea what he was saying."[6]

What if the ailing Chernenko had to make a decision about nuclear attack? For the Soviet leadership, the ultimate catastrophe would be a bolt-from-the-blue first strike that would destroy the Kremlin in minutes. There was a special underground train out of the Kremlin to the war bunkers—but what if they were facing sudden death, if the missiles were only minutes away, a decapitation? With the leaders gone, who would order retaliation? Who would transmit the orders? How would they communicate to the remote missile command posts and submarines? If decapitation were swift and powerful, perhaps they would not be able to retaliate; and if so, they were vulnerable. Soviet fears of decapitation were real, fed by actions in the United States. The directive signed by President Carter in 1980 for protracted nuclear war, P.D. 59, had deliberately singled out the Soviet leadership as a target. The deployment of Pershing II and ground-launched cruise missiles in late 1983 seemed to further reinforce the threat of weapons that could reach the Soviet Union in a matter of minutes.

In early 1984, just as Chernenko took power, Valery Yarynich, then forty-seven, a colonel in the elite Strategic Rocket Forces, was quietly transferred to a new position as a deputy department chief in the Main Rocket Armaments Directorate. Yarynich was a master of communications channels and methods who had worked for two decades setting up cables, radio systems and satellites which linked the rockets, troops, commanders and the political leaders in Moscow. He had a serious demeanor and a sense of purpose. When there was a break in a vital communications link for the Strategic Rocket Forces, Yarynich was the one they trusted to fix it quickly. He was transferred to a sensitive, ultra-secret new project for decision making and communications in the event of nuclear war.

In the early days of the Soviet nuclear weapons program, communications were primitive. Getting word to the troops—and the missiles—was time-consuming. Yarynich witnessed the cumbersome procedures. Born in 1937 to the family of a Soviet naval officer at Kronshtadt, near Leningrad, Yarynich graduated from the Leningrad Military Academy of Communications in 1959, two years after Sputnik. That December, the Strategic Rocket Forces was established as a separate service, and the giant, cumbersome R-7 liquid-fueled intercontinental missiles were put on combat duty. Khrushchev was boasting that the Soviet Union was turning out missiles like sausages. Yarynich served in the first Soviet division of intercontinental ballistic missiles, at Yurya, north of Kirov. They were just building the rocket base when he arrived, carving it out of the forest. At the end of 1960, Yarynich moved up to the corps headquarters in Kirov, where five new missile divisions were being formed.

At the time, the Soviet general staff transmitted orders to the missile commanders by radio and cable, using code words in a system called "Monolit." The system relied on special packets prepared in advance and kept under strict control in a safe at the command posts, to be opened in an emergency. Yarynich recalled that during drills, in a decisive moment, an unfortunate duty officer often failed to open the packet fast enough with scissors because his nervous hands were shaking so badly. Precious minutes were wasted. The problem of using scissors was considered serious enough that experts were asked to come up with a new method. "The packet was constructed with a pull-string, on which an operator could tug to immediately open it up," Yarynich recalled. The whole system was slow and cumbersome. Monolit had another, more serious shortcoming. The orders could not be recalled—there was no way to cancel.[7]

In late October 1962, during the Cuban missile crisis, Yarynich was sent as a communications officer to supervise at a rocket division near Nizhny Tagil, 860 miles east of Moscow in Siberia. At the peak of the confrontation, the crews received an unmistakable signal through the Monolit system. The code word was "BRONTOZAVR." The word was a signal: switch the command system from peacetime to combat alert status. A telegraph typed it out, and Yarynich took the paper tape from one of the young women who served as operators. The word was unmistakable, he remembered. "Oh God," he said. "BRONTOZAVR!"

"Never before had we sent it out," he recalled. "It was a signal to cut open the packages."

Inside the packages were new call signals and frequencies for radio communications in the event of nuclear war. "It was a wrong idea in my view, because to change frequencies and call signals when the war is breaking out meant to mess everything up," Yarynich said. "Still, that was the procedure. So, our job was to introduce this new radio information immediately, everywhere, on receiving the order."

Yarynich recognized immediately the message was not a drill. He handed the tape to a colonel on duty. "You understand?" Yarynich asked. The man was shaking. They had never received this command, even during exercises. The missiles at Nizhny Tagil were not yet fueled, so they would not be launched soon, yet the switch to combat alert was met with dread. "It was strangely quiet," Yarynich recalled. "I cannot forget the mixture of nervousness, surprise and pain on the faces of each operator, without exception—officers, enlisted men, women telephone operators." In the end, the Cuban crisis was defused, and in Nizhny Tagil, the "BRONTOZAVR" alert expired. But the problem of command and control of nuclear weapons grew more intense as the Soviet leaders threw their resources into building a new generation of missiles, which required new methods of control—the paper packets were obsolete.

The first attempt to automate the command and control system was ready by 1967. It was called "Signal," and it could transmit thirteen fixed commands from headquarters to the troops, such as telling them to escalate to a higher readiness. The new system could also transmit a cancel order. While a vast improvement over the paper packets, the Signal system did not command the weapons, but rather sent orders to the troops, and they in turn had to operate the weapons. This was still cumbersome and time-consuming. As pressure increased for more speed and streamlining, a second stage of automation was developed in the mid-1970s, known as "Signal-M." It reached all the way from the top decision-makers to the lowest level in the field. The installation of the new, faster

Signal-M came as the Soviet Union put on duty the new generation of missiles, including the giant SS-18. This was the first time the Soviet nuclear command and control featured a remote-control button that could be pushed to launch.[8]

In the Soviet system of the 1970s, the General Staff oversaw the weapons at sea and on bombers, while the Strategic Rocket Forces supervised land-based missiles. At the time, Soviet leaders sitting in the Kremlin did not have a nuclear "football" carried around everywhere they went. The launch apparatus remained with the military branches. The political leaders shared control with the generals.

Yarynich, who worked on Signal-M, often pondered the profound psychological calculus of nuclear weapons command and control. How would real people behave when they had to press the button? How would they make a decision about whether to inflict utter devastation in just minutes? Yarynich recalled another episode he experienced in the mid-1970s when he was working on command and control systems for nuclear weapons. A malfunction occurred in the alert system. An erroneous message was automatically transmitted from the top down to the command posts of all rocket divisions: go one step to a higher alert. Most duty officers in the command posts failed to obey. "People didn't believe it," Yarynich said. "We were not at war." Instead of summoning troops from their barracks to combat sites, they began telephoning their superiors to find out if the message was genuine. Only a lone duty officer, a lieutenant colonel, actually put his unit on alert. The incident revealed a great deal of reluctance in the rocket forces to push any buttons. The duty officers knew, Yarynich said, that "one could not act blindly."

In order to give a Soviet leader additional precious minutes to make a launch decision, the military strove to build super-fast communications to carry messages from the headquarters right to the missiles themselves. In 1985, Signal-M was upgraded to a computerized system known as Signal-A, which allowed missiles in remote silos to be retargeted directly by the Strategic Rocket Forces main staff. Several different flight plans were stored at the launcher and could be chosen remotely. It would take only ten or fifteen seconds to load a flight plan.[9] The significance of this was that Soviet authorities would gain speed and bypass uncertainty—the human kind—on the ground. They would skip over any troops who, lacking discipline and burning with curiosity, might be tempted to pick up the phone to ask what was going on. The military designers were being pushed all the time to make the launch system as fast as possible. "The designers said we need it—now it is five minutes, then it will be three, and soon it will be 20 seconds," Yarynich recalled.

In addition to speed, the designers wanted fail-safe, ironclad security. They knew the flaws of Soviet industry, and the potential for error. Yarynich said they devoted just as much effort to guarding against failure or cheating as they did to gaining speed; they built in rigid procedures, constantly checking for anomalies, up and down the chain.

In 1985, the Soviet designers finished work on a nuclear "football," in this case a briefcase known as the *Cheget*. Three were prepared: to accompany the general secretary of the party, the defense minister and chief of the General Staff. However, the *Cheget* was for information only; it could not be used to launch, and did not have a button to press. The officer carrying the *Cheget* would plug into a wider communications network, known as *Kavkaz*, designed just for the national leadership. Then the general secretary could give permission to the military, also plugged into *Kavkaz*, to launch. This "permission command" would then be transformed into a "direct command" by the General Staff. The direct commands were authenticated, and if proven correct, would become "launch commands" sent to the missiles.

Over the years, as Yarynich worked to build and strengthen these communications systems, he came to see the hair trigger as a dead end, that neither side could gain an edge by just shaving minutes off the decision process. But in 1984, he was doing his job, caught up in the quest for speed.

In the event of nuclear explosions, communications links would be vulnerable to disruption, especially between the headquarters and the missile silo. The Soviet military designers wanted to eliminate that uncertainty. All the previous experience had shown that the traditional cables, radio and satellite channels they had built to carry the data might be suddenly incinerated. They also feared the electromagnetic pulse that would precede a nuclear attack could wipe out all standard communications equipment. Some other means to control the missiles in time of war had to be found.

———

One answer was the survivable underground command post in the Ural Mountains, known as *Grot*, carved out of a mass of granite. The designers had searched long and hard for a site that would allow radio signals to penetrate through the rock. The granite was perfect. *Grot* was situated at a mountain place known locally as Kosvinsky Kamen, east of Moscow and north of Sverdlovsk.[10] While the mountain bunker was intended to shield the commanders from nuclear war, the designers also created a parallel plan for safely broadcasting the launch orders—via missiles soaring high above the earth.

Missiles had always been a Soviet strength, so it was natural to turn to them to solve the problem of wartime communications. The designers conceived robot-like command missiles that could be kept in super-hardened silos, and then launched quickly at the onset of nuclear war. Instead of a warhead, the command missiles would carry a special nose cone of electronics. Once in flight, safely above the war conditions on the ground, the command missiles would broadcast a message to all the remaining nuclear-armed intercontinental ballistic missiles in their silos below: "launch!" Should all else fail, the retaliation command would get through. There was one drawback: the command missiles might take thirty minutes to complete the mission; at that point, all the intercontinental ballistic missiles might be destroyed. Nonetheless, a decision was made to build the system. In utmost secrecy, the Soviet military and civilian designers won approval to start work in 1974. The Yuzhnoye Design Bureau, one of the leading Soviet missile builders in Dnepropetrovsk, Ukraine, was given responsibility for the command rocket.[11] The electronics were created at the Special Design Bureau of the Leningrad Polytechnic Institute, an elite engineering and computer institute. Colonel General Varfolomei Korobushin, first deputy chief of the rocket forces main staff, was in charge of the project for the military. Taken together, the new bunkers and rockets were one of the most creative, astonishing and frightening inventions of the Cold War. It was called Perimeter.[12]

When Yarynich was transferred to the new job in January 1984, he was assigned to Perimeter—then approaching the final year of testing.

———

In the logic of nuclear alert, the fate of the Earth would rest on human decisions made in a few fleeting minutes. If Soviet leaders feared an imminent attack, they had three choices. The first option was preemption, to attack first. But such a strike had almost no chance of success—it was just not possible to wipe out the land and sea legs of the American missile force with a preemptive strike. The second option was to launch immediately when a warning was received that enemy missiles were on the way—a warning that would come from the infrared satellites, and then, ten to fifteen minutes later, from ground-based radars. To launch on a warning was to take extraordinary risks. What if the warning was wrong? What if a radar had mistakenly seen a flock of geese? Or if an early-warning satellite had mistakenly seen a glint off the clouds? These kinds of errors were common to both superpowers. No one wanted to launch nuclear missiles because of a flock of geese. Nonetheless, in the tense standoff of the early 1980s, launch on warning was not dismissed out of hand. The third option was to retaliate only when under attack. Among the Soviet leadership, this was also considered a realistic scenario, especially after they achieved rough parity in missiles with the United States in the 1970s. But launch under attack carried its own risks: what if they didn't survive to retaliate? In this supreme test of human behavior, a hair-trigger decision to launch a nuclear missile attack was one that theorists and planners simply could not fathom nor reliably predict. It was almost impossible to know whether a leader would launch on warning, and take the risk of firing too soon, or wait for an attack, and take the chance of decapitation and destruction.

Out of such imponderable choices arose yet another aspect of Perimeter. What if the ailing Chernenko could not decide whether to shoot first, or be shot? What if he was wiped out before he could decide? The Soviet designers responded with an ingenious and incredible answer. They built a Doomsday Machine that would guarantee retaliation—launch all the nuclear missiles—if Chernenko's hand went limp.

In effect, the designers created a command system—a switch—that gave Chernenko the option not to decide on retaliation. If he turned on the switch, the system would pass the decision to someone else. Thus, an ailing general secretary might avoid the mistake of launching all missiles based on a false alarm. Should the enemy missiles actually arrive and destroy the Kremlin, the general secretary could be certain there would be retaliation. According to Yarynich, the logic was to take the immense burden of a sudden, shoot-or-die decision off the shoulders of the Soviet leader, especially someone as feeble as Brezhnev or Chernenko. If retaliation was necessary, that decision would be slightly delayed and transferred to a survivor. The immense burden was shifted to a few duty officers who might still be alive in a concrete bunker. They would face the big decision about destroying what remained of the planet.

This was not only a concept, but an elaborate program which took a decade to build. It was Perimeter.

Buried within the idea was an even deeper and more frightening concept that the Soviet leaders considered: a totally automated, computer-driven retaliatory system known as the Dead Hand. It would still function if *all* the leaders and *all* the regular command system were destroyed. Computers would memorize the early-warning and nuclear attack data, wait out the onslaught, and then order the retaliation without human control. This system would turn over the fate of mankind to computers. The details remain very sketchy. Katayev, the Central Committee staff man, described it as a "super project," but said it was eventually abandoned. The Soviet designers and leaders could not go that far. Yarynich confirmed that a totally automatic system that would work without the participation of any human element at all was considered in the early 1980s, but the military rejected the idea of launching without one last human firewall. "It was complete madness," Yarynich said.[13]

The Perimeter system, however, was constructed. In the early moments of a nuclear crisis, the order might come from the General Staff, or perhaps from the underground command post at *Grot*, to activate the system. The actual switching-on mechanism is not known. In peacetime, relatively junior duty officers sit in the specialized bunkers. In a crisis, they might be augmented or replaced by experienced high-level officers, but, more likely, under a surprise attack, regular duty officers would be present. The bunkers are known as *shariki*, spheres or globes. Built of hardened concrete, they were buried so far underground that they could survive a nuclear attack on the surface.[14]

Deep in the globes, the officers had a checklist of three conditions to monitor as the minutes ticked by. Condition 1: Verify the Perimeter system was activated. This activation meant that the military commanders or the Kremlin had given advance permission for the system to fire. Condition 2: Check whether contact had been lost with the military and political leaders. If the lines went out, if the hand was dead, this meant decapitation. Condition 3: Determine whether nuclear detonations were being felt by a network of special sensors that measured light, radioactivity, seismic shocks and atmospheric overpressure.

If all three of these conditions were met—the system was activated, the leaders were dead and the nuclear bombs were detonating—then from inside the globe, the officers were supposed to issue a command to launch the Perimeter command rockets, which would fly for about thirty minutes and order all the remaining nuclear-armed missiles of the Soviet Union to launch, aimed at the United States.[15]

The officers buried in the globe were the last human decision-makers in a chain that was now ultrafast and largely automated. If they acted as they had been ordered, Perimeter would unleash a spasm of destruction. "Thus, there was no need for anyone to push a button," said Korobushin. Much would rest on the thinking of the officers in the globe. Yarynich often wondered whether the men in the bunkers at this point would follow orders or defy them. Did the men in the bunker give it one last layer of sanity, the possibility of saying no to mass destruction? Yarynich thought they did. "We have a young lieutenant colonel sitting there, communications are destroyed, and he hears 'boom,' 'boom,' everything is shaking—he might fail to launch. If he doesn't begin the launching procedure there will be no retaliation. What's the point of doing it if half the globe has already been wiped out? To destroy the second part? It makes no sense. Even at this point, this lieutenant colonel might say, 'No, I won't launch it.' No one will condemn him for it or put him before a firing squad. If I were in his place, I wouldn't launch." But Yarynich added that no one could predict how the duty officer would react in such an extraordinary moment, at the edge of the abyss.

Another way to look at Perimeter, however, is more ominous: the duty officers are just another cog in an automatic, regimented system. If the duty officers are drilled over and over again to follow the checklist, and if the highest authorities had given the permission from the top, and if all three conditions on the checklist are met, wouldn't they naturally do as they had been trained to do? In the *sharik*, there would be no communications with the outside world, no negotiations or appeals, no second-guessing, and no recalling the command rockets once they were launched.

If the Americans had known of Perimeter—if they realized that decapitation of the Kremlin would trigger near-automatic retaliation—it might have given them pause. It might have been a deterrent. But in the peculiar dark world of the arms race, the Soviets treated the Perimeter project as super-secret, and tried to mask what they had invented. The Perimeter command missiles were cleverly disguised to look like ordinary missiles so they could not be detected by satellites.

"We hid it," Yarynich said. "We should have announced from the very beginning, here it is, we are having trials. But we hid it. If you don't know about it, it's bad. It means you might take a decisive step, and then what?" This prospect worried Yarynich for many years.

On November 13, 1984, the Soviet military carried out a major test of Perimeter. The Leningrad design bureau simulated the General Staff command post. A signal was sent to a low-frequency transmitter in Moscow. Then the signal was transmitted to the command rocket at the Kapustin Yar test range on the banks of the Volga River in southern Russia. The command rocket took off and flew toward Lake Balkhash in Kazakhstan. Along the entire flight, the command rocket delivered the launch order, as a test, and receivers were listening across the country. During the test, Yarynich watched reports come in; some signals were stronger, others weaker.

Among other locations, the command rocket signal was received by an intercontinental ballistic missile located at the Tyuratam test range, also in Kazakhstan. The missile was poised to launch. In conditions of nuclear war, it would have lifted from the silo immediately, but the Soviet officials delayed it during the test because they suspected American satellites were monitoring every move. A while later, the big missile launched and flew to the Kamchatka Peninsula, hitting a target there.[16]

The test was a success, and the system was put on combat duty in the new year, 1985.

MORNING AGAIN IN AMERICA

Ronald Reagan opened 1984 with bold declarations of an American renaissance. "America is back" with "renewed energy and optimism," he said in the State of the Union address on January 25. He urged the American people to "send away the hand-wringers and doubting Thomases," and added, "The cynics were wrong—America never was a sick society." Polls showed Reagan enjoyed high public approval ratings. The mood of the country was upbeat despite the collapsed nuclear arms talks with the Soviets, a misadventure in Lebanon and record budget deficits. Reagan's optimism had been a tonic for the debilitating years of Vietnam, Watergate, the Iran hostages and the energy crises of the 1970s. A deep recession had wrung hyperinflation out of the economy, and growth was rebounding. An American high-technology revolution was taking hold. Reagan formally announced he was seeking reelection January 29. His campaign was framed by inspirational television commercials, including one titled "Morning Again in America," which opened with glimpses of a farmhouse, followed by scenes of a wedding party and of an elderly man raising the American flag while young faces watched in adoration. As the flag filled the screen to the sounds of soft and stirring music, an announcer said, "It's morning again in America . . . And under the leadership of President Reagan, our country is stronger, and prouder, and better. Why would we ever want to return to where we were less than four short years ago?"

After the tense months of the previous autumn, Reagan wrote repeatedly in his diary early in 1984 that he had come to realize Soviet leaders might have a genuine fear of the United States, and he yearned to talk them out of it. He acknowledged "my own attitudes toward the Soviets were changing a little."[1] The president of Yugoslavia, Mika Spiljak, visited Reagan at the White House February 1, and the president asked a lot of questions about the Soviet Union. "He believes that coupled with their expansionist philosophy they are also insecure & genuinely frightened of us," Reagan wrote in his diary. "He also believes that if we opened them up a bit their leading citizens would get braver about proposing changes in their system. I'm going to pursue this."

At Andropov's funeral in Moscow, Chernenko had sent a conciliatory signal during a talk with Vice President Bush, saying, "We are not inherently enemies." Reagan had yet to see a Soviet leader face-to-face and wondered if he should meet Chernenko. "I have a gut feeling I'd like to talk to him about our problems man to man & see if I could convince him there would be material benefit to the Soviets if they'd join in the family of nations, etc.," he wrote February 22.

When Suzanne Massie, author of several books on Russian culture and history, came by to see Reagan on March 1, after a trip to Moscow, Reagan expressed admiration for her insights and said "she reinforced my gut feeling that it's time for me to personally meet with Chernenko."[2]

The next day, Reagan held a high-level meeting to plan next steps with the Soviets. The secret gathering, kept off Reagan's public schedule, brought together all of Reagan's top cabinet and staff advisers on Soviet affairs. Reagan announced at the opening of the meeting he wanted to arrange a summit, to show Chernenko he was not the sort of person who would "eat his own offspring." But the session wandered off, and ended without a decision.[3] "I'm convinced the time has come for me to meet with Chernenko along about July," Reagan wrote that night.[4] On March 5, Reagan met West German Chancellor Helmut Kohl. Reagan recalled, "He confirmed my belief the Soviets are motivated, at least in part by insecurity & a suspicion that we & our allies mean them harm. They still preserve the tank traps & barbed wire that show how close the Germans got to Moscow before they were stopped. He thinks I should meet Chernenko."

Reagan concluded that he needed a "more hands-on approach" to the

Soviets. He sent a seven-page letter to Chernenko. "I tried to use the old actor's technique of empathy: to imagine the world as seen through another's eyes and try to help my audience see it through my eyes," he said. "I said it was my understanding that some people in the Soviet Union felt a genuine fear of our country." The letter ended with a hand-written postscript, recalling "Soviet losses in warfare through the ages." He added, "Surely those losses, which are beyond description, must affect your thinking today. I want you to know that neither I nor the American people hold any offensive intentions toward the Soviet people."[5]

But Chernenko didn't reciprocate, and rejected a summit. Reagan and Chernenko exchanged a half-dozen letters in the spring of 1984, to no effect. After a strategy session on the Soviets March 23, Reagan con-cluded: "I think they are going to be cold & stiff-necked for a while."

In Moscow, the KGB director, Vladimir Kryuchkov, opened a conference at headquarters saying that RYAN—spotting preparations for nuclear attack—was still the overwhelming overseas intelligence priority. Kryuchkov declared that the risk of nuclear war had reached "dangerous proportions," the Pentagon was driven by "the fantastic idea of world domination" and the White House was engaged in "the psychological preparation of the population for nuclear war." Kryuchkov's speech text landed on Gordievsky's desk in London. It said the top priority was to get a copy of the secret war plans of the United States and NATO.[6] Another urgent priority for Gordievsky and the London office was to monitor field exercises involving the cruise missiles stationed at the Royal Air Force base at Greenham Common. But according to Gordievsky, the London office had no intelligence sources for this; they sent British press reports to Moscow instead.[7]

Early in 1984, Reagan had signed an order formally launching the research effort into his Strategic Defense Initiative.[8] In the Kremlin, however, Soviet leaders were still worried about the threat from Pershing IIs and the ground-launched cruise missiles. The Pershing IIs were fast, but the cruise missiles more numerous. While 108 Pershing IIs would be deployed in West Germany, the plan was to station 464 cruise missiles in Belgium, Britain, Italy, Netherlands and West Germany. The cruise missile was a modified navy sea-launched Tomahawk, about twenty-one feet long, each carrying a single nuclear warhead. It would fly at 550 miles per hour to a target as far as 1,350 miles away. The ground-launched cruise missile was a wonder of technology. It could soar at high altitudes over hostile territory and then swoop down to fifty feet above ground level and be steered toward its target with a sophisticated, terrain-sensitive and radar-avoiding guidance system. The Soviets had nothing like it.[9]

In Moscow, Anatoly Chernyaev, deputy director of the International Department of the Central Committee, attended a briefing June 4 given by Marshal Sergei Akhromeyev, who was then deputy chief of the Soviet military's General Staff. "It was amazing," Chernyaev said, with "missiles homing in on their targets from hundreds and thousands of kilometers away; aircraft carriers, submarines that could do anything; winged missiles that, like in a cartoon, could be guided through a canyon and hit a target 10 meters in diameter from 2,500 kilometers away. An incredible breakthrough in modern technology. And, of course, unthinkably expensive."[10]

On June 28, Herbert E. Meyer, vice chairman of the National Intelligence Council, a think tank inside the CIA, sent a memo to CIA director William Casey titled "What Should We Do About the Russians?" Meyer noted the war scare of the previous year, and the paralysis in Moscow. He also saw the Soviet system under deep internal strain. "Decades of overemphasis on military production have wrecked the country's civilian industrial and technological base," he said.

> More precisely, the Soviets have failed miserably to generate the kinds of innovations on which modern economies are increasingly dependent: robotics, micro-electronics, computerized communications and information-processing systems. Even if the Soviets could develop such systems, they could not deploy them without losing the political control on which the Communist Party depends for its very survival. For after 40 years of fear among Western intellectuals that technology would lead inexorably to Big Brother societies throughout the world, it now turns out that technology, in the form of personal computers and the like, has put communications and information processing beyond the control of any central authority. Unwilling and unable to develop and deploy

innovations like these—as we in the West are doing with such robust enthusiasm—the Soviet Union can now produce little but weapons.[11]

Reagan tried a back-channel gambit to reach Chernenko in April. Brent Scowcroft, who had been President Ford's national security adviser, carried a letter from Reagan to Chernenko on a private trip to Moscow.[12] He never got to see Chernenko, however. The letter went undelivered. "He believes the Soviet cold shoulder is due in part at least to their not wanting to help me get re-elected," Reagan noted after talking to Scowcroft on his return.[13] Scowcroft told reporters, "If you compare the political or psychological atmosphere between the two powers, it's as bad as it's been in my memory."[14]

When the Soviets announced May 8 they would boycott the upcoming Olympic Games in Los Angeles, Reagan concluded that Chernenko wasn't completely in control, and the lion of the old guard, Gromyko, was running foreign policy.[15] In June, the Soviets proposed opening talks on space weapons, but when Reagan asked to include ballistic missiles, Chernenko refused. "They are utterly stonewalling us," Reagan wrote in his diary. Reagan cared about his reelection campaign, but his horizon was longer than just the vote. If "America was back," then in his own mind, it was time to engage the Soviet Union. Reagan still did not have a Soviet partner, his first term was almost over and the paralysis in the Soviet elite was even worse than Reagan could have imagined at the time.[16]

On August 11, 1984, at Rancho del Cielo in California, Reagan prepared for his Saturday radio address. He often made wisecracks in the warm-up, considered off the record by reporters and technicians present. Asked for a microphone check on this day, the president said, "My fellow Americans, I am pleased to tell you today that I've signed legislation that will outlaw Russia forever. We begin bombing in five minutes." The remark soon leaked, and made headlines around the world, once again reinforcing the caricature of Reagan as a reckless gunslinger. TASS denounced the remark as "unprecedentedly hostile toward the USSR and dangerous to the cause of peace." The president was chagrined. "Doing a voice level with no thought that anyone other than the few people in the room would hear I ad-libbed jokingly something about the Soviets," he admitted in his diary. "The networks had a line open & recorded it and of course made it public—hence an international incident."

On August 13, two days after the radio gaffe, at a lunch in Los Angeles, Shultz suggested, very tentatively, that Reagan invite Gromyko to the White House after the opening of the United Nations General Assembly in September. The president quickly agreed. "It's the right thing to do," Reagan said. "Try to work it out."[17] The meeting was arranged; it would be Reagan's first with any member of the Soviet Politburo since becoming president. Reagan wrote in his diary, "I have a feeling we'll get nowhere with arms reductions while they are suspicious of our motives as we are of theirs. I believe we need a meeting to see if we can't make them understand we have no designs on them but think they have designs on us. If we could once clear the air maybe reducing arms wouldn't look so impossible to them."

Reagan spent most of Saturday, September 22, working on the speech he was to give the following Monday at the United Nations. It was "ticklish," he acknowledged. "I don't want to sound as if I'm going soft on Russia but I don't want to kill off the Gromyko meeting before it takes place." In his speech, Reagan offered not a word of criticism of the Soviet Union; the "evil empire" was gone. As he spoke from the podium, Reagan was watching the faces of Gromyko and the Soviet representatives, sitting in the front row, right below the microphone. "I tried to catch their eyes several times on particular points affecting them," he recalled. "They were looking through me & their expressions never changed."

Reagan finally got his chance to talk to Gromyko eye-to-eye in the Oval Office on September 28. They lectured each other. At one point, Gromyko recalled, Reagan reached into a side drawer and pulled out some charts on nuclear weapons. As the meeting broke for lunch, Reagan asked Gromyko to remain behind in the Oval Office. They spoke alone, in English, without interpreters. Gromyko had said the world was sitting atop a huge mountain of nuclear weapons that should be reduced. "My dream," Reagan said, "is for a world where there are no nuclear weapons."[18]

Reagan escorted his guest down the long colonnade from the West Wing to the main White House mansion for a reception. Gromyko was amazed at the number of "English long-case clocks" in the White House and wondered if Reagan was a collector. A small chamber orchestra played classical music. Reagan introduced Nancy. At the end of the reception, Gromyko took Nancy aside and said, "Does your husband believe in peace?"

"Of course," she replied.

"Then whisper 'peace' in your husband's ear every night," he said.

"I will, and I will also whisper it in your ear," she said. And with that she leaned over with a smile and whispered softly, "Peace."[19]

At the end of the visit, the Soviet Embassy called Don Oberdorfer, diplomatic correspondent of the *Washington Post*, and asked for a photograph of Reagan talking to Gromyko that appeared in the morning paper. It showed Reagan's hands on both of Gromyko's arms. The photo was rushed over to Gromyko before his departure. Gromyko had first come to Washington forty-five years earlier. Although no one knew it then, this was his last trip to the White House. Reagan had finally met a member of the Soviet Politburo, but had yet to find one with whom he could do business.[20]

Although Reagan wanted to talk to the Soviet leadership, he also approved policies to directly challenge the Soviet Union. At the behest of CIA director Casey, he vastly expanded proxy wars against Soviet influence in the Third World. In 1984, covert U.S. support for the *mujahedeen* fighting the Soviet army in Afghanistan reached a major turning point. The secret aid pipeline from the United States and Saudi Arabia, through Pakistan, suddenly bulged; by one account the total had tripled to hundreds of millions of dollars, in a matter of weeks.[21] At the same time, Reagan wanted to channel money to guerrilla fighters, known as *contrarevolucionarios*, or contras, who were opposing the Sandinista government of Nicaragua. Reagan called the contras the "moral equivalent of our Founding Fathers" and he cast Nicaragua's Sandinista junta, led by Daniel Ortega, as the front line in the war on communism. But Congress had cut off the aid to the contras, and money was running out in 1984. Reagan instructed McFarlane, his national security adviser, to keep the contras alive, "body and soul." That summer, McFarlane reassured

Reagan that Saudi Arabia had pledged $1 million a month into a secret bank account for the contras. The driving force in Afghanistan and Central America was Casey. "By the end of 1984, Casey's covert war in the Third World against the Soviet Union and its surrogates was in full swing," recalled Gates, who was then his deputy.

In the summer of 1984, the RYAN operation seemed to expire. Gordievsky said anxiety in Moscow about nuclear war "was visibly declining."[22] Chernenko didn't share Andropov's sense of alarm and paranoia about nuclear attack. Although there were no arms control negotiations that year, Soviet officials protested with increasing frequency about what they called "militarization of space." Shultz said Dobrynin brought up *kosmos*—the Russian word for outer space—at every meeting.[23] This was aimed directly at Reagan's Strategic Defense Initiative, although the actual program was barely getting started. By one account, that summer the program comprised two dozen people working out of a dilapidated office building in Washington.[24]

Reagan's dream got a lucky break that summer. The army, in a program started in the 1970s, was studying rocket interceptors, and created an experiment, using a test interceptor with an infrared homing device and computer. It was called the Homing Overlay Experiment. The first three tests had failed. In the fourth and last test on June 10, 1984, the interceptor was launched from Meck Island in the Kwajalein Islands, and more than one hundred miles high, it locked onto a Minuteman missile carrying a dummy warhead. The interceptor found the Minuteman in part because the dummy warhead was heated up for the test, and the Minuteman turned sideways, to be easier to detect. The missile was destroyed. The Pentagon announced the test was a stunning success. "We do know that we can pick them up and hit them," a spokesman said. The Kremlin was rattled.[25]

Reagan's reelection campaign aired one commercial that hinted at voter fears about the arms race. It was a thirty-second spot written by the same team that created "Morning Again in America." But this commercial had a darker undertone, one that warned of uncertainty. The goal was to acknowledge the danger but also suggest there might be a way out. The ad shows a grizzly bear wandering in the forest. "There is a bear in the woods," the announcer says in a tone of seriousness and authority. "For some people, the bear is easy to see. Others don't see it at all. Some say the bear is tame. Some say it's vicious. Since no one knows, isn't it smart to be as strong as the bear, if there is a bear?"[26]

On November 6, 1984, Reagan was reelected in the largest electoral-vote landslide in U.S. history. He won 59 percent of the popular vote, carried 49 states and received 525 electoral votes to 10 for Walter Mondale.

Between the summer vacation and the election, Shultz had been talking privately to Reagan about the work of a second term. Shultz could not tell if Reagan absorbed what he said, but he kept lecturing. He told Reagan the Soviet Union was caught in an inconclusive leadership struggle, from one generation to another, bound up in a stagnating economy and "extreme distrust verging, in some instances, on paranoia" about the United States. It wasn't clear how the leadership succession would be resolved, Shultz said, but one of the most promising candidates was a member of the younger generation, a man with a broader view—Mikhail Gorbachev.[27]

PART

TWO

"WE CAN'T GO ON LIVING LIKE THIS"

Five weeks after Reagan was reelected, Mikhail Gorbachev and his wife, Raisa, were driven from London through rolling English farmland to Chequers, the elegant official country residence of the British prime minister. Margaret Thatcher and her husband, Denis, greeted the Gorbachevs just before lunch on Sunday, December 16, 1984. It was a highly unusual gesture for a Soviet official to take his wife abroad. Gorbachev had asked Chernenko's approval before doing so. On their arrival, Thatcher noticed Raisa had chosen a well-tailored, Western-style suit, gray with a white stripe, "just the sort I could have worn myself." After posing at the entrance for the press photographers, with Gorbachev standing at the far left of the group next to Raisa, Thatcher very conspicuously repositioned the group so she would be standing next to Gorbachev. Then she extended a welcoming handshake.[1]

For more than a year, Thatcher had been searching for clues to the next generation of Soviet leaders. Thatcher was intrigued about whether the dour older generation would give way to a new, younger field. She had enormous faith in the power of the individual, and believed that in a dictatorship that repressed individual initiative, some could still make a difference, as had dissidents Alexander Solzhenitsyn, Andrei Sakharov and others. Thatcher wondered if one person at the very top could change the Soviet system from within. In her memoir, she recalled that

she was determined to "seek out the most likely person in the rising generation of Soviet leaders and then cultivate and sustain him." Her foreign
secretary, Geoffrey Howe, said Thatcher carried out a "deliberate campaign to get inside the system."[2] Thatcher remembered what Professor
Archie Brown had told her at the Chequers seminar: Gorbachev was the
most open and promising man in the leadership. She invited Brown to
come back to No. 10 Downing Street on December 14, just before Gorbachev's visit, to brief her again.[3]

"I spotted him," Thatcher said of Gorbachev, "because I was searching
for someone like him."

In the KGB residency in London, Oleg Gordievsky worked hard for
weeks in advance of Gorbachev's arrival. So many demands poured in
from headquarters in Moscow! Gordievsky realized the KGB chiefs saw
Gorbachev as a rising star and wanted to demonstrate they were behind
him. "The KGB was backing him because he was a new man, a man for
the future, an honest man who would fight corruption and all the other
negative features of Soviet society," Gordievsky recalled. Moscow bom-
barded the London residency with requests for material that could be
useful for the visit: about arms control, NATO, the economy, Britain's
relations with the United States, China and Eastern Europe. Although he
had never met Gorbachev, Gordievsky sensed a voracious appetite for
new information. "He wanted to be brilliant, know all about Britain, and
make an impression, and then come to Moscow and show everybody that
after Chernenko he was the best candidate," Gordievsky said.[4]

Gordievsky was not only writing reports for Moscow, but also feeding
information to his British handlers. They, too, were intensely interested
in Gorbachev, the rising star. Gordievsky gave the British valuable early
warning about what Gorbachev would ask and what he would say. At
the same time, Gordievsky passed back to Moscow the materials he was
given by the British. Gordievsky was a channel for both sides at a critical
moment in history. He was almost perfect for Thatcher's mission. The
British knew what their agent was doing, but the Soviets did not.

The days of Gorbachev's visit were frantic for Gordievsky. "Every
evening we were under pressure to produce a forecast of the line the next
day's meetings would take, and this of course was impossible to discover

from normal channels. I therefore went to the British and asked urgently for help: could they give me an idea of the subjects Mrs. Thatcher would raise? They produced a few possibilities, from which I managed to concoct a useful-looking memorandum; but the next day's meeting was much more fruitful. When I asked for a steer on Geoffrey Howe, they let me see the brief which the foreign secretary would be using in his talks with Mr. Gorbachev. My English was still poor, and my ignorance was compounded by nervousness and lack of time, so that I had to concentrate hard to remember all the points."

"Back at the station, full of excitement at my little *coup*, I sat down at a typewriter . . . and hacked out a rough draft, allegedly based on my general sources and what I had gleaned from newspapers," Gordievsky said. He was momentarily deflated when it was rewritten by another KGB man into something much less precise. He appealed to the acting chief, Leonid Nikitenko, who saw Gordievsky's version and sent it direct to Gorbachev, "verbatim."

After stepping into the mansion at Chequers, Gorbachev spoke to Thatcher over drinks in the Great Hall. He had risen to become Soviet agriculture chief, and inquired about farms he'd seen on the drive from London. The lunch table was set with Dover sole, roast beef and oranges, but they hardly touched the food. Gorbachev and Thatcher immediately fell into a vigorous debate. Gorbachev claimed the Soviet Union was reforming its economy. Thatcher, skeptical, lectured him about free enterprise and incentives. Gorbachev shot back that the Soviet system was superior to capitalism, and, according to Thatcher's account, he declared that the Soviet people lived "joyfully." Thatcher pointedly asked: then why are so many denied permission to leave? Gorbachev replied these people were working on national security matters. Thatcher didn't believe it.

When they got up and left the dining room, Raisa went with Denis to look at the Chequers library, where she took down a copy of Hobbes's *Leviathan*. Malcolm Rifkind, who accompanied her to the library, recalled she discussed her favorite contemporary British novelists, including Graham Greene, W. Somerset Maugham and C. P. Snow.[5]

In the main sitting room, Thatcher and Gorbachev got down to business. Thatcher recalled that the content of Gorbachev's remarks was unsurprising. What grabbed her attention was the refreshingly open style. "His personality could not have been more different from the wooden ventriloquism of the average Soviet *apparatchik*," she said. "He smiled, laughed, used his hands for emphasis, modulated his voice, followed an argument through and was a sharp debater." They talked for hours. Gorbachev did not consult prepared papers—he referred only to a small notebook of jottings, handwritten in green ink. "As the day wore on," she added, "I came to understand that it was the style far more than the Marxist rhetoric which expressed the substance of the personality beneath. I found myself liking him."

Gorbachev was well prepared. He quoted Lord Palmerston's famous dictum that Britain had no permanent allies or enemies, only permanent interests. "This was remarkable most of all for the precisely effective way it was deployed—and by this 'non-expert' in foreign policy," said Howe, who attended. He quoted Gorbachev as adding, "It is up to us to identify the interests we have in common."[6] Thatcher steered Gorbachev toward the topic of the arms race. After a year of impasse, the negotiations were to reopen in Geneva in three weeks, the first since the Soviets had walked out during the 1983 war scare.

At this moment, Gorbachev reached into his suit pocket. He unfolded a diagram he had brought with him, the size of a newspaper page. The page was filled with 165 boxes containing five thousand small dots, except for the center box, which had only one. The single dot in the center represented the explosive power of 3 million tons of bombs dropped by the Allies during the six years of World War II. The other dots represented the 15 billion tons of explosive power in the American and Soviet nuclear arsenals.

Gorbachev's diagram, which had been published in the *New York Times* as an advertisement by antinuclear businessmen the previous February, might have been dismissed as a piece of agitprop, a gimmick.[7] What was significant was not so much the dots and squares on the page, but the obvious enthusiasm of the man who was using it to make his point. Gorbachev was knowledgeable, unhesitating and demonstrative.

In Moscow, Gorbachev at this point had participated in the high-level internal discussions of military and foreign policy issues, such as the war in Afghanistan, the deployment of the Pioneer missiles, the shooting down of KAL 007 and the strategic arms negotiations. But little was known outside the Soviet Union of his views. He had never spoken out so openly on disarmament and foreign affairs as he began to do in Britain. Throughout the visit, he called attention to the dangers of nuclear war and emphasized Soviet fears of an arms race in space. He promised "radical reductions" in nuclear weapons and signaled that the Soviets were serious about returning to the Geneva talks. He confidently parried criticism about human rights and Afghanistan. In substance, Gorbachev did not change Soviet policy, and in the meeting with Thatcher, he went out of his way to cite Chernenko as the source of his authority.[8] But his style spoke volumes. He seemed to promise a more flexible approach, a sharp contrast with the rigidity of the past.

Gorbachev felt the conversation with Thatcher was a personal turning point.[9] He recalled vividly the diagram he presented at Chequers. He said he told Thatcher that all the weapons in one box on that page would "suffice to blow up the foundation of life on Earth. And it turns out that it can be done another 999 times—and what's after that? What, blow it up one million times? That is absurd. We were possessed by the absurd."

"It had been accumulated already, stored already—including inside of me—that something needed to be done," he said of the threat of nuclear war. "To describe it in one word, or one sentence: *that something needs to be done.*" But Gorbachev acknowledged it was difficult for him, back then, to imagine what that would be. Even as he unfolded the paper with all the squares and dots in front of Thatcher, he had no idea how to reduce the nuclear arsenals. He wondered, "How could all of it be stopped?"

Thatcher wasn't impressed with the Gorbachev diagram, but remembered he carried off the presentation with "a touch of theatre." Gorbachev also warned of the dangers of a "nuclear winter" that would follow a war with atomic bombs.[10] But Thatcher said, "I was not much moved by all this." She responded with a heartfelt lecture on the virtues of nuclear deterrence: the weapons, she said, had kept the peace. This was one of her core beliefs. Thatcher was "eloquent and emotional," Gorbachev remembered.

Thatcher also knew Gorbachev might give her a message for Reagan. She listened closely when he spoke about Reagan's Strategic Defense Initiative. Privately, Thatcher had little confidence in Reagan's dream of making nuclear weapons obsolete, but kept her counsel. What caught her ear at Chequers was the urgency in Gorbachev's voice. The Soviets, she concluded, "wanted it stopped at almost any price." She told Gorbachev there was no way Britain would be split from the United States. Gorbachev was supposed to leave at 4:30 P.M., but remained until 5:50 P.M. As his car pulled away, Thatcher recalled, "I hoped that I had been talking to the next Soviet leader."

Officially, Gorbachev came to London as head of a Supreme Soviet delegation, but his reception and performance were anything but low-key. He charmed his hosts and captured the imagination of Britain. Television had never looked kindly on any Soviet leader, but Gorbachev thrived on the attention. "Red Star is born," the *Daily Mail* said of Raisa. The Gorbachevs stopped in the cavernous reading room of the British Museum to see the place where Karl Marx had written *Das Kapital*, and they toured Westminster Abbey, seeing the graves of medieval kings, memorials to national poets, taking interest in the stained glass windows and the architecture.

On Monday, Thatcher gave an interview to the BBC. In her first answer to a question, she declared:

"I like Mr. Gorbachev. We can do business together."[11]

Gorbachev's visit was interrupted by news of the sudden death in Moscow of Dmitri Ustinov, the defense minister. Gorbachev flew home. Without Ustinov, there would be a new leadership vacuum. Chernenko was so ill he could not attend Ustinov's funeral, and Gorbachev faced still more uncertainty in the Kremlin. "The leadership of the country was in a deplorable state," he said.

Thatcher visited Reagan at Camp David on December 22, 1984. In preparation for the visit, the president had in his pocket seven note cards of talking points. The second card said, "Understand Gorbachev was impressive." And, "What are your impressions?"[12] Thatcher delivered a detailed report on the lunch at Chequers: human rights, economics, arms control. Thatcher said Gorbachev was more charming and more open to discussion and debate than his predecessors. She recounted how Gorbachev had zeroed in on the Strategic Defense Initiative. In response, Reagan opened up with a fulsome description of his great dream as both a technological quest and a moral imperative, with an ultimate goal of eliminating nuclear weapons. It was the first time Thatcher had heard Reagan talk about it directly, and she later confessed she was "horrified." But she listened.

She also relayed to Reagan what Gorbachev had said to her: "Tell your friend President Reagan not to go ahead with space weapons."[13]

To understand the rise of Mikhail Gorbachev, who, with Reagan, would change the world in the years ahead, we must first reach back a half century into the tumultuous events that confronted his people and his country, from Stalin's terror and the unimaginable losses of World War II, through the hardships, thaws, triumphs and stagnation of the postwar years. All of these directly touched Gorbachev. In his early life, there are few clues he would later become a catalyst of immense change. He was a child of the Soviet system, hardly a radical. But one thread is visible through it all. Gorbachev, over a long period of time, saw a reality that was strikingly different from the artificial world portrayed by the party and the leadership. As he rose through the ranks, he accumulated insights and revelations about the huge chasm between how people actually lived and the stuffy slogans of those who ruled. Raisa, too, grasped the depth of this chasm, and reinforced Gorbachev's determination to change it.

Gorbachev's doubts were sown incrementally, over a generation, and for many years kept to himself. His first reaction to a disappointment or failure was always to strive to improve the system. He was never in a frame of mind to tear it down. By the time he became Soviet leader, he had fully absorbed the abysmal reality, but had limited understanding of how to fix it. His greatest skill was in political maneuvering to achieve his goals. He tried to rescue the system by unleashing forces of openness and political pluralism, hoping that these would heal the other maladies. They could not.

Gorbachev's achievements in ending the Cold War—braking what he called the speeding locomotive of the nuclear arms race, allowing a revolution in Europe to unfold peacefully, ending the confrontation in the Third World—were not his first objectives. They grew out of his desire for radical change at home, rooted in his experience as a peasant son, a young witness to war, a university student during the thaw, a party official in the stagnation years and, most importantly, out of his own deep impressions about what had gone wrong.

Gorbachev did not set out to change the world, but rather to save his country. In the end, he did not save the country but may have saved the world.

Mikhail Sergeyevich Gorbachev was born March 2, 1931, in the small village of Privolnoye, in the black earth region of Stavropol in southern Russia. His parents, Sergei and Maria, worked the land; life in his village was little changed over centuries. From childhood, Gorbachev remembered "adobe huts with an earthen floor, and no beds at all"—people slept near the oven for warmth.[14] Gorbachev spent much of his childhood as the favorite of his mother's parents; he often lived with them. They kept books of Marx, Engels and Lenin on a shelf, but also a Russian Orthodox religious icon. His maternal grandfather, Pantelei, was remembered by Gorbachev as a tolerant man, and immensely respected in the village. In those years, Gorbachev was the only son; a brother was born after the war, when he was seventeen years old. He seems to have had a happy childhood. "I enjoyed absolute freedom," he recalled. "My grandparents made me feel like the most important member of the family."

The country was soon plunged into suffering and tragedy. Famine struck the Stavropol region in 1933, when Gorbachev was just two years old. Stalin had launched the mass collectivization of agriculture, a brutal process of forcing the peasants into collective farms and punishing those known as *kulaks*, who were somewhat better off. A third to half of the population of Privolnoye died of hunger. "Entire families were dying, and the half-ruined ownerless huts would remain deserted for years," Gorbachev remembered. Stalin's purges took millions of lives among the peasantry in the 1930s.

Gorbachev's family was touched by the purges, too. His grandfather on his father's side, Andrei, rejected collectivization and tried to make it on his own. In the spring of 1934, Andrei was arrested and accused of failing to fulfill the sowing plan set by the government for individual peasants. "But no seeds were available to fulfill the plan," Gorbachev recalled of the absurdity of the charge. Andrei was declared a "saboteur" and sent to a prison camp for two years, but released early, in 1935. On his return, he became a leader of the collective farm.

Two years later, grandfather Pantelei was also arrested. The charges were similarly absurd, that he had been a member of a counterrevolutionary organization and sabotaged the collective farm's work. The arrest was "my first real trauma," Gorbachev recalled. "They took him away in the middle of the night." His grandfather was treated badly. Pantelei was finally released one winter evening in 1938, and returned to Privolnoye. Sitting at a hand-planed rustic table, he told the family how he had been beaten and tortured. Pantelei said he was convinced that Stalin did not know of the misdeeds of the secret police, and he did not blame the Soviet regime for his misfortunes. Pantelei never discussed it again. Gorbachev was only seven years old at the time, but later said the events left a deep, lasting impression on him. He held the secret of Pantelei's ordeal privately, and only discussed it in the open a half century later.

By the late 1930s, both grandfathers were back at home, and village life seemed to be on an upswing. The families spent Sunday picnics in the woods. Then, on one of these Sundays, June 22, 1941, came terrifying news. A radio announced: the Germans had invaded the Soviet Union.

Gorbachev's father was soon off to the front. He bought his ten-year-old son an ice cream, and a balalaika for a keepsake. Women, children and old men sobbed as the soldiers left. A massive snowfall that first winter put Privolnoye into deep isolation. There were no radios and newspapers seldom arrived. Gorbachev remembered that he "skipped from childhood directly into adulthood." In the summer of 1942, the village fell under German occupation for four and a half months. The war devastated the countryside; they had no seed, no machines, no cattle. Famine spread in the winter and spring of 1944. The family was saved when Gorbachev's mother, then thirty-three years old, sold his father's last belongings, two pairs of boots and a suit, in a neighboring town for a 109-pound sack of corn.

In the summer of 1944, the family received a letter from the front. It contained family photographs and an announcement that Sergei Gorbachev had been killed in battle in the Carpathians. "The family cried for three days," Gorbachev recalled. Then another letter came from his father saying he was alive. Both letters were dated August 27, 1944. Four days later, yet another letter—Sergei was indeed alive! How did it happen? His father later told Gorbachev that after an ambush, his unit had found his bag alone. He was missing and assumed dead. They sent the first letter to the family. Only days later did they discover him alive, but seriously wounded. Sergei told his son this confusion was typical of the chaos of war. "I have remembered this all my life," Gorbachev later wrote.

In the early spring of 1943, Gorbachev was with other children, roaming the countryside, when they came to a remote stretch of forest between Privolnoye and a neighboring village. "There we stumbled upon the remains of Red Army soldiers, who had fought their last battle there in summer 1942. It was an unspeakable horror: decaying corpses, partly devoured by animals, skulls in rusted helmets, bleached bones, rifles protruding from the sleeves of rotting jackets. There was a light machine gun, some hand grenades, heaps of empty cartridges. There they lay, in the thick mud of the trenches and craters, unburied, staring at us out of black, gaping eye-sockets. We came home in a state of shock."

Gorbachev was fourteen years old when the war ended. "Our generation is the generation of wartime children," he said. "It has burned us, leaving its mark both on our characters and on our view of the world."

After the war, Gorbachev worked in the fields each summer, "backbreaking labor twenty hours a day." In high school, he was a good student and threw himself into the drama club and sports. School records showed Gorbachev had received top grades in Russian literature, trigonometry, history of the Soviet Union, the Soviet constitution, astronomy. He graduated in 1950 with a silver medal.[15] For those long summers in the fields, he had also won an award, the Order of the Red Banner of Labor. This was a rare award for a schoolboy and most certainly helped Gorbachev win a place at Moscow State University, the most prestigious in the country, in the law department.[16]

Arriving in the capital in September 1950, at nineteen years old, the peasant boy was disoriented for the first few months in the bustling metropolis. Freshmen students lived twenty-two to a dorm room; for a few kopeks they could buy tea in the cafeteria, with unlimited free bread on the tables.

Gorbachev joined the Communist Party in 1952. To be a Communist then was to be a Stalinist. The first two years of his university life coincided with Stalin's anti-cosmopolitan campaign, aimed at Jewish scholars and writers. This was an eye-opener for Gorbachev. He recalled that one morning, a friend, a Jew, had been confronted by a shouting, taunting mob and then crudely shoved off a tram. "I was shocked."

By his own account, Gorbachev was taken with Soviet ideology, like many of his generation. "Communist ideology was very attractive for young people then," he recalled. "The front-line soldiers came back from the war, most of them young people, filled with the pride of victory." The younger generation hoped that war, famine and the Great Terror were things of the past, and believed they were building a new society of social justice and people power.[17]

Stalin was part of this fabric of belief. Stalin's "Short Course" of the history of the party was held up to students as "a model of scientific thought," Gorbachev recalled.[18] The students "took many of the professed theses for granted, sincerely convinced of their truth." Gorbachev was a leader of the Communist Youth League, known as the Komsomol. In high school he had written a final exam paper in which the title was borrowed from a song, "Stalin—our combat glory."

But Gorbachev also was restive, and twice caused a stir by mildly speaking out against authority at the university. Once he wrote an anonymous note to a lecturer who mechanically droned on by reading Stalin's work verbatim to the class. This was disrespectful to the students, Gorbachev said, since they had already read the book. Gorbachev admitted to writing the note, which touched off an investigation, but no action was taken.

When Stalin died on March 5, 1953, Gorbachev joined the huge mourning crowds in Moscow's streets. He was "deeply and sincerely moved by Stalin's death." But in the years that followed, Gorbachev came to see Stalin differently. On February 25, 1956, Khrushchev delivered his famous "secret speech" at the 20th Party Congress denouncing Stalin's personality cult and use of violence and persecution. Only after the speech, Gorbachev recalled, "did I begin to understand the inner connection between what had happened in our country and what had happened to my family." His grandfather Pantelei had said that Stalin didn't know of his torture. But maybe Stalin was the one responsible for the family's pain.

"The document containing Khrushchev's denunciations circulated briefly within the party, and then it was withdrawn. But I managed to get my hands on it. I was shocked, bewildered and lost. It wasn't an analysis, just facts, deadly facts. Many of us simply could not believe that such things could be true. For me it was easier. My family had itself been one of the victims of the repression of the 1930s."[19] Gorbachev later frequently called Khrushchev's speech "courageous." It was not a total break with the past, but it was a break nonetheless. He felt once again as if illusions about the system were falling away. Gorbachev saw this as a reason to be hopeful, but he was also aware that many people, especially those in an older generation, were skeptical and downright confused. Not everything was clear for Gorbachev, either. How could everything they had believed in be wrong?

While at the university, Gorbachev met and married Raisa Titorenko, a bright philosophy student. In the two years after Stalin's death, Moscow began to open up to new ideas, often expressed in literature. Ilya Ehrenburg's novel *The Thaw*, a title that came to define the era, was published in 1954. Gorbachev met a young Czech student at the university, Zdeněk Mlynář, who became Gorbachev's best friend in those years, and they enjoyed stormy debates late into the night in their dormitory room. The university experience began to open Gorbachev's eyes, but at the same time, "for me and others of my generation the question of changing the system in which we lived did not arise."

Upon graduation in the summer of 1955, Gorbachev returned to Stavropol, where he found new evidence of the gap between rhetoric and reality. Many saw this but did nothing; what was different about Gorbachev was his capacity to be shocked by it. During his university days he held a summer job in a local procuracy in Stavropol, but was appalled by the arrogant behavior of the apparatchiks.[20] In a letter to Raisa written then, he described them as "disgusting." He added, "Especially the manner of life of the local bosses. The acceptance of convention, subordination, with everything predetermined, the open impudence of officials and the arrogance. When you look at one of the local leaders you see nothing outstanding apart from his belly."

Gorbachev decided on a career with the Komsomol, the party's youth division, as deputy head of the "agitation and propaganda department." This was a conformist career path. Gorbachev threw himself into the work, honing his speaking skills, often making trips around the region to exhort young people to believe in the party.[21] The job brought him face-to-face with the bleakness of daily life, especially in the backwater rural corners of the Soviet Union. On one trip, he went to the most remote cattle farm in the region. After hiking through thick mud, Gorbachev arrived at a village of low, smoke-belching huts and blackened fences along the River Gorkaya Balka, and was shocked at what lay before him: poverty and desolation. "On the hillside, I wondered: 'How is it possible, how can anyone live like that?'" Gorbachev's impressions were shaped and deeply reinforced by his strong-willed wife, Raisa, who researched and wrote a thesis on peasant life in these years. She may have seen more of these desolate villages than he did. She trudged in boots and rode by motorcycle and cart through the bleak Russian countryside to carry out her research.[22]

Gorbachev moved up in Stavropol, first through the city organization and then to become the highest-ranking party official in the region. In these years, in the 1960s and 1970s, he again felt the disparity between the way people lived and the empty party slogans and rhetoric. In farming and industry, the heavy hand of the state stifled individual initiative. Theft, toadying, incompetence and malaise were everywhere. Central planning was both intrusive and woefully inefficient. Once, he toured a collective farm in Stavropol. There were "magnificent crops of both grain and fodder." Gorbachev was pleased, but asked the chairman of the collective farm, "Where did you get the pipe to do the irrigation?" The man just smiled. He had diverted the pipe from somewhere, on his own, and Gorbachev knew that his success had nothing to do with socialism.[23]

It is important to recall that the most daring changes in the centrally controlled Soviet economic system at the time were extremely modest, such as demonstrations of self-financing, or *khozraschyot*, the idea that a factory or farm could retain its own profits. Sweeping challenges to the system were just not possible; even minor experiments in individual initiative were snuffed out. This is the world Gorbachev knew. The bureaucrats at central planning in Moscow arrogantly issued orders to do this and that, and on the ground in farms and cities, the orders often made no sense. The demands were ignored, statistics faked, budgets swallowed up with no result, and anyone who deviated was punished. From 1970 to 1978, Gorbachev was first secretary of the Communist Party in Stavropol, the highest-ranking official in the region, an expanse between the Black and Caspian Seas with the most fertile lands in all of Russia. Gorbachev was essentially the governor, but wielded much more power than an American governor. Regional party bosses were a key power bloc in the Soviet system and could affect how Moscow decisions were implemented. As first secretary, Gorbachev joined an elite group at the pinnacle of Soviet society. He was eligible for special privileges—good housing, food, transport—and was a full member of the Central Committee in Moscow. In the Brezhnev years, a party first secretary was "a prince in his own domain," as Robert G. Kaiser of the *Washington Post* described it.[24] But Gorbachev was something of a populist. By one account, he often walked to his office and informally listened to people on the streets. He was a regular at theater performances and encouraged the local press to be less driven by party ideology.[25] Gorbachev was "as pragmatic an innovator as the conservative temper of the times allowed."[26] For example, he supported a farming plan to give autonomy to groups or teams of workers, including families, even though it was viewed with suspicion by the Moscow bureaucrats. In 1978 Gorbachev wrote a lengthy memo on the problems of agriculture that called for giving "more independence to enterprises and associations" in deciding key production and money issues. But there is no evidence that these ideas ever took root very widely, and Gorbachev was definitely not a radical. He joined other party bosses in lavishing obsequious praise on the 1978 volume of Brezhnev's ghostwritten memoirs of war, *Malaya Zemlya*, a blatant effort at self-glorification. Words of the state and party lost their meaning, but it was mandatory for Gorbachev and others to keep repeating them.

Gorbachev realized as regional party boss that something much more serious was wrong with the Soviet system than just inefficiency, theft and poor planning. The deeper flaw was that no one could break out with new ideas. Gorbachev bridled at being "bound hand and foot by orders from the center."[27] He concluded that a "hierarchy of vassals and chiefs of principalities was in fact the way the country was run." In a reflection many years later, he said bluntly, "It was a caste system based on mutual protection."

The outside world, too, offered Gorbachev fresh evidence of the contrast between reality and the party line. When his university friend Mlynář visited Stavropol in 1967, he surprised Gorbachev with a warning that Czechoslovakia was "on the verge of a major upheaval." In the year that followed, Mlynář became a figure in the liberalizing movement in Czechoslovakia, headed by Alexander Dubček, which led to the Prague Spring and the drive to create "socialism with a human face." This fling with democracy was crushed by Soviet tanks and Warsaw Pact troops on the night of August 20–21, 1968. Gorbachev has acknowledged that in 1968 he supported the invasion as a party official in Stavropol. But Gorbachev saw a different reality a year later when he visited Prague. On this trip, he did not see Mlynář, but he realized people sincerely believed in the liberalization and hated the Soviet leadership in Moscow. While the KGB line was that external factors were at work, Gorbachev saw that the impetus was internal. On a factory tour in Brno, workers refused to even talk to Gorbachev. "This was a shock to me," Gorbachev said. "This visit overturned all my conceptions." In Bratislava, he saw walls densely covered with anti-Soviet slogans. "From that time on, I began to think more and more about what was going on in our country, and I came to an unconsoling conclusion: there was something wrong . . ." But he kept these thoughts to himself, and Raisa.[28] Throughout the 1970s, Gorbachev traveled several times to the West, including Italy, France, Belgium and West Germany. What he saw in these relatively prosperous democracies was far different from what he had been shown in Soviet propaganda books, films and radio broadcasts. "People there lived in better conditions, and were better off than in our country. The question haunted me:

why was the standard of living in our country lower than in other developed countries?"

The Stavropol town of Kislovodsk was favored by the Soviet elite for its soothing spas and mineral springs. The Soviet KGB chief, Yuri Andropov, who suffered kidney ailments, often retreated to a KGB lodge there. He and Gorbachev shared a holiday at the mineral springs in August 1978. Andropov had taken notice of Gorbachev as a potential future leader. They climbed in the nearby mountains, and spent many hours sitting around an open bonfire, cooking shashlik under the star-studded skies. Andropov, who had wide-ranging interests, often talked to Gorbachev about affairs of state, and they listened to tape recordings of Vladimir Vysotsky and Yuri Vizbor, who strummed a seven-string guitar and sang of people's everyday problems. This must have been an amazing scene: two party bosses enjoying the music of bards whose works were largely distributed on bootleg tapes. Andropov, head of the secret police since 1967, became one of Gorbachev's mentors and tutors.

In Moscow, Gorbachev was elected a secretary of the Central Committee and put in charge of agriculture.[29] Full of enthusiasm, he went to see Brezhnev about farm policy. But Gorbachev, forty-eight years old, found the Soviet leader, then seventy-one, almost lifeless in his Kremlin office. "Not only did he not take up the conversation, but he showed no response at all, neither to my words nor to myself," Gorbachev recalled.

As a junior member of the Soviet ruling elite, Gorbachev soon discovered that the final years of Brezhnev's rule were filled with such scenes. Some Politburo meetings lasted no longer than fifteen or twenty minutes, so as not to tire the chairman. "It was a sad sight," recalled Gorbachev. The country was in serious trouble economically as the oil boost of the late 1970s began to give out. The war in Afghanistan, launched by a coterie around Brezhnev, turned into a quagmire. The hopes of détente in the 1970s evaporated, and the superpower tension escalated. Food shortages grew at home. During the first four years that Gorbachev was secretary for agriculture in Moscow, there were four successive bad harvests and massive Soviet grain purchases abroad.[30]

From the time Gorbachev arrived in Moscow in November 1978,

through the early 1980s, a simmering power struggle unfolded between an old guard, bastions of the party and military, and a handful of reformers, most of whom were academics with fresh ideas but no power base. When Brezhnev died, Andropov promoted a group of younger officials, including Gorbachev and Nikolai Ryzhkov, an experienced factory manager from Sverdlovsk. Andropov put Gorbachev in charge of economic policy for the whole country. Gorbachev solicited ideas from the academic reformers. Now, at least the reformers had an umbrella—Gorbachev would listen to them.[31]

True to his background in the KGB, Andropov tried to rejuvenate the country with police-state methods, such as arresting people seen as loafers on the street during working hours. Gorbachev told him this was a dubious practice, that people were making jokes about it, but Andropov wouldn't listen. He brushed Gorbachev off, saying, "When you get to my age, you'll understand."

What brought these two men together was a shared understanding of the plight of the system. Gorbachev recalled that Andropov was determined to root out the ills of the Brezhnev era, including "protectionism, in-fighting and intrigues, corruption, moral turpitude, bureaucracy, disorganization and laxity." But as historian Robert English pointed out, it was extraordinarily hard to make change "in an ossified, militarized Party-state system," especially given the latent power of the hard-liners.[32] In the end, Andropov ran out of time. Gorbachev wrote later that Andropov could not have really carried out drastic change; the years with the KGB left him unable to break out. "He was too deeply entrenched in his own past experience; it held him firmly in its grasp," Gorbachev said.

It fell to Gorbachev to become the agent of change, and his time was coming.

A turning point came in May 1983, when Gorbachev went to Canada for a seven-day visit as head of a parliamentary delegation. Alexander Yakovlev, the Soviet ambassador there, saw an opportunity to show Gorbachev how the West worked, and to offer his own deep concerns about the direction of the Soviet Union. In Alberta, Gorbachev was fascinated by a discussion with a wealthy farmer who had a 4,942-acre spread. Gorbachev quickly got to talking and discovered the farmer's herd produced a milk yield of 4,700 kilograms each cow per year. The yield of Soviet cows was 2,258 kilograms.[33] The farmer had two homes, cars and aluminum grain towers, and told Gorbachev he worked a long, hard year without vacations. Canada offered Gorbachev a prosperous counterpoint to Soviet agricultural failure.

The key moment of the visit was out of public view, on the evening of May 19, at the Ontario farm of Eugene Whelan, the Canadian agriculture minister. Whelan had invited Gorbachev for dinner, but was delayed in arriving. His wife, Elizabeth, greeted the Soviet guests after they drove in on a long, bumpy dirt road. Waiting around, Gorbachev and Yakovlev decided to take a private stroll, alone, in a nearby orchard. Yakovlev had been the Central Committee propaganda chief in the early 1970s, but had written an article with radical ideas for a newspaper—and was sent to diplomatic exile in Canada. He was a reformist whose enthusiasm for change only deepened as he witnessed the collapse of détente and the stagnation of the late Brezhnev years. Yakovlev, then fifty-nine years old, was angered by the over-militarization of Soviet society, and he believed markets could offer improvements to socialism. Most of all, he later recalled, he had made freedom his "religion." In the walk in the orchard, it all spilled out.

"We had a lot of time together," Yakovlev recalled. "So we took a long walk on that minister's farm and, as it often happens, both of us were just kind of flooded, and let go. I somehow, for some reason, threw caution to the wind and started telling him about what I considered to be utter stupidities in the area of foreign affairs, especially about those SS-20 missiles that were being stationed in Europe and a lot of other things. And he did the same thing. We were completely frank. He frankly talked about the problems in the internal situation in Russia. He was saying that under these conditions, the conditions of dictatorship and absence of freedom, the country would simply perish. So it was at that time, during our three-hour conversation, almost as if our heads were knocked together, that we poured it all out."[34]

Two weeks later, Yakovlev was asked to return to Moscow to head up a prestigious think tank, the Institute of World Economy and International Relations, where he would become a pioneer of the new thinking.

The Kremlin paralysis under Chernenko was grave. Politburo meetings were difficult to convene. Fifteen or twenty minutes before the start time,

11 A.M., a phone call came and Gorbachev was told that Chernenko was so sick he could not attend. Would Gorbachev take the chair? This left Gorbachev little time to prepare, and it was awkward in front of the other, more senior members. By the end of 1984, "Chernenko had dropped out altogether," Gorbachev recalled. With no one in charge, the suspicions and infighting worsened. According to Yakovlev, hard-liners launched an offensive against some of the liberal think tanks, threatening a purge that would have silenced them.[35]

Gorbachev's sense of gloom was reinforced at a December soul-searching talk with Eduard Shevardnadze, who was the first secretary of the party in the republic of Georgia, just to the south of the Stavropol region. Like Gorbachev, Shevardnadze was a high-ranking official and a man with clear vision about the country's problems. They met at a barren park on the deserted shore near the Black Sea's Cape Pitsunda. Strolling down a path beneath the trees, they talked openly, holding nothing back. "Everything's rotten," Shevardnadze said. "It has to be changed."[36]

That winter was terrible. Yegor Ligachev recalled that because of massive snows and bitter cold, industry in the country began to break down. Fifty-four of the largest electric plants were on the verge of shut-down because 22,000 freight cars carrying coal were stopped dead on the tracks, their cargo frozen solid.[37]

In early December 1984, Gorbachev prepared to give a critical speech at a party conference on ideology. The Soviet elite was dejected and Gorbachev wanted to offer badly needed new ideas. Months of work had gone into refining his speech, with help from Yakovlev. The participants had already arrived in Moscow. Then Gorbachev got a call from the ailing, cautious Chernenko at 4 P.M. Alarmed at the new ideas Gorbachev planned to offer in the speech, Chernenko insisted the conference should be postponed for some vague reason about not being fully prepared. Gorbachev was indignant. The participants had already arrived! What was Chernenko thinking? "OK," the Soviet leader backed down. "Have it, but don't make too much noise." In fact, Gorbachev's December 10 address offered hints of dramatic change to come. He talked about restructuring—*perestroika*.

On February 24, 1985, Chernenko was shown voting on television in an election. Chernenko was seen accepting his ballot, voting, accepting flowers from a well-wisher and shaking hands. He raised his hand up to his brow and said "Good." End of broadcast. Anatoly Chernyaev, the deputy of the International Department at the Central Committee, watched with disgust. "A man half-dead. A mummy," Chernyaev wrote in his diary. Two days later, Chernenko was shown on television again. This time he appeared wan and held on to a chair for support as an election official handed him a document. He was wheezing. "It was a terrible show," Chernyaev wrote.[38] The only other official in the room in both broadcasts was Viktor Grishin, seventy, the Moscow party chief, a member of the Politburo's old guard who seemed to be making a bid for power, positioning himself standing next to Chernenko. But Grishin's move swiftly backfired. The sight of the ill Chernenko was a reminder, if one was needed, that it was time for change.

On the evening of Sunday, March 10, Gorbachev returned home from work and took a call from the Kremlin doctor, Yevgeny Chazov. Chernenko had died of heart failure and complications from emphysema at 7:20 P.M. Gorbachev, who had been passed over in the transition after Andropov, wasted little time. A Politburo meeting was called at the Kremlin for 11 P.M. Three voting members, including two old Brezhnevites, were out of the country and would not make it back.

About twenty minutes before the meeting started, Gorbachev met Gromyko, the foreign minister, lion of the old guard, in the Walnut Room, where full voting members of the Politburo often gathered before formal sessions. Gromyko was the key figure in deciding who would be the next general secretary. Earlier, Gromyko had sent a private emissary to Gorbachev with the message that he would back him in the succession struggle, in exchange for being allowed to retire as foreign minister and take up a sinecure position as chairman of the Supreme Soviet. The back channel was through Gromyko's son, Anatoly, and Gorbachev's reformist adviser, Yakovlev.[39]

When Gorbachev and Gromyko met in the Walnut Room, they reconfirmed the understanding reached earlier.

"Andrei Andreyevich, we have to consolidate our effort, the moment is crucial," Gorbachev recalled saying to Gromyko.

"I believe everything is clear," Gromyko replied.

When they had all assembled, Gorbachev informed the Politburo of

Chernenko's death. Usually, the person chosen to head up the funeral commission was the one who would be the next general secretary. The question of the funeral commission arose. There was momentary hesitation in the room: Would Grishin make a play for it?

In fact, before the meeting, Gorbachev had already made a gesture to Grishin, who declined to head the commission.

"Why the hesitation about the chairman?" Grishin said now, in front of the Politburo members. "Everything is clear. Let's appoint Mikhail Sergeyevich."

The old guard had died. Gorbachev became head of the commission and the next day would become the new general secretary. Precisely why Grishin did not fight is not known, but he may well have realized, or sensed, that he had no chance, that Gromyko would support Gorbachev.

Gorbachev was a shining light in a dusky hall. Five of the ten voting members of the Politburo that day were over seventy, three in their sixties and only two in their fifties. Not only was Gorbachev, at fifty-four, the youngest member of the Politburo by a full five years, he was thirteen years younger than the average age of the voting membership.[40] Plans were hurriedly made through the night for the transition, which would include a Politburo meeting and then a Central Committee plenum March 11 to ratify the choice.

Gorbachev went home at 4 A.M. He was then living at a large dacha outside of Moscow. Raisa was waiting up. Suspicious of KGB listening bugs, they went out in the garden, as they did almost every day. They strolled the paths for a long time just before dawn. Spring had not yet come, there was snow on the ground. Raisa recalled the air felt very heavy. They talked about the events and the implications. Gorbachev told her he had been frustrated all the years in Moscow, having not accomplished as much as he wanted, always hitting a wall. To really get things done, he would have to accept the job.

"We can't go on living like this," he said.

At the next day's session, Gromyko delivered a strong testament to Gorbachev, speaking in a way that was not customary on such occasions, without notes and without hesitation. "I shall be straight," Gromyko began. Gorbachev is the "absolutely right choice." Gorbachev had "indomitable creative energy, striving to do more and do it better." Gorbachev respected "the interests of the party, the interests of the society, the interests of the people" above his own, he said. Gorbachev would bring experience of work in the regions and the center, and ran the Politburo while Chernenko was ill. This required knowledge and stamina. "We won't make a mistake if we choose him," Gromyko said.

After the agonizing years of stagnation, death and disappointment, Gorbachev was chosen first and foremost as the best hope to get the country moving.[41] Georgi Shakhnazarov, who had served Andropov and would later advise Gorbachev, recalled that Gorbachev's rise was not a certainty. Gorbachev did not have a sterling biography that made him the natural choice, and the Politburo might have chosen another, such as Grishin, to muddle through. But Shakhnazarov felt there was one factor that, while not official, could not be ignored. "People were desperately tired of participating in a disgraceful farce . . . They were tired of seeing leaders with shaking heads and faded eyes, knowing the fate of the country and half the world was entrusted to the care of these miserable semi-paralytics."[42]

YEAR OF THE SPY

When Reagan was awakened March 11, 1985, at 4 A.M., with word that Chernenko had died, he asked Nancy, "How am I supposed to get anyplace with the Russians if they keep dying on me?" Four leaders—Lenin, Stalin, Khrushchev and Brezhnev—had guided the Soviet Union over its first six decades. Now it had the third new leader in three years. Perhaps no one really knew at this early point that Gorbachev would become a revolutionary. But at first, Reagan missed the signs. He was blinkered by his own deep anti-communism and his own long-held ideas about the Soviet system, and hampered by lack of good intelligence. To the United States, the Kremlin remained a black box. Reagan and many of those around him could not imagine a Soviet leader carrying out radical reform from above. Shultz saw promise in Gorbachev, as had Thatcher in Britain, but Reagan's circle was riven by disagreement, and there was no consensus that this was a man they could do business with.

Among the hard-liners, Robert Gates, then the deputy CIA director for intelligence, felt that Gorbachev was a tough guy wearing a well-tailored suit. Underneath, he saw trouble, and did not want to be fooled. In the weeks before Gorbachev took power, in February 1985, Gates wrote a memo to one of the CIA's leading Soviet experts. "I don't much care for the way we are writing about Gorbachev," Gates said. "We are losing the thread of what toughness and skill brought him to where he is.

This is not some Gary Hart or even Lee Iacocca. We have to give the policymakers a clearer view of the kind of person they may be facing." Gates said he felt that Gorbachev was the heir to Andropov, the former KGB chief, and to Suslov, the onetime orthodox ideology chief. Thus, Gates said, Gorbachev "could not be all sweetness and light. These had been two of the hardest cases in recent Soviet history. They would not take a wimp under their wing."[1]

Reagan found this analysis very appealing. The assumption was based on years of imagining a Soviet monolith—that all leaders were alike, that the system could not change. Reagan met with U.S. Ambassador to Moscow Arthur Hartman. "He confirms what I believe that Gorbachev will be tough as any of their leaders," Reagan recalled. "If he wasn't a confirmed ideologue he never would have been chosen . . . by the Politburo."[2]

Yet Reagan was capable of holding multiple views at the same time. He still dreamed of eliminating nuclear weapons, even if he had doubts about the new Soviet leader. He mentioned elimination of nuclear weapons as "our common goal" in one of his first letters to Gorbachev.[3] Reagan also listened to Shultz, who urged him to use "quiet diplomacy" with the new Soviet leader. As Reagan recalled it, this meant "the need to lean on the Soviets but to do so one on one—not in the papers."[4]

Five years into his presidency, Reagan was still surrounded by intense feuds and conflicts among those who served him. Tempers were raw over a Soviet blunder in East Germany. On March 24, an American army officer, Major Arthur D. Nicholson Jr., was shot by a panicky Soviet sentry while in a restricted area. As with the Korean airliner, the clumsy Soviet response to the incident made it even worse. The shooting "has to be called murder," Reagan wrote in his diary.[5]

At a White House breakfast April 27, Reagan's top cabinet members argued over whether to allow the secretary of commerce to visit Moscow on a trade mission. Casey and Weinberger were opposed. Shultz wanted to engage Moscow, and thought Reagan did too. "The scene was bizarre," Shultz said. "Here was the president ready to lead the charge to engage with the Soviets. At the same time, his secretary of defense and director of central intelligence were leading their own charge in exactly the opposite direction."[6] Tired of the disputes, Shultz told Reagan he wanted to resign by summer. Reagan talked him out of it, saying he needed Shultz to deal with the Soviets.[7] Reagan decided to let the trade mission go ahead, but sent a tough, private message to Gorbachev.[8]

The Central Intelligence Agency devoted about 45 percent of its analytical manpower to the Soviet Union.[9] But for all the attention to weapons and research programs, the agency had little understanding of the new man in the Kremlin. Shultz later recalled that "our knowledge of the Kremlin was thin, and the CIA, I found, was usually wrong about it."[10] Gates acknowledged that the CIA had scant inside knowledge. "We were embarrassingly hungry for details" from the British and Canadians who had met Gorbachev on his visits, and others who knew him, Gates said. These sources described Gorbachev as stylistically more open than Soviet leaders had been, but "unyielding" on the issues. Gorbachev was "an innovative, dynamic communist, not a revolutionary," Gates concluded. The CIA's first assessment of Gorbachev, titled "Gorbachev, the New Broom," was sent to Reagan on June 27. The study portrayed Gorbachev as gambling on a campaign against corruption and inefficiency, but "not radical reform," at home. The study said Gorbachev had already demonstrated that he was "the most aggressive and activist Soviet leader since Khrushchev."[11] When this paper went to Reagan, however, Casey attached a cover note that was far more skeptical. Casey wrote that Gorbachev and those around him "are not reformers and liberalizers either in Soviet domestic or foreign policy."[12]

He could not have been more wrong.

Inside the Kremlin, the tune was changing. Gorbachev demanded a rewrite of a Communist Party program. "It must not be propagandistic babble about endless achievements," Gorbachev wrote on the document, "the kind of stuff that you used to write for Brezhnev and Chernenko, but rather include specific proposals for a truly radical transformation of the economy."[13] This was just the beginning. Anatoly Chernyaev, the deputy head of the International Department of the Central Committee, who received this note, wondered, "Is this really happening? It's too good to be true."

The day after Gorbachev became general secretary, on March 12, he received an important memorandum from Alexander Yakovlev, the reformist thinker who had the soul-searching talk with Gorbachev in the orchard in Canada. The title was simply "On Reagan."[14] In tone and substance, Yakovlev offered a stark contrast to the Soviet rhetoric of the past. Yakovlev's analysis of Reagan, while imperfect, was pragmatic, not ideological. He described Reagan as striving to grasp the initiative in international affairs, to go down in history as a peacemaking president. He said Reagan had fulfilled his promises to rebuild the American military; Reagan "practically gave to the military business everything he promised." This reflected an early misconception of Yakovlev and Gorbachev about the power of the defense industry in the United States. But Yakovlev did not make Reagan out to be a reckless cowboy, as Soviet propaganda had done so often. Rather, he said, the president was seeking to improve his political standing, facing off against many different forces, including global competition from Japan, domestic budget pressure and restive European allies. Reagan had invited Gorbachev to a summit, and Yakovlev told Gorbachev, ". . . from Reagan's point of view, his proposition is thoughtful, precisely calculated, and contains no political risk." There had not been a superpower summit in six years. Yakovlev's advice to Gorbachev was: go to a summit, but not hastily. Make it clear to Reagan, he said, that the world does not spin every time he pushes a button.

This was a moment when Reagan could have used fresh and penetrating insights into Gorbachev's thinking and life experiences. If he had seen Gorbachev's notes about radical economic reform, if he had read Yakovlev's memo, he might have realized immediately that Gorbachev had people around him who were thinking in new ways. The United States deployed remarkably accurate satellites to collect technical data on missiles, but it lacked the textured and revealing intelligence on the new leader that came only from human sources. Reagan would have benefited from knowing that Gorbachev nurtured a lifetime of lessons and convictions about the gap between the Soviet party-state and society. Reagan would have found fascinating Gorbachev's comment to Raisa that "we can't go on living like this." Reagan would have been surprised to know of Gorbachev's reluctance to use force, and his determination there would not be another Prague Spring.[15] But Reagan did not know these things. The United States had never recruited a spy who provided political information at a high level inside the Kremlin.[16] And just when the United States could have used some good human intelligence about the new leader in Moscow, the CIA suffered a series of blinding catastrophes.

A month after Gorbachev took office, on April 16, 1985, a man with a mustache and heavy eyeglasses waited at the bar of the Mayflower Hotel in Washington for a meeting with a Soviet diplomat. The man was Aldrich Ames, a forty-four-year-old CIA counterintelligence official who was supposed to be keeping track of, and looking for, Soviet spies working in the United States. Ames often met Soviet officials at downtown restaurants to talk about arms control and U.S.-Soviet relations. This was part of his job in the hunt for spies. Ames was permitted by the CIA to have these contacts, as long as he reported them afterward.

Ames was waiting for Sergei Chuvakhin, a specialist on arms control, who failed to show up. Ames walked two blocks to the ornate Soviet Embassy on 16th Street N.W. and entered. The building was constantly being monitored by the FBI, which Ames knew, but he may have assumed that he would not raise suspicions because he was known to meet with Soviet officials for his work. Inside, Ames went to the reception desk and asked for Chuvakhin. At the same time, he silently handed an envelope to the duty officer at the desk.

The envelope was addressed to Stanislav Androsov, the KGB resident, the most senior KGB man in the embassy. Ames didn't say so specifically, but motioned to the duty officer that he wanted the envelope given to the KGB boss. Chuvakhin then showed up briefly, apologized for the no-show at the hotel, and Ames departed.[17]

Ames was a spy hunter, but in the envelope he offered to become a spy himself for the Soviet Union. Inside, he left a note that described two or three cases involving Soviets who had approached the CIA to offer their services. These were double agents. He thought that by identifying them, he would establish his own credentials as a CIA insider who had something to offer. He also included a page from a CIA phone directory of the Soviet and Eastern Europe division that identified him as the chief counterintelligence official in the division. For the KGB, this was a potential gold mine—a person in this position would know the names of all the CIA spies inside the Soviet Union. Ames asked for $50,000, and said nothing more.[18]

A few weeks later, Chuvakhin called and scheduled another meeting with Ames. On May 15, Ames entered the Soviet Embassy and asked for

Chuvakhin, but was escorted instead to another, soundproofed room. There, a KGB officer passed him a note saying they had agreed to pay him $50,000.

The very next day in London, May 16, a cipher clerk walked into the office of Oleg Gordievsky and handed him a handwritten telegram from Moscow headquarters.

Gordievsky had done much to help the West: revealing Andropov's paranoia about nuclear war with the RYAN operation, and paving the way for Gorbachev's successful visit to Britain. In April, Gordievsky moved up to become KGB chief in London, in position to do even more for the West. But the message from Moscow hit him like a "thunderbolt," he recalled. The telegram was a summons for him to come back to Moscow right away "in order to confirm your appointment as resident," and to meet top officials of the KGB. It was strange—he had already done that a few months earlier.[19] He was terrified. He went to his British handlers and told them of the request. They were relaxed and urged him to go ahead with the trip. But just to be sure, Gordievsky rehearsed a plan the British had developed for him to escape if he felt in danger. He left his family behind in London.

On May 17 in Washington, Ames met in a restaurant with Chuvakhin, who handed him $50,000 in cash, in $100 bills.

When Gordievsky arrived in Moscow May 19, he grew even more worried. At passport control, the border guard scrutinized his documents for a long time, made a phone call and examined some papers before letting him pass. When he reached his apartment, a third lock on the door, for which he long ago had lost the key, was turned shut. The apartment had been searched.

On Sunday, May 20, late in the evening in a wooded area of Montgomery County, Maryland, John Walker stopped his van and left an empty 7-Up can by the side of the road, then drove away. At another spot, he left a brown paper bag. For a decade, Walker had run a navy spy ring for the

Soviets, feeding them top-secret communications documents stolen from American warships. Walker's partners in espionage included Jerry Whitworth, who had served on the U.S.S. *Enterprise* and leaked classified communications from the Pacific Ocean exercises in 1983. Walker did not realize it on this night, but the FBI, after months of investigation, was closing in on him and watching his every move in the woods. When Walker drove away, an FBI agent picked up the 7-Up can, intended as a signal to the Soviets that Walker had left them something and wanted to pick up money. Then the FBI found the brown paper bag, and in the bottom of it was an inch-thick package, wrapped in a white plastic garbage sack. The corners were neatly folded over and taped. Inside were 129 secret documents stolen from the U.S.S. *Nimitz* and a letter, "Dear Friend," outlining the activities of others in his spy ring, including Whitworth, using coded letters of the alphabet to disguise their identities.

Walker expected a payment that night, and was puzzled when his Soviet contact did not leave it. The Soviet man with the money had been in the vicinity, looking for the 7-Up can—when he did not find it, he left without dropping the cash. Walker drove back to the woods later that evening, apparently realizing his brown bag had disappeared. Did the Soviets pick it up? Where was his money? It was late, so he went to the nearby suburb of Rockville and checked into a Ramada Inn. At 3:30 A.M., he was awakened by an apologetic clerk at the front desk of the hotel, saying someone had accidentally smashed into his van in the parking lot. Could he come down with his insurance forms? It was a ruse. At the elevator, Walker was arrested by the FBI. Soon, U.S. intelligence and military officials began to unravel the incredible story of how Walker had given away some of the deepest secrets of the Cold War.

On May 28, in Moscow, Gordievsky took some pep pills the British had given him in London to fight fatigue. At the office, he was summoned to meet agents from KGB counterintelligence who wanted to talk about possible penetration of the KGB in London. Gordievsky was driven several miles from headquarters to a small bungalow, where he met the agents. They had lunch, and a servant poured them all a brandy. Gordievsky took his and passed out. He had been drugged. When he awoke, Gordievsky realized what had happened. He had been interrogated while in a drugged stupor. He was "more depressed than ever before in my life. I kept thinking, '*they know*,' I'm finished.' How they had found out, I could not tell. But there was not the slightest doubt that they knew I was a British agent."

It was not clear how much the KGB knew, or from what source. Gordievsky had no idea how he was betrayed. He recalled in his memoir that during the drugged interrogation he had given no ground, and strenuously denied working for the British. Gordievsky did not know if they had any proof, but the interrogators clearly had some information to start with. The KGB "hounds were hot on my scent," Gordievsky said.

One of the most valuable human sources the CIA had ever tapped in the secretive Soviet military-industrial complex was Adolf Tolkachev, a quiet, stooped man in his fifties. He was a senior research scientist in a Russian military aerospace program at a Moscow institute, helping design radars, air defenses and new jet fighters. The CIA had given him the code name GTVANQUISH. Tolkachev quietly worshipped America from afar, although he had never left Russia. For seven years, Tolkachev had provided the CIA a huge volume of sensitive and valuable intelligence on military research and development, including plans for the next generation of Soviet fighter aircraft. The information saved the United States billions of dollars and allowed the air force to develop planes that would prevail in any military confrontation with the Soviets.

In April 1984, meeting his handler in Moscow, Tolkachev turned over schematics of Soviet radar systems, rolls of film containing ninety-six frames of secret documents and thirty-nine pages of handwritten notes. He sometimes made the photos of documents in the bathroom at the institute. In October 1984, Tolkachev gave his CIA handler two miniature cameras containing ninety frames and twenty-two pages of written notes.[20] For his meetings with the Americans, Tolkachev had worked out a system in which he would signal whether he was ready by opening one of the *fortochkas*, small ventilation windows above the main window in his apartment, between 12:15 and 12:30 P.M. He lived on the ninth floor of a tall wedding-cake tower that had long housed the Soviet aviation elite, among others.[21] The distinctive building was also just down the street from the American Embassy, and CIA officers could check the window on a walk by the building.

On June 5, 1985, the window was open. But when the CIA officer came by, he grew uneasy at what seemed to be heavy surveillance, often a problem for the agents in Moscow, who were constantly being watched. The next date planned for a rendezvous was June 13. Again, the window was open. The CIA case officer didn't see any surveillance—the only thing he noticed was a woman talking loudly on a pay phone. According to CIA veteran Milt Bearden, the case officer was carrying two plastic shopping bags. One contained 125,000 rubles in small notes, the equivalent of $150,000, as well as five new compact subminiature cameras concealed in key chain fobs, preloaded with microfilm. The other had books with concealed messages giving Tolkachev instructions for communications and secrets the CIA wanted him to steal.[22]

At the exact time of the planned meeting, 9:40 P.M., the CIA case officer was jumped and seized by more than a dozen KGB personnel in military camouflage uniforms, who had been hiding in nearby bushes. The case officer, Paul M. "Skip" Stombaugh Jr., was taken off to Lubyanka, the hulking prison and KGB headquarters. Once there, in front of him, the packages that he was planning to deliver to Tolkachev were opened piece by piece, with a video camera rolling. A note in the package thanked Tolkachev for the "very important written information" he had provided earlier, but added that due to low light, some of the photographs he had made could not be read. The note suggested that the CIA could get Tolkachev a new security badge, fabricating it "as we did in 1980." That was the end.

Tolkachev had already been arrested. He was later executed.

On the same day Stombaugh was seized outside of Tolkachev's apartment in Moscow, the CIA's Soviet operations suffered another devastating setback in Washington. Ames arrived at a small restaurant, Chadwicks, located on the Georgetown waterfront. Ames had wrapped up five to seven pounds of classified messages in his CIA office and carried them out of the headquarters building in Langley without being stopped.

Ames carried the documents into the restaurant in a plastic bag. He was met there by Chuvakhin from the Soviet Embassy, and Ames gave him the bag. It held the largest batch of sensitive documents and critical information ever turned over to the KGB in a single meeting. Ames identified more than ten top-level CIA and FBI sources who were then reporting on Soviet activities. Among them were Gordievsky and Tolkachev. If the KGB had earlier been suspicious about them, they now had proof.

Two days after Ames gave away the bag filled with secrets, Gordievsky, still fearful and uncertain, went to a KGB sanatorium outside of Moscow. He was told to wait there while the KGB decided his fate. Gordievsky's family was safely headed to their summer vacation in Azerbaijan. Despite the risks, Gordievsky decided to escape. He returned to his apartment in Moscow and retrieved from his bookshelf an English novel that had his exfiltration instructions on a cellophane sheet under the flyleaf.

The instructions were: signal to the British that he had a message, and then meet a British agent in a "brush by" encounter that would be unobtrusive. Frantic, Gordievsky gave the signal that he had a message. Then he went to Red Square, crowded with tourists. He went into the men's room at Lenin's tomb, closed the door to the stall and wrote a note to the British. "AM UNDER STRONG SUSPICION AND IN BAD TROUBLE. NEED EXFILTRATION SOONEST. BEWARE OF RADIOACTIVE DUST AND CAR ACCIDENTS." The last line referred to common KGB methods for following people or eliminating them. Gordievsky failed to deliver the note—he couldn't find the agent.

At the next assigned meeting, he was looking for someone who would have an unmistakable British look, and would acknowledge having spotted Gordievsky by chewing something. After twenty-four minutes of waiting on a designated street corner, Gordievsky noticed a man with a British appearance carrying a dark-green Harrods bag and eating a Mars candy bar. "I gazed into his eyes shouting silently, 'Yes! It's me! I need urgent help!'"

Gordievsky then took a train to Leningrad and a bus almost all the way to the border with Finland. Thatcher approved a daring plan to whisk him away from the Soviet Union. Gordievsky said he was picked up by British agents in a forested area near the border and driven out in the trunk of a car. Passing through checkpoints, he cowered inside the trunk, but it was not opened by Soviet guards. When the lid finally popped open once safely in Finland, Gordievsky recalled, "I saw blue sky, white clouds and pine trees above me." Thanks to his British handlers, he had escaped. "I had outwitted the entire might of the KGB! I was out! I was safe! I was free!"[23] For a while, however, the British kept to themselves the news of their triumph.

On August 1, in Rome, Vitaly Yurchenko, forty-nine, a beefy KGB official who had recently been named deputy director of the department that ran spies in the United States and Canada, went for a walk and never came back. He called the U.S. Embassy, said he wanted to defect to the United States and in a matter of days was flown back to Andrews Air Force Base, in suburban Maryland, outside of Washington. Yurchenko had previously spent five years in KGB counterintelligence.

To meet Yurchenko at the airport, the CIA assigned several people, among them its own top Soviet counterintelligence expert, Ames. However, Ames was late arriving at Andrews, and his behavior was odd. When he saw Yurchenko, in a crowd of CIA and FBI officials, Ames went right up to him and delivered a pompous greeting: "Colonel Yurchenko, I welcome you to the United States on behalf of the President of the United States." Bearden speculates that Ames did this because he was afraid Yurchenko might already know he was working for the KGB. Ames then sat in the car with Yurchenko as the defector was driven to a townhouse in Oakton, in the northern Virginia suburbs, for debriefing.[24]

The debriefings were, in retrospect, one of the most bizarre chapters in the Cold War. Ames had just recently given the KGB the largest dump of secrets in the CIA's history. He was sitting across the table and debriefing one of the most significant defectors ever to come offering the KGB's secrets to the United States. The details Yurchenko told them were then being transmitted by Ames back to the KGB, and the CIA didn't know it.

Yurchenko made two stunning disclosures. The first was that a former

CIA trainee was selling secrets to the Soviets. Yurchenko said he knew the contact only by his KGB code name, "Robert," and one identifying characteristic: he had been slated to go to Moscow but did not. A thunderbolt hit the CIA. The description could only fit a disgruntled trainee they had fired in 1983, Edward Lee Howard.[25] Then came a second bombshell. The KGB, he recalled, harvested a rich crop of secrets from a walk-in to the Soviet Embassy in 1980, an employee of the National Security Agency, which ran American global electronic eavesdropping. Yurchenko said he only knew of this agent as "Mr. Long," and gave his debriefers some details. He said Mr. Long sold to the Soviets the details of the U.S. operation to tap the Soviet undersea cables in the Sea of Okhotsk. This was the monitoring operation known as Ivy Bells, which had been discovered and removed by the Soviets in 1981. (A second undersea cable-tapping operation in the Barents Sea had not been compromised.) The FBI launched a manhunt for Mr. Long, and four months later arrested Ronald Pelton, a communications specialist with the NSA who sold the classified data to the Soviets for $35,000.

Casey, the CIA director, took huge delight in the Yurchenko defection. "Casey was like a child with a new toy with Yurchenko," Gates said. "Not only was he eager to hear, virtually on a daily basis, about the debriefings: he also could not help bragging about this great CIA coup. He met with Yurchenko, had dinner with him, couldn't get enough of him."[26]

On October 1, 1985, Robert Hanssen, an FBI analyst on Soviet intelligence, dropped a letter into a mailbox in Prince George's County, outside of Washington. Hanssen was based in the New York office but was working that day in the capital. The letter was addressed to the home of a KGB operative, Viktor Degtyar, who lived in Alexandria, Virginia. The letter arrived October 4. Inside an outer envelope was a second envelope that Hanssen marked "DO NOT OPEN. TAKE THIS ENVELOPE UNOPENED TO VICTOR I. CHERKASHIN." The KGB man took the letter to Cherkashin, the second-ranking KGB official in Washington at the time, who was already running Ames.

When Cherkashin opened it, he found a second letter:

DEAR MR. CHERKASHIN,

SOON, I WILL SEND A BOX OF DOCUMENTS TO MR. DEGTYAR. THEY ARE FROM CERTAIN OF THE MOST SENSITIVE AND HIGHLY COMPARTMENTED PROJECTS OF THE U.S. INTELLIGENCE COMMUNITY. ALL ARE ORIGINALS TO AID IN VERIFYING THEIR AUTHENTICITY. PLEASE RECOGNIZE FOR OUR LONG-TERM INTERESTS THAT THERE ARE A LIMITED NUMBER OF PERSONS WITH THIS ARRAY OF CLEARANCES. AS A COLLECTION THEY POINT TO ME. I TRUST THAT AN OFFICER OF YOUR EXPERIENCE WILL HANDLE THEM APPROPRIATELY. I BELIEVE THEY ARE SUFFICIENT TO JUSTIFY A $100,000 PAYMENT TO ME.

I MUST WARN YOU OF CERTAIN RISKS TO MY SECURITY OF WHICH YOU MAY NOT BE AWARE. YOUR SERVICE HAS RECENTLY SUFFERED SOME SETBACKS. I WARN THAT MR. BORIS YUSHIN (LINE PR, SF), MR. SERGEY MOTORIN (LINE PR, WASH.) AND MR. VALERIY MARTYNOV (LINE X, WASH.) HAVE BEEN RECRUITED BY OUR "SPECIAL SERVICES."[27]

Hanssen then described a sensitive intelligence collection technique used by the United States. He told the Soviets that he would be in touch. He didn't sign the letter. On October 15, Degtyar received in the mail, at his home, a package from Hanssen containing a large number of classified documents. The next morning, Degtyar was seen by FBI agents carrying into the Soviet Embassy a large black canvas bag that he did not usually carry. About ten days later, Degtyar received another letter from the agent, whom the KGB was calling "B," in an envelope postmarked New York City. This letter proposed a dead drop site under a wooden footbridge in Nottoway Park in northern Virginia, near where Hanssen had earlier lived. On Saturday, November 2, the KGB put $50,000 for Hanssen under the bridge.[28]

The CIA moved Yurchenko to a new, larger safe house on a piece of wooded lakefront near Fredericksburg, Virginia. But Yurchenko was increasingly disillusioned. Word of his defection had leaked to the press, even though he asked the CIA to keep it secret. And his hopes to be reunited with a Russian woman he had known years earlier were dashed.[29] When he defected in August, Yurchenko thought he might have been suffering from stomach cancer, although later tests in the United States showed he was not. On November 2, while at Au Pied de Cochon, a restaurant in Georgetown, Yurchenko simply walked away from his inexperienced CIA handler. When the CIA man realized what had happened, the agency and the FBI launched a manhunt all over Georgetown. They didn't find Yurchenko. On Monday, November 3, he showed up at the Soviet Embassy, where he held a strange press conference in which he claimed he had been abducted in Rome, drugged and held against his will. "Something smells fishy," Reagan observed in his diary on November 4.

Yurchenko boarded a flight back to Moscow on November 6. His defection and return have long been one of the unsolved puzzles of the Cold War. Was he a deliberate plant by the KGB? For what purpose? Or did he just grow disillusioned with his treatment by the CIA? The truth is unknown. His return to Moscow brought with it one grim footnote. On the plane escorting Yurchenko home was KGB agent Valery Martynov, the officer in the Soviet Embassy working on Line X, stealing Western technology. Both Ames and Hanssen had, by this time, identified Martynov as a spy for the United States. Martynov was arrested the day he arrived in Moscow, and later executed.

American intelligence operations in the Soviet Union were collapsing, but the CIA was not aware of the enormous damage it had suffered in 1985. Ames and Hanssen had only just begun their espionage, which went on for years. Later investigations showed how severely the American intelligence operations in Moscow had been compromised. Gates said that Howard was the "CIA's most devastating counter-intelligence setback up to that point," and "many of our Soviet operations were compromised and either rolled up by the KGB or shut down by us." According to a damage assessment by the CIA, nine of the agents whom Ames identified on June 13 were executed. The Senate Select Committee on Intelligence later found that more than twenty operations were compromised, a "virtual collapse of the CIA's Soviet operations." John Deutch, the CIA director, told Congress that Ames not only caused the execution of agents who worked for the United States but "made it much more difficult to understand what was going on in the Soviet Union at a crucial time in its history."

The year of the spy, as 1985 became known, blinded American intelligence operations against the Soviet Union just as Gorbachev was coming to power. Reagan simply did not have the assets to help him understand what was happening behind the Kremlin walls. In the end, there were more powerful agents of change than the agents of espionage. Those forces—rooted in Gorbachev's convictions about what his country needed, in the overpowering burden of the arms race, in Reagan's desire to eliminate nuclear weapons—were about to unleash a momentous revolution.

OF SWORDS AND SHIELDS

In his early days in office in the spring of 1985, Gorbachev worked feverishly. Vladimir Medvedev, the Kremlin security director who had served since Brezhnev, watched in amazement. "After Brezhnev's many years of illness and lethargy," he recalled, "there was suddenly a volcano of energy near you." Gorbachev worked until 1 or 2 A.M. and got up the next morning at 7 A.M. He was on his way to the Kremlin at 9:15 in the ZIL limousine. Gorbachev sat in the backseat, closing the glass sliding partition behind Medvedev and the driver, making notes, and placing calls on the two phones in the car. "Over this short period of time he managed to talk to 3 or 4 people," Medvedev recalled. "Walking from the car to the office, he gave several orders, advice, promises—not a moment to catch his breath. Still walking, he gave concrete advice to the military, to civilians—whom to talk to, what to say, what to pay attention to, what to insist on, what to ignore. He spoke in short, precise sentences."[1]

Gorbachev sent a shock wave of excitement through a moribund society. At a time when people were accustomed to flowery but empty official pronouncements, when portraits of leaders were dutifully hung from every wall, when conformity suffocated public discussion, Gorbachev's style was refreshingly direct.[2] Often he talked too much, wavered on important decisions and was slow to break out of the old Soviet mind-set. Yet the absolute core of his early drive was to halt the decay in Soviet living standards and rejuvenate society. He believed that open discussion was essential to the survival of socialism. He didn't fear what people had to say. He believed in Lenin's ideals, but concluded that leaders after Lenin had gone off track, and he wanted to set things right. It would have been so much easier to fall back into the old habits, to take the well-worn old pathways, but Gorbachev did not.

On a visit to Leningrad in May, he bantered with a large, jostling crowd on the street. It was an extraordinary sight to see a Soviet leader talking spontaneously with people. "I'm listening to you," he told them. "What do you want to say?"

Someone shouted back, "Continue as you began!"

A woman's voice broke in, "Just get close to the people, and we'll not let you down." Gorbachev, hemmed in tightly, responded with a smile. "Can I be any closer?" The crowd loved it.

In a combative speech to Leningrad Communists at Smolny Institute on the same visit, Gorbachev spoke largely without notes, insisting that the economy be reenergized, demanding that people who could not accept change must step aside. "Get out of the way. Don't be a hin-drance," he declared.[3] Gorbachev was skilled at manipulating the elders of the Politburo; he didn't tell them in advance about the speech, in which he spilled out some of their closed deliberations in March and April. He was thrilled with the enthusiastic response, and took a video home from Leningrad. The following weekend he watched it with his family at the dacha. Then he ordered it to be shown on national television.[4] Crowds lined up to get a pamphlet of the text at newsstands. Anatoly Chernyaev, the deputy chief of the International Department of the Central Committee, who played a key role in the great Gorbachev drama, recalled that in the past such texts would lie on the floor of the newsstands until the leader died. "The people are flabbergasted at the TV coverage of Gorbachev's meetings and speeches in Leningrad," Chernyaev wrote. "The question of the day is: Did you see it? At last we have a leader who knows what he is doing and enjoys it, who can relate to the people, speak in his own words, who doesn't avoid contact and doesn't worry about appearing magisterial. He really wants to get our wheels out of the rut, wake the people up, get them to be themselves, to use their common sense, to think and act."[5]

At a Politburo meeting April 11, Gorbachev's impatience was on full display. He was furious at the dreadful state of Soviet farming and at the food supply, which often spoiled in storage and transport. There were only enough warehouses for 26 percent of the fruit, vegetables and potatoes, and they were rotting; only a third of the storage facilities for produce had refrigeration. The loss of agricultural raw materials was running at 25 percent. As Chernyaev later lamented, any leader would see "the country was on the verge of collapse." Gorbachev threatened the ministers that he would take away Kremlin privileges—an eatery and special food store—which allowed them to avoid exposure to the misery in most food shops.[6]

Even in his first blunder, a campaign against alcohol abuse, Gorbachev showed his determination to save the country from itself.[7] The campaign was widely ridiculed and eventually dropped, but Gorbachev knew, correctly, that alcoholism had become a scourge. Per capita, the amount of alcohol consumed was two and a half times greater than it had been under the tsars. Gorbachev recalled that the saddest part was that vodka helped fill the consumer goods deficit; there was nothing else for people to buy with their rubles. Chernyaev sensed right away the campaign was doomed. One day he stopped by a grocery. "Everyone there from the manager to the saleswoman is drunk. The anti-alcoholism law is nothing for them. Try to fire them. Who are you going to find to replace them?"[8]

Less than two weeks after Gorbachev took power, two military men came to his office. Both held the rank of Marshal, the highest in the Soviet military. One was the unremarkable new defense minister, Sergei Sokolov, who had been appointed after Ustinov's death. The other was Sergei Akhromeyev, chief of the General Staff. Lean and muscular, not very tall, with a strong chest like an athlete and a thin face, Akhromeyev carried himself very straight, was known as an exacting commander and rarely smiled. He had joined the Red Army at age seventeen, just before the outbreak of World War II, fought to lift the siege of Leningrad and later commanded a tank battalion in Ukraine. He ended the war as a major. His generation went into the war surprised and outgunned, fighting the Nazi tanks with only rifles and Molotov cocktails. After the war, they graduated from the military academies and devoted their lives to the belief, as Akhromeyev put it, that "everything the Soviet Union achieved in the post-war organization of Europe and the world must be protected."[9] Their determination was only strengthened by the development of nuclear weapons.

By contrast, Gorbachev was a boy when the Germans invaded. He never served as a soldier, nor in the military-industrial complex or the defense establishment. Nor was Gorbachev in thrall to the great designers and scientists who had built the missiles and warheads that turned the Soviet Union into a nuclear superpower. Gorbachev simply did not share the worldview that the generals so deeply cherished and fervently protected. He did not see military power as decisive in global competition; he realized economic power was more potent. "We are encircled not by invincible armies," he later concluded, "but by superior economies."[10]

In the meeting with Sokolov and Akhromeyev, Gorbachev got his first look at the true size and scope of the Soviet defense machine, and it was enormous. As they finished, Gorbachev turned to Akhromeyev. "We begin to work together in difficult times," he said. "I speak to you as a Communist. I know what I must do in the area of economics to correct the situation. I know where and what to do. But the area of defense is new for me. I count on your help." Akhromeyev, who had been chief of the General Staff for only six months, and before that deputy chief, held sway over military policy and planning. He promised to give Gorbachev his help.[11]

Gorbachev realized that the sprawling defense establishment—the Army, Navy, Air Force, Strategic Rocket Forces, Air Defense Forces and all the institutes, design bureaus and factories that supported them—were a monumental burden on the country. How the military-industrial complex functioned, how far it ranged and how much it cost were concealed by deep secrecy, what Gorbachev called the "closed zones."[12] But Gorbachev's travels around the country had provided him with hints. "Defense spending was bleeding the other branches of the economy dry," he recalled. "When I visited defense plants and agricultural production complexes, I was always struck by the same picture. The defense production workshop making modern tanks, for example, had the newest equipment. The one working for agriculture was making obsolete models of tractors on old-time conveyor belts."

"Over the previous five-year plans, military spending had been grow-

ing twice as fast as national income. This *Moloch* was devouring everything that hard labor and strain produced . . . What made matters worse
was the fact that it was impossible to analyze the problem. All the figures
related to the military-industrial complex were classified. Even Politburo
members didn't have access to them."[13]

On the staff of the Central Committee, one man knew the secret inner
workings of the military-industrial complex. Vitaly Katayev had the
appearance of a thoughtful scientist or professor, with a long, angular
face and wavy hair brushed straight back. As a teenager he loved to
design model airplanes and ships. He spent two decades in aircraft and
missile design and construction bureaus in Omsk and Ukraine, and took
part in some of the largest missile projects of the Cold War before coming to the Central Committee headquarters in Moscow in 1974 to work
on defense issues. In private, Katayev was a funny, quirky man who
loved to sing and play musical instruments.[14] But in his work at the Central Committee, he was very serious and precise. The Central Committee
position was located in the heart of power, perhaps roughly equivalent
to serving at the White House National Security Council. Katayev
worked in the Defense Industry Department, later renamed just the
Defense Department, which oversaw the military-industrial complex.
Over many years, Katayev kept detailed records in large bound notebooks, often jotting down rows of numbers, drawing schematics of
weapons systems, recording major decisions and debates. His notebooks
and writings, revealed here for the first time, offer an unparalleled window on the inner workings of the Soviet military-industrial colossus.[15]
Katayev described it once as "a sort of Soviet Texas—everything existed
on a grand scale." But Katayev knew it was not as fearsome as often portrayed. The defense establishment was run in a way that was extremely
random, ad hoc, and subjective. Katayev knew that Soviet central planning did not work. Weapons were not built because they were needed,
but rather because of the power of vested interests, of prominent designers, generals and Politburo members. To meet the artificial benchmarks
of progress, everything had to increase every year, so the military was
often saturated with weapons it did not need. The factories often lacked

the necessary precision and reliability to produce high-technology weapons. Katayev recalled that while the Soviet Union had advanced science and a high level of design expertise, many projects were wrecked by miserable materials and sloppy production, for which no one was ever fired. Even such a simple ingredient as metals were often of unpredictable quality, so designers had to allow for wide margins. And it was not possible to fix the problems in electronics and high technology by design alone. A circuit board couldn't be made more reliable by making it twice as large. There was a "permanent gap," he said, between the drawing boards and the factories. This was the underside of the Soviet military machine.

Katayev's notes show that the military-industrial complex was indeed as large as Gorbachev feared. In 1985, Katayev estimated, defense took up 20 percent of the Soviet economy.[16] Of the 135 million adults working in the Soviet Union, Katayev said, 10.4 million worked directly in the military-industrial complex at 1,770 enterprises. Nine ministries served the military, although in a clumsy effort to mask its purpose, the nuclear ministry was given the name "Ministry of Medium Machine Building," and others were similarly disguised. More than fifty cities were almost totally engaged in the defense effort, and hundreds less so. Defense factories were called upon to make the more advanced civilian products, too, including 100 percent of all Soviet televisions, tape recorders, movie and still cameras and sewing machines.[17] Taking into account all the ways the Soviet military-industrial complex functioned and all the raw materials it consumed and all the tentacles that spread into civilian life, the true size of the defense burden on the economy may well have been even greater than Katayev estimated.

Gorbachev would need deep reserves of strength and cunning to challenge this leviathan. At one Politburo meeting, he lamented, "This country produced more tanks than people." The military-industrial complex was its own army of vested interests: generals and officers in the services, designers and builders of weapons, ministers and planners in the government, propaganda organs, and party bosses everywhere, all united by the need, unquestioned, to meet the invisible Cold War threat. For decades, the threat had been the overriding reason to divert resources to defense and impose hardship on the Soviet people.[18]

In title, Gorbachev was the top man in this system: general secretary of the party, supreme commander and chairman of the defense council. But when he came to power in 1985, he was not really in control. The military-industrial complex was in the hands of Akhromeyev's generation.

Gorbachev's thinking about security was influenced by a group of progressives, outsiders to the military-industrial complex. They were academics from the institutes, people who, like Gorbachev, had been excited by the Khrushchev secret speech, but had grown fatigued by the stagnation in the Brezhnev years.[19] They did not trust the military but knew of its immense power. Now they hoped to see reform rise again, and Gorbachev listened to them.

An important figure in this inner circle was Yevgeny Velikhov, an avuncular and open-minded physicist who was then deputy director of the Kurchatov Institute of Atomic Energy. As a child, Velikhov had devoured books about science. He entered Moscow State University just after Stalin died in 1953. After graduation, he joined the institute, headed by Igor Kurchatov, leader of the Soviet atomic bomb project. Velikhov was lucky to be assigned to a famous physicist, Mikhail Leontovich, who supervised theoretical research on controlled nuclear fusion and plasma physics. "The atmosphere was wonderful," Velikhov recalled. "Plasma physics was just emerging, and we felt that we had very few rivals anywhere in the world." Velikhov was allowed to travel, and in the summer of 1962, he visited universities in New York, Boston and Chicago, and stopped at Los Alamos. He built his own network of contacts with American scientists.[20]

When Velikhov became a vice president of the Academy of Sciences in 1977, he was the youngest to hold the position. His first assignment was to focus on cybernetics and computer technology in the Soviet Union, and he found they were in "very bad shape." One day in the early 1980s, Velikhov invited Gorbachev, then a Politburo member, to his office at the academy. He recalled telling Gorbachev about the Apple computer on his desk, which he had brought from overseas. "I showed him and I said, 'Look, this is a revolution.'" Once in power, Gorbachev continued to listen to Velikhov.

Others in Gorbachev's circle were Yakovlev, the reformist thinker who walked with Gorbachev in the orchard in Canada in 1983 and was now at the Institute of World Economy and International Relations, and Georgi Arbatov, director of the Institute for the Study of the U.S.A. and

Canada, who was a critical channel of ideas and information for Gorbachev in the early years.

Gorbachev was desperate for real information, cutting through the mountains of artificial data. "We especially need objective information, showing not what we would like to see but what really is," Gorbachev appealed to the Politburo.[21] Georgi Shakhnazarov said the military tried to manipulate the leadership. "They reported to the leadership one thing, while thinking and doing something totally different," he said. "It was a cat and mouse game."[22]

In Afghanistan, the military was sinking deeper and deeper into a losing quagmire. In Gorbachev's first months, angry letters flooded into the Central Committee from around the country decrying the war. In April 1985, Reagan wrote to Gorbachev, "Isn't it long overdue to reach a political resolution of this tragic affair?" Just weeks before he wrote this, Reagan signed a classified order, National Security Decision Directive 166, which provided the legal basis for a massive escalation of the CIA's war against the Soviets in Afghanistan, setting a new and more ambitious goal. Instead of just supporting resistance to the Red Army, now the CIA decided to push the Soviets out.[23] Arbatov gave Gorbachev a memo that included far-reaching ideas, including that "we must cease with Afghanistan." On June 19, 1985, Gorbachev called Arbatov to the Kremlin and told him Afghanistan was a "paramount issue" for him.[24] In August, Soviet soldiers revolted on a train headed to Afghanistan; they did not want to be shipped off to a war where ten soldiers were killed every day. Gorbachev began planning a retreat, but it took years.

Looking back, Gorbachev recalled that he had to "clear up the 'snow drifts' left over from Cold War times." Afghanistan was just one. In foreign policy, he said, what he had in mind were "not simply cosmetic changes, but practically a U-turn."

Yet the outside world did not see this right away. Gorbachev's early overtures to Reagan were given the brush-off. When Gorbachev proposed April 7 to freeze the Pioneer missiles in Europe that had stirred the West to deploy the Pershing IIs and cruise missiles, Reagan and Thatcher immediately refused, saying it was a propaganda gambit. Their deployments were only getting started, so a freeze would leave the two sides unequal.[25] "Unhelpful," Reagan wrote to Gorbachev on April 30. "I cannot help but wonder what the purpose could have been in presenting a proposal which is, in its essence, not only an old one, but one which was known to provide no basis for serious negotiation."[26] What Reagan may not have known was that, in the Kremlin, the Pioneer missiles, also known as the SS-20s, were already viewed as a mistake. "Why do we need these SS-20s?" Chernyaev asked in his diary two weeks before Reagan's letter. "Their installation was as foolish as Khrushchev's missiles in Cuba in 1962."[27]

On April 17, Gorbachev proposed a moratorium on nuclear tests. The United States again said no. The arms control negotiations in Geneva, which resumed in early 1985, soon stalled.[28] Out of frustration, Shultz quietly put together a secret overture to Moscow. With Reagan's approval, he met with Dobrynin in Washington in June and offered a trade-off: if both sides made deep cuts in offensive nuclear weapons, perhaps Reagan's Strategic Defense Initiative could be slowed down. Shultz also proposed that negotiations be started through a confidential back channel, bypassing the deadlocked Geneva talks. In two weeks, the answer came back from Moscow: unequivocally no. "The Soviets wanted to stop SDI in its tracks, not just moderate it," Shultz recalled.[29] Dobrynin later said there was another reason: Gromyko had killed the idea because he feared the back channel would bypass him.[30]

It was Gromyko's last chance to say "nyet." On June 29, Gorbachev replaced Gromyko as foreign minister, moving him to be chairman of the Supreme Soviet. Gromyko, who held the post twenty-eight years, was a custodian of the old thinking—the world as a collision of two opposing camps—which Gorbachev was about to demolish. Gorbachev then stunned everyone by naming Eduard Shevardnadze, the Georgia party leader, as foreign minister. "This was like a bolt from the blue," recalled Chernyaev.[31] Shevardnadze, who had spent his entire career in Georgia, shared Gorbachev's understanding of the poverty of the Russian heartland. They stood out from others in the leadership—they did not have experience in heavy industry or the military-industrial complex.[32] Shevardnadze had little familiarity with diplomacy, but he was a politician, and he had Gorbachev's trust. He was promoted immediately to a full Politburo member. In the same session, Gorbachev appointed Lev

Zaikov, a Leningrad party official, to oversee the military-industrial complex. Katayev would be one of Zaikov's key staffers at the Central Committee. "There are many obstacles in this area of our work," Gorbachev said. "We need to fix things here."[33]

Chernyaev said Soviet propaganda was so stale, no one believed it, "and the root of the Geneva deadlock is this. Revolutionary approaches to talks are needed, identical to the one Gorbachev demonstrated in Leningrad."

"The question is about the fact that we must stop treading water," Chernyaev concluded, "as the arms race is about to shoot out of control."[34]

Just after Gorbachev took office, in the spring and early summer of 1985, the directors, designers and constructors of satellites, space boosters, radars and lasers produced a colossal new plan for Gorbachev's approval. Unknown to the outside world, the Soviet military-industrial complex laid on Gorbachev's desk a plea for their own "Star Wars." It came two years after Reagan had announced his Strategic Defense Initiative. It would propel the Soviet Union on the path of previous decades, faithful to the Cold War trajectory of two worlds in collision and ceaseless competition.

Since 1984, the Soviet leadership had been increasingly anxious about Reagan's dream, and Reagan gave them plenty to worry about. In his second inaugural speech in early 1985, Reagan offered a high-flying description of his program, calling it a global shield to make nuclear weapons obsolete. "I have approved a research program to find, if we can, a security shield that will destroy nuclear missiles before they reach their target," he said. "It wouldn't kill people. It would destroy weapons. It wouldn't militarize space, it would help demilitarize the arsenals of the Earth. It would render nuclear weapons obsolete."

In Moscow, the KGB made its highest priority gathering intelligence about "American policy on the militarization of space." That was the title of a ten-page directive issued three and a half weeks after Reagan's inaugural speech. Soviet spies were ordered to gather intelligence on all the American programs that might deploy systems in space for nuclear and conventional war. They were asked to watch the use of the American space shuttle for deploying weapons in space, the U.S. effort to build an anti-satellite weapon; and they were given extensive tasks to spy on the Strategic Defense Initiative. Woven into the KGB's instructions were details already plucked from newspapers about Reagan's program, such as the budget sums and the broad direction, along with ample doses of fear and skepticism about the unknowns. Perhaps Reagan's program would never work? Perhaps there was a hidden purpose? The KGB was "very anxious to know," the instruction said, precisely what were the Reagan administration's plans, how they were evolving, and the "targets, dates and expected financial outlay." The KGB wanted to know what technical results were achieved in tests, whether it was possible to shoot down a missile using "kinetic weapons," such as hitting it with another missile or solid object. And what were Reagan's intentions for negotiating? Was Star Wars really a "large-scale disinformation operation" designed to force the Soviet negotiators into making concessions?[35]

An avalanche of intelligence reporting began to flow to Moscow, and stacks of it crossed Katayev's desk. He observed that the spies were lazy and passive; they often simply sent along press clippings as intelligence. What the agents and Soviet military analysts feared the most, Katayev realized, was to underestimate the seriousness of the threat, so they overestimated it. No one could honestly declare that Star Wars would not work, so they reported that it might. The spies flooded the system with reports of the threat; before long, the military-industrial complex geared up to counter the threat. Starting in 1985 and continuing through the decade, Katayev recalled that about ten cables a day came through his offices in the Central Committee on political-military and technical issues. Of them, 30–40 percent dealt with Star Wars and missile defense. Katayev wondered if the Americans were deliberately trying to choke Moscow with fear by leaking a flood of information.[36] In the two years since Reagan's announcement, the Strategic Defense Initiative was not even close to blueprints—it was still little more than a dream—but it had grabbed the attention of the Soviet leadership.

To build a Soviet Star Wars would mean enormous, lucrative new subsidies for work at the design bureaus, institutes and defense factories. Many of these designers and workers already enjoyed better living conditions than the general population. It was, Katayev recalled, like a hunting dog sensing a new quarry. By summer of 1985, the weapons chiefs pulled together a comprehensive plan for a Soviet missile defense system. According to Katayev's notebooks and papers, there were two major umbrella programs, each of which included a sprawling array of separate projects ranging from fundamental exploratory research to building equipment ready for flight tests. The two umbrella programs had code names. The first was "D-20," which included research on ground-based missile defenses and was assigned to the Ministry of Radio Industry, which traditionally had worked on early warning, command and control and the Moscow anti-ballistic missile system. The second was "SK-1000," a product of the design bureaus of the Ministry of General Machine Building, which oversaw missile and space-related research, development and production. Katayev calculated that altogether the programs would have involved 137 projects in the *opytno-konstruktorskie raboty* phase, or design and testing; 34 projects in *nauchno-issledovatelskiye raboty*, or scientific research; and 115 in fundamental science. The estimates of the costs ran into the tens of billions of rubles, enough to keep the design bureaus working full tilt into the late 1980s. Given obscure code names such as Fundament-4 and Integral-3, Onega E, Spiral, Saturn, Kontakt, Echelon and Skif, the programs went on for pages and pages in Katayev's notebooks. Most of the proposals brought to the Kremlin that summer were intended to produce initial results in 1987–1988; Katayev kept track of goals and targets through 1990.[37]

For all the imposing scope and cost, the grand package concealed deep cracks in the system. Some of the programs, started years earlier, lacked results or purpose, or were starved for resources. Some of them were nearly abandoned or obsolete, hoping for a rebirth. SK-1000 included virtually all the space launcher and satellite programs that were underway in the Soviet Union at that time.

One program that illustrated the ambitions, haste and deficiencies that plagued Soviet space weapons builders was an anti-satellite craft known as Skif. The goal of Skif, started in 1976, was to carry a laser in space that could shoot down enemy satellites. The original idea was to build nothing less than a space battle station. It would be hoisted into orbit by the Energia, an enormous booster then under development, and perhaps serviced by the Buran, the planned Soviet space shuttle. By 1984, the Skif program had yet to produce any hardware because there was no laser that would be suitable for space weaponry. The Soviets were shaken that June by news of the successful American missile interception over the Pacific, the lucky single hit, known as the Homing Overlay Experiment, described earlier. Even without a space laser, the government in August ordered creation of a "demonstration" spacecraft, the Skif-D, which would carry a smaller, substitute laser, one that could not shoot down satellites but would at least replicate the original idea. Then, in 1985, came the renewed planning for a Soviet Star Wars. The Skif-D was modified once again. This time it was to be put on an accelerated schedule to fly by the following year. However, the designers still lacked a laser. So they decided to create a mock-up with no functioning laser equipment on board, and called it "Skif-DM." The vessel was to be 36.9 meters long and weigh 77 tons. The Skif mock-up demonstrator was among those programs offered to Gorbachev for accelerated work in the summer of 1985.[38]

Roald Sagdeev, a physicist and director of the Space Research Institute, a leader in the Soviet deep-space exploration effort, recalled attending a small meeting in Gorbachev's office. Gorbachev was still on a learning curve, asking questions and absorbing details about complicated arms control issues. According to Sagdeev, a top official of the Soviet space industry appealed to Gorbachev to build his own Star Wars. "Trust me," the official said. "We are losing time while doing nothing to build our own counterpart to the American SDI program."

"I almost died from suppressing my laughter," Sagdeev recalled. He realized that the Soviet Union could not afford billions of rubles to do it and lacked critical technology, especially high-speed computers and precision optics.[39]

These were still early days for Gorbachev, and he was clearly not yet fully in control. The list of D-20 and SK-1000 could only have added to his fears about the military-industrial complex. On July 15, 1985, the Central Committee approved the huge list of proposals for a Soviet missile defense. What is significant here is not so much the approval—most of the programs were years away from materializing—but the unbridled ambitions of the designers and builders. They wanted to construct a massive and expensive response to Reagan's dream. In the past, they had been the driving force behind Soviet weapons systems. Gorbachev would have to outfox them.

Velikhov, by his own experience and outlook, was ready to help navigate the forbidding obstacle course Gorbachev faced. Both open-minded and entrepreneurial, Velikhov was the right man at the right time. His specialty was nuclear and plasma physics. When the Soviet weapons designers gave Gorbachev their grand plan, he spotted the faults. Velikhov knew the top-secret history of Soviet efforts to build missile defenses, dating back to the 1960s, because he had participated in it. Certainly, they had achieved scientific and engineering breakthroughs against great odds, but the Soviet Union fell short of building next-generation weapons in space.[40]

The most concrete achievement was completion of a ground-based missile defense system around Moscow, as permitted by the 1972 Anti-Ballistic Missile Treaty. In the event of an attack, interceptor rockets were poised to shoot up from locations around the city and knock out the incoming warheads. The Soviets had also launched a relatively primitive anti-satellite weapon, first designed in the 1960s, which would position itself into the same orbit as a target satellite and shoot conventional weapons at it. The system had largely ceased to work by 1983.[41]

But there were also many setbacks, especially in the quest for exotic laser and space weapons, which consumed huge expenditures in the 1960s and 1970s. A testing ground was constructed for this work at Sary Shagan, near the eastern shores of Lake Balkhash in Kazakhstan. Scientists, designers and their military patrons dreamed of building powerful beams capable of striking satellites from space battle stations or stopping missiles in flight. They drew designs of lasers in space and on the ground, long before Reagan's dream was unveiled. But they never knocked anything out of the sky.

One of the legendary Cold War designers was Vladimir Chelomei, architect of the SS-19 intercontinental ballistic missile, the Proton launcher, the Soviet cruise missile and the early anti-satellite weapon. In 1978, near the end of his career, he proposed to build and launch "baby" space shuttles carrying anti-satellite weapons. Velikhov, a rising star in a younger generation, served on a commission to examine Chelomei's baby shuttle. The commission rejected it, and in the process Velikhov gained a much deeper appreciation of the difficulty of missile defense. "The Chelomei affair was killed," Velikhov said. "And this was a very good inoculation for Russia against the Star Wars proposal by Reagan, because five years before, we had already had all these internal discussions, with a very detailed analysis on the technical engineering level."

The challenges of stopping a missile in flight were a technical nightmare. Scientists and engineers in the Soviet Union struggled from 1962 to 1978 to build super-powerful lasers that could knock out satellites and missiles. The first major project, known as LE-1, was a ruby laser, built at Sary Shagan, that eventually proved capable of tracking airplanes about one hundred kilometers away, but not in space, and the laser was not capable of shooting down objects.[42] A more advanced laser, code-named Terra-3, was also on the drawing boards for a decade, and the plan was to test it at Sary Shagan, where a structure was built for the power source and laser-beam-pointing system. Although Soviet scientists made advances in laser technology during Terra-3, it never worked as a weapon. The reentry vehicles that the system was supposed to shoot down are very difficult targets. The project was abandoned by 1978.[43] A follow-up called Terra-3K was also planned, with a goal of using a high-power laser to attack low-orbit satellites, but it never worked.[44]

Despite the Herculean efforts, the designers ran into difficulty when they reached the limits of Soviet technology and innovation and the vexing physics of missile defense. Laser weapons demanded enormous energy sources, superb optics and precision targeting. The designers and scientists struggled with the tendency of a beam to dissipate as it shot into space. Velikhov, as a physicist and vice president of the academy, knew the designers and their troubles. In his own research, he had helped build a magneto hydrodynamic generator, which created huge amounts of electricity in a short burst, a potential laser power supply. Velikhov knew as well that an almost insurmountable roadblock for Soviet designers was the primitive state of their computers. Massive amounts of fast calculations would be necessary to hit a bullet shooting through space. Velikhov was in charge of the academy's department for computer science. He knew the Soviet Union was a decade or more behind in computer technology.

While many Soviet weapons scientists worked in secrecy and isolation, Velikhov benefited from much broader horizons. When Pope John Paul

II called for an examination of the dangers of nuclear war by scientists from around the world, Velikhov was chosen by the authorities to represent the Soviet Union. At the Pontifical Academy of Sciences in the autumn of 1982, Velikhov had extensive contacts with scientists in debates over nuclear war and weapons in space. The Vatican declaration called on global powers never to use nuclear weapons in war. "The catastrophe of nuclear war can and must be prevented," the declaration said.[45] This was consistent with Soviet disarmament propaganda, but the experience in Rome and other meetings gave Velikhov a better understanding of the West that would help him guide Gorbachev. Also, in May 1983, two months after Reagan's speech on missile defense, Velikhov was named head of a group of twenty-five Soviet scientists intended to warn of the dangers of nuclear war.[46] Again, promoting Soviet disarmament propaganda may have been the intent, but Velikhov and the scientists steered their own course.

Velikhov was asked by the Kremlin in late 1983 to once again evaluate the Reagan missile defense proposal from a technical standpoint. The conclusion was that Reagan's dream would not work. The Soviet scientists knew this from their own hard labor and failures. When Gorbachev came to power two years later, Velikhov dusted off the same document. He had accumulated all the knowledge and experience necessary to give an honest and cold-eyed appraisal of the reality of missile defense.[47]

He used that experience at a key turning point in the summer and early autumn of 1985. Velikhov urged Gorbachev *not* to build a Soviet version of Star Wars. He suggested they abandon the Cold War approach of toe-to-toe competition. Gorbachev was naturally open to this argument; he also wanted, in principle, to move away from the zero-sum game. But it was Velikhov who helped lead Gorbachev to something different.

The Soviet weapons designers wanted to match what Reagan was doing, a symmetrical response. By contrast, Velikhov argued for an "asymmetrical response," one that would answer Reagan but not be the same. To stop ballistic missiles in flight, an American defense system would have to target and destroy a thousand speeding points in space almost perfectly and simultaneously. To counter it, one idea for "asymmetrical response" was to unleash so many speeding points—warheads, either real or fake—that the American defense system would be overwhelmed. Some of the Soviet missiles would penetrate and get through to their targets.

There were different ideas among Soviet experts about the hardware for "asymmetrical response." According to Katayev's records, Soviet engineers came up with technological tricks to fool the anti-missile system. For example, they could launch decoys or chaff, to imitate the warheads and deceive the defenses. They could spin and maneuver warheads to avoid detection, or blind the American satellites and command centers, knocking out the eyes of the defensive system.

Another method was more ominous: build more missiles and an avalanche of additional nuclear warheads. The Soviet Union was good at missiles, and it would be easier and cheaper to double or triple the missile warheads than to build an entirely new defense against them. This approach was hypothetical, but not entirely. Katayev recalled that the latest version of the SS-18 intercontinental ballistic missile carried ten warheads each. This was the biggest, most feared, multiple-warhead weapon in the Soviet arsenal. But if the missile's range was shortened somewhat, and the warheads made smaller, he wrote, the SS-18 could actually be modified to carry "up to 40 nuclear warheads. And this one missile alone!" In a separate, more precise chart in his files, Katayev noted the modified SS-18 could carry thirty-eight warheads. At the time, the Soviet Union deployed 308 of these missiles. If they were modified, the fleet would go from 2,464 warheads to a total of 12,084. It would be much more difficult for American defenses to stop. This was only a concept that had been discussed in earlier years by missile designers, but it illustrated what could become a potent Soviet response to Reagan's Star Wars.[48]

Gorbachev would most certainly not favor this version of "asymmetrical response." He wanted to eliminate weapons, not propagate them. In his memoir, he avoided talking about the details of this option. When the author questioned Gorbachev in an interview in 2006, he was still uneasy about discussing it. "We did have a project," he said. "There was one. It existed. But it is closed down. And destroyed. It's only tens of billions" of rubles. "But it's a horrible project, it's a horrible response." He added, "What is one missile, SS-18? It's a hundred Chernobyls. In one missile."[49]

More weapons were not the only answer. There was a third approach to "asymmetrical response." Words were Gorbachev's stock-in-trade, and his best weapon. He was a robust if long-winded orator. Could he simply say "no" to the Reagan dream, persuade Reagan of his folly and talk it into oblivion? Perhaps he could strike a deal to cancel a giant weapons machine that the United States did not yet possess, that the Soviet Union would have great trouble matching, and exchange it all for something they both wanted: deep reductions in existing nuclear weapons.

Gorbachev realized this was his best answer. If he could talk Reagan out of his dream of missile defense, it would prevent stiff competition on a field—high technology—where the Soviet Union lagged years behind. There was an important domestic component too. The military-industrial complex constantly pressed for more resources, saying the United States was a threat. If Gorbachev could persuade Reagan not to build "Star Wars," he would find it easier to resist the generals and the missile designers at home. By slowing the arms race, Gorbachev might find time and resources to begin modernizing the country.

Yet in the summer of 1985, the military and defense industries were powerful forces. Velikhov saw Gorbachev was buffeted by crosscurrents. He was a man of the party who depended on the Central Committee bureaucracy; he had no choice but to listen to the generals, the ministers and the KGB; and the military establishment distrusted Velikhov, Yakovlev and other progressive thinkers around the general secretary. Gorbachev was personally wary of the military and defense industry, and surrounded himself with advisers who shared his caution, but he did not, and could not, move overtly or swiftly against them.[50]

Behind the scenes, however, Gorbachev was starting to lead the country in a radical new direction. A leader's courage is often defined by building something, by positive action, but in this case, Gorbachev's great contribution was in deciding what not to do. He would not build a Soviet Star Wars. He averted another massive weapons competition.

Gorbachev didn't show his hand right away. The full dimensions of this change in direction took time to appear. If anything, Gorbachev was good at tactics.

In late July, he announced the Soviet Union, by itself, would stop nuclear testing, and invited the United States to follow suit. Reagan did not.

———

To Velikhov's confident assertion that the Strategic Defense Initiative would not work, his Soviet colleagues often posed a difficult question: if it was not possible to create an effective missile shield with America's best technology, if Reagan was utterly dreaming when he talked about making nuclear weapons obsolete, then why was the United States devoting so much money to it, year after year? As Katayev recalled it, the Soviet analysts saw "a clear discrepancy between the goals and the means" of Reagan's announced intentions. "What is it being done for?" the Soviet specialists asked themselves, according to Katayev. "In the name of what are the Americans, famous for their pragmatism, opening their wallet for the most grandiose project in the history of the United States when the technical and economic risks of a crash exceed all thinkable limits?"

"Or," Katayev wrote, "is there still something different behind this curtain?" To the Soviet specialists on strategic weapons, Katayev said, Reagan's zeal for his dream led them "from the very beginning to think about the possibility of political bluff and hoax." They pondered whether it was a "Hollywood village of veneer and cardboard." The question went unanswered.

According to Katayev, a few Soviet experts—he doesn't say exactly who—held an even darker view of Reagan's goals. They concluded that the Americans were always distinguished by their systematic approach to problems, that they "do nothing in vain." Rather than a hoax or bluff, they decided the Strategic Defense Initiative was a cover story for a gigantic, hidden effort to subsidize American defense contractors, save them from "bankruptcy" and produce a fresh surge of superior military high technology. Perhaps, Katayev said, this "was the major underwater part of the SDI iceberg." This analysis was woefully misguided. While Reagan did fatten the defense contractors with record military budgets in the early 1980s, defense spending was a relatively small slice of the overall American economy. While there was a fresh surge of high technology, much of it was sprouting in the private sector, in the entrepreneurial spirit of Silicon Valley. And in the United States, defense contractors simply did not play the same role as the outsized military-industrial complex in the Soviet Union. The Soviet analysts were mistakenly applying their own experience—in which the military-industrial complex was at the center of decisions—to what they could not explain in the United States. Each side in the Cold War remained a mysterious black box to the other. The Americans could not see Gorbachev's radical intentions. The Soviets could not understand Reagan's dream.

In late August 1985, Gorbachev gave an interview to *Time* magazine, his rhetoric offering a refreshing change from the decades of Cold War confrontation. When asked about the Strategic Defense Initiative, Gorbachev said Soviet experts believed it was "sheer fantasy and a pipe dream." His progressive brain trust had helped prepare his remarks.[51] Two weeks later, Reagan wrote in his diary, "I made a decision we would not trade away our program of research—S.D.I. for a promise of Soviet reduction in nuclear arms."[52] Arriving in Washington for the first time on September 27, Shevardnadze gave Reagan a letter from Gorbachev offering to cut long-range nuclear arsenals of the two superpowers by 50 percent in exchange for "a complete ban on space attack weapons." The offer didn't fly; Reagan could not accept the limits on Star Wars. But he was ready for deep cuts in existing nuclear arsenals.[53]

In Washington, both the Defense Department under Weinberger and the CIA under Casey and Gates were deeply skeptical of Gorbachev. The Pentagon published a glossy annual booklet, *Soviet Military Power*, a propaganda piece designed to help boost congressional support for Reagan's military spending. The fourth edition, published in April 1985, contained the claim that the Soviets had "two ground-based lasers that are capable of attacking satellites in various orbits."[54] This was a gross exaggeration; neither the LE-1 nor the Terra-3 lasers could attack anything. An artist's conception, a black-and-white pencil sketch, appeared across the top of page 58, showing what purported to be the Sary Shagan proving ground. A building with a dome on top was shown firing a white laser beam into the heavens. The caption said, "The directed-energy R&D site at the Sary Shagan proving ground includes ground-based

lasers that could be used in an anti-satellite role today and possibly a
BMD role in the future." The key words were "could" and "possibly." In
fact, the long, expensive search to build laser weapons against targets in
space had, up to this point, totally fizzled. The Soviets had not given up
hope, but the glossy Pentagon booklet took old failures and hyped them
into new threats.

In October, the State and Defense departments published a new report
titled "Soviet Strategic Defensive Programs." The pencil sketch of Sary
Shagan appeared again. The text claimed that Soviet achievements in
laser weapons "have been impressive." It was true the Soviet scientists
had scored advances in lasers, but they had not created an exotic weapon
that worked. The text said that the Soviets "may also have the capability
to develop the optical systems necessary for laser weapons to track and
attack their targets." In fact, they could track, but not attack.

Reagan picked up the theme in a radio speech October 12. "The Soviets have for a long time been doing advanced research on their version of
SDI," the president said. "They're doing so well, our experts say they may
be able to put an advanced technology defensive system in space by the
end of the century." One might dismiss this as just standard rhetoric, but
Reagan's words suggest that he never really grasped the impact on the
military of the economic decay and stifling leadership in the Soviet system. Through superhuman striving, against all odds, the Soviet Union
managed to reach superpower status, and yet there were massive internal
stresses and agonizing fissures. The Soviet Union was not ready to put a
missile defense system in space as Reagan claimed. They were not ready
to knock out a satellite with lasers—and would never do so. It was a
tragedy that a country that had spawned some of the great minds in
mathematics and physics, that had produced chess champions and
launched Sputnik, was by the 1980s behind in the computer revolution,
sinking in economic backwardness and totally unprepared for the next
century. But Reagan saw weakness only on the domestic side of the Soviet
Union. He saw the military as ten feet tall.

In one of the more notable errors of judgment, the October report on
Soviet strategic defenses accused leading Soviet scientists, including
Velikhov, of being hypocrites. In one passage, the document noted that
many of them had signed a letter published in the *New York Times* in
opposition to Reagan's Strategic Defense Initiative in 1983. Velikhov was

named and singled out with a photo. It was noted accurately that Velikhov had been head of the Institute of Atomic Energy at Troitsk, a branch of the Kurchatov Institute, located outside of Moscow, "where lasers for strategic and tactical applications are being developed." The connotation was that Velikhov was a mindless propaganda puppet of the regime and a secret weaponeer. The Americans missed the point. While Velikhov had worked on laser weapons, that was precisely the reason he could tell Gorbachev the unvarnished truth about missile defense.

Reagan was eager to meet Gorbachev and try out his one-on-one persuasive powers as a November summit in Geneva drew near. No summit had been held since 1979; Reagan had only three years of his presidency remaining. He did not want to lose time. "Starting with Brezhnev, I'd dreamed of personally going one-on-one with a Soviet leader," Reagan later wrote in his memoirs, saying he believed if the leaders agreed on something, all else would fall into place. Now, he was at last going to get his chance.

Reagan, who liked one-page briefing papers, was buried under a mountain of information in preparation for the summit. McFarlane and Matlock assembled two dozen briefing papers from the CIA and State Department, about eight to ten pages each, single spaced. McFarlane said Reagan received them eagerly, jotting notes in the margins.[55] But Reagan privately complained, "I'm getting d--n sick of cramming like a school kid."[56] The experts told the president that Gorbachev represented a fresh style of Soviet leader, that dramatic changes were underway, but none threatening the system itself.[57] Shultz recalled that "word from the intelligence community and other Soviet specialists around the government was that the Soviet Union would never, indeed *could* never, change no matter how bad their internal economic and social problems were."[58] The CIA briefing paper given to Reagan, titled "Gorbachev's Personal Agenda for the November Meeting," said Gorbachev had "little expectation of any major substantive breakthrough on arms control or regional issues." Gates, a longtime Soviet specialist, who also briefed the president, predicted that Gorbachev wasn't going to be pushed around. His conclusion: "Gorbachev simply intended to outwait Reagan."[59]

For Reagan, one CIA briefing proved riveting, by specialist Kay Oliver, who had just drafted a National Intelligence Estimate titled "Domestic Stress on the Soviet System." She told Reagan of the decay in everyday life in the Soviet Union—alcoholism, alienation, drug abuse, economic decline—and explained how the "ruling elite had become stagnant, cynical, outrageously corrupt and ineffective" in the 1970s and early 1980s.[60] These themes reinforced Reagan's lifelong assumptions. He wrote approvingly in his diary that Oliver "confirmed things I had heard from unconfirmed sources. The Soviet U. is an ec. basket case & among other things there is a rapidly spreading turn by the people to religion."[61]

Reagan was attentive to Suzanne Massie, the author and Soviet culture expert, and read her book *Land of the Firebird: The Beauty of Old Russia*. Massie recalled that when she met Reagan, he seemed hungry to learn more about the Russians as people than he was getting from the briefing papers. "He was an actor: actors like to absorb from feeling, and he just wasn't getting that . . . kind of juice, if you want, that helped him make sense of affairs, from his official sources." In her briefing, Massie tried to counter the Hollywood stereotypes of the Russians. She told him Gorbachev had been called to rule a country that was unruly and fractious, "not a whole lot of Communists marching in locked step, that it was far from that." Massie also told Reagan not to worry about the contrasts being made between himself and the younger Gorbachev—that in fact Reagan was in a stronger position.[62]

Summing up his impressions, Reagan wrote by hand on a yellow pad a four-and-a-half page memo. The note, which was typed up and then corrected by Reagan in ballpoint pen, offers a valuable snapshot of his thinking before the meeting. Reagan accepted the cautious view that Gorbachev would not bring radical change.

"I believe," he wrote, "Gorbachev is a highly intelligent leader totally dedicated to traditional Soviet goals."

Reagan added, "He will be a formidable negotiator and will try to make Soviet foreign and military policy more effective. He is (as are all Soviet General Secretaries) dependent on the Soviet-Communist hierarchy and will be out to prove to them his strength and dedication to Soviet traditional goals." On arms control, Reagan wrote that Gorbachev wished to "reduce the burden of defense spending that is stagnating the

Soviet economy," and that "could contribute to his opposition to SDI" since "he doesn't want to face the cost of competing with us."[63]

The economic pressures on the Soviet system had gravely worsened that autumn. Saudi Arabia increased oil production in a radical change in policy that was undertaken to boost its market share. A glut of crude hit world oil markets, prices collapsed and so did Soviet foreign currency earnings. By one estimate, Moscow had just lost $20 billion a year. Gorbachev's backward country suddenly became a lot poorer.[64]

Reagan's memo also included a curious statement about the Soviet military. In the original memo, he wrote that an internal study "makes it plain the Soviets are planning a war. They would like to win without it and their chances of doing that depend on being so prepared we could be faced with a surrender or die ultimatum." The surrender-or-die ultimatum was one of Reagan's old chestnuts from his anti-communism speeches. Reagan's comment seemed to be lifted right out of his late-1970s slogans warning of a "window of vulnerability."

According to Matlock, Reagan "had not been advised that the Soviets were planning to start a war, but that they were planning so that they could fight one and prevail."

When he read what he had written, Reagan felt misgivings, and crossed out the part about the Soviets planning a war. He substituted instead: "They would like to win by being so much better prepared we could be faced with a surrender or die ultimatum." It was still a skeptical, fearsome, dark view of the other side.

To prepare for the summit, Shultz and McFarlane went to Moscow and met Gorbachev on November 5. They found Gorbachev in a feisty, uncompromising mood. Gorbachev's remarks followed the broad outline of the "asymmetrical response," but he was clumsy. He attacked Reagan's Strategic Defense Initiative, saying at one point the purpose was to bail out the military-industrial complex in the United States, which Gorbachev claimed employed 18 million Americans. Shultz, an economist and former labor secretary, was surprised at Gorbachev's bad information, and responded that defense was only a small part of the American economy. He delivered a mini-lecture to Gorbachev—which he had composed in his mind before the trip—about how the global economy was turning to a new information age. Gorbachev was stubborn and unmoved. "We know what's going on," he insisted. "We know why you're doing this. You're inspired by illusions. You think you're ahead of us in information. You think you're ahead of us in technology and that you can use these things to gain superiority over the Soviet Union. But this is an illusion." If Reagan went ahead with the plan for Star Wars, Gorbachev warned, "We will let you bankrupt yourselves."

Then he added, "We will engage in a buildup that will break your shield."[65]

Shultz called Reagan afterward. Reagan wrote in his journal that night, "Gorbachev is adamant we must cave in our S.D.I.—well, this will be a case of an irresistible force meeting an immovable object."[66]

After Shultz flew back and briefed Reagan, the president added, "It seems Mr. G. is filled with a lot of false info about the U.S. & believes it all. For example, Americans hate the Russians because our arms manufacturers stir them up with propaganda so they can keep selling us weapons."[67] Reagan vowed, "In Geneva I'll have to get him in a room alone and set him straight."[68]

In the weeks before the summit, Roald Sagdeev, the space institute director who had been skeptical about a Soviet Star Wars, was invited to a meeting at the Central Committee with others from the academic and arts elite. They were told that, from now on, they were totally free to meet foreigners without asking permission. "It was a thrilling sensation," Sagdeev recalled. "In a society where everything was under strict control and tight regulation, even phone numbers could not be given to foreigners." He was ordered to join Velikhov and other leading advisers to Gorbachev on a plane to Geneva one week before the summit. The instructions: be open, give press interviews.[69] Hundreds of reporters called, and the group kept busy. A total of 3,614 journalists, including television technicians, registered for the summit. They were drawn by the sense of unpredictability—rarely in the history of superpower summits had there been a meeting without a prearranged script and treaty to be signed; adding to the uncertainty was Reagan's long history of anti-communism and the curiosity stirred by Gorbachev's first months in power. The CIA was there, too. The agency "pulled out all the stops to make Gorbachev feel unwelcome in Geneva," Gates recalled. The CIA sponsored anti-Soviet demonstrations, meetings and exhibits.[70]

When he arrived in Geneva November 16, Reagan, then seventy-four years old, was full of anticipation. "Lord I hope I am ready and not overtrained," he wrote. The first meeting was to be held at Maison Fleur d'Eau, a twenty-room, nineteenth-century villa on the western shore of Lake Geneva. He and Nancy Reagan toured it in advance, spotting a cozy pool house on the lakeshore. Reagan made sure the White House advance team knew he wanted to steer Gorbachev there for a private chat, with a fire blazing. In the preparations, Reagan held a mock summit session, with Matlock playing Gorbachev, speaking in Russian and trying to mimic Gorbachev's gestures.[71] In another briefing, Reagan seemed to glaze over. There was a long silence. "I'm in the year 1830," the president suddenly said, startling his aides. "What happened to all these small shopkeepers in St. Petersburg in the year 1830 and to all that entrepreneurial talent in Russia? How can it have just disappeared?" The aides realized he was absorbed in thought about Massie's book.[72]

Cold winds blew off Lake Geneva as Reagan bounded down the steps to greet Gorbachev without an overcoat just after 10 A.M. on November 19. Gorbachev, then fifty-four years old, in office less than a year, stepped out of his black ZIL limousine, bundled up in a blue patterned scarf and overcoat, and took off his fedora, asking Reagan: "Where is your coat?" "It's inside," Reagan replied as he motioned toward the glass doors and the warmth of the chateau, guiding Gorbachev by the elbow. As they shook hands for the photographers, Reagan later recalled, "I had to admit . . . that there was something likeable about Gorbachev. There was a warmth in his face and his style, not the coldness bordering on hatred I'd seen in most senior Soviet officials I'd met until then."[73]

Once inside, the original plan called for a short tête-à-tête, fifteen minutes, then a larger session, but Reagan and Gorbachev spent an hour with just interpreters in their first encounter. Reagan declared right away he wanted to ease mistrust between them. They held the fate of the world in their hands, he said. He offered bromides and aphorisms collected from a lifetime of speeches. Countries do not mistrust each other because of arms, but arm each other because of mistrust, he said. People do not get into trouble when they talk to each other, but when they talk about each other. Gorbachev responded with an unemotional, reasoned appeal. The two superpowers could not ignore each other, he said. They were too interrelated. Gorbachev said he had come to improve their relations despite the differences of the past. They needed to create a concrete "impetus," he said, to show the world they were serious about ending the arms race. Gorbachev, in a preplanned gesture to Reagan, told the president that Soviet scientists had recently calculated there was a high probability of a big earthquake within the next three years in California. Reagan said he realized a quake was overdue. The two leaders had broken the ice.

In the formal meeting that followed, flanked by aides, they turned to the arms race. In both countries, "the military is devouring huge resources," Gorbachev said. The "central question is how to halt the arms race and disarm." Reagan brought up Eisenhower's speech "Atoms for Peace," offering to internationalize the atom. The United States was always giving, and the Soviet Union rejecting, Reagan complained. While earlier the superpowers reached agreements to slow the growth in weapons, Reagan said, now he wanted to actually reduce the "mountains of weapons." Reagan then launched into an exposition of his dream of "an anti-missile shield which would destroy missiles before they hit the target." Reagan said he didn't want to call it a weapon, but a defensive system, and if it worked, he would share it with the Soviet Union. This was a small preplanned surprise Reagan had decided to offer Gorbachev. The Soviet leader did not have time to respond before they broke for lunch, but he was downbeat as he went back to his residence.[74]

"Reagan appeared to me not simply a conservative, but a political 'dinosaur,'" he recalled of his first impressions.[75]

But the president was chipper. "Our gang told me I'd done good."[76]

In the afternoon, Gorbachev came roaring back, this time deploying the "asymmetrical response" with energy and verve. Gorbachev fired volley after volley of arguments against the Strategic Defense Initiative. It would lead to an arms race in space, not just a defensive one, but an offensive one, he said. Scholars say any shield can be pierced, he added, so why create it? He threatened retaliation; if Reagan went ahead, there could be no reduction of existing offensive weapons. The Soviet response "would not be a mirror," Gorbachev added, but "a simpler, more effective system."

"We will build up to smash your shield," he said.

If there were "seven layers" of space defenses, Gorbachev added, it would require automation, putting important decisions in the hands of computers. Political leaders would just be hiding in bunkers with computers making the decisions. "This could unleash an uncontrollable process. You haven't thought this through, it will be a waste of money, and also will cause more distrust and more weapons," he told Reagan.

Reagan responded the best way he knew how, by articulating his visions and his dream. "There is something uncivilized" about the idea of mutual assured destruction, he said. He told Gorbachev a story. The American ambassador to the United Nations had met some Chinese. They had asked him: what happens when a man with a spear that can penetrate anything meets a man with a shield that is impenetrable? The ambassador said he didn't know, but he did know what happens when a man with no shield meets that same opponent who has the spear. Neither wants to be in the position of having no shield, Reagan insisted.

At this point, Reagan invited Gorbachev to get some fresh air and go down to the pool house. Gorbachev "leaped out of his chair," eager to go, Reagan remembered.[77] When they reached the small room in the pool house, a fire was already roaring. They sat in easy chairs, only interpreters present.

Immediately, Reagan took papers out of a manila folder and handed them to Gorbachev. These are goals for arms control talks, Reagan said, which could be the seeds of a future agreement. Gorbachev started to read and the room was quiet for a few minutes. Soon they had resumed the most difficult disagreement—missile defense, weapons in space. Gorbachev demanded to know: why was there nothing on Reagan's list about that? Reagan repeated his dream was defensive and would not aggravate the arms race. Back and forth they went—Gorbachev seeking to talk Reagan out of his dream, Reagan striving to get Gorbachev to feel the magic. The dialogue was captured in the interpreter's notes:

Gorbachev: If the goal was to get rid of nuclear weapons, why start an arms race in another sphere?

Reagan: These are not weapons that kill people or destroy cities, these are weapons that destroy nuclear missiles.

Gorbachev: Let's ban research, development, testing and deployment of space weapons, then cut offensive arms by 50 percent.

Reagan: Why do you keep speaking about space weapons? We certainly have no intention of putting something into space that would threaten people on Earth.

Gorbachev: A defense against one level of missiles is one thing, but a defense against a much larger number would not be reliable at all.

Reagan: Our people overwhelmingly want this defense. They look at the sky and think what might happen if missiles suddenly appear and blow up everything in our country.

Gorbachev: The missiles are not yet flying. If S.D.I. is actually implemented, then layer after layer of offensive weapons, Soviet and American, would appear in outer space and only God himself would know what they were. And God provides information only very selectively and rarely. Please understand the signal we are giving you—we now have a chance which we must not miss!

They walked back to the main house, having settled nothing. But something had happened to both of them. They had finally taken the measure of the other. "He's adamant but so am I," Reagan wrote that night in his diary. "The 'human factor' had quietly come into action," Gorbachev recalled. "We both sensed that we must maintain contact and try to avoid a break."[78]

Gorbachev was chilled suddenly in the air on the walk back. But he told Reagan this would not be their last meeting. Reagan suggested they visit each other's country. Gorbachev agreed before they got to the door.[79]

On the second day, tempers rose even higher. Gorbachev said a Soviet scientist had done research and found out the explanation for Reagan's determination to build the Strategic Defense Initiative was that it would add $600 billion to $1 trillion in new military expenditures. Reagan said the scientist was dealing in fantasy. If a defensive system could be found, it would be available to all. This would end the nuclear nightmare for the people of the United States, the Soviet Union, indeed for "all people."

Gorbachev started to interrupt Reagan. Why wouldn't Reagan believe him when he said the Soviet Union would never attack? Before Reagan could answer, Gorbachev repeated the question. He again interrupted Reagan's answer to insist on a response. Gorbachev questioned Reagan's sincerity in offering to share research, saying the United States did not even share advanced technology with its allies.

Reagan tried to overcome the interruptions, and in exasperation at one point spilled out one of his deepest hopes—nuclear weapons could be eliminated altogether. At another point, he asked Gorbachev whether he believed in reincarnation and then speculated that perhaps he, Reagan, had invented the shield in an earlier life.

Listening to one of Reagan's pitches for cooperation on Star Wars, Gorbachev lost his cool. Don't treat us as simple people! Reagan said he did not see how he had shown disrespect in any way. It was an open debate.

Reagan captured the spirit of the day in his diary that night: ". . . the stuff really hit the fan. He was really belligerent & d--n it I stood firm."

That evening, after dinner, Reagan and Gorbachev met in the study over coffee to consider how they would present the summit to the world the next morning. Shultz complained angrily to Gorbachev, his voice rising, finger pointing, that Soviet negotiators—especially the deputy foreign minister Georgi Korniyenko—were backpedaling on agreements. Shultz said the negotiators should stay up all night, if necessary, to hammer it out.

At this point, Reagan and Gorbachev, listening while sitting side by side on a red silk couch, decided to intervene. Reagan insisted they should take matters into their own hands and order the negotiators to go back to the table and work out their differences. Gorbachev agreed. The next morning, November 21, the joint statement was ready. When Reagan and Gorbachev came to the international press center to read their statements, Reagan turned to Gorbachev and whispered, "I bet the hardliners in both our countries are bleeding when we shake hands." Gorbachev nodded in agreement.[80]

The headline from the summit was that Reagan and Gorbachev would meet again. But in retrospect, it was not the most important news. Much more significant was a short, innocuous phrase in the joint statement. The two superpowers agreed, the statement said, that "a nuclear war cannot be won and must never be fought."

These words could be dismissed as nothing more than a feel-good slogan, and Reagan had spoken them before.[81] Not a single nuclear warhead was eliminated at Geneva; Reagan was not any closer to his cherished goal of building a missile defense system; Gorbachev was no closer to stopping it. But in so openly announcing that a nuclear war could not be won and must never be fought, the radical reformer from Stavropol and the dreamer from Hollywood had called a halt to years of extraordinary tension and fright. They had put behind them the terrible worries of the RYAN operation and Andropov's fears of imminent attack. They had buried the idea that the Soviets were planning to fight and win a nuclear war. Both of them wanted a world with fewer nuclear weapons, and they had jointly made Geneva their first waypoint on that path. Words had power, and they had found the words. Now they had to find the deeds.

On New Year's Day, Reagan and Gorbachev exchanged simultaneous televised greetings to people in each other's countries, an historic first. Reagan's address appeared at the opening of the main evening news program, and many people in the Soviet Union saw Reagan directly for the first time. "A nuclear war cannot be won and must never be fought," Reagan said.[82]

THE ROAD TO REYKJAVIK

On Sunday, January 5, 1986, very late in the evening, Marshal Sergei Akhromeyev, the chief of the Soviet military's General Staff, telephoned one of his deputies, Colonel General Nikolai Chervov, head of the legal department, which handled arms control negotiations. Both men were products of the World War II generation who rose to the General Staff in the Cold War years. Akhromeyev, the ramrod-straight commander who had promised to help Gorbachev, asked Chervov to report to headquarters at 6 A.M. the next morning. "You will fly to Mikhail Sergeyevich Gorbachev," Akhromeyev said. The Soviet leader was vacationing on the Black Sea coast.

"What must I have with me and what uniform must I wear?" Chervov asked.

"Have your wits about you," Akhromeyev said. "And wear your military uniform."

The next morning, Akhromeyev gave Chervov an envelope for Gorbachev, ordered his personal driver to take him to the airport and said Gorbachev would be expecting him at 10 A.M.

"Can I ask a question?" Chervov said, nervously. "What's inside the envelope?"

Akhromeyev told him it was the draft of the program on global disarmament. "Report all details to the General Secretary."[1]

———

After the Geneva summit with Reagan, Gorbachev was searching for something new. When Chervov arrived with the envelope, Gorbachev greeted him warmly. Gorbachev was vacationing in a house on the coast at Pitsunda, in the republic of Georgia, set in a pine grove, with wood-paneled interiors, spacious rooms and an office. It was a restful place in the solitude of a nature reserve; outside, waves swept across a fine pebble beach. Without wasting words, Gorbachev asked right away, "What have you brought?"[2]

The envelope contained a written proposal to eliminate all nuclear weapons—*all*, including those of the United States, the Soviet Union and other countries—by the year 2000, in three stages, with specific deadlines. Akhromeyev had been working on the idea ever since the Soviets walked out of the Geneva talks in late 1983. He brought in weapons scientists and the staff of different branches of the military, who debated in secret. Once the proposal was drafted, Akhromeyev put it in his desk drawer. In Gorbachev's first year, Akhromeyev kept it to himself, thinking the time was not right to bring it out. By the end of 1985, when Gorbachev was searching for new initiatives, Akhromeyev opened the drawer. The file was titled "Proposal of the USSR for a Program of Full Liquidation of Nuclear Weapons in the Whole World by the Year 2000." It was a sweeping proposal that could grab headlines and win sympathy from anti-nuclear forces around the world. After a year as chief of the General Staff and eight months working with Gorbachev, Akhromeyev could see pressures were building to reduce nuclear arsenals. He personally wanted to scale back the huge stockpiles of warheads, and he felt that Gorbachev's proposal might at least bring about significant cuts, if not lead all the way to total elimination. He could see, too, that Gorbachev was a man of action. The Soviet Union had been calling for general disarmament for decades. But what was new in Akhromeyev's plan was a certain date—the turn of the century.[3]

When Chervov took out the papers, Gorbachev expressed skepticism at first. "What can there be that's new in your initiative?" he asked. "We have been harping on this since 1945. Gromyko has been constantly talking about this at the United Nations. Should the General Secretary repeat this all over again?"

"Mikhail Sergeyevich, everything that you say is correct," Chervov replied. "However, in the past there were only general declarations and wishes to liquidate nuclear weapons. There was nothing concrete. We only came out with a general idea, like 'We are for the liquidation.' . . . This is a completely new program that gives a detailed description of all the possible problems. The nuclear issue is becoming a more burning problem by the day. I ask you to have a look at the document." Gorbachev was in no hurry to take the papers. As if he were talking to himself, he asked Chervov, "And *should* we liquidate all the nuclear weapons? In the West they keep saying that the more nuclear weapons there are, the stronger a country's security is. Should we accept such a concept? What do you think?"

"Mikhail Sergeyevich, everyone has heard the Western leaders' statements to this effect, such as Thatcher, for example. I believe these are dangerous statements. There is a saying, *when there are too many guns, they begin to shoot by themselves.* Today, so many nuclear weapons have been stockpiled in the world, they can explode by themselves . . . the nuclear danger is growing in proportion to the stockpiles." The proverb was familiar; Gorbachev had recalled a similar one to make the same point to British Foreign Minister Geoffrey Howe in late 1984. Gorbachev listened, asked a few more questions and took the envelope. He read the documents in silence. Chervov thought Gorbachev fell into deep thought. Then he said, "This is it. This is what's needed." But Gorbachev wanted to add more. Why not add something about stopping nuclear tests? Banning chemical weapons? Gorbachev took a blank sheet of paper and began writing instructions. When he was finished, Chervov gathered up the papers and flew back to Akhromeyev in Moscow.[4]

Gorbachev's grand plan was visionary, dramatic and dreamy. He proposed in the first phase, five to eight years, to halt all nuclear testing, cut the superpower strategic arsenals by 50 percent, to no more than 6,000 warheads each, and eliminate U.S. and Soviet medium-range missiles in the European zone, including the Pioneers, the Pershing IIs and the ground-launched cruise missiles. He also demanded that the United States and Soviet Union mutually renounce "space strike weapons," a reference to Reagan's Strategic Defense Initiative. In the second stage, to begin in 1990 and last five to seven years, the United States and Soviet Union would continue to reduce their arsenals, joined by the other nuclear powers, France, Britain and China, and the United States and Soviet Union would also eliminate the small battlefield, or tactical, nuclear weapons. Finally, in the third stage, by 2000, all nations would get rid of nuclear weapons and sign a universal pact that nuclear weapons would never return again.[5]

For all its sweeping ambition, the plan was unveiled January 15, 1986, in an oblique Soviet fashion. On the regular Soviet evening news program *Vremya*, an expressionless announcer picked up a sheaf of papers and began droning through a statement on disarmament by the general secretary. Gorbachev was nowhere to be seen. TASS distributed the 4,879-word text. The next morning, the full statement was printed in the official newspapers, *Izvestia* and *Pravda*. The declarations were grand: "The Soviet Union proposes at the beginning of 1986 the implementation of a program for freeing mankind from the fear of nuclear catastrophe." A reader or television viewer might have been excused for asking: so what? Disarmament had been a time-worn Soviet slogan for decades, while the arms race zoomed ahead, ever faster.[6]

Yet this time it was different. Anatoly Chernyaev, the deputy director of the International Department at the Central Committee, writing in his diary after the statement was announced, could sense that Gorbachev was reaching for the stars. "My impression is that he's really decided to end the arms race no matter what. He is taking this 'risk' because, as he understands, it's no risk at all—because nobody would attack us even if we disarmed completely. And in order to get the country on solid ground, we have to relieve it of the burden of the arms race, which is a drain on more than just the economy."

"My God!" Chernyaev wrote. "What luck that there was a man in the Politburo [Andropov] who showed the wisdom of a true 'tsar,' finding Gorbachev and dragging him out of the provinces—and in a country which has 95 such regions! And now we have a real find of a leader: intelligent, well-educated, dynamic, honest, with ideas and imagination. And bold. Myths and taboos (including ideological ones) are nothing for him. He could flatten any of them."[7]

When the television announcer began reading Gorbachev's statement on *Vremya* on January 15, 1986, it was still early in the day in Washington. Dobrynin, the Soviet ambassador, called Shultz in the morning to alert him that an important announcement was about to be made in Moscow. Shortly before the call, a letter from Gorbachev to Reagan arrived, accompanying the new proposal. Shultz and his advisers puzzled over the text, which had both new ideas, such as tackling some disputes one by one rather than all together, and some old roadblocks, such as Soviet demands to stop Reagan's Strategic Defense Initiative. Paul Nitze was fascinated. "I wonder whose work of art on the Soviet side this is," he said.[8]

Weeks earlier, Reagan had appointed a new national security adviser, John M. Poindexter, a retired admiral, to replace McFarlane, who resigned. On the day of the Gorbachev proposal, Poindexter telephoned Matlock, the Soviet expert on the National Security Council, who was across town at that moment. Matlock rushed to the White House, where Poindexter showed him the text and asked whether he thought Gorbachev was serious. "Have they put it on TASS yet?" Matlock asked. Poindexter called the duty officer in the Situation Room and was told the text was coming over the wires at that moment. Matlock said that making the initiative public so quickly "raised the suspicion" that Gorbachev "had nothing more than propaganda in mind." Most government agencies who looked at the proposal, Matlock recalled, thought it was "nothing more than smoke and mirrors and advised a flat rejection." A White House official told reporters, "The language is eerie; it's so extremely flexible that it may look better than it really is." Doubts were everywhere in Washington that day. "A clever propaganda move," said Senator Sam Nunn, Democrat of Georgia.[9]

Shultz went to see Reagan at 2 P.M., and found the president already liked what he had been told about Gorbachev's statement. "Why wait until the end of the century for a world without nuclear weapons?" Reagan asked.

That night, Reagan wrote in his diary that Gorbachev "surprisingly is calling for an arms reduction plan which will rid the world of nuclear weapons by the year 2000. Of course he has a couple of zingers in there which we'll have to work around. But at the very least it is a h--l of a propaganda move. We'd be hard put to explain how we could turn it down." At a White House photo session the next day, Reagan told reporters, "It is just about the first time that anyone has ever proposed actually eliminating nuclear weapons."[10]

But once again, in official Washington, the president was largely alone. Nuclear deterrence had sunk its roots deep into American strategic thinking for four decades. "The naysayers were hard at work, even in my own building . . ." Shultz said. "No one could accept the thought of a world moving toward the elimination of nuclear weapons." Richard N. Perle, an assistant secretary of defense and relentless critic of détente, told the White House Senior Arms Control Group that "the president's dream of a world without nuclear weapons—which Gorbachev had picked up—was a disaster, a total delusion," Shultz recalled. "Perle said the National Security Council should not meet on the idea, because then the president would direct his arms controllers to come up with a program to achieve that result. The Joint Chiefs' representative agreed with Perle. They feared the institutionalization and acceptance of the idea as policy."

Two days after Gorbachev's proposal, Shultz told his staff to face facts; yes, they were all skeptical about elimination of nuclear weapons, but "the president of the United States doesn't agree with you." In fact, Shultz said, "he thinks it's a hell of a good idea."

Shultz set up a small steering group of insiders, starting January 25, in a deliberate effort to bypass the rigid interagency process for making policy in Washington. They met every Saturday morning. Shultz and Gates faced off in these sessions. Shultz thought Gorbachev was for real, "bold and agile." Gates, deputy CIA director, thought Gorbachev was cut from the old Soviet mold. Gates wrote to Shultz at the time, saying "all we have seen since Gorbachev took over leads us to believe that on fundamental objectives and policies he *so far* remains generally as inflexible as his predecessors." Gorbachev's new proposal to eliminate nuclear weapons, Gates said, was "tactically a clever stroke" but "did not change any basic Soviet position."[11]

On Monday, February 3, Reagan met in the White House Situation Room with his top advisers to discuss a response to Gorbachev's proposal. "Some wanted to tag it a publicity stunt," Reagan wrote afterward. "I said no. Let's say we share their overall goals & now want to work out the details. If it is a publicity stunt this will be revealed by them. I also propose to announce we are going forward with SDI but if research reveals a defense against missiles is possible we'll work out how it can be used to protect the whole world not just us."[12]

Gorbachev hurtled forward. He telephoned Chernyaev, the deputy director of the International Department at the Central Committee, and asked him to become his adviser on national security. Chernyaev was a liberal but not yet part of Gorbachev's inner circle. He was known for an encyclopedic mind. He was intensely curious, outspoken and fearless. He loved drama, memorized poetry and read Western literature, even when prohibited. Chernyaev had been schooled in Russian culture and had the best schools and teachers. He went to the front as a volunteer at the outbreak of the Great Patriotic War, fought and was seriously wounded. After the war he graduated from and taught at Moscow State University. In the 1950s, Chernyaev had served in Prague on the staff of a new party journal, *Problemy mira i sotsializma,* or Problems of Peace and Socialism, where the environment was relatively open, compared to Moscow. This left an enduring impression on Chernyaev, who returned to Moscow to spend two decades in the Central Committee apparat, harboring hopes for liberal reform despite the deep disappointments of the era, including Moscow's crushing of the Prague Spring and the invasion of Afghanistan.

When Gorbachev called, Chernyaev hesitated at first, because it seemed an almost overwhelming responsibility. He was sixty-five years old, and feared he would disappoint Gorbachev. He wanted more time for reading, theater, exhibitions, the conservatory, a steady and quiet life.

"What do you say?" insisted Gorbachev.

"One does not refuse such offers, Mikhail Sergeyevich," Chernyaev replied.[13]

In the critical years that followed, Chernyaev remained at Gorbachev's elbow, a key member of the reformist brain trust who offered candid advice to Gorbachev as well as unblemished loyalty. He joined the other intellectuals who generated the ideas and firepower behind *glasnost* and *perestroika.* Chernyaev's diary, detailed and revealing, is perhaps the single most important contemporaneous account of Gorbachev's decision making and thinking.[14]

Change was coming fast in 1986. Boris Yeltsin, the party chief in

Sverdlovsk, was brought to the capital, and soon plunged into a populist drive to improve living standards. Alexander Yakovlev, a strong proponent of democratization, was brought from his think tank to head the Central Committee department on ideology, becoming another preeminent adviser to Gorbachev and the heart and soul of "new thinking." Chernyaev began to take notes at meetings with Gorbachev. Later, other Gorbachev advisers, including Yakovlev, Shakhnazarov and Vadim Medvedev, contributed their notes, making up another valuable contemporaneous account.[15]

Soon after Chernyaev was appointed came the 27th Party Congress, a mammoth affair in which 4,993 delegates from across the country packed into Moscow hotels and assembled in the scarlet-bedecked hall of the Kremlin Palace of Congresses from February 25 to March 6, 1986. Held every five years to approve the membership of the three-hundred-member Central Committee and ratify the next five-year program, the congress was Gorbachev's stage for a premiere of "new thinking" and *perestroika*. In his speeches, Gorbachev referred to the war in Afghanistan as a "bleeding wound," and described a Soviet foreign policy based on living with the non-Communist world rather than endless confrontation of military blocs. Gorbachev's words were spoken in billowing paragraphs, wrapped in old rhetoric about American imperialism, and he still attempted to give socialism a boost rather than destroy it. But "new thinking" was on display nonetheless.[16]

Chernyaev recalled that Gorbachev was in a state of "extreme enthusiasm" when the party congress ended. But just as he savored this success, a chill wind blew in from Reagan. In the wake of the Walker spy ring discovery the year before, Reagan had signed a secret directive in late 1985 to curb Soviet espionage activity, but action had been delayed. On March 7, the day after the party congress ended, the United States ordered the Soviet Union to sharply reduce its diplomatic mission to the United Nations in New York, from about 270 diplomats to 170. Gorbachev took this as an unexpected jab from Reagan. The Soviet mission at the United Nations was believed by U.S. officials to be a headquarters for KGB spies.[17] In fact, two of the most devastating spies of all time were not at the Soviet mission but deep within the U.S. government—Ames and Hanssen.

In another setback for Gorbachev, on March 13, U.S. warships carrying sophisticated electronic gear sailed six miles inside the Soviet Union's twelve-mile territorial limit in the Black Sea, a clear provocation, which the Soviets protested. On March 20, Gorbachev was exasperated when he met aides to plan a speech in the Volga River manufacturing city of Togli-atti. According to Chernyaev's notes, Gorbachev said he hoped to give the Americans a good swift kick. He could not understand European or American indifference to his initiatives and speeches. "What do we see on the part of Europe and the United States?" he asked. "Excuses, evasive-ness, attempts to get away with half-measures and promises."[18]

Gorbachev had prolonged the Soviet self-imposed moratorium on nuclear testing by three months, but Reagan refused to go along. On March 22, the United States set off a twenty-nine-kiloton underground nuclear explosion, code-named Glencoe, two thousand feet below the Nevada desert.[19] Gorbachev continued to hold off on Soviet tests, but bit-terly complained to his inner circle on March 24 that the moratorium showed the Americans "have no intentions to disarm." Gorbachev asked that day, "What does America want?" Chernyaev recalled, "It seemed we were sliding back toward confrontation."

Gorbachev turned again to Reagan's stubborn Star Wars dream. He vowed that the Soviet asymmetrical response could nullify it for just 10 percent of the cost. "Maybe we shouldn't be so afraid of SDI?" he asked. This was a change in tune from his vigorous campaign against missile defense at the Geneva summit just months earlier. "Of course we cannot just disregard this dangerous program," Gorbachev said. "But we should overcome our obsession with it. They're banking on the USSR's fear of SDI—in moral, economic, political and military terms. Therefore they're pursuing this program in order to wear us out."[20]

Speaking just among his top aides, Gorbachev said: "We should do everything not to impoverish our country further through defense spend-ing."

Gorbachev could not grasp why the spirit of the Geneva summit was fading. He wrote to Reagan on April 2, saying, "More than four months have passed since the Geneva meeting. We ask ourselves: what is the rea-son for things not going the way they, it would seem, should have gone? Where is the real turn for the better?" He complained "we hear increas-ingly vehement philippics addressed to the USSR." On April 3, he lamented to the Politburo: "The whole world sees that Gorbachev makes a suggestion in the evening and the next morning the Americans quickly say 'no.'" On April 4, he had a long talk with two influential congressional leaders—Dante Fascell, Democrat of Florida, and William Broomfield, Republican of Michigan—who were visiting Moscow. "Disarmament issues cannot be postponed," Gorbachev said.

"The locomotive is rushing forward at great speed. Today there is still a chance to stop it, but tomorrow it might be too late."

In the marshy flatlands and forests of the Ukraine, spring breezes arrived early that April, carrying scents of cherry blossoms. A giant nuclear electricity-generating plant with a red-and-white candy-striped smokestack stood astride the Pripyat River, ten miles north of the town of Chernobyl and nestled next to a small town, Pripyat. The station housed four 1,000-megawatt reactors, and two more reactors were under construction that, when finished, would make it the largest nuclear power plant in the Soviet Union. In the early-morning hours of Saturday, April 26, a test was getting underway at Reactor No. 4.[21]

The reactor core was a mammoth block of graphite 23 feet high and 38 feet in diameter, weighing 1,700 tons, honeycombed with 1,661 holes for rods filled with uranium fuel. When lowered by a crane into the holes, the fuel rods set off nuclear fission, which gave off heat, turning water into steam to power turbines generating electricity. Another 211 holes in the graphite were drilled for control rods. When lowered into the reactor, the control rods absorbed neutrons and slowed or stopped the nuclear fission. Six pumps, capable of moving up to 18.6 million gallons an hour, forced coolant water through the reactor, with two pumps in reserve. Seventeen of the Soviet RBMK-1000 reactors were built in the Soviet Union between 1973 and 1990; the RBMK acronym stood for *Reaktor Bolshoi Moshchnosti Kanalnyi,* or High-Power Channel Reactor. Unlike reactors in the West, such as the one at Three Mile Island, where an accident occurred in 1979, the Soviet RBMK-1000 design lacked a containment shelter, the overarching, concrete shell to hold radioactivity inside in the event of a disaster.

The rods, pumps and gears used to control and moderate the nuclear fission inside the Chernobyl reactor were dependent on electricity. If outside power were suddenly cut off, it would take forty seconds to kick-start auxiliary diesel engines. Without power for forty seconds, however, the pumps would not force water through the reactor, which would quickly overheat. This forty-second gap was something that Soviet designers knew about and worried over; they were still trying to fix it. On the night of April 26, an improvised work-around was being tested. The operators knew that after a power outage, the spinning turbine blades would keep rotating under their own momentum. So they reasoned: why not use the still-spinning blades to generate enough power to keep the water pumps going for forty seconds? The goal of the test was to see how much power the rotating blades could generate, but the duty operators were ill prepared and the reactor design badly flawed.

One operator, arriving at his station, was confused by the logbook. He called someone else to inquire.

"What shall I do?" he asked. "In the program there are instructions of what to do, and then a lot of things crossed out."

The other person thought for a minute, then replied, "Follow the crossed out instructions."[22]

After midnight Saturday, the reactor was powered down to very low levels for the test. Then, apparently because power was too low, the operators tried to power it up again, perhaps too quickly. Nuclear fission creates by-products that must be allowed to dissipate before the reactor is powered up again, but this danger was ignored.

As they powered up the reactor, a chain reaction began to spin out of control.

A foreman who entered the reactor hall at about 1:23 A.M. saw an unforgettable sight. The reactor had a massive lid. It was the "upper biological shield," intended to prevent radiation exposure to workers during routine operations. The lid was a circle forty-nine feet in diameter, consisting of cubes, each sitting on top of a channel. When the foreman looked down, he saw the 770-pound cubes start to rumble and dance on top of the channels, "as if one thousand seven hundred people were tossing their hats into the air."[23]

The operators hit the red panic button, marked "AZ," for the emergency power reduction system. But it was too late. They desperately tried to lower the control rods to stop the fission, but the rods, by some accounts, got stuck, perhaps because the holes in the core had warped.

Also, there was a design flaw in the rods, which had a section of water and graphite at each end known as the displacer, while the absorber was in the middle. When the rods got stuck, the absorber didn't make it far enough down into the core to be useful in moderating the fission. Moreover, the rods also may have forced water out from the channels, increasing the heat and steam. In the RBMK-1000 reactor design, excessive steam caused the nuclear chain reaction to accelerate. As the heat inside the graphite core skyrocketed, more of the water then turned to steam, which caused the reactor to get even hotter. More steam, more heat, and the reactor went out of control.

At 1:23 A.M., two explosions rocked Chernobyl. These were extremely powerful, caused by the chain reaction generating huge amounts of heat and pressure. The reactor blew apart, and the explosions were followed by fire. The blast blew a hole straight upward through the roof of Reactor No. 4. The weighty lid was tossed aside like a cocked hat, and radioactive materials—gases, graphite and bits of broken fuel rods—were thrust into the atmosphere. Some debris fell down near the site. Radioactive elements were carried by the winds across Europe. The initial contamination was one nightmare, then came another: the graphite core was on fire and burned for ten days, spewing more dangerous materials into the air.

Hours after the disaster, with the graphite core burning, an "urgent report" arrived at the Central Committee in Moscow from Deputy Energy Minister Alexei Makukhin, who had once been minister of energy in the Ukraine when Chernobyl was first being built. The report said that at 1:21 A.M. on April 26 an explosion occurred in the upper part of the reactor, causing fire damage and destroying part of the roof. "At 3:30, the fire was extinguished." Personnel at the plant were taking "measures to cool the active zone of the reactor." No evacuation of the population was necessary, the report said.

Almost everything in Makukhin's report was wrong. The reactor was still burning and was not being cooled, and the population should have been evacuated immediately. What the report did not say was even worse: at the scene, radiation detectors failed, firefighters and others were sent in without adequate protection and officials were debating—but not deciding—about evacuation.[24]

Gorbachev recalled many years later that he first heard of the disaster in a phone call at 5 A.M., but he insisted he did not learn until the evening of April 26 that the reactor had actually exploded and there had been a huge discharge into the atmosphere. "Nobody had any idea that we were facing a major nuclear disaster," he recalled. "Quite simply, in the beginning even the top experts did not realize the gravity of the situation."[25] Chernyaev, who was at Gorbachev's side throughout the crisis, recalled that "even our top leadership did not fully realize the difficulties and dangers associated with nuclear energy." He acknowledged that "one can blame Gorbachev for trusting those responsible," but added, "since nuclear energy was directly linked to the military-industrial complex, it was taken for granted that everything was in perfect order. And that there was no chance of a 'surprise' like Chernobyl."[26]

The reason for the lack of information was the Soviet system itself, which reflexively buried the truth. At each level of authority, lies were passed up and down the chain; the population was left in the dark; and scapegoats were found. Gorbachev was at the top of this decrepit system; his biggest failure was that he did not break through the pattern of cover-up right away. He reacted slowly, a moment of paralysis for this man of action. He seemed unable to get the truth when he needed it from the disaster scene or the officials responsible for nuclear power. While Gorbachev's personal charisma had sparked excitement on the streets of Leningrad the year before, he did not appear in public for eighteen days after the explosion. While he disdained the secrecy of the military, he was just as silent before his own people and much of Europe in a situation of real peril. Gorbachev, who in January called for the elimination of all nuclear weapons, suddenly was faced with a real-time, catastrophic example of what the world might be like after a nuclear explosion, and it was even more frightening than he could have guessed.

Without a containment shelter, radioactive isotopes soared into the atmosphere. Winds carried the contamination north, and by Sunday, radiation was detected in Sweden at the Forsmark nuclear power station, one hundred miles north of Stockholm. The Swedes confronted the Soviets at midday Monday, April 28. Gorbachev had assembled an emergency Politburo meeting at 11 A.M., but the Kremlin had not said a word about the accident, at home or abroad. In notes from the emergency meeting, aides to Gorbachev wrote: "The information was alarming but scant."[27] According to Volkogonov, the historian, as the Politburo discussed how to handle the accident, Gorbachev said, "We must issue an announcement as soon as possible, we must not delay . . ." Alexander Yakovlev also said, "The quicker we announce it, the better it'll be . . ." Other accounts suggest some Politburo members wanted to keep silent.[28] The announcement was delayed for hours and hours. But people with radios that could pick up foreign broadcasts in Moscow already knew something truly horrible had happened; the reports were alarming.

Gorbachev later claimed there were two reasons for the delay: he lacked information and didn't want to create panic. The Kremlin eventually instructed the news media to distribute a statement so terse as to relay none of the catastrophic nature of the event. The announcement was issued at 9 P.M. on April 28:

> An accident has occurred at the Chernobyl Nuclear Power Plant, damaging one of the reactors. Measures are being taken to eliminate the consequences of the accident. The injured are receiving aid. A government commission has been set up.[29]

On the next day, April 29, Gorbachev called another Politburo meeting. According to Volkogonov, Gorbachev now realized "that he had anything but a routine problem on his hands," given the global alarm about the accident. He began consulting with physicists and security officials. Gorbachev opened the Politburo meeting with a terse remark, "Perhaps we aren't reacting as sharply as the states around us?" Gorbachev proposed they create an operational group to manage the crisis. He then asked, "How are we to deal with the population and international public opinion?" He paused and added a somewhat contradictory remark: "The more honestly we conduct ourselves, the better. To ensure that a shadow of suspicion should not fall on our equipment, we must say that the power station was undergoing a planned repair . . ."

After more discussion, the Politburo decided to issue another public statement, which Volkogonov described as "terms that might have been used to announce an ordinary fire at a warehouse."[30] The announcement said the accident had destroyed part of the reactor building, the reactor itself, and caused a degree of leakage of radioactive substances. Two people had died, the statement said, and "at the present time, the radiation situation at the power station and the vicinity has been stabilized." One section was added for socialist countries saying that Soviet experts had noted radiation spreading in the western, northern and southern directions from Chernobyl. "Levels of contamination are somewhat higher than permitted standards, however not to the extent that calls for special measures to protect the population."[31]

In the early weeks, firefighters and "liquidators," people called from all over the country to help mitigate the disaster, fought bravely and worked with amazing courage and dedication in the face of danger. Firefighters recalled standing on a roof so hot their boots melted; helicopter pilots braved the smoldering ruins to dump 5,020 metric tons of sand and other material in an effort to suffocate what appeared to be a red glow, the burning graphite reactor below.[32] But while individuals performed acts of heroism, the bosses of the Soviet state obfuscated. One of the first actions of the plant director was to cut nonessential telephone lines around Chernobyl.[33] An evacuation of Pripyat was begun only thirty-six hours after the explosion; the second stage of the evacuation, including a wider zone that eventually displaced 116,000 people, did not begin until May 5. The Communist Party in Ukraine insisted that May Day parades should carry on as usual in Kiev even though winds were blowing in that direction. On May 1 in Moscow, Nikolai Ryzhkov, the prime minister, signed an instruction to take Soviet news correspondents to areas adjacent to the Chernobyl power station with a goal of preparing reports in newspapers and television showing the "normal vital activity of these areas."[34] But the truth was dawning at the highest levels in Moscow. The same instruction from Ryzhkov admitted the Health Ministry "failed" to provide full information from the scene and insisted that the ministry "take urgent measures to bring order into this affair."

Reagan wrote in his diary, "As usual the Russians won't put out any facts but it is evident that a radioactive cloud is spreading beyond the Soviet border."[35]

Vladimir Gubarev, the science editor of *Pravda*, who had good contacts in the nuclear establishment, heard of the accident soon after it happened and called Yakovlev, Gorbachev's close adviser and champion of new thinking. But Yakovlev told him to "forget about it, and stop meddling," Gubarev recalled. Yakovlev wanted no journalists to witness the scene. But Gubarev was persistent, and kept calling Yakovlev every day. Yakovlev finally authorized a group of journalists to go to Chernobyl, including Gubarev, who had a physics degree but also wrote plays and books. He arrived May 4 and returned May 9. His private report to Yakovlev depicted chaos and confusion. One hour after the explosion, the spread of radiation was clear, he said, but no emergency measures had been prepared. "No one knew what to do." Soldiers were sent into the danger zone without individual protective gear. They didn't have any. Nor did helicopter pilots. "In a case like this, common sense is required, not false bravery," he said. "The whole system of civil defense turned out to be entirely paralyzed. Even functioning dosimeters were not available." Gubarev said, "the sluggishness of local authorities is striking. There were no clothes, shoes, or underwear for victims. They were waiting for instructions from Moscow." In Kiev, the lack of information caused panic. People heard reports from abroad but didn't get a single word of reassurance from the leaders of the republic. The silence created more panic in the following days when it became known that children and families of party bosses were fleeing. "A thousand people stood in line in the ticket office of the Ukraine Communist Party Central Committee," Gubarev said. "Naturally, this was perfectly well known in the city." When Gubarev returned to Moscow, he gave Yakovlev his written report. It was passed to Gorbachev.[36]

Gorbachev finally spoke about the disaster on May 14, two and a half weeks after it happened, in a nationally televised address. He looked "like a man bereaved," recalled Angus Roxburgh, the BBC correspondent. "His face showed that he knew he had lost credibility." His speech dodged the reasons for the catastrophe, and advanced the line that people had been alerted "as soon as we received reliable initial information." Gorbachev seemed to lose his cool entirely at some of the wild accusations that spread in the West while the Kremlin had bottled up information, such as early reports of mass casualties in the thousands. He also took umbrage at criticism of his sincerity as a reformer. The United States and Germany "launched an unrestrained anti-Soviet campaign," he complained.

In the weeks after Chernobyl, Gorbachev began to shake off his early inertia. At the Politburo meeting July 3, his fury boiled over at the nuclear establishment.

> For 30 years you've been telling us that everything was safe. And you expected us to take it as the word of God. This is the root of our problems. Ministries and research centers got out of control, which led to disaster. And, so far, I do not see any signs that you've learned your lesson from this . . . Everything was kept secret from the Central Committee. Its apparat didn't dare to look into this area. Even decisions about where to build nuclear power stations weren't made by the leadership. Or decisions about which reactor to employ. The system was plagued by servility, bootlicking, window-dressing . . . persecution of critics, boasting, favoritism, and clannish management.
>
> Chernobyl happened and nobody was ready—neither civil defense, nor medical departments, not even the minimum necessary number of radiation counters. The fire brigades don't know what to do! The next day, people were having weddings not far away from the place. Children were playing outside. The warning system is no good! There was a cloud after the explosion. Did anyone monitor its movement?[37]

In Gorbachev's anger after the disaster, he did not turn the spotlight of blame on the Soviet party or the system itself. Rather, he responded by blaming individuals and finding scapegoats, including the plant operators, who were later put on trial. Gorbachev wanted to shake off the lethargy of the system, not challenge its legitimacy. Yet the inescapable truth was that Chernobyl offered a glimpse of how the Soviet Union was rotting from within. The failures, lassitude and misguided designs that led to the disaster were characteristic of much else. "The great glowing crater at Block 4 had revealed deep cracks in the state," Volkogonov said. "After the Afghan fiasco, which Gorbachev condemned but which dragged on for another four years, Chernobyl was the next bell tolling for the system."

Gorbachev's emphasis on *glasnost*, or openness, grew significantly when he finally came to grips with what happened at Chernobyl. The word *glasnost* eventually became a signature of his reforms, along with *perestroika*, which referred to the idea of rebuilding society, politics and the economy. At the July 3 Politburo meeting, he declared, "Under no conditions will we hide the truth from the public, either in explaining the causes of the accident nor in dealing with practical issues." He added, "We cannot be dodging the answers. Keeping things secret would hurt ourselves. Being open is a huge gain for us." Shevardnadze's assistant Sergei Tarasenko said Gorbachev and Shevardnadze were shamed by the way the radioactive cloud floating over Europe had revealed what they failed to announce. "For the first time, they understood that you cannot cover up anything," Tarasenko said. "You can say, 'Nothing happened there,' but with radiation you cannot hide it. It will go in the air, and anyone will know it is there."[38] Shevardnadze wrote in his memoirs that Chernobyl "tore the blindfold from our eyes and persuaded us that politics and morals could not diverge."[39]

Akhromeyev, the chief of the General Staff, recalled that Chernobyl changed the entire country's view of nuclear danger. "After Chernobyl, the nuclear threat stopped being an abstract notion for our people. It became tangible and concrete. The people began to see all the problems linked with nuclear weapons much differently."[40] This was especially true for Gorbachev. In his televised address, he said Chernobyl showed "what an abyss will open if nuclear war befalls mankind. For inherent in the nuclear arsenals stockpiled are thousands upon thousands of disasters far more horrible than the Chernobyl one." Gorbachev's words struck some as hollow at the time he spoke, a propaganda diversion from the real crisis of what had just occurred and his bungled response. But once again, as with the January 15 proposal to eliminate nuclear weapons, propaganda reflected what Gorbachev believed. He may well have asked himself, if there were no working dosimeters at Chernobyl, if soldiers lacked proper uniforms, if operators were relying on crossed-out instructions, what would happen to a city hit by a nuclear weapon? The smoldering Chernobyl site held portents more grave.

"In one moment," he told the Politburo on May 5, "we felt what a nuclear war is." In a secret speech at the Foreign Ministry on May 28, which was only published years later, Gorbachev implored the diplomats to make all possible effort "to stop the nuclear arms race."[41]

Thirty-one people were killed as direct casualties of the Chernobyl accident. Twenty-eight died in 1986 due to acute radiation syndrome, two more from injuries unrelated to radiation and one suffered a heart attack. While it is much more difficult to determine long-term cancer mortality from the contamination, one estimate is that up to four thousand additional cancers may have resulted among the six hundred thousand people exposed to higher levels of radiation, such as liquidators, evacuees and residents of the most contaminated areas.[42]

Reagan never lost his antipathy to Soviet communism, but now, in early summer of 1986, he wanted to do business with Gorbachev. Reagan mentioned in a letter to Gorbachev that "we have lost a full six months in dealing with the issues which most merit our personal attention." Suzanne Massie, the author and cultural expert, came to give Reagan her impressions from a recent visit, and reported "the Soviet Union was on the road to collapse," recalled Shultz, who attended with the president. "There were shortages of everything, and people now realized they had to turn to free enterprise. Chernobyl was of great symbolic importance, she felt: it showed that Soviet science and technology were flawed, that the leadership was lying and out of touch, that the party could not conceal its failures any longer. Chernobyl means 'wormwood,' a reference to bitterness and sorrow from the Book of Revelation. There are many biblical allusions in Russia now."[43] While the shortages had been a feature of Soviet life for years, Massie's description dramatized the situation for Reagan and clearly left a deep impression on him. "She is the greatest student I know of the Russian people," he wrote that evening.[44]

On May 14, the same day as Gorbachev's televised speech about Chernobyl, Shultz had a long talk with Reagan. He planted a small seed that would grow large in the months ahead. "The Soviets," he said, "contrary to the Defense Department and the CIA line, are not an omnipotent, omnipresent power gaining ground and threatening to wipe us out.

> On the contrary, we are winning. In fact, we are miles ahead.
> Their ideology is a loser. They have one thing going for them:
> military power. But even then they have only one area of genuine
> comparative advantage—the capacity to develop, produce, and
> deploy accurate, powerful, mobile land-based ballistic missiles.

There's only one thing the Soviet Union does better than we do:
that is to produce and deploy ballistic missiles. And that's not
because they are better at engineering. They're not . . . So we must
focus on reductions in ballistic missiles. Reductions are the name of
the game.[45]

Shultz urged Reagan to begin to think about what he would give up at
the bargaining table. "This is the moment when our bargaining position
is at its strongest." Shultz wanted to signal to the Soviets that Reagan
would trade limits on his Strategic Defense Initiative for deeper cuts in
offensive weapons, like ballistic missiles, but Shultz was opposed at every
turn by Weinberger, the defense secretary, who urged Reagan not to even
hint at compromise of his dream.

On June 12, Weinberger surprised everyone. At a small, secret meeting in the White House Situation Room, Weinberger made a radical proposal. He suggested that Reagan should ask Gorbachev to eliminate *all
ballistic missiles*. These were the guns of the nuclear age, the fast-flying,
no-return, nuclear-tipped weapons that Reagan worried about after he
visited Cheyenne Mountain in 1979. It was a radical idea that would go
right to the heart of Soviet military strength—the Soviets were most
powerful in land-based missiles like the SS-18, while the United States
forces were stronger at sea. "Everyone was astonished," Shultz recalled of
the Weinberger proposal. Reagan just smiled. He reflected in his diary
that night that the proposal would show whether the Soviets are "for real
or just trying for propaganda."

Since Hiroshima and Nagasaki, a nuclear weapon had never been used in
combat, but hundreds of explosive tests shook the Earth. Kennedy and
Khrushchev halted all tests in the atmosphere, in outer space and in the
oceans with the 1963 limited test ban treaty, but underground explosions
were frequent. The 1974 threshold test ban treaty limited underground
tests to less than 150 kilotons, although it was never ratified. Testing was
a subject of constant suspicion; the United States carried out its own
secret tests and accused the Soviets of violating the treaties.

When Gorbachev announced a unilateral Soviet moratorium on testing in 1985, marking forty years since Hiroshima, he challenged the

United States to follow suit. Gorbachev hoped the moratorium would crimp research for Reagan's Strategic Defense Initiative. Tests would be needed to develop an effective nuclear-pumped X-ray laser. "If there is no testing, there will be no SDI," Chernyaev wrote.[46] Reagan refused to go along with Gorbachev's moratorium, saying a test ban could not be effectively verified. Thus, the dispute over "verification," whether or not a test ban was being observed, became both a scientific and political issue. Reagan had a second reason for refusing to go along with Gorbachev: American designers wanted to test a new generation of warheads that would be able to survive the radiation effects of a nuclear blast.[47] Gorbachev's moratorium was brushed off as propaganda. From 1949 until the start of the moratorium, the Soviet Union had carried out 628 nuclear explosions, 421 of them at the remote Semipalatinsk test site in Kazakhstan in Central Asia. The United States had carried out its 978th test, code-named Jefferson, just days before Chernobyl.[48]

By the spring of 1986, Gorbachev was under pressure from the Soviet nuclear weapons establishment to resume testing. His peace overture, the unilateral moratorium, had borne no results. "It is hard to tell when the new thinking will arrive," he lamented in a meeting with advisers. "But it will come, and maybe unexpectedly fast."

In those exhausting days, Velikhov, the open-minded physicist, once again showed the way. His contacts in the West proved critical. Velikhov knew of Americans outside the U.S. government who were skeptical of Reagan's policies and who were independent thinkers. One of them was Frank von Hippel, a physicist and professor of public and international affairs at Princeton University, who was chairman of the Federation of American Scientists. The group was founded in 1945 by atomic scientists concerned about control of the technology they had helped create, and von Hippel practiced what he called "public interest science," attempting to influence government policy. In the early 1980s, he was caught up in the nuclear freeze movement and sought to provide an analytical basis for some of its initiatives. He had met Velikhov several times at conferences, and they enjoyed brainstorming together.[49] Riding together in the back of a bus at a conference in Copenhagen, Velikhov suggested to von Hippel: perhaps independent, nongovernment scientists from the United States could help demonstrate the feasibility of seismic verification, which had deadlocked the superpowers?[50]

A similar notion was gaining ground among American scientists. One who was keenly interested in building such a bridge was Thomas B. Cochran of the Natural Resources Defense Council, an environmental group. Cochran, a nuclear specialist who had opposed the U.S. plutonium breeder reactor program in the 1970s, was digging into evidence of secret U.S. nuclear tests. When Reagan came into office, he became interested in branching out from strictly environmental issues. In March 1986, Cochran was attending a Federation of American Scientists conference in Virginia. During a coffee break, he talked with von Hippel about a seismic verification experiment.

Then, in April, von Hippel was in Moscow and sought out Velikhov. "Do you have any good ideas?" Velikhov asked him, as he always did when he met the Americans. Velikhov was disorganized—von Hippel once found his desk drawer filled with unsorted business cards—but he restlessly sought new ideas. Velikhov and von Hippel decided to hold a workshop in Moscow on seismic monitoring. Three different proposals were aired at the workshop, held in May. A few days after the workshop ended, Velikhov, a vice president of the Academy of Sciences, signed an agreement with Cochran's group to allow a team to position seismic monitoring equipment adjacent to the Semipalatinsk nuclear weapons test site.[51] This was one of the Soviet crown jewels, the counterpart to the Nevada Test Site. Velikhov urged Cochran to get back within a month; the test moratorium was scheduled to expire soon. They needed to do something big to help Gorbachev keep the moratorium in place.

There was just one hitch: Velikhov did not have official permission for the Americans to make the trip to such a secret location. (The Semipalatinsk site was totally closed; during the Cold War, the United States deployed radioactivity-sniffing aircraft and other methods to monitor Soviet weapons tests.) Velikhov took a gamble—if Cochran could somehow show verification was possible, it would strengthen Gorbachev's hand in prolonging the moratorium.

The Scripps Institution of Oceanography loaned the first seismic gear, relatively unsophisticated surface monitors. Cochran and his team lugged them to Moscow in early July.[52] The plan was to set them up at three locations outside of Semipalatinsk, within 150–200 kilometers from the center of the testing area, but not actually on the site. The Soviets were not conducting tests at the time. Cochran's goal was simply to show that the Soviets would allow American seismologists to set up stations inside the

Soviet Union, record data, and bring it out. This would be immensely symbolic, calling into question the Reagan argument that a test ban could not be verified, and helping support Velikhov's effort to get Gorbachev to extend the moratorium.[53]

The American team arrived in Moscow on July 5, but before they could unpack their equipment, Velikhov ran into trouble.

"All of our military was completely against it," Velikhov said. Gorbachev got cold feet and decided to ask the Politburo to rule whether Velikhov could allow the Americans to get close to the secret test site. The Soviet leadership was still struggling with the Chernobyl aftermath. "It was a very, very tense meeting on Chernobyl," Velikhov recalled. "And after this meeting, everybody was tired, and there was a discussion of Semipalatinsk. Gorbachev was tired, and as usual, he wished somebody else would make this decision, not him. I made the case, but he didn't give me any indication of strong support."

Then, abruptly, two prominent figures turned against Velikhov. They were Dobrynin, the former ambassador to the United States, and Zaikov, the Politburo member for the military-industrial complex. They demanded: Why isn't the measuring reciprocal? Why are we not putting our equipment in Nevada at the American test site?

Look, replied Velikhov impatiently, you have it all wrong. Reagan wants to continue testing. We are trying to impose a moratorium. We should help the scientists who will show the world that a test ban can be verified!

"After the meeting, it was inconclusive," Velikhov recalled. He had no authority to sign the papers and give permission to Cochran. When the meeting was over, Velikhov was sitting with Gorbachev. What should he do?

Gorbachev replied, in his maddeningly vague way: "Follow the line of discussion of the meeting."

"As I understood it?" Velikhov asked.

"Yes," said Gorbachev.

Velikhov took that to mean "yes." He gave a green light to Cochran's team. The only condition, apparently to satisfy the military, was that the American scientists turn off their monitors in the event of any Soviet weapons test. Cochran agreed.[54] The team began to set up the first station on July 9. It was an amazing moment, a toe into a closed zone, accom-

plished by an environmental group, not by the United States government. It demonstrated that scientists could, on their own, break through
the Cold War secrecy and mistrust. It also underscored the unusual clout
of Velikhov. "Not only his clout," Cochran said, "but his chutzpah."[55]

When Cochran, von Hippel, Velikhov and other scientists went to
Gorbachev's offices at the Central Committee in Moscow on July 14, they
urged him to extend the moratorium. Cochran carried back from the test
site the first seismic record, made by a scratchy needle moving across
smoked paper fastened to a drum recording device. *Pravda* played up the
meeting in a front-page article the next morning.

A few days later, on July 18, former president Richard Nixon held a
private talk with Gorbachev in Moscow. Gorbachev told Nixon he
wanted to send a signal to Reagan: he was eager to move ahead, he would
not seek to postpone action until Reagan left office. "In today's tense
atmosphere, it means we cannot afford to wait," Gorbachev said. Nixon
reinforced the idea, saying Reagan was also primed to move. Nixon
transmitted the message to Reagan, writing up a twenty-six-page memo
for the president on his return.

On July 25, Reagan sent Gorbachev a seven-page formal letter, an outgrowth of the meeting at which Weinberger had proposed eliminating all
ballistic missiles. The language of the Reagan letter was convoluted. It
proposed that either the United States or the Soviet Union could research
missile defense, and if they succeeded in creating it, would share, but only
if both sides also agreed on a radical idea: "eliminate the offensive ballistic missiles of *both* sides." If they didn't agree to share-and-eliminate, then
either side could, after six months, build missile defense on its own. Thus,
Reagan had taken his dream of missile defense and hammered it together
with Weinberger's improbable proposal to get rid of the missiles.

On testing, Reagan firmly refused to stop.

On August 18, Gorbachev once again extended the Soviet nuclear-testing
moratorium. Velikhov's efforts had paid off. But Gorbachev was restless.
When he went on vacation at the end of the month, Gorbachev was
accompanied by Chernyaev, his national security adviser, as a one-man
staff. They sat on the veranda or in Gorbachev's office before lunch,

reviewed the cables and made telephone calls to Moscow. Gorbachev asked the Foreign Ministry to provide an outline of ideas for the next meeting with Reagan. When the document came from Moscow, the suggestions were dry repetitions of what had been offered at the stalled arms control negotiations in Geneva.

Gorbachev threw it on the table. "What do you think?" he asked Chernyaev.

"It's no good," Chernyaev replied.

"Simply crap!" Gorbachev said.

Gorbachev asked Chernyaev to draft a letter to Reagan inviting him to a summit very soon, suggesting one venue might be Reykjavik, the capital of Iceland, perhaps in September or October. When Chernyaev asked why Reykjavik, Gorbachev said, "It's a good idea. Halfway between us and them, and none of the big powers will be offended."[56] Shevardnadze subsequently took the invitation to Washington on September 19. In the letter, Gorbachev offered a choice of London or Iceland; Reagan agreed to Iceland. The letter proposed "a quick one-on-one meeting . . . maybe just for one day, to engage in a strictly confidential, private and frank discussion (possibly only with our foreign ministers present)."[57] Gorbachev said the talk "would not be a detailed one," but designed to prepare a few issues for a later summit agreement. Reagan wrote in his diary, "This would be preparatory to a Summit."[58]

But what was going through Gorbachev's mind was something far more ambitious. He began to plan for a grand overture. He wanted to move very far, and fast. In their private discussion and memos, Gorbachev and Chernyaev plotted a dramatic turning point in the arms race. The summit must bring "major, sweeping proposals" to the fore, Chernyaev wrote. On September 22, Gorbachev told the Politburo he was willing to consider releasing twenty-five dissidents on a list demanded by Reagan, a move to assuage the president.[59] In early October, a paper on the summit came to Gorbachev from Akhromeyev and others, offering guidelines for what Gorbachev should do. Gorbachev rejected it; he wanted to be bolder.[60] Chernyaev offered his views to Gorbachev, which captured the mood: "The main goal of Reykjavik, if I understood you correctly in the South, is to sweep Reagan off his feet by our bold, even 'risky' approach to the central problems of world politics."[61] Chernyaev urged Gorbachev to make strategic weapons—

missiles, bombers, submarines—his main topic, seeking a 50 percent reduction. Gorbachev agreed on the need for sweeping change, but did not want to get bogged down in arithmetic. "Our main goal now is to prevent the arms race from entering a new stage," he said. "If we don't do that, the danger to us will increase. If we don't back down on some specific, maybe important issues, if we don't budge from the positions we've held for a long time, we will lose in the end. We will be drawn into an arms race that we cannot manage. We will lose, because right now we are at the end of our tether."

By contrast, Reagan approached the Reykjavik meeting casually, without any of the careful study he had applied before Geneva. There was no precooked agenda, as in previous summits. The Americans had little inkling of what Gorbachev was planning. Shultz wrote Reagan on October 2 that arms control would be central, but the Soviets "are largely talking from our script." A Soviet specialist at the State Department wrote a two-page memo that opened: "We go into Reykjavik next week with very little knowledge of how Gorbachev intends to use the meeting." Poindexter wrote "talking points" that he gave to Reagan, including "anticipate no substantive agreements per se," and "meeting is in no sense a substitute or a surrogate for a summit."[62]

But in Moscow, in his instructions to his summit aides October 4, Gorbachev was once again clear and direct about his ambitions—they were sky high. He talked about finding something to offer Reagan with "breakthrough potential," and at the top of Gorbachev's list was "the liquidation of nuclear weapons." As a more immediate goal, he wanted to be rid of the arms race in European missiles, to remove the threat of the fast-flying Pershing IIs. "In our mind we must hold the priority task to kick the Pershing IIs out of Europe," he said. "This is a gun at our temple."

Gorbachev mentioned "liquidation of nuclear weapons" repeatedly.

He also told the aides he had a strategy. He would push for bold achievements, and "if Reagan does not meet us halfway, we will tell the whole world about this. That's the plan."

"If we fail, then we can say—Look, here's what we are prepared to do!"

Reagan and Gorbachev met at Hofdi House, an isolated, two-story white structure overlooking the bay with a reputation for being haunted—it had been sold by the British ambassador in 1952 after pictures kept falling inexplicably off the walls. The North Atlantic weather cast cold, driving rain squalls—and brief splashes of brilliant sunshine—across the city on Saturday, October 11. Reagan and Gorbachev met at 10:40 A.M., sitting in brown leather armchairs opposite a small table in a room on the first floor, with a window on the gray and turbulent sea just beyond, and, on another wall, a dark blue oil painting, a seascape of waves crashing onto the rocks. In their initial meeting alone, Reagan repeated his favorite Russian proverb, "trust, but verify," and Gorbachev wasted no time telling Reagan that the arms negotiations were stalled and they needed to give them an "impulse." Suddenly, there was an awkward moment. Reagan dropped his note cards. Gorbachev deflected the embarrassment by suggesting they invite their foreign ministers to join them; Shultz and Shevardnadze entered the room. Shultz remembered the scene: "Gorbachev was brisk, impatient and confident, with the air of a man who is setting the agenda and taking charge of the meeting. Ronald Reagan was relaxed, disarming in a pensive way, and with an easy manner."

Gorbachev launched into his dramatic proposals right at the outset. He proposed a 50 percent reduction in what he called "strategic offensive arms," a very broad definition that could cover many weapons. He pledged the Soviets would accept deep cuts in the giant land-based missiles. He proposed to eliminate all medium-range missiles in Europe, including the Pioneers and the Pershing IIs. He called for "full and final prohibition of nuclear testing." Gorbachev proposed that both sides promise for ten years to stick by the 1972 Anti-Ballistic Missile Treaty. This would put restraints on Reagan's dream: research on missile defense would have to be confined to the laboratory.[63]

Reagan then replied to Gorbachev rather formally, reading from his cards. They used consecutive translation, which meant each remark was translated after it was spoken, which took time. Reagan's presentation repeated the idea in his July 25 letter that once his Strategic Defense Initiative was ready, he would share it, and the ABM treaty would disappear, replaced by a new agreement, while both sides would reach "total elimination of strategic missiles." From this very first exchange, Reagan clung tenaciously to his vision.

At the first break, "excitement was in the air," Shultz said. He realized that Gorbachev had offered extraordinary and unexpected concessions. "He was laying gifts at our feet," Shultz said. Shultz and other U.S. officials crowded into the secure "bubble" at the embassy, a small, vaultlike soundproof enclosure. Reagan then joined them, joking, "Why did Gorbachev have more papers than I did?" Nitze said, "This is the best Soviet proposal we have received in 25 years."

In the afternoon session, Reagan and Gorbachev debated the 50 percent cut in weapons. Gorbachev wanted a simple 50 percent slash, while Reagan was worried that it would still leave the Soviets with advantages. But their talk was businesslike, and Gorbachev passed to Reagan a data sheet of Soviet weapons. "Let us cut this in half," he said. "You are troubled by our SS-18 heavy missiles, and they will be reduced by 50 percent." They agreed to leave the details to their staffs to hammer out overnight. Then Reagan returned to his missile defense dream. He told Gorbachev that it would "make missiles obsolete," and "provide a guarantee against the actions of any madman," and is "the best possibility for ensuring peace in our century." Gorbachev took the lecture in stride, but he had heard it all before, and Reagan was giving no ground at all on Gorbachev's demand to keep the research in the laboratory.

Gorbachev's temper flared, and he warned Reagan that if he built the Strategic Defense Initiative, there would be a Soviet response—an "asymmetrical" one. He did not say what it would be, only that it would be "different."

Reagan apparently did not realize that Gorbachev, in talking about a response, was contemplating a massive, offensive assault of nuclear warheads to overwhelm Reagan's defenses. Rather, Reagan imagined Gorbachev's system as something benign, like his own. "If you find that you have something a little better, then perhaps you could share it with us," Reagan suggested.

"Excuse me, Mr. President," Gorbachev replied sternly, "but I do not take your idea of sharing SDI seriously. You don't want to share even petroleum equipment, automatic machine tools or equipment for dairies, while sharing SDI would be a second American revolution. And revolutions don't occur all that often. Let's be realistic."

They decided to continue the next day, Sunday, which had not been part of the original plan—and ordered their staffs to work all night on compromises.[64]

Shultz later recalled that "the whole nature of the meeting we had planned at Reykjavik had changed." Instead of a quick meeting, it was now becoming a full-scale summit. Through the night, American and Soviet officials sought common ground. The conditions were trying; without photocopying machines, they used carbon paper. Two U.S. officials, Colonel Bob Linhard of the National Security Council staff, and Richard Perle, an assistant secretary of defense, had nowhere else to work, so they put a board on a bathtub and got down to business. One of the surprises of the marathon overnight talks was that the U.S. officials for the first time got to know Akhromeyev, the chief of the General Staff who had pledged to help Gorbachev, and they found him to be a formidable negotiator. At one point, in an informal moment, Akhromeyev told Shultz, "I'm the last of the Mohicans." When Shultz asked what he meant, Akhromeyev said he was the last active Soviet commander who had fought the Nazis in World War II. Shultz then asked him where he had learned the phrase. "In boyhood," Akhromeyev said. "I was raised on the adventure tales of James Fenimore Cooper." Shultz recalled that Akhromeyev seemed "far more at ease with himself, more open, more ready for real conversation" than earlier Soviet negotiators.[65]

By morning, as a result of the dramatic all-night conversations, breathtaking agreements to slash nuclear arsenals were drafted on paper. If the summit had just stopped there, if the two leaders had signed the papers, it would have been the climactic turnaround of the arms race. The Euromissiles would be dismantled except for one hundred on each side, and long-range or strategic weapons cut by 50 percent, a stupendous achievement when compared with the strategic arms treaties negotiated by Nixon and Carter. The 1972 SALT I accord, for example, had only put a freeze on missile launchers; now Reagan was slicing into the metal of the feared SS-18. Reagan agreed to negotiations on a nuclear test ban, too.

"We were getting amazing agreements," Reagan later wrote in his memoirs. "As the day wore on, I felt something momentous was occurring."[66]

But then Gorbachev turned up the heat. "Now I am testing you," Gorbachev said, as he insisted they take up missile defense. He told Reagan that he wasn't demanding that he abandon his dream, just keep it in the laboratory. This meant Reagan could "show the idea is alive, that we are not burying it," Gorbachev said. But Reagan would not budge. "The genie is already out of the bottle. Offensive weapons can be built again. I propose creating protection for the world for future generations, when you and I will no longer be here."

Gorbachev begged for a concession. "As the American saying goes, it takes two to tango," he insisted.

Soon, perhaps out of fatigue, the two leaders began to shadow-box with their old slogans. Reagan brought out his Marx and Lenin aphorisms, and Gorbachev replied disdainfully, "So you are talking about Marx and Lenin again." For his part, Gorbachev bristled at the memory of Reagan's 1982 speech at Westminster, and the prediction that the Soviet Union would wind up on the ash heap of history. "I will tell you, that is quite a terrifying philosophy," Gorbachev said. "What does it mean politically, make war against us?"

"No," Reagan replied.

Then, almost as quickly, they gave up and turned back to the danger of nuclear weapons. Reagan launched a defense of his dream. "It appears at this point that I am the oldest man here," Reagan said. "And I understand that after the war the nations decided they would renounce poison gases. But thank God that the gas mask continued to exist. Something similar can happen with nuclear weapons. And we will have a shield against them in any case."

Exasperated, Gorbachev concluded, "The president of the United States does not like to retreat." He seemed resigned to failure. "I see that the possibilities of agreement are exhausted."

They didn't give up, however. Gorbachev hammered away at the idea of keeping missile defense confined to the laboratory. Reagan was alternately insistent and unfocused. He told Gorbachev, "I can imagine both of us in ten years getting together again in Iceland to destroy the last Soviet and American missiles under triumphant circumstances. By then I'll be so old that you won't even recognize me. And you will ask in surprise, 'Hey, Ron, is that really you? What are you doing here?' And we'll have a big celebration over it."

"I don't know whether I will live till that time," Gorbachev said.

"I know I will," Reagan replied.

During a break, Shultz attempted to craft new language in an effort to keep alive the hope of some kind of agreement. Reagan offered it to Gorbachev: a ten-year commitment to the ABM treaty, during which there would be "research, development and testing" of missile defenses.

Gorbachev immediately saw what was missing. The new formula omitted any mention of the word *laboratory*. Was it done on purpose? Yes, Reagan said.

Reagan also proposed two five-year periods for weapons elimination—exactly the same time frame as Gorbachev had suggested in January. But in Reagan's version, there would be a 50 percent cut in "strategic offensive arms" in the first five years and the remaining 50 percent of "offensive ballistic missiles" in the second. Gorbachev said, correctly, the two five-year periods each eliminated a different category of weapon—how could that make sense? The first phase was all strategic arms, the second phase was only missiles. These were obviously different categories. "There is some kind of confusion here." Indeed there was. The U.S. draft had been inexact in an effort to satisfy both sides.

Reagan was also confused. "What I want to know is, will all offensive ballistic missiles be eliminated?" he asked.

Gorbachev suggested that in the second phase, the wording should say "strategic offensive weapons, including ballistic missiles." Perhaps they could improve the language later on, he said.

Then Reagan suddenly took everything further than it had ever gone before. An incredible moment in the history of the Cold War arrived abruptly, without any warning, without preparation, without briefing papers or interagency process, without press conferences or speeches, in the small room overlooking the bay.

"Let me ask this," Reagan inquired. "Do we have in mind—and I think it would be very good—that by the end of the two five-year periods all nuclear explosive devices would be eliminated, including bombs, battlefield systems, cruise missiles, submarine weapons, intermediate-range systems, and so on?"

Gorbachev: "We could say that, list all those weapons."

Shultz: "Then let's do it."

Reagan's proposal was, by any measure, the most concrete, far-reaching disarmament initiative by a U.S. president ever to be formally submitted in a superpower summit negotiation. It was not a throwaway line. If earlier he had talked about eliminating ballistic missiles, or been imprecise or cloudy about what was under discussion, at this moment he swept away any doubts and clearly proposed total nuclear disarmament. There was no confusion. Reagan had reached the very core of his beliefs at the very peak of his power.

But Reagan and Gorbachev did not take out a paper and sign it at that moment. It was a huge missed opportunity.

Gorbachev, while saying there was a chance for such an agreement, again insisted that research on missile defense must be confined to the laboratory. "The question of laboratories is of fundamental importance."

Reagan refused, saying his aim was "to make a kind of gas mask against nuclear missiles" and a system to protect against "the danger of nuclear maniacs."

Gorbachev: "Yes, I've heard all about gas masks and maniacs, probably ten times already. But it still does not convince me." He added, again, that he only wanted to keep missile defense research in the laboratory.

Reagan: "You're destroying all my bridges to continuation of my SDI program."

Gorbachev: "In regard to laboratories, is that your final position? If so, we can end our meeting at this point."

Reagan: "Yes it is."

More verbal jousting followed, with no progress. Gorbachev appealed to Reagan's sense of history. If they could sign an agreement containing all the Soviet concessions, "you will become, without exaggeration, a great president. You are now literally two steps from that." If they could sign, Gorbachev pleaded with Reagan, "it will mean our meeting has been a success." And if not, "then let's part at this point and forget about Reykjavik. But there won't be another opportunity like this. At any rate, I know I won't have one."

Both men seem to have sensed their historic moment was slipping through their fingers.

"Are you really going to turn down a historic opportunity for the sake of one word in the text?" Reagan demanded. The word was "laboratory."

"You say that it's just a matter of one word," Gorbachev shot back. "But it's not a matter of one word, it's a matter of principle." If he went back to Moscow having allowed Reagan to deploy his missile defense, Gorbachev added, "they will call me a fool and irresponsible leader."

"Now it's a matter of one word," Reagan lamented. "I want to ask you once more to change your viewpoint, to do it as a favor to me so that we can go to the people as peacemakers."

"We cannot go along with what you propose," Gorbachev responded. "If you will agree to banning tests in space, we will sign the document in two minutes. We cannot go along with something else . . . I have done everything I could." Shultz recalled that Gorbachev said, "It's 'laboratory,' or good-bye."

Reagan passed a note to Shultz: "Am I wrong?" Shultz whispered back, "No, you are right."

Reagan stood up to go and gathered up his papers, as did Gorbachev, according to Shultz. "It was dark when the doors of Hofdi House opened and we all emerged, almost blinded by the klieg lights. The looks on our faces spoke volumes," Shultz recalled. "Sad, disappointed faces," said Chernyaev.

"I still feel we can find a deal," Reagan said to Gorbachev as they parted.

"I don't think you want a deal," Gorbachev replied. "I don't know what more I could have done."

"You could have said 'yes,'" Reagan said.

"We won't be seeing each other again," Gorbachev said, meaning that they would not see each other again in Reykjavik. The remark was overheard and set off a rumor that the talks had failed terribly.

Shultz joined Reagan back in the residence, where the president and his top advisers slumped in easy chairs in the solarium. "Bad news. One lousy word!" Reagan said.[67]

That evening, he summed it up briskly in his diary. "He wanted language that would have killed SDI," Reagan wrote. "The price was high but I wouldn't sell & that's how the day ended. All our people thought I'd done exactly right. I'd pledged I wouldn't give away SDI & I didn't but that meant no deal on any of the arms reductions. I was mad—he tried to act jovial but I acted mad and it showed. Well the ball is in his court and I'm convinced he'll come around when he sees how the world is reacting."[68]

"I was very disappointed—and *very* angry," Reagan recalled years later in his memoirs.

Gorbachev was also fuming. "My first, overwhelming, intention had been to blow the unyielding American position to smithereens, carrying out the plan we had decided in Moscow: if the Americans rejected the agreement, a compromise in the name of peace, we would denounce the U.S. administration and its dangerous policies as a threat to everyone around the world." Chernyaev later noted this was the Politburo's instructions to Gorbachev: to come out blasting Reagan if the Americans refused to give the Soviets what they wanted.

But as Gorbachev walked to a press conference, he was unsure. Had they not accomplished a lot, even if they failed to reach a final agreement?

"My intuition was telling me I should cool off and think it all over thoroughly. I had not yet made up my mind when I suddenly found myself in the enormous press conference room. About a thousand journalists were waiting for us. When I came into the room, the merciless, often cynical and cheeky journalists were waiting for us. I sensed anxiety in the air. I suddenly felt emotional, even shaken. These people standing in front of me seemed to represent mankind waiting for its fate to be decided."

In another dramatic turn, Gorbachev decided not to follow his instructions from the Politburo. He decided not to smash Reagan to smithereens, and instead he sounded optimistic.

"We have already reached accord on much," he told the journalists. "We have come a long way."[69]

FAREWELL TO ARMS

When George Shultz entered the pressroom on the evening of October 12, 1986, in Reykjavik, the secretary of state had disappointment etched in his face. Shultz opened his remarks with a strained voice. Max Kampelman, one of the American negotiators, was nearly in tears. The two leaders had come so close to a deal—and then departed empty-handed. The *Washington Post* carried a two-line banner headline the next morning: "Reagan-Gorbachev Summit Talks Collapse as Deadlock on SDI Wipes Out Other Gains." Lou Cannon of the *Post* wrote that the summit ended "gloomily" and Gorbachev was described as giving a "bleak assessment" of the prospects for the future. But in capturing the drama of the moment, the press corps failed to grasp the long-term significance. Reagan and Gorbachev had debated, negotiated and in some cases reached agreement on the most sweeping disarmament proposals of the nuclear age. Both men realized very quickly they had reached a turning point in the Cold War. "Let us not despair," Gorbachev told Chernyaev on the plane home to Moscow, saying he was still a big optimist.[1]

Gorbachev reported to the Politburo two days later that the negotiating positions of the past had been "buried" once and for all. "A totally new situation has emerged," he said, a "new, more elevated plateau from which we now have to begin a struggle for liquidation and complete ban on nuclear arms . . . This is a strong position. It reflects new thinking."[2]

Chernyaev quoted Gorbachev as saying in the weeks that followed: "Before, we were talking about limitations on nuclear arms. Now we are talking about their reduction and elimination."[3]

Yet for all his optimism, Gorbachev knew a huge opportunity had been missed at Reykjavik. Not a single nuclear warhead had yet been dismantled, not a single treaty had been signed. Gorbachev needed results—and he felt time was slipping away. His dreams of nuclear disarmament were driven by very genuine fears of the danger. But there were other, pragmatic reasons, too. His tentative efforts at *perestroika* had failed to improve Soviet living conditions, and a gathering storm loomed over the economy. Oil prices tumbled in 1986, and so did hard currency revenues. The country was forced to import grain and meat and borrow heavily from abroad. A huge budget deficit opened up. Gorbachev acknowledged at a Politburo meeting: "Now the situation has us all by the throat."[4]

The overriding goal for Gorbachev was to transform the Reykjavik summit talk into concrete gains that might alleviate the military burden. Gorbachev seized the brake handles on the hurtling locomotive and threw himself into bringing about real change. Internal documents and evidence from memoirs suggest that it was not at all evident to the generals, or the weapons builders, or the old guard in the leadership, how radical a turnabout Gorbachev was contemplating after Reykjavik. After Gorbachev's report to the Politburo, the ruling body acted cautiously. They issued an instruction to the military to prepare for possible deep cuts in strategic arms. But at the same time, the Politburo considered it entirely possible the Soviet Union would remain locked in Cold War competition, that there would be no deep cuts and they would have to retaliate against Reagan's Strategic Defense Initiative, "especially its outer space components." For all Gorbachev's enthusiasm, they thought, the arms race might not end soon.[5]

Although the Politburo members did not see where Gorbachev was headed, Akhromeyev, the chief of the General Staff, most certainly did. Akhromeyev was above reproach by the military elite for his long service to the country, and he gave Gorbachev the cover and legitimacy he needed to attempt a radical farewell to arms.

In 1986, after helping Gorbachev with the January 15 proposal to eliminate all nuclear weapons, Akhromeyev concluded that it was time to create a new Soviet military doctrine to match Gorbachev's era.

The military doctrine was the foundation of all the assumptions, goals and preparations of the sprawling Soviet defense machine, from front-line troops to the General Staff, from research institutes to arms factories. The old doctrine declared that the United States and NATO were the main adversaries of the Soviet Union; that the Soviet Union must strive for parity with the West in weapons. In the late autumn and early winter of 1986, Akhromeyev tore up the old doctrine. This was an excruciatingly difficult moment for him, requiring a reversal of all he had been taught. "The doctrine that had existed before 1986 was an indisputable truth for me and the General Staff," he recalled. "It was bequeathed to us by the World War II commanders . . . who taught and molded me and people like me, whose names we pronounce when we take an oath to serve our Fatherland! How can all this be changed? Everything I had been taught for many years in the academies, on maneuvers. To change things I myself had been teaching to the younger generation of generals and officers, for many years already. A substantial segment of our military experience, theory and practice was being ditched."

Just after Reykjavik, Akhromeyev delivered a lecture on the new doctrine at the Academy of the General Staff in Moscow, where the best and brightest officers studied. He spoke to an elite audience, which included military specialists, professors and strategists. The changes were stark. While the United States would still be the main adversary, Akhromeyev said, "we are prepared to dismantle the mechanism of military confrontation with the United States and NATO in Europe." While a war would still be contemplated with nuclear and conventional weapons, he said, "we stand for complete liquidation of nuclear weapons in the world." Instead of striving for parity, he said, the Soviet Union would reduce its forces, either by agreement or unilaterally if necessary.

"While I was speaking, there was absolute silence in the hall," Akhromeyev recalled. "The faces reflected incomprehension, bewilderment and alarm." When he was finished, "all restraints broke loose. The decorum of our military scientists was gone! Many of them seemed to forget that it was the head of the General Staff who was speaking to them. Accusations just short of treason were hurled at me. A number of points of the report were called erroneous and unacceptable." What had taken months for Akhromeyev to think over was delivered in about ninety minutes. "One could understand why they were in a state of shock," he said. "I had to answer questions for another two hours."[6]

A grand retreat had begun.

Right after the Reykjavik summit, Reagan was at the top of his game. In a nationally televised speech October 13 and in campaign appearances across the country before the November election, Reagan launched one of the most extraordinary—and persuasive—public relations campaigns of his presidency. He boasted that he had stood up to Gorbachev. On the campaign trail, he evoked enthusiastic cheers from audiences when he declared that at Iceland, "I just said, 'No!'" Reagan portrayed his refusal to give up the Strategic Defense Initiative as a triumph, even though SDI did not even exist.

Soon, however, Reagan was plunged into a season of troubles. Serious questions were raised about what was actually said at Hofdi House. Gorbachev noted in a televised speech from Moscow on October 22 that he and Reagan had agreed to the complete elimination of *all strategic offensive weapons* by 1996.[7] This seemed to differ from Reagan's claim, in his own televised speech after the summit, that he had discussed elimination of *all ballistic missiles* in ten years.[8] In an embarrassing moment for Reagan, the Soviets made public part of their note takers' minutes of the summit, showing that in fact Reagan had discussed elimination of all strategic weapons. The White House reluctantly acknowledged that Gorbachev was right, saying it was a goal, not a proposal. Reagan was lambasted by critics for sloppy handling of nuclear policy. Next, it turned out he had gone to Reykjavik without consulting the chairman of the Joint Chiefs of Staff, Admiral William J. Crowe Jr., about the sweeping proposals made to Gorbachev, nor had anyone reported back to the nation's military leaders about what happened at Reykjavik. The joint chiefs were apparently never notified of Reagan's July 25 letter containing the Weinberger formula for "zero ballistic missiles." After the summit, Crowe asked the other service chiefs what they thought. "The unanimous answer was that from a national security perspective it was completely unacceptable. The chiefs were quite disturbed," he recalled. Crowe lost sleep for several nights worrying about how to proceed.

Although Crowe feared he would lose his job, he decided to speak up at the White House National Security Planning Group meeting October 27. It was unusual for a military man to rise at such a meeting, but Crowe delivered a four-page statement. "Mr. President," he said, "we have concluded that the proposal to eliminate all ballistic missiles within 10 years time would pose high risks to the security of the nation." This was a bombshell—the nation's top soldier telling the president he had risked the nation's security by giving away too much. Crowe waited for the reaction.[9]

"Admiral," the president said, "I really love the U.S. military. I have always loved it. Those young men and women do a wonderful job for our country, and everywhere I go I tell people how proud I am of our armed forces." The meeting ended.

"If the president was angry, it was not obvious to me," Crowe recalled later. "If he had heard my remarks, it was not obvious to me. If he simply did not wish to respond, that was not clear to me either. Nor did I know where the controversial proposal stood now." Reagan had not only heard Crowe, but thought he had answered him. That night in his diary, Reagan wrote, "The Joint Chiefs wanted reassurances that we were aware of the imbalance with the Soviets in conventional arms & how that would be aggravated by reduction in nuclear weapons. We were able to assure them we were very much aware & that this matter would have to be negotiated with the Soviets in any nuclear arms reduction negotiations."[10] Once again, Reagan kept his eye on the very big picture and blithely skipped over the unpleasant details.

On November 4, Republicans lost the Senate majority they had held for six years. And in the weeks and months that followed, Reagan was engulfed by the biggest scandal of his presidency. The Iran-Contra affair centered on secret operations, run in part out of the White House National Security Council, in which the United States sold missiles and missile parts to Iran to secure the release of American hostages in Lebanon, and then diverted some of the proceeds from the arms sales to help the Nicaraguan contras, circumventing a ban on aid imposed by Congress. The scandal went to the heart of a contradiction in Reagan's thinking. In rhetoric, he stood tall on principles and pledged never to make deals with terrorists or the states that backed them. But in private, he could be deeply moved by individual human suffering, and sold the weapons to Iran out of his emotional reaction to appeals from the families of the American captives. The diversion of aid to the contras also reflected the wild and woolly side of the CIA under Casey, which seemed eager to launch swashbuckling covert wars against communism on every continent, blatantly disregarding laws passed by Congress. The scandal caused Reagan's popularity at home to drop suddenly in late 1986 and early 1987. His presidency went into a deep freeze.

Gorbachev was puzzled and irritated. He thought he had put Reagan in a box at the summit. He had made an irresistible all-or-nothing offer, and he was sure Reagan would come around to accept it. Gorbachev repeatedly called it the "package": concessions on the intermediate-range missiles and on the long-range weapons must be contingent on limiting the Strategic Defense Initiative. "We will stand on this, firmly," Gorbachev confidently told the Politburo on October 14. "We do not need any cheap tricks, only the package." But to Gorbachev's consternation, Reagan gave no signs of flexibility in the weeks after the summit. "What is it that America wants?" Gorbachev asked at the Politburo on October 30. "I have more and more doubts about whether we can achieve anything at all with this administration."[11]

Gorbachev also had his own troubles, especially the war in Afghanistan.[12] The war had become a morass for the Soviets, and provided a fresh test of whether Gorbachev could withdraw from the military burdens he inherited. On November 13, 1986, a restless Gorbachev told the Politburo he wanted to get out of Afghanistan. "We must not waste time!" he said. "We have been fighting for six years! Some say, if we continue the same way, it may be going on for another 20 or 30 years. And this is what's going to happen. People have raised the question: are we going to stay there forever? Or should we end this war? If we don't it will be a complete disgrace. Our strategic goal is to wrap up the war in one, maximum two years, and pull out the troops."

Yet, as Chernyaev recalled later, "We carried the heavy burden of Afghanistan into the new year. For all of Gorbachev's determination to end the war . . . no significant steps were yet taken. And this, like the aftermath of Chernobyl, was a huge weight on all his further reform activities. It greatly restricted his freedom of political and economic maneuver, including his efforts to realize the idea of Reykjavik."[13]

Another setback for Gorbachev came on his nuclear testing moratorium. The Soviet test sites had been silent for eighteen months, but the United States refused to join, and conducted some twenty tests during the period. The moratorium was good for propaganda, but it brought Gorbachev no tangible results. The Soviet nuclear weapons establishment was eager to resume explosions. On December 18, Gorbachev threw in the towel. The Soviet Union announced it would resume testing in 1987, right after the next American weapons test. Gorbachev was discouraged by having to give up one of his cherished initiatives, and dispirited at the continued signs of backsliding by Reagan on other issues.[14] Gorbachev said the Iran-Contra scandal "pushes them to do it in order to save the president." He worried about more surprises from Reagan. "We are dealing with political dregs," he said. "One can expect anything from them."

In December, Gorbachev approved the new military doctrine Akhromeyev had forged, but he heard grumbling from the military. "We should not become like the generals, who are trying to scare us," Gorbachev said. "They are already hissing among themselves: what kind of leadership do we have? 'They are destroying the defense of the country.' They say that Ogarkov is very upset. To him it is just give, give more. Cannons should be longer!"[15]

With small steps, those around Gorbachev began slowly to reverse the secrecy and deceit so deeply woven into the hypermilitarized Soviet system. Fresh streams of candor began to run through the corridors of the Kremlin. The new thinking—honest, but still cautious—was evident in the detailed reference papers that Vitaly Katayev prepared for his superiors in the Central Committee defense department, especially Lev Zaikov, the Politburo member in charge of the military-industrial complex. The style of the typewritten reports reflects Katayev's precision and background as an engineer: three neat columns across, often many pages long, each row addressing a new issue, or question. At the top, he typed "S P R A V K A," or information.

On December 24, 1986, Katayev finished another *spravka* that showed he was candid—at least to his bosses in the system—about shortcomings in the Soviet military machine. In this document, Katayev carefully dissected the points in a speech made in San Francisco four weeks earlier by Gates, the deputy CIA director. Gates claimed that a radar station being constructed north of Krasnoyarsk, in Siberia, violated the 1972 Anti-Ballistic Missile Treaty, a charge the United States had made before in the glossy annual booklet *Soviet Military Power*.[16] The Americans claimed the station could be used for "battle management" of a nationwide anti-missile system. This was not the case. The Soviets claimed the radar was for civilian space tracking. This was also not true. In fact, it was a permitted type of radar for early warning against missile attack, but the Soviets had put it in a prohibited location. The treaty said that early-warning radars could only be built around the periphery of a country, facing outward. The Soviet leaders had put this radar station inland, 1,669 miles from the Pacific Ocean and nearly five hundred miles north of the border with Mongolia, clearly not at the perimeter. The radar antenna faced northeast, too, which was not exactly outward. The real reason it faced this way was to plug another Soviet shortcoming, a hole in the early-warning network—to watch out for American missiles coming from submarines in the northern Pacific Ocean. Katayev candidly acknowledged the Soviet violation in his *spravka*: "The building of the radar in the city of Krasnoyarsk indeed contradicts the Article 6b of the ABM Treaty because the antenna curtain is oriented toward the inside of the territory." Although Katayev had admitted it internally, it was a violation the Soviets would not acknowledge publicly for more than two years.

On another point in the speech in San Francisco, Gates warned that the Soviet Union was "laying the foundation" for a nationwide missile defense system, which would be prohibited by the treaty, and pursuing advanced technology to do it, such as laser, particle beam, kinetic energy and microwave electronics. This argument was often made by U.S. officials to build support for the Strategic Defense Initiative. But it was hype. Katayev wrote in his *spravka* the Soviets were in fact way behind the level of technology suggested by Gates. The alarmist charges were greatly exaggerated. The most advanced Soviet research on laser and other exotic technology "are at the initial stage of laboratory stand experiments," he said. Prototypes of such weapons could not be created any sooner than the year 2000. The Soviets were unable to shoot down anything with a laser.[17]

Another important voice for *glasnost*, and against the long tradition of military secrecy, was Velikhov, the open-minded physicist and adviser to Gorbachev. In January 1987, four weeks after Katayev's *spravka*, Velikhov came up with an idea. He wrote to the Central Committee defense department—Katayev's office—proposing to challenge the misleading American statements about Soviet laser weapons. A showcase nuclear disarmament conference was scheduled for later in the month in Moscow, and Velikhov was one of the organizers. Scientists, celebrities and antinuclear activists were being brought in from all around the world. Velikhov suggested: what if Gorbachev himself announced at the conference that the Soviet Union would open up the top-secret test facility at Sary Shagan that was so often at the center of American propaganda? What if the Americans were invited to see for themselves that Gates and *Soviet Military Power* were wrong? Velikhov suggested that a group of five to eight American scientists and journalists be taken on a "spontaneous" four-hour visit. Contrary to American claims about the lasers, their actual power was "thousands of times less than required" for shooting down missiles, he said. "There exists a complete and unique chance to demonstrate the false nature of the official American claims," Velikhov insisted. "An exposure of the lie with one concrete example may have big political consequences."

Velikhov was a vice president of the Academy of Sciences, and his proposal immediately commanded the attention of top security and defense officials, including Zaikov, Akhromeyev and the head of the KGB, Viktor Chebrikov. A staff report dumped cold water on Velikhov's idea, saying the American visitors would quickly realize the Soviet equipment was really quite old. The two lasers at the complex were experimental samples using components from the early 1970s, the staff report said. The visiting scientists and journalists might think the Soviets were insincere, or covering up something, the report added. Akhromeyev worried that the Americans—seeing the size of buildings and the nature of the test range—might try to prove that the Soviets were planning to build missile defenses in the future. There was also worry that the visitors might see a secret project called "Gamma" to build an anti-satellite weapon in the future. In fact, Gamma never materialized. The only thing to hide at Sary Shagan was the painful truth: Soviet technology was way behind.

On February 12, the Central Committee answered Velikhov: proposal rejected. No Americans could see the secret test range. But Velikhov had opened the door a crack, and did not give up.

Another key moment in Gorbachev's drive for change came December 16, 1986, when he telephoned Andrei Sakharov, who was watching television with his wife, Yelena Bonner. Sakharov, the 1975 Nobel Peace Prize winner and dissident physicist who had helped design the Soviet hydrogen bomb, was banished to Gorky in 1980 without trial for speaking out against the Soviet invasion of Afghanistan and Soviet human rights violations. Reagan had raised the question of Sakharov in a letter to Gorbachev delivered at the Reykjavik summit. Gorbachev did not want to seem to be under pressure, but in December he told Sakharov on the phone, "You can return to Moscow." Sakharov stepped off the train in Moscow at the Yaroslavl station on December 23.

In February, Sakharov appeared in public for the first time since his return, attending the international disarmament conference, "The Forum for a Nuclear-Free World and the Survival of Mankind." The conference was jam-packed with celebrities invited from around the world, but Sakharov's presence cast a special glow. Even more significant was Sakharov's message: it was time to get on with reducing dangerous missiles and break the deadlock over the Strategic Defense Initiative. It was time to crack open the Gorbachev "package" from Reykjavik.[18]

Gorbachev had earlier been certain the package deal would bring results. But now, in late February 1987, the Soviet Union was preparing to set off its first nuclear explosion since the end of the moratorium. Gorbachev needed something new, and bold. Sakharov's speech at the conference has been credited by some as pushing Gorbachev to move. But there was another strong impetus. On February 25, Gorbachev's influential adviser, Alexander Yakovlev, wrote an extensive memo to him, arguing the time had come to unbundle the "package" and make separate deals to reduce nuclear weapons.

Yakovlev, the paragon of new thinking who had walked with Gorbachev in the orchard in Canada, said Gorbachev needed to pay attention to the political dynamics. "In politics, maximum freedom of maneuver is always valuable," he wrote. "The 'package' in its present form only ties our hands." At the top of Yakovlev's list of priorities, if the package were dropped, was to seek a separate agreement on the intermediate-range missiles that would ease the threat posed by the American Pershing II missiles in Europe. "For us, this would be tantamount to removal of a very serious threat," he said. Yakovlev expressed a sense of urgency. "It is extremely important now not to lose the tempo we have developed, and not to lose time. If we want to untie the package, we need to do it right now, because later the effect of it will be much weaker." A public speech making the announcement "could compensate, in the eyes of the world public, for the fact of our reciprocal resumption of nuclear testing."[19]

If Gorbachev untied the package, it would mean the very real concessions he made at Reykjavik—such as eliminating all the Pioneers—would be pocketed by Reagan, without any slowdown in the missile defense plan. But Gorbachev also realized that, since Reykjavik, they had been treading water. His package tactic wasn't working. Gorbachev desperately wanted to get results, not shadow-box over the future.

On the day after Yakovlev's memo, February 26, 1987, the Soviet Union set off its first nuclear explosion since 1985, in tunnel No. 130 at the Semipalatinsk testing range in Kazakhstan. Gorbachev had absorbed Yakovlev's argument by the time he addressed the Politburo that day. "The biggest step that would make an impression on the outside world, on public opinion, would be if we untie the package and agree to cut 1,000 of our most powerful missiles," he said.

"Let's untie the package."

On February 28, he made the announcement. "The Soviet Union suggests that the problem of medium-range missiles in Europe be singled out from the package of issues, and that a separate agreement be concluded on it, and without delay." Reagan took the news cautiously, saying it was "progress" toward a "new opportunity," speaking to reporters in his first visit to the White House pressroom since disclosure of diversion of the Iran money to the contras two months earlier.

The Pioneer missile had a brutish silhouette and carried three warheads, each 150 kilotons and independently targetable. The missile's range was called intermediate or medium: less than the giant missiles that flew across the oceans, but more than those designed for use on battlefields. The Pioneer was a modern, mobile missile, transported on huge six-axle vehicles, which could keep the weapon in a state of constant combat readiness and launch it. Between 1978 and 1986, 441 Pioneer systems were deployed, including a version with improved accuracy and range in 1980, but they created a terrible problem the Soviet leadership had not anticipated. "The Soviet leadership at the time failed to take into account the probable reaction of the Western countries," Gorbachev recalled. "I would even go so far as to characterize it as an unforgivable adventure, embarked on by the previous Soviet leadership under pressure from the military-industrial complex." The NATO response—the Pershing IIs and the ground-launched cruise missiles—became "a pistol held to our head," as Gorbachev put it. "Not to mention the exorbitant and unjustifiable costs of developing, producing and servicing the SS-20—funds swallowed up by the insatiable Moloch of the military-industrial complex."[20]

Katayev, the Central Committee staff man with long experience in the missile design bureaus, knew how the Soviet leaders fell into such a blunder. As he toured the archipelago of factories, bases and institutes under his supervision, Katayev found excess everywhere. Missiles were built because the design bureaus and factories needed to keep production lines open, not because the military wanted them. He recalled meeting with the directors of two factories building submarine-launched missiles. When he suggested they were wasting money manufacturing weapons no one would use, the factory bosses objected. "The order for missiles is given, it is included in the plan, funds are given, and so we make them," Katayev recalled of their response to his protest. "And the way these missiles are used by the military—this is not our problem."

The navy was the worst. At one point Katayev calculated there were between four and eight missiles manufactured for each submarine launching tube, compared to a ratio of 1.2 or 1.3 missiles per tube in other countries. "A vast number of sea-launched missiles in the Soviet Union were kept in poor conditions, reducing the combat reliability of the weapons," Katayev said. He took a three-day voyage on a Project 941 submarine, the Typhoon, a huge vessel with two separate pressure hulls, which carried twenty solid-fuel missiles with a range of more than six thousand miles. As he watched, the crew launched four missiles toward the test range in Kamchatka. Katayev turned to the Typhoon chief designer, Sergei Kovalyov.

"Sergei Nikitich, four missiles flew, this is roughly the cost of a residential building of 200 apartments. What do you need this for?" Katayev asked.

Kovalyov replied simply that it was a training exercise. But he admitted that once the missile left the tube, he was finished with it. The point was just to train for the launch. Katayev said a concrete-filled trainer missile would work just as well, and make no difference for the crew. As Katayev recounted the conversation, Kovalyov replied, "Why not? Somehow this idea never occurred to me. There were always plenty of missiles, we didn't give it a thought. Because this new solid-fuel missile is certainly a little expensive for training novices." From then on, they started to use a concrete-filled missile for training.

Katayev, precise and careful, loved lists and charts. He filled his notebooks with them, in neat handwriting, often accompanied by notes and drawings. He saw in his own records proof that missile production was excessive. He took the charts to his superiors. He implored Zaikov: they had far more missiles than the country needed. The missile overproduction was not increasing the security of the country; rather, in the case of the Pioneers, it had led to a "dangerous, strategic dead end." But Katayev knew that his conclusion was not shared by either the generals or the legendary missile designers. The Pioneers were the newest Soviet missile, the best technology, with twenty or thirty years of useful service duty ahead of them—and all those involved were appalled at the idea of sacrificing them. Katayev recalled one particularly emotional meeting in 1985 when the idea of reducing the missile arsenal was debated. There were shouts of protest: "Sabotage!" and "The Fifth Column!" and "Remember Khrushchev!" (for the Cuban missile crisis fiasco). "I tried in vain to defuse the emotions with the help of technical arguments in favor of reducing the number of missiles," Katayev recalled. After the stormy meeting, he remained in the conference room with one of Akhromeyev's deputies. Katayev attempted in earnest to argue his point. "Unbeknownst to everybody," Katayev told the deputy, "the time has arrived when the accumulation of nuclear weapons has outgrown its own level of safety and when it reached the zone where both our own nuclear weapons and those of the Americans have turned from being a means of deterrence into an instrument of increased danger. And first of all, for the Soviet Union, not for the Americans. Nobody in this country has considered it! They thought, the more missiles the better. We are the ones who have to step away from the danger—not Reagan." They talked past midnight. Katayev recalled that although Akhromeyev's office was right next door, he never once came into the room.[21]

If Akhromeyev heard the discussion, he must have been personally torn. He hated to think they were wasting what they had built at such cost. But he was committed to Gorbachev, and perhaps even more important, Akhromeyev understood the folly of the original decision to deploy the Pioneers aimed at Western Europe. Chernyaev concluded, "As a military professional, he realized the danger Pershing II missiles posed to us, and he had always disapproved of the policy of targeting SS-20s on the U.S.'s NATO allies. A 'local nuclear war' was by definition impossible."[22] Other military leaders were not so farsighted. "Gorbachev had to go through a difficult struggle with his own generals," Chernyaev said. "It took a long time to convince them to get rid of the SS-20s in Europe."

When Thatcher came to Moscow, March 23 to April 1, 1987, she told Gorbachev that it was folly to eliminate nuclear weapons. Sitting across the table from each other in Saint Catherine's Hall, they had a vigorous argument, not unlike their first one at Chequers. "You, Madam Thatcher, with your stance on nuclear weapons, hamper the negotiations and hinder efforts to start a process of genuine disarmament," Gorbachev said. "When you solemnly declare that nuclear weapons are beneficial, it's clear that you are an ardent supporter of them—prepared to accept the risk of war."

Thatcher "got very tense, blushed, and her expression hardened," Chernyaev recalled. "She reached out and, touching Gorbachev's sleeve, began to talk without letting him get in a word." She insisted that nuclear weapons had kept the peace. "She became so excited that the discussion got completely out of hand. They started to interrupt each other, repeat themselves, assure each other of their best intentions." When Thatcher flew home, she described it as the most fascinating and important overseas visit she had ever taken; she realized "the ground was shifting underneath the communist system."[23]

Gorbachev revealed his deep frustrations to Shultz on April 14. At a Kremlin meeting, he complained the Reagan administration was behaving as if nothing was going on in the Soviet Union, when in fact it had a better opportunity to improve relations than any U.S. administration in decades. "Where do we go from here?" he wondered.[24] They immediately began to wrestle over details of how to eliminate the Pioneer and Pershing II missiles. The negotiations to eliminate intermediate-range missiles were to cover those with a range of between approximately 300 and 3,500 miles. The Pershing IIs had a maximum range of 1,100 miles, and Pioneers about 3,100 miles. The Soviet Union had also deployed a relatively new short-range missile, the SS-23, named after the Oka, a Russian river. The single-stage, solid-fueled Oka was easily moved around on trucklike launchers, which could erect and fire it. The Soviet military calculated the range of the SS-23 as only 250 miles, and thus felt it should not be included in negotiations on intermediate-range missiles. American experts guessed it might have greater range, given the size of the projectile.[25] The missile was prized by the Soviet military because of its mobility, and it was capable of carrying either nuclear or conventional warheads. Earlier, Gorbachev had offered to freeze the level of these missiles, and he went still further and proposed negotiating deep cuts, and ultimately elimination.

But in the Kremlin meeting, Shultz suggested the United States first wanted to build up its arsenal of short-range systems to match Soviet levels, after which they could negotiate.

Gorbachev unexpectedly offered, on the spot, to eliminate the Oka missiles altogether, if the United States would agree to a "global zero," or none on either side.

When Gorbachev made the offer, Akhromeyev, the chief of the General Staff, was not in the room. He was scheduled to arrive only later, after a break.

Shultz replied to the offer by saying he would consult with the NATO alliance.

"Why can't you make a decision?" Gorbachev insisted.

Shevardnadze interjected, "I am amazed that the United States is objecting to unilateral Soviet elimination of operational short-range missiles."

Gorbachev had just made an extremely sensitive concession. By the time Akhromeyev entered the hall later for a discussion of strategic weapons, Gorbachev had abandoned a whole weapons system. Akhromeyev only found out the next day, when he saw his name was on the list of attendees at the meeting, put there because Gorbachev wanted to show he had approved. Akhromeyev later said the concession was a "miscalculation" that infuriated the generals. "The military leadership was indignant at the incident with the Oka," Akhromeyev recalled. "The Foreign Ministry didn't give any appropriate explanation of the one-sided deal. The first serious split appeared between the military and Shevardnadze." The generals tried to fight back in the months that followed, but were reprimanded. Gorbachev had maneuvered skillfully to get his way against his own military, but he still lacked any tangible result from the Americans. Appearing before the Politburo days later, Gorbachev sputtered in frustration that Shultz could not make a decision on the spot. The conversation was good, he said, but "essentially empty—we did not move anywhere."[26]

"We have to recapture the initiative," said Shevardnadze.

From his office at the Central Committee, Katayev, the precise and careful staffer, slowly came to a profound conclusion: the leadership of the country—hierarchical, centrally planned, rigid and hidebound by long practice—simply had no process for deciding how to abandon and destroy the weapons it had built at such enormous cost, even if disarmament had been a propaganda line for decades. The previous strategic arms control treaties from the Nixon and Carter era had only limited the growth of weapons, and destroyed none of them. The Biological and Toxin Weapons Convention had outlawed an entire class of weapons and the Soviet Union secretly built them anyway. There was no road map for retreat. Katayev recalled it was an enormous psychological barrier, as well as a practical roadblock to decisions.

Katayev, who understood the excesses, quietly set about changing the way defense decisions were handled in the Kremlin. In the Brezhnev years, designers and builders filled the power vacuum. Once Gorbachev came into office, specialists like Katayev and others gained a greater voice. For the most part, in their private discussions, Katayev found the specialists favored disarmament, and were cognizant of the Soviet overkill. At the top, a group of powerful decision-makers remained from earlier times. They were known as the "Big Five": the Defense Ministry, Foreign Ministry, KGB, the Military Industrial Commission, and the Central Committee. Katayev elevated the role of technical experts like himself as a "working group" serving the Big Five. It marked a shift in the way arms control was handled in the Kremlin, giving the technocrats and specialists more input, although few knew about it outside. All the documents describing the change were stamped "Top Secret." On May 6, 1987, members of the Big Five sent Gorbachev a recommendation to make Katayev's arrangement permanent. Gorbachev signed it.[27]

Another shoot of fresh thinking about how to brake the arms race came to the surface at the military's General Staff headquarters in Moscow. Valery Yarynich had been assigned to work at the headquarters of an internal think tank, the Center for Operational-Strategic Research, established just as Gorbachev took power. Yarynich, the communications expert who had once witnessed the Cuban missile crisis panic, arrived at the center in 1985 after finishing with Perimeter, the semiautomatic nuclear missile retaliatory system. As *glasnost* blossomed, Yarynich enjoyed a freedom to raise issues with relative openness inside the heart of the Soviet military, and he devoted himself to analyzing the risks of nuclear war. "We had a chance to think and say what we thought without fear of punishment," he said. The research center was given a difficult task—to find the theoretical justification to support lower levels of nuclear weapons. It was a forward-thinking idea born of Gorbachev's new era. He was assigned to run a research project called Kupol. The project used mathematical models to study scenarios of a possible first-strike nuclear attack from the United States.

Yarynich and his coworkers on Kupol found a very important insight in the mathematical models. When considering a possible nuclear attack, it was not enough to just measure the number of warheads that would probably reach their targets, or the number that could retaliate. The

Soviet command and control systems, which were reliable and split-second, also had to be figured into the calculation. If one took command and control into account, then mathematical models showed the goal of deterrence could be guaranteed with a drastic reduction of nuclear arsenals. This was because it was likely there would always be at least *some* retaliation for an attack. Even the smallest retaliation in a real nuclear war meant pretty massive destruction. The attacker always faced this uncertainty. Thus, Yarynich concluded, the massive overkill of the arms race was unnecessary.

Yarynich was seized with an idea—what if the two superpowers could open up and share such mathematical models? What if the leaders could see what he and his coworkers had discovered in Kupol? But the reaction from Soviet military leaders was not very encouraging. They could not imagine exchanging top-secret command and control data with the United States. "The old thinking prevailed over the new," Yarynich recalled.

At the same time, he saw on the streets that the "new thinking" and *glasnost* of Gorbachev were spreading. Barriers were collapsing everywhere. One day, the experts, including Yarynich, got a translated copy of a book published in the United States in 1985. The book, *The Button: America's Nuclear Warning System—Does It Work?* by Daniel Ford, questioned whether command and control was the weak link in the American nuclear deterrence. Yarynich said the Russian experts were "astounded by the degree of openness, detail and healthy criticism which the author used to describe the American system. And it dealt no harm to America whatsoever!" Yarynich suggested that his staff prepare a similar work. Once again, his suggestion went nowhere.[28]

By summer 1987, nearly two years had passed since the space designers and rocket builders had put on Gorbachev's desk their blueprints for a sprawling Soviet version of the Strategic Defense Initiative. To see their handiwork, Gorbachev flew to the Soviet cosmodrome at Baikonur, in Kazakhstan, on May 11. The next day, he toured the launch pad for the giant two-stage, four-engine heavy space booster, *Energia*. Wearing a hard hat and in a business suit, Gorbachev walked in a broad circle clockwise around the enormous white booster, which stood 190 feet tall and weighed 2,400 tons fully fueled. It was full at that moment. For weeks, the launcher had been kept in two-day readiness for takeoff. The *Energia* had never flown before and was built to carry the Soviet space shuttle, the Buran, but the shuttle was not ready, so designers planned instead to use the first launch of the Energia to carry aloft a mysterious black cylinder. On the black vehicle was painted the name *Polyus*, or Pole, in white letters on the outside, but inside it carried the Skif-DM, the demonstration model of the space laser weapon, the most tangible result so far of the drive to build a Soviet Star Wars. The Skif-DM was among those projects that had been touted to Gorbachev by the space designers in 1985, shortly after he took office. Since then, work had been rushed. In fact, there was no laser inside; the Skif-DM was a mock-up, a placeholder for a possible future weapon. The Soviet builders had not mastered the technology.

Gorbachev had spent the last two years warning the United States against weapons in space—precisely the purpose of Skif-DM. As Gorbachev was briefed, walking around the huge booster on May 12, with other Politburo members trailing behind, examining the white rocket and black cylinder, he abruptly told the designers: "The Politburo is not going to allow you to launch this rocket." Gorbachev had said many times he did not want an arms race in space—and he meant it.

Boris Gubanov, the chief designer, was dumbfounded, but tried to carry on. He explained to Gorbachev details of the heavy launcher: fuel, tremendous pressures and temperatures at launch. In the next hour or so, Gorbachev softened. He asked if they could wait a few months. Gubanov said it was impossible: the rocket was ready, it was fueled, people worked around the clock, they could not sustain such a pace. At lunchtime, Gubanov recalled, the word came back: permission to launch. The next day, Gorbachev praised the workers at Baikonur. And he reminded them, as he had done so often before, "We are categorically against moving the arms race into space."

Gorbachev left the cosmodrome on May 14. At 9:30 P.M. the next day, the *Energia* roared into the night sky with the Skif-DM payload inside the mysterious black container, *Polyus*.

The *Energia* booster performed flawlessly. Four hundred and sixty seconds after launch, the *Polyus* separated from the *Energia*.

Then something went wrong. The *Polyus* was supposed to turn 180 degrees and fire engines to push itself into higher orbit. Instead, it kept turning all the way to 360 degrees, so when the engines fired, it was in the wrong direction. It shot itself back down toward Earth. The *Polyus* flew straight for the Pacific Ocean.

The black *Polyus* cylinder fell into the sea. All work on the Skif project came to a halt.

Gorbachev did not attempt to revive the Skif. He did nothing—another step toward his goal of slowing the arms race.[29]

The most devastating defeat for the Soviet military in 1987 came not directly from Gorbachev, but he exploited it. It came at the hands of a dreamy nineteen-year-old youth who lived in Hamburg, Germany. Mathias Rust was deeply disappointed by the failure of Reagan and Gorbachev to make a deal at Reykjavik. He decided to make a personal protest. He rented a single-engine Cessna 172P, a sports airplane, and told his family he was going to tour Scandinavia. He flew it to the Faroe Islands on May 13, and the next day to Keflavik, Iceland, the airfield from which Reagan and Gorbachev had departed after the summit.

After further travel, on May 28, he took off from Helsinki, having filed a flight plan for Stockholm. Twenty minutes into the flight, he switched off his communications gear and turned east. Finnish air traffic controllers feared he had crashed and launched a rescue effort. Rust disappeared into the clouds.

It was a holiday in the Soviet Union: "Border Guards Day."[30] At 2:25 P.M., the Cessna, with a small German flag on the tail, flying low, crossed a beach into Estonia and Soviet airspace. Thirty-one minutes later, Rust passed near the town of Kohtla-Yarve, at approximately three thousand feet. He set a course for Moscow. The Soviet air defense system picked up the plane, alerted the antiaircraft batteries and scrambled a fighter jet. The Soviet jet pilot zoomed past the small Cessna—flying seven times the speed of the small craft—and reported that it was a light plane, white, with a blue stripe, at under three thousand feet. Rust saw the Soviet jet, recognized the red star, and could spot the oxygen mask and coveralls of the pilot. He feared he would be shot down. "My heart fell into my pants," he recalled. But then nothing happened, the fighter disappeared and Rust flew on toward Moscow.

On the ground, Soviet air and ground defenses, built up over decades to warn of American bomber fleets bearing nuclear weapons, went limp. Radar operators made no effort to determine the type of airplane that had just invaded their space. They made no immediate report to the headquarters of the Air Defense Forces. The rapidly changing weather and a certain blurriness on the radar screen caused the operators to doubt whether it was a plane at all; they thought it might be a flock of birds.[31] The fighter jet had only forty minutes of fuel at low altitudes, and could not remain aloft longer to search. Another group of jets were scrambled; one spotted Rust, but they did nothing. Then the radar operators lost track of Rust altogether at 3:58 P.M. No further action was taken. At 6:38 P.M., the Moscow regional air defenses switched to "routine watch duty."

At exactly that moment, Rust was approaching Moscow, confused by its sprawling size. He spotted the cubelike Rossiya Hotel, and near it, Red Square. He approached for a landing, but there were people in the square, and he feared casualties, so Rust pulled up and circled again, and again.

On the third approach, Rust spotted a wide, open road bridge, and landed on it at 6:45 P.M., taxiing the plane toward Red Square and St. Basil's Cathedral. A crowd gathered around as Rust, with oversized aviator eyeglasses and an orange jacket, climbed out and announced he was on a mission of peace. He was arrested by the KGB and taken away.

Rust's solo flight riveted the attention of the country and the world. Jokes were told in Moscow in the days that followed: a group of citizens gathered in Red Square with their luggage. When a policeman asked why they were there, they answered, "We are waiting for the flight to Hamburg." But Rust's daring stunt was no joke for the military. It came at the dawn of the age of low-flying, radar-evading cruise missiles. If he could make it all the way to Moscow and be mistaken for a flock of birds, then what of the country's defenses against cruise missiles? The Soviet military was red faced. The rules after the Korean Air Lines disaster in 1983 were not to shoot at civilian intruders, but to force them to land. They had not even tried.

Gorbachev was in Berlin meeting with Warsaw Pact leaders—telling them of the new Soviet military doctrine—when he got word. He told the Soviet allies that Rust's stunt "was no reason to doubt the efficiency of our technology or the reliability of our defense," but in private, he was floored. "I was utterly shaken and completely at a loss as to how this could have happened," he recalled.[32] As Gorbachev stepped off the plane back in Moscow, Chernyaev recalled, his eyes were "flashing with anger." Chernyaev wrote Gorbachev a note before a Politburo meeting the next day. "A great military power was reduced to a joke in the space of a minute," he said. "What happened forces us to reflect again on the state of the army. Our equipment wasn't at fault. To spot such a tiny aircraft, 1930s-era technology would suffice. Rather it was a broader carelessness and lack of responsibility that was to blame, not an episodic problem but something endemic that reflects a much more serious illness in the armed forces." Chernyaev pleaded with Gorbachev to consider undertaking a reform of the military and to fire the defense minister, Sokolov. "Maybe I'm blinded by anger and emotion over this shameful incident, which, in one moment, devalued not only our air defenses but our entire military structure. But I believe that *perestroika* and *new thinking* cannot be successful without a reform of the army."[33]

At the Kremlin, the Politburo meeting was tense. Gorbachev, mocking and furious, said the Rust intrusion showed the impotence of the defense ministry. The first deputy minister of defense, Pyotr Lushev, began to brief the Politburo on what happened. He described how the plane had flown undetected toward Moscow.

Gorbachev: And this lasted for two and a half hours during which time the intruder aircraft was within the zone of the 6th Army? Did they report it to you?

Lushev: No. I learned about it after the aircraft's landing in Moscow.

Gorbachev: Learned from the traffic police?

Lushev described the existing orders not to shoot down a civilian plane but force it to land. The jet fighters were going too fast to do this. Ryzhkov, the head of the government, asked, "And helicopters, wasn't it possible to use them?" Lushev replied, "There are no helicopters" in the Air Defense Forces.

Summing up, Lushev said the reasons for the episode were "a loss of vigilance and a dulled sense of responsibility, especially on duty shifts," and "carelessness of the duty officers, who had grown used to routine action and were unprepared to operate in non-standard circumstances."

Gorbachev: "And then how are we going to operate in combat conditions, when non-standard situations occur?"

Gorbachev fired the head of the Air Defense Forces and accepted

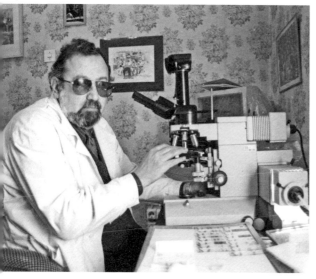

Lev Grinberg (left) and Faina Abramova, the pathologists who autopsied victims of the 1979 Sverdlovsk anthrax outbreak. [David E. Hoffman]

The Chkalovsky district, where the outbreak occurred. [David E. Hoffman]

Sergei Popov, the bright young researcher who worked on genetic engineering of pathogens, and his wife, Taissia, at Koltsovo in 1982. [Sergei Popov]

Lev Sandakhchiev, the director of Vector, who pushed to create artificial viruses for weapons. [Andy Weber]

Igor Domaradsky, the "troublemaker" at Obolensk who attempted to alter the genetic makeup of pathogens. [David E. Hoffman]

Vitaly Katayev (in eyeglasses at left), an aviation and rocket designer by profession, began in 1974 to work for the Central Committee in Moscow. In the years leading up to the Soviet collapse, he kept detailed notebooks, filled with technical information about weapons systems and key decisions. Here, he attends a May Day celebration, date unknown. [Ksenia Kostrova]

Katayev in the 1990s. [Ksenia Kostrova]

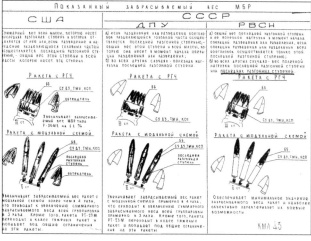

A Katayev drawing on modular missiles. [Hoover Institution Archives]

President Ronald Reagan and the Joint Chiefs of Staff discussed the concept of missile defense on February 11, 1983. The president wrote in his diary that night, "What if we tell the world, we want to protect our people, not avenge them…?" [Ronald Reagan Library]

Reagan unveiled his vision for the Strategic Defense Initiative in a televised speech on March 23, 1983. [Ray Lustig/*Washington Post*]

The nuclear accident at Chernobyl in April 1986 was a turning point for Soviet leader Mikhail Gorbachev. [Reuters]

Marshal Sergei Akhromeyev, chief of the Soviet General Staff, played a key role in Gorbachev's drive to slow the arms race. [RIA Novosti]

A poster outlining Gorbachev's proposal in 1986 to eliminate all nuclear weapons by the year 2000. Akhromeyev is identified on the reverse as the main author. [Hoover Institution Archives]

At the Reykjavik summit, October 11–12, 1986, Gorbachev and Reagan came closer than any other leaders of the Cold War Period to agreements that would slash nuclear arsenals. [Ronald Reagan Library]

They parted without a deal after Reagan insisted that his cherished dream of missile defense could not be limited to research in the laboratory. [Ronald Reagan Library]

Yevgeny Velikhov (right), an open-minded physicist, helped break through the walls of Soviet military secrecy. With Thomas B. Cochran of the Natural Resources Defense Council, near the Semipalatinsk nuclear test site, July 1986. [RIA Novosti]

Velikhov and Cochran arranged an unprecedented joint experiment to verify the presence of a nuclear warhead on a missile aboard the *Slava*, a Soviet cruiser off the coast of Yalta, July 1989. [Thomas B. Cochran]

Anatoly Chernyaev, who harbored hopes for liberal reform in the Soviet Union, became Gorbachev's top foreign policy adviser in 1986 and remained at his side until 1991. [Photograph courtesy of Dr. Svetlana Savranskaya, National Security Archive, Washington, D.C.]

Valery Yarynich, who spent thirty years in the Soviet Strategic Rocket Forces and General Staff, helped bring to fruition the semi-automatic missile launch system known as Perimeter, a modified "Dead Hand." [Valery Yarynich]

Gorbachev returns to Moscow on August 21, 1991, after the failed coup attempt during which he lost control of the nuclear command system. [TASS via Agence France-Presse]

Secretary of State James A. Baker III closely questioned Russian President Boris Yeltsin about who controlled the nuclear weapons as the Soviet Union neared collapse. [AP Photo/Liu Heung Shing]

Gorbachev concludes his resignation speech on December 25, 1991. [AP Photo/Liu Heung Shing]

Pasechnik's business card.

Vladimir Pasechnik, the director of the Institute of Ultra-Pure Biological Preparations in Leningrad, defected to Britain in 1989 and revealed the true size and scope of the Soviet biological weapons program. [Photograph courtesy of Raymond Zilinskas at the Monterey Institute]

In this memo to Gorbachev about biological weapons on May 15, 1990, Politburo member Lev Zaikov wrote the word *biological* by hand, due to its sensitive nature. [Hoover Institution Archives]

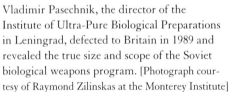

Senators Sam Nunn, Democrat of Georgia (right), and Richard Lugar, Republican of Indiana, saw the dangers of loose nuclear materials and weapons in the former Soviet Union. [Ray Lustig/*Washington Post*]

Andy Weber, a U.S. diplomat, located 1,322 pounds of highly-enriched uranium in Kazakhstan. Here, an image of the uranium, which was airlifted out in Project Sapphire. [Andy Weber]

Loading the uranium onto cargo planes to be flown to the United States. [Andy Weber]

President George H. W. Bush raised questions about biological weapons in a private
talk with Gorbachev at Camp David, June
2, 1990. [George Bush Presidential Library
and Museum]

Christopher Davis, the senior biological
warfare specialist on the British Defense
Intelligence Staff, makes a video recording
during a second visit to Pasechnik's institute in November 1992. Yeltsin promised
end the biological weapons program, but i
continued nonetheless. [Christopher Davis]

Ken Alibek was chief of the anthrax factory built at Stepnogorsk, and later served as deputy director of Biopreparat, the Soviet biological weapons system. [James A. Parcell/*Washington Post*]

The Stepnogorsk anthrax facility, with underground bunkers in the foreground. [Andy Weber]

Inside the Stepnogorsk complex, machines were ready to create tons of anthrax for weapons if the Kremlin had given the order. [Andy Weber]

Dry, deserted Vozrozhdeniye Island as seen by Weber and his team as their helicopter approached for the first time in 1995. The island held clues to years of biological weapons testing. [Andy Weber]

Searching for buried anthrax on Vozrozhdeniye Island. [Andy Weber]

Weber, who helped uncover the secrets of the Soviet biological weapons program, found rusting cages once used to hold primates for germ warfare testing on the island. [Andy Weber]

In a tin can of peas at a lightly guarded institute, Weber once found samples of plague agent. [Andy Weber]

The graves of the Sverdlovsk anthrax victims. [David E. Hoffman]

Defense Minister Sokolov's resignation on the spot. About 150 senior officers were also fired. Dmitri Yazov, a mild-mannered former deputy
defense minister, was appointed to succeed Sokolov. The one top military
man who was untouched by the affair was Akhromeyev.

Gorbachev called Chernyaev at home that evening. "We discredited
the country, humiliated our people," Gorbachev said, according to
Chernyaev's account. Gorbachev wondered if he should have resigned
too. Then he added, "But fine, at least everyone here, and in the West,
will know where power lies. It is in the hands of the political leadership,
the Politburo. This will put an end to gossip about the military's opposition to Gorbachev, that he's afraid of them, and they are close to ousting
him."[34]

On June 12, 1987, in Berlin, Reagan stood before the Brandenburg Gate,
a symbol of Europe's division between East and West, and addressed
Gorbachev directly. "We hear much from Moscow about a new policy of
reform and openness," he said. "Are these the beginnings of profound
changes in the Soviet state? Or are they token gestures, intended to raise
false hopes in the West or to strengthen the Soviet state without changing it?

"General Secretary Gorbachev," Reagan declared, "if you seek peace—
if you seek prosperity for the Soviet Union and Eastern Europe—if you
seek liberalization, come here, to this gate. Mr. Gorbachev, open this gate.
Mr. Gorbachev, tear down this wall!"

The speech was classic Reagan, infused with his powerful faith in freedom and prosperity and the link between the two. Reagan recalled in his
memoir that when he saw the wall, he spoke with genuine anger in his
voice. Gorbachev still did not entirely understand Reagan, nor his rhetoric, and called Chernyaev a few days later. "He is trying to provoke us, to
make us snap, which would help them get the Soviet threat back. If, like
Reagan, I was giving interviews every week, I would say that he hasn't
forgotten his previous occupation over these eight years."[35]

Gorbachev's retreat from the arms race led to confusion not only in the military but in the prestigious defense institutes and design bureaus. They needed to find new justifications for their programs. And Reagan's missile defense dream still flummoxed some of them. Katayev recalled that in August, Alexander Nadiradze, the missile designer who created the Pioneer, sent a panicky letter to the Central Committee. Four years after Reagan had first announced the Strategic Defense Initiative, Nadiradze declared he had figured out the truth: it was a plan to use space to shoot a nuclear warhead back down to Earth! This was worse than first strike. He said the missile defense plan should be exposed as an "aggressive weapon that gives the USA a new possibility to deliver an instant nuclear strike against the Soviet Union." He claimed his research showed "an undersized missile 'Space-Earth' will be capable of carrying a nuclear charge of 0.1–0.15 megaton, a solid-fueled rocket engine will allow it to accelerate toward Earth—at about 4–5 kilometers per second—in 30 seconds." He added, "From the moment of the order to launch, the time of the rocket's flight to Earth will be only 1–2 minutes." Nadiradze said if Reagan's program were deployed, then the Soviet Union should destroy American satellites in space. The Polyus and the Skif might be dead, but the hopes of the missile designers burned on.[36]

In early September, Velikhov, the open-minded physicist, struck another hammer blow against Soviet military secrecy.

Thomas B. Cochran, the American scientist who had set up the seismic monitoring stations around Semipalatinsk, was traveling with three members of Congress, several aides and a *New York Times* journalist, showing them the equipment. On a stopover in Moscow, Velikhov telephoned Cochran at the Sovietskaya Hotel, about 6 P.M., and told him to get the delegation to the airport by midnight. Velikhov had won permission to take them to see the disputed Krasnoyarsk radar that the Reagan administration said was a treaty violation.

Velikhov was attempting exactly the kind of *glasnost* gamble the Central Committee had rejected in February. The group took off for Siberia at 4 A.M., reached the radar site in late afternoon and slowly circled the entire radar site by helicopter, looking down on two large concrete structures, one a transmitter and the other a receiver. The receiver, nearly thirty stories tall, had a long, sloping side, facing northeast. Both structures were unfinished; the receiver's radar face appeared to be partially covered with corrugated metal sheets. At first the Soviets said the Americans could not go inside the structures. After a meal of roasted pig, fruit and vodka toasts in a large white tent, the Americans pleaded for a chance to go inside, and the Soviets relented. The Americans discovered the project was years from completion, just empty shells, empty rooms and no electronics. Judging by what they could see, the visitors concluded it would not be a battle management system, as the Reagan administration claimed. For one thing, a battle management system would be hardened against a nuclear blast; this structure was not. Nor did it look like it was dedicated to space-tracking, as the Soviets claimed.[37] Although they could not be sure, the visitors surmised it was probably an early warning radar, pointing in the wrong direction. It was not facing outward, as required by the ABM treaty. What was most remarkable was that the congressmen got an eyewitness look at a top-secret site. The team took over one thousand photographs and made an hour of video, and no one tried to interfere. Velikhov's openness undercut both the American propaganda and the Soviet lie. "It's the beginning of military *glasnost*," said Representative Tom Downey, D-N.Y., who led the delegation. In their report, the congressmen said the chances that it was a battle management radar were "extremely low." Yet even with such an extraordinary firsthand look, Downey and the others did not change the Reagan administration's view.

In Moscow, the top level of the Soviet leadership was privately at a loss about what to do with Krasnoyarsk. They knew the radar was a violation of the treaty, but they had not admitted it. They also knew that their public explanation of its purpose (space-tracking), as well as Reagan's claims (battle management), were both untrue. On October 23, Gorbachev told Shultz that there would be a one-year moratorium on construction. Shultz replied that the United States would accept nothing short of dismantlement. A month after that, on November 21, an internal memo from the Big Five ministers suggested that the Soviet Union should continue to attempt to pressure the United States for some concessions in exchange for giving up the radar. The prospect of dismantling the whole thing was already being discussed internally. But the memo did not suggest an admission that the radar was in violation of the treaty.[38]

When Shultz saw Gorbachev in Moscow in October, the Soviet leader seemed feisty, and there was more acrimony in their discussion than in the past. Shultz failed to secure agreement on a summit date to sign a treaty on intermediate-range weapons. Shultz wrote in his memoirs that Gorbachev appeared to have been through a tough period.[39] In the days before Shultz arrived, Gorbachev had suffered a major crisis, an outbreak of open criticism in the Politburo. On October 21, Yeltsin, in a rushed, short speech before a Central Committee plenum, complained that reform was moving too slowly, and that Gorbachev was starting to enjoy the adulation of a "cult of personality," a reference to Stalin. Yeltsin resigned on the spot from the Politburo. His speech and resignation stunned the hall. Gorbachev found himself squeezed between Yeltsin's demands for faster reform and Politburo member Yegor Ligachev, who resisted it.[40] Then, a few days after Shultz left Moscow, Gorbachev agreed to the summit dates. "The Soviets blinked," Reagan wrote in his diary.

The yawning gulf of misunderstanding between Washington and Moscow had remained. Despite all that happened in 1987—the new military doctrine, the Rust affair and its aftermath, the abandonment of the Oka missile, the failure of the Soviet Star Wars, the achievement of eliminating the INF weapons—the Defense Intelligence Agency sent a report to Congress stating that "all evidence points to continuity in the Soviet Union's military policy."[41]

Two weeks before Gorbachev arrived in the United States, Gates, the deputy CIA director, wrote a memo to Reagan about the Soviet leader that failed to grasp the essence of Gorbachev's attempts to reverse the arms race, and miscast his goals and motivations. There is a "continuing extraordinary scope and sweep of Soviet military modernization and weapons research and development," Gates said, offering not even a brief acknowledgment of Gorbachev's efforts to change course. "We still see *no* lessening of their weapons production. And, further, Soviet research on new, exotic weapons such as lasers and their own version of SDI continues apace." In fact, the Soviet version of SDI was a shambles and would never be built. Gates concluded that despite "great changes underway" in the Soviet Union, "it is hard to detect fundamental changes, currently or in prospect, in the way the Soviets govern at home or in their principle objectives abroad." Gates told the president, amid the summit excitement, that "a sober—even somber—reminder of the enduring features of the regime and the still long competition and struggle ahead will be needed."[42]

Still, the December summit in Washington was far from somber, and crackled with energy. Gorbachev spontaneously stopped his limousine on Connecticut Avenue and began shaking hands with thrilled passersby. Reagan and Gorbachev signed the Intermediate-range Nuclear Forces treaty with a brisk exchange of pens and handshakes in a ceremony in the East Room of the White House. The treaty would eliminate 1,846 Soviet Pioneers and 846 American Pershing IIs, the first time in the nuclear age that an entire class of Soviet and U.S. weapons was wiped out, and under stringent verification provisions. It was not the end of nuclear danger, but it was the most concrete joint accomplishment of Reagan, the dreamer, and Gorbachev, the radical, nuclear abolitionists who found each other at the right moment. In remarks before they signed the treaty, Reagan said, "We have listened to the wisdom of an old Russian maxim, *doveryai, no proveryai*—trust, but verify."

"You repeat that at every meeting," Gorbachev said.

"I like it," Reagan replied, smiling.

GERMS, GAS AND SECRETS

In the thick woods south of Moscow, at Obolensk, the microbiologist Igor Domaradsky redoubled his search for agents of death. He experimented with genetic engineering, combining the gene of diphtheria with the agents of plague or tularemia to make a hybrid pathogen. He turned his results over to the military, never to hear of them again. He labored to engineer a tularemia strain resistant to antibiotics. If used in a weapon, once spread, the disease would be difficult to treat. He created two strains that retained their virulence, but with only limited resistance to antibiotics. This was always the challenge—Domaradsky had never been able to achieve a high resistance and, simultaneously, sufficient virulence. If he got higher resistance, he got less virulence. One of the strains was tested on monkeys, but proved unsatisfactory. Domaradsky was adrift, and his conflict with the institute director, Nikolai Urakov, worsened as the months went by. Urakov blocked one of Domaradsky's students from receiving a doctorate, questioned Domaradsky's salary, gave Domaradsky piles of paperwork and insisted Domaradsky move out of his breezy flat in Protvino and into the dark woods at Obolensk. Domaradsky at one point took a daring step, writing a letter of complaint about Urakov to the Politburo. The letter resulted in an internal investigation and more conflict. Finally, Domaradsky asked to be transferred to another job in Moscow. He left Obolensk in the summer of 1987, having done much to launch the biological weapons program, but never to return.

Domaradsky thought his research on genetically modified agents fell short. He believed the search for a tularemia agent was a stopgap idea. It wasn't contagious and the military wanted more virulent and dangerous pathogens that could spread. Overall, he said, "Very little was done to develop a new generation of these weapons, as had been the original goal" of the interagency council he had joined in Moscow in 1975. "I have to say that it has justified neither the hopes nor the colossal investment of material. Essentially nothing remarkable was ever produced . . ."[1]

Domaradsky's conclusion was premature. As he left, others took up the quest to create the agents of death.

In Domaradsky's final year at Obolensk, a new scientist arrived. Sergei Popov was the bright young researcher who had worked on genetic engineering at Koltsovo, figuring out how to make the immune system turn on itself. At the time he arrived at Obolensk, the new building for working on dangerous pathogens was rising out of the forest. Popov recalled seeing Domaradsky roaming the halls, a bitter outcast. They did not talk. Popov believes he was brought in as Domaradsky's successor in the intensifying search for genetically altered agents to be used in a biological weapon. When he departed Koltsovo in 1986, Popov turned over to other scientists his "construct," the piece of DNA that would be inserted into a genome. Once at Obolensk, he began to look for ways to broaden his early discovery, using bacteria as the vehicle instead of viruses. "New, improved constructs had been provided to me in Obolensk," he recalled. "My mission was to continue what had been started in Koltsovo." The goal was to create agents with new and unusual characteristics, causing death in ways that would be unfathomable, and unstoppable.

For Popov, the Obolensk lifestyle seemed a welcome change from Koltsovo. With Moscow only an hour away, Popov drove north and loaded up his car with food and goods unknown in Koltsovo. But at work, Popov ran into resistance from Urakov, who was not pleased. "Urakov did not want me there," Popov said. "Why would he? It was recognized that he had not kept up with the problem, and that microbiology was underdeveloped at the institute. Domaradsky also failed to meet the goal, and Biopreparat decided to assign a new person who would solve the problem. And imagine, a military general who was told some-

thing like this. He was against me from the very beginning! But Biopreparat insisted."

In the years that followed, Popov sought to engineer some of the most
hazardous biological agents ever imagined. Using his earlier experience
with the smallpox virus, he sought to create a pathogen that would
deceive the victim. With genetic engineering, he hoped to create a deadly
one-two punch: a first wave that would cause illness, followed by recovery, then a second wave that would be unexpected and fatal. It was a profoundly evil idea, to manipulate the very smallest building blocks of life,
creating a germ that could not be stopped by remedies known to
mankind. Nor was the idea his handiwork alone. It was the deliberate
policy of the Soviet state.

The method Popov took was to construct a pathogen within a
pathogen; the second one would deliver the deadly assault. He told
Urakov he wanted to try five different microbes as the vehicle, or the first
stage of the illness. Each of the agents was under control of a different
group at the institute, and Popov would have to work with them all. The
five were: *Burkhholderia mallei*, which causes glanders, an infectious disease primarily affecting horses; *Burkholderia pseudomallei*, which causes
melioidosis, an infectious disease prevalent in tropical climates; *Yersinia
pestis*, which causes plague; *Bacillus anthracis*, which causes anthrax;
and *Legionella*, which leads to legionellosis, or Legionnaires' disease.
Although Popov was at the center of the research, thousands of people
participated in it. The best and brightest graduates from Soviet universities were recruited for Obolensk. Each floor of the new building was outfitted for work on different pathogens. Popov scrutinized each for signs
that it would make a good carrier. Anthrax didn't work; plague was not
good enough. Eventually, Popov found that only *Legionella* would succeed. The amount needed was small; a lethal dose was only a few
Legionella cells. But there were technical obstacles; it wasn't easy to grow
enough *Legionella* to experiment with and, if weaponized, it would be
very difficult to mass-produce.

For the second stage, Popov returned to the lessons of Koltsovo and his
discovery there. He inserted into *Legionella* the genetic material that
would cause the body to attack its own nervous system. Nerves are covered with a myelin insulation that helps them transmit impulses. Popov's
plan was to cause the body's immune system to destroy the myelin. This
would cause paralysis and, eventually, death. If the new genetically engi-

neered pathogen worked, the victim would first come down with Legionnaires' disease, a form of pneumonia. "Some of the infected would die, and some recover, absolutely recover. However, in two weeks the recovered person would develop paralysis and would die," Popov explained. The paralysis and death were caused by the destruction of the myelin insulation. In effect, the body would wreck its own nervous system. "When your body tries to heal itself," Popov said, "it actually does the reverse."

"It was deceptive," Popov said. "The first wave disease would disappear or would never be an acute disease. It could be a little bit of coughing, or nothing, you don't feel it, that's it. And then two weeks later, the disease would be hardly treatable, actually there would be no way to effectively treat it."

The idea took him years to perfect. But the result was so terrible that when Popov saw what happened to guinea pigs during testing, he was overwhelmed with doubt.[2]

On the bleak steppe of Kazakhstan, new workers streamed into the massive new factory at Stepnogorsk. By 1986, Ken Alibek, the chief of the anthrax assembly line, recalled that he supervised nine hundred people, and the Soviets had created "the most effective anthrax weapon ever produced." He remembered working at a frenzied pace, spending all his days and nights in the laboratories. "I still shuddered occasionally when I looked at the bacteria multiplying in our fermenters and considered that they could end the lives of millions of people. But the secret culture of our labs had changed my outlook."

The pressure-cooker environment took a heavy toll, and accidents happened every week. Once, he recalled, a technician was infected with anthrax. The man's neck began to bulge, closing off his breathing. Antibiotics did not work. Within days, death seemed inevitable. At the last minute, they injected the man with a huge dose of anthrax antiserum and saved him. "The technician's narrow escape drove home the potency of our new weapon," Alibek recalled in his memoir. "Our powdered and liquid formulations of anthrax were three times as strong as the weapons that had been developed at Sverdlovsk."

In 1987, the anthrax was tested on Vozrozhdeniye Island, according to

Alibek. With the success of the tests, the old facility in Sverdlovsk, where the accident had occurred eight years earlier, was no longer needed. The massive new factory at Stepnogorsk was far superior. "Our factory could turn out two tons of anthrax a day in a process as reliable and efficient as producing tanks, trucks, cars or Coca-Cola," Alibek said. "With the creation of the world's first industrial-scale biological weapons factory, the Soviet Union became the world's first—and only—biological super-power."[3]

But not everything was quite as efficient as Alibek claimed. Popov recalled that Stepnogorsk suffered "huge problems." Among them, "People in charge were drunkards, and they didn't care very much about what they did. The only requirement was that anthrax had to kill; they tested the product on animals. From the microbiological standpoint, they did a dirty work. As a result, the facility was very unproductive, and the results were often miserable—sometimes good, but sometimes they harvested no anthrax. The anthrax cells dissolved in the process we call phage lysis." This is a virus that attacks the bacteria. "So, quite often the anthrax microbe just didn't survive in those huge fermenters. And Biopreparat people often complained about it. They asked if we could help Alibek with his problem . . . They could not solve it. They thought the reason was the poor sterility of the components."

Nonetheless, Alibek recalled, the larger goal was achieved. "Stepnogorsk demonstrated our ability to wage biological warfare on a scale matched by no other nation in history. We had taken the science of biowarfare further in the previous four years than it had traveled in the four decades since World War II."

Alibek was promoted and transferred to Moscow in September 1987. After just a few months, he was given his first major assignment at Biopreparat headquarters. He was to supervise creation of a new smallpox weapon. He spent an afternoon reading over a top-secret document that he described as a five-year plan for biological weapons development, signed by Gorbachev in February 1986. The document carried a line for what kind of weapon, what kind of systems and when each would be tested between 1986 and 1990, he said. Among other things in the plan, Alibek saw a line for funding a 630-liter viral reactor to produce smallpox at Koltsovo. "Our military leaders," he recalled in his memoir, "had decided to concentrate on one of the toughest challenges of bioweaponeering—the transformation of viruses into weapons of war." He added, "Gorbachev's Five Year Plan—and his generous funding, which would amount to over $1 billion by the end of the decade— allowed us to catch up with and then surpass Western technology."[4]

When Alibek visited Vector, the smallpox project was just getting off the ground. "Vector's prize acquisition was the expensive new viral reactor authorized by Gorbachev's decree," he recalled. "Designed by one of our Moscow institutes . . . it was the first of its kind in the world. It stood about five feet high and was enclosed within thick stainless steel walls. An agitator at the bottom kept the mixture inside churning like clothes in a washing machine. Pipes led out in several directions, both for waste matter and weapons-ready material. A window on its convex roof allowed scientists to observe the viral culture at all times."

Popov also knew of the five-year plan for biological weapons and was certain it had been approved at the highest levels. "We didn't have any doubt the Central Committee was behind all of this. Not a single doubt," he said. Once, in Moscow, Popov also read a top-secret document in a folder that described the long-term program. "I remember that I misplaced the document and took it somewhere as I was walking through Biopreparat offices, and they chased me because it was a top-secret document. I had it in my folder, it wasn't even a briefcase, they gave it to me in a folder, there was a special table I had to sit at. I don't know how it happened, maybe I went to the restroom or something." The guards grabbed him and returned him to the table.

In all of Gorbachev's struggle for disarmament—his determination to push back the military and its powerful designers, his willingness to abandon the doctrine of two blocs inexorably at odds, his rhetoric about a world free of nuclear destruction and danger—there was one unexplained gap. Hidden in secret institutes, referred to obliquely even in the Kremlin as "works on special problems," the biological weapons drive was going at full speed at the same moment that Gorbachev reached the apex of his cooperation with Reagan. Gorbachev abhorred nuclear weapons, and he declared his intention to eliminate chemical weapons. Did he also fear the pathogens?

One key question is how much Gorbachev knew about the program. The record suggests that some members of the Politburo knew in great detail what kinds of horrors were being cooked up at Obolensk and Vector. Lev Zaikov, the Politburo member in charge of the military-industrial complex, who was Katayev's boss, certainly knew. Gorbachev must have become aware of the program when he became general secretary in 1985, and perhaps before. There is a document in Katayev's files that lists a Central Committee resolution on biological weapons on November 18, 1986. This was in effect an order from the Politburo that Gorbachev certainly would have known about. Three sources—Alibek, who built the anthrax assembly line; Popov, who worked at both Koltsovo and Obolensk; and Vladimir Pasechnik, a well-informed institute chief in the system who later defected to Britain—claim that Gorbachev and the Politburo were kept abreast of the program in the late 1980s. Alibek claims to have seen the specific five-year plan signed by Gorbachev. Chernyaev, perhaps the closest aide to Gorbachev, also confirmed in an interview that Gorbachev knew the Soviet Union was in violation of the biological weapons treaty. Chernyaev insisted that Gorbachev wanted to end the biological weapons program, but the military misled him, promising to shut it down, although they did not.[5] "Not even Gorbachev was fully informed about the activities of our military-industrial complex," Chernyaev wrote in his memoirs.

It is also not known what intelligence Gorbachev received from the KGB. The United States had abandoned offensive biological weapons in 1969, but scientists in the Soviet program have insisted they were told by the KGB for many years that the American offensive germ warfare program did exist; it was just well hidden.

If Gorbachev knew of the Soviet program, and if he was so determined to slow the arms race in missiles, why did he not take stronger action to slow the arms race in test tubes? He had done so much else with *glasnost* to unearth the misdeeds of the Soviet past—admitting the mass repressions of Stalin, for example—why could he not expose or stop the dangerous germ warfare efforts that began long before he came to power? This is difficult to answer.

One explanation may be that the biological weapons program was so entrenched that Gorbachev might have decided it was impossible to tackle, or at the very least, as a tactical matter, that he should wait until later to deal with it. In other cases it took Gorbachev years to bring about a change in course and overturn past errors and deep secrecy involving military affairs.

Also, Gorbachev might have felt himself unable to challenge the authority of those who ran the biological weapons empire. The Chernobyl experience was relevant—it showed him how hard it was to confront the nuclear priesthood, and surely the biological weapons scientists and generals could be just as difficult. In Gorbachev's last two years, as his power waned, he may simply have lacked the willpower or stature to take on a new power struggle. "He didn't know how to exercise his control," Chernyaev said. Gorbachev may have been reluctant to admit the full scope of Soviet violations out of fear of what it could do to his public image and that of his "new thinking" all over the world. He may have opted to avoid the whole subject because he had no idea how to handle the impact of such a damaging disclosure.

One reason that has been suggested by Soviet officials for Gorbachev's inaction is that biological weapons may have been seen as some kind of military asset, to be held in reserve, perhaps to compensate for other shortcomings in defense. But it is doubtful Gorbachev preserved the pathogens out of any sense of their strategic or military value. Gorbachev was clearly determined to ease the threat of war, not build new weapons of such comparable power and danger.

Still, it remains a puzzle why, given Gorbachev's dedication to *glasnost* and his enormous effort at disarmament in the nuclear field, he did not do more to stop the dangerous biological weapons program. In all the years of Gorbachev's drive for change and openness, the Soviet Union continued to cover up Biopreparat and all it encompassed.

One of the most elaborate deceptions involved the 1979 Sverdlovsk anthrax leak, the worst disaster of the Soviet biological weapons program. Through the decade of the 1980s, the Soviets fabricated details about the outbreak to suggest it had explicable, natural causes, such as tainted meat. Soviet officials spread these falsehoods around the world. They lied in international meetings, to other scientists and to themselves. They misled the distinguished Harvard molecular biologist Matthew

Meselson, who had been called in by the CIA to puzzle over the early reports about the Sverdlovsk accident in 1980.

Meselson had been trying through the 1980s to answer the questions he first raised when studying the intelligence reports. An effort in 1983 to organize an expedition to Sverdlovsk fell apart after the Korean air-liner shoot down that year. In 1986, he was invited to come to Moscow by officials at the Ministry of Health. On that visit, Meselson met with sev-eral top Soviet health officials, including Pyotr Burgasov, the deputy health minister who, at the time of the outbreak, spread the story that contaminated meat was the cause of the anthrax epidemic. Burgasov probably knew better; he had been involved with the Soviet biological weapons program since the 1950s and had served in the Sverdlovsk facil-ity from 1958 to 1963. In the meetings in Moscow with Meselson, August 27–30, 1986, Burgasov repeated that contaminated meat was the cause and added that contaminated bone meal had been fed to cattle and caused the epidemic. Meselson also met with Vladimir Nikiforov, chief of the infectious diseases department at the Central Postgraduate Insti-tute, located within the Botkin Hospital in Moscow, and Olga Yampol-skaya, a specialist in infectious diseases there, who had been present during the Sverdlovsk epidemic. Nikiforov was the courtly scientist who had courageously told the Sverdlovsk pathologists to hide and preserve their autopsy results in 1979. But now he was advancing the official line. Nikiforov showed Meselson fourteen photographic slides from the autopsies that, he insisted, supported the argument that anthrax had been ingested by eating the contaminated meat. The lungs of the victims, he claimed, were "undamaged and free of hemorrhage." Before leaving Moscow on August 29, Meselson told the chargé d'affaires at the U.S. Embassy what he found in his discussions. The Soviet officials had insisted victims had died from intestinal anthrax; Meselson said he had no way of knowing if the story was true, but it "did seem to hang together."[6]

In September 1986, the Soviet officials offered the same false explana-tion in Geneva at the Second Review Conference for the Biological Weapons Convention. Soviet officials prepared a briefing for Gorbachev warning him that suspicions were deepening in the West that the Soviet Union had something to hide. Nonetheless, the cover-up continued at the conference and afterward.[7] On October 10–12, 1986, Joshua Lederberg, president of Rockefeller University, who was chairman of the Committee on International Security and Arms Control of the National Academy of Sciences, visited Moscow. Lederberg was a pioneering microbiologist, recipient of the 1953 Nobel Prize for the discovery that bacteria engage in a form of sexual reproduction and thus possess a genetic mechanism similar to those of higher organisms. Lederberg was presented with the story that anthrax bacteria had been spread by contaminated meat from cattle fed a bonemeal supplement that was improperly sterilized, and produced from naturally infected carcasses. Like Meselson, Lederberg was deceived. "My personal conclusion," Lederberg later wrote, "is that the present Soviet account of the epidemic is plausible on its face and internally consistent." The Soviet explanations are "very likely to be true."[8]

In Moscow, on November 18, 1986, the Central Committee and the Council of Ministers approved a measure, proposed by the Defense Ministry, to move the secret formulas for biological weapons and the manufacturing plants away from the military. Specifically, the measure called for action by 1992—in the course of the next six years—to eliminate "the stockpile of biological recipes and industrial capacities for production of biological weapons located at the sites of this ministry." This appears to mean that over the next six years, the Defense Ministry would transfer the formulas and production facilities to the better-concealed Biopreparat complex. Such a move was already undertaken with the anthrax facility at Sverdlovsk, which was moved to Stepnogorsk. The reason for the move, according to the documents, was to meet the goal "of insuring openness of work in conditions of international verification." This was code for the fact that Soviet leaders wanted to keep the program alive—and well hidden—at a time when international inspectors might be nosing around. It seems extremely likely that such a high-level action by the Central Committee, which was led by members of the Politburo, would have come to Gorbachev's attention.[9]

———

In 1987, a fresh worry arose in Moscow among the top echelons of Bio-preparat and the military. For all their efforts at secrecy, a speech on chemical weapons treaty verification by Foreign Minister Eduard She-vardnadze threatened to crack open the door to their empire. During Gorbachev's *glasnost,* Soviet diplomats in several negotiations had expressed a willingness to allow more intrusive verification of arms con-trol treaties, to show they were not cheating. This new openness was the spirit of a speech August 6, 1987, by Shevardnadze at the Conference on Disarmament in Geneva. In the spring, Gorbachev had announced the Soviet Union would stop manufacturing chemical weapons. Now, She-vardnadze went further and promised support for "the principle of mandatory challenge inspections without right of refusal." This was a "vivid manifestation" of Soviet commitment to "genuine and effective verification," he said. For years, the United States had accused the Soviet Union of violating treaties and demanded effective verification. It was the essence of Reagan's favorite Russian slogan, "trust, but verify." While Shevardnadze's overture was made for chemical weapons, it dawned on Soviet biological warfare experts back in Moscow that it could easily be applied to them, too. The inspections could take unpre-dictable turns. If the West wanted to peek into a suspect facility—say, Obolensk or Koltsovo or Stepnogorsk—how could they refuse? Nikita Smidovich, an aide to Shevardnadze who wrote the Geneva speech, said the biological weapons chiefs realized the chemical inspections threat-ened their closed world. They concluded, he said, if the inspectors "can go everywhere, they will probably get to us as well, so we need to get prepared."[10]

On October 2, 1987, after Shevardnadze's speech, the Central Com-mittee and Council of Ministers issued an order to speed up preparations for possible international inspections. The goal was not to be open, but the opposite: continue the secret germ warfare program by moving the formulas and factories to a more secret place. And do it quicker.[11]

The Sverdlovsk deception reached a new level of audacity April 10–17, 1988, when Burgasov, Nikiforov and a third Soviet medical official, Vladimir Sergiyev, came to the United States with a presentation of their theory about contaminated meat and bonemeal. Meselson said he arranged the visit in hopes that the Soviet officials would be exposed to expert questioning from American scientists. The Soviets delivered their bogus story to distinguished audiences three times: at the National Academy of Sciences in Washington, the Johns Hopkins School of Hygiene and Public Health in Baltimore and the American Academy of the Arts and Sciences in Cambridge, Massachusetts. "It was clear to us that infectious meat was the cause," claimed Burgasov. "The whole idea of some sort of aerosol is impossible," he said. He dismissed the possibility of a leak of anthrax bacteria from Compound 19. "I couldn't imagine that in the midst of the highly populated area that there could be any work on highly dangerous pathogens," he said, although he knew that was probably what happened. Nikiforov, who also knew the truth, narrated autopsy slides that portrayed great black intestinal sores, which pointed toward contaminated meat, not inhalation. In all, the Soviet officials had addressed more than two hundred private and government medical scientists and arms control experts, delivering untruths to all of them. Afterward, summarizing the Soviet presentations, Meselson wrote that he found the Soviet explanation "plausible and consistent with what is known from previous outbreaks of human and animal anthrax in the USSR and elsewhere, including the US." Meselson still hoped to send a group of American scientists to Sverdlovsk.[12]

Alibek, who had built the anthrax assembly line at Stepnogorsk and was now working in Moscow at the Biopreparat headquarters, sensed the tension over possible international inspections. "Once knowledgeable foreign scientists set foot in one of our installations, our secret would be out," he wrote in his memoir. When Alibek became first deputy director of Biopreparat in 1988, he was put in charge of hiding the evidence. The assignment soon crowded out his other duties. A special task force for the deception plans was set up at the Moscow Institute of Applied Biochemistry. Even the name of the institute was itself a deception. "The institute had no connection with biochemistry: its function was to design and manufacture equipment for our labs," he said. The task force was given the equivalent of $400,000 to create a cover story, or "legend," for Biopreparat operations and to demonstrate the "civilian" character of the work, that they were making medicines to defend against disease, or pesticides.

"Nevertheless, some of us worried that foreign inspectors would see through our schemes." By 1988, Biopreparat had produced an instruction manual for employees on how to answer questions for inspectors, Alibek said. "Every conceivable question—What is this room for? Why is this equipment here?—was followed by a prepared reply, which workers were expected to memorize."

"I was most concerned about our smallpox project," he said. "If foreign inspectors brought the right equipment to the Vector compound in Siberia, they would immediately pick up evidence of smallpox." As part of the global smallpox eradication effort, in which the Soviet Union had played a leading role, there were supposed to be only two repositories for the remaining smallpox strains, one in the United States and the other in Moscow at the Ivanovsky Institute of the Ministry of Health. This is what the Soviet Union had pledged to the World Health Organization. What the world didn't know until years later was that the Soviet Union had broken its word.[13]

In 1988, worried about foreign inspections, an order was given by the Soviet military to get rid of a large supply of anthrax spores that had been removed from Sverdlovsk after the accident. This *Bacillus anthracis* had been in storage at the town of Zima, near Irkutsk, in Siberia. When the order came to destroy it, more than one hundred tons of anthrax solution, in 250-liter stainless steel containers, was taken by train, and then by ship, to Vozrozhdeniye Island, where it was mixed with hydrogen peroxide and formic acid, and then buried in eleven graves dug in the earth. The graves, four to six feet deep, were unlined, so nothing would prevent the anthrax from seeping deeper into the ground. As they lay there under the earth, the anthrax spores were not all destroyed. Some remained active for many years to come.[14]

One thousand miles east of Moscow, in a flatlands beyond the industrial city of Chelyabinsk, stood a nondescript rectangle-shaped compound, more than a mile long and nearly a mile wide, situated almost precisely on a north-south axis, with orderly rows of low-lying wood-plank warehouses and corrugated metal rooftops, surrounded by trees and traversed by rail lines. Inside the warehouses, berths cradled row upon row of projectiles, from 85mm artillery rounds to larger warheads for Scud missiles. They were set on racks like so many wine bottles in a dark cellar. In this one remote compound, near the town of Shchuchye in western Siberia, 1.9 million projectiles were filled with 5,447 metric tons of the nerve agents sarin, soman and a Soviet analogue of the nerve gas VX. All told, it was 13.6 percent of the Soviet chemical weapons arsenal.[15] The projectiles were the legacy of a shadowy era of the arms race in which the United States, Great Britain and the Soviet Union stockpiled massive amounts of chemical weapons, while negotiations to restrict them dragged on for two decades in Geneva without result. From the beginning of his disarmament drive, Gorbachev wanted to be rid of these chemical weapons.

The killing power of chemical weapons is monstrous. Less than ten milligrams of the American nerve agent VX—a small drop of fluid on the skin—could kill a grown man in fifteen minutes or less. A liter of such an agent contains enough lethal doses, theoretically, to kill one million people.[16] Such nerve agents serve no peaceful purpose—they are solely agents of death. The author Jonathan Tucker described them as colorless, odorless liquids that enter the body through the lungs or skin and attack the nervous system. The victim falls to the ground, convulses and loses consciousness, after which inhibition of the breathing center of the brain and paralysis of the respiratory muscles cause death by asphyxiation within minutes.

The Soviets had amassed at least forty thousand tons of chemical agents, and the United States thirty-one thousand tons. While silent about biological weapons, Gorbachev openly sought to get rid of the chemical arms. He announced in Prague on April 13, 1987, that the Soviet Union would stop manufacturing them. He mothballed the Soviet factories for making the chemicals and filling the munitions.

After his speech on surprise inspections in Geneva, Shevardnadze invited foreign observers to a top-secret Soviet chemical weapons testing facility at Shikhany, on the Volga River 560 miles southeast of Moscow.

Shevardnadze said he wanted to "build an atmosphere of trust." On October 3–4, 1987, a delegation of 110 experts from 45 countries and 55 journalists were flown there in four airplanes. At the facility, on a freshly poured concrete slab, the delegation saw nineteen projectiles and containers, including hand grenades, rocket and artillery rounds, and a nine-foot-tall chemical warhead for the Scud.[17] The visit seemed to be another sign of the Gorbachev *glasnost*. Yuri Nazarkin, the Soviet representative at arms control talks, declared, "We have nothing to hide."[18] This was not quite true. Missing from the lineup on the concrete pad was a new type of chemical weapon Soviet scientists were desperately trying to develop to keep pace with the United States.

Until the 1980s, both the United States and Soviet Union built chemical weapons that contained a single agent that would be dispersed when detonated. This was called a unitary chemical weapon. The agents tended to degrade over time. The United States stopped manufacturing them in 1969, when potential hazards were discovered in the U.S. arsenal. In 1985, Congress approved destroying the older weapons while authorizing the creation of a new type of chemical weapon, known as a binary. It would have two parts, each a stable ingredient that, when combined at the last minute in the shell or bomb, would turn into a toxic cocktail. This was a tricky engineering feat, but a binary weapon might have a longer shelf life. Reagan approved production of the new binary weapon right after the December 1987 summit with Gorbachev. "Maybe that will get the Soviets to join us in eliminating chemical warfare," he wrote in his diary.[19] The Soviets were already rushing—in secret—to create the same thing. They experimented with binary weapons in the 1970s, but failed to come up with a successful model. Then, in the 1980s, they launched another quest. One part of this new drive was to create a binary weapon out of ordinary chemicals that might be used in fertilizer or pesticides. These were called the *novichok* generation of agents, or the "new guy."

Vil Mirzayanov was a witness to the potential power of these deadly nerve agents. He had worked for many years at the headquarters of chemical weapons research in Moscow. In May 1987, one of his friends, an experienced military chemist, Andrei Zheleznyakov, suffered an accident. He was a test engineer whose job was to check finished products. He was working on a binary weapon, one of the *novichok* generation.

According to Mirzayanov, there was a chemical reactor under a fume hood, and then a pipe carrying the substance to a spectrometer, which was too big to put under the hood. It was in the room, with ventilation on the ceiling, but not protected by the hood.

The pipe somehow broke, and the poison leaked into the air. Zheleznyakov quickly sealed the leak, but it was too late. He felt the impact immediately—myosis, the constriction of the pupil of the eye. "I saw rings before my eyes—red, orange," he later recalled. "Bells were ringing inside my head. I choked. Add to this the feeling of fear—as if something was about to happen at any moment. I sat down and told the guys: I think it has 'got' me. They dragged me out of the room—I was still able to move—and took me to the chief. He looked at me and said, 'Have a cup of tea, everything will be fine.' I drank the tea and immediately threw up.

"They took me to the medical unit," he added, "where I was injected with an antidote. I felt a little better. The chief told me: 'Go home and lie down. Come back tomorrow.' They assigned me an escort, and we walked past a few bus stops. We were already passing the church near Ilyich Square, when suddenly I saw the church lighting up and falling apart. I remember nothing else."

His escort dragged Zheleznyakov back to the medical unit. They called an ambulance and took him to the hospital, accompanied by KGB agents, who told doctors he had suffered food poisoning from eating contaminated sausage. The KGB agents made the doctors sign a pledge never to discuss the case. After eighteen days in intensive care, doctors managed to save his life.

At the end of the hospitalization, he was given a pension and told to remain silent. Zheleznyakov suffered aftereffects for a long time, including chronic weakness in his arms, toxic hepatitis, epilepsy, severe depression and an inability to concentrate. Zheleznyakov had been a jovial man and was known as a talented woodcarver, but the accident left him unable to work or be creative. He died five years after the accident.[20]

Novichok had shown its teeth.

THE LOST YEAR

Reagan's last hurrah with Gorbachev came on a warm spring day, May 31, 1988. Having finished the third plenary meeting of their fourth summit, they stepped out into the lilac-scented breezes for a walking tour around the Kremlin and Red Square, trailed by aides and journalists. They stopped near a thirty-nine-ton cannon dating from 1586 that stands in a plaza in the center of the Kremlin. Asked if he still considered the Soviet Union to be an evil empire, Reagan replied, "No." Surprised, reporters asked why. Reagan paused, and tilted his head to one side. "You are talking about another time, another era," he said.

The moment marked the end of Reagan's cold war. On his first visit to the Soviet Union after so many decades of antipathy, Reagan and Gorbachev did not sign any nuclear arms treaties, a missed opportunity for deep cuts in strategic weapons, and they would not eliminate any more weapons together in the eight months remaining in Reagan's term.[1] But they began to put the superpower rivalry to rest, in a vivid and symbolic way, walking the cobblestones of Red Square for twenty minutes under the afternoon sun. Gorbachev, in a light business suit, showed Reagan, in a darker one, the onion-shaped domes of St. Basil's Cathedral, the GUM department store, the State Historical Museum and Lenin's tomb. At one point, Reagan and Gorbachev put their arms around each other's waists, like two tourists posing for photos. "What we have decided to do," Reagan said, "is talk to each other and not about each other, and that's working just fine."

Later in the day, Reagan delivered one of the most powerful speeches of his presidency to students at Moscow State University. He spoke in the lecture hall standing under a large white bust of Lenin with a mural spreading out behind him depicting the Bolshevik Revolution. Reagan articulated his themes of democracy, capitalism and freedom, ideas that had so animated his anti-communism. Reagan declared the world stood at the start of a new revolution "quietly sweeping the globe without bloodshed or conflict." This was the "information revolution," Reagan said, describing the power of one computer chip, and "its effects are peaceful, but they will fundamentally alter our world, shatter old assumptions, and reshape our lives." Reagan celebrated freedom, entrepreneurship and dissent. And, quoting Boris Pasternak, he championed "the irresistible power of unarmed truth" to the students. Reagan endorsed Gorbachev's drive for change, and voiced anew his goal of abolishing nuclear weapons. Those days in May marked the zenith of his extraordinary partnership with Gorbachev.

Reagan's enthusiasm was not shared by his vice president, George Bush, who was watching the spectacle at his home in Kennebunkport, Maine. Bush was campaigning that year to be Reagan's successor, running against a liberal Democrat, Governor Michael Dukakis of Massachusetts. Bush was profoundly cautious by character. His guiding principles were good stewardship—public service in an old-fashioned sense—and avoiding mistakes. He had doubts about whether the changes in Moscow were real, and he was uneasy at the scenes from Red Square. A few weeks later, speaking in San Francisco to the World Affairs Council of Northern California, he expressed this uncertainty. "We must be bold enough to seize the opportunity of change," he said, "but at the same time be prepared for what one pundit called 'The Protracted Conflict.'" Bush clearly had not made up his mind. He was more certain about the past than the future. "The Cold War is not over," he declared.[2]

The next few months underscored how wrong he was. Gorbachev rushed toward fundamental change. The Soviet leader announced troops would begin a pullout from Afghanistan by May 15, 1988, and they did. In private conversations in the Kremlin, the Cold War was being tossed into the waste bin of history. For example, on June 20—nine days before Bush said the Cold War was not over—Gromyko, once the hardest of the hard-liners, gave strong voice to the new thinking, declaring at a Politburo meeting that decades of competition in the arms race had been senseless. "And so we made more and more nuclear weapons," he said, according to a transcript of the meeting. "That was our mistaken position, absolutely mistaken. And the political leadership bears the entire blame for it. Tens of billions were spent on production of these toys; we did not have enough brains" to stop.[3]

By autumn, Gorbachev was preparing his most daring proposal yet, a major speech to the United Nations announcing a massive Soviet troop pullback from Europe. Meeting with a small group of his foreign policy advisers October 31, he recalled Winston Churchill's famous speech, "Sinews of Peace," at Fulton, Missouri, in March 1946. In the address, Churchill warned that "an iron curtain has descended across the Continent" with Soviet control tightening over "all the capitals of the ancient states of Central and Eastern Europe." Gorbachev declared his own ambition was to mark the end of the era. "In general, this speech should be an anti-Fulton—Fulton in reverse," Gorbachev said.

On November 3, after a Politburo meeting, Gorbachev brought up his plan with a wider group of senior officials. Chernyaev recalled that Gorbachev was "clearly nervous." He carefully maneuvered so as not to ignite opposition from the military. He did not disclose the full details of the planned one-sided pullback. He noted that the Soviet military was far larger than would be required under the new doctrine Akhromeyev had drafted. This would be difficult to admit publicly. "If we publish how matters stand, that we spend over twice as much as the United States on military needs, if we let the scope of our expenses be known, all our new thinking and our new foreign policy will go to hell," Gorbachev said. "Not one country in the world spends as much per capita on weapons as we do, except perhaps the developing nations that we are swamping with weapons and getting nothing in return."[4]

Gorbachev's address to the United Nations on December 7 was a milestone in his retreat from the Cold War. He condemned the "one-sided reliance on military power" that had been a pillar of Soviet foreign policy, and he announced unilateral reductions in the Soviet armed forces of five hundred thousand men, including six tank divisions in Eastern Europe. It was a profound break from the past to make such a sizable one-sided pullback. Gorbachev said the Soviet Union would no longer hold the nations of Eastern Europe in its grip, another breathtaking change in approach. "Freedom of choice is a universal principle," he said. "It knows no exceptions."

After the speech, Gorbachev took a ferry to meet Reagan for a farewell lunch on Governor's Island, joined by Bush, who had just been elected president. In the twilight hours of his presidency, Reagan was ebullient, and wrote in his diary that the meeting was a "tremendous success" and Gorbachev had "a better attitude than at any of our previous meetings. He sounded as if he saw us as partners making a better world."[5] Yet on substance, Reagan did not discuss Gorbachev's remarkable speech in any detail, and they parted without having realized their most cherished goal, eliminating the long-range nuclear weapons, the brass ring they had nearly grasped at Reykjavik. The hope of cutting the arsenals by 50 percent was bogged down in negotiations.[6]

At the Governor's Island meeting, Bush, the president-elect, kept quiet, not wanting to upstage Reagan.[7] Gorbachev noticed the hesitation. "We should take into account that Bush is a very cautious politician," Gorbachev told the Politburo on his return to Moscow. Georgi Arbatov, director of the Institute for the Study of the U.S.A. and Canada, the leading Soviet specialist on America, was more blunt. Gorbachev read out to the Politburo group Arbatov's assessment that the United States has "suddenly sent a trial balloon: we are not ready; let's wait, we will see. In general, they will drag their feet, they want to break the wave that has been created by our initiatives."[8]

Bush did not share Reagan's hopes of eliminating nuclear weapons. He decided against an early summit with Gorbachev. Two days after Bush was inaugurated, Brent Scowcroft, his national security adviser, said, "I think the Cold War is not over."[9] Within a month of taking office in January 1989, Bush ordered a series of internal foreign policy studies, including one on U.S. policy toward the Soviet Union, which produced little and wasted months. "In the end, what we received was mush," said Bush's close friend and his new secretary of state, James A. Baker III.[10] In general, Bush saw Gorbachev's dynamic of change, but interpreted it as a competitive threat to the United States rather than an opportunity. "I'll be darned if Mr. Gorbachev should dominate world public opinion forever," Bush wrote to a friend March 13.[11]

Baker recalled many years later that Bush paused in early 1989 primarily to put his own stamp on foreign policy, and because slowing down the pace with the Soviets would also help calm the right wing of the Republican Party. Baker said the pause was driven by these needs, and was not a response to Gorbachev or the situation in Moscow. The administration soon came up with the idea of "testing" Gorbachev, setting up hoops and demanding that Gorbachev jump through them.[12]

On April 29, Defense Secretary Dick Cheney predicted in a televised appearance that Gorbachev would "ultimately fail."[13] Bush also found reinforcement from Scowcroft, who was extremely cautious because he feared that Gorbachev was trying to rope the United States into another period of détente in order to gain some advantage, as many felt had happened in the 1970s. "Once burned, twice shy," Scowcroft said later.[14]

When Baker visited Moscow on May 10, Shevardnadze told him Gorbachev was eager to eliminate the whole class of tactical, or short-range, nuclear weapons in Europe. "Do not dodge" the issue, Shevardnadze warned Baker. A day later, Gorbachev announced he was unilaterally withdrawing five hundred warheads from Eastern Europe, and promised even more if the United States would take similar steps. But Baker brushed off the proposal as a political ploy.[15] On May 16, Marlin Fitzwater, the White House press secretary, told a press briefing that Gorbachev was throwing out arms control proposals like a "drugstore cowboy," a slang term meaning someone who makes promises they can't keep.[16]

On July 20, the U.S. ambassador in Moscow, Jack F. Matlock Jr., met with Alexander Yakovlev, one of the leading architects of Gorbachev's new thinking. "There is only one danger—nuclear weapons," Yakovlev insisted, imploring the United States to accelerate negotiations. Matlock replied that Reagan's dream of nuclear abolition was no longer on the table. "Reagan believed in the possibility of liquidation of nuclear weapons," Matlock said. "Bush thinks that we need to reduce them to a minimum, but not liquidate them. He believes that without nuclear weapons the risk of war being unleashed would increase."[17]

While Bush delayed, Gorbachev's ambitions for disarmament were as keen as ever. Katayev's files contain a Politburo work plan on arms control and defense issues for 1989—with dozens of instructions and tight deadlines, starting in early January and running well into the next year—which underscored how the Kremlin wanted to move briskly on many fronts. The list, ten pages long, included the new initiative to reduce tactical or short-range nuclear weapons; the elimination of chemical weapons; publication of once-secret data on Soviet military spending; creating a global space organization; reducing foreign aid to other states in the Soviet bloc; boosting science and technology for the civilian sector; and downsizing the military-industrial complex. The list included directives to various ministries and agencies aimed at jump-starting defense conversion, or switching military production to civilian goods, with an aim of creating better living standards for a society staggering under shortages and economic hardship.[18]

Katayev drafted a five-page instruction, prepared for the Central Committee's approval in January 1989, laying out the rationale for a dramatic cut in Soviet weapons. The document is yet another powerful piece of evidence that Gorbachev at this point was pushing to slash military spending. The goal of defense cuts, the instruction said, was to free up resources "for accelerated development of the national economy" and provide for the most urgent everyday needs of the Soviet people.[19] Another document in Katayev's files shows that Soviet military spending peaked in 1989 and began a sharp decline thereafter.[20] As promised, the Soviet army retreated from Afghanistan by February 15, when the last Soviet commander of the 40th Army, Lieutenant General Boris Gromov, walked back across the Amu Darya River bridge at Termez.

By late 1988 and early 1989, just as Bush was taking office, Gorbachev may have reached the zenith of his powers as a leader. It would have been an ideal time to seize the initiative and lock in a 50 percent cut in strategic weapons, as well as reductions in other systems, such as tactical nuclear weapons. A strategic arms treaty also might have been easier because Bush was not dazzled by Reagan's grand dream of a defense against ballistic missiles that had proven so contentious in earlier years. But Bush hesitated.

In Moscow, Gorbachev's room for maneuver soon began to shrink. The forces of freedom and openness he had unleashed began to overtake him, creating obstacles and open resistance: new forces of democracy at home; a sweeping tide of change in Eastern Europe; the reawakening of old nationalist dreams in the Soviet republics. On March 26, the first relatively free election since the Bolshevik Revolution was held for a new Soviet legislature, the Congress of People's Deputies. In the balloting, the Communist Party leadership in Leningrad was turned out, pro-independence parties won in the Baltics and Yeltsin, the radical reformer, triumphed in Moscow. The Communist Party establishment took a shellacking. When the new legislature met for the first time from May 25 through June 9, Gorbachev ordered the proceedings broadcast on television. People stayed home from work to watch the broadcasts; the country was transfixed by debates that broke new ground in freedom of speech. One result was that Gorbachev, the party, the KGB and the military were lambasted with open and often trenchant criticism. The virus of freedom seemed to be spreading fast.

In China, Gorbachev's visit in May brought the student protests for democracy in Tiananmen Square to a new level of intensity. They were suppressed by the massacre a few weeks later. Across Eastern Europe, ferment spread, especially in Hungary and Poland, where the Solidarity movement came out from the underground and won in the elections to parliament. On July 7, Gorbachev affirmed to leaders of the Warsaw Pact that the Soviet Union would not intervene to stop the juggernaut, and they were free to go their own way. During the same week, Akhromeyev, in his new capacity as an adviser to Gorbachev, had a remarkable tour of U.S. military installations during which he and Admiral William Crowe, chairman of the U.S. Joint Chiefs of Staff, openly debated how to end the arms race.[21] Bush's trip to Poland and Hungary in July exposed him to the torrent of change there.[22] In his diary, Chernyaev captured the madness and the drama of these months. "All around Gorbachev has unleashed irreversible processes of 'disintegration' which had earlier been restrained or covered up by the arms race, the fear of war . . ." he wrote. Socialism in Eastern Europe is "disappearing," the planned economy "is living its last days," ideology "doesn't exist any more," the Soviet empire "is falling apart," the Communist Party "is in disarray" and "chaos is breaking out," he wrote.[23]

In September, Shevardnadze flew with Baker on the secretary's air force plane to a meeting in Jackson Hole, Wyoming. In a long talk on the flight, Shevardnadze drove home to Baker the urgency of Gorbachev's problems at home, especially the forces of disintegration pulling the republics away from the center. Baker had not realized in the spring that Gorbachev's situation was so precarious and the window of opportunity was closing. "Our CIA was way, way behind the curve," he said. Baker recalled the first hints came only that summer, and by September, on the flight to Jackson Hole, it "really became obvious."[24] One concrete outcome of the Baker and Shevardnadze meeting in Wyoming was an agreement to exchange data about chemical weapons stockpiles. However, the Soviet Union did not disclose the secret research on the new binary weapon, the *novichok* generation.

Chernyaev called 1989 "The Lost Year." It was also the beginning of the crack-up. A gargantuan superpower was starting to come unglued, with nuclear, chemical and biological weapons strewn across the landscape.

As authority weakened in the Soviet Union, secrets leaked out of the military's most carefully guarded citadels. Velikhov, the progressive physicist and Gorbachev's adviser, personally exposed some of them in another amazing *glasnost* tour. In July, he brought a group of American scientists, led by Cochran of the Natural Resources Defense Council, to the Black Sea to conduct a verification experiment involving a Soviet cruise missile, armed with a nuclear warhead, on a navy ship.[25] It was rare for Americans to get so close to a Soviet weapon. The point was to determine if radiation detectors could spot the presence or absence of a nuclear warhead. While some theoretical studies had been done, the experiment offered a chance to check the radiation detectors against a real weapon. The question was important because of the larger debate at the time about whether there could be effective verification of sea-launched cruise missiles. The United States claimed it was impossible to verify nuclear warheads on naval cruise missiles, and insisted they should be left out of the negotiations on strategic arms. The Soviets wanted to count them— and limit them—because of the American advantage. Velikhov wanted to pierce the veil of secrecy, in hopes it would reduce the danger of the arms race, just as he had done in 1986, bringing Cochran to the secret Semipalatinsk nuclear-testing site, and again in 1987 to the disputed

Krasnoyarsk radar. This time, the KGB tried to stop Velikhov, but Gorbachev overruled them.[26]

On a sunny July 5, 1989, the Americans, joined by a group of Soviet scientists, lugged their radiation detectors aboard the *Slava*, a 610-foot Soviet cruiser at Yalta on the Black Sea. At that moment, the ship held a single SS-N-12 nuclear-armed cruise missile, NATO code-named "Sandbox," stored in the forward, exterior starboard launcher. The Soviets were so nervous about the visit that they had rehearsed it for weeks. They feared the Americans might learn too much about the design of the warhead. The sea was a sparkling blue, and Cochran wore shorts, a baseball cap and a T-shirt as he and his team wrestled the test equipment onto the missile tube to measure the radiation. The evening before the experiment, the Soviets had insisted that, by the plan, the Americans could take only a very short reading, but Cochran got a longer one and plenty of data. Soviet scientists carried out their own tests, too. In one extraordinary *glasnost* moment, the hatch was opened and the Americans took photographs of the dark, menacing tip of the cruise missile, lurking just inside the cover.[27]

No sooner were the scientists back in Moscow on July 7 than Velikhov bundled them off to the airport to see another secret installation. They flew 850 miles east to Chelyabinsk-40, near the town of Kyshtym, a nuclear complex built in Stalin's day, where reactors had churned out plutonium for nuclear weapons. The complex was top secret, but when Velikhov appeared at the gates, they swung open. "It was the first time foreigners were in a town whose whole existence was to destroy America," Velikhov recalled.[28] Von Hippel, the Princeton professor who had known Velikhov since the early 1980s, said that Velikhov wanted the Americans to see a plutonium reactor being shut down, fulfilling a promise Gorbachev had made earlier. After the tour, "We had a fairy-tale-like dinner on an island in the middle of this lake, with a long table with white tablecloth and silver laid out under the birch trees," Von Hippel remembered. Boris Brokhovich, the seventy-three-year-old director of Chelyabinsk-40, stripped naked and plunged into the lake. Several of the Americans then followed him. Not far from the lake was the scene of a devastating accident more than three decades earlier, when a storage tank exploded, throwing 70–80 metric tons of waste containing 20 million curies of radioactivity over the surrounding area. The total release of long-lived fission products, almost comparable to Chernobyl, had contaminated thousands of square kilometers. The accident, September 29, 1957, was hushed up for decades, but revealed after the Soviet collapse.

The last stop on Velikhov's *glasnost* tour was the most daring, the one he had first suggested to the Central Committee, and which they had rejected: the Sary Shagan laser test site. This was the facility the Reagan administration claimed "could be used in an anti-satellite role" and might also be used for missile defense. It was the subject of the ominous illustration in *Soviet Military Power* showing a beam shooting straight up into the heavens. The Soviet leadership knew the claims were untrue but had been embarrassed to admit it. Velikhov brought the Americans to see for themselves on July 8. Von Hippel quickly realized the U.S. claims had been vastly exaggerated. "It was sort of a relic," he said of the lasers he saw there, which were the equivalent of industrial lasers, easily purchased in the West. There was no sign of the war machine the Reagan administration had conjured up. "These guys had been abandoned, a backwater of the military-industrial complex. It was from an earlier time. It was really pitiful." The one "computer" consisted of transistor boards wired together—built before the personal computer. "They had been trying to see whether they could get a reflection off a satellite," he recalled. "They never succeeded."[29]

Velikhov's campaign for openness paid one of its most surprising dividends in 1989, when the Soviet leadership finally admitted that the Krasnoyarsk radar was a violation of the ABM treaty, as Katayev's candid internal *spravka* had indicated in 1987. Shevardnadze acknowledged the treaty violation in a speech to the Soviet legislature, and claimed, "It took some time for the leadership of the country to get acquainted with the whole truth and the history about the station." This was a dubious claim, since Shevardnadze had signed a document laying out the issues two years before. The larger point was clear, however. Gorbachev was coming clean.[30]

The *glasnost* championed by Velikhov did not extend to Biopreparat. On July 27, 1989, the masters of biological weapons met in Moscow at the office of Lev Zaikov, the Politburo member who oversaw the military-industrial complex. According to minutes and handwritten notes in Katayev's files, the meeting began at 6:30 P.M. and was attended by sixteen other officials in addition to Zaikov. The meeting was a Politburo "commission," a formal high-level committee of members of the ruling body of the Soviet Union, and although Gorbachev was not present, he must have known about the discussions. Among those present were Yuri Kalinin, the head of Biopreparat; Valentin Yevstigneev, the head of the military's 15th Main Directorate, which oversaw biological weapons; Foreign Minister Shevardnadze; Vladimir Kryuchkov, head of the KGB, and his predecessor, Viktor Chebrikov, who remained a member of the Politburo; Mikhail Moiseev, chief of the General Staff; and others. Akhromeyev was originally on the list, but his name was crossed out.[31]

The first item on the agenda was listed as "About measures for modernizing the organization of work on special problems." The term "special problems" was a euphemism for biological weapons. The officials were once again worried about the arrival of international inspectors and how to cover up the illegal work. The goal of the meeting was to prepare a Central Committee resolution, which would be a major policy instruction.

Katayev's notes of the meeting are fragmentary and leave unanswered questions. But they also open a window on high-level discussions about the illicit germ warfare program—evidence of a remarkable back-and-forth discussion that was kept utterly secret.

Kalinin opened the meeting, suggesting that biological weapons were cheap.

The Katayev notation:

Per 1	conventional	2,000 doll.
	Nuclear	800 "
	Chem	60 "
	Bio	1 "

The unit of measurement is not stated, but apparently was dollars. Experts in nonproliferation had worried about the same thing for many years—biological weapons could be the poor man's atomic bomb.

Then, according to Katayev's handwritten notes, Kalinin complained that the United States had concealed the location of work on biological weapons.

Next, Kalinin reported to the group on the status of preparations for international arms inspections. Some facilities were being modified so they could be displayed as centers for civilian medicines. According to Katayev's notes, Kalinin said the cleanup would have to remove any speck of evidence that would point to a weapons program. "Today we are not finding spores," Katayev wrote. "But possibly in pockets."

If inspectors came, Kalinin said, they would be given the explanation "these are for manufacturing vaccines."

Kalinin said he needed eighteen months to bring two more sites into order, and appeared to be seeking permission.

Shevardnadze, who had endorsed the idea of surprise inspections in his speech in Geneva, interjected. "Violation or not?" he demanded, according to Katayev's notes. "What is the purpose of legends?" or cover stories. "There will be a convention in a year's time—any enterprise will be under verification." This was a reference to a chemical weapons treaty, or international convention, which would include provisions for surprise inspections as a verification measure. It was being hammered out by negotiators.

Zaikov asked why Kalinin needed the eighteen months. Couldn't he be ready sooner?

Kalinin said something about "secret designs," perhaps hinting that more time was needed to hide the true purpose of the facilities. Katayev noted, cryptically, and without specifying which facilities were being discussed: "All recipes are destroyed. Stockpiles liquidated . . . Equipment is multi-purpose—remains. It serves to manufacture medications. We are going to preserve the equipment for the time being."

Zaikov wanted the equipment taken down, too. He was also worried about documents, and wanted them destroyed. At one point he suggested all the documents be "liquidated" in three months. Katayev wrote another cryptic line in his notes, quoting Shevardnadze: "What we violate and what we don't."

A little more than two months after the meeting in Zaikov's office, the Central Committee issued the resolution, ordering more cover-up activity, with an eye toward possible future inspections, according to records in Katayev's archives. This instruction was to recall all documentation from sites "connected with manufacturing of special-purpose product," design new means of disguising them and modernize facilities so they could appear to be manufacturing defensive biological agents, such as vaccines. The goal, according to the resolution, was to preserve "the achieved parity in the field of military biology."[32]

A very small group of intelligence officials in the United States and Great Britain worked on biological weapons. They were mainly technical specialists, and they were outnumbered in the intelligence and policy community, where vast staffs worked on nuclear and strategic weapons, and on topics such as the Soviet economy. The CIA even had a full-time analyst devoted to monitoring canned goods in Soviet stores. The germ warfare experts felt like a lonely band, warning of dangers that were often not taken seriously by others and for which they could not offer absolute proof. Christopher Davis, who served on the British Defense Intelligence staff for ten years as the senior specialist on biological weapons, said that methods that had worked for counting nuclear missile silos were virtually useless when it came to assessing a biological weapons program. The missiles and hardware could be tracked from above, but not the pathogens. "A building is a building at the end of the day," he explained. "It might have some strange features but there is little one can conclude about its function without x-ray eyes. You can't tell what anyone is doing inside, and that's the key question. In intelligence terms, it's a very hard target."[33]

The claims of the biological weapons experts met with deep skepticism by other defense, intelligence and policy officials. "The biological weapons clique inside Washington was so doomsdayish, that they tended to undermine their own credibility," said Doug MacEachin, who had become arms control director at the CIA in March 1989. "It never had a whole lot of credibility. They went beyond the evidence too many times." MacEachin was also influenced by his own calculation that biological weapons would have little use on the battlefield; thus no one would go to all the trouble, certainly not in the nuclear age.[34]

In the autumn of 1989, Ken Alibek, deputy director of Biopreparat, recalled visiting Obolensk, south of Moscow. On the first floor of the big

new building, in the auditorium, the annual review of work at the institute was held. "We were not allowed to bring briefcases or bags inside the
room," Alibek recalled. "We could take notes, but they were gathered up
by security guards after each meeting. We had to get special permission to
see them again."

The next-to-last speaker was Sergei Popov, the young researcher who
had worked at both Koltsovo and Obolensk. He approached the lectern
to give a report on a project that Alibek called "Bonfire."

"Few paid attention at first. Work on Bonfire had dragged on for some
fifteen years, and most of us had given up hope of ever achieving results."

But Alibek added that his attention perked up when Popov
announced that a suitable bacterial host had been found. This was the
two-punch weapon in which one agent would be the vehicle and the
attack on the immune system would be the second, deadly strike. Alibek
recalled watching an experiment involving animals. Alibek wrote in his
memoir they were rabbits, but Popov said later they were guinea pigs.
Behind glass walls in a laboratory, a half-dozen were strapped to boards
to keep them from squirming free. Each was fitted with a masklike
mechanical device connected to a ventilation system. Watching from the
other side of the glass, a technician pressed a button, delivering small
bursts of the genetically altered pathogen to each animal. When the
experiment was over, the animals were returned to their cages for examination. They all developed symptoms of one sickness, such as high temperatures. In one test, several also developed signs of another illness.
"They twitched and they lay still," Alibek recalled. "Their hindquarters
had been paralyzed—evidence of myelin toxin."

It was Popov's two-punch killer agent on display. "The test was a success," Alibek recalled. "A single genetically engineered agent had produced symptoms of two different diseases, one of which could not be
traced." The room fell silent. "We all recognized the implications of what
the scientist had achieved. A new class of weapons had been found."[35]

Popov vividly recalled working with the guinea pigs. By 1989, the scientists at Obolensk had reached a period of uncertainty. There was less
money than before. "It was a frustrating time of disappointment and

moral challenge," he said. "And at that time, I made a commitment to myself. I committed myself to never deal with animal experiments again. The trigger was my last huge experiment with guinea pigs. Something like a few hundred guinea pigs had been held in a containment facility. I and my colleagues visited them every day. Wearing space suits, we fed the survivors and took out the dead. I was very shocked with how it went. Nothing new, but it was unpleasant. Absolutely unpleasant.

"I just couldn't stand any more the conditions the animals were held in. We saw animals dying, awfully, starving, experiencing paralysis and convulsions in conditions neglecting the very sense of life. The agent paralyzed half of the animal's body. I did not want to be involved in this any more."[36]

THE GREATEST BREAKTHROUGH

Vladimir Pasechnik was reserved, diffident and modest, but his face brightened when talk turned to science. In a photograph taken in the 1980s, when he was an institute director in Leningrad, he was wearing a corduroy jacket, glancing up from his desk, creases across his forehead, his hair receding, eyes inquiring, one hand holding down a notebook or journal. Born in 1937, Pasechnik lost both his parents in the siege of Stalingrad. He had overcome many obstacles to study as a physicist, and graduated at the top of his class at the Leningrad Polytechnic Institute. But the sacrifices of the war left a deep scar on Pasechnik, and he was determined to use his science for peaceful purposes. After graduation, he became a researcher at the Institute of Higher Molecular Compounds in Leningrad, attracted by the chance to create new antibiotics and treat diseases like cancer.[1] In 1974, one of Pasechnik's professors was asked to recommend a young researcher for a special assignment. Pasechnik was selected to set up a new scientific research facility, the Institute of Ultra Pure Biological Preparations in Leningrad.[2] It seemed a promising opportunity—the new institute would have resources for the best equipment and could attract the finest talent. He took the job, and in the years that followed he demonstrated ability as a talented and strong-willed manager. By 1981, the institute had become one of the most advanced microbiology facilities in the Soviet Union. It was also part of Biopreparat, the secret Soviet biological weapons machine. Pasechnik later told people that it was about this time that he realized the research could not be just for defensive purposes, as he originally believed, but was for offensive weapons.

While Domaradsky and Popov attempted to modify the genetic makeup of pathogens, Pasechnik's mission was more practical: to optimize the pathogens for use in combat, and to build superefficient industrial methods to produce them. If anthrax or other agents were to be deployed in wartime, they needed to be manufactured in large batches, remain stable, survive dissemination into the air and be effectively dispersed. Pasechnik's job was to find ways to prepare and manufacture the pathogens so they could be weaponized without losing effectiveness and virulence. Working with models of the deadly agents, he sought to master the complex process of how to concentrate the pathogens and turn them into aerosols.[3]

Soviet biological weapons builders were bedeviled with complications. Before being deployed as an aerosol, a pathogen must be mixed in a proper "formulation," with the addition of chemicals and other substances, specific for each germ. If done correctly, it will maintain the pathogen's virulence or toxicity while in storage or in the weapon. But if done incorrectly, the agents may die or lose their power. They can also clog nozzles or clump up inside a weapon, which would make it ineffective, or they can be neutralized by the environment once disseminated. Also, they can face other complications that render them ineffective, such as the anthrax spores killed by phage lysis bacteria in Stepnogorsk. Moreover, it was essential to keep the particles small, to penetrate deep into the lungs of the victims. According to U.S. estimates, the ideal size is one to five microns; a micron is one-millionth of a meter. If larger, they would be filtered out by the upper respiratory tract before reaching the lungs; larger particles also settle out of the air more quickly. However, Biopreparat and the Soviet military produced agents up to twelve microns, knowing that, even if they did not reach the lungs, they would still infect the victim once trapped inside the body in the upper respiratory tract.[4]

One of Pasechnik's most important inventions was a "milling" machine that used a powerful blast of air to turn batches of dried agent into a fine powder. He also developed new methods of microencapsulation—covering the tiny particles containing the infectious agents in polymer capsules to preserve and protect them from ultraviolet light. Pasechnik frequently accompanied the officers from the 15th Main Directorate of the Defense Ministry when they visited the research institutes. Popov recalled that Pasechnik sat in the front row, writing everything down in his notebooks.

Alibek, then first deputy director of Biopreparat, recalled in his memoir how he had once spent a long, tiring day in Leningrad with Pasechnik, going over projects at the institute. "Pasechnik seemed sad and a bit depressed as he drove me to the railway station, where I planned to catch the overnight train back to Moscow. I asked him if anything was wrong. Posing such a personal question to a man like Pasechnik was risky. He was one of our senior scientists, twelve years older than me, and he had always been somewhat aloof. I worried that he might take offense."

"Can I be honest with you," Pasechnik replied. "It's like this. I am fifty-one years old, and I am going through a strange time in my life. I don't know if I have accomplished what I want to. And they're going to make me retire soon." Alibek knew that fifty-five was the mandatory retirement age in Biopreparat, but recalled that he clapped Pasechnik on the shoulder and told him not to worry. "Four years is a long time, and they could be your best years!"

Pasechnik smiled thinly, Alibek said.[5]

But this conversation did not even begin to reveal the depth of Pasechnik's despair. According to those who knew him and later spoke with him, Pasechnik had found it increasingly difficult to justify his work devoted to weapons. Each year, the tasks assigned to him by the military were more demanding, as they sought still more virulent and effective agents and ever-larger industrial capacity for producing them.

Foremost among his tasks, Pasechnik worked on creating models of a plague agent that would be resistant to antibiotics. If the models worked, they could easily be adapted for the real *Yersinia pestis*. His dream of working on a cure for cancer was fading. His promise to himself to use science for peaceful goals was unfulfilled. His personal crisis was profound. Pasechnik felt trapped, and began to plan an escape.

In October 1989, Pasechnik went to France on a business trip to purchase laboratory equipment. Alibek had approved the trip and forgotten about it. While in France, Pasechnik received a message to return for an urgent meeting of all Biopreparat institute directors in a few days' time. Pasechnik told a colleague traveling with him to go on ahead, he would follow the next day. When the colleague arrived back in Moscow, alone, he found Pasechnik's wife waiting at the airport—and she was surprised Pasechnik was not on the plane. In Paris, Pasechnik walked to the Canadian Embassy, knocked on the door and announced that he was a scientist at a secret biological weapons laboratory in the Soviet Union and wanted to defect. The Canadians shut the door in his face. Pasechnik felt desperate. He feared going to the United States or Britain, thinking either country might force him to go back to work on biological weapons. But with few options left, he reluctantly called the British Embassy from a phone booth and repeated that he was a Soviet germ weapon specialist and wanted to defect.

The British Secret Intelligence Service responded with alacrity. He was picked up in a car, flown to Heathrow on a British Airways shuttle flight and taken to a remote safe house on the English coast.[6]

It was a rather miserable, cold and wet Friday afternoon in London, October 27, 1989. The workday was nearly over and dark had fallen. Christopher Davis, a surgeon commander in the Royal Navy, educated at Oxford and London universities, and the senior biological warfare specialist on the Defense Intelligence Staff, recalled that he was looking forward to the weekend. He had cleared his desk. There was not a piece of paper on it, everything locked away, as required. Then his phone rang around 5 P.M., and his boss, Brian Jones, was on the line.

"Chris, you better come to my office," Jones said. Davis went to the small office, not much larger than his own. Jones handed Davis a one-page document, a message from the British Secret Intelligence Service, known as MI6, describing the arrival of a Soviet defector, and a brief summary of what the defector was telling them.

"Oh, shit," Davis said. His eyes were riveted on one word on the page, "plague." He immediately realized the significance. He told Jones, "The Soviet Union is developing strategic biological weapons. Plague is not a battlefield weapon!"[7]

———

In Moscow, Alibek's secretary rushed into his office on Monday morning. Pasechnik's deputy, Nikolai Frolov, was on the line from Leningrad and needed to talk to Alibek immediately. Alibek recalled he was so overworked, he felt like putting his head on his desk and going to sleep.

"We've got a problem," Frolov said, sounding strained. "Pasechnik hasn't come."

Alibek replied reassuringly, saying it was no problem if Pasechnik was a little late to the meeting of institute directors. "No! No!" Frolov nearly yelled into the phone. "I mean, he hasn't come back from France!"

Frolov's account of what happened spilled out in a torrent of excited words, Alibek recalled. In France, Pasechnik had been up all night, lying in bed, fully dressed, before telling his colleague to go on ahead without him. When the colleague got ready to leave for the airport, Pasechnik hugged him and said *proshchai,* or farewell, rather than the usual *do svidaniya,* or until we meet again.

"I listened to the entire story with a knot tightening in my stomach," Alibek said. He went down the hall to see Kalinin, the director of Biopreparat. When told of Pasechnik's disappearance, Alibek said, it was as if Kalinin had just heard about the death of a close relative. Kalinin went pale. He told Alibek he would call Gorbachev immediately.[8]

In the days after he defected, Pasechnik was constantly nervous. He had left his family behind. He was frightened that he would be tried as a war criminal, or pilloried in public, or forced to go back to work on the pathogens, or returned to the Soviet Union. He knew volumes about the research at Biopreparat and was terrified of the British reaction. "It must have been like walking the plank and not knowing if the waters are going to be shark infested or you are going to make it to shore and be okay," recalled Davis. "That's what made it all the more brave, I think, in making the decision he could no longer do what he was doing. It was an exceptional move."

The case was given a code name, Truncate. Davis became one of the two main debriefers, along with a man from MI6, and periodically they were joined by David Kelly, who was head of microbiology at Porton Down, the British chemical and biological defense research facility. Davis was among the small band of allied biological weapons experts who had puzzled for years over Soviet activities. When Pasechnik was interviewed, an invented name was always used, such as "Michael," but Davis knew Pasechnik's real identity. They spoke English, although sometimes Davis had to ask for a translation, as when Pasechnik tried to describe a hamadryas baboon. When he wasn't speaking about the Soviet system, Pasechnik was curious about Britain, asking questions about family life and communities, and marveling, for example, that Kelly had a personal computer at home.

What Davis and his colleague learned from Pasechnik was more revealing than all the fragments of information they had accumulated over the years. "It was an extraordinary moment," Davis said. "If you're an intelligence officer, this doesn't happen but once in a lifetime. Maybe never in a lifetime. It was just one of those exceptional moments. Prior to the time when he came, there were no defections of any note. Neither were there any good, high-level human intelligence sources in place." He added, "The fact that Vladimir defected was one of the key acts of the entire ending of the Soviet Union and the end of the Cold War. It was the greatest breakthrough we ever had."

What Pasechnik told them was remarkable. The Soviet Union had not only weaponized classic pathogens, but was seeking to create new agents designed to be resistant to antibiotics and to break down the defenses of the victim. The Soviets were also working on vaccines that would shield their germ warfare operators from harm, and they were developing detectors to sense a possible attack. Not only was there a large program devoted to battlefield weapons, which were for short-range attacks, but the emphasis on plague and smallpox suggested a focus on long-range, strategic weapons. Pasechnik noted that the Soviets had not yet achieved one of their prime goals, the creation of a new biological warfare agent completely resistant to treatment, but the work was still underway.

Pasechnik also revealed how the Soviet program might ultimately be concealed, perhaps with small, mobile laboratories that could never be found. Pasechnik told them about the sprawling network of laboratories and production facilities hidden in Biopreparat that had cost in excess of

1.5 billion rubles over fifteen years and employed tens of thousands of scientists and support workers. He told them how the Interbranch Scientific and Technical Council, where Domaradsky had once worked, was responsible for coordinating and administering the germ warfare effort with money from the military. He revealed that the Soviets had created a system of false financial plans for the institutes, purporting to show they were working on innocent civilian biotechnology projects, in order to cover up the actual military biological weapons work.

While hesitant at first, Pasechnik gained confidence over time, and his knowledge was relayed in a way that was calm and precise. "He was a very frank source," said Jones. According to Davis, Pasechnik was clear about "what he knew personally, or as a result of data that he was aware of, and what he had been told, and what he had just found out chatting with other people. He never, ever stretched things."

Only three months after the Politburo commission met in Zaikov's office to discuss the cover-up, Pasechnik was sitting in Britain, laying the Kremlin's darkest secrets on the table. His information helped the British draw up a list of twenty excuses the Soviets might use to hide their illegal work. As Pasechnik talked, British policy-makers began to realize that some of their core assumptions in recent decades had been wrong.

Jones, who earned his doctorate in metallurgy, had just two years earlier become head of unit DI-53, which analyzed nuclear, chemical and biological weapons intelligence data, from all sources, for the U.K. Defense Ministry. The focus was overwhelmingly on nuclear weapons materials and chemistry; Jones recalled that his unit had just two people who specialized in chemical and biological warfare. One of them was Davis.

When the British gave up their biological weapons program in the late 1950s, the central assumption then, and since, had been that nuclear weapons were the most effective deterrent. "The same year our nuclear capability became active, we dropped our biological weapons program and chemical weapons program," Jones said. "Nuclear would do for us." Then, in the early 1970s, the Biological Weapons Convention was signed; British diplomats played a major role. The popular assumption, he added, was that biological weapons had no utility in modern warfare.

"They are not a deterrent, they are difficult to use defensively, they didn't fit, as it were, into Western perceptions of useful military material," Jones recalled. An added factor was Nixon's 1969 decision to close the U.S. program. Jones added, "The Russians had nuclear weapons—why on earth would they need biological weapons?" The British postulated that, if the Soviets were doing anything, it might be trying to create an improved battlefield chemical or biological weapon that would emit toxins, perhaps a sort of hybrid chemical-biological weapon. They assumed such a new weapon would be used for close-in battlefield combat against troops. "There was this idea that this is what the Russians were really after," Jones said.[9]

But Pasechnik's debriefing opened up the British thinking to a much broader spectrum of weapons, ranging from tactical to strategic. The Soviet program was far more ambitious than the West had ever imagined. This was evident from the moment Pasechnik began talking about the pathogens he knew the most about, such as *Yersinia pestis*, the agent that causes plague. Pasechnik said that great emphasis had been placed on the perfection of pneumonic plague as a weapons agent by optimizing its production, storage, aerosol dissemination and resistance to antibiotics. Pasechnik said his institute had worked on models of the plague agent to create a kind of super-plague.

One of the most chilling disclosures Pasechnik made was that the Soviet military had already weaponized plague and was pouring it into some kind of warheads, which had to be refilled every few months. In order to produce enough agent, the industrial capacity had been scaled up, reaching two metric tons a year. He revealed the Soviets had tested the plague agent on baboons on Vozrozhdeniye Island in the Aral Sea as recently as 1989.

As the secrets spilled out, the mention of plague carried special weight. "You do not choose plague to put on a battlefield," Davis said. "You choose plague because you're going to take out the other person's country. Full stop. That's what it is about."[10]

"Plague is highly transmissible. Remember, one third of the population of Europe disappeared in the 13th Century with plague. And it's quick. If you don't get treatment within 12–24 hours at best, after symptoms appear in pneumonic plague, you will die, whether we give you antibiotics or not. It's over."

This was Pasechnik's message. The target of the plague weapon was unprotected populations. "That was the gift, to realign the thinking, to move it back to the traditional use of biological weapons as a weapon of mass destruction," Jones said.

Later, Pasechnik told the British his institute was tackling an assignment to develop a method of aerosol distribution that would work from a vehicle flying two hundred feet above the ground. Pasechnik did not work on the vehicle itself, only the dissemination system, but the British had no difficulty guessing what kind of weapon flew at two hundred feet: a cruise missile. The fast-flying, low-altitude cruise was a modern weapon, feared for its ability to fly under radar. A cruise missile carrying deadly biological agents could be launched from a submarine, release the pathogens somewhat away from the target, and then disappear. The thought of it startled Pasechnik's debriefers.

Over months of conversations, a picture emerged not only of the traditional pathogens, but also of the more advanced genetic engineering underway at Koltsovo and Obolensk. Although Pasechnik's institute had only a specialized role, he was aware of the broader effort to boost resistance to antibiotics. Pasechnik also told the British of the work being done to fool the body's immune system. Pasechnik was careful to delineate where the research had not borne fruit; he noted that improved plague had not been the result of genetic engineering, but rather of conventional genetic selection techniques. Pasechnik also told the British that genetic engineering of tularemia—Domaradsky's dream—had been a goal, but was unsuccessful in the field tests.[11]

Pasechnik knew the people in the system, including the bosses, Alibek and Kalinin, at the Biopreparat headquarters on Samokatnaya Street. He knew the names and missions of the separate military biowarfare facilities in Kirov, Sverdlovsk and Zagorsk. He knew of the massive anthrax factory at Stepnogorsk. Pasechnik's information showed conclusively the Soviet Union had violated the Biological Weapons Convention and deceived the outside world. The Soviets concealed their misdeeds under layers and layers of disguise, and Pasechnik peeled it away.

The disclosures soon led to a quiet debate in British intelligence and policy circles: did Gorbachev and Shevardnadze, the Soviet reformers, know about the dangerous agents in the test tubes? Pasechnik was perplexed by the frequent questions he got from his debriefers about Gorbachev. He said Gorbachev *must* have known if Shevardnadze knew. That was how the system worked. And Pasechnik was certain that Shevardnadze had attended some of the high-level meetings in 1988. Davis's assessment strongly supported this view as well.

If Gorbachev knew, then the British had to question their assumptions about him, too. Thatcher was the first Western leader to declare that Gorbachev was a man with whom she could do business. In Washington, after nearly a year of dithering, Bush was also planning his first summit with Gorbachev. Was this a man they could do business with, or was he the leader of a country and a system that created—and was still creating—the most destructive biological weapons mankind had ever known, in violation of all treaty promises?

In London, the revelations from Pasechnik were summarized into a quick note for the Joint Intelligence Committee. The first recipient of such reports is always Her Majesty, The Queen. The second is the prime minister, who at the time was Thatcher.

In early November 1989, while Pasechnik was still being debriefed, the Berlin Wall crumbled. Over the previous summer, Hungary had opened its border with Austria. Thousands of East Germans had flooded West German embassies in Budapest and Prague. In October, Gorbachev had visited Berlin and signaled that the Soviet Union would not intervene, a lesson drawn from his searing visit to Prague after the Soviet invasion in 1968 and his soul-searching talks with his best friend Mlynář. In an evening torchlight ceremony on that Berlin visit, handpicked party youth activists had stunned Gorbachev by ignoring the hard-line party boss Erich Honecker on the reviewing stand and instead shouting to Gorbachev, "*Perestroika!* Gorbachev! Help us!"[12] Gorbachev had become a beacon of change that was now shaking the very pillars of the empire he ruled. In early November, roiled by public protests, a new government in East Germany permitted travel to the West through Czechoslovakia, prompting tens of thousands of people to crowd the roads. Hastily, new rules for travel were drafted by the government, and the plan was to announce them November 10, but inadvertently the decision was read aloud at a government press conference at the end of the day November

9.[13] News reports vaguely suggested that East Germans could get visas to leave the country immediately through border crossings, touching off a frenzy of excitement. Rumors spread that all travel restrictions were being lifted. Thousands of people gathered at the Berlin Wall in the evening. The guards, who had no instructions, just opened the gates, and the Berlin Wall was breached twenty-eight years after it was first erected. The long division of Europe was over.

In Washington, reporters were summoned to the Oval Office at 3:34 P.M. Bush was nervously twisting a pen in his hands. He later recalled feeling awkward and uncomfortable. Ever cautious, he was worried that any comments he made could trigger a Soviet crackdown. The memory of the Tiananmen Square massacre was still fresh. Lesley Stahl of CBS News remarked that "this is a sort of great victory for our side in the big East-West battle, but you don't seem elated. I'm wondering if you're thinking of the problems."

"I am not an emotional kind of guy," Bush said.[14]

In Moscow, Chernyaev wrote in his diary the next day, November 10, "The Berlin Wall has collapsed. This entire era in the history of the socialist system is over."

After the fall of the wall, even more threatening storms were on the horizon for Gorbachev. The Soviet economy plummeted in 1989; there were acute shortages of goods, along with a grain crisis and declining oil production. *Perestroika* had not produced better living standards. At a Politburo meeting on the day the Berlin Wall fell, Gorbachev was preoccupied not with Eastern Europe, but the possibility that the Soviet Union would disintegrate, as internal republics began to consider breaking away. The leaders of Estonia and Latvia, two tiny Baltic republics, had told Gorbachev in recent days "they have a feeling that there is no other way than to leave the USSR," Gorbachev told the Politburo.[15]

After Bush had waited almost a year to engage Gorbachev, he was now confronted by a confluence of serious troubles: the future of Germany, and indeed Europe, was up for grabs; Gorbachev was in deeper and deeper trouble at home; and arms control negotiations were going nowhere. When Bush and Gorbachev finally met in a summit December 2–3 on the Mediterranean island of Malta, severe winds and high waves lashed the harbor as they talked aboard the Soviet cruise liner *Maxim Gorky*. Bush reassured Gorbachev that he supported *perestroika*, but he also defended his words of caution when the Berlin Wall came down. "I do not intend to jump up on the Wall," Bush said, mangling one of his favorite aphorisms, that he would not "dance on the wall" to embarrass the Soviet leader. "Well," Gorbachev replied, "jumping on the Wall is not a good activity for a president." They laughed. For eight hours, they talked about a ban on chemical weapons; how to accelerate negotiations on strategic nuclear weapons and reduce troop levels in Europe; the revolution in Central Europe; Nicaragua; Afghanistan; and Soviet economic and trade woes. Not once did they mention biological weapons.[16]

In Moscow in late 1989, Pasechnik's defection sent shock waves through the small group of Soviet officials who knew. On December 6, the Kremlin made an urgent decision. According to a *spravka* in Katayev's files, the Ministry of the Medical Industry, which had jurisdiction over Biopreparat, was ordered by a Central Committee resolution—effectively a decision by the Politburo—to accelerate the preparation of facilities for possible foreign inspection. The order said the facilities must be ready by July 1, 1990, "to prevent undesirable consequences" from the defection of Pasechnik.[17]

Alibek recalled in his memoir that "we took comfort in the fact that there were many things Pasechnik didn't know. He had not been personally involved in weapons production, and much of what he could tell Western intelligence agencies was likely to be hearsay at best, thanks to our internal security regime. Nevertheless, Pasechnik's interrogators would have learned the secret that had been kept hidden for so long: the real function of Biopreparat."[18]

Alibek was right that Pasechnik did not bring the British information about weapons production. But Pasechnik had spent many hours visiting the microbiology institutes and taking notes about their activities. His memory was sharp.

In early 1990, a very modest effort inside the Soviet system at more openness about the Sverdlovsk anthrax epidemic was immediately crushed.

By this time, Gorbachev and Shevardnadze had deeply antagonized the military. They negotiated the destruction of hundreds of the most modern Soviet nuclear warheads and missiles and slashed military spending. The Warsaw Pact was disintegrating as Soviet troops made an unceremonious and precipitous retreat. All of these actions were in keeping with Gorbachev's intention to end the hypermilitarized state and ease the burden of defense on the economy and society, but the military took it hard, very hard. They were furious, especially at Shevardnadze.

On January 5, Shevardnadze's ministry tried to force a little openness about biological weapons. The ministry distributed a draft Central Committee resolution stating that the best way to deflect outside demands about biological weapons, in the wake of the defection of Pasechnik, would be to propose an exchange of data with the Americans in two areas: weapons work before the Biological Weapons Convention went into effect in 1975, and information on how any biological weapons development since then was being converted to civilian purposes. The Foreign Ministry also suggested that if specific questions came up about the Sverdlovsk anthrax incident, the Americans should be told that "indeed, an accident took place," an investigation was underway and the results might be shared with them. Shevardnadze's deputy for arms control, Viktor Karpov, circulated this document. He sent the draft to officials at Biopreparat (Alibek was on the list), the military (including the 15th Main Directorate, which handled bioweapons), the KGB, the Health Ministry, the Academy of Sciences and others.

Five days later, the military exploded. Dmitri Yazov, the defense minister, wrote a letter to all who had received the draft proposal. He complained the military had been left totally out of the loop. The military realized, correctly, that the offer of a data exchange would "radically contradict" previous statements that "the Soviet Union has never worked on nor produced nor possessed stockpiles of biological weapons," Yazov said. In other words, the Foreign Ministry had proposed to open the window on the lie, and the military wanted to slam it shut before it got out.

On Sverdlovsk, Yazov insisted "there were no explosions and accidents" at the facility. The epidemic was caused by tainted meat, a government commission had determined at the time, and "at the present time there exists no new information or circumstances that would force a doubt about the correctness of the conclusions."

The military was so alarmed that it demanded Karpov recall all fifteen copies of the draft resolution. The documents show the military prevailed. The language in the Foreign Ministry draft was immediately changed. Karpov sent out the amended instructions the next day, January 11.[19]

From October 1989 through January and February 1990, the British worked long hours to sift through the mountain of new information they received from Pasechnik. Details began to be shared with the United States. At the CIA headquarters, Doug MacEachin, the arms control director, received a file of reports coming in from London, not yet formally circulated in the CIA, summarizing the debriefings with Pasechnik, concluding that the Soviets were building strategic biological weapons. Joshua Lederberg, the Nobel Prize–winning microbiologist, went to Britain to interview Pasechnik, and came away shocked by the revelation of the smallpox program and convinced that Pasechnik was genuine. MacEachin asked the CIA's technical teams to help him corroborate what the defector was saying, using satellite data to locate facilities and other details.

Like the British policy staff, MacEachin had long assumed the Soviets would not build germ weapons if they had nuclear ones. "We also had authoritative information that the common view amongst the professional Soviet military, the line officers, was that biological weapons and chemical weapons are not weapons, they're terrorism devices," MacEachin said. "You know, they're no good in the battlefield. How are you going to deploy a BW weapon on the battlefield?" He said that while biological weapons would cause mass casualties in a city, "bugs and gas are not the weapons that professional soldiers use. And we had plenty of evidence the Soviet military was very professional. One of the major arguments against putting a BW weapon on a SS-18 was: what a waste of time. It didn't track."

MacEachin took the new information to a meeting of the key arms control policy-makers at the White House, known as the "ungroup." Out of a fear of leaks and bureaucratic infighting over arms control, the Bush White House had decided to handle the most sensitive matters in a very small circle. The members came from the departments of State and Defense, the CIA, the Joint Chiefs of Staff, the Arms Control and Disarmament Agency and the Energy Department as well as the National Security Council. No assistants were allowed to sit on the back benches, no leaks were tolerated and the very existence of the group was known to only a few people. It was called the "ungroup" because formally it did not exist.[20]

After the Malta summit, the group had plenty to deal with: troop reductions in Europe, chemical weapons negotiations and pressure to reach a new strategic arms treaty by early June, when Bush and Gorbachev had scheduled a full summit in Washington. When all the regular business was finished at the ungroup one day in February, MacEachin asked everyone to wait. They had a frightening new problem which he described as "a turd in the punchbowl."

What he told them next was astounding: a high-level human source had provided the outlines of a vast, secret Soviet biological weapons program, concealed in a civilian organization, Biopreparat. For the members of the ungroup, this was a potential time bomb. Every day, Gorbachev was sinking deeper. Bush had already put U.S. diplomacy on pause for a year. MacEachin told the ungroup, referring to the defector, "If what he says turns out to be even partially corroborated, it is of sufficient significance that, if we don't resolve this problem, we ain't going to get a single arms control agreement." MacEachin believed that hawks in Congress, including the conservative senator Jesse Helms of North Carolina, who was the ranking Republican on the Senate Foreign Relations Committee and was already attacking Gorbachev for violations of other treaties, would seize on the news to block any more agreements with Moscow. "Can you imagine Jesse Helms sitting up there with that in his hand?" MacEachin recalled. The senator would say, he predicted, "You can't deal with the Soviets, they're liars, cheaters, bums, rats, scums—and I've got the list right here in my hand." MacEachin told the ungroup that the British defector was credible and "we're going to try and make sure we corroborate. He's given us so many details that we've got to be able to do some corroboration."[21]

Bush decided to keep the story of Biopreparat under wraps, just as the Soviets had themselves done for so many years. The United States and Great Britain at last possessed tangible evidence that had so long eluded the experts on Soviet biological weapons, but because of all the pressures building up on Gorbachev, because of the dramatic rush of events in Europe, the president decided not to go public. To do so would not only trigger outrage in Congress, it might also severely damage Gorbachev and Shevardnadze at a time when the Soviet leaders could ill afford it. Dennis Ross, who was director of the Policy Planning office at the State Department and a top assistant to Baker, recalled, "Gorbachev and Shevardnadze were under enormous pressure. We wondered, what can *their* traffic bear? And we were trying to get [a unified] Germany into NATO. Germany in NATO is a strategic architecture for the next generation. Germany is bigger than anything else. And you're going to introduce *this*? There were competing objectives and we had to make a choice."[22] When Baker met Gorbachev on February 9, not a word was said about biological weapons. MacEachin said that in the spring the CIA briefed only a small circle of lawmakers on Capitol Hill, and swore them to maximum secrecy. The story did not leak.

Alibek recalled in his memoir that disclosure might have forced Gorbachev to abandon the whole biological weapons enterprise on the spot. But that is not what happened. Bush's decision "gave us unexpected breathing space," Alibek said. "We continued to research and develop new weapons for two more years."

Gorbachev's power ebbed in the spring of 1990. Mass protests were held against his rule, the Baltic republics declared independence and Yeltsin became the chairman of the Russian parliament. The Congress of People's Deputies, the legislature that Gorbachev's reforms had created, repealed the Communist Party's monopoly on political power. Chernyaev, Gorbachev's closest adviser, was riddled with doubt. "I was deeply worried about what was happening in the country," he said. "Most of all because nothing was working out the way Gorbachev intended, much less how it really ought to have."[23] Gorbachev wanted to save his country with his reforms, but instead it was coming apart at the seams. When Shevardnadze came to Washington April 4–6, the Americans realized the Soviet military was in a state of near rebellion against its civilian leadership. At one point, Shevardnadze retracted a concession about cruise missiles he had made to Baker in February. "I had the image of a diplomat with a political gun to his head," Baker recalled. "Any step forward could lead to suicide."[24]

Alibek at this point was still a company man, deputy director of Bio-preparat, working at the headquarters. But he also had a change of view, and wondered how much longer they could go on covering up the biological weapons program. "Like everyone else, I was furious with Pasechnik and believed he had put our security at risk," he said. "But where others desperately wanted to preserve the status quo, I saw no choice but to change course." He thought they should mothball the pathogen production lines, while preserving the sample strains and research facilities. The laboratories would be easier to hide—they could be portrayed as making vaccines—than the factories mass-producing anthrax and small-pox. "If circumstances required, we could always recover our strength. So long as we had the strains in our vaults, we were only three to four months away from full capacity."[25] Alibek said that the KGB chairman, Vladimir Kryuchkov, sent a memorandum to Gorbachev recommending the "liquidation of our biological weapons production lines" because of the Pasechnik defection. The memorandum argued that the germ warfare program was no longer a secret from the West, so the Soviet Union should "cut our losses" and close down the factories.[26]

But rather than shut down the biowarfare machine, the system applied more camouflage. A detailed plan to deflect American questions about biological weapons was approved at a Politburo meeting April 25, 1990. The plan was to offer what would seem to be more openness, an exchange of *visits*. These would not be intrusive, formal inspections, but rather choreographed visits to select Soviet laboratories that had already been well scrubbed, as well as demands to see American sites and an exchange of information about defensive work, such as vaccines. The written plan, contained in five pages of "additional directives" and three appendixes approved by the Politburo, included an assertion that the Soviet side sincerely wanted to establish more "openness" and "trust" about biological weapons. One appendix was a draft agreement for both sides to sign, titled, in part, "measures to strengthen trust and broaden openness." But it was all doublespeak. The true intent was to take the heat off Biopreparat. To deflect questions about the 1979 anthrax accident, another appendix offered "informational material about the Sverdlovsk facility." This three-page document claimed Sverdlovsk had worked on vaccines against anthrax. It said nothing about the 1979 accident, nor about work on offensive biological weapons.[27]

At one point, Alibek recalled, he was given the job of getting a signature on the document about an exchange of visits from Karpov, the Foreign Ministry official for arms control. "I headed through the midday Moscow traffic to Smolenskaya," the square where the ministry, in one of the distinctive Stalin-era wedding-cake towers, looms over the city.

"I didn't need an armed guard, since there were no state secrets in my briefcase," Alibek said. "Just a portfolio of lies."

Karpov read the papers, then looked up at Alibek, he recalled. "You know, young man, I see a troubled future ahead of you."

"I was taken aback," Alibek recalled in his memoir. He protested that others had signed the documents. "I am just the courier."

Karpov shook his head wearily, Alibek recalled.

"I know who you are and I know what you do," Karpov said. "And I know that none of what is written here is true." He signed.

Alibek persuaded his boss, Kalinin, that they should mothball some of the pathogen-making industrial plants and preserve the research laboratories. Alibek recalled he drafted a decree for Gorbachev to sign. There were just four paragraphs. The decree said Biopreparat would cease to function as an offensive biological weapons agency and would be made into an independent organization. A few weeks later, on May 5, Alibek said the decree came back from the Kremlin. "We've got it," Kalinin told him. When Alibek looked at the document Gorbachev had sent back, however, "I went numb." He explained, "Every paragraph I had drafted was there, but an additional one had been tacked on at the end. It instructed Biopreparat 'to organize the necessary work to keep all of its facilities prepared for further manufacture and development.'"

The first part ended Biopreparat's functioning as an offensive biological warfare organization, Alibek recalled in his memoir. The last part resurrected it.

Alibek protested, but Kalinin dismissed his worries with a flutter of his hand. "With this paper," Kalinin said, "everyone gets to do what he wants to do."

Using the Gorbachev order, Alibek said he sent a message to Stepnogorsk, the anthrax factory, and ordered the destruction of an explosive test chamber he had spent much time and effort to create. He also talked to Sandakhchiev at Vector about converting some facilities to civilian use. Alibek said he went to Siberia several times to oversee the conversion, which was completed by the end of 1990. But at the very same time, Sandakhchiev built a new facility for cultivating viruses for weapons, he said. "Similar double games were being played around The System," he said. "While I closed production lines down," Alibek said, another Biopreparat official "was authorizing new railcars for the mobile deployment of biological production plants."[28]

The United States and Great Britain, now in possession of Pasechnik's detailed and frightening overview, quietly confronted the Soviets. On May 14, 1990, the British and American ambassadors in Moscow, Sir Rodric Braithwaite and Jack F. Matlock Jr., delivered a joint démarche, or formal protest. In separate meetings that afternoon, they took the protest to the heart of the leadership, meeting with Chernyaev, who was Gorbachev's assistant, and Alexander Bessmertnykh, a deputy to Shevardnadze.

Matlock said Chernyaev "was not at all polemical" when the ambassadors delivered the protest. "He said immediately that there were three possibilities," Matlock recalled. One was that the information was incorrect. "We of course interjected that we were certain it was correct," Matlock said. Second, Chernyaev said, perhaps there was such a program and Gorbachev knew about it but had not told Chernyaev. Third, he said, it was possible such a program existed but neither he nor Gorbachev knew about it. "Chernyaev's reply, allowing the possibility of a program with or without Gorbachev's knowledge, was the first time I heard such a comment" from a Soviet official, Matlock recalled.[29]

At the Foreign Ministry, Bessmertnykh took detailed notes. He recorded that Matlock and Braithwaite said the West had "new information" on specific Soviet biological weapons facilities, personnel and programs. They added, according to his notes, "We have a basis to suggest that in the USSR a large-scale secret program in the field of biological weapons is being carried out and there exists significant stockpiles of such weapons far in excess of the reasonable requirements for research purposes."

The ambassadors insisted they did not want "public agitation" over the issue. Braithwaite appealed to Bessmertnykh to resolve it "without additional fuss." Matlock said it was being handled only in top-secret channels, and the United States was "absolutely not interested in burdening our relations with a new problem on the eve of the most important negotiations at the highest levels." The planned summit between Bush and Gorbachev in Washington was just weeks away. Bessmertnykh promised to inform Shevardnadze.[30]

The démarche got the Kremlin's attention. The next day, May 15, 1990, Zaikov sent a typewritten letter to Gorbachev. The letter, found in the Katayev archive, is a milestone in the story of the Biopreparat deception. It shows that Gorbachev personally instructed another Politburo member to report to him on biological weapons work.

Zaikov's response was sent to Shevardnadze, too. "This is for your eyes only," warned a small cover note to Shevardnadze, signed by Zaikov.[31]

"In accordance with your instructions," Zaikov wrote to Gorbachev, "I report to you on the subject of *biological* weapons." The word *biological* was neatly handwritten in blank spaces throughout the letter, apparently because the issue was so ultrasensitive he did not want a typist to know.

Zaikov put a very selective spin on the past and present history of the biological warfare program. It is evident from the letter that Soviet officials lied not only to the world, but to each other, including to the president of the country. "In our country," Zaikov told Gorbachev, "the development of *biological* weapons began in the 1950s at three USSR Ministry of Defense organizations, located in Kirov, Zagorsk, and Sverdlovsk." In fact, the Soviet work on biological weapons dated back to the late 1920s. Zaikov had identified three of the military's chief facilities in the postwar period, including Sverdlovsk.

"In 1971," Zaikov continued, "they were joined in this work by another 12 organizations of the USSR Ministry of the Medical Industry and the former USSR State Agroindustrial Committee. By 1985, they had developed 12 recipes and means for using them. These were produced in suitable quantities, stored, and destroyed after the expiration of useful life (an average of 6 months.)"[32]

Zaikov's description hardly did justice to the ambitious quest for genetically engineered microbes, production and weaponization, and the string of laboratories and factories built by Biopreparat and the military. Zaikov then reviewed the history of the treaty, noting it "had no effective inspection mechanism for ensuring compliance, nor was there a precise definition of the difference between developing biological weapons and defensive means against them."

Zaikov was correct that the boundary between offensive and defensive biological weapons work was sometimes unclear. But the Soviets had not just stepped over the line, they had taken giant and deliberate strides into activity clearly prohibited by international treaty. Zaikov did not inform Gorbachev of the Soviet violations. He instead claimed it was the West that may have violated the agreement.

Next, Zaikov described the high-level Soviet decision making on biological weapons in the last few years. He told Gorbachev that Soviet officials had concluded there was a possibility of inspections under a forthcoming global ban on chemical weapons, and even "possible" inspections to check on compliance with the 1972 biological weapons treaty. He reminded Gorbachev of the Central Committee decision of October 6, 1989, a few weeks before Pasechnik defected. That decision, Zaikov said, was that "all research capacity for *biological* weapons be redirected and used to develop defensive means against these weapons so as not to contradict our international obligations." What Zaikov neglected to tell Gorbachev was that the October 6 decision also stated that the Soviet Union would try to "preserve" its "parity" in "military biology."

Zaikov then told Gorbachev, "In 1988, the stocks of special recipes were destroyed, production of active materials at industrial facilities was halted, and special processing and munitions-assembly equipment was dismantled."[33] Zaikov went on to remind Gorbachev of the high-level decisions made earlier to accelerate the process of getting some facilities scrubbed for possible inspection.[34] Three research laboratories "are currently being prepared for international inspection," he said—Obolensk,

where Popov and Domaradsky had worked on genetic engineering of
bacteria and where Popov saw the guinea pigs die; Koltsovo, where
Popov had first experimented with genetically modified viruses; and
Pasechnik's facility in Leningrad, where, among other things, he had
explored how to produce agents more effectively and to make them even
more potent. These three laboratories were at the heart of the Biopreparat program.

"It is possible that some Western circles have a heightened interest in
our country's compliance with the 1972 Convention after the defection of
V. A. Pasechnik in France in October, 1989," Zaikov wrote. Pasechnik, he
added, "had knowledge of the content of special biological research
work, as well as the locations of organizations involved in this work."

"However," he reassured Gorbachev, "any possible leak of information by Pasechnik, who is a narrow specialist, will not cause damage in
revealing our scientific and technical achievements in this field, but might
provide a basis for Western countries to question the Soviet Union's compliance with the Biological Weapons Convention." Zaikov told Gorbachev that the Soviet Union had given the United Nations

a complete list of the names and locations of 17 facilities that
handle high-risk infectious materials, including facilities
developing defensive means against biological weapons. At the
same time, the USA disclosed only six such facilities, although
some data indicate there are far more than that.

In fact, the Soviet declarations to the United Nations were woefully
incomplete, failing to include some of the secret mass-production facilities or the offensive nature of the Soviet program.

Zaikov closed the letter by telling Gorbachev that "if the issue arises"
of mutual visits to biological facilities "in order to lessen concerns about
their activity," the Americans could be invited to Koltsovo, Obolensk and
the older military laboratory at Kirov. Zaikov said the Soviets should
demand access to three American sites.[35]

Gorbachev's reaction to the Zaikov letter is not known, but events
moved quickly after he received it. Baker had just arrived in Moscow for
meetings to plan the upcoming summit in Washington. He did not raise
biological weapons at any of the regular negotiating sessions in the Soviet

capital. But on May 17, Shevardnadze invited Baker on a sightseeing trip to Zagorsk, a town forty-three miles northeast of the Kremlin with a famous Russian Orthodox monastery. At Baker's request, MacEachin, who was also in Moscow, assembled a short paper outlining what the United States knew, and he gave it to Baker. As they cruised to Zagorsk in Shevardnadze's ZIL limousine, flying Soviet and American flags on the front, with no aides but two interpreters in the car, Baker raised the issue of biological weapons and handed the paper to Shevardnadze. Baker recalled that Shevardnadze said, in the present tense, "he didn't think it could be so, but he would check it out." Ross recalled the paper was a special effort to make sure Shevardnadze knew Baker took the issue seriously and wanted a response.[36]

The next day, May 18, the British defense secretary, Tom King, was in Moscow and held formal talks with Dmitri Yazov, the Soviet defense minister. King also pressed Yazov about biological weapons. Yazov said it was inconceivable that the Soviet Union would have a policy of developing biological weapons. Yazov's manner was hopelessly clumsy, recalled Braithwaite, the British ambassador, who was present. "Yazov muttered to his aide that the British had presumably learned something from 'that defector,' went red in the face, but blandly denied all knowledge," Braithwaite recalled.[37]

Before his departure for Washington, Baker saw that the Gorbachev revolution was running aground. Negotiations on nuclear arms control—the unfinished business of Reykjavik—were "going nowhere slowly." Baker wrote to Bush from Moscow: "The economic problems, the public mistrust, the sense of losing control, the heat of the nationality issue, and concerns about Germany, are all weighing very heavily." Baker said he left "with an overriding impression that Gorbachev was feeling squeezed." Germany was "overloading his circuits," and "the military now seemed in charge of arms control."[38]

A troubled Gorbachev returned to Washington for a summit May 31, 1990. Two years had passed since his sunny walk in Red Square with Reagan. Bush had finally come around to the belief that Gorbachev was a genuine reformer. In the weeks before the summit Bush called Gorbachev a "tremendous statesman" and "bold Soviet leader" who tried to "initiate daring reforms." But the hour was late. On Saturday, June 2, Bush and Gorbachev helicoptered together to Camp David, the 143-acre presidential retreat in the Catoctin Mountains of Maryland. Bush recalled they were each accompanied by military aides carrying the briefcases that would link each of them to their command posts in the event of nuclear war.

Bush persuaded Gorbachev to change out of his suit and tie into a sweater for an informal discussion at Aspen Lodge, sitting at a glass table on the veranda, overlooking the pool, golf course and putting green. Gorbachev was joined by Akhromeyev and Shevardnadze; Bush by Baker and Scowcroft. The sky was clear and a breeze rustled through the trees. Much of the discussion was about regional conflicts around the world, including Afghanistan.[39] Gorbachev recalled that at one point during the day, Bush called him aside for a very private chat. "It was just the two of us and my interpreter," Gorbachev said.

Bush told Gorbachev that the CIA was reporting that the Soviet Union had not destroyed all its biological weapons and production facilities.

"I said," Gorbachev recalled, "my intelligence people report that *you* have not destroyed all your biological weapons. I believe you, I said, but why don't you believe me?"

Bush: "Those are the reports I get."

Gorbachev: "Well, you are not an expert on biological weapons. And I am not an expert on biological weapons. Let us have mutual verification, mutual verification of whether biological weapons have been destroyed. Let your people come to our weapons facilities, we also know where your facilities are, and we will come to your country. Let's have an exchange."

Gorbachev was trying to deflect Bush, just as Zaikov had suggested.

According to Gorbachev's account, Bush responded to the idea of an exchange by proposing that the Americans should check the Soviet Union first.[40]

Years later, when Gorbachev was asked directly whether he knew that Biopreparat existed, he seemed uneasy. His reply was vague. "No, I can't say I remember dealing with that organization," he said. "But there was medical research and they make vaccines against epidemics. Where is the line, the point where research becomes biological weapons and production? This is still controversial, even today, because you need cooperation, you need the kind of international relationship to make it possible to get rid of those weapons." Gorbachev then quickly changed the subject.[41]

When Thatcher met Gorbachev in Moscow on June 8, he was similarly vague. Thatcher said a biological weapons program "naturally causes us grave concern." Gorbachev replied that "this information does not correspond to reality." He added the Soviet Union had "facilities working in this field, but not quite in this direction." It was an artful dodge.[42]

In July 1990, Baker gave Shevardnadze another paper outlining American concerns about biological weapons.[43] Shevardnadze had invited Baker for a relaxing visit to a scenic area of Siberia in early August. Before they met, however, Shevardnadze needed to come up with an answer to the Western protests. On July 27 and again on July 30, a group of officials gathered at Zaikov's office in Moscow to draft talking points that Shevardnadze would use to respond to Baker. According to the talking points, found in Katayev's files, the group decided to preserve the facade.[44]

Baker and Shevardnadze spent most of August 1 boating and fishing on idyllic, mile-deep Lake Baikal. When they got around to discussing arms control, Shevardnadze was guided by the papers written in Zaikov's office: six neatly typed, double-spaced pages. Shevardnadze opened with a solemn declaration that he took the American and British complaints with "utmost seriousness." Then he said, "I can state that at the present time no activity is being carried out in the Soviet Union that would violate the articles of the convention on prohibition of biological weapons. We have no biological weapons."

Shevardnadze claimed the issue of Soviet compliance had been taken up "by the political leadership of the country," and "special decisions were taken" followed by instructions "to take all measures to provide rigorous compliance with this international agreement." In fact, the decisions were taken to hide the incriminating evidence. Shevardnadze also said, in a bit of window dressing, the Soviet Union was thinking about enacting new legislation that would make it a crime for any actions that "will" violate the convention—in the future.

Shevardnadze, following the script, promised Baker that the Soviet side was ready "to arrange a visit to any of the biological facilities named by the American side in the U.S. memo." And, he said, the Soviets would even go so far as to allow American scientists to "work at the Soviet biological facilities." In a page that was not numbered, but apparently added at the end of his presentation, Shevardnadze suggested both sides work out a program of joint scientific work on defense against biological weapons. Shevardnadze also gave Baker a written paper containing the Soviet response to his questions.

Shevardnadze had been aware of, and participated in, discussions of the scrub-down and cover-up strategy to hide Biopreparat in 1989. In his memoir, Shevardnadze alluded to this moment. "If anything, Jim could have had some doubts about my honesty, in connection with an unpleasant story I do not intend to tell here." He added, "Lying is always unproductive."[45]

Back at the CIA in Washington, a decision was made not to punish the Soviets but to take up their offer of visits. "We said to ourselves, about Shevardnadze, he's lying, but let's not decide to ram it up their ass," MacEachin recalled. "The number one objective for U.S. national security is to eliminate, and get onsite inspections. We knew if we accused, there would be 900 meetings of finger-pointing without anything happening."[46] In the months that followed, working in total secrecy, Baker and Shevardnadze negotiated the details of the first visits to suspected Soviet biological weapons sites.[47] But they had many other pressing demands to cope with.

On August 2, while Baker and Shevardnadze were meeting privately, they were interrupted by Baker's spokeswoman Margaret Tutwiler, who handed Baker a message saying that Iraq had invaded Kuwait. Baker enlisted Shevardnadze and Gorbachev in what became a concerted, months-long effort to build a diplomatic coalition against Iraq. Gorbachev was reluctant to see the use of force and kept hoping that Saddam could be talked into pulling out of Kuwait. Nevertheless, when Baker came to Gorbachev's official country residence at Novo-Ogaryovo on November 7, the Soviet leader said, "What's really important is that we stick together."[48]

In these hectic months, a treaty reducing troop levels in Europe was signed, an agreement was reached on the unification of Germany and Gorbachev won the Nobel Peace Prize. At home, Gorbachev sank. He tried to fashion a new Union Treaty to hold the restive republics together, while Yeltsin urged them to grab all the independence they could. Chernyaev observed that "Gorbachev seemed truly at a loss, the first time I'd ever seen him in that state. He could see power slipping from his hands."[49] Shevardnadze brooded over the growing strength of reactionary forces, especially the "men in epaulets," and felt Gorbachev was abandoning their shared cause of democratic reform. "The only thing I needed, wanted, and expected from the President was that he take a clear position: that he rebuff the right-wingers, and openly defend our common policy," Shevardnadze recalled. "I waited in vain."

On the morning of December 20, after a sleepless night, Shevardnadze wrote out a resignation. He called his daughter in Tbilisi and told her, then informed two of his closest aides. He left for the Kremlin.[50] The Congress of People's Deputies fell into a stunned silence as he spoke. Shevardnadze complained bitterly of a lack of support; the reformers had scattered. "Dictatorship is coming," he warned. Gorbachev, sitting nearby, listened impassively. When the speech was over, he clutched his forehead and looked down at his papers.[51]

In the autumn of 1990, another Soviet defector, a medical biochemist, sought asylum at the British Embassy in Helsinki. He had once had top-secret clearances in the Soviet system and worked at Obolensk in the very early years when it was being carved out of the forest. He later worked in the anti-plague system, and described to the British how pathogens were harvested from it for use in biological weapons. The defector's information reinforced Pasechnik's revelations.[52]

Very early in the morning on Monday, January 8, 1991, Davis and Kelly stood in Moscow in the bone-chilling cold. Seven American and five British representatives—experts on biotechnology, microbiology, virology, arms control verification and the structure of the Soviet program—

were about to begin the very first visit to suspected biological weapons sites. Davis, usually sharp and no-nonsense, was a bit groggy. It was deep winter, absolutely frigid, and he had uncharacteristically overslept. The British-American team had arrived in total secrecy; Davis had not even told his wife where he was going or why. Standing in front of an aging yellow bus, Davis was introduced for the first time to Alibek, who was put in charge of the visit. Alibek, smoking a cigarette, wore a brown wool sweater while everyone else on the Soviet side was in suits and ties. Alibek spoke no English and had never met an American or Briton. He recalled his surprise that the Westerners "knew a lot about us," and one asked why "Biopreparat chief Kalinin" wasn't present. Alibek lied, "Unfortunately, Mr. Kalinin is extremely busy." Kalinin had instructed him never to even mention his name.[53]

The bus set off for the Institute of Immunology at Lyubuchany, 35 miles south of the Kremlin, which did support work for Obolensk. The bus crawled in a snowstorm, and suddenly Davis heard a loud bang. The bus windshield shattered from the cold. "It was bloody awful," Davis recalled. "This is the big game. This is day one. We haven't even reached the place yet, and we have to slow down because we can't keep going at speed, or we'd all die of exposure. We're shivering now, probably doing 15 miles per hour, and we arrive late, frozen to death." Alibek said the Soviet strategy for the visits, worked out over the previous weeks, was to hide as much as possible, and "waste as much time as possible" with meals, drinks and official speeches, to limit time for the visitors to carry out inspections. Vodka and cognac were ordered up at every stop. Popov said "there was a huge training program" before the visits so that every employee knew to repeat the "legend" that they were working only on defense against pathogens. "Every department and every lab had several meetings," Popov recalled. The first stop was easy—the institute had no dangerous pathogens on hand.

Next came Obolensk, the compound in the woods that had played such a central role in the work of Domaradsky and Popov. When they arrived January 10, Davis noted that, although thousands of people worked there, the halls were eerily empty. Urakov, the stern director who had clashed with Domaradsky, welcomed them with a long speech, sandwiches and drinks. When the Westerners pressed to get to work, Urakov warned them that if they wanted access to the floor containing *Yesenia pestis*, they would have to be quarantined for nine days on site. The point was to discourage the visitors from asking for access. Alibek had actually given orders the previous weekend for Obolensk and Vector to be totally disinfected, so the risk of exposure to dangerous pathogens was very low. Still, Urakov's threat worked, and they did not ask to go there.[54]

The Westerners had brought their own plan of action for the visit to the complex, which had more than thirty buildings, and they split up into small teams. Davis was the person on the delegation with the most complete knowledge, and he needed to be in several places at once. He went with one team to Korpus 1, the large cubelike modern building in which each floor was dedicated to a different pathogen. But when another team in the older part of the complex found something interesting, he was asked to come over, and was driven there by the Russian hosts.

Davis happened upon an unmarked door that, he recalled, looked like that of a restroom. This opened into a shower changing room, and eventually a high-ceiling room containing a large freestanding hexagonal steel chamber, which Pasechnik had told them about. Biological bombs would be exploded inside the chamber, and animals, pinned down at one end, were exposed to the pathogens. Pasechnik had said the facility was used to test whether pathogens remained effective after being released by an explosive device.

They climbed inside the chamber. It was dark.

"Can we turn the lights on, I can't see," Davis asked. The Soviets said the bulb was burned out.

Davis reached for a small flashlight held by his trusted friend and deputy, Major Hamish Killip. Before Davis could turn the flashlight on, a Soviet official accompanying them grabbed his wrist and stopped him, saying it was a prohibited electronic device. They struggled back and forth. Davis protested strongly that he was on an officially sanctioned mission by the president of the Soviet Union. "We are your guests," he insisted. "This is not the way to behave!"

"I wasn't letting go of the flashlight, and he has ahold of me, and we're in a standoff here. It was tense. They didn't know what to do, and I wasn't going to back off." Eventually, the laboratory officials relented and managed to turn on the overhead light.[55] Davis noticed the steel walls appeared to have been recently burnished, to erase any marks that would indicate explosive fragments. But when Davis looked at the door, which seemed to be double-skinned and made of a softer metal, he saw the tell-tale dents. What's this? he asked.

The laboratory officials said it was poor workmanship with a hammer when the door was installed. "They knew that we knew this was laughable rubbish," Davis said. Alibek remembered that Davis spoke up directly, saying, "You have been using explosives here." Davis said the visit to the chamber was "pay dirt" showing the Soviets had an offensive biological weapons program, as Pasechnik had so painstakingly described. "It was quite chilling," he said. The size of the equipment at Obolensk was a tip-off to the American and British experts that offensive weapons work was underway, and not just vaccines or defensive research. "You've got this gigantic building. You're brewing up large quantities. You're beginning to smell a rat here."

Next, on January 14, the team went to Vector, the facility at Koltsovo where Popov had first experimented with genetic engineering. Sandakhchiev, the driven, chain-smoking Armenian who had once dreamed of creating a new artificial virus every month, began to give the foreigners a dull lecture on the latest advances in Soviet immunology, but the visitors, now alert to the Soviet delay strategy, cut him off. Davis and Kelly wanted to see the laboratories. "I could see their eyes widen with astonishment as we took them past enormous steel fermenters, larger than what any Western pharmaceutical firm would ever use for the mass-production of vaccines," said Alibek. They were not permitted, however, to enter the most sensitive floors where virus research was being done.

At one point, a midlevel researcher let slip to Kelly that the laboratory was working on smallpox. Kelly asked him, quietly, through the interpreter, to repeat what he had just said. The researcher repeated it three times: *Variola major.* Kelly was speechless. The World Health Organization had eradicated smallpox, and samples were supposed to exist in only two official repositories, at the Centers for Disease Control in Atlanta and at the Ivanovsky Institute of Virology, a Ministry of Health facility in Moscow. Vector was not supposed to be working with smallpox; it was not supposed to *have* any smallpox. When Kelly later confronted Sandakhchiev, the director denied that offensive work was being carried out, and then refused to answer any more questions.

Alibek knew that one of Vector's prize possessions was the 630-liter smallpox reactor, standing five feet tall, which could manufacture great quantities of the virus. The visitors took note of the reactor and other equipment, including the most advanced aerosol-testing capability any of them had ever seen. There could be no justifiable explanation other than an offensive biological weapons program, they concluded.

At the last stop, Pasechnik's institute in Leningrad, Alibek thought he could relax. "The worst was behind us," he later wrote. "Nothing at Pasechnik's old institute would pose a threat. Or, so I thought." All the incriminating equipment had been moved, and the laboratories scrubbed down.

Then, during the tour, one of the visitors stopped by an imposing machine and asked, "What's this?"

"I groaned inwardly," Alibek said. "I had forgotten about Pasechnik's jet-stream milling equipment. It had been too heavy to move." This was the machine that used a powerful blast of air to turn agents into a fine powder. An institute official proffered an explanation. "For salt," he said. "That's where we mill salt."

The visitors saw machinery for preparing biological aerosols that would be the perfect size for sticking in the human upper respiratory system. And they saw equipment Pasechnik had alerted them about for disseminating pathogens from a low-flying craft, such as a cruise missile.

After the visitors left, Alibek felt victorious. Although the Westerners had suspicions, he recalled, "they could prove nothing, and we had given nothing away."

The delegation knew they did not get a full view of Biopreparat, but they had seen enough. They wrote in their report: the sheer size and scope of the program, the configuration of the facilities, the nature and extent of the work on pathogens, the guards and physical security and the large aerosol experiments—all of it pointed to an offensive germ warfare effort that was far beyond anything needed for civilian purposes.

Pasechnik had told them the truth.

THE YEAR OF LIVING DANGEROUSLY

In the winter months of early 1991, nearly six years after the Politburo had chosen him as a younger, energetic standard-bearer who could save the party and state, Gorbachev, approaching his sixtieth birthday, felt exhausted. His attempt to create real, competitive politics gave rise to a potent rival, Boris Yeltsin, who became a rallying point for many who opposed Gorbachev, the establishment and the party. Nationalities long suffocated inside the Soviet Union began to awaken, with aspirations for independence, something Gorbachev had never foreseen.

Gorbachev's *perestroika,* or restructuring—which began with a goal of rejuvenating socialism, and later was aimed at creating a hybrid of socialism and capitalism—was never a full-throated drive to free markets. Gorbachev had experimented with capitalism, and given permission for the first private entrepreneurs to set up their own businesses, known as the cooperatives. But shortages, disruption and hardship spread across the country. A catastrophic drop in oil extraction, along with low oil prices, took a heavy toll; foreign currency reserves were almost exhausted, and a lack of commercial credits made imports almost impossible. Flour was rationed. Gorbachev announced at a meeting of the Security Council one day in the spring that, in two or three months, the government would no longer be able to feed the country.[1] And his halting half-steps away from the centrally planned economy led to demands, championed by Yeltsin, for a more radical leap to the free market.

"There were already bread lines in Moscow like those for sausage two years before," Chernyaev recalled. "I took a car on Saturday and drove all around Moscow. Bread stores were closed or absolutely empty—not figuratively, but literally!"[2] He wrote in his diary on March 31, "I don't think Moscow has seen anything like this in all its history—even in the hungriest years." And, he added, "on that day, certainly, nothing remained of the image of Gorbachev."[3]

The aggrieved losers in this vortex of change began to resist. They included the military, which felt humiliated as soldiers and tanks retreated from Europe, only to discover they were almost destitute at home; the party elite, which lost its monopoly on power; and the security agencies, primarily the KGB, who saw themselves as guardians of a power structure under siege and a country near disintegration. Gorbachev attempted to buy time. He tried to satisfy the disillusioned old guard while hanging on to the allies of *perestroika*, the progressive intellectuals, but he could not do both, and succeeded at neither. The progressives abandoned him for Yeltsin, a more promising agent of change. The hard-liners pushed Gorbachev to use force, and declare a state of emergency to reassert control in the old Soviet tradition. A coterie of the hard-liners, from the KGB, the military and the party, would soon take matters into their own hands.

In earlier years, Gorbachev and Reagan, in a courageous break with the past, managed to slow the speeding locomotive of the Cold War arms race. After some hesitation, Bush also realized Gorbachev was a man to do business with, a negotiating partner, an anchor in a stormy sea.

Then the anchor broke loose. Gorbachev lost control.

Very early on the morning of Sunday, January 13, Soviet tanks, led by members of Alpha Group, an elite KGB special forces unit, attacked pro-independence demonstrators at the television tower in Vilnius, Lithuania. The troops opened fire and killed more than a dozen people in a massacre that caused a wave of apprehension and revulsion. The assault had been secretly orchestrated in Moscow by the hard-liners around Gorbachev, perhaps in expectation that Gorbachev would have no choice but to order a crackdown and state of emergency. On the night of the assault, Kremlin records showed the hard-liners met in the office of Gorbachev's chief of staff, Valery Boldin, from 7:15 P.M. until 2:30 A.M., shortly after the shooting began.[4]

The day after the Vilnius massacre, speaking to parliament, Gorbachev insisted he had known nothing about the violence until it was over, "when they woke me up." He blamed independence leaders in Lithuania for provoking it. His comments didn't answer the central question: either Gorbachev, as commander in chief, was in control of his own security forces or he wasn't. Both were disturbing possibilities. Liberals who had been at Gorbachev's side, appalled by the use of force, quit the party, including the entire editorial board of *Moscow News*, a leading voice of *perestroika*, which published a devastating joint statement from the intellectuals. Chernyaev wrote in his diary on January 14 that Gorbachev's address to parliament was "a disorganized, confusing speech full of rambling digressions . . ."[5]

"I was in complete despair," said Chernyaev, perhaps Gorbachev's most loyal adviser. He wrote a letter of resignation, admonishing Gorbachev that ". . . you chained yourself to policies that you can only continue by force. And so you contradict your own philosophy." The hard-liners were "pathetic and shameful," Chernyaev said. "They discredit you, making the center look ridiculous. And you're following their logic, which is basically the code of the streets—you beat me up . . . so now I'll call my big brother and you'll get it!"

"You're losing the most important thing that we've gained from new thinking—trust," he wrote. "You'll never be trusted again, no matter what you do." Chernyaev reminisced about his partnership with Gorbachev "the great innovator and father of *perestroika*." But "now I don't recognize or understand him."[6]

However, Chernyaev never gave Gorbachev the letter, and did not resign. In the days that followed, Gorbachev did not order more repression, as the hard-liners hoped he would. But at the same time, Chernyaev said, Gorbachev never figured out that his public appeals to reason and negotiation could not halt the Baltic secession. It was all but inevitable.

The American and British biological weapons team departed the Soviet Union on the weekend of January 19–20, even more worried than when they arrived. In the weeks that followed, the teams wrote a report of what they had seen. On March 5, the new British prime minister, John Major, told Gorbachev of his concerns during a tête-à-tête meeting in Moscow. Then, on March 15, Baker met Gorbachev in the Kremlin, and delivered a strong protest, saying he believed there was a "colossal" biological weapons program. Gorbachev did not admit it. "Maybe all this is fantasy?" he suggested. Baker replied, "No, we don't think so." On March 25, Baker sent papers to Gorbachev that outlined the concerns raised by the January visits.[7]

Neither Major nor Baker said a word about it in public. They did not want to undercut Gorbachev, who was increasingly vulnerable at home. Also, a new U.S.-Soviet strategic arms treaty, years in the making, was finally nearing completion. If the illicit germ warfare program became public, it would wreck any chance for Senate ratification.

On April 5, Braithwaite, the British ambassador, came to see Chernyaev, this time with a formal, written message from the prime minister, a detailed, damning and very accurate list based on the January visits.[8] On May 11, Foreign Minister Bessmertnykh delivered an answer to Baker's papers from March, continuing the cover-up on every point.

In late May, Margaret Thatcher, now out of office, visited Gorbachev in the Kremlin. After a dinner with him, she returned to the British ambassador's residence, where Braithwaite was waiting, along with the American ambassador, Matlock, whom Thatcher had invited. With an after-dinner drink in her hand, Thatcher settled into a chair in Braithwaite's study, turned to Matlock and said, "Please get a message to my friend George," meaning the president.

"We've got to help Mikhail," she pleaded. "Of course, you Americans can't and shouldn't have to do it all yourselves, but George will have to lead the effort, just as he did with Kuwait." She paused, Matlock recalled, and then explained why she felt so strongly. "Just a few years back, Ron and I would have given the world to get what has already happened here." She wanted Bush to invite Gorbachev to the Group of 7 summit in

London in July and deliver a massive Western aid package. Matlock hesitated. The Soviet economy was a shambles, and pouring aid into it might be a waste, he said. Thatcher glared. "You're talking like a diplomat!" she responded. "Just finding excuses for doing nothing. Why can't you think like a statesman? We need a political decision to support this process, which is so much in everyone's interest."

Matlock sent Thatcher's message to Bush that night. Then he wrote in his own journal, "I think that Mrs. Thatcher is right."[9]

On June 17, Valentin Pavlov, the prime minister and one of the hardliners who had planned the Vilnius attack, asked the Supreme Soviet to give him extraordinary powers that were granted only to the president. He did not tell Gorbachev beforehand. It was a daring power grab, but Gorbachev reacted only with a statement that he hadn't endorsed the proposal. In a closed meeting of the assembly, other hard-liners at the center of the gathering storm—KGB Chairman Vladimir Kryuchkov, Defense Minister Dmitri Yazov and Interior Minister Boris Pugo—also backed Pavlov's move.

Matlock was surprised at Gorbachev's timidity. Why didn't he fire these appointees trying to usurp his power? On June 20, Matlock had coffee with Gavriil Popov, a close ally of Yeltsin who had just been elected mayor of Moscow on the shoulders of the growing democratic movement. When they were alone in the library at Spaso House, the ambassador's residence, Popov took out a sheet of paper, scribbled a note and handed it to Matlock. In a large, uneven Russian scrawl, it said:

A COUP IS BEING ORGANIZED TO REMOVE GORBACHEV.
WE MUST GET WORD TO BORIS NIKOLAYEVICH.

Yeltsin was at that moment in the United States.
Matlock then wrote on the same sheet:

I'LL SEND A MESSAGE. BUT WHO IS BEHIND THIS?

Popov wrote on the paper and shoved it back to Matlock:

PAVLOV, KRYUCHKOV, YAZOV, LUKYANOV

Popov took the paper back when Matlock had read it, tore it into small pieces and put them in his pocket.[10]

Matlock sent an urgent message to Washington for Bush, who was to meet with Yeltsin at the White House later that day. Within hours, Matlock was instructed to take a warning to Gorbachev. About 8:20 P.M. in Moscow, early evening but still broad daylight at this time of year, Matlock arrived at Gorbachev's office. Chernyaev was present. Gorbachev greeted him as "Comrade Ambassador!" and lavished praise on Matlock, which made him uncomfortable. Matlock sat at the long table in Gorbachev's office facing the window, with Gorbachev and Chernyaev on the other side.

"Mr. President," Matlock said, "President Bush has asked me to notify you of a report we have received which we find greatly disturbing, although we cannot confirm it. It is based on more than rumor but less than hard information. It is that there is an effort under way to remove you, and it could happen at any time, even this week."

Matlock did not name his source. He was trying to convey that the information was not from intelligence sources, but that was just what Chernyaev and Gorbachev assumed he was saying. On his notepad, Chernyaev wrote, "American services" had given the warning the coup would be the next day.[11]

Both Gorbachev and Chernyaev laughed. Matlock recalled that Gorbachev then grew serious. "Tell President Bush I am touched. I have felt for some time that we are partners, and now he has proved it. Thank him for his concern. He has done just what a friend should do. But tell him not to worry. I have everything well in hand. You'll see tomorrow."

According to Chernyaev, Gorbachev also said, "It's a hundred percent improbable."[12]

After Matlock spoke, Gorbachev lapsed into a soliloquy, saying that things were unsettled, Pavlov was inexperienced and had realized the mistake of his power grab earlier in the week, Yeltsin was being more cooperative, a new union treaty would soon be signed and Gorbachev's visit to the London summit would be a further step into the world economy.

Looking back, Matlock said later that Gorbachev may have wrongly interpreted what he was saying, and assumed he was referring to the reactionary forces in parliament as the source of trouble. Chernyaev's notes confirm Gorbachev mistakenly thought Matlock was referring to the parliamentary hard-liners, not Kryuchkov of the KGB and Yazov from the military.

The next day Pavlov's power-grab proposal was defeated in parliament. Talking to reporters afterward, Gorbachev was flanked by a grim Yazov, Pugo and Kryuchkov, and said, with a large grin, "The 'coup' is over."[13] But Matlock was not sanguine about Gorbachev. "He was the one with the most to lose, and yet he was acting like a somnambulist, wandering around oblivious to his surroundings." In fact, Gorbachev got warnings from other sources, too. Just after Matlock left, Gorbachev told Chernyaev that he'd received a warning the day before from his special envoy, Yevgeny Primakov.

"Beware!" Primakov had insisted. "You're trusting the KGB and your security service too much. Are you sure you are safe?"

Gorbachev replied, "What a chicken! I told him, 'Zhenya, calm down. You of all people shouldn't yield to panic.' "[14]

Two nights after Matlock's warning, Bush phoned Gorbachev, who brushed off the chances of a coup.

"A thousand percent impossible," he said.[15]

On June 21, Valery Yarynich walked into a small conference room with a single wood table on the upper floors of the Institute for World Economy and International Relations, a prestigious Soviet research institute in Moscow. Yarynich was the expert on communications who had worked many years in the Strategic Rocket Forces. He worked on Perimeter, the semiautomatic system for launching a retaliatory nuclear strike. Perimeter was still ultra-secret. After Perimeter was finally put into operation in 1985, Yarynich served during the Gorbachev years at a think tank inside the military's General Staff headquarters in Moscow, where he concluded, based on mathematical models, that deterrence could be guaranteed with far fewer nuclear weapons.

Yarynich was invited to the conference room to participate in a meeting between Russian and American civilian experts on the problems of command and control of nuclear forces. Such a meeting would have been unheard of in earlier years, but in the atmosphere of greater openness, it was possible to talk about subjects that had long been strictly off-limits. Waiting in the conference room was one of the foremost civilian experts in the United States on nuclear command and control, Bruce Blair, a senior fellow at the Brookings Institution, a leading Washington think tank. Blair came in a coat and tie, and carried a small notebook. He had a lot of questions. During service in the Air Force, he spent two years as a Minuteman missile launch officer in the early 1970s, working shifts in underground silos. Subsequently, he carried out top-secret research on the vulnerability of American command and control of nuclear weapons for the Congressional Office of Technology Assessment. At Brookings, Blair wrote a book about American nuclear systems, *Strategic Command and Control*. For his next book, Blair had been searching, since 1987, for clues about Soviet command and control. While Blair had valuable sources in the United States, it was excruciatingly difficult to learn the truth in the Soviet Union; anything about nuclear command and control was top secret. Often, Blair gathered fragments of information but could not figure out the larger picture. Day after frustrating day, in countless smoke-filled rooms, he conducted interviews. When he met with Yarynich in the conference room, Blair realized he had finally connected with a real expert, someone who shared Blair's depth of knowledge about launch systems and procedures. Yarynich emphasized that he was speaking only for himself, not for his superiors. "He's here on his own, a confidential meeting," Blair wrote in his notebook. He also noted that Yarynich was from the Center for Operational and Strategic Research in the General Staff, a specialist on command and control. However, Blair didn't write down Yarynich's name; in his view it was still too sensitive.

Blair found it took hours and hours of conversation to extract anything useful from Soviet military officers. But Yarynich was surprisingly assertive; he seemed to be "someone who had a lot on his mind." Yarynich told Blair a Kremlin leader might have only two to four minutes to make a decision about retaliation if warned of a missile attack. The Soviet leader might have to make a decision in the dangerous situation known as "launch on warning," in other words, firing off nuclear missiles based entirely on a warning. If a false warning, it could be a disastrous decision. Blair took careful notes.

From his American sources, Blair had heard of a Soviet system called the Dead Hand, a computer-driven machine that would, in the event the Soviet leadership were wiped out, launch a retaliatory attack without human hands on the button. When Blair asked about it, Yarynich responded that there was no Dead Hand in the Russian system. Blair wrote those words in his notebook. But Yarynich was careful to tell Blair something else, too. There was no *automatic* Dead Hand, but there was a *semiautomatic* system of some kind. Blair didn't fully comprehend that day what Yarynich was telling him, but some details were in his notes. He didn't connect the dots, at first.[16]

A year and a half had passed since Pasechnik's defection. Gorbachev had been the recipient of repeated, specific complaints from the Americans and British about Biopreparat. The latest came in a letter June 19 from Bush to Gorbachev, which once again asserted that the Soviet Union had a large-scale biological weapons program and called for another meeting of experts.[17] Gorbachev wrote back to Bush in mid-July. His letter pledged to keep up the spirit of "frank dialogue" between them. But Gorbachev was not forthcoming. He followed the script of the Soviet cover-up—deny the weapons program, proclaim a desire for openness and refer to the narrow line between offensive and defensive biological research.

Soon after sending Bush the letter, Gorbachev joined leaders of the Western industrial democracies in London, as Thatcher had urged. On July 17, Gorbachev met Bush at Winfield House, a mansion in Regent's Park used as the official American ambassador's residence. Gorbachev made an appeal to Bush for economic assistance, but Bush felt the Soviet Union was not ready.[18] After lunch, Bush and Gorbachev sat alone, with only interpreters and aides, to again take up the thorny issue of biological weapons. "Gorbachev categorically denied all the accusations," Chernyaev said. According to Chernyaev, an exchange between Bush and Gorbachev followed:

Bush: Mikhail, I received your letter. I don't know what's going on; either we're misinterpreting things, or your people are doing something wrong or misunderstanding something . . . Our specialists continue to alarm us . . . It's hard for me to figure it out.

Gorbachev: George, I have figured it out. I can tell you with confidence: we aren't making biological weapons . . . I asked for a report on this matter. The report is ready, it's been signed by Minister of Defense Yazov and other people. I told you the essence of this report, its main conclusions. I suggest we finish with this.

Bush: Let's do that. If our people are mistaken, or misleading us, they're in trouble. But we need clarity. Maybe another meeting of experts would help.

Chernyaev said he, too, was concerned about being misled. "And I broached it in a memo to Gorbachev: Did he know himself exactly where matters stood, was he sure he wasn't being misled as had happened with the Krasnoyarsk radar station and in some other cases?" Gorbachev replied that he was confident. "I know!"[19]

Nearly five years after Reykjavik, the United States and the Soviet Union finally agreed on a treaty to reduce the most dangerous strategic nuclear weapons. But the agreement, more than seven hundred pages long, was not as sweeping as Reagan and Gorbachev had envisioned at Reykjavik. Instead of the elimination of all ballistic missiles, or 50 percent fewer nuclear warheads, the treaty left the two superpowers with forces about 30 percent lower. Each had plenty of firepower: even after the treaty, the two countries would be allowed a total of eighteen thousand nuclear warheads. There were some notable gains: the agreement sliced deeply into the largest Soviet missiles. The number of SS-18s would be cut in half, to 154, and stringent new compliance measures would be imposed to prevent cheating—including twelve types of on-site inspections.[20]

When Bush and Gorbachev signed the agreement in St. Vladimir's Hall at the Kremlin on the afternoon of July 31, there was almost no trace of the old dispute over the Strategic Defense Initiative, the single issue on which the Reykjavik summit foundered. Gorbachev, who had protested so long and so loudly about weapons in space, did not mention it once. Bush noted it only in passing. Gorbachev had been urged to build a Soviet Star Wars machine by the military-industrial complex. He did not. Gorbachev had also been urged to build a massive retaliatory missile force—the "asymmetric response"—to overwhelm the American defensive shield. He did not. One of Gorbachev's greatest accomplishments was in the things he did not do.

An argument was often made in later years that it was the Strategic Defense Initiative that bankrupted the Soviet Union. It is true that Reagan's vision gave Soviet leaders a fright—it symbolized the unbridled nature of American ambitions and technological superiority. But in the end, Reagan did not build it. The Soviet Union did not build one either. Gorbachev was determined to avoid an arms race in space, and Soviet technology could not possibly have met the challenge. The early plans for a Soviet "Star Wars" never reached fruition. The Soviet system bankrupted itself, and by late 1991, the end was near. When Gorbachev and Bush signed the strategic arms treaty, the Soviet economy was imploding, sucking oxygen out of everything, including the military-industrial complex. The fabled design bureaus and defense factories ran out of cash, and gradually ground to a halt. The powerful riptide of the economy pulled everything down with it.

On August 3, the eve of his annual vacation, Gorbachev offered some private, candid thoughts to Chernyaev. Chernyaev remembers him sitting on the wing of an armchair. "I'm tired as hell, Tolya," he said. "And tomorrow, right before I leave, I have another government meeting. The harvest, transportation, debts, communications, no money, the market falling apart." He added, "Everywhere you look, things are in a bad way." Gorbachev brightened when he remembered the agreement with Yeltsin July 23 on a new union treaty. Gorbachev and Yeltsin had discussed replacing some of the hard-liners, including Yazov, the defense minister, and Kryuchkov, the KGB chief, as they restructured the highest levels of government. Gorbachev planned to formally sign the new union treaty on August 20 at a Kremlin ceremony. "But his overall mood was still dark," Chernyaev recalled.

"Oh, Tolya," Gorbachev said, "everything has become so petty, vulgar, provincial. You look at it and think, to hell with it all! But who would I leave it to? I'm so tired."[21]

Gorbachev took Chernyaev with him on the holiday to Foros in the Crimea. After lunch on Sunday, August 18, Gorbachev went to work on his speech about the new union treaty. He planned to fly back to Moscow on Monday for the ceremony on Tuesday. The treaty would radically decentralize the Soviet Union by giving the republics broad new powers, including control over their own resources.

On Sunday, the hard-liners swung into action.[22]

On the grounds of Gorbachev's resort compound, code-named Zarya, or Dawn, duty officers stood by with a suitcase for command of the Soviet nuclear forces. The suitcase was known as the *chemodanchik*, or little suit-case, and formally called the Cheget. It connected to a special communi-cations network, Kavkaz, that would enable the Soviet leader to authorize the launching of nuclear weapons. There was also a small port-folio with written codes. In the Soviet command and control system, as it stood in 1991, three leaders—the president, the defense minister and the chief of the General Staff—would have to give a permission to launch. All three were accompanied by the Cheget suitcases. This permission would be passed simultaneously to the General Staff headquarters in Moscow and the three commanders-in-chief: of land-based rockets, naval and air forces. Once permission was given, the actual launch order would be issued by the General Staff to the three commanders-in-chief. Thus, Gorbachev's suitcase was not a nuclear button but a communications link for monitoring and decision making. There was also the option of switching on the secret Perimeter system. The nuclear suitcase and Perimeter were put into operation shortly before Gorbachev took office. Akhromeyev had played a key role in making sure the modernized sys-tem was on duty and ready. But Gorbachev regarded the whole appara-tus with disdain. He abhorred the thought of nuclear war.

At the Zarya compound, nine duty officers worked shifts in groups of three, two operators and one officer, squeezed into small rooms in a guest house about one hundred yards from Gorbachev's lodge. The doors were always closed, and they took turns leaving for meals. When off duty, they left the compound and bunked several miles away at an isolated military lodge, which had only a local phone and no communications.

At 4:30 P.M. on Sunday, Gorbachev talked over the phone with Georgi Shakhnazarov, one of his leading advisers, who was at a nearby compound, about the forthcoming speech.

At 4:32 P.M., Lieutenant Colonel Vladimir Kirillov, the commander of the nuclear watch, was startled by a signal from his equipment that all communications links were down. The television in his room went off too. The only working line was a radio-phone connected to a government phone exchange in Mukholatka, a nearby small town. Kirillov called there and asked to be connected to the commanders in Moscow. They said it was impossible, they had no communications with anyone. At 4:35 P.M., another duty officer called Mukholatka and asked why there was no line to Moscow. "Accident," he was told.

Ten meters away, in the same building as the duty officers, Chernyaev was in his small room, with the windows closed and the air-conditioning running. An assistant interrupted him to say a high-level delegation had arrived unexpectedly from Moscow and was entering Gorbachev's building. "Something strange is going on," the assistant said. "Did you know they cut off communications?" Chernyaev immediately picked up the phone to call Moscow. All three receivers at his desk—to the government exchange, the satellite line and the ordinary internal phone for the compound—were dead.

At 4:40 P.M., Kirillov was summoned out of the duty officers' room. In the hall, he saw General Valentin Varennikov, commander of Soviet ground forces, standing with several other men. Varennikov asked about the status of the communications. Kirillov said the lines were dead. "That's the way it should be," Varennikov said, adding that it would remain so for twenty-four hours and that the president knew about it.

Kirillov went back to the room and continued to try to get in touch with Moscow. The government exchange at Mukholatka stopped answering altogether.

The Soviet nuclear forces were cut off from their civilian commander.

At 4:40 P.M., Gorbachev, wearing shorts and a sweater in his study, was interrupted by his chief bodyguard, Vladimir Medvedev, who said a group had come from Moscow, demanding to see him immediately. Gorbachev rarely invited visitors to his working vacation, and was baffled how they had penetrated the tight security around him. Medvedev said they had been let in by Lieutenant General Yuri Plekhanov, chief of the 9th Main Directorate of the KGB, responsible for Gorbachev's overall protection. One by one, Gorbachev picked up the phones at his desk— the government line, the satellite line, the internal line and the city line. All dead. Finally, he picked up the red phone to the strategic nuclear forces. Silent. Gorbachev found Raisa, who was reading a newspaper on the veranda, told her what was happening and to expect the worst. She was shaken but remained cool, he recalled. They went into the nearby bedroom and called in their daughter, Irina, and her husband, Anatoly, and explained. They all knew Russia's terrible history of leaders assassinated, imprisoned and exiled. The last reformer, Khrushchev, had been forced from office. "You must know," Gorbachev told his family, "that I will not give in to any kind of blackmail, nor to any threats of pressure and will not retreat from the positions I have taken."[23] Raisa said, "It's up to you to make a decision, but I am with you whatever may happen."

When Gorbachev climbed the stairs to his second-floor study, he saw the visitors had already entered the small room. They were Varennikov, who had been in charge of troops in Vilnius; Boldin, Gorbachev's trusted chief of staff; Oleg Shenin, a Politburo member; and Oleg Baklanov, the party secretary for the military-industrial complex. Plekhanov was also with them, but Gorbachev threw him out.

Gorbachev demanded, "Who sent you?"

"The committee," they said.

"What committee?"

"The committee set up to deal with the emergency situation in the country."

"Who set it up?" Gorbachev insisted. "I didn't create it and the Supreme Soviet didn't create it. Who created it?"

Baklanov said the committee—which became known as the State Committee for the Emergency Situation, known by its Russian acronym GKChP—was established because the country was sliding toward disaster. Baklanov added, "You must sign a decree on the declaration of a state of emergency." The visitors demanded Gorbachev hand over his powers to the vice president, Gennady Yanayev. Baklanov said Yeltsin had been arrested, then corrected himself and said Yeltsin *will be* arrested. He also suggested that perhaps Gorbachev's health had deteriorated terribly. He told Gorbachev that other members of the committee included Yazov, the defense minister; Pugo, the interior minister; Kryuchkov, the head of the KGB; Pavlov, the prime minister; and Yanayev. Most of them had been present in Boldin's office before the Vilnius crackdown in January. Gorbachev seethed at the personal treachery. "I had promoted all these people—and now they were betraying me!" He refused to sign anything, and told the delegation of plotters to go to hell. Varennikov demanded Gorbachev's resignation. Gorbachev insulted him by pretending not to remember his name. "Oh yes," he said. "Valentin Ivanovich, is it?"

Gorbachev said he would not resign.

Boldin, Gorbachev's longtime chief of staff, said, "Mikhail Sergeyevich, you don't understand what the situation in the country is." Gorbachev shot back, "Shut up, you prick! How dare you give me lectures about the situation in the country!"[24]

Gorbachev swore at them as they left.

For the next three days, Gorbachev and his family were effectively prisoners of their own compound, tormented and sleepless. Gorbachev feared Baklanov's statement about his health meant they might poison him, so the family and staff refused to accept food from outside and lived off compound supplies. Raisa took charge of looking out for their safety. Gorbachev strolled openly around the compound to show anyone who saw him that he was healthy. Armed guards had appeared at the garage, gates to the compound and the helicopter pad. The exit road was blocked by trucks. They listened to a tiny Sony transistor radio, and heard on the BBC that in Moscow the coup plotters had announced Gorbachev was ill and his duties taken by Yanayev. Gorbachev's own security detail managed to rig up a television antenna and they saw a press conference in Moscow at which Yanayev appeared drunk. They heard that Yeltsin had called on people to resist the coup. "I was sure, quite convinced that the whole business could not continue for long—they would not get away with it," Gorbachev said. He and Chernyaev walked outside, where they could not be bugged. Gorbachev called the plotters "agents of suicide" and "scoundrels." Gorbachev found it hard to believe Yazov and Kryuchkov had betrayed him.

On Monday, August 19, Chernyaev found Gorbachev resting his back, lying on the bed, writing in a notebook. Chernyaev sat down next to him and began swearing about all that had happened in the last day. Gorbachev looked at him sadly, he recalled, and said, "Yes, this may not end well. But you know, in this case, I have faith in Yeltsin. He won't give in to them, he won't compromise. But that means blood." Later in the day, Gorbachev, Chernyaev and Raisa huddled in a small pavilion at the beach, a place they hoped did not have KGB bugs. Raisa tore a few sheets of clean paper from a notebook and gave them to Chernyaev with a pencil. Gorbachev dictated a statement of demands for the outside world: turn on the phones and give me back the plane to return to Moscow and to work. In the middle of the night, they drew the curtains. With help from Irina and Anatoly, Gorbachev made a videotape denouncing the coup plotters. Raisa wrote in her diary, "Whatever happens to us, the people should know the truth about the fate of the President." They took apart the videocassette and cut the tape into four pieces using manicure scissors. Each piece of tape was wrapped in paper and sealed with tape, hidden around the house until they could smuggle them out. The cassette was reassembled so it would not show that it had been taken apart.

In Moscow on Monday morning at 8 A.M., Colonel Viktor Boldyrev, commander of the division in the General Staff that oversaw the nuclear system, was ordered by his superiors to bring the *chemodanchik* and the nuclear suitcase duty officers back to Moscow. Boldyrev replied that there was no way to communicate with them. The lines were still down.

In Foros, at 9 A.M., the next regular shift of duty officers for the nuclear suitcase showed up at Gorbachev's gate. They had been isolated at the military lodge and had no idea what had happened. At the gate, they were informed their passes were no longer valid. A radio played broadcasts from the GKChP. After an hour, they were told to go back.

Boldyrev finally got through to Foros, with help from the KGB, and instructed all the duty officers to return to Moscow with the nuclear suitcase. That afternoon, at 2 P.M., the officers gathered up their equipment—including the president's Cheget and the portfolio with the codes—and boarded a jeep for the airfield. They flew back to Moscow on Gorbachev's plane, the one that was supposed to bring him to the Kremlin for a ceremony signing the new union treaty on Tuesday. The duty officers were met in Moscow by representatives of the General Staff, who took the suitcase.[25]

Yeltsin had been elected president of the Russian republic, the largest of the internal Soviet republics, in June. Combative and iron willed, he rallied the people of Moscow against the plotters. At his dacha on the morning of August 19, Yeltsin and a few allies wrote a statement of resistance. Then he donned a bulletproof vest under his suit, and sped into town. Tanks were rolling toward the nineteen-story building on the banks of the Moscow River known as the Russian White House, where Yeltsin had his offices. Yeltsin walked out of the White House toward a mass of people who had come to defend the building. As journalist Michael Dobbs recalled, "A roar went up from the crowd when they spotted the towering figure of the Russian president striding purposefully down the ceremonial steps in front of the White House." Yeltsin climbed up Tank No. 110 of the Taman Division and read out his statement. "The use of force is absolutely unacceptable," he declared. "We are absolutely sure that our compatriots will not permit the tyranny and lawlessness of the putschists, who have lost all sense of shame and honor, to be confirmed. We appeal to military personnel to display their high sense of civil courage and refuse to participate in the reactionary coup."[26]

The coup attempt collapsed Wednesday, August 21. Tanks and troops were poised for action on the streets of Moscow, but the KGB's crack special forces troops, who were supposed to attack the White House, refused to do so.

Gorbachev lost control of the nuclear suitcase, but the nuclear commanders in the military kept their cool. At least one of the three who would have to launch an attack, Air Force General Yevgeny Shaposhnikov, was openly against the putsch. He recalled in his memoir that he told Yazov that the other two commanders-in-chief, of the rocket forces and the naval forces, also backed him. Most likely, they would not have followed any orders from the clownish coup plotters.[27] Yarynich, who knew well the workings of nuclear command and control, was inside the defense ministry during the days of the coup. "The vast number of people in the military were awaiting positive changes in the country, sympathized with the changes, and did not fall into a panic," he said. "The military understood the danger of rocking the boat in this storm, and did everything to prevent the boat from keeling over."[28]

As Gorbachev flew triumphantly back to Moscow, Chernyaev recalled a sense of euphoria on the plane. But when Gorbachev landed at Vnukovo Airport at 2 A.M., August 22, it became clear the tension had taken a terrible toll on his family. On the last day in Foros, Raisa had suffered a small stroke. In the car from the airport, Gorbachev's daughter Irina suffered a nervous breakdown, throwing herself on the seat in wracking sobs as her husband, Anatoly, tried to console her.

"I have come back from Foros to another country, and I myself am a different man now," Gorbachev declared. But Gorbachev did not realize how deeply the country had been transformed in those three days. The old system—the party and state that shaped his life and that he had led to *glasnost* and *perestroika*—was now dead. Gorbachev later admitted, "At the time I was not yet fully aware of the extent of the tragedy." Perhaps shell-shocked or preoccupied with his family's trauma, Gorbachev fumbled. He did not go directly to the White House, where crowds were waiting, nor to the huge victory demonstration the next day. He was unaware of how people had changed, wanting a complete break with the old system. Gorbachev told a press conference August 22 that the Communist Party remained a "progressive force," despite the betrayal of its bosses. Two days later, under pressure from Yeltsin, he retreated, resigning as general secretary of the party and calling for dissolution of the Central Committee. Yeltsin suspended actions of the Communist Party of the Soviet Union. Gorbachev was still president, but the country was rapidly disintegrating as the republics asserted independence, some before and some after the coup attempt.[29]

Chernyaev was working in the offices of the Central Committee on Old Square one day right after the coup when he heard the public address system urgently instruct everyone to leave immediately. He ignored the announcement and worked on for several hours. Then, when he reached the door to leave, he saw crowds outside. For his personal safety, he was evacuated through an underground tunnel to the Kremlin. The offices of the Central Committee were turned over to the Moscow city government as thousands cheered. The party heaved its last breath.

Sergei Akhromeyev, who had come to those same Central Committee offices six years earlier and promised to work with Gorbachev, who had been through so much with Gorbachev on arms control, pulling troops out of Afghanistan, revising the military doctrine and negotiating at Reykjavik, was despondent. He did not know about the coup attempt in advance, but once it began, he flew back to Moscow from his vacation and helped prepare the military for the assault on the White House that never came. Akhromeyev was not one of the original coup plotters, but he gave them an assist. After the putsch collapsed, Akhromeyev hanged himself by a white nylon cord in his Kremlin office. He left a note on his desk.

> I cannot live when my motherland is dying and everything that I ever believed in is being destroyed. My age and previous life give me the right to leave this life. I fought to the end.[30]

PART

THREE

A GREAT UNRAVELING

A day after the failed coup, Senator Sam Nunn, chairman of the Senate Armed Services Committee, squeezed his way through a crowd on the streets of Moscow. He had flown there from a conference in Budapest after receiving a phone call from Andrei Kokoshin, deputy director of the Institute for the Study of the United States and Canada. They had known each other for years, and there was urgency in Kokoshin's voice. Kokoshin wanted Nunn to come to Moscow immediately. Kokoshin "said there were big things happening in Russia," Nunn recalled. "He said *Russia* about four times. Always before it had been the Soviet Union. The bells went off in my head." In Moscow, Kokoshin picked up Nunn in his cramped little car and they drove directly to the White House. Yeltsin's supporters thronged streets still strewn with stone slabs and construction debris hastily erected as barricades against the tanks. Kokoshin introduced Nunn to several people he described as the new leaders of Russia. The next day, Kokoshin took Nunn to listen to the debates in parliament about the breakup of the Soviet Union. When Nunn left the building, he pushed his way through a crush of people. There was an atmosphere of intense excitement. "A new country was being created," he recalled. The crowd was shouting, "Down with the Soviet Union!"

Next, Nunn went to see Gorbachev in the Kremlin. They talked for about an hour. "I thought he looked shaken," Nunn recalled. "Obviously, he had been through quite an experience. And we talked a good bit about what was going to happen to the Soviet Union. He was still saying it was going to stay together. He was still the president." Nunn brought up the issue of command and control over nuclear weapons. In the back of his mind, he was worried about all the small, easily transportable tactical nuclear weapons that were spread among the republics. Gorbachev "tried to reassure me that the Soviet Union was going to remain intact, and that things were under control," Nunn recalled.

As he was leaving, Nunn turned to Gorbachev. "Did you lose command and control while you were in captivity?" he asked.

Gorbachev would not answer the question.[1]

Nunn grew up in a leading Methodist family in Perry, Georgia, population 11,000, in red dirt farm country. His father was a lawyer-farmer who was mayor of Perry when Nunn was born, and had served in the State Legislature and on the State Board of Education. After graduating from Emory University law school in 1962, Nunn went to Washington for a year, as a staff counsel on the House Armed Services Committee, returned to Georgia, served in the State Legislature and won a race for the U.S. Senate in 1972. Nunn had been mentored and influenced by powerful southern Democrats of an earlier generation, conservatives who were bulwarks of the military, among them Carl Vinson and John Stennis.[2] In the Senate, Nunn was a moderate-conservative, wary of Soviet intentions; he voted for Reagan's military buildup but was also an advocate for arms control agreements, especially to reduce the dangers of accidental nuclear war. Arms control, he once said, should "take the finger of both superpowers off the hair-trigger."[3]

What Nunn saw in Moscow after the coup brought back a personal memory from a Cold War flashpoint many years earlier. In 1974, when he had been in the Senate for only a year, Nunn toured NATO headquarters in Brussels and American military bases in Germany and Italy.[4] If war were to come in Europe, the first battlefield would be divided Germany. Soviet war plans called for a massive sweep of sixty divisions from East Germany and Czechoslovakia into West Germany, reaching the German-French border within thirteen to fifteen days.[5] They would face

NATO's tactical or battlefield nuclear weapons. American scientists and engineers had created tiny warheads that could fit into small missiles and artillery shells. The firepower of these miniature nukes was an alternative to using massive numbers of troops. The West had deployed seven thousand nuclear weapons in Europe during the period when Nunn visited. A substantial number of U.S. aircraft and missiles were on five-minute alert in case of a crisis.

At a U.S. tactical nuclear weapons base in Germany, where bunkers held warheads and shells, Nunn was shown the relatively small devices, including warheads that could be easily moved by one or two men. Nunn was reassured by the commanders that all the weapons were secure. As he left the building, a sergeant shook hands with him. In his hand, Nunn felt a piece of folded paper. He slipped it into his pocket.

"Senator Nunn," it said, "please meet me and some of my guard buddies at the barracks around 6 tonight after work. I have very important information for you."

That night, Nunn and his staff director, Frank Sullivan, went to the barracks. The sergeant and "three or four of his fellow sergeants related a horror story to me," Nunn later recalled. "A story of a demoralized military after Vietnam. A story of drug abuse. A story of alcohol abuse. A story of U.S. soldiers actually guarding the tactical nuclear weapons while they were stoned on drugs. The stories went on and on for over an hour." Nunn left "thoroughly shaken," he said.[6]

In Europe, Nunn also saw how easy it would be to stumble across the trip wire to nuclear war. In his report to the Senate, Nunn wrote, "There is a considerable danger that tactical nuclear weapons would be used at the very outset of a war, leading to possible, or even probable, escalation to strategic nuclear war." Nunn recalled that NATO briefers had told him they would want nuclear weapons released "as soon as necessary," but "as late as possible." Nunn felt they didn't put enough emphasis on *as late as possible*.

For many years, Nunn worried that the small, tactical nuclear weapons were even more fraught with danger than the huge intercontinental ballistic missiles. What if there was a minor skirmish over Berlin that got out of hand? "All of a sudden, bang, you've got a request on an American president's desk to be able to use battlefield nuclear weapons," Nunn said. "I was convinced nobody in the world had any idea what was going to happen after that started. You can sit around and read all the analytical stuff in the world, but once we start firing battlefield nuclear weapons, I don't think anybody knew." In the 1980s, Nunn added a new dimension to his concerns about accidental nuclear war. He realized the superpowers could be drawn into confrontation by gaps in the early-warning systems. A lone missile, perhaps from a third-country submarine, if mistaken for a first strike, could unleash a retaliatory onslaught before anyone would know how it began. Nunn asked the U.S. Strategic Air Command whether they could detect the origin of a submarine missile launch rapidly and accurately. After a top-secret study, they reported to Nunn that while the United States had a "fair" capability to pinpoint the origin, the Soviet Union's warning systems were much worse. If the Soviets spotted a missile from, say, China, and thought it was really from the United States, a terrible miscalculation could follow.[7]

Now, on a crowded street in Moscow in August 1991, all of Nunn's experience, knowledge and fears about nuclear danger came together once again. Who would protect thousands of small atomic bombs spread all over the Soviet Union? What if the Soviet Union plunged into chaos and civil conflict? Who was responsible for command and control? What if the Russian military were as demoralized as the American soldiers had been after Vietnam? As he flew home, Nunn said, "I was convinced of two things. One, that there would be no more Soviet empire. And two, that they and we had a huge, huge security problem."

Sitting on the deck of his family home at Walker's Point, Maine, with a sweeping view of the Atlantic Ocean, Bush pondered the aftermath of the coup at the end of his summer holiday. In a morning press conference September 2, he said he would not "cut into the muscle of defense of this country" to provide aid to the faltering Soviet Union. At lunch, alone on the deck, writing in his diary, he recalled that on this day forty-seven years before, he had been shot down in the Pacific during World War II. So much had changed. Just that morning, he had recognized the independence of the Baltics.

In these days, Bush raised with Scowcroft the possibility of a sweeping new initiative to reduce the danger of nuclear war.[8] For all his emphasis on prudence and his characteristic caution, Bush acted boldly. Within three weeks, he launched a significant pullback of U.S. nuclear weapons, both land and sea. He did it without drawn-out negotiations, without a treaty, without verification measures and without waiting for Soviet reciprocity. Raymond L. Garthoff, the historian, called it an arms race in reverse—and downhill. In a nationally televised address from the White House on September 27, Bush said, "The world has changed at a dramatic pace, with each day writing a fresh page of history before yesterday's ink has even dried." Bush announced the United States would eliminate all of its ground-launched battlefield or tactical nuclear weapons worldwide, and withdraw all those on ships; stand down the strategic bombers from high-alert status; take off hair-trigger alert 450 intercontinental ballistic missiles; and cancel several nuclear weapon modernization programs.[9] The announcement meant a pullback of 1,300 artillery-fired atomic projectiles, 850 Lance missile nuclear warheads, and 500 naval weapons. In one stroke, Bush pulled back naval surface weapons that the United States had earlier refused to even discuss as part of strategic weapons negotiations.

On October 5, Gorbachev joined the downhill arms race. He announced a pullback of all ground-based tactical nuclear weapons and removal of tactical nuclear weapons from ships and submarines, took strategic bombers off alert and removed 503 intercontinental ballistic missiles from combat readiness. Again, the world witnessed real disarmament at lightning speed. The CIA noted in a report that Gorbachev's initiative would essentially eliminate the nuclear capability of Soviet ground forces.[10] Only weeks before, in St. Vladimir's Hall in the Kremlin, Bush and Gorbachev had signed a strategic arms treaty that took nearly a decade to negotiate and allowed seven years to implement; now they both acted immediately, without a single negotiating session. Nothing was binding, and nothing was verifiable, but it was the most spontaneous and dramatic reversal of the Cold War arms race.[11]

On October 21, Bush wrote a note to Scowcroft, his national security adviser. "Please discuss," he said. "Does Mil Aide need to carry that black case now every little place I go?" He was asking about the "football" with the codes for managing a nuclear war. Bush did not think it was still necessary for a military aide to shadow him with the suitcase. Scowcroft and others persuaded him it was still necessary. At the State Department, a new policy memorandum informed Baker: "The Soviet Union as we know it no longer exists. What matters now is how the breakup of the Soviet Union proceeds from this point onward. Our aim should be to make the crash as peaceful as possible."[12]

It is hard to overstate the sense of relief, triumph and fresh possibility that arose from events in the Soviet Union that autumn. Forty-five years after George Kennan had written the Long Telegram, which laid the foundation for the Cold War strategy of containment, the protracted, draining competition that had shaped so much of the world abruptly came to an end, without cataclysm. "Today, even the most hard-eyed realist must see a world transformed," said the CIA director, Robert Gates, who had voiced grave doubts about Gorbachev for years. "Communism has at last been defeated."[13]

Yet even in these days of euphoria, when one could forget about the movie *The Day After* and the horror of nuclear winter, a danger appeared on the horizon. The threat was still masked by layers of Soviet secrecy and overshadowed by the celebratory mood. But an early hint came with Gorbachev's pullback of tactical nuclear weapons. The warheads were hastily moved to new storage depots by train. Could a weakened Soviet military, barely able to feed hungry troops, adequately protect the nuclear charges? With so many competing power centers—republics breaking away into new nations—could the Soviet system of centralized command and control remain intact? No one knew the answers to these questions, but signs of chaos and upheaval were everywhere. The Soviet rail cars were relatively primitive, lacking sophisticated alarm systems. The warheads were deactivated before being put on the trains, but there were no armored blankets to protect them from a bullet or shrapnel. The warhead depots were filled to capacity. Sometimes the trains just stopped dead on the tracks. There was an acute shortage of containers to protect the uranium and plutonium removed from dismantled weapons. The Soviet system did not have a suitable, secure warehouse to store these dangerous materials over the long term. When a Soviet official visited Washington that autumn, he was insistent on the need for help from the West to build a secure warehouse for the plutonium from warheads. Thousands of plutonium pits, the essential chunk of material used to cause the nuclear explosion, were stored like so many boxes in a furniture warehouse. "The containers are sticking out of the windows!" he warned.[14]

No one was prepared for an arms race in reverse.

As he flew home, Nunn pondered what he had seen. He felt the United States had to help Russia and the other new states just emerging from the Soviet breakdown. "We could end up with several fingers on the nuclear trigger," he thought. It was a nightmare of the nuclear age, yet concrete action was difficult to envisage. The dangers seemed pressing, but details were still scarce. One of the best-informed American experts about the Soviet system was Bruce Blair, the scholar at the Brookings Institution in Washington, who had asked many of the key questions about Soviet nuclear command and control during his research in Moscow. Although Blair felt the old Soviet system of rigid, central controls was reliable, he shared Nunn's worry about what would happen if it broke apart.[15] Another informed expert was Ashton B. Carter, a physicist, professor and director of the Center for Science and International Affairs at Harvard University. During the 1980s, Carter had served at the Pentagon, and understood the complexity of the American nuclear command and control systems.[16] Carter recalled telling Nunn that keeping a lid on nuclear weapons was not purely a technical matter. "A nuclear custodial system is only as stable as the social system in which it is embedded," he added. "And it's really made up of people and institutions and standard operating procedures and so forth, not just gizmos. When all of that is in the middle of a social revolution, you've got big trouble."

A social revolution was just what Nunn had seen on the streets of Moscow.

Soon after his return, Nunn walked across the Capitol to the office of Representative Les Aspin, a Wisconsin Democrat, who was chairman of the House Armed Services Committee. Aspin earned a reputation when he first came to Congress as a publicity hound and a maverick who delighted in exposing wasteful Pentagon spending. In later years, he moved to the center, and, like Nunn, became an influential voice on military and defense issues. Right after the coup, on August 28, Aspin proposed a dramatic shift of guns to butter: take $1 billion from the $290

billion Pentagon budget and spend it on humanitarian assistance for the
Soviet people. Two weeks later, on September 12, Aspin issued a white
paper, "A New Kind of Threat: Nuclear Weapons in an Uncertain Soviet
Union." The United States should make sure that "the first winter of
freedom after 70 years of communism isn't a disaster," Aspin declared.

When Nunn and Aspin met, the conversation was respectful, and at
first, tactful. Nunn hoped to coax Aspin to change his approach. In Russia, Nunn said, the most pressing need was helping the Soviet Union dismantle its arsenal. They agreed on one bill that would provide $1 billion
for transport of medicine and humanitarian aid, which was Aspin's idea,
as well as money for demilitarization, destroying warheads and converting defense factories to civilian purposes, which were Nunn's priorities.[17]

Nunn and Aspin, both experienced politicians, seriously miscalculated
the public mood.[18] A recession was setting in at home, and voters were
tired of overseas commitments. In early November, Democrat Harris
Wofford upset Republican Dick Thornburgh for a Senate seat from
Pennsylvania with an angry populist campaign, saying "it's time to take
care of our own people." The Nunn-Aspin bill came at just the wrong
moment. Polls showed Americans were opposed to sending direct aid to
the Soviet Union. Aspin recalled, "You could feel the wind shift."[19]

"It was clearly a firestorm, it wasn't like it was mild opposition," Nunn
recalled. He was deeply frustrated. With his own eyes he had seen the
chaos on the streets of Moscow, and he knew of the potential for nuclear
accidents and proliferation, but the politicians in Washington seemed
oblivious to the dangers. Some senators told Nunn they could not explain
in one-minute sound bites why they should support his legislation, so
they would not vote for it. Nunn went to the Senate floor November 13
and tried to break through the mood of indifference with a powerful
speech. He said that even after the strategic arms treaty signed earlier in
the year, the rapidly disintegrating Soviet Union, including the republics
outside of Russia, still had fifteen thousand nuclear warheads to destroy,
and needed help. "Unfortunately, nuclear weapons do not just go away
when they are no longer wanted," he said. The Soviet Union was short of
storage space, transportation, dismantlement plants and equipment for
radioactive materials handling. Nunn had learned these details from
Viktor Mikhailov, the deputy minister of atomic energy, who had visited
Washington and pleaded for help.[20]

"Do we recognize the opportunity we have today during this period in history and the great danger we have of proliferation, or do we sit on our hands and cater to what we think people want to hear in this country?" Nunn asked.

"What are the consequences of doing nothing?"

Nunn wondered what kind of one-minute explanation his colleagues would need if the Soviet Union fell into civil war like Yugoslavia, with nuclear weapons all over. "If helping them destroy 15,000 weapons is not a reduction in the Soviet military threat, why have we been worrying about these 15,000 weapons for the last 30 years? I do not see any logic here at all," he said. The United States had spent $4 trillion during the Cold War, so $1 billion to destroy weapons "would not be too high a price to pay to help destroy thousands and thousands of Soviet nuclear weapons," Nunn insisted.

"We have the opportunity for an unprecedented destruction of the weapons of war," Nunn declared. Yet he warned, "We are going to sleep—to sleep—about a country that is coming apart at the seams economically, that wants to destroy nuclear weapons at this juncture but may not in the months and years ahead."

"Are we going to continue to sit on our hands?" Nunn then pulled back the legislation. [21]

At this critical moment, the president was nowhere to be seen. Bush did not want to take political risks for the Nunn-Aspin legislation. But a handful of influential voices from Moscow made a difference in the Senate. Hours after Nunn pulled back the bill, Alexander Yakovlev, the architect of Gorbachev's *perestroika*, spoke with senators in the Capitol at an early-evening reception, impressing on them the urgency of the crisis. Two days later, Nunn relaunched his efforts. Two top officials of the Institute for the Study of the United States and Canada—Andrei Kokoshin, who had met Nunn with his little white car in Moscow, and Sergei Rogov—were both at that moment in Washington. The institute had long been a meeting point between American and Soviet experts on defense and security issues. Nunn invited them to a small lunch, to which he also brought Senator Richard Lugar of Indiana, a leading Republican voice on foreign affairs. At the lunch, Kokoshin and Rogov warned that power was slipping away from Gorbachev by the minute, and that in a "worst-case scenario," nuclear weapons could be caught up in the struggle for power among the Soviet republics. This was a volatile, dangerous situation, they said, urging America to "wake up." Lugar told journalist Don Oberdorfer that the lunch with Kokoshin and Rogov was "a very alarming conversation."[22]

On November 19, Ashton B. Carter, the Harvard physicist, came to Nunn's office for a brainstorming session, along with Lugar; William J. Perry of Stanford University, who had been examining the Soviet military-industrial complex; David Hamburg of the Carnegie Corporation of New York; and John Steinbrunner of the Brookings Institution. Carter drove home the point that a Soviet collapse, now clearly visible from the daily news reports coming out of Moscow, was an immense security threat. "This is completely unprecedented," Carter recalled saying. "Never before has a nuclear power disintegrated." Carter had just completed a study of the potential dangers, *Soviet Nuclear Fission: Control of the Nuclear Arsenal in a Disintegrating Soviet Union*, and it was a snapshot of the frightening dilemma that Nunn and others confronted at the time. The study pointed out that nobody really knew what lurked behind the curtain of Soviet secrecy on nuclear weapons. But, the study warned, there were "three cardinal dangers": the dispersal of control over nuclear weapons to different republics; the chance that weapons, components or fissile materials "will fall into unauthorized hands"; and the possibility that outside groups, including terrorists and other nations, might seek to obtain weapons, materials or knowledge from the chaotic Soviet complex, "through theft or sale." While Nunn feared a rogue general grabbing control of the launch system, Carter responded that the threat was "all kinds of motives, all kinds of people, the wayward general to the wayward scientist to the wayward clerk, custodian and sergeant." The next day, November 20, Lugar announced his support for immediate action on legislation in a floor speech. He decried the "quarrelsome" mood in Congress in the face of "strategic danger" to the country. "Nuclear weapons do not simply fade away; they must be disabled, dismantled and destroyed," he said.

On November 21, at an 8 A.M. breakfast, Nunn brought sixteen senators from both parties to the Senate Armed Services committee room, where the trillions of defense spending had been authorized over the years. He told them what he had seen in Moscow and turned the floor over to Carter, who delivered a presentation without notes. Carter said command and control over nuclear weapons could not be isolated from the troubles of society. "It's not something that you can take for granted, that it's all wired up in some way, and it will be okay," Carter recalled telling the senators.[23] The clarity of his presentation had an instant impact. The addition of Lugar was critical. Within days, Nunn and Lugar had turned around the Senate and gathered the votes for new legislation to set aside $500 million to deal with the Soviet nuclear dangers. The outcome was a remarkable and rare example of foreign policy leadership by Congress. The Bush administration was indifferent. Ross, who was the State Department's policy planning director, said he saw the need but recalled a sense of fatigue and exhaustion in the administration; they had just been through the Gulf War and the Middle East peace conference, and could not summon the energy for another major initiative. There was also a lingering Cold War mind-set, especially at the Defense Department under Secretary Dick Cheney. Carter recalled making a presentation of his concerns to Donald Atwood, deputy secretary of defense. "His position was very clear, which was that we had spent 50 years trying to impoverish these people, and we'd finally done it, and at this moment you want to assist?" Carter recalled. "In fact, Don had a phrase, which was *freefall*. He wanted them in freefall. And I felt that freefall was not safe. It was not a safe position given that they had nuclear weapons."

Visiting Bush at the White House, Nunn and Lugar found him ambivalent. "I remember that he wasn't saying no," Nunn said. "He just was very cool to the whole idea. I think he was sensing the political dangers of it." While Bush stood on the sidelines, Congress moved swiftly. The Senate approved the Nunn-Lugar bill by a vote of 86–8. Later, the total was reduced to $400 million, and it passed the House by a voice vote. To secure enough support, the legislation did not mandate that the United States spend the money, it only said the administration *could*. It did not require that it be new money, but rather funds shifted from other programs.

Bush's cautious national security adviser, Brent Scowcroft, shrugged at the prospect that there would be more than one finger on the nuclear trigger. After all the years of the Soviet Union as the singular source of danger, he thought it wouldn't hurt if the central command and control were broken up into several smaller nuclear powers.[24] But Baker, the secretary of state, was more alarmed than others about the prospect of nuclear bedlam after a Soviet crackup. "I wanted to make sure we didn't have a proliferation of nuclear weapons states," he recalled. "The more nuclear weapons you have, the less stability you have. The more chance of accidental launches, and all the rest of it, or just having little countries that have nukes, like Pakistan, getting pissed at India and letting loose."[25]

On December 1, voters in Ukraine approved a referendum on independence. Then, on December 8, at Belovezhskaya Pushcha, a hunting resort outside the city of Brest in Belarus, Yeltsin and the leaders of Ukraine and Belarus declared the Soviet Union dissolved and formed a new Commonwealth of Independent States without telling Gorbachev. The collapse of the center was accelerated by Yeltsin's fierce determination to wrest power from Gorbachev. Back in Moscow, Yeltsin went to the Soviet defense ministry in a conspicuous effort to woo the military. Baker recalled, "These moves were the stuff of a geopolitical nightmare. Two Kremlin heavyweights, jockeying for political power, calling on the army to follow them, and raising the specter of civil war—with nuclear weapons thrown into the mix." The situation was so unsettled that Baker, due to give a speech at Princeton on December 12, could not decide what to call the dying Soviet Union. In the end, he settled for the awkward phrase "Russia, Ukraine, the republics, and any common entities." Baker said in the speech, "If, during the Cold War, we spent trillions of dollars on missiles and bombers to destroy Soviet nuclear weapons in time of war, surely now we can spend just millions of dollars to actually destroy and help control those same nuclear weapons in time of peace."[26] Bush signed the Nunn-Lugar bill the same day.

The worst fears of Nunn, Baker and others were that loose nukes, fast money and a weak state would all come together, perhaps in some kind of proliferation-for-profit syndicate. A glimpse of this possibility materialized at 15 Ulitsa Varvarka, a pleasant street near the old Central Committee offices in the heart of Moscow. There, the International Chetek

Corporation opened a makeshift but bustling one-room office in 1991. The name of the company was derived from the Russian words for man, *chelovek*, technologies, *tekhnologii*, and capital, *kapital*. The capital came from several leading enterprises in the military-industrial complex, including Arzamas-16, the nuclear weapons design laboratory based in the closed city of Sarov, 233 miles east of Moscow, where the Soviet Union had first developed a nuclear weapon and Andrei Sakharov had worked on the hydrogen bomb. Chetek was offering to sell a special service: underground nuclear explosions to destroy chemical and toxic industrial wastes, munitions, nuclear reactors or anything else by incinerating it with thermonuclear blasts two thousand feet underground—for a fee.[27]

This was the first known case of Soviet weapons scientists seeking to privatize their knowledge. A frequent booster of the enterprise in 1991 was Viktor Mikhailov, the chain-smoking deputy atomic energy minister, who had visited Washington in October, warning of the need to build safe storage for nuclear warheads. Mikhailov had spent years in the Soviet nuclear-testing program. Peaceful nuclear explosions—using blasts for digging canals, mining or other purposes besides war—had been carried out by both the United States and Soviet Union, but eventually discarded, in part because of environmental hazards.[28] The last Soviet explosion was in 1988. What was startling about Chetek was the idea that nuclear explosions were for sale from a weapons laboratory.

In December, a group of American experts on arms control and nuclear weapons arrived in Moscow for a joint workshop with Soviet specialists on warhead verification and dismantlement. On their first night, they were surprised to find that Chetek was hosting a banquet for them at a former Communist Party training school. The toastmaster was Alexei Leonov, a commander of the joint Apollo-Soyuz missions in the 1970s and the first Soviet cosmonaut to walk in space. Mikhailov was there, too, along with officials from Arzamas-16. On entering the banquet room, each member of the delegation was handed a plastic bag containing small souvenirs and a press release, at the top of which was printed both the name of the private company and the government ministry. Mikhailov signed as deputy atomic energy minister, along with Vladimir Dmitriev, president of Chetek. The press release was defensive in tone—responding to news reports about Chetek's activities in recent months—but it also confirmed some of the worst fears of the Americans.

It said that Chetek had signed a deal with Arzamas to use nuclear explosions for the destruction of highly toxic industrial wastes. And the nuclear devices? Just to be clear, Chetek "did not have, does not have, and can not have access to nuclear devices, their components or any knowledge about them." The press release said that "practical work" in nuclear weapons would still be done by the government.[29]

When they entered the hall, the Americans saw right away what was happening. "Various elements of the national security establishment were maneuvering to privatize themselves and go into business," recalled Christopher E. Paine, of the Natural Resources Defense Council, who attended. "The elements of the Soviet state that you would almost least expect to be rushing into business were in fact the ones that were doing it, and trying to earn a buck off whatever asset they had, including surplus nuclear weapons. A lot of the people we met from the weapons laboratories were kind of innocent in a strange way, innocent in the ways of the world. They lived in this bubble all of their lives, and they didn't have an idea of business, they didn't know what it was."

One of the Soviet officials at the banquet was Alexander Tchernyshev, who had worked for many years with Mikhailov on Soviet nuclear tests. Tchernyshev headed an office at Arzamas-16, but also represented Chetek. It was hard to see where the government-operated nuclear weapons laboratory ended and the private company began. Tchernyshev presented the Americans with a Chetek business card that also carried his Arzamas affiliation.

When Fred Hiatt of the *Washington Post* went to the Chetek offices in Moscow a few weeks later, he interviewed Tchernyshev, who explained that the nuclear weapons establishment, long hidden behind barbed wire in closed cities, was falling on hard times with the collapse of the Soviet economy. "Representatives of our institute are running around the region looking for food, but everything is for barter," he said. "Does it mean we will have to trade bombs for meat? It's absurd."[30]

According to its advertising literature, Chetek planned to bring in clients and finance the research for blasting the wastes, while the government would actually handle the explosions. The first demonstration was planned for 1992 at Novaya Zemlya, the Soviet nuclear weapons testing range in the Arctic. In the end, Chetek never carried out the demonstration because of a test ban that remained in place, but it was an early and ominous example of what could happen if desperate weapons scientists went into business. It was also a harbinger of a phenomenon that would spread like wildfire in Russia in the 1990s: the hijacking of state resources and expertise for private gain.

As the Soviet economy nose-dived in the autumn of 1991, Nunn and others wondered whether the gargantuan Soviet military-industrial complex could be transformed to serve the civilian economy. This idea was known as "defense conversion" and Gorbachev once harbored great hopes for it: retooling tank factories, shipyards and missile design bureaus to churn out refrigerators, washing machines and computers. Gorbachev had first begun to push for conversion in earnest after his United Nations speech in 1988, but it proved difficult to convert swords to plowshares. The military and its complex of factories stiffly resisted. Typical was Alexander Sarkisov, chief engine designer for Soviet fighter jets. "Look, in the world market, a kilo of a modern fighter plane costs over $2,000, and a kilo of saucepans, $1." It didn't make sense, he added, to switch from jet fighters to saucepans. Some defense factories made shoddy civilian goods; others simply atrophied.[31]

In the end, Gorbachev ran out of time. By late 1991, the radical reformers around Yeltsin were determined to make the leap toward free markets and destroy the Soviet state. In a landmark speech October 28, Yeltsin said he would set prices free, and pledged "deep conversion," shutting down defense enterprises altogether and converting others totally to civilian purposes. The new market system, just taking shape, injected yet another wild card into the chaos of the reverse arms race. For decades, the sprawling military-industrial complex was dependent on the state, fed subsidies from the center and protected by the Communist Party. Factory bosses did not worry about prices, markets or efficiency. But now, they had to rethink everything: not only how to reengineer themselves to construct a washing machine, but how to accomplish it in an entirely different and unfamiliar economic system, without subsidies and without the godfathers of the party. The CIA produced a classified report in early October that captured all the doubts: "Soviet Defense Industry: Confronting Ruin."[32]

On a freezing day in the remote industrial city of Perm, William F. Burns got a glimpse of the reality, and it was not promising. A retired army major general, Burns had served as an arms control negotiator, and later director of the Arms Control and Disarmament Agency at the State Department.[33] In December 1991, the National Academy of Sciences sent him to examine Soviet defense factories and evaluate their potential for conversion. "The whole point was to see if this was an irreversible transition, or whether it was just sort of a sideline," he said. Burns toured a decrepit former munitions factory in Perm where the managers were trying to manufacture bicycles. Inside the U-shaped building, low-wattage electric lightbulbs hung from the ceiling, the factory floor was cold, workers were dressed in winter clothes, wearing gloves with their fingers protruding, as bicycle parts moved about on a conveyor that used to hold 203-mm artillery projectiles.

As Burns recalled later, the factory manager didn't have a clue what would happen to the bicycles. Rather plaintively, he asked Burns if they might sell in the United States. Burns thought to himself the primitive bicycles looked like his own bike when he was eight years old in 1940. "He was trying to be a western businessman," Burns recalled of the manager, "but he didn't know the language."

Burns asked what price the manager would set for the bicycles. "Three hundred eighty rubles," he replied.

"How did you arrive at the price?" Burns asked.

"Well, I did it the capitalist way," the manager replied. "I added up the cost of production. I added up the wages and divided by the number of bicycles. It comes to 380 rubles." He smiled, Burns recalled, pleased with himself.

"Well, how about investment?" Burns asked.

"Investment?" the manager replied. "What is investment?"

"What about profit?" Burns asked. "If you are trying to run a business the capitalist way, then profit is a very important thing."

"How do you calculate the profit?" the manager asked.[34]

At Obolensk, Sergei Popov sat in his office, depressed. He had given the system years and years of his best efforts, but by 1991, government funding was running out. Salaries were paid late, or paid in kind with sugar, or eggs from a local poultry farm. Biopreparat was no longer isolated from the economic collapse in the rest of the country. The scientists were told by the government to convert to civilian research.

Popov felt fortunate that his laboratory could generate some ideas for projects beyond biological weapons, but he knew others who could not. "It was just impossible if you dealt with anthrax or plague weaponization," he remembered. "What could you suggest would be the practical purpose?" Popov joined a cooperative, the pioneering, small private businesses created by Gorbachev's reforms. They developed a microbial powder for veterinary use, using the facilities at Obolensk. Instead of growing plague or other pathogens, they cultivated intestinal bacteria and sold it as a supplement to cattle and chicken feed. They made a profit right away, since their overhead was free. Popov also created a new variety of interferon that could boost the immune system response against viruses. "We found it could be a good additive to chicken feed, because chickens suffered heavily from viral infections," he said. They could even aerosolize the preparation to spray whole poultry houses, just as they had considered doing with biological weapons. Popov applied for a patent.

In the laboratories, the weapons research lapsed into a twilight zone. It wasn't stopped, but as scientists struggled to survive, they spent less time creating agents for the military. Popov said he was "almost completely refocused" on trying to make ends meet. "We were still under serious restrictions. We could not tell anybody what we did before. We could not disclose our secrets. But the overall situation was that nobody cared very much about it anymore." Popov and his wife planted potatoes and vegetables, picked forest mushrooms and ferns. One winter day, wolves attacked and killed rabbits being kept for biological weapons experiments at the laboratory. The wolves didn't eat the rabbits, just killed them for sport, and left an awful scene, spattered with blood. Popov gathered them up, skinned them and put them in the freezer to feed his family.

Then the chicken feed business collapsed. "It ended very suddenly because these farms had no money to feed chickens at all," he said. "There was no sense adding anything to the chicken feed, because there was no money. It was a time of financial crisis, cash was in short supply, nobody paid anybody. There was a bank crisis and no honest business had

a chance to survive. The cooperatives and those poultry farms went bankrupt simply because there was no means to pay, and no means to get a
profit."

Popov and his wife, Taissia, were desperate. "I realized that all my
efforts were fruitless," he said, "and I saw no future for myself." She
feared for their daughters, then seven and seventeen. "I realized there
was no money to support the children," she said. "I was scared. I said to
Sergei, we need to do something."

Twelve years earlier, when he had spent six months in Cambridge,
England, Popov worked in the laboratory of a microbiologist, Michael
Gait. In the summer of 1991, Gait came to Moscow for an international
scientific conference and was delighted to see Popov again. Popov had
driven all the way into the city to see Gait, and invited him to visit his
home and meet his family. They headed south, driving an hour to
Obolensk in Popov's white Zhiguli car. As they approached the restricted
zone around the institute, Popov warned Gait to be absolutely silent as
they drove through the checkpoints. No one stopped them. They didn't
go to the institute, but to Popov's apartment, where Gait enjoyed a meal
with the family, sampling homemade brandy and listening to the Beatles.
Gait recalled that the Popovs told him their money was drying up. Taissia was in tears. They asked for help in getting a postdoctoral appointment for Sergei in the United Kingdom. Gait promised to do everything
he could. In the autumn, he received a letter from Sergei saying they were
down to their "last sack of potatoes."[35]

Alibek finally got a chance to see America. At the last minute, he was
added to the Soviet delegation making a reciprocal visit to the United
States for the one in January to the Soviet Union by the British and
American experts. (Davis and Kelly came, too, representing the United
Kingdom.) For many years, the KGB had claimed there was a hidden
U.S. germ warfare effort. Now Alibek could check for himself. The thir-
teen-member Soviet delegation arrived in Washington on December 11,
1991. The delegation also included Sandakhchiev, director of Koltsovo,
and Urakov, director of Obolensk. They were two of the most important
institute directors in the Soviet biological weapons program.

The first stop was Fort Detrick, Maryland, where biological weapons research had been halted in 1969 by Nixon's decision. "We didn't believe a word of Nixon's announcement," Alibek recalled. "We thought the Americans were only wrapping a thicker cloak around their activities." In the first building the Soviet team wanted to see, white-coated technicians explained that they were working on antidotes to toxins from shellfish and animals. Alibek thought they were too friendly. "I despaired of ever penetrating beneath the surface," he wrote in his memoirs. Next, the Soviets asked to inspect a large structure on the grounds at Fort Detrick, which looked like an upside-down ice cream cone. Their bus took them there, and through a pair of open bay doors, they saw a gray powder. They asked the Americans what it was.

"Salt," they were told, for treating icy roads in the winter.

One member of the Soviet delegation went up to the pile, put his finger in it and put it to his mouth. He looked embarrassed. "It's salt," he said.

They went on to visit another laboratory, which they were told was developing vaccines against anthrax. "The small size of the operation made it clear that weapons production was out of the question there," Alibek recalled. "The Americans had just two specialists in anthrax. We had two thousand."

They flew to Salt Lake City, Utah, to see the Dugway Proving Grounds, where germ warfare experiments were halted in 1969. On the way, Alibek said, "I stared in wonderment at the well-paved highways, the well-stocked stores, and the luxurious homes where ordinary Americans lived." While some of the buildings at Dugway seemed similar to those used in Soviet test sites, Alibek saw "there were no animals, no cages, not even the footprint of experimental weapons activity."

Then they flew to Pine Bluff, Arkansas, where the United States once had a stockpile of pathogens, which were destroyed after Nixon's decision. Alibek realized as he walked through the buildings that the facilities were now solely for civilian use. On the second day, the Soviet delegation was on a bus, passing various structures, when one of the military officers shouted, "Stop the bus! Stop the bus!" The officer pointed to a tall metal structure on a rise. "We have to check that out," he insisted.

"Don't be ridiculous," Alibek replied. "It's a water tower."

"I don't think so," the officer said, running to the tower. He climbed it all the way to the top. Alibek could hear some of the Americans stifle a laugh. "At this point," Alibek concluded, "the absurdity of our quest was clear to me."

There was no American biological weapons program, as Alibek had believed for years. "It was a shock," Alibek said. "When you spend 17 years doing something, you considered it important, and—suddenly you realize, you have been lied to for 17 years! I was really offended, and I started hating the system." Alibek was instructed to write a report about the trip, saying he found evidence of biological weapons in the United States, the exact opposite of the truth. At this point, he decided to quit Biopreparat. He returned to Moscow on December 25. As he entered the hallway of his apartment, arms full of gifts from the United States, his wife told him some startling news about Gorbachev.[36]

Gorbachev fought to hold the Soviet Union together, but could not. Soon after Baker had arrived on December 16 for meetings with Gorbachev and Yeltsin, he learned that Yeltsin had already signed decrees effectively taking over the Soviet Foreign and Interior ministries. Yeltsin went out of his way to display his preeminence, making sure he met with Baker in Saint Catherine's Hall in the Kremlin, the gilded chamber where Baker had often held talks with Gorbachev.[37] Yevgeny Shaposhnikov, the defense minister for the new commonwealth, was at Yeltsin's side. Baker saw the end was near for Gorbachev. "I was really saddened," he recalled.[38]

Baker and Yeltsin were left alone at the end of their meeting to talk about nuclear command and control. Yeltsin gave Baker a description of how the system would work: in effect, only he and Shaposhnikov, commander of strategic forces with control over all the nuclear weapons, would possess the briefcases, the Cheget. The three other republics with nuclear weapons, Ukraine, Belarus and Kazakhstan, would get a "hot line," a telephone, but not a nuclear briefcase. Gorbachev still had a briefcase, but his would be taken away by the end of December, Yeltsin said. The system was one of "consultation," Yeltsin said, "not coordination."

According to Baker's notes of the conversation, Yeltsin told him the leaders of the other republics didn't understand how nuclear command and control worked. "They'll be satisfied with having telephones," he said. And once Russia got all the nuclear weapons back on its soil, even the telephones would be removed. Baker wrote in his notes:

"5 tele.—2 briefcases for now

Only Pres. of Russia can launch—Def. Min. won't be able to alone."

Later, in a private meeting with Shaposhnikov, Baker asked him to go over, once again, the nuclear command and control arrangements. Shaposhnikov confirmed what Yeltsin had told Baker.

"Who gives you orders today?" Baker asked.

"Gorbachev," Shaposhnikov replied. He would not speculate about the future.

But Baker was worried. He had written at the top of his notepad a question: "Who gives Shaposhnikov his orders?"[39]

About 5 P.M. on December 25, Gorbachev called Bush, who was at Camp David celebrating Christmas morning with his family. The Soviet president said he planned to resign, stepping down as commander in chief and transferring his authority to use nuclear weapons to Yeltsin. "I can assure you that everything is under strict control," he said. "There will be no disconnection. You can have a very quiet Christmas evening."[40]

At 6:55 P.M., Gorbachev entered the crowded Kremlin television studio, Room No. 4, crammed with network cameras and bright lights. He was carrying a briefcase with his departure speech, and a decree giving up his role as commander in chief of the armed forces. He put the decree on the small table and asked Andrei Grachev, his press secretary, for a pen. He tested it on a sheet of paper and asked for one with a smoother tip. The head of the CNN crew reached over Grachev's shoulder and offered his own pen to Gorbachev. With a flourish, he signed the document just before he went on the air.

His short address reflected his long, remarkable journey. When he took office in 1985, Gorbachev said, he felt it was a shame that a nation so richly endowed, so brimming with natural resources and human talent endowed by God, was living so poorly compared with the developed countries of the world. He blamed the Soviet command system and ideology, and he blamed the "terrible burden of the arms race." The Soviet people had "reached the limits of endurance," he said. "All attempts at

partial reform—and there were many—failed, one after another. The
country was losing its future. We could not go on living like this. Everything had to be drastically changed."

After the speech, Gorbachev went back to his office, where Shaposhnikov
was waiting for him, along with the duty officers carrying the suitcase
with the nuclear command codes and communications links. Yeltsin earlier agreed to come to Gorbachev's office to get the Cheget. But Yeltsin
was upset by something in Gorbachev's speech and changed his mind,
refusing to come, proposing instead they meet halfway, in Saint Catherine's Hall. Gorbachev thought this was a stupid game, and brusquely
decided to dispatch Shaposhnikov and the duty officers off with the suitcase without him. "They disappeared into the corridors in search of their
new boss," recalled Grachev.[41]

The Soviet hammer-and-sickle came down after the speech, and the
Russian tricolor flag was hoisted over the Kremlin.

The collapse of the Soviet Union marked the end of seven decades of a
failed ideology, hypermilitarization and rigid central controls. It left
behind 6,623 nuclear warheads on land-based intercontinental ballistic
missiles, 2,760 nuclear warheads on sea-based missiles, 822 nuclear bombs
on planes and 150 warheads deployed on cruise missiles, as well as perhaps another 15,000 tactical nuclear warheads scattered in depots, trains
and warehouses.[42] It left behind at least 40,000 tons of chemical weapons,
including millions of shells filled with nerve gas so deadly that one drop
would kill a human being. It left behind tons of anthrax bacteria spores,
buried on Vozrozhdeniye Island, and perhaps as much as 20 metric tons
of smallpox in weapons, as well as pathogens the world had never known,
stashed in the culture collections at Obolensk and Koltsovo. It left behind
hundreds of thousands of workers who knew the secrets, and who were
now embittered, dispirited, and, in some cases, down to their last sack of
potatoes.

THE SCIENTISTS

In a televised speech on December 29, 1991, Boris Yeltsin promised to rule an entirely new country. "We are abandoning mirages and illusions," he declared. "We are ridding ourselves of the militarization of our life, we have stopped constantly preparing for war with the whole world, and much more besides." Yeltsin described the grim inheritance from the Soviet Union: devastated farmlands, the economy "gravely ill," and towering external debt.[1]

In a gamble with history, Yeltsin attempted to make a rapid leap from failed socialism to a market economy, setting prices free and putting the colossal stock of state property into private hands. Yeltsin believed it was the only route for Russia to become a normal country, tap into global markets, modernize aging factories and lift living standards. But there were stark, unsettling dislocations. A few tycoons, known as oligarchs, grew wealthy, while millions of workers got their wages months late, if at all, or were paid in barter goods, such as socks and jars of pickles. Even though the new capitalism featured stock markets, private banks, expensive restaurants, luxury cars and sparkling new office towers, the deeper transformation—creating a modern industrial base, building rule of law, civil society and a diversified economy—was excruciatingly difficult and did not come about at first. The sad reality of these years was that many people could not adapt to the new world, and were set adrift. The weapons scientists and workers of the sprawling Soviet defense complex were among them.

Yeltsin deliberately let the military-industrial complex atrophy. He viewed the old defense establishment as a relic of the hypermilitarization that had so doomed the Soviet Union, and had little faith the aging institutes and factories could ever be converted to peaceful purposes or be of much use in the new capitalism. Yeltsin and his team were determined to completely raze the Soviet system and build a new one. There were many reasons for this approach, not the least of which was that Yeltsin possessed a much stronger view of what he wanted to tear down than what he wanted to build. He sought to eliminate the overweening state that he knew at first hand, while he had no model, just instincts, for constructing a modern free-market democracy. It was an enormous task. As Yeltsin biographer Leon Aron pointed out, Yeltsin's first revolutions were carried out against the party and the Soviet empire, both with a rising tide of popular support. This time, Yeltsin had only "the shallows and fetid waters of the 'command economy,' choked with decomposing and toxic debris."[2]

On February 14, 1992, in a car speeding through the forests of western Siberia, James A. Baker III, the U.S. secretary of state, witnessed a breathtaking tableau: white snow, frozen lakes, birch stands and a storybook *troika*—a sleigh pulled by three horses—in the distance. Then he passed through several checkpoints and barbed-wire perimeter fences to arrive at the citadel of Soviet nuclear bomb builders, the All Union Scientific Research Institute of Technical Physics, Chelyabinsk-70, one of two Soviet nuclear weapons design laboratories, a facility so secret it was not on any Soviet map. Chelyabinsk-70 was established in 1955 as a competitor to the first Soviet nuclear weapon design bureau at Arzamas-16. The scientists at Chelyabinsk-70 had pioneered miniaturization of nuclear warheads for the Soviet Union, allowing many small explosives to be placed atop a giant intercontinental ballistic missile, or put inside shells so small they could be fired as artillery on the battlefields of Europe.[3] The two labs were analogous to Los Alamos National Laboratory in New Mexico and Lawrence Livermore National Laboratory in California.

As Baker pulled up to the main building at Chelyabinsk-70, about eight stories tall, hundreds of technicians and scientists pressed against every available window, shouting and waving. Their jubilation took Baker by surprise. "I felt a bit as though I had landed from Mars," he recalled, "an alien curiosity that these men and women just had to see with their own eyes." The facility itself was another shock, shabby and threadbare. Whereas Livermore and Los Alamos were champions of supercomputing, there were no computer monitors in sight. When Baker was escorted to a small lecture hall to meet with twenty-five of the institute's senior scientists, he sat with his back to a dusty chalkboard. It reminded him of a Princeton undergraduate classroom in the 1950s. He told the scientists, seated in front of him, "This is every bit as remarkable for us as it is for you." Later, he recalled in his memoir, "As we sat down, I thought, here are the men that designed the weapons that defined the Cold War, and we're about to discuss how we in the West can help them secure their future."

The scientists and engineers talked openly of their deteriorating living standards. This once-insular elite was in trouble, and reaching beyond the barbed wire for help. Yevgeny Avrorin, the scientific director, standing at the end of the table by the blackboard, said the laboratory faced a "difficult, trying situation" as government subsidies dwindled. The scientists didn't want handouts, he said; they wanted productive and challenging work. They possessed an enormous storehouse of knowledge and equipment, and felt they had much they could give back to society. The deputy director, Vladislav Nikitin, said that salaries for top scientists were no more than fifteen hundred rubles a month, or $15 at the official exchange rate. Chelyabinsk-70 employed sixteen thousand people, about nine thousand technicians and about seven thousand scientists and engineers. "We have no shortage of ideas," Avrorin said, presenting Baker with a long list of commercial products they could produce if they had Western investors: artificial diamonds, fiber optics, food irradiation, nuclear medicine. But they had no investors, and no way to reach any. Avrorin didn't yet have e-mail. Avrorin then handed Baker the paper he had been reading from, apologizing for a hasty translation into English.[4]

Baker appealed to them not to lose hope. "We know that right now your options at home are limited and outlaw regimes and terrorists may try to exploit your situation and influence you to build new weapons of war." As the physicists and engineers scribbled in tiny notebooks, Baker added, "Some talk about the brain drain problem. But I think we should talk about the brain gain solution, and that is a solution of putting you to the work of peace, to accelerate reform and build democracy here, to help your people live better lives for decades to come." He described plans by the West to establish a new center, with international funding, to support their science and technology work.

Baker's visit offered a hint of a crisis that was gathering force and would persist for years. If Chelyabinsk-70, located 1,118 miles east of Moscow, was at all emblematic of the Soviet military-industrial complex, then the potential for disaster was greater than anyone had imagined: scientists with knowledge to build weapons of mass destruction were wanting for food and medicines.[5]

Anne M. Harrington arrived in Moscow with her family just after the August 1991 coup attempt. Her husband was a foreign service officer in the political section of the U.S. Embassy, and the State Department was starting a new program to provide more opportunity to spouses, offering them positions as analysts. Harrington, eager to help, became the science and technology analyst in the Moscow embassy. Her office was dreadful, located in an underground, windowless annex. After a recent fire in the main embassy building, sacks of wet, burned documents were piled nearby. The odor of cinders lingered. Harrington worked on a desktop thrown over two wooden sawhorses. She volunteered to track the "brain drain" problem because no one else was interested. "I put up my hand and said, 'I can do that,'" she recalled. In the first weeks after the Soviet Union collapsed, Harrington met with science counselors from other Western embassies, and sent a cable back to Washington. "Is brain drain good or bad?" she wrote, adding:

Should Western countries be concerned if Russia loses its best scientists? After all, we all spent 74 years fighting the Soviet system, why should we let them maintain the capability to rebuild a threat? It was largely agreed that stripping Russia of its scientific potential is not constructive if the country is ever to stabilize. It was also agreed that nonproliferation is the major concern and that no one really worried about departing botanists. Soviet science was highly compartmentalized and there was strict control over the relatively small number of scientists whose knowledge presents a real threat.[6]

But would that "strict control" hold? It was unimaginably difficult to estimate the scope of the problem, since there were thousands and thousands of individuals, only a vague understanding in the West of the jobs they held and the institutes where they worked, porous borders and unknown temptations. One small leakage of highly skilled bomb-builders could lead to disaster. Reports surfaced of Soviet nuclear scientists traveling to Libya and Iraq. President Saddam Hussein of Iraq, just a year after the Persian Gulf War, was still trying to hold on to nuclear weapons know-how, and the specter of even a single bomb-builder making his way to Baghdad caused real concern.[7] Iran also had nuclear ambitions. Harrington said she was well aware that Russians could easily travel through Kazakhstan or Moldova, and perhaps far beyond, without being noticed. "You could go anywhere, leave, come back, and who would be the wiser? We were critically aware of the fact that people could move around without anyone knowing where they were going." Moreover, leaving the country was not the only proliferation threat. Knowledge could be sold to outsiders who came to Russia. Bomb or missile designers could leak their knowledge from inside the country, perhaps under the cover of giving "lectures" to eager "students" from abroad, or through business transactions. The potential disguises were almost infinite, and the secret police were no longer watching everyone. All the major defense factories and design bureaus included a Soviet internal security office, known as "the regime," but they, too, were desperate for survival and often eager to help the scientists make business deals. By one informed estimate, a core of sixty thousand people had developed and designed weapons of mass destruction and their delivery systems. About half learned their trade in the aerospace industry, twenty thousand in nuclear and ten thousand in chemical and biological warfare. Perhaps half of these minds were located in institutes around Moscow. No one knew for sure how many could become wayward weaponeers, nor which, nor how to reach them quickly, nor how to stop them.[8]

On February 17, 1992, after a three-hour meeting in the Kremlin,
Baker and Yeltsin announced formation of the International Science and
Technology Center to help weapons scientists shift to civilian projects.
The United States pledged $25 million.[9] Germany also proposed to enlist
aid from the European Union. Given the desperate straits of the Russian
scientists, the money might have had an immediate impact had it been
distributed to those who were surviving on $15 a month. But the center
proved far more difficult to organize and launch than anyone expected.
Soviet laws were still on the books, Soviet-era bureaucrats still in their
offices and the weapons scientists were still shrouded in the secrecy and
mistrust of the Cold War. The U.S. government could hardly begin distributing cash to Russian bomb designers. The State Department needed
a coordinator in the Moscow embassy to work through all the bureaucratic obstacles. Harrington got the job.

As Harrington visited institutes around the capital in 1992, searching
for office space to set up the new science center, she found the corridors
dark for lack of lightbulbs, and stepped gingerly around gaps in the floor-
ing. She toured the nuclear institute at Troitsk, south of the city, where
Velikhov had once done pioneering laser work. "I have lots of people,"
the institute director lamented. "Just no money." Eventually, the science
center offices were opened at the Scientific Research Institute of Pulse
Technique.[10] The science center was not ready to offer grants in 1992, nor
in 1993, but as Harrington struggled with logistics and paperwork has-
sles, she listened patiently to the laments of the weaponeers who came to
see her. "People would come in and just pour their hearts out to you about
conditions in the laboratories, and what it was like trying to support their
families and not knowing what they were going to do," she recalled. "I
remember one scientist, a Russian scientist, a prominent physicist, he had
come to discuss a project and had to break off the meeting early. He had
been paid in vacuum cleaners for that month and he had to go out and
figure out how to sell the vacuum cleaners in order to get food for his
family. He's there, in his suit and tie." Another time, at an elite aerospace
institute, Harrington and a group of Americans were taken on a tour
from building to building, and then to a yard full of what looked like
rusting metal scrap, huge pipes and disks. The engineers explained, excit-
edly, that during the Persian Gulf War they had seen the Kuwaiti oil
fields ablaze, and invented a way to douse the fires. They built an enor-

mous metal disk—like a Frisbee—that would be launched by an airplane into the sand and crimp the underground oil pipe. After many failed attempts, they had finally managed to make it work, and were very proud, but the war ended before they could market the idea. Harrington recalled she and her colleagues just looked at each other in amazement. "My God," she thought, "these people just have no idea what to do with their intellect. They have no direction whatsoever. They spent thousands of hours trying to come up with this absolutely crazy scheme to crimp oil pipes."[11]

By the time the International Science and Technology Center began funding projects in March 1994, the outlook for scientists was still bleak. The first wave of grants were aimed at those who could be the biggest proliferation risk: nuclear weapons and missile scientists and engineers.[12] Among them was Victor Vyshinsky, a specialist in fluid dynamics who worked at the Central Aerohydrodynamic Institute in Moscow, a world-renowned facility that carried out wind-tunnel tests on cruise missiles. Vyshinsky, head of a department at the institute, had been eager to make it in the new Russian economy. He searched for commercial applications for his team. "There was this feeling of huge freedom, sort of inspiration and searching. It was a wonderful time," he recalled. They knew how to test a cruise missile in a wind tunnel, so they came up with an idea to use wind tunnels to dry timber. But they could not sell it. Then they proposed to use their mathematical models to predict the course of overflowing rivers. Again, a dead end. Soon they realized nothing was working. Vyshinsky turned to the science center, and his group of experts put together a proposal to study vortex wakes caused by airplanes at civilian airports, a project with widespread application that the science center supported. "I wanted to remain in Russia," Vyshinsky said. But he knew others were tempted to leave, or to sell their knowledge to the highest bidder. He was aware of contracts with Iran inside his own institute. "The only thing that keeps you from doing things like that are scruples," he said. "If someone takes it into their head to sell something, I don't think there will be a problem."[13]

Proliferation was a shady business. The vultures from abroad moved in to pick over the carcass of the dying military-industrial complex in the early 1990s.[14] In one extraordinary case, North Korea attempted to recruit an entire missile design bureau: in 1993, the specialists at the V. P.

Makeyev Design Bureau in the city of Miass, near Chelyabinsk, were invited to travel to Pyongyang. The bureau designed submarine-launched missiles, but military orders had dried up. Through a middle-man, North Korea recruited the designers, who were told they would be building rockets to send civilian satellites into space. One of them, Yuri Bessarabov, told the newspaper *Moscow News* that he earned less than workers at a local dairy, while the Koreans were offering $1,200 a month. About twenty of the designers and their families were preparing to fly out of Moscow's international airport in December when they were stopped by the Russian authorities and sent home. "That was the first case when we noticed the North Korean attempts to steal missile technology," a retired federal security agent said years later in an interview. If you look at a missile, the security agent said, the North Koreans recruited a specialist to help them with every section, from nose cone to engine.[15]

Agents for Iran and Iraq, warring rivals in the Persian Gulf, also scoured the former Soviet Union for scientists and military technology. Iran was especially active. A special office was opened in Tehran's embassy in Moscow to search for and acquire weapons technology. The Iranians approached the prestigious Moscow Aviation Institute, a school for missile and rocket technology. One of the professors at the school was Vadim Vorobei, a department head and an engineer, a teacher with big workingman's arms, solid fists and balding hair, who coauthored a text-book on how to build liquid-fueled rocket engines. In his classrooms, graduate students from Iran started to appear. They enrolled to study rocket engineering. Then the students pressed Vorobei to come lecture in Tehran. It was the beginning of a larger underground railroad of Russian rocket scientists who went to Iran in the 1990s. Vorobei was among the first to go. Although the Iranians made a show of keeping the scientists apart, Vorobei said, they frequently bumped into each other at hotels and restaurants. One day, he would spot a leading Russian missile guidance specialist; the next, a well-known missile engineer from Ukraine. All had been brought to Tehran on the pretext of giving lectures on rocket tech-nology. Vorobei did deliver the lectures, but was also often asked to examine missile blueprints and help Iran spot flaws in their plans. Vorobei eventually made ten all-expense-paid trips to Tehran starting in 1996. He was paid $50 a lecture, compared to the $100 a month he received at home. According to Vorobei, the underground railroad was a bit of a circus. The Iranians brought more scientists and engineers from the former Soviet Union than they knew what to do with. Tehran also suffered from a lack of critical raw materials and technology for rockets, which slowed their progress in building missiles. "It was a mess," Vorobei recalled.[16]

Russia was a leaking sieve in these years. Iraq, seeking to build a more accurate long-range missile in defiance of the United Nations arms embargo, dispatched a thirty-two-year-old Palestinian-Jordanian hustler and middleman, Wiam Gharbiyeh, to Moscow.[17] He managed to pass easily in and out of the secret military institutes, signing deals for a wide array of missile goods, technology and services. Gharbiyeh's biggest triumph came in 1995 with the purchase of gyroscopes and missile guidance components extracted from SS-N-18 submarine-launched intercontinental ballistic missiles under the strategic arms control treaty. Gharbiyeh took ten of them as samples back to Baghdad, and had about eight hundred more packed up and delivered to Sheremetyevo, the main international airport in Moscow. The gyroscopes were then flown out of Russia on two Royal Jordanian flights to Amman. From there, at least half the gyroscopes made their way to Baghdad.[18]

On Wednesday evening, October 30, 1996, Vladimir Nechai returned to his office on the third floor at Chelyabinsk-70. He opened the door and locked it behind him. A square-jawed man who wore V-neck sweaters under his sport coat, Nechai was a theoretical physicist who arrived at the institute in 1959, just four years after it was founded, and became director three decades later. It had now been four years since Baker had visited the institute.

The mood inside was dark, and conditions were grim. Nechai kept notebooks on his desk with details of a desperate search for money to pay the nuclear weapons designers and keep the laboratory from falling apart. On September 9, 1996, Nechai wrote an appeal to Viktor Chernomyrdin, the Russian prime minister, saying, "At the present time, the state of the institute is catastrophic." The government owed the facility the equivalent of $23 million for work it had already done, including $7 million for salaries, which had not been paid since May. The institute was saddled with $36 million in debts for utilities and other needs. The nuclear bomb-builders were unable to carry out orders for the government, or convert to projects for peaceful purposes, Nechai wrote. Long-distance phone lines were cut off for failure to pay the bills. Parents could not buy basic school supplies for their children. "There isn't even enough money to buy food," he said. In some of the smaller departments, he added, "Lists are being put together for the distribution of bread on credit, and the enterprise isn't in a condition to provide even this for everyone."[19]

Nechai informed Chernomyrdin that he had taken matters into his own hands. He could not bear to see what was happening to a laboratory that had once been among the most prestigious in the country. In a gamble, he started borrowing money from private banks. The laboratory owed $4.6 million on these loans but could not pay them back. Boris Murashkin, a colleague who had known Nechai since they both arrived at Chelyabinsk-70, said that Nechai's appeal for help was met with silence by Chernomyrdin. On October 3, Murashkin and other employees of the Russian nuclear complex joined a protest for back wages in Moscow outside the Ministry of Finance. "Pay the Nuclear Center of Russia!" said one of their placards. "Don't Trifle with Nuclear Weapons!" said another. The ministry agreed to pay some of the back wages later in the month, but by the end of October, far less than promised had trickled out. Nechai told Murashkin he was sympathetic, although as director he could not join the workers in street protests.

On that Wednesday night, Nechai went to a small study off to the side of his office, with chairs, a tea table and television. He wrote that he could no longer look his people in the eye, that he could no longer bear the strain. The last thing that Nechai wrote in his notes was that he wanted to be buried on Friday.

Then he shot himself with a pistol.

Nechai was remembered at a subdued funeral service two days later. Grigory Yavlinsky, leader of the Yabloko Party, one of the pioneers of Russian democracy whose bloc included many scientists and professionals, recalled the mourners had gathered in a cafeteria that looked more like a railroad station waiting room. Not a single official of the government came, not one sent telegrams or wreaths for a man who led the designers of the nuclear shield. On the tables were boiled potatoes, blini, as well as *kutiya*, a traditional funeral dish of raisins and nuts, and a half-glass of vodka for each person. The scientists spoke softly, in bitterness at the hardships and the loss. "Someone else might take another way," Yavlinsky recalled the scientists saying. "Everyone knew what that meant. It was clear to everyone what 'another way' could be. They were nuclear scientists, after all. Didn't Moscow understand, they asked, how dangerous it is to drive people who hold the nuclear arsenal in their hands to this state?"

REVELATIONS

I n the dawn of a new Russia, people stood up without fear to confront the lies and disinformation of the past. In acts of conscience, curiosity and determination, they began to expose secrets of the arms race. It was a haphazard process of discovery, and often did not attract the public attention of the earlier years, when Gorbachev began to fill in the "blank spots" of history, admitting the truth about Stalin's mass repressions. But the stories that surfaced in the early 1990s were no less startling to those who heard them: nuclear reactors dumped at sea, exotic nerve gas cocktails and a mysterious machine for retaliation in the event of nuclear attack.

These were exhilarating moments that no one ever expected to see in a lifetime. Siegfried S. Hecker, the director of Los Alamos National Laboratory, flew to Arzamas-16 in late February 1992 for his first trip ever to the Soviet Union.[1] When he landed on the tarmac, a short, elderly man approached him. It was Yuli Khariton, who had designed the first Soviet atomic bomb under Igor Kurchatov, and who later became the first scientific director of Arzamas-16. Khariton extended his hand and said, "I've been waiting forty years for this."

That night, at a dinner, Khariton delivered a remarkable lecture on the early days of the Soviet atom bomb. These were the deepest secrets of the Cold War, long protected by fear and hidden in vaults, now spilling out over the banquet table. Speaking in his British-accented English, which he had learned while studying at the Cavendish Laboratory at Cambridge University before World War II, Khariton recounted in detail the story of how physicists had designed and built the weapon. He recalled how they worked on their own design but kept a stolen American blueprint in their safe, which they had been given by the spy Klaus Fuchs. Khariton claimed the Soviet scientists designed a device that was half the weight and twice the yield of the American bomb. Hecker asked Khariton—sitting directly across from him—why did they use the American design instead of their own? Khariton reminded Hecker that the Soviet program was run by Stalin's ruthless security chief, Lavrenti Beria. "The reason we tested yours," he said, "is that we knew yours worked—and we wanted to live."[2]

The next morning, Hecker went for a jog through the gray apartment blocks of the once-secret city. He marveled at how American and Russian weapons scientists had swapped stories and experiences, and he wondered how many billions of dollars were spent for intelligence during the Cold War to get the kind of details that were casually being exchanged now. "We were received with open arms," Hecker said. "It was just mind-boggling to sit there and have the Russians explain their nuclear weapons program, how they actually put the pieces together, between the physics and the computational capabilities."

The Russian scientists told Hecker they saw themselves as exact equals of the Americans and only wanted to take part in scientific cooperation on that basis. Hecker could not solve their financial plight, but he established a vital line of communications to the Soviet weaponeers, a lab-to-lab program of joint projects and an early bridge over the Cold War mistrust.

From 1959 until 1992, the Soviet Union dumped nuclear waste and reactors into the Arctic Ocean. Twelve submarine reactors, six of them containing fuel, were discarded, even though the Soviet Union had signed an international treaty that prohibited dumping waste in the oceans.[3] The nuclear dumping might have remained forever concealed were it not for Alexander Zolotkov, a radiation engineer in Murmansk, the largest city on the Kola Peninsula in the Russian Far North. The rocky ice-free coastline of the peninsula harbored the Northern Fleet, with two-thirds of the Soviet navy's nuclear-powered vessels, including 120 submarines. Zolotkov also represented Murmansk in the Congress of People's Deputies, the parliament in Moscow.

In 1987, the environmental group Greenpeace had launched the Nuclear Free Seas campaign to challenge the arms race at sea. When the Greenpeace activists came to Murmansk and met Zolotkov, they invited him to join one of their voyages. On board the boat, he read a report from the International Atomic Energy Agency in which the Soviet Union declared it had never dumped, was not dumping and had no intention to dump nuclear wastes into the ocean. "This came as a big surprise to me," Zolotkov said, "because I knew for sure that this had been going on for a prolonged period of time."

He participated in one dumping shortly after he got a job in 1974 at the Murmansk Shipping Company, which operated nuclear-powered ice-breakers in the Arctic. On the *Lepse*, an auxiliary maintenance vessel, he heaved liquid nuclear wastes into the Barents Sea. Later, he worked on two atom-powered icebreakers, the *Lenin* and *Artika*, and was working on the *Imandra*, a vessel that serves icebreakers, when he met the Greenpeace team.

As a member of parliament, he could ask probing questions. Zolotkov learned there were secret orders and instructions to carry out dumping of radioactive wastes in the Barents and Kara Seas, and that no one in the shipping company was bothering to monitor or control the wastes. He also talked to company workers. Then Zolotkov discovered the records of radioactive waste dumping kept aboard the *Lepse*. He made a map and a small graph, showing the coordinates in the sea where the dumping occurred, the number of containers and the volume of wastes.

Zolotkov was asked to speak at a seminar being set up by Greenpeace in Moscow. John Sprange, one of the Greenpeace activists, recalled being uncertain whether Zolotkov would dare to take such a step, which could wreck his career, get him arrested or worse. All the documents Zolotkov had examined were labeled secret—he was taking a big risk. The night before the seminar, Zolotkov and the Greenpeace people gathered in the kitchen of a Moscow apartment and drank a lot of vodka. Zolotkov hesitated. He was deeply worried about going public. But the next day, September 23, 1991, he did not disappoint. The seminar, held in a long and narrow conference room that Greenpeace had rented, was packed with journalists, environmentalists and more than a few military and defense people. Zolotkov showed them a map of harbors and marine regions where dumping took place between 1964 and 1986. He revealed that when the waste barrels sometimes floated to the surface, workers shot holes in them. They sank, unprotected. Zolotkov spoke out against the secrecy that hid the reckless dumping for so many years. "The Chernobyl experience shows that all attempts to hide the truth are doomed to failure," he said.[4]

Yeltsin appointed a commission to investigate, chaired by Alexei Yablokov, a prominent environmentalist who had become one of Yeltsin's advisers. The commission, digging into the official records, confirmed there had been decades of dumping, and found the greatest hazards were the reactor cores, tossed overboard into the shallow inlets of Novaya Zemlya in the Kara Sea. No monitoring had been done in the disposal areas for twenty-five years.[5] When the report was finished, the commission members assumed it would be labeled "top secret," locked up and forgotten, as was the practice in earlier times. Yablokov appealed to Yeltsin. "I said, let's disclose all the data. It is not Russia's fault. This is a dirty practice typical of the Soviet Union, this is a convenient time to say, our hands are clean, we are not going to do it any longer." Yeltsin agreed. The report was published in 1993. The military was furious, Yablokov recalled.

One day not long afterward, Josh Handler, research director for the Greenpeace campaign, came by Yablokov's office to see if he could obtain the report. Yablokov said yes—but he had no photocopier.

Could Handler make him five more copies?[6]

On Friday, March 1, 1992, William Burns, the retired major general who had inspected the bicycle factory in Perm a few months earlier, took a phone call at home in Carlisle, Pennsylvania, where he was teaching at the Army War College. The caller, from the State Department, asked Burns to drop everything and take charge of the faltering American efforts to help Russia with the dismantlement of nuclear weapons. He was told he would have to leave for Moscow in just a few days.

Burns agreed, but his task was formidable. The Russians were

swamped with nuclear warheads and wanted financial help, but suspicion and hostility ran strong through the military, bureaucracy and
nuclear weapons establishment, where officials had been conditioned by
decades of service to the secretive Soviet state. Whenever the discussion
turned to the most basic details about nuclear weapons—such as how
many and how quickly they would be dismantled—the Russians went
silent.[7] After eight days of meetings in January 1992, one U.S. official
cabled back to the State Department and the White House: "The Russians refused to tell us the locations of their dismantlement facilities or
their rates of dismantlement. They said everything was fine with these
plants and no help was needed." The official quoted a Russian proverb,
"We have been talking about how to share the skin of a bear that is still
loose in the forest."[8]

At the State Department, Burns was handed seven short memos
describing areas where the Russians needed assistance. One said the Russians wanted one hundred secure rail cars for transporting nuclear warheads. The Soviet Union had always used rail to move their nuclear
bombs, but now the pace was quickening as the warheads were returned
to Russia from the periphery. The United States had twenty-five surplus
secure cars in storage, but no one knew whether they could operate on
Russian rails, or how quickly. Russia had pledged to complete the pullout
of tactical nuclear warheads from other republics by July 1. There wasn't
much time left.[9]

As soon as Burns arrived in Moscow, he ran headlong into the wall of
mistrust. Across the table sat Lieutenant General Sergei A. Zelentsov,
who commanded the 12th Main Directorate of the Ministry of Defense,
custodian of the nuclear weapons. Zelentsov told Burns he believed the
Americans had come to spy and learn secrets about Russian weapons.
"All you want to do is get out and see our stuff. I'm not sure you really
want to help us at all," Burns recalled the general told him. In fact, what
Zelentsov suspected was partially true. The American delegation of
sixty-four people included a fair number from the intelligence agencies.
The Russian side had their share of security people, too. "We met for a
period of about two and a half weeks, and got nowhere," Burns recalled.

In an attempt to break through the mistrust, Burns arranged for a
Russian delegation to visit Sandia National Laboratory in Albuquerque,
New Mexico, from April 28 to May 1, 1992. The visitors were given two

briefings that described how the United States had reacted to nuclear weapons emergencies, including a 1966 accident over Spain in which a B-52 lost four nuclear bombs. "They were really taken aback that we were so frank and open in explaining how we screwed up, and here are the lessons learned," Burns said.[10] Zelentsov softened. The Russians were impressed at how motivated the Americans were, and how dispirited their own people were.[11]

A few weeks later, Burns brought U.S. railroad experts to Moscow to examine one of the Russian nuclear weapons rail cars, under control of the Ministry of Defense. When the American experts arrived at a remote siding outside of Moscow, the nuclear transport car, model VG-124, was surrounded by a platoon of infantry, raising fixed bayonets. The Americans were told: not one step closer! Burns placed a phone call, and when the Americans returned the next day, the bayonets were down. Inside, the experts saw the rail cars were vulnerable. There was flammable insulation that might burn and threaten the weapons; the bombs were mounted on a movable platform that might come loose; the rail car had no structural reinforcement and would provide little protection. The warheads were being moved in what was essentially a modified but basic cargo boxcar, with only primitive communications. Burns realized it would take too long to adapt the American rail cars. With approval from Moscow, the United States quietly grabbed a single Russian nuclear weapon transport car, without the wheel sets, and shipped it by sea from St. Petersburg to Houston, and then overland to Sandia National Laboratories in New Mexico. There, specialists built an upgrade to improve the security of the rail car and shipped it back to Russia.

Given the mistrust that Burns had faced, and the deep secrecy about nuclear weapons, it was another extraordinary moment of cooperation.[12]

Vil Mirzayanov had witnessed the suffering of his colleague, Andrei Zheleznyakov, who was poisoned by nerve gas in an accident in 1987 at the chemical weapons research institute in Moscow. Mirzayanov had worked at the institute for many years. Behind the high walls, the Soviet Union and later Russia secretly developed and tested a new binary nerve gas known as *novichok*, or the "new guy." Binary weapons are those in which two nonlethal chemicals are mixed together at the last minute to become a deadly agent.

Mirzayanov had heard the lofty disarmament speeches about chemical weapons. Gorbachev pledged in April 1987 that the Soviet Union would no longer produce them. Yeltsin, in one of his first announcements as the new Russian president in January 1992, promised to support the global treaty then under negotiation in Geneva that would outlaw chemical weapons.[13]

Yet Mirzayanov knew that the Soviet Union—and Russia after it— had never given up work on the new binary weapon. He discovered the truth one day when he noticed a new poster in the hallway of the institute in Moscow. The poster proclaimed that scientists had invented a "pesticide" for use in agriculture, and it presented the chemical formula. Mirzayanov recognized immediately that it was actually the formula for something else—a *novichok* agent. The pesticide was a cover story. Despite all the promises of disarmament, Mirzayanov realized there was a plan to conceal the new generation of chemical weapons in ordinary industrial and agricultural compounds. This way, the Kremlin could sign the global ban on chemical weapons while keeping a hidden arsenal at the ready. Mirzayanov decided he had to tell the world.[14]

A lean, compact man who gestured often with his hands when he talked, Mirzayanov landed a job in 1965 at the State Scientific Research Institute of Organic Chemistry and Technology, located on the Highway of the Enthusiasts in Moscow. He was a specialist in chromatography, a laboratory technique for the separation of mixtures, and he became an expert in detecting tiny traces of chemicals in nature.

During his many years there, Mirzayanov came to have profound doubts about the military usefulness of chemical weapons. Nevertheless, in 1985, at fifty years old, he was given a sensitive job as chief of the department of foreign technical counterintelligence, responsible for checking the air and water at all the facilities for telltale leaks and, more broadly, protecting them from foreign spies. Mirzayanov had a rebellious streak, so the job was an odd fit, but he hoped to stick to the technical side. It could mean he would get scarce hard-currency resources to purchase new equipment. In his position, Mirzayanov was told the secrets of the *novichok* agents. He saw field tests at first hand. He was put on the scientific councils and allowed to read the piles of reports.

As the Gorbachev revolution took hold, Mirzayanov found himself drawn into the democracy protests, especially Yeltsin's call for radical change. "From the very first days, I went to the streets," he recalled. He quit the Communist Party on May 4, 1990, and became still more active in the pro-democracy movement. As a result, he was kicked out of his counterintelligence post.

His indignation about the *novichok* deception erupted in April 1991. He learned of a banquet to celebrate the award of the Lenin Prize to the institute director, Viktor Petrunin, and to Anatoly Kuntsevich, a general who had been in charge of a chemical weapons test installation at Shikhany. The prize was for creating a binary chemical weapon—long after the Soviet Union had promised to halt the chemical weapons production.[15]

Mirzayanov hoped Yeltsin's growing prominence and power in 1991 would bring a new direction. He read newspapers every day, but saw nothing about chemical weapons. He knew the institute was still functioning. "I was suffering from the agonizing burden I carried," he recalled, "feeling personal responsibility for participating in the criminal race of chemical weapons.

"I decided, I was ready to speak openly."

He sat down at home one night and typed out an essay, pouring out criticism of the whole chemical weapons enterprise. The next day he hand-carried his essay to the editor of a popular Moscow weekly newspaper, *Kuranty*, which published the article on October 10, 1991. Mirzayanov titled the essay "Inversion," referring to the process by which a chemical unnoticeably changes from one form into another without changing its chemical formula. He meant it as a commentary on the duplicity of the generals and their determination to continue building chemical weapons.

In the article, Mirzayanov disclosed that the chemical weapons chiefs were "busy developing a more modern type of chemical weapon, and its testing was carried out at an open test site in one of the most ecologically unsafe regions." He did not call it *novichok* but had spilled the beans. And he hinted that the generals were trying to hide their misdeeds. "The question is: why are we misleading the West again?" he wrote.

Mirzayanov called the essay a "cry from the heart," but there was little public reaction. Mirzayanov knew people were preoccupied with survival through a difficult winter. Inside the institute, his bosses were furi-ous. They fired Mirzayanov on January 5, 1992. He was soon struggling to make a living selling Snickers and jeans in a Moscow open-air market. "It wasn't very good for a professor with a Ph.D.," he recalled.

Yet he could not forget about the *novichok* agents. He decided to speak out again, and wrote another essay. On September 16, 1992, it was pub-lished in *Moscow News*, a progressive weekly tabloid.[16] The article, head-lined "A Poisoned Policy," was accompanied by photographs of the administration building of the institute on the Highway of Enthusiasts that had never before been identified in public. Mirzayanov revealed more about the dark secrets of the *novichok* generation of weapons. He said "a new toxic agent" had been developed at the institute, more lethal than the American VX gas. Injury from the new agent is "practically incurable," he said. He disclosed that the toxic agent was the basis for a brand-new binary chemical weapon, and that field tests of the new binary agent were being carried out in Uzbekistan as recently as the first three months of 1992—*after* Yeltsin's pledges in January.

Instead of destroying chemical weapons, Mirzayanov said the generals were developing new ones. The people of Russia "have no reason whatso-ever to entrust the destruction of chemical weapons to those who devel-oped them," he insisted. The promises of Gorbachev and Yeltsin to the West were completely betrayed by work going on inside the country. Who was in charge?

Mirzayanov was arrested October 22, 1992, for revealing three state secrets: the new toxic agent that was more deadly than VX gas; the devel-opment of the binary weapon; and the recent field tests. On October 30, he was indicted. Mirzayanov pleaded not guilty, was imprisoned and then released as his case dragged on.[17]

On January 13, 1993, the global treaty banning the development, pro-duction, stockpiling and use of chemical weapons was signed in Paris—with Russia among the signatories.[18]

In the legal proceedings, Mirzayanov and his lawyer were entitled to see the record of the investigation, including top-secret documents. Mirzayanov painstakingly copied documents in his own hand, took the notes home and typed them up. As a precaution, he faxed some of the documents to Gale Colby, an environmental activist in Princeton, New Jersey, who was organizing Western support for him.[19] One day, prosecutors put in the record a document that described the development, manufacture and delivery of *Novichok 5* for field tests. Mirzayanov copied it. According to the document, the field tests were scheduled for 1991–1992, well after Gorbachev and Yeltsin had pledged to stop making chemical weapons.

Only in 1994, after he had been twice imprisoned, did the case against Mirzayanov fall apart.[20] At great personal risk, Mirzayanov had revealed the duplicity of the generals and the development of the *novichok* generation of chemical weapons.

Bruce Blair, the Brookings Institution scholar, finished his second book, *The Logic of Accidental Nuclear War*, and it was published early in 1993. Blair's research in Moscow had paid off—he was able to write a detailed account of the Soviet nuclear command and control system. But one small detail eluded him. In Moscow, he had been told by his sources that the Soviet Union created a special system of command rockets that would fly across the country in the event of a nuclear attack, and issue launch orders to the intercontinental ballistic missiles. But when he checked the U.S. data on flight tests for these command rockets, in some thirty examples, nothing seemed to happen when they flew. No large ballistic missiles rose out of their silos as a result of the presumed commands. Blair wrote in his book, on page 78, that what the Soviets told him could not be corroborated by evidence.

Still, he wondered: what were the rockets for, if the commands were not followed?[21]

Blair sent a copy of his new book to Valery Yarynich, the nuclear command and control specialist whom he had met in Moscow nearly two years before. Back then, Yarynich had impressed Blair with his knowledge, and Blair had been careful not to write down Yarynich's name, out of an abundance of caution. Yarynich had given Blair a clue about the control rockets, but Blair didn't quite grasp it.

When Blair's book was published, he invited Yarynich to Washington.[22] Yarynich believed strongly in openness. He brought with him to Washington a typewritten document, single-spaced, dated February 24, 1993. One page was titled, at the top, "Reserve commanding rockets system." Under this, Blair saw a half-page, hand-drawn diagram, Figure 1. The drawing was labeled "Emergency Rocket Command System." It depicted satellites in the air, missiles in silos, submarines, command centers and strategic bombers. Blair tried to figure out, what did it all mean?

Under the diagram was a half-page of text. As Blair read on, it dawned on him. Yarynich had told him earlier that there was no *automatic* Dead Hand in the Russian system, but there was a *semiautomatic* system of some kind.

And here it was, on the typewritten page: the Doomsday Machine.

Yarynich, who had personally worked on the system in 1984, had been very careful not to write down any technical data, nor numbers or locations of the system, and did not use the real name, Perimeter, in the document. Rather, he sketched its broad principles. Blair examined the paper closely. It outlined how the "higher authority" would flip the switch if they feared they were under nuclear attack. This was to give the "permission sanction." Duty officers would rush to their deep underground bunkers, the hardened concrete globes, the *shariki*. If the permission sanction were given ahead of time, if there were seismic evidence of nuclear strikes hitting the ground, and if all communications were lost, then the duty officers in the bunker could launch the command rockets. If so ordered, the command rockets would zoom across the country, broadcasting the signal "launch" to the intercontinental ballistic missiles. The big missiles would then fly and carry out their retaliatory mission.

In May 1993, Blair visited Yarynich again in Moscow. This time, Yarynich gave him an eleven-page, single-spaced review of Blair's book. It was a thoughtful document, and near the end of it, Yarynich mentioned a few errors he had found in the book, and thus helped Blair resolve the riddle of page 78. Yarynich told Blair the reason the command rocket test flights were not followed by launches of the huge intercontinental ballistic missiles was this: the Soviets knew that the Americans were watching. So they waited, delaying launches by forty minutes or up to twenty-four hours to fool the Americans, and hide Perimeter.

Blair took notes. When he got home, he called his sources and checked the U.S. flight test data again. He was especially interested in the test of November 13, 1984, right after Reagan's election.

Sure enough, Yarynich was right. The heavy missiles did fly, just forty minutes after the command rockets.

Yarynich believed Perimeter had a positive role. If it were turned on, the leaders in the Kremlin would feel less pressure to make a dangerous, hair-trigger decision to launch on receipt of the first warning. They could wait. It might help them avoid a terrible, impulsive mistake. But Blair had a different view. He knew from his own experience that in the American system of command and control, people were the essential fire-wall. People ruled machines. The Soviet Union seemed to have built a Doomsday Machine by removing all but a few people. Blair was uneasy that it put launch orders in the hands of so few, and with so much automation.

Blair revealed the amazing system in an op-ed published in the *New York Times* on October 8, 1993, headlined "Russia's Doomsday Machine," describing "a fantastic scheme in which spasms of the dead hand of the Soviet leadership would unleash a massive counter-strike after it had been wiped out by a nuclear attack."

"Yes," Blair wrote, "this doomsday machine still exists."

Blair was inundated with phone calls from around the world. The very next day he was visited by Larry Gershwin, the national intelligence officer for Soviet strategic weapons, who was the man most responsible in the intelligence community for tracking Soviet missiles, bombers and submarines. Gershwin was intensely interested in what Blair had discovered. American intelligence had known some pieces of the puzzle, but they had not understood the command and control aspects of the Dooms-day Machine.

Blair had connected the dots.[23]

YELTSIN'S PROMISE

After he became Russian president, Yeltsin quickly and privately admitted the truth about Soviet biological weapons. On January 20, 1992, he met the British foreign secretary, Douglas Hurd, in Moscow. The British ambassador, Rodric Braithwaite, passed a note to Hurd during the meeting, suggesting he ask Yeltsin about germ warfare. For nearly two years, Braithwaite had been demanding answers about the program. He had been stonewalled. This time, Yeltsin said something "spectacular," Braithwaite recalled.

"I know all about the Soviet biological weapons program," Yeltsin told Hurd.

> It's still going ahead, even though the organizers claim it's merely defensive research. They are fanatics, and they will not stop voluntarily. I know those people personally, I know their names, and I know the addresses of the institutes where they're doing the work. I'm going to close down the institutes, retire the director of the program, and set the others to work designing something useful, such as a cow with a yearly yield of 10,000 liters. When I've checked for myself that the institutes have in fact stopped work, I'm going to ask for international inspection.

"Those people," Yeltsin said, expressing disgust, "can even make a cow grow an extra leg."

"We were stunned," Braithwaite recalled. "We could do no more than thank him."[1]

When Yeltsin met Baker in Moscow on January 29, the American secretary of state was equally impressed. Yeltsin proposed another major leap in the downhill arms race, reducing strategic weapons still further. "I saw a different Yeltsin from the man I'd seen before," Baker recalled. "Whereas in the past he had often seemed vague and rather glib, now he spoke at greater length, with no notes, about highly technical issues." Yeltsin admitted a Soviet biological weapons program had existed, and he promised to dismantle it "within a month." He repeated his pledge to British Prime Minister John Major in London on January 30, and to President Bush at Camp David on February 1. Celebrating his sixty-first birthday at Camp David, Yeltsin said, "There has been written and drawn a new line, and crossed out all of the things that have been associated with the Cold War." Neither Yeltsin nor Bush said anything in public about biological weapons, but Dmitri Volkogonov, the historian, who was advising Yeltsin then, relayed word to reporters during the Camp David summit that they had discussed it. This didn't make the headlines, which were dominated instead by word of deeper cuts in strategic arms and pledges of cooperation in other areas, but it was noted in news accounts that day. Volkogonov said that Yeltsin promised "a number of centers and a number of programs dealing with this issue have been closed," and "from 1992 there will be no budget allocations to that program."[2]

Sergei Popov, who had carried out some of the most ambitious experiments in genetic engineering at Vector and Obolensk, saw the economic despair all around him. He wasn't interested in selling his knowledge, he just wanted to escape the hardship. "When it started to collapse," he said, "people started selling everything from the shelves in the labs. So what we ended up with was almost empty labs. Whatever we had, reagents, equipment, everything had been sold."

His friend in Cambridge, Michael Gait, sent him an application for a postdoctoral fellowship in England. Popov carefully completed all the paperwork. On his résumé, he stated that in Obolensk, among other things, he was working on "microbiology of pathogens," but he didn't say more. He identified himself as a "department chief" who was carrying out studies "on recombinantly produced proteins." He was careful not to say he was genetically engineering pathogens for weapons. Popov worried that if he mailed the application from Obolensk, the KGB would intercept it, so he drove to Moscow and mailed it from the main post office, figuring it would not be noticed. The letter got through; Gait then wrote back with the news—a grant was awaiting him from the Royal Society.

Popov needed KGB permission to travel out of the country, even temporarily. He told the Obolensk director, Urakov, that he had a grant from the Royal Society, and that he was going to England "to set up connections" for possible business deals. Privately, Popov knew that Urakov wanted to get his son out of Russia. When Popov promised to help with the son, the director did not decline. Urakov turned to the KGB boss in his office. Shall we let him go? Urakov asked.

The KGB man nodded yes. They gave Popov his travel documents.[3]

Ken Alibek decided to quit the military after the eye-opening visit to the United States in December 1991. "The last straw," he said, came when a ten-page "summary" of the trip, prepared by Kalinin, the Biopreparat boss, was attached to Alibek's trip report. Kalinin's summary falsely claimed the visit "proved the continued existence of an American offensive weapons program." Alibek now realized that the generals hoped to continue their offensive weapons research, even after the Soviet collapse and the discovery that the United States did not have a program. Alibek took his letter of resignation, dated January 13, 1992, to Kalinin.

"I lived in a country called the Soviet Union," Alibek recalled telling him. "I served it loyally. It doesn't exist anymore. So now I'm free." Kalinin grew angry, and they quarreled. Kalinin accused Alibek of betrayal. Alibek recalled he stalked out of Kalinin's office. The building was quiet. He went to the personnel office and turned in his badge. He cleaned out his office and never saw Kalinin again.[4]

Yeltsin had told Bush the truth about the existence of the Soviet biological weapons program, but back in Moscow, the high-ranking generals did not want to tell the whole truth. In words, Yeltsin had finally come clean; but in deeds, what happened next was something else entirely.

When he got home from Camp David in February 1992, Yeltsin appointed a government commission to oversee the disarmament of chemical and biological weapons. Inexplicably, he put two generals from the old guard in charge of it. Anatoly Kuntsevich, a retired lieutenant general who had devoted his entire career to chemical weapons, was named chairman, and Valentin Yevstigneev, the general who was head of the 15th Main Directorate of the Defense Ministry—the biowarfare directorate—was appointed deputy chief. For ten years Kuntsevich had been boss of the Shikhany chemical weapons complex, where, in 1987, reporters and international experts were given the show of chemical weapons. Yevstigneev was directly in charge of the military biological weapons program, which took pathogens from the Biopreparat laboratories and turned them into weapons. Yeltsin had put men of the past in charge of the future.

Yeltsin was a revolutionary and a populist. He enjoyed making a dramatic flourish, but left the hard work of governing to others. When he received the American and British ambassadors in Moscow on April 4, 1992, he was in a confident and expansive mood. On biological weapons, Braithwaite made this notation in his journal of the meeting:

> Yeltsin says he is determined to fulfill the promise he made to
> the Prime Minister in January. He has already retired the general
> in charge, and will be closing down the production facilities
> and test sites, and retraining the scientists. I remark that I
> started badgering the previous government two years ago, but
> nothing happened: perhaps Gorbachev found the politics too
> intractable. Yeltsin says with a grin that he has had a lot of
> trouble with his generals: but they find it difficult to stand up to
> him.[5]

What happened next was that the generals stood up to Yeltsin. Russia faced an important deadline on April 15, 1992, for disclosing its past offensive biological weapons program to the United Nations. All parties to the 1972 Biological Weapons Convention—including the Soviet Union—had agreed to make a full declaration by that date as a "confidence building measure."[6] Just four days before the deadline, Yeltsin signed a presidential decree, No. 390, making it illegal to work on biological weapons in violation of the 1972 treaty. Yeltsin instructed his commission within a month to prepare measures for "strengthening openness, trust and broadening international cooperation in the framework of the convention."[7] But then Russia missed the deadline for submitting a declaration about past activity to the United Nations. On April 22, a British diplomat was summoned to the Foreign Ministry and offered a copy of the draft Russian declaration. Looking at the draft, Braithwaite was pleased that it acknowledged an offensive biological weapons program had existed from 1946 to March 1992. "The programme is now closed by Presidential decree, and the sites will be open to inspection. It is at least as much as we could have hoped for," Braithwaite wrote in his diary. At the same time, Braithwaite worried that experts in London and Washington "will find loopholes in the small print."[8]

The gaps were enormous. The draft declaration did not mention Biopreparat, nor the Sverdlovsk anthrax outbreak, nor the genetic engineering of pathogens. The generals had subverted Yeltsin's promise of full openness.[9] On May 5, Braithwaite and an American diplomat, James Collins, delivered a private protest to the Russian Foreign Ministry. On May 7, Braithwaite again badgered a Kremlin official about the biological weapons. According to Braithwaite's journal, the official acknowledged that Yeltsin was having a hard time "because of the degree of secrecy" in the program "and the number of 'fanatics' involved who have a vested interest in keeping it going."[10]

On May 27, Yeltsin took another stab toward openness in an interview with the mass-circulation newspaper *Komsomolskaya Pravda*. The interviewer stated that Yeltsin had known biological weapons were being developed in Sverdlovsk, and only mentioned it in public recently. Why? "First," Yeltsin replied, "nobody asked me about it. And, second, when I learned these developments were under way, I visited Andropov . . . when there was an anthrax outbreak, the official conclusion stated that it was carried by some dog, though later the KGB admitted that our military development was the cause."[11]

Yeltsin's six words—"our military development was the cause"—were as close as the Soviet Union or Russia had ever come to a formal acknowledgment that the 1979 epidemic was caused by the military.

When he appeared June 17 before a joint session of Congress in Washington, Yeltsin was once again bold and unequivocal. "We are firmly resolved not to lie any more," Yeltsin declared, to applause. "There will be no more lies—ever." This also applied to "biological weapons experiments," he said.[12] After their summit meeting, Yeltsin and Bush also announced agreement on still-deeper cuts in strategic nuclear weapons.

Yet even as Yeltsin promised "no more lies," the deception went on. A fresh jolt came when a junior scientist from Pasechnik's institute began talking to the British in the spring or early summer. The scientist was given the code name Temple Fortune. What alarmed the British was that the scientist described a biological weapons program continuing even *after* Yeltsin had promised to shut it down. The defector said that Pasechnik's old facility, the Institute of Ultra-Pure Biological Preparations in the former Leningrad, now St. Petersburg, had continued to develop an antibiotic-resistant *Yersinia pestis*, the plague agent. Moreover, the defector said all the research and development was completed by the spring, and the agent was being prepared for large-scale production. The factory would be located about two miles north of the institute in Lakhta. The defector said a cover story was being prepared that it was for making civilian pharmaceuticals. Once again, it appeared that Yeltsin was not in control.

The question of Russia's honesty about biological weapons was important not only because of the past violations of an international treaty but also for the future of the Nunn-Lugar legislation to clean up the legacy of the Cold War. If Russia was found to be violating the biological weapons treaty, under the provisions of the law it could not qualify for money from Nunn-Lugar. The money was flowing already, but a violation of the treaty would be seized upon by critics to turn off the spigot.

In meetings in June with British and American officials, the Russians offered three different drafts of their proposed United Nations declaration. Kuntsevich, the general Yeltsin had put in charge of compliance, insisted the declaration met all the legal requirements. But all three drafts were woefully incomplete. It was clear to American officials that the Russians were divided: Yeltsin wanted nothing to do with the germ weapons, but his powerful generals protected their empire, as they had done successfully in the Soviet years.[13]

At meetings in London on August 25, Douglas Hurd, the British foreign minister, and Lawrence Eagleburger, the acting U.S. Secretary of State, delivered yet another strong and private protest about the biological weapons to Russia's foreign minister, Andrei Kozyrev, a soft-spoken career diplomat who shared Yeltsin's ideals. Faced with this, Kozyrev invited American and British officials to come to Moscow, perhaps hoping if they laid out their evidence it might help Yeltsin overcome the generals. The Americans accepted, also hoping a high-level mission might pry open some doors. The U.S. delegation was led by an experienced diplomat, Undersecretary of State Frank Wisner. When he arrived at the Foreign Ministry September 10, 1992, Wisner carried a meticulous, ten-page, double-spaced brief. It was one of the most direct and forceful protests the West had ever made to Moscow on biological weapons. The mood was tentative and tense in the conference room as Wisner began to tell the Russians what was known. Kuntsevich was not present, but Yevstigneev, his deputy and head of the military biowarfare directorate, was there.

Wisner correctly identified the massive operation of Biopreparat, the genetic engineering research at Obolensk and Koltsovo, and the critical link played by Pasechnik's institute in preparing pathogens for delivery. Wisner pointed out the huge manufacturing plants ready to spring into action, including Stepnogorsk, the anthrax factory—none of which were in the draft declaration. He identified the secret role of antiplague institutes in helping the offensive weapons program. And he told the Russians that the official explanations for the Sverdlovsk outbreak were untrue.

Then, on the eighth page, in the most dramatic turn in his presentation, Wisner referred to the information that had come from the informer Temple Fortune—information that work on biological weapons was going on "over the past year," which meant the months Yeltsin was in power.

We have reports that the All Union Institute of Ultra-Pure Biological Preparations in St. Petersburg is constructing, equipping, and staffing a facility at Lakhta designed to do scale-up work to allow industrial production of a strain of plague—a strain developed to be resistant to cold and heat and to 16 antibiotics—for offensive purposes.

Wisner also revealed that the United States now knew exactly how the Soviets had covered up the germ warfare activity at Ultra-Pure when the American-British team had first visited in January 1991. He said they knew that information was destroyed that would be incriminating; laboratories were cleaned to remove traces of plague bacteria; employees who knew what was going on were sent away; and microphones were installed to monitor every conversation. After the visit, the institute continued to refine the plague agents. Wisner said the United States believed that "by the spring of this year, according to the information we have been provided, research and development was completed and the question of the suitability for large-scale production resolved." This added a note of super-urgency; Wisner was accusing the Russians of getting ready to manufacture a super-plague weapon.

Wisner's bill of particulars identified the cities, the programs, the institutes and the disease agents in the Soviet biological weapons program. He hoped this approach would, quietly, begin to pry open the closed doors. But the Russians didn't flinch. They listened to his presentation stone-faced, and insisted they did not have biological weapons. Among those most recalcitrant was Yevstigneev, the general in charge of the military's biological weapons program. "They gave not an inch in the face-to-face," Wisner recalled. No one admitted that the Russian declaration to the United Nations was incomplete. When the Sverdlovsk incident was raised, Yevstigneev once again stuck by the cover-up of previous years. He said it may have been caused by contaminated meat, and he insisted that it was not from Compound 19. He also said that Biopreparat had nothing to do with offensive germ warfare.[14]

The next day, Wisner and the Russians reached an agreement on a new round of inspections between Russia, the United States and Britain, which became known as the Trilateral Agreement. The Russians had again insisted any inspections be reciprocal, although it was Russia, and not the United States or Britain, that had violated the treaty. As they had done before, the Russian generals essentially played for time. There had already been one round of inspections in 1991 that had deepened suspicions in the West that the Russians were not telling the full story.

Had Wisner's indictment become fully public, it might have ignited a firestorm of demands from around the world that Russia simply close everything down at once. But Wisner believed in quiet diplomacy rather than open confrontation. "We came without believing we would get a whole loaf, and over time we got half a loaf," he said. "Trying to force a public embarrassment, shock, confrontation wasn't going to get you a thing, and chipping away at the internal contradictions on the Russian side, nudging, pushing along was a better strategy."

The Trilateral Agreement was unveiled at a press conference in Moscow September 14, 1992. In a joint statement, the three countries "reaffirmed their commitment to comply fully" with the Biological Weapons Convention and "declared their agreement that biological weapons must have no place in the armed forces." Russia said it had taken measures to "remove concerns over compliance," including "the cessation of offensive research," budget cuts and closing of facilities. The statement said Yeltsin had ordered a "checkup" of Ultra-Pure in St. Petersburg "in response to expressed U.S. and British concerns."

At the press conference, the Russians insisted everything was just fine. Grigori Berdennikov, the deputy foreign minister who led the Russian side in the talks, said that after Yeltsin's decree, "activities that would be running counter to the convention are not undertaken in this country." Yevstigneev brushed aside any suggestion that plague research was conducted at Pasechnik's institute. They were actually making "a vaccine to prevent chicken plague," he insisted.

The new Russia was not yet completely open, and Wisner said he realized the mission had not been a total success. "The Russians didn't say, 'Ah hah! You got us! We'll comply.'" In fact, in the private meetings as well as the public the Russians had lied to the Americans repeatedly.

The collapse of the Soviet Union opened a door for Matthew Meselson, the microbiologist at Harvard University, to further investigate the Sverdlovsk anthrax epidemic. He had been consulted about it by the CIA in 1980, visited Moscow to inquire in 1986 and brought the Soviet officials to the United States in 1988, when they claimed contaminated meat had been the cause. But Meselson had never been allowed to go to the scene of the epidemic.

In the autumn of 1991, a local legislator in Sverdlovsk, Larissa Mishustina, demanded that Yeltsin organize a new investigation. Mishustina represented families of the deceased; she said they had received only fifty rubles each, and the military continued to deny any responsibility for the deaths. "I think you know not less than I do that the death of 70 people was the consequence of a leak of bacteriological weapons," she wrote to Yeltsin. Following her appeal, on December 6, 1991, Alexei Yablokov, the prominent environmentalist whom Yeltsin had appointed to be his counselor on ecology and health care, wrote out a *spravka*, or information memorandum, on the situation and then a separate letter to Yeltsin, saying the official version of events had hidden the truth about the military's role. Beyond a doubt, Yablokov wrote, the epidemic was linked to Compound 19. Yablokov also said he had learned that the primary official documents had been destroyed by the KGB a year earlier.[15]

When Meselson heard of Yablokov's interest, he sent a letter January 22, 1992, offering to help any investigation. Yablokov replied February 5, saying he had doubts "that after all these years you can find scientific evidence" of what happened at Sverdlovsk. Meselson pressed him again. On March 23, Yablokov responded, referring to the case as "skeletons" in the closet. By coming to Sverdlovsk to investigate, "You can only catch some rumors and visit cemetery with 64 graves," he wrote. Nevertheless, Yablokov helped pave the way for a visit, writing letters of introduction for Meselson.

Meselson led an expedition that included Jeanne Guillemin, a medical sociologist, and other experts.[16] They arrived in the city—now back to its original name, Yekaterinburg—in June 1992. They were able to examine the slides and samples from the victims, hidden in 1979 by Grinberg and Abramova. The two pathologists had written a scientific paper, based on their preserved materials on the forty-two cases, which concluded that "these patients died because of inhalation of aerosols containing B. anthracis."[17]

The expedition made important discoveries. Mishustina, the local legislator, had obtained from the KGB a list of sixty-four people who were killed in the outbreak, and was able to locate eleven who had survived.

Guillemin, assisted by colleagues at the Ural State University, then interviewed relatives and friends of the victims, walking the streets of the
area where they were exposed, examining headstones in the cemetery,
and investigating medical records. Using this data, she and Meselson
mapped where the anthrax victims worked and lived at the time of the
epidemic. They also plotted on the map the direction of the wind on
Monday, April 2, 1979, using meteorological records. The results were
revealing: most of the people who contracted anthrax in those days either
worked, lived or attended daytime military reserve classes in a narrow
zone downwind from Compound 19 and stretching southward about 2.5
miles. And for another thirty miles or so beyond, sheep and cows died of
anthrax.

More than a decade earlier, when he was first called in to consult by the
CIA, Meselson had written a question in his notes: "How many persons
might have been present within an ellipse fitted to the facility and the various sites where early cases were presumably exposed? How many of
those became ill? Where did later cases reside and/or work?"

Now he had answers. The people were *inside* the ellipse. The victims
were under the plume. Meselson, Guillemin and their team had not gone
inside Compound 19 nor identified the precise reason for the outbreak,
but they peeled away the secrecy that the U.S. government could not penetrate in years of official diplomatic protests to the Soviet and Russian
leaders. They found solid evidence that anthrax spores had come from
the military facility at Compound 19.[18]

Alibek, leaving Biopreparat behind, worked for a while as the Moscow
representative of a Kazakh bank. But he felt the security services were
watching his every move. "My phones soon started to click and crackle
every time I made a call," he said.

In September 1992, Alibek decided to flee to the United States. He got
in touch with a Defense Department official whom he had met while on
the U.S. inspection tour the year before. In September he and his family
left Russia through a third country, and he defected to the United States.
It wasn't a classic defection, since the Soviet Union had collapsed and
Russia was still in the first year of its rebirth. But Alibek's arrival was an

intelligence coup for the United States. He was the highest-ranking official of Biopreparat ever to come out.[19]

Just a week or two later, Sergei Popov also left Russia for the last time. Before buying his plane ticket, he exchanged his monthly salary from rubles to dollars: in his hand he held only $4. He used his savings to buy the ticket. When he arrived at Heathrow Airport in London, no intelligence agents were waiting for him. They never bothered to contact him. On October 1, Popov took up a six-month visiting postdoctoral fellowship at the Laboratory of Molecular Biology at Cambridge University, where Michael Gait was a senior staff scientist. "I had nothing with me, just a small suitcase," he recalled. Realizing he had no money, his hosts offered a small loan. "I couldn't tell them what I did before," Popov recalled. "And I had no intention to tell them." Popov knew of Pasechnik's defection, but that role was not what he wanted. "I never contemplated defecting and disclosing secrets," he said. "My intention was to start a new life and not talk about the past."

In November, the first results of the Trilateral Agreement, a new round of inspections, got underway. The target was the Institute of Ultra-Pure Biological Preparations in St. Petersburg, where Pasechnik had been director and where the United States and Great Britain feared the Russians were scaling up to manufacture super-plague. Kuntsevich, who was Yeltsin's point man on chemical and biological weapons, appointed a Russian "Commission of Inquiry," which met at the institute from November 18 to 21, 1992. A team of American and British observers were invited, but they soon found the whole exercise was a "pathetic set-up job," one of them recalled. The Russian participants, who were hand-picked from Biopreparat, the Ministry of Public Health and the Ministry of Defense, mostly watched and listened. Rather than dig into the truth, they were apologists. They announced that there was no biological weapons work going on. The institute director said there never had been any. This was ludicrous in light of the fact that Pasechnik had pioneered such work there, and told the British about it. Among those on the visit was Christopher Davis, who had been one of the leading debriefers of Pasechnik. David C. Kelly, the British microbiologist, later recalled that "it was the American and British observers who actually asked the questions," rather than the appointed Russian commissioners.

During the November visit, the three buildings that made up the institute were examined again, as they had been in 1991 when Alibek attempted his clumsy cover-up. Again, American and British observers—this time accompanied by the Russian commissioners—spotted a large dynamic aerosol test chamber, a telltale sign of biological weapons research. They asked about its purpose; the answers didn't add up. The visitors also saw Pasechnik's milling machine, designed to produce particles of a particular size without damaging the pathogen used in the weapon. It also could not be explained. The "checkup" was over and the Russians had conceded nothing. Their denials made the American and British officials even more suspicious that weapons work was still going on—despite Yeltsin's orders to stop it.[20]

The Trilateral process dragged on. At the next stage of the visits, another team of American and British experts went to the All-Union Scientific Research Institute of Veterinary Virology in Pokrov, sixty-one miles east of Moscow, in October 1993. Kelly was among them. At Pokrov, his suspicions were rekindled that a massive Soviet—and now Russian—biological weapons program lay just beneath the surface. While Russian officials insisted they were making vaccines at Pokrov, Kelly saw telltale signs of biowarfare activity. "There were nuclear hardened bunkers and incubators for thousands of eggs. That's the standard method for growing smallpox virus," he said. Kelly saw that Pokrov had far more capacity than was needed for vaccines, and the hardened bunkers also seemed to be a giveaway that it was designed for wartime mobilization. But the Russians stuck by the vaccine story, and ducked questions about the past. The visitors were prevented from visiting a sister plant in Pokrov.[21]

By late 1993, intelligence analysts in the United States and Britain were growing worried that the Russian biological weapons program was still ongoing in defiance of Yeltsin's orders. One secret intelligence report quoted Yeltsin himself as complaining that the biological weapons work was continuing at three facilities despite his decree. In 1993, Alibek was also being debriefed by the intelligence agencies in the United States.

In the autumn, the United States prepared an overview of the situation—and the evidence—in a top-secret National Intelligence Estimate, a report pulling together information from many different sources.

Soon after the estimate was distributed in the U.S. government, it passed into the hands of Aldrich Ames, who was still spying for Russia from within the CIA. Ames's last operational meeting with the Russians was on November 1, 1993, in Bogotá, Colombia. According to one source, either at this moment or soon thereafter, he turned over to the Russians the National Intelligence Estimate describing what the United States knew about Moscow's biological weapons program, including specific locations. If the Russians wanted to conceal their germ warfare effort with even greater effectiveness, they had just received a helping hand: Ames delivered to them *everything* the Americans knew.

There were no more visits to Russian laboratories for a long time. The Trilateral process stumbled on in 1994, when the Russians demanded two visits to facilities of the American pharmaceutical giant, Pfizer. The company was reluctant, but eventually agreed, under pressure from the White House. The Russians also demanded a visit to the Vigo plant in Indiana, where, at the end of World War II, the United States had built the capability for large-scale fermentation of anthrax and a bomb-filling line. It was now abandoned, and as Kelly put it, "the archeological evidence was clearly of 1940s vintage." The Trilateral process ground to a halt.

On April 7, 1994, Yeltsin abruptly dismissed Kuntsevich, the general whom he had appointed two years earlier to head his committee on chemical and biological weapons. The Kremlin press service said Kuntsevich was relieved of his duties for a "one-time gross violation of work responsibilities." Details were not disclosed at the time, but came to light the following year when Kuntsevich ran for the lower house of parliament, the State Duma, on the party list of ultranationalist Vladimir Zhirinovsky. Russian officials revealed that he was under investigation for helping arrange an illegal delivery of about seventeen hundred pounds of nerve gas precursor agents to Syria and for planning a much bigger shipment. However, Kuntsevich was never prosecuted in Russia. He insisted he had run afoul of internal politics. But the United States thought the charges were serious enough to impose sanctions on Kuntse-vich for "knowingly providing material assistance" to Syria's chemical weapons program.[22]

The weapons of the Cold War had been spread around the globe by an insider who was supposed to be protecting them.

PROJECT SAPPHIRE

The United States opened eleven new embassies in the far reaches of the former Soviet Union in the year after its implosion, and a younger generation of diplomats volunteered for hardship assignments in remote outposts. Andy Weber was among them. On a long airplane flight, reading the *Wall Street Journal*, he saw a page-one article with the headline "Kazakhstan Is Made for Diplomats Who Find Paris a Bore." The article described how Ambassador William Courtney was working out of a dingy hotel in the capital, Almaty, with phones so bad he often could not place a call to Washington. "America is busy," the operators would say. It sounded like an adventure, and Weber jumped at the chance. With tours in the Middle East and Europe under his belt, he asked the State Department if his next assignment could be Kazakhstan. They signed him up on the spot. After Russian-language training, he arrived in July 1993 to take up the embassy's political-military portfolio. He found Kazakhstan's landscape a breathtaking tableau of steppe, lakes, forests and mountains, but Almaty was dismal. He threaded his way through fetid corridors without lightbulbs in the apartment blocks, and went to markets where pensioners stood forlornly offering to sell a vacuum tube.[1]

Weber took a recently built house in the foothills of the Tien Shan Mountains that resembled a Swiss chalet, with a large fireplace, paneled walls and a sauna. When he needed to meet Kazakh officials, he invited them home for lunch or dinner. Weber had a cook and a few guards, and he relied on an auto mechanic and all-round fixer, Slava, at a time when everything was difficult to obtain. Slava was also an avid hunter, and Weber learned to stalk pheasant, moose and elk in the secluded wilds. One day not long after he arrived, Slava came to him and said, "Somebody wants to meet you." Weber realized that whoever it was wanted a discreet meeting.

He was picked up on a street corner, taken to an apartment building and shown to the door of a company that sold hunting rifles, scopes and night-vision equipment. Inside, he found a lively former Soviet navy submarine commander, Vitaly Mette, who wore a leather jacket. Mette's thick hair was combed back from an angular face, and he carried himself with a self-confident air. Standing nearby was a large man with a polished head like a bullet, introduced as Colonel Korbator, and a very attractive blonde woman. Weber sat on a chair in the small room. The colonel left, then so did the blonde.

When they were alone, Mette turned serious. He said he wanted to discuss the possibility of selling uranium to the U.S. government.

Mette was vague about the nature of the uranium, except that it was stored at the Ulba Metallurgical Plant, an enormous industrial complex that fabricated reactor fuel in the grimy city of Ust-Kamenogorsk, in Kazakhstan's northeast. Mette was the factory director. As he listened, Weber was curious, but his training told him not to rush. He wanted to talk to Courtney, the ambassador, an experienced foreign service officer who knew something about the Soviet military-industrial complex. That night, Weber and Courtney drove together to see Mette at a guesthouse in Almaty. Courtney asked questions about the material Mette was offering, but Mette just said "uranium."

Then Mette turned to Weber. Please come hunting with us, he asked.

Kazakhstan, the second largest of the former Soviet republics, suffered as a Cold War proving ground and arms depot. In the remote steppe, the Soviet Union built test sites and factories for nuclear, chemical and biological weapons. The most spectacular was Semipalatinsk in the northeast, where 456 nuclear blasts were carried out from 1949 until

1989. Eighty-six of them were exploded in the air, 30 at the surface, and 340 underground in tunnels and boreholes.[2] Contamination poisoned the population.[3] Fallout from a 1956 explosion drifted over Ust-Kamenogorsk. Also in the north, at Stepnogorsk, anthrax was weaponized at the mammoth factory Alibek once led. A third facility in the north, built at Pavlodar on the banks of the Irtysh River, was a dual-purpose plant to make chemicals for civilian use and, if needed upon war mobilization, for weapons.[4] Farther to the west, missiles were launched from the Soviet space complex at Scientific Research Test Range No. 5, at Tyuratam, later named Baikonur. And in the southwest was the Aral Sea, where the Soviet biological weapons testing site was built on Vozrozhdeniye Island. When the Soviet Union collapsed, Kazakhstan inherited the world's fourth-largest nuclear arsenal, including 104 SS-18 intercontinental ballistic missiles with ten warheads each.[5]

Richly endowed with natural resources, Kazakhstan's greatest treasure was 70 trillion cubic feet of natural gas and 16.4 billion barrels of oil reserves. But despite this wealth, as author Martha Brill Olcott has observed, the new Kazakhstan was a fragile state, crippled by history and geography and born entirely out of the collapse of an empire, without a cohesive national identity.[6] About 37 percent of the population was Russian, concentrated in the north, and 40 percent Kazakh, among a total of nearly one hundred ethnic groups and nationalities. In Soviet times, the Russians were the elite, but after the collapse many felt shipwrecked there. The newly minted country was ruled by Nursultan Nazarbayev, a onetime steelworker whom Gorbachev had named Communist Party leader of the republic. An ethnic Kazakh, Nazarbayev gradually transformed himself after the Soviet collapse into a Central Asian potentate, mixing authoritarianism, oil wealth and crony capitalism. Now Nazarbayev wanted to be rid of the scourge of weapons that had so disfigured the landscape. He had no use for the uranium at Ust-Kamenogorsk.[7]

A few weeks after their first meeting, Weber flew to join Mette for a hunting expedition. They drove in a jeep for hours to a base camp in the Altai Mountains of eastern Kazakhstan, near the borders of Russia and China, an ideal territory for hunting. Weber enjoyed the *banya* steam baths, chewed on smoked pork fat and shivered in the early-morning cold with the Russians, speaking their language, hunting with them and earning their trust. He also shot a moose. He did not ask them about the uranium then. At the end of the trip, returning to the city, Mette volunteered to show Weber the plant in Ust-Kamenogorsk. They drove him around the gargantuan factory, fenced off, dark and brooding. Mette's workers were making fuel for Russian nuclear power plants. If they weren't exactly thriving, Weber saw they were not starving either. The entire town seemed to be a "little Russia"—Weber saw no Kazakhs there. Just before leaving, Weber inquired gently about the uranium. "If it is not a secret," he asked, "do you have any highly-enriched uranium?" Highly-enriched uranium could be used for nuclear weapons. Mette was still evasive.

The former Soviet Union was brimming with highly-enriched uranium and plutonium. Viktor Mikhailov, the Russian atomic energy minister, revealed in the summer of 1993 that Russia had accumulated much more highly-enriched uranium, up to twelve hundred metric tons, than was previously thought.[8] Outside of Russia, in the other former republics, less was known about stockpiles, but much was feared about the Iranians and the Iraqis hunting for material to build nuclear bombs. "We knew that Iran was all over Central Asia and the Caucasus with their purchasing agents," recalled Jeff Starr, who was principal director for threat reduction policy at the Pentagon.

At the same time, all the former Soviet lands were awash in scams and deceptions—people offering to sell MiGs, missile guidance systems or fissile material, real and imagined. There was such a frenzy to strike gold that it was hard to detect what offer was genuine. "A lot of people thought it was a scam," Weber recalled of the initial reaction to his reports of finding enriched uranium.

He went back to Mette. "Look," he remembered saying, "for us to take this seriously, you have to tell me what the enrichment level is, and how much of it there is."

In December 1993, Weber was extremely busy. Vice President Al Gore visited Kazakhstan in the middle of the month. During the bustle, Slava, the mechanic, came to Weber and said, "Colonel Korbator wants to meet you." Weber quickly agreed. On a snowy day, he went back to the same small office where he had first seen Mette and Korbator a few months earlier.

Korbator said, "Andy, I want to talk to you. Let's take a walk."

They walked through the snowy, dim courtyard of the apartment complex. Korbator spoke first. "Andy, I have a message for you from Vitaly," he said. "This is the answer to your question."

Korbator handed Weber a piece of paper. Weber unfolded it. On the paper was written:

U^{235}

90 percent

600 kilos

Weber calculated that was 1,322 pounds of highly-enriched uranium, enough to make about twenty-four nuclear bombs. Weber closed the piece of paper and put it in his pocket. He said, "Thank you very much. Please tell him, thank you. This is very important."

Weber sent a cable to Washington, with very limited distribution. Then for a few days he was preoccupied by the Gore visit. Immediately after Gore departed on December 14, Weber was awakened after midnight by the embassy communications officer, who called saying a night action cable from Washington had arrived, requiring his immediate attention. Weber drove back to the embassy. The cable asked a thousand questions about the uranium. What was Mette's motivation? They wanted to make sure Weber was confident of his source. Weber answered the questions as best he could.

Nothing happened for about a month. Weber's response languished in the State Department until one day in January 1994, when it came up as an afterthought at a White House meeting. Ashton B. Carter, who had helped frame the Nunn-Lugar legislation in 1991 and was now an assistant secretary of defense, volunteered to take over the issue. Shortly after the meeting, he called Starr into his office. "Your job is to put together a team and go get this stuff out of Kazakhstan," Carter said. "Whatever you need—do it." Carter said to get the uranium out within a month. Starr quickly put together a top-secret "tiger team," an ad hoc group of action-oriented officials from different agencies.[9]

On February 14, 1994, Nazarbayev made his first visit to see President Bill Clinton. In a White House ceremony, Clinton praised Nazarbayev's "great courage, vision and leadership," and announced that American aid to Kazakhstan would be tripled to over $311 million. In their public remarks, neither Clinton nor Nazarbayev, nor the official who briefed reporters that day, used the word "uranium." But when Nazarbayev was at Blair House, the guest residence across the street from the White House, Weber and Courtney quietly paid him a visit. They asked Nazarbayev if the United States could send an expert to verify the composition of the uranium at Ust-Kamenogorsk. He agreed, but insisted it be kept under wraps.[10]

Starr's tiger team was uncertain of conditions at the plant in Kazakhstan. They needed someone who could quickly lay "eyes on target," as Starr put it, and know exactly what was stored there, and how vulnerable it was. They couldn't be sure if they could take samples, or photographs, so it had to be someone who could mentally absorb everything, who would know about canisters and metals. The job went to Elwood Gift of the National Security Programs Office at the Oak Ridge National Laboratory in Tennessee. A chemical-nuclear engineer, Gift had experience in most of the nuclear fuel cycle, including uranium enrichment.

Gift arrived in Kazakhstan March 1 amid swirling snowstorms, and for several days holed up at Weber's house. When the weather cleared, they boarded an An-12 turboprop for Ust-Kamenogorsk. The Kazakh government purchased tickets in false names to hide their identity. Fuel was scarce. Just ten minutes after takeoff, they unexpectedly landed again—the tanks were almost empty and the pilot attempted to coax more fuel from a military airfield. Gift and Weber spotted old Soviet fighter jets parked on the tarmac. After an hour or so, they took off again for the 535-mile flight north.

By this time, Weber had come to know Mette better. As plant director, Mette was perhaps the most powerful person in Ust-Kamenogorsk. Weber found him charismatic, gutsy and intelligent, the opposite of an old Soviet bureaucrat. When Weber and Gift showed up the first morning and proposed to take samples of the uranium, Mette consented, knowing that they had Nazarbayev's approval, and he told them the story of how it got there. The Soviet Union had designed and built a small attack submarine, known as Project 705, given the code name Alfa by NATO. The sub was distinguished by a sleek design, titanium hull and relatively small crew. The most futuristic part of Project 705 was the nuclear power plant, which used an unusual liquid lead-bismuth alloy to moderate heat from the reactor. The subs were completed in the late 1970s, but the reactors proved troublesome—the lead-bismuth alloy had to be kept molten at 275 degrees Fahrenheit—and designers scrambled to build a new reactor. The uranium at Mette's factory was to be used to make the fuel for the new reactor, but Project 705 was scrapped altogether in the 1980s. Mette was left with the highly-enriched uranium.[11]

When they approached the building where the uranium was stored, Weber saw the doors were protected by what he later described as a Civil War padlock. The doors swung open into a large room with concrete walls, a dirt floor and high windows. Knee-high brick platforms stretched from one end to the other. On top of the platforms, sheets of plywood were laid out, and resting on the wood, about ten feet apart, were steel buckets and canisters holding the highly-enriched uranium, separated to avoid a chain reaction. Each container had a small metal dog tag stating the contents and quantity. Weber and Gift, working with plant technicians, randomly selected a few containers and took them to a small laboratory area. They weighed them to verify the dog tag was correct. In one canister they found uranium rods wrapped in foil, like so many ice packs in a picnic cooler. From another container, they took a rod-shaped ingot, and Weber hefted it, surprised at how heavy the uranium felt. Gift wanted to break off a piece and bring it back as a sample. He asked a technician to take a wood-handled hammer and a chisel to it, but the ingot would not break.

Weber went off with another worker to watch him file off some shavings they could take as samples. At first, the technicians handled the uranium in a glove box, but one of them took it out and placed it on an open table in the center of the room. The technician slid a piece of paper under it and began to file the ingot. Sparks flew, like a child's holiday sparkler.

"My eyes are lighting up, because I've had this chunk of metal in my hand," Weber recalled. "I know it is bomb material. This uranium metal would require nothing—just being banged into the right shape and more of it to make a bomb. It didn't need any processing. This is 90 or 91 percent enriched uranium 235, in pure metal form. And I remember thinking that dozens of nuclear weapons could be fabricated from this, easily fabricated from this material, and how mundane it is. It was just a piece of metal. And just looking at these buckets, how could something this mundane have such awesome power and potential for destruction? So, as he started filing, and sparks are coming off, you can imagine what's going through my head. What is this bomb material going to do?"

Gift was on the other side of the room, dealing with another sample. When he saw the sparks, Weber said, "Elwood! It's sparking!" Gift didn't realize they had taken the uranium out of the glove box, but he didn't look up. "Don't worry," he said, "that's just normal oxidation."

Gift collected eight samples of highly-enriched uranium while at the plant. Portions of four samples were dissolved in acid and analyzed by mass spectrograph while Gift and Weber were still there, and they confirmed it was 90 percent enriched uranium. Three of the dissolved samples and the eight original samples were taken by Gift for further analysis.[12]

Gift carried a miniature dosimeter in his shirt pocket while they were inside. He and Weber wore face masks to protect against dust with beryllium, which is highly toxic and carcinogenic. Weber felt comfortable that they were protected—the dosimeter didn't issue any alarms. Mette reassured them that the uranium was fabricated from natural sources, not reprocessed, so in its present state, although highly enriched, it was not very radioactive. After they finished taking the samples, Weber cheerfully suggested that Gift show the little dosimeter in his pocket to Mette. Gift took it out and discovered that he had forgotten to turn it on. "I thought, *oh great!*" Weber recalled. In his briefcase, Gift placed the small glass vials that held the eleven samples into holes cut in foam cushioning and snapped it shut. When they walked away from the uranium warehouse, Gift, carrying the briefcase, suddenly slipped and fell hard on the ice. Weber and Mette helped him to his feet but looked at each other. "Both of us, our initial reaction was, *Oh my God, the samples!*" Weber said. Both Gift and the samples were fine. Back in Almaty, they told the ambassador they had verified the uranium was highly enriched. Courtney immediately sent a cable to Washington, noting the ancient padlock on the door. The cable, Weber recalled, "hit Washington like a ton of bricks." Starr, who was in Washington, said the cable "established there was a potentially serious proliferation issue."

Weber thought there was only one thing to do. "In my mind it was a no-brainer," he said. "Let's buy this stuff as quickly as we can and move it to the United States." He knew there was a risk Iran might buy it. Later, it was discovered the plant had a shipment of beryllium, which is used as a neutron reflector in an atomic bomb, packed in crates. Stenciled on the side was an address: Tehran, Iran. Apparently a paperwork glitch was the only thing that had kept the shipment from being sent.[13]

Gift could not carry the samples on a commercial flight—orders from Washington had arrived saying it was too risky. Weber locked the samples in his safe and waited for instructions. Soon, three boxes came addressed to him on the embassy's regular resupply flight. Weber put Gift's briefcase with the samples in his jeep and drove out to greet the arriving C-130. He opened the first two boxes and carefully packed the samples in them, and resealed them to be shipped back home. Then he opened the third box: it was the gloves, dosimeter and protective gear he was supposed to have worn while packing the first two boxes.

When the samples got back to the United States, an analysis confirmed the uranium was 90 percent enriched. The tiger team went into high gear, and Starr looked at all the possible options. One was to do nothing, but that was quickly rejected. Another was to secure the uranium in place; that too was rejected on grounds that no one knew what would happen at the plant, or to Kazakhstan, in a few years. A third option was to turn the uranium over to Russia. A tense debate unfolded on this point. The Pentagon representatives wanted nothing to do with the Russians. The State Department people thought it would be an opportunity to show some goodwill and make a point about nonproliferation. A few low-level queries were sent to Moscow. The first went unanswered. A second triggered a reply that Russia would, naturally, want millions of dollars from the United States. After more internal arguments, a decision was made to have Gore raise the issue at his next meeting with Russian Prime Minister Viktor Chernomyrdin, in June. Gore carried with him a set of talking points that did not ask, but informed, the Russians that the United States would take the uranium out of Kazakhstan. Everyone held their breath, but Chernomyrdin did not object. Nazarbayev at one point picked up the phone and called Yeltsin, who agreed not to interfere. The tiger team wrestled with other difficult issues over the summer, such as how much to pay Kazakhstan, and how to prepare an environmental impact statement for the arrival of uranium at Oak Ridge. They went over every detail to make sure the mission would succeed. Weber, waiting for action in Almaty, was frustrated by the delays. "It was absurd because the Iranians probably would have paid a billion dollars for just one bomb's worth of uranium, and we were talking about dozens of bombs' worth," he recalled.

By early 1994, there were signs of progress in the struggle to avert a nuclear nightmare. Russia managed to bring its tactical nuclear weapons back from Eastern Europe and the outlying former Soviet republics. The rail cars carrying warheads were upgraded. Ukraine, Belarus and Kazakhstan were moving toward giving up their strategic nuclear weapons. The United States announced plans to buy 500 tons of highly-enriched uranium from Russia and blend it down into reactor fuel. In the first year of his presidency, Clinton appointed several architects of the Nunn-Lugar legislation to high-level policy positions. He named Les Aspin his first defense secretary. William Perry, the Stanford professor, was appointed deputy defense secretary, and became secretary in February 1994. Carter was appointed assistant secretary of defense for international security policy, overseeing the Nunn-Lugar legislation.[14] In Russia, after a violent confrontation with hard-liners in October 1993, Yeltsin won a new constitution giving him broad powers and a new legislature.

Nonetheless, what Andy Weber had seen in one factory in Kazakhstan existed across Russia. Kenneth J. Fairfax, an officer in the environment, science and technology section of the U.S. Embassy in Moscow, had arrived in July 1993, assigned to work on improving nuclear power plant safety. He soon discovered the Russian nuclear establishment was showing the same signs of deterioration as the rest of the country. Some of the worst conditions were at facilities that Russia considered civilian, but which held large quantities of weapons-usable uranium and plutonium. The materials were so poorly protected as to be up for grabs. Fairfax sent a series of startling cables from Moscow to the State Department describing what he saw.

Fairfax reported that almost everyone in the atomic sector, from maintenance workers to world-class scientists, was in distress. He started a personal effort to help nuclear scientists link up with American firms. "I would try to get scientists to show me what they could do, to really display their most outstanding talents," he said. Then he would seek out American companies that could pay for their skills. "I had no big program or budget," he said. "Just a rolodex and a head for business." When a few early efforts succeeded, scientists who had been receiving a paltry $7 a month soon were bringing in $3,000 or $4,000. They told colleagues, leading to new contacts, and Fairfax was soon a welcome visitor at the once-secret nuclear cities across Russia. He was even granted an official security pass to enter Minatom's headquarters in Moscow, the nerve center of the nuclear empire. More than once he recalled waltzing into Minatom while frustrated bureaucrats from Russia's Ministry of Foreign Affairs were stuck at the security desk at the entrance.

While looking for jobs for nuclear scientists, Fairfax began to notice security standards for some nuclear materials were at times "shockingly poor," he recalled. One of his early visits in Moscow was to the Kurchatov Institute, the prestigious nuclear research facility led by Velikhov. While on the grounds one day, looking at reactor research, he was shown Building 116, which held a research reactor powered by highly-enriched uranium. The building was surrounded by overgrown trees and bushes. "It was literally a wooden door, with a wax seal on it, with a piece of string. You break the wax seal and open it," he recalled. Inside, the Kurchatov workers brought out the highly-enriched uranium in the shape of large heavy washers. Fairfax picked up some of them. It was the first time he had ever held highly-enriched uranium in his hands.

Fairfax received "lots of scary information" from technicians and scientists in laboratories and from the security people—including sources in the 12th Main Directorate of the Defense Ministry, responsible for guarding the nuclear arsenal. Fairfax wrote cables describing what he witnessed: holes in fences, storerooms full of materials for which there was no proper inventory, heaps of shipping and receiving documents that had never been reconciled.

Fissile material was scattered across thousands of miles and tucked inside hundreds of institutes and warehouses, much of it in ingots, pellets and powder, held in canisters and buckets, poorly accounted for by longhand entries in ledger books, or not accounted for at all. Fairfax wrote in his cables that the weakest security was often found for highly-enriched uranium and plutonium, usable for weapons but intended for civilian use or basic scientific research. Since it was not headed for warhead assembly, it got less protection. Large quantities of weapons-usable material was stored in rooms and warehouses easy for an amateur burglar to crack: unguarded windows, open footlockers, doors with a single padlock, casks with a wax seal and a near-total absence of sophisticated monitors and equipment.

In Soviet times, the nuclear security system depended on closed fences, closed borders, a closed society, as well as the surveillance and intimidation of everyone by the secret police. In the Soviet system, people were under stricter control than the fissile materials. When the material was weighed or moved, it was tracked in handwritten entries in ledger books. If material was lost, it was just left off the books; no one wanted to get in trouble for it. And factories would often deliberately keep some nuclear materials off the books, to make up for unforeseen shortfalls.[15]

One of Russia's leading nuclear scientists at the Kurchatov Institute told a group of visiting U.S. officials in March 1994 that many facilities had never completed a full inventory of their bomb-grade materials, so they might not know what was missing.[16] The single greatest obstacle to building a bomb—whether for a terrorist or an outlaw state—was obtaining enough fissile material. Now it was evident from the Fairfax cables that in some places the former Soviet Union was turning into a Home Depot of enriched uranium and plutonium, with shoppers cruising up and down the aisles.

The same month as the Kurchatov briefing, three men were arrested in St. Petersburg trying to sell 6.7 pounds of weapons-usable highly-enriched uranium. The material was smuggled out of a facility in an oversized laboratory glove. Separately, two navy officers and two guards used a crowbar to rip off the padlock on a nuclear fuel storage facility on the Kola Peninsula, stole two fuel assemblies, fled to an abandoned building, and used a hacksaw to open one—and extract the core of uranium.[17]

Although many of Fairfax's sources were clearly working outside official channels and taking risks in talking to him, Fairfax felt none of them were spies or traitors; most were scientists, police and even a few former KGB agents who understood the nuclear dangers. Fairfax recalled that one officer in the 12th Main Directorate of the Defense Ministry explained his motives by saying he had worked on nuclear weapons his entire life to defend the Soviet Union, and by helping to point out the deficiencies in Russia, he was still keeping the country safe.[18]

When the Fairfax cables landed in Washington, Matthew Bunn read them with fascination. "It was just incredible stuff," Bunn recalled. He was a staff member at the White House Office of Science and Technology Policy. While the cables were distributed to the White House and elsewhere in Washington, not everyone recognized the warning signs. But

Bunn was totally floored. The cables, plus a string of nuclear smuggling cases in 1994, showed him that a crisis was coming, and he was standing at the bow.

His father, George Bunn, had been a pioneer in arms control and nuclear nonproliferation, helping to negotiate the nuclear Nonproliferation Treaty of 1968, and serving as the first general counsel of the Arms Control and Disarmament Agency. Matthew graduated from MIT and followed in his father's footsteps in Washington during the 1980s. He became editor of a magazine, *Arms Control Today*. Then, just as the Soviet Union was collapsing, he took on a new assignment at the National Academy of Sciences, to direct an in-depth study of the dangers of excess plutonium coming from dismantled Cold War nuclear weapons. Bunn concluded the risks were not only plutonium, but also the much larger supply of highly-enriched uranium. Bunn broadened his study, and the two-volume report recommended that, to the extent practical, every kilogram of the uranium and plutonium should be locked up as securely as the nuclear warheads.[19]

With the research project complete, in January 1994 Bunn was recruited to come to the White House by Frank von Hippel, the Princeton physicist. Von Hippel, a self-described citizen-scientist, had joined the new Clinton administration, working in the White House Office of Science and Technology Policy. Bunn saw there was little he could do to influence arms control, so he decided to devote almost all his time, with von Hippel, to fighting the leakage of uranium and plutonium in the former Soviet Union.

Bunn's early days in the White House were discouraging. The government was moving at a glacial pace. The plans at the time were to build one or two pilot projects in Russia over several years to show how to secure fissile material, and hope Russian specialists would learn from the experience. The pilot projects were for low-enriched uranium facilities that didn't even pose a proliferation risk. Bunn practically shouted his impatience. "We haven't *got* several years," he said, "the thefts are happening *now*!" The U.S. government was typically caught up in its own maddening budget and turf wars. Should the Defense Department or the Energy Department deal with nuclear materials policy? What about the national laboratories, such as Los Alamos, which were building their own bridges to the laboratories in Russia with some success?

To make matters worse, suspicions from the Cold War still ran deep on both sides. The Russians steadfastly refused to give the Americans access to facilities handling highly-enriched uranium or plutonium. Russia and the United States were prisoners of their old habits. "As long as you approach this from the point of view of arms control—let's negotiate for 20 years and make sure everything is reciprocal and bilateral—then you are left with a situation when you can't get anything done," Fairfax recalled. He suggested, radically, that they simply work together immediately, since neither would benefit from a nuclear bomb in the wrong hands. "My attitude was: does a fence make us more secure?" he said. "If so, build the fence." In a similar mind-set in Washington, Bunn came up with a scheme he called "quick fix." The idea was to ask the Russians to identify five to ten of their most vulnerable or broken-down facilities, rush in and improve the security, then identify the next worst, attack those, and so on. But the Russian response was: no way. "They were just not at all interested," Bunn said. The chief obstacle was the Ministry of Atomic Energy, known as Minatom, the nuclear empire lorded over by Mikhailov.[20]

On May 10, 1994, in the small town of Tengen-Wiechs, near Stuttgart, police searching the home of a businessman, Adolf Jaekle, unexpectedly discovered in the garage a cylinder containing 56.3 grams of powder. On testing, about 10 percent was extraordinarily pure plutonium. Jaekle was arrested and jailed, and the source of the plutonium never identified. Then, on August 10, Bavarian criminal police at Munich's Franz Joseph Straus Airport confiscated a black suitcase being unloaded from a Lufthansa flight arriving from Moscow. Inside was a cylinder containing 560 grams of mixed-oxide fuel that included 363.4 grams of plutonium-239, 87.6 percent pure. The suitcase also included a plastic bag with 201 grams of nonradioactive lithium-6, a metallic element used in making tritium, a nuclear weapons component. Bavarian authorities arrested the apparent owner of the suitcase, Justiniano Torres Benitez, and two Spaniards, one of whom came to meet Benitez at the airport. The arrest was the culmination of a sting operation set up by the Bavarian police and the German federal intelligence service, the BND, and had a huge impact on thinking about fissile material in Russia, seeming to confirm that it was leaking, badly. "We were going crazy worrying about this stuff though much of 1994," Bunn recalled.[21] Fairfax, writing from Moscow, sent a message to Washington that pointed to four Russian nuclear facilities as "my best guesses on where to look" to find the origins of the material.[22]

A month after the Munich arrests, Fairfax drove von Hippel to the Kurchatov Institute. Again, they visited Building 116, where Kurchatov employees poured out onto a tray some of their seventy kilos of highly-enriched uranium, pressed into washer shapes. Von Hippel noticed it was stored in what looked like high school lockers. "I was dumbfounded," von Hippel said. There were no motion detectors, no guards. Anyone could have walked off with the uranium.

In October, von Hippel returned to Mayak, near Chelyabinsk, which he had visited five years earlier on Velikhov's *glasnost* tour. The facility was one of those on the Fairfax list of possible sources of the material seized in Munich. On this visit, von Hippel was taken to a building he had not seen before, No. 142, a single-story warehouse, originally built in the 1940s. A lone Interior Ministry guard held a key. Inside the building were stored 10,250 containers, each about the size of a hotel coffeepot. Each held 2.5 kilos of plutonium oxide. They were lined up in trenches. The cans were double-sealed to avoid leaks, but the warehouse was so hot with radioactivity that employees were allowed inside for only short periods each week. Moreover, the building was an easy target for theft. There were no security cameras; a ventilation shaft would have made an escape route. The building "would not offer much resistance to penetration," von Hippel wrote after the visit. "The walls have multiple windows and doors and the roof is lightweight. The plutonium containers within are easily accessible by simply cutting the sealing wire, removing a 20-kg cover, and reaching down and pulling out the canisters. The seals are easily defeated lead seals. The guards do not have radios . . ." After the containers are put in the trenches, he added, "no inventories are made to check that the canisters are still there." Von Hippel figured there was enough plutonium in the warehouse to make several thousand bombs.

By autumn 1994 it was clear the entire former Soviet Union was awash in fissile material, and the United States had yet to do much about it. Von Hippel noted in a memorandum, "progress in gaining cooperation from the Russian side has been extremely slow" although "scores of facilities and hundreds of tons of weapons-usable material" were at risk.[23]

———

After months of preparation, the covert mission to remove the uranium in Kazakhstan was almost ready in October. The winter snows were coming. "I kept pressing and pressing to get this thing going, knowing full well that winter comes early in this part of the world," Weber said. "It would get messy if we didn't get it finished before the first snowfall." A small group of Americans slipped unnoticed into Ust-Kamenogorsk during the summer to check whether the airport runway could handle C5 Galaxy airlifters, and to examine the containers inside the Ulba warehouse. The Oak Ridge Y-12 laboratory built a mobile processing facility. A team of twenty-nine men and two women were recruited for the mission, including Elwood Gift, who made the first visit. On October 7, President Clinton signed a classified presidential directive approving the airlift, and the final briefing was held at Oak Ridge. The next day, three C5 aircraft, among the largest planes in the world, lifted off from Dover Air Force Base, Delaware, carrying the team and their processing facility. They flew to Turkey, and then, after some delays, to Ust-Kamenogorsk. Weber was waiting for them in the control tower of the small airport. "This was one of those bizarre post–Cold War experiences you have to live through to believe, but I'm in the control tower, nobody in the control tower speaks English," Weber recalled. "So they said, 'Andy, can you talk to the planes and guide them in?'" The C5s needed a six-thousand-foot runway, and landed like a "bucking bronco," in the words of one pilot, on the bumpy eight-thousand-foot strip at Ust-Kamenogorsk. The planes were unloaded, and flew off to bases elsewhere until it was time to return.

On the ground, at the Ulba factory, the team began its arduous work. Twenty-five members were from Oak Ridge; the others were a communications technician, a doctor and four military men, including three Russian-speaking interpreters. Each day, they left their hotel before dawn and returned after dark, spending twelve hours packaging all the uranium into special containers suitable for flying back to the United States. The total material to be packed up was 4,850 pounds, of which approximately 1,322 pounds was the highly-enriched uranium. There were seven different types of uranium-bearing materials in the warehouse, much of it laced with beryllium.[24] Altogether, the team discovered

1,032 containers in the warehouse, and each had to be methodically unpacked, examined and repacked for transport into quart-sized cans that were then inserted into 448 shipping containers—55-gallon drums with foam inserts—for the flight. Laborious checking was necessary, each can compared with the Ulba handwritten logs. In the end, the Americans discovered several canisters lying in the warehouse without dog tags. Some of the uranium had to be heated in special ovens to remove water to facilitate the repacking. The entire process required precision, endurance and secrecy. If word leaked, the whole effort might have to be aborted. The tiger team in Washington had worked out a cover story—if the Americans were discovered, they were to say they were helping Kazakhstan prepare declarations for the International Atomic Energy Agency. Working conditions were stressful; many of the team members had never been outside the United States. Some were so homesick they broke the rules and called home from local telephones. From a distance, Kazakh special forces troops kept a watchful eye to protect the Americans inside the plant.

By November 11, the job was finished and the 448 barrels loaded onto trucks. The team was determined to get home for Thanksgiving, but then winter weather set in. The original air force order was for five C5s to evacuate the uranium and the team. But only three planes were ready when the right moment came. Mechanical problems and bad weather caused delays. Finally, on November 18, one plane left Turkey for Kazakhstan. While it was in the air, at 3 A.M., the uranium was driven from the Ulba plant to the airport, with Weber in the lead security car, a Soviet-era Volga. "It was black ice conditions," Weber said. "And these trucks were sliding all over the place, and I'm thinking, I don't want to make the call to Washington saying one of the trucks with highly-enriched uranium went off the bridge into the river, and we're trying to locate it. But somehow, miraculously, we made it all safely to the airport."

The plane took three hours to load. But before it could take off, the runway had to be cleared of snow. A pilot recalled the airfield was being pummeled by sleet, ice and rain. There were no snowplows to be seen. Then the local airport workers brought out a truck with a jet engine mounted on the back. They fired up the engine and blasted the runway free for takeoff. The Galaxy heaved itself into the sky. The next day, two more C5s flew out the remaining uranium, the gear and the team. The enormous transports, operating in total secrecy, flew twenty hours straight through to Dover with several aerial refuelings, the longest C5 flights in history. Once on the ground, the uranium was loaded into large, unmarked trucks specially outfitted to protect nuclear materials and driven by different routes to Oak Ridge.

Weber remained on the tarmac until the last plane took off.

When it was announced to the public at a Washington press conference on Wednesday morning, November 23, Project Sapphire caused a sensation. Defense Secretary William Perry called it "defense by other means, in a big way." He added, "We have put this bomb-grade nuclear material forever out of the reach of potential black marketers, terrorists or a new nuclear regime."[25] With imagination and daring, Sapphire underscored what could be done. The United States had reached into another country, which was willing to cooperate, removed dangerous material and paid for it.[26] But that method could not be replicated inside Russia, where there was far more uranium and plutonium, and much more suspicion. It was hard to imagine landing C5s in Moscow and emptying out Building 116 at the Kurchatov Institute.

The U.S. government has long run a secretive intelligence committee, spanning different agencies, which studies nuclear developments overseas. In late 1994, the Joint Atomic Energy Intelligence Committee prepared a report about the extent of the Russian nuclear materials crisis. The top-secret report concluded: not a single facility storing highly-enriched uranium or plutonium in the former Soviet Union had adequate safeguards up to Western standards. Not one.

In the White House science office, Bunn felt he had "zero power" and worked "10 tiers down from the top." His quick-fix idea was dead on arrival. In late 1994, on advice from his staff, Clinton asked for a blueprint for action on nuclear smuggling and loose fissile material, to be written by the President's Committee of Advisors on Science and Technology. The study was chaired by Professor John Holdren, then of the University of California at Berkeley, and Bunn was named study director. When finished in March 1995, the study, classified secret, called for a multifront war. The study identified approximately one hundred sites handling sizable quantities of weapons-usable nuclear materials in the former Soviet Union.[27] Then, to drive home their point, Bunn and Holdren lobbied for, and won, permission to give a briefing to President Clinton and Vice President Gore in the Oval Office.

They stayed up until 2 A.M. the night before preparing. On May 1, 1995, just weeks after the Oklahoma City bombing, they told Clinton and Gore the fissile material crisis was one of the gravest national security problems the country faced. Holdren described to Clinton the serious gaps: how Russian facilities had no idea, or precise records, of the amount of uranium and plutonium lying about; the weak links in buildings, fences and guard forces; and the threat that terrorists could walk off with a bag or bucket of uranium or plutonium. In a clever move, Holdren had brought an empty casing from one of the fuel pellets used at the nuclear power and engineering institute at Obninsk, south of Moscow. He tossed it on a table and told Clinton there were perhaps eighty thousand of those filled with uranium or plutonium, and not one with an inventory number on it. The institute had no monitors to stop someone from carrying one out in their pocket. Bunn thumped on the table a two-inch stack of press clippings he'd assembled, including a *Time* magazine cover with the headline "Nuclear Terror for Sale." At the end of the presentation, they showed Clinton a diagram of what would happen to the White House if the Oklahoma City bomb had been set off on Pennsylvania Avenue— superficial damage. Then they showed what would happen if it was a one-kiloton nuclear "fizzle"—a bomb that didn't work very well. In that case, the White House was at the edge of the crater.

Clinton said he realized that security was bad, but he had no idea that the Russians didn't even know if something had been stolen.[28]

In the weeks after Clinton's briefing, a delegation from the United States Department of Energy arrived in Ukraine, including a young logistics assistant, Erik Engling. He had landed a job in the department just the year before, doing administrative chores for the office of National Security and Nonproliferation, which required a security clearance. Engling possessed the right credentials from an earlier job working in a government library. He helped with visas, cables, and chores for government officials struggling to cope with the fissile materials crisis in the former Soviet Union. One day, he recalled, a senior policy-maker came and sat down in his office. Engling was twenty-nine years old then, a large young man, blunt-spoken and eager to learn more about the nuclear problems they were discovering. "The problem is so huge," the senior policy-maker said, "your grandchildren won't be able to work this out."[29]

In June, Engling made his first visit to the former Soviet Union, accompanying the delegation to Ukraine. The team went to the Kharkiv Institute of Physics and Technology, once a premier research institute. Engling wound his way through a labyrinthine corridor, up and down stairs and then through a door. "And we went through the door, and into that room, and there's 75 kilos of highly-enriched uranium lying on the floor. *On the floor!* You've got it on racks, too. There's an oversized dumbwaiter that goes up and down to one of the rooms above where they were doing experiments. The uranium is in all sorts of configurations. Some in tubes, some in boxes. And we all had this sinking feeling, like, *why?* Why do you guys even have this shit?" The uranium was entirely unprotected. "We walked up a couple of stairs, we're out in a parking lot. This is where the nuclear materials are stored, and not a thing between the parking lots and these doors. The stuff was sitting just 55 feet from the back door. You could just walk in, and walk out."[30]

FACE TO FACE WITH EVIL

O n a brilliant summer day, June 2, 1995, a chartered white and blue Yak-40 jet descended to the remote city of Stepnogorsk in northern Kazakhstan, landing on a bumpy airstrip of concrete slabs. The plane, emblazoned with the name Kazakhstan Airlines, carried Andy Weber and a team of biological weapons experts from the United States. About nine miles away stood the anthrax factory Alibek had built in the 1980s. Never before had a Westerner set foot in the secret plant, where, in the event of war, anthrax bacteria was to be fermented, processed into a thick brown slurry, dried, milled and filled into bombs—by the ton.

Weber's flight to Stepnogorsk was the culmination of months of careful preparation. His mission was to find a new entryway into the secret empire of Biopreparat. In Russia, attempts by American and British officials to penetrate the biological weapons program had been blocked, made even more difficult after Aldrich Ames gave the U.S. National Intelligence Estimate to the Russians in late 1993. Moreover, Yeltsin's promises of openness had been subverted by his own generals.

But now, there was another chance. A colossal anthrax-processing machine stood intact at Stepnogorsk, and if Weber could get inside, it might hold a key to the larger Soviet biological weapons story.

Weber began laying the groundwork for this mission days after Project Sapphire was over. In November 1994, he started a series of inoculations against potential pathogens he might encounter at Stepnogorsk, including anthrax and tularemia. Then he lobbied the Kazakh government for permission to visit three facilities with a team of experts: the chemical weapons plant at Pavlodar, in the northeast near the Russian border; the biological weapons plant at Stepnogorsk, also in the north; and a testing grounds for germ warfare agents at Vozrozhdeniye Island, in the Aral Sea, which borders Kazakhstan in the far west. The hulking industrial works were frozen in time, equipment mothballed or rusting, the halls and laboratories monitored by Russians who remained the stewards long after the Soviet Union imploded.

When Weber discovered the highly-enriched uranium in Ust-Kamenogorsk, he had followed a single tip on a small piece of paper. This time, he had much more information, thanks to Alibek, who was debriefed for more than a year by American intelligence and military agencies, meeting daily in a second-floor conference room in an office building in northern Virginia. Alibek sketched out the sprawling Biopreparat and military germ warfare complex: the facilities, pathogens, history, scientists, directors, structure, accomplishments and goals. While Pasechnik had done the same for the British in London, Alibek held a higher-ranking position.

To the Americans, there were still many unknowns—not only the hidden history, but also the urgent questions about whether the Russians were actually closing down the Soviet biological weapons program, as Yeltsin had promised. The earlier visits to Obolensk, Vector and other facilities had all been frustrated by the cover-up. The Trilateral Agreement reached a dead end. The Americans wanted to know: which pathogens and laboratories could still be a proliferation threat?[1]

Alibek provided a gold mine of new data about the laboratories and factories of Biopreparat. He knew a great deal about Stepnogorsk, which he had directed in the 1980s: the layout, building numbers, pipelines, processes, machinery, fermenters and bunkers. Thanks to Alibek, Weber had a road map.[2]

In the last days of May 1995, Weber made final appeals to the Kazakh government. When he got the green light, the American team immediately flew in from overseas to join him. On the first leg of the journey, Weber headed to Pavlodar, the abandoned chemical weapons plant, where he was given open access and cooperation. "They showed us everything," he recalled. The main engineer explained that Pavlodar was a war mobilization plant, designed to produce sarin and soman for bombs in a matter of weeks if the orders came from Moscow. But the factory showed signs of having been left behind years earlier. "It was a wreck," Weber remembered.

Then, on Friday, June 2, they took off for Stepnogorsk, 261 miles to the west of Pavlodar. The Stepnogorsk plant was alerted—by someone in the Kazakh government—that an American delegation was coming to town and should be met at the airstrip. Weber was accompanied by a security official from the president's office, in case there were any questions about his authority to be there. When he climbed down the stairs of the plane, Weber ran into trouble.

"Remember, it's a chartered plane, this is Stepnogorsk. The airport no longer operates. They didn't get a lot of flights coming in. So they came right out to our plane," Weber said. The first person he met was Gennady Lepyoshkin, director of the plant. A Soviet army colonel, Lepyoshkin had first come to Stepnogorsk in 1984 as Alibek's deputy, and took over when Alibek went to Moscow in 1987. He was shorter than Weber, with dark hair combed straight over, and thick glasses. Lepyoshkin brought his own security man, who offered Weber a finger-crushing handshake. Lepyoshkin left no doubt about his attitude.

"You're not welcome in our city," Lepyoshkin told Weber. "Leave!"[3]

Weber insisted he had come at the invitation of the Kazakh government. Lepyoshkin demanded to see documents. Weber had brought none. After more back-and-forth, Lepyoshkin allowed Weber and his team to come into the town—but not the factory—and check into a guesthouse.

They next met at the mayor's office. Weber recalled that the Russians regarded their installation as a satellite of Moscow, not under the authority of Kazakhstan. The town was largely populated by Russians, too. "I had entered Brezhnev-era Russia," Weber recalled. "This was going back in a time warp." He made a forceful case for the visit, saying that Nazarbayev had approved it. "Gennady and the locals didn't really care" about the Kazakh president, however. Weber then called Courtney, the ambassador in Almaty. "We need something on paper," he told him, "or this visit is not going to happen."

The lone fax machine in the city was in the mayor's office, and a few hours later a letter arrived from Vladimir Shkolnik, the Kazakh minister of science and new technologies, who had been the atomic energy chief at the time of Project Sapphire. Shkolnik urged Lepyoshkin to open up everything to the visitors. "When Lepyoshkin had the approval on paper, he was covered," Weber said. "He didn't like it but he couldn't stop us."

The next morning, Weber and his team drove out to the plant from the guesthouse. First they went to Lepyoshkin's office, where Lepyoshkin gave them a briefing. He said they were making vaccines at the plant. Weber figured it was the cover story. At this moment, both Weber and Lepyoshkin knew more than they said aloud. Lepyoshkin knew that Alibek had gone to the United States. Weber knew the details of the Alibek debriefings, in which he had described the anthrax factory. Weber then gave a brief summary of what he believed the plant had been used for in the past.

Suddenly, Lepyoshkin's deputy for security, Yuri Rufov, burst out, "That's all lies! It's a vaccine production plant! That's all. We never had anything to do with biological weapons."

At this point, Lepyoshkin's manner changed. "Let's end this discussion," he said. "We'll show you everything, and you can make your own judgments."

On the first full day, Saturday, June 3, Weber and his team started by examining the complex from the exterior. Spanning the top of one building were letters spelling out "Progress" in Russian, the name of the civilian enterprise that served as cover for the biological weapons plant. When they alighted from a jeep they saw bunkers, with thick concrete walls, nestled deep into earthen mounds. Pipes snaked from building to building atop concrete pillars. Behind the bunkers, a crane and rail line marked the location where anthrax munitions would be loaded onto trains in the event of war. Lightning arrestors—another telltale sign of weapons work—were stacked up to one side. At the end of the first day, there were still many mysteries. At 9 P.M. that night, they spread out a schematic of the basement of the main production plant, wondering what was inside the rooms they had not yet seen.

The second day, Sunday, June 4, 1995, they returned and probed deeper inside. Most of the equipment had been mothballed but looked well preserved. Pipes and valve handles were color-coded blue, green and red. Storage tanks stood silent, connected by miles of tubes and wires. The whole complex seemed to be waiting to spring to life. While the interior was in good order, outside the facility had gone to seed. Roads were potholed and junk strewn everywhere. Sheep fed from a trough outside one building. A stiff wind blew across the steppe.

From what he saw, Weber realized that Alibek's descriptions matched everything they found. One of the most important discoveries was in Building 600, the main laboratory. They located the pad where Alibek recalled there had been a giant stainless steel aerosol chamber for testing the most dangerous agents, such as anthrax, Marburg and Ebola on monkeys and other animals. The high-ceilinged hall was painted an institutional green, eerily empty save for pipes and wires around the periphery, disconnected from the bulbous experimental chamber that once filled up the middle. A crane loomed overhead—maybe to lift the stainless steel ball? In the center of the pad they found a drainage hole. Weber and his team carefully swabbed it for samples. Then they found what looked like a latched, plastic traveling cage for a pet dog, with a handle on top. But it wasn't for traveling. A hole was cut in the front, and two V-shaped supports protruded from the hole. Here was where the dog's head would be strapped down during biological weapons experiments.

They combed Building 211, the facility to prepare nutrient media for growing bacteria, with a capacity of thirty thousand metric tons a year. They checked out underground bunkers with reinforced concrete walls two meters thick for weaponization of the agents. The bunkers contained compressors and refrigerators to store agents, and special lines where the pathogens would be filled into bombs and sealed. They swabbed Building 231, where the anthrax bacteria would be dried and milled before being put into the bombs. It appeared never to have been operational.

The most important discovery was the main production facility, Building 221. Several stories tall, on the inside it resembled a scene from a very old science fiction movie, crammed full of pipes, tanks, valves, coils and wires. Most was not active, just standing in place. The building contained a high-level containment facility for handling dangerous pathogens. In a three-day production cycle, the facility could make 1.5 tons of bacteria. The nutrient media was pumped from Building 211 to the upper floors of Building 221, where small fermenters were inoculated with anthrax bacteria. After a period of growth, the content of the small chambers was drained downward into ten massive fermenters, each four stories tall. After further fermentation, the mixture was spun in centrifuges to remove culture medium and waste. The bacterial slurry was then pumped to Building 231 for drying and milling, and then to the bunkers for munitions filling or storage. The finished weapons would then be loaded onto waiting railway wagons for transport.

Of all the amazing discoveries, Weber recalled the day he saw the large fermenters as one of the most disturbing of his life.

"This is a plant that could produce and load onto weapons—targeted at the United States—300 metric tons of anthrax during a war-time mobilization period," he said. "It looked like a plant right out of the 1930s. There was nothing high-tech about it. It was like when I held the uranium ingot in my hand. It was just metal. These were just big vessels that looked like something out of a 1930s movie. Yet we knew it had the capability of wiping out a big portion of population. It was just scary to think that you didn't need some super-high sophisticated technology to produce these horrible weapons in massive quantities."

In Building 221, Weber climbed to the top of one of the twenty-thousand-liter fermenters and looked down into it with a flashlight. The cylinder was made of specialty steel with a resin lining. He could see the impellers attached to a central rod that would stir the anthrax spores. He could not see the bottom in the dark, four floors below, but he got a full sense of the incredible volume, the trillions of spores of anthrax bacteria that would be swirling inside the chamber, enough to wipe out entire populations. Weber, taciturn, methodical and careful, felt a chill run up and down his spine. "I think more than any other day in my life," he said, "this was my introduction to two things. First, to biological weapons. I had read about them. I had taken courses. But this was the real thing. And second, to the Soviet Union. I had never bought into Reagan's 'Evil Empire' thing. I was a product of liberal eastern schools, I went to Cornell, but there it was. I was face to face with evil."[4]

On Sunday, Lepyoshkin invited Weber and his team to the plant's dacha, an A-frame cottage on the Seleti River, for a closing feast. It was a sunny afternoon and they went fishing and swimming, ate shish kebab and enjoyed fish soup, and Lepyoshkin poured vodka. They wore baseball caps in the bright sun that glinted off the reeds and blue surface of the river. Lepyoshkin opened the feast by declaring, "Now the official meeting is over." Weber recalled, "What he really meant was, now we can talk to you. Now we can tell you the truth. Everything we said until now has been part of a script."

Lepyoshkin then told them the full story of Stepnogorsk. "They were open about the whole history, the whole purpose," Weber recalled. The anthrax factory was built after the 1979 Sverdlovsk accident. The goal was to give the Soviet Union the ability to wage biological war within a few weeks after the mobilization order was given. Pasechnik and Alibek had been right, and all those years, the Soviet and Russian generals and diplomats had lied about it. Indeed, Weber remembered, these men had lied to his face only two days before, saying the plant made vaccines.

The teams bonded over vodka on the riverbank; the Russians were candid about their own experiences inside the system. As Weber recalled it, they told him: "At the time we didn't know it was wrong. We didn't know it was illegal. We didn't know there was a Biological Weapons Convention. We just thought we were defending our country. Now we know enough to know it was wrong, and we want to work together to do positive things for the rest of our lives." Lepyoshkin said activity at Stepnogorsk had come to a halt four years earlier with the Soviet collapse. There had been nothing, officially, from Moscow since then. They had made halting attempts on their own to convert to civilian products. He hoped they would succeed someday.

"They just poured their souls out to us," Weber said. "For these people to meet Americans, who they had been taught to hate, to meet their counterparts and find out that they actually liked them, I think it was a big event for them, too. There was no more isolated place in the world than Stepnogorsk, Kazakhstan. It's this poor, little, isolated, artificial military city that was created in the middle of Kazakhstan on purpose to be as far away from life forms as possible. They knew we were the main enemy. And all of a sudden, we're there, and we don't have horns and we're having fun with them. We're laughing at their jokes and they are laughing at ours."

Weber had broken through the secrecy. The trip produced proof that Biopreparat and the Soviet military envisioned manufacturing germ weapons by the metric ton in the event of war. The Soviets had grossly violated the Biological and Toxin Weapons Convention. He had seen, too, that the anthrax factory, while not operating, remained intact. The fermenters were still there, mothballed but ready. "By the end of that day we had gone from almost failing, the team not even being allowed in, to the exhilaration of succeeding in our mission beyond our wildest expectations," Weber recalled.

Weber asked Lepyoshkin if he would come with them the next day as they headed to Vozrozhdeniye Island, where the germ weapons had long been tested. Weber thought it would be useful to have Lepyoshkin as a guide. The island had been at the heart of the Soviet germ warfare program. Lepyoshkin readily agreed. In the morning, they took off together in the Yak-40. On the flight, Weber wore a plaid open-necked shirt and took a window seat. Lepyoshkin sat next to him, in a sport coat and tie with red-white-and-blue stars and stripes. They lifted a toast to cooperation, Weber holding a small American flag in one hand.

They could not fly a fixed-wing jet to Aralsk, the closest city to the island, so they took the chartered Yak-40 to Kyzil Orda, a city to the east. Much to Lepyoshkin's surprise, Weber, on the spot, chartered a Soviet-built Mi-8 helicopter from a medical rescue service, for $8,000, to make the flight to the testing range. Weber plunked down a stack of $100 bills for the chopper. "You're quite a cowboy!" Lepyoshkin said, surprised at Weber's determination and resourcefulness. "No, Gennady," he replied, "you're the cowboy."

Boarding the chopper, fitted out with stretchers and emergency medical equipment, they flew about 228 miles west to the city of Aralsk, which had once been a fishing port on the edge of the Aral Sea, where the smallpox outbreak had occurred in 1971. Since then, the sea had dramatically receded, and Aralsk was now thirty miles from the nearest shore-line.

After the collapse of the Soviet Union, Vozrozhdeniye Island was inside the borders of the newly independent nation of Uzbekistan. Weber realized he needed to get Uzbek approval for his flight to the testing ground. He and his team spent a night in a hot, miserable hotel in Aralsk, and then he worked the phones. It took hours and hours of effort. Weber also visited the former military support facility for the testing ground, based in Aralsk, which was now being used as a leper colony.

Finally, they took off. As the blue-and-white chopper with a bright Red Cross insignia lumbered through the air, the noise was deafening. Lepyoshkin, now in a white T-shirt, sat alone, gazing out the porthole window of the chopper. Below, the island appeared to be as devoid of life as the surface of the moon, a dull gray-brown with patches of vegetation. A cluster of low-lying buildings, bleached white with the sun and heat, marked the headquarters of the testing range, but there was no sign of inhabitants, not a person, not a car. Weber did not know if anyone remained on the site—maybe it was still guarded by the Russian mili-tary? Were there Uzbek border guards? They circled once in the helicop-ter, slowly, to make sure. Nothing. They landed near the headquarters and residential buildings, all with windows blown out. As the chopper engines came to a quiet halt, the only thing Weber heard was a dog bark-ing in the distance. "It was all totally abandoned," Weber said. "Like *Planet of the Apes.*"

They walked away from the chopper and toward the buildings. A rusting, abandoned truck, without wheels, lay where it last stopped. A faded Communist Party propaganda book was picked off the sidewalk. The first building they saw had a sign over the door: MEDICAL CLINIC. The door creaked open to desolate rooms, stripped, the paint peeling. Lizards skittered away in the grass. After another short chopper flight, they landed in the laboratory area. In the stifling heat, the Americans put on their white hazardous materials suits. Lepyoshkin, who had worked with pathogens for so many years, thought they were being overly cau-tious and did not suit up.

In these buildings they found traces of what had gone before. Hun-dreds of gas masks tumbled out of a storage room. Another room held a large supply of flasks and Petri dishes. They found glove boxes for handling dangerous pathogens. Weber was surprised to discover some equipment in the labs was mothballed carefully. Placards were hung from it in Russian, saying "in conservation." But mothballed for what? He wondered: was someone planning to come back another day?

In earlier times, Lepyoshkin spent seventeen summers on Vozrozhdeniye Island, helping carry out tests of Soviet biological warfare agents, and he knew it even better than Alibek. The proving ground was run by the military's 15th Main Directorate, the one in charge of germ warfare. The scientists had lived in barracks, forbidden to tell anyone, including their families, where they were going. Alibek recalled in his memoir, "Winds swirling off the desert steppes provided the only respite from the heat. There were no birds and the dust settled everywhere, getting into clothes, hair, and eyes, sweeping through the animal cages and into the food and scientists' notebooks.

"We used to say that the most fortunate inhabitants of the Soviet Union were the condemned monkeys" on Vozrozhdeniye Island, he added. "They were fed oranges, apples, bananas and other fresh fruits rarely seen by Soviet citizens."

Now, as Weber walked through the laboratories, all that remained of the monkeys were cages—hundreds of them, including one large enough for a human to stand up in. Weber found reams of blank paper forms used to record the symptoms of biological weapons agents on the monkeys. On the left of the page was an outline of the primate with key places to check, and on the right were blanks for listing data gathered from those points. At the top of the form was written "Top Secret, When Filled In."

In their hazardous materials suits, Weber and his team took samples of the filters in the laboratory, hoping to find pathogens trapped in them. On the windswept proving grounds, they saw the bleak poles where animals were harnessed for outdoor tests.

Alibek had told the Americans that the anthrax removed from Sverdlovsk, and later stored at the town of Zima, near Irkutsk in Siberia, had been buried on Vozrozhdeniye Island in 1988, but he had not said precisely where. Weber and his team extracted sample cores from the earth adjacent to the laboratory, where they thought the anthrax might be buried, and on the test grid. They didn't find the anthrax that day; the pink powder was buried in eleven unmarked graves nearby. It would be discovered on a later expedition. But in finding the weathered buildings and discarded primate cages, in taking the samples and photographs and exploring the island, Weber had broken through the Soviet lies once again.

Weber and Lepyoshkin flew out together. They posed for a picture on the tarmac, both giving a thumbs-up. Lepyoshkin had nowhere to stay in Almaty; Weber invited him to be his houseguest in the mountains. By chance, there was a reception at the American Embassy for visiting officials from Washington. Among them was Carter, an assistant secretary of defense, who was an architect of the Nunn-Lugar legislation, and Starr, the principal director of the Pentagon's threat reduction office, who led the "tiger team" for Project Sapphire. They met Lepyoshkin for the first time. Lepyoshkin seemed to have unmoored himself from the Soviet past. He was eager to meet the American officials. They talked in the leafy courtyard of the embassy. Lepyoshkin had only one request: he wanted them to help clean up Stepnogorsk and convert it to peaceful purposes. "I promise," Carter told him, "we will."

In Russia, Weber discovered the footprints of Iranians—and they were reaching for the germs.

In 1997, back from overseas, he was working at the Pentagon on the Nunn-Lugar programs, which had become known as Cooperative Threat Reduction. He was trying to find a new approach to dealing with the danger of biological weapons inside Russia. Weber's first trip there came in June 1997, when he took a train fourteen hours from Moscow to Kirov, five hundred miles east, to attend a scientific conference, accompanied by several other American experts. In a stroke of good luck, Weber met researchers from both Obolensk and Vector, the laboratories at the heart of Biopreparat's research on bacteria and viruses. Late one afternoon, after the formal conference sessions, a small group of scientists from Obolensk invited Weber to share some beers in the *banya*, a traditional Russian sauna. Joining the scientists in the steam room, with his Russian-language skills and knowledge of biological weapons and pathogens, Weber made a personal connection, as he had done earlier with Mette and Lepyoshkin. In these discussions, Weber learned that

scientists from Obolensk and Vector had recently participated in an officially sponsored Russian trade fair in Tehran, and very quickly, the Iranians had shown up at the Russian institutes. The Iranians were
somewhat rough-cut agents of influence, and the Russians found them
off-putting, the scientists said. From this informal talk in the *banya*,
Weber realized the Iranians were trying to scoop up know-how for biological weapons. What really alarmed him was a discussion with a senior
scientist at Obolensk who had been on the trip to Tehran. "They talk
about pharmaceuticals," the scientist said, "but it's clear their interest is
in dual use equipment that can be used for biological weapons." The scientist said the Iranians had offered him thousands of dollars to teach
in Tehran. And then the scientist took a business card from his wallet,
which had been given to him by the Iranians. He showed it to Weber,
who immediately recognized the name and the office: a front for the
military and intelligence services in their drive to procure Russia's
weapons.

A few weeks later, Weber met Lev Sandakhchiev, the compact,
intense, chain-smoking director of Vector, who had once pushed to create
artificial viruses for biological weapons. Sandakhchiev had come to
Washington for the first time. Weber took Sandakhchiev on an hour-
long drive to Fort Detrick, Maryland, once the home of the American
biowarfare effort, and now headquarters of the work on defense against
dangerous pathogens. In the car, Sandakhchiev revealed to Weber the
Iranians had come to Vector, hunting for technology and know-how.
Weber sensed that Sandakhchiev wanted to cooperate with the United
States, to open the Russian system to joint projects. He also realized that
conditions at Vector were increasingly desperate, with salaries unpaid
and subsidies drying up.

Weber and Sandakhchiev met again in October 1997 at a NATO conference in Budapest, and this time, in a hotel room, they had a knock-
down, drag-out argument over Iran, as Sandakhchiev ate sausage and
drank vodka. Sandakhchiev wanted to know: why was Iran such a buga-
boo to the Americans? Weber replied, "You have to understand, they
kept our Embassy and our diplomats hostage for 444 days!" Sandakhchiev looked puzzled. When was that? Weber reminded him it was
1979. Sandakhchiev, sounding sincere, told Weber that, isolated in his
laboratory in Siberia, he had never heard of the Iran hostage-taking.

Weber thought to himself it was an astonishing example of how closed the world of biowarfare had been in Soviet times, apparently so tight that not even the news of the hostage crisis had penetrated. Weber implored Sandakhchiev to stop the cooperation with Iran. Sandakhchiev was reluctant to give up the big money the Iranians had offered, but the Iranians were also very unpleasant partners—they made promises up front, but delivered money late, and constantly tried to bargain for less. Weber and Sandakhchiev went back and forth, arguing for hours. Weber found that Sandakhchiev was open with him, and Weber learned that in addition to work at Vector, there was probably a large, separate stockpile of *Variola major* virus at the military laboratory at Zagorsk. Later, on a tour in Budapest, they walked past the confessional in an old church, and Sandakhchiev turned to Weber and joked, in Russian, "Andy, let's go in there and I'll confess all my sins about biological weapons!"

Back in Washington, Weber searched for a way to act, to offer Sandakhchiev something to preempt the Iranians. But up to this point, the Nunn-Lugar program was largely devoted to nuclear materials and strategic weapons, and there was tremendous resistance in the U.S. government, especially in the intelligence agencies, to using any of it to stop the spread of biological weapons. The long history of Soviet and Russian deception about germ warfare had left a deep reservoir of mistrust in Washington. "There was this real fear of our funds being misused by these clearly dangerous, bad actors," Weber recalled. At a meeting at the White House one day in late 1997, a decision was made to engage Vector, as Weber had urged. After the meeting, he walked to the State Department with Anne M. Harrington, who had helped establish the International Science and Technology Center in Moscow, and was now working on nonproliferation issues at the department. Harrington shared Weber's goal of reaching out to the scientists at Vector. She knew they were in financial trouble; a few years earlier, the science center held workshops at Vector and Obolensk for possible grant recipients, and scientists at Obolensk said they hadn't been paid for months. Many just stayed home to grow food or find other ways to support their families; to produce enough income to cover minimal salaries, Obolensk boasted a brewery and an assembly line for men's suits, and was planning to start a vodka distillery. Harrington thought the beleaguered germ warfare scientists should get as much attention as had the nuclear engineers.[5]

When they reached the office, Weber and Harrington decided to take a chance and reach out to Sandakhchiev on their own. They would not go through the usual bureaucratic channels: embassies, cables, government ministries. On Harrington's office computer, they tapped out an e-mail to Sandakhchiev. It was brief, noncommittal, but inviting, suggesting closer cooperation and asking if Weber could visit Vector. They didn't know what would happen. "What are your employment options if this doesn't work?" Harrington asked Weber.

But the gamble paid off. Sandakhchiev responded with an invitation. Weber made several visits to Vector, and on one of them, Weber asked to see Buildings 6 and 6A, where the research on smallpox had been done years earlier, and about which Sandakhchiev had earlier deceived the British and American visitors. This time, Weber was allowed a close look at the building, and to take photographs. "It was clear the place was just a wreck, crap all over the floors, the equipment was in terrible shape," Weber recalled.

He went to Frank Miller, then acting assistant secretary of defense for international security policy, a longtime civil servant working on threat reduction. "I think we can break Vector's ties with Iran," Weber said. "They're desperate for limited cooperation and investment." Miller asked him how much money it would take. "Three million dollars," Weber replied. Miller went to work and eventually found the money. They persuaded Sandakhchiev to curtail the deals with the shady agents of Tehran.

On each trip and with each passing year, it was more and more apparent to the Americans who visited the former Soviet Union that the Cold War legacy of danger far exceeded what anyone had imagined at first. Years had gone by since the Soviet collapse, yet pathogens in flasks, unguarded fissile materials, idle weapons scientists and marooned defense factories were still being discovered for the first time in the late 1990s.

In a lightly guarded building at the Anti-plague Institute in Almaty, Kazakhstan, Weber once discovered a clutch of test tubes, with plague strains, stored in an empty tin can of peas. In 1997, in Tashkent, Uzbekistan, Weber and another U.S. official were scouting out weapons specialists for the International Science and Technology Center. They explained to a group of institute directors at the Uzbek Academy of Sciences that grants were intended for those who had worked on Soviet weapons programs. How many in the room thought they might qualify? One by one, they stood up. Among them, Weber met the director of an institute that, in Soviet times, worked on plant pathogens intended to wipe out the entire American wheat supply. The director invited Weber to visit, and Weber found, to his amazement, they were also working on how to grow crops *after* a nuclear holocaust. Weber brought back to Washington a whole new list of dangerous pathogens to worry about.[6]

In 1998, Weber made contacts at the Research Center for Molecular Diagnostics and Therapy in Moscow. The institute, which worked with dangerous pathogens in the Soviet years, had fallen on hard times in the 1990s. A scientist from the institute confided to Weber he had just received an e-mail from a postdoctoral student in Tehran who wanted to come work there. Weber told him: don't reply. Within weeks, Weber helped arrange grants from the International Science and Technology Center for some of the hard-pressed researchers to begin working on civilian projects.

Over the next few years, more secrets of Biopreparat spilled into the open. In 1998, Alibek published his memoir, describing his career in the germ warfare system. In May 2000, Nikolai Urakov, the director of Obolensk, hosted a conference cosponsored by the International Science and Technology Center. In an extraordinary day, journalists were shown around parts of Korpus No. 1, where Sergei Popov and Igor Domaradsky had worked on genetic engineering. Urakov complained the laboratory was receiving only 1 percent of the government budget of Soviet times—the rest they had to earn on their own. Urakov, director of the largest facility for developing bacteria for biological weapons in the old days, announced a new mission: "We have to protect humans from diseases."[7]

Over and over again, Weber found the key was forging relationships with scientists, respecting their dignity, their desire to carry out useful research, and building their trust. Governments and agreements had their purpose, but the real success started when they could look you in the eye and speak directly. The *banya* talks worked wonders.

For Weber and many of those Westerners who went to the former Soviet Union to staunch the threats, there was also a frustrating unknown. They could tally up the success stories, measure the number of fences built and grants given, but could only guess at what had slipped through their fingers. It was the nature of threat reduction that it was always risky business, devilishly challenging, often defying a chance to declare absolute success. In trying to prevent something, the most consequential and terrifying metric was failure.

EPILOGUE

When Mikhail Gorbachev shook hands for the first time with Ronald Reagan at Geneva on November 19, 1985, the two superpowers had amassed about sixty thousand nuclear warheads. The arms race was at its peak. "We looked at each other on the threshold, in front of the building where the negotiations were to take place, the first meeting," Gorbachev recalled more than two decades later. "Somehow, we extended a hand to each other, and started talking. He speaks English, I speak Russian, he understands nothing, and I understand nothing. But it seems there is a kind of dialogue being connected, a dialogue of the eyes." At the end of the summit, when they shook hands again on a statement that a nuclear war could not be won and must never be fought, Gorbachev was astonished. "Can you imagine what that meant?" Gorbachev told me. "It meant that everything we had been doing was an error."

"Both of us knew better than anyone else the kind of weapons that we had," he said. "And those were really piles, mountains of nuclear weapons. A war could start not because of a political decision, but just because of some technical failure." Gorbachev kept a sculpture of a goose in his Moscow office as a reminder that a flock of geese was once briefly mistaken for incoming missiles by the early-warning radars.

At Reykjavik, Gorbachev and Reagan went further toward eliminating all nuclear weapons than anyone had gone before. But a generation later, the great promise of Reykjavik remains unfulfilled. The "absolute weapon" is still with us. While the total number of nuclear warheads has shrunk by about two-thirds, thousands are still poised for launch. The United States maintains at the ready about 2,200 strategic nuclear warheads, and 500 smaller, tactical nuclear weapons. Another 2,500 warheads are held in reserve, and an additional 4,200 are awaiting dismantlement. Russia still maintains 3,113 warheads on strategic weapons, 2,079 tactical warheads and more than 8,800 in reserve or awaiting dismantlement. That's more than 23,000 nuclear warheads.

Since the end of the Cold War, the world has changed dramatically. Amorphous and murky threats—failed states, terrorism and proliferation—have grown more ominous. Nuclear weapons will hardly deter militias such as the Taliban, or terrorists such as those who attacked New York, Washington, London, Madrid and Mumbai in recent years. The terrorists and militias seek to frighten and damage a more powerful foe. So far they have employed conventional weapons—bombs, grenades, assault rifles and hijacked airliners—but they also want to get their hands on more potent weapons of mass casualty. Driven by intense zeal, they are not intimidated by a nuclear arsenal, nor deterred by fear of death. A lone suicidal terrorist carrying anthrax bacteria or nerve agents in a plastic pouch is not an appropriate target for a nuclear-armed missile. And while nuclear weapons worked as a reliable deterrent for leaders in the Kremlin and the White House, two experienced adversaries, they may not work so well if one of the protagonists is an untested nuclear power, nervous and jittery.

After the collapse of the Soviet Union, the United States twice reexamined its nuclear weapons policies and deployments in formal studies, known as the Nuclear Posture Review. Both times, in 1994 and 2002, the reviews acknowledged that the world had changed after the Cold War, but neither report was followed by radical change. The main reason was fear of the future; nuclear weapons were needed as a "hedge" against uncertainty. At first, the uncertainty was the chaos in the former Soviet Union, and later it was the prospect of some other nation or terrorist group obtaining nuclear weapons.

But the arsenals of the last war seem a poor hedge against new threats. Four elder statesmen of the nuclear age issued an appeal in 2007 to take action toward "a world free of the nuclear threat." They were Sam Nunn,

Chairman of the Senate Armed Services Committee 1987–1994; George Shultz, Secretary of State 1982–1989; Henry Kissinger, Secretary of State 1973–1977; and William J. Perry, Secretary of Defense 1994–1997. Gorbachev soon joined them. All were intimately involved with decisions about the nuclear balance of terror. The time has come to listen to them.[1]

One of their recommendations is to eliminate the short-range battlefield or tactical nuclear weapons left over from the Cold War. The United States has five hundred of these weapons deployed, including two hundred in Europe. They were originally intended to deter a Warsaw Pact invasion; the Warsaw Pact is history. Little is known about the disposition in Russia of the thousands of tactical nuclear weapons removed from Eastern Europe and the former Soviet republics after the 1991 Bush-Gorbachev initiative. They may be in storage or deployed; they have never been covered by any treaty, nor any verification regime, and the loss of just one could be catastrophic.[2]

Another step would be to take the remaining strategic nuclear weapons off launch-ready alert. When Stanislav Petrov faced the false alarm in 1983, launch decisions had to be made in just minutes. Today, Russia is no longer the ideological or military threat the Soviet Union once was; nor does the United States pose such a threat to Russia. Americans invested much time and effort to assist Russia's leap to capitalism in the 1990s—should we aim our missiles now at the very stock markets in Moscow we helped design? Bruce Blair has estimated that both the United States and Russia maintain about one-third of their total arsenals on launch-ready alert. It would take one to two minutes to execute the launch codes and fire Minuteman missiles in the central plains of the United States, and about twelve minutes to launch submarine-based missiles. The combined firepower that could be unleashed in this time frame by both countries is approximately 2,654 high-yield nuclear warheads, or 100,000 Hiroshimas. Procedures could easily be put in place that would de-alert the missiles and create deliberate launch delays of hours, days or weeks to prevent a terrible mistake. And it would be wise for Russia to disconnect and decommission Perimeter, the semiautomatic command system for nuclear retaliation. The Doomsday Machine was built for another epoch.[3]

After these steps, the United States and Russia could begin working— ideally in a renewed partnership—toward the goal of total, verified elimination of nuclear weapons around the globe. The United States and Russia together hold 95 percent of the world's warheads. The Moscow Treaty of 2002, signed by President George W. Bush and President Vladimir Putin, called for between 2,200 and 1,700 warheads "operationally deployed" on each side by the year 2012. Neither nation would suffer from radical reductions from this level. In today's world, thousands of nuclear warheads on each side do not provide thousands of times more deterrence or safety than a small number of warheads. A drive toward liquidation of the arsenals would be a fitting way to bury the Cold War. So would a determined effort to halt the spread of nuclear weapons and fissile materials elsewhere, as well as ratification of the Comprehensive Test Ban Treaty. We should remember the wisdom of Bernard Brodie, the pioneering early thinker about atomic weapons, who wrote that they are "truly cosmic forces harnessed to the machines of war." The war is over. It is long past time to scrap the machines.

In 1992, Senators Nunn and Lugar took a gamble with history. Back then, skeptics suggested it would be best to let the former Soviet Union drown in its own sorrows—to go into "free fall." Nunn and Lugar did not agree. They helped Russia and the other former Soviet republics cope with an inheritance from hell. The investment paid huge dividends. In the years that followed, Kazakhstan, Belarus and Ukraine completely abandoned nuclear weapons. A total of 7,514 nuclear warheads, 752 intercontinental ballistic missiles, and 31 submarines were deactivated.[4] These were required by arms control treaties, but Nunn-Lugar provided the resources that made dismantlement a reality.

Many of the facilities with unguarded fissile material in the mid-1990s underwent security upgrades. By 2008, more than 70 percent of the buildings in the former Soviet Union with weapons-usable nuclear materials had been fortified, although the uranium and plutonium were still spread across more than two hundred locations.[5] After Project Sapphire, highly-enriched uranium was removed, often quietly, from an additional nineteen research reactors and sensitive installations around the former Soviet bloc.[6] The International Science and Technology Center, started after Baker's visit to Chelyabinsk-70, made grants over fourteen years that benefited, at one time or another, about seventy thousand scientists and engineers involved in building weapons.[7] The anthrax factory at Stepnogorsk was destroyed, including the giant fermenters in Building 221. On Vozrozhdeniye Island, eleven graves where anthrax was buried were pinpointed; the substance, pink with a texture of wet clay, was excavated and the pathogens neutralized.[8] On the steppe near Russia's southern border, a $1 billion factory has been constructed that will destroy the huge stockpiles of chemical weapons, including sarin, stored in the nearby warehouses. At the Mayak Chemical Combine in the city of Ozersk, a massive fortified vault was built by the United States at a cost of $309 million to store excess Russian fissile materials. With walls twenty-three feet thick, the Fissile Material Storage Facility answered the need so starkly evident after the Soviet collapse—a Fort Knox to guard uranium and plutonium.

It was never going to be easy for a country so turbulent as Russia to accept the hand of a rich and powerful rival, and it wasn't. Suspicions, delays, misunderstandings and errors were abundant in the years after the Soviet collapse.[9] But overall, given the immense size of the Soviet military-industrial complex and the sprawling nature of the dangerous weapons and materials, the Nunn-Lugar gamble paid off. The world is safer for their vision and determination. It was also a bargain. The yearly cost for all facets of Nunn-Lugar was about $1.4 billion, a tiny sliver of the annual Pentagon budget of more than $530 billion.[10]

In a cemetery in Yekaterinburg, the city that was Sverdlovsk in Soviet times, on a cold snowy December day, I found a cluster of graves amid tall pines and birches. Wilted roses lay upon some of the tombstones, while others showed signs of neglect. What they all shared were the same dates of death: April and May 1979. These were the victims of the anthrax outbreak, their names a roll call from a long-forgotten battlefield of the Cold War. Andrei Komelskikh was sixty-seven years old when he died April 13. He was a grandfather. "You are always in our hearts, from your wife, children and grandchildren," his headstone was inscribed. Neither Andrei nor the other victims knew why they died in those horrific weeks of 1979. Except for a brief, one-sentence comment by Yeltsin, neither the Soviet Union nor Russia has ever admitted, either to the families or to the world, how or why the biological weapons disaster occurred.

On February 10, 2005, I was admitted to the once-secret Biopreparat headquarters at No. 4a Samokatnaya Street in Moscow. This was the same building where Ken Alibek worked as first deputy director. I went to the second floor to interview Valentin Yevstigneev, the retired lieutenant general who once headed the 15th Main Directorate of the Ministry of Defense, which supervised germ warfare. Yevstigneev was part of the old guard that had participated in the cover-up of Biopreparat activities in earlier years. Now wearing a business suit in a modern office, he handed me his card: first deputy general director of a privatized company, Biopreparat, a commercial enterprise. On a table, I picked up a glossy brochure about the new Biopreparat, containing photographs of test tubes, syringes and pills, describing the company's activity manufacturing medicines and medical technology. There was no mention of the pathogens of the past.

When I asked Yevstigneev about the anthrax outbreak in Sverdlovsk in 1979, he repeated the story that it was spread by contaminated meat. Then he suggested it was caused by sabotage or terrorists from outside the Soviet Union. This was another line of disinformation that had been floated by the military in earlier years.[11]

Telling the whole truth about the Sverdlovsk outbreak would be a good first step toward putting the terrible secret history of Biopreparat to rest.

The truth matters. Deception is a tool of germ warriors. The same disguise that concealed the Soviet biological weapons program as civilian research could be used today to hide a dangerous germ warfare program anywhere. The anthrax letter attacks in the United States in 2001, the outbreak of Severe Acute Respiratory Syndrome in 2003 and the dramatic advances in biosciences have all underscored the destructive nature of biological agents. The National Academy of Sciences concluded in a report in 2009 that closed cities like Obolensk with a relatively large footprint are no longer necessary to house an illicit biological weapons program. A dangerous pathogen, say a virus, could be spread with no discernible signature. The workspace of a biological weaponeer or terrorist could be safely nestled inside a university or commercial laboratory, impossible to discover by satellite reconnaissance. People are the key, as Vladimir Pasechnik demonstrated by following his conscience and revealing Soviet misdeeds. To detect such dangers in the future requires human contacts, networks, transparency and collaboration, the painstaking building of bridges that Andy Weber pursued.

In the 1990s, Russia seemed vulnerable and desperate, but starting in the year 2000, a surge of oil wealth fueled a new sense of independence. Also, Russia was led into another period of authoritarianism under President Putin, during which it grew hostile to outsiders. Under Putin, Russia increasingly shut down cooperation with the West on biological weapons proliferation. Russian officials have insisted that since the country has no offensive biological weapons program, there is no need to cooperate. But it also appears Russia is reverting back to Soviet-era habits. Putin's security services went on a hunt for suspected spies among scientists, which put a chill on joint projects with the West.

Russia has long refused to open the doors of three military biological research facilities. To this day, it is unknown how far the Soviet Union went in creating warheads and bombs from the bacteria and viruses that were developed at Obolensk and Vector. Did the Soviet scientists produce a super-plague resistant to antibiotics? Did they create a cruise missile capable of disseminating anthrax bacteria spores? Or warheads for an intercontinental ballistic missile to carry smallpox? And if they did these things, all in violation of an international treaty they signed in 1972, should the details at last be brought to light?[12] A string of Russian anti-plague institutes and stations that once fed into the germ warfare program also remain closed to Western cooperation. If there are no weapons, no offensive program, as Russia claims, then what is behind the closed doors? What formulas for weaponization remain in the military laboratories? And most importantly, what has become of the scientists with know-how to create pathogens that can be carried in a shirt pocket?

What are they working on today?

If it wasn't worrisome enough that Russia was weak and vulnerable after the Soviet collapse, another jolt came in the 1990s: terrorists and cults were in search of weapons of mass destruction. The people who would commit mass terror lacked the resources or industrial base of a government or military, but they burned with the ambition to kill in a large and theatrical way. Terrorism certainly wasn't new, but terrorists in possession of the arsenals of the Cold War would be devastating.

In 1995, the Aum Shinrikyo cult released the deadly nerve agent sarin on three Tokyo subway trains, killing twelve people, injuring over one thousand and causing mass panic. Technical problems, leaks and accidents plagued the cult. But the Tokyo subway attack showed what only a small amount of dangerous material could do. The Tokyo calamity resulted from 159 ounces of sarin. By contrast, in Russia, in a remote compound near the town of Shchuchye in western Siberia, there are still 1.9 million projectiles filled with 5,447 metric tons of nerve agents.[13]

Osama bin Laden was reportedly impressed with the Tokyo subway disaster and the chaos it generated. In 1998, Al Qaeda leaders began to launch a serious chemical and biological weapons effort, code-named Zabadi, or "curdled milk" in Arabic. Details of the effort were later revealed in documents found on a computer used by the Al Qaeda leadership in Kabul. Ayman Zawahiri, the former Cairo surgeon who that year merged his radical group, Islamic Jihad in Egypt, with Al Qaeda, noted that "the destructive power of these weapons is not less than that of nuclear weapons."[14] In 1999, Zawahiri recruited a Pakistani scientist to set up a small biological weapons laboratory in Kandahar. Later, the work was turned over to a Malaysian who knew the 9/11 hijackers and had helped them, Yazid Sufaat. He had been educated in biology and chemistry in California, and spent months at the Kandahar laboratory attempting to cultivate anthrax. George Tenet, the former CIA director, said the anthrax effort was carried out in parallel with the plot to hijack airplanes and crash them into buildings.[15] He believed, he said, that bin Laden's strongest desire was to go nuclear. At one point, the CIA frantically chased down reports that bin Laden was negotiating for the purchase of three Russian nuclear devices, although details were never found. "They understand that bombings by cars, trucks, trains, and planes will get them some headlines, to be sure," Tenet wrote. "But if they manage to set off a mushroom cloud, they will make history . . . Even in the darkest days of the Cold War, we could count on the fact that the Soviets, just like us, wanted to live. Not so with terrorists."[16]

It is difficult to build a working nuclear bomb, but less difficult to cultivate pathogens in a laboratory. A congressional commission concluded in 2008 that it would be hard for terrorists to weaponize and disseminate significant quantities of a biological agent in aerosol form, but it might not be so difficult to find someone to do it for them. "In other words," the panel said, "given the high-level of know-how needed to use disease as a weapon to cause mass casualties, the United States should be less concerned that terrorists will become biologists and far more concerned that biologists will become terrorists."[17]

The tools of mass casualty are more diffuse and more uncertain than ever before. Even as securing the weapons of the former Soviet Union remains unfinished business, the world we live in confronts new risks that go far beyond Biopreparat. Today one can threaten a whole society with a flask carrying pathogens created in a fermenter in a hidden garage—and without a detectable signature.

The Dead Hand of the arms race is still alive.

ACKNOWLEDGMENTS

I had the good fortune to be a White House correspondent for the *Washington Post* during the presidency of Ronald Reagan, and then bureau chief in Moscow in the 1990s. This book had its origins in those experiences, and I am grateful to many friends, colleagues, sources and participants who provided insights, recollections and materials.

My insights into Reagan were drawn from several interviews as well as his eventful eight years in office, and my understanding further enriched by publication of his memoir and private diary. Mikhail Gorbachev granted two interviews for this book, and I benefited from his memoir and extensive writing and public speaking. Anatoly Chernyaev gave me his personal recollections, and his diary is one of the single most valuable accounts of the years of *perestroika* and *glasnost*.

Pavel Podvig shared his knowledge of Russian weapons systems and helped decipher the Katayev papers. Svetlana Savranskaya guided me with precision and patience through Cold War memoirs and documents. For additional insights and comments on the manuscript I am grateful to Bruce Blair, Christopher J. Davis, Milton Leitenberg, Thomas C. Reed, Mikhail Tsypkin, Andy Weber, Valery Yarynich and Ray Zilinskas.

I am very much in debt to Ksenia Kostrova, who assisted with the papers of her grandfather, Vitaly Katayev. After the Soviet collapse, Katayev tried to adapt, establishing a private company. He was not very successful, but he continued to dream. One of his more spectacular ideas was to use surplus intercontinental ballistic missles to assist stranded sailors, fishermen or mountain climbers. The missiles would release a rescue package tethered to a parachute. Katayev drew charts and trajectories for his ambitious plan, which he called "Project Vita." His dream was never realized. Katayev passed away in 2001. His papers are deposited at the Hoover Institution Library and Archives, Stanford University.

Masha Lipman has long been my guiding light on Russia and offered valuable comments on the manuscript. My thanks also go to Irina Makarova, Vladimir Alexandrov and Sergei Belyakov.

At the *Washington Post*, I am deeply indebted to Katharine Graham and Donald Graham for their trust. They built a newsroom of creativity and dynamism under the leadership of Benjamin C. Bradlee and Leonard Downie Jr. Four gifted colleagues at the *Post* provided years of inspiration as well as valuable comments on the book: Rick Atkinson, Steve Coll, Michael Dobbs and Glenn Frankel. In addition, Robert G. Kaiser and Philip Bennett were unceasing in their friendship and encouragement, for this project and many others, over all the years we worked together.

Lou Cannon was my partner and tutor in Reagan's time. My thanks also go to *Post* colleagues Laura Blumenfeld, Jackson Diehl, David Finkel, Peter Finn, Mary Lou Foy, Michael Getler, Jim Hoagland, Don Oberdorfer, Keith Richburg, Julie Tate, Gene Thorp, Joby Warrick and Scott Wilson. For support in a thousand ways, I am indebted to Rebekah Davis. My thanks also to Katja Hom, Kate Agnew and Terissa Schor.

Robert Monroe shared far more about chemical demilitarization than I could ever absorb, and I am deeply grateful for our long conversations. For research, my thanks to Alex Remington, Josh Zumbrun, Robert Thomason and Anna Masterova. Maryanne Warrick and Abigail Crim transcribed interviews.

An important contribution came from Thomas S. Blanton and the National Security Archive in Washington, which provided key historical documents and analysis. I am also grateful to Anne Hessing Cahn for access to her collection of papers at the archive.

I have been enriched by years of guidance and teaching by Archie Brown at St. Antony's College, Oxford University.

Valuable contributions were also made by Ken Alibek, Martin Anderson, James A. Baker III, Rodric Braithwaite, Matthew Bunn, Joseph Cirincione, Thomas C. Cochran, Dick Combs, Igor Domaradsky, Sidney Drell, Erik Engling, Kenneth J. Fairfax, Andy Fisher, Chrystia Freeland, Oleg Gordievsky, Tatiana Gremyakova, Jeanne Guillemin, Cathy Gwin, Josh Handler, Anne M. Harrington, Laura Holgate, Richard Lugar, Matthew Meselson, Vil Mirzayanov, Kenneth A. Myers III, Sam Nunn, Vladimir Orlov, Sergei Popov, Theodore A. Postol, Amy Smithson, Margaret Tutwiler, Yevgeny Velikhov, Frank von Hippel and Lawrence Wright.

I am grateful for a media fellowship at the Hoover Institution, Stanford University, in 2004, which allowed me time for research. At the Hoover Library and Archives, I was assisted with great professionalism by Carol Leadenham, Lara Soroka, Heather Wagner and Brad Bauer.

At the Liddell Hart Centre for Military Archives, Kings College, London, my thanks to Caroline Lam and Katharine Higgon, and at the Ronald Reagan Presidential Library, my gratitude to Lisa Jones. I also profited from research at the British National Archives at Kew, and the U.S. National Archives at College Park, Maryland.

To Esther Newberg, my deepest appreciation for unflagging commitment and enthusiasm. At Doubleday, Bill Thomas gave the project a life. From our first conversations, Kristine Puopolo provided wise counsel and was a thoughtful, inspiring editor. And my thanks also to Stephanie Bowen.

To my wife, Carole, who read the entire manuscript many times over, to my sons, Daniel and Benjamin, and to my parents, to whom this book is dedicated, I express profound appreciation for loving support on the long and winding road.

ABBREVIATIONS IN NOTES

DNSA	Digital National Security Archive, *http://nsarchive.chadwyck.com*
EBB	Electronic Briefing Book of the National Security Archive
FOIA	Freedom of Information Act
FBIS	Foreign Broadcast Information Service
Katayev	The papers of Vitaly Katayev at the Hoover Institution Library and Archives, Stanford University, and in author's possession
NIE	National Intelligence Estimate
TNSA	The National Security Archive, *http://www.gwu.edu/~nsarchiv/index.html*
RRPL	Ronald Reagan Presidential Library

ENDNOTES

Prologue

1 Margarita Ivanovna Ilyenko, interview, Nov. 30, 1998. Roza Gaziyeva is quoted by Sergei Parfenov in *Rodina,* no. 5, Oct. 24, 1990.

2 Matthew Meselson, Jeanne Guillemin, Martin Hugh-Jones, Alexander Langmuir, Ilona Popova, Alexis Shelokov, Olga Yampolskaya, "The Sverdlovsk Anthrax Outbreak of 1979," *Science,* 1994, vol. 266, pp. 1202–1208; Jeanne Guillemin, *Anthrax: The Investigation of a Deadly Outbreak* (Berkeley: University of California Press, 1999); Ken Alibek, with Stephen Handelman, *Biohazard: The Chilling True Story of the Largest Covert Biological Weapons Program in the World—Told from Inside by the Man Who Ran It* (New York: Random House, 1999), Ch. 7.

3 Theodore J. Cieslak and Edward M. Eitzen Jr., "Clinical and Epidemiologic Principles of Anthrax," in *Emerging Infectious Diseases,* vol. 5, no. 4, July–Aug. 1999, p. 552.

4 Alibek was told the accident resulted from failure to replace a filter, but this account has never been confirmed. Alibek, pp. 73–74. Alibek said the release occurred on Friday, March 30. Given wind patterns, Monday April 2 seems more likely. Alibek told the author Monday was possible.

5 The children may have been indoors, in schools, or had a different immune system reaction, or been less susceptible to airborne anthrax than adults.

6 Lev M. Grinberg and Faina A. Abramova, interviews, Nov. 30, 1998. Abramova's account also appeared in *Rodina.*

7 Guillemin, p. 14.

8 Vladlen Krayev, interview, Nov. 1998. It was later realized the incubation period could be much longer.

9 Some months after the epidemic, the KGB searched Hospital No. 40 for materials. Abramova hid unlabeled samples on a high shelf. The KGB did not find them.

10 Petrov interviews, January 1999; Jan. 22, 2006, May 29, 2007.

11 Pavel Podvig, "History and the Current Status of the Russian Early Warning System," *Science and Global Security,* October 2002, pp. 21–60.

12 Podvig, p. 31.

INTRODUCTION

1 Bernard Brodie, ed., *The Absolute Weapon: Atomic Power and the World Order* (New York: Harcourt Brace and Co., 1946).

2 Albert Carnesale, Paul Doty, Stanley Hoffmann, Samuel P. Huntington, Joseph S. Nye Jr., and Scott D. Sagan, *Living with Nuclear Weapons* (New York: Bantam Books, 1983), pp. 31–32.

3 Admiral G. P. Nanos, "Strategic Systems Update," *Submarine Review,* April 1997, pp. 12–17. Nanos quoted another admiral but affirmed this was a "reasonable, unclassified scale." See "The Capabilities of Trident Against Russian Silo-based Missiles: Implications for START III and Beyond," George N. Lewis, Theodore A. Postol, Massachusetts Institute of Technology, Feb. 2–6, 1998.

4 David Alan Rosenberg, "The Origins of Overkill, Nuclear Weapons and American Strategy, 1945–1960," in *Strategy and Nuclear Deterrence,* Princeton University Press, 1984, pp. 113–181. Also see William Burr, ed., "The Creation of SIOP-62: More Evidence on the Origins of Overkill," EBB No. 130, doc. 23, "Note by the Secretaries to the Joint Chiefs of Staff on Strategic Target Planning," Jan. 27, 1961.

5 McGeorge Bundy, *Danger and Survival: Choices About the Bomb in the First Fifty Years* (New York: Random House, 1988), p. 354.

6 "History of the Joint Strategic Target Planning Staff: Preparation of SIOP-63," January 1964. "New Evidence on the Origins of Overkill," TNSA EBB No. 236, doc. 2. Also see McNamara commencement address at the University of Michigan, June 16. McNamara may have been influenced by the fact that, through improved satellite intelligence, the United States had obtained the first comprehensive map of the Soviet missile bases, submarine ports, air defense sites and other military installations. Desmond Ball and Jeffery Richelson, eds., *Strategic Nuclear Targeting* (Ithaca: Cornell University Press, 1986), p. 65. Also see Alfred Goldberg, "A Brief Survey of the Evolution of Ideas about Counterforce," Rand Corp., Memorandum RM-5431-PR, October 1957, rev. March 1981, p. 9. DNSA, No. NH00041.

7 Alain C. Enthoven and K. Wayne Smith, *How Much Is Enough?: Shaping the Defense Program, 1961–1969* (New York: Harper & Row, 1971), rev. ed. (Santa Monica: RAND Corp., 2005), pp. 67 and 207.

8 The acronym was advanced by Donald G. Brennan of the Hudson Institute to capture what he thought was the folly of the idea of MAD. Brennan was an advocate of missile defense and finding a way out of mutual vulnerability. See "Strategic Alternatives," *New York Times,* May 24, 1971, p. 31, and May 25, 1971, p. 39.

9 Arnold L. Horelick and Myron Rush, "Deception in Soviet Strategic Missile Claims, 1957–1962," RAND Corp., May 1963. DNSA NH00762.

10 An exception to this was Europe, where the Soviets knew that tactical nuclear strikes were possible early in any war, and they planned for preemptive nuclear attack. See Vojtech Mastny and Malcolm Byrne, eds., *A Cardboard Castle: An Inside*

History of the Warsaw Pact, 1955–1991 (Budapest: Central European University Press, 2005), pp. 406–412.

11 John Hines, Ellis M. Mishulovich, John F. Shull, *Soviet Intentions 1965–1985,* BDM Federal Inc., for Office of Secretary of Defense, Sept. 22, 1995, offers a good overview of Soviet thinking based on interviews with Soviet participants. See Vol. I, *An Analytical Comparison of U.S.-Soviet Assessments During the Cold War.* Also see Aleksander Savelyev and Nikolay Detinov, *The Big Five: Arms Control Decision-making in the Soviet Union* (Westport, Conn.: Praeger, 1995), pp. 1–13.

12 The end result of the competition was a turn toward hardened silos and reliance on a retaliatory posture, which Keldysh favored. Hines, Vol. II, p. 85; Savelyev, pp. 18–19; Vitaly Katayev, unpublished memoir, *Some Facts from History and Geometry,* author's possession; Pavel Podvig, communication with author, March 27, 2009; and Podvig, ed., *Russian Strategic Nuclear Forces* (Cambridge: MIT Press, 2001).

13 The plan still incorporated the counterforce idea. Task Alpha would use 58 percent of the arsenal to hit Soviet forces. By contrast, task Charlie—cities and industrial targets—was to use only about 11 percent of the weapons. See "The Nixon Administration, the SIOP, and the Search for Limited Nuclear Options, 1969–1974," TNSA EBB No. 173, doc. 3.

14 For Kissinger on Nixon, see TNSA EBB 173, doc. 22. H. R. Haldeman, *The Haldeman Diaries* (New York: G. P. Putnam's Sons, 1994), p. 55. Kissinger pushed for the creation of limited nuclear war options, saying that threats of a massive attack were just not credible. On January 17, 1974, Nixon signed National Security Decision Memorandum 242, a top-secret directive that laid out a desire for a "wide range" of limited nuclear war attack options. The directive was the result of Kissinger's prodding. See TNSA EBB 173 and Burr, "The Nixon Administration, the 'Horror Strategy,' and the Search for Limited Nuclear Options, 1969–1972," *Journal of Cold War Studies,* vol. 7, no. 3, Summer 2005, pp. 34–78.

15 Hines, vol. II, p. 27.

16 The treaty limited each side to two sites with one hundred launchers. This was cut in 1974 to one site each. The United States built one around North Dakota missile fields, but later dismantled it. The Soviet Union built one around Moscow.

17 Lawrence Freedman, *The Evolution of Nuclear Strategy* (New York: St. Martin's Press, 1981), p. 363. Kissinger press conference, July 3, 1974.

18 Nitze, "Assuring Strategic Stability in an Era of Détente," *Foreign Affairs,* January 1976, vol. 54, no. 2.

19 Hines asked Soviet participants about key conclusions in the Team A-Team B experiment. While he found support for a Soviet desire for superiority, he also found U.S. assessments had overstated Soviet intentions as aggressive. Hines, pp. 68–71. For the Team B report, see "Intelligence Community Experiment in Competitive Analysis: Soviet Strategic Objectives, An Alternative View: Report of Team 'B,'" December 1976, DNSA SE00501. Pipes later claimed Team B's conclusions were based on a deeper insight into Russian history and mind-set. See Richard Pipes, *VIXI: Memoirs of a Non-Belonger* (New Haven: Yale University Press, 2003), p. 137. For Team A, see "Soviet Forces for Strategic Nuclear Conflict through the Mid-1980s," NIE 11-3/8-76, Dec. 21, 1976, Vol. 1, Key Judgments and Summary, p. 3. Also see Anne Hessing Cahn, *Killing Détente* (University Park:

Pennsylvania State University Press, 1998); and Cahn, "Team B: The Trillion Dollar Experiment," *Bulletin of the Atomic Scientists,* April 1993, vol. 49, no. 3, pp. 22–27. For evidence Team B erred, see Raymond L. Garthoff, "Estimating Soviet Military Intentions and Capabilities," Ch. 5 in Gerald K. Haines and Robert E. Leggett, eds., *Watching the Bear: Essays on CIA's Analysis of the Soviet Union* (Washington, D.C.: Center for the Study of Intelligence, Central Intelligence Agency, 2003). Through the late 1970s and early 1980s, many hawks warned about the "window of vulnerability" for American land-based missiles. This argument, made by Nitze, Pipes and eventually Reagan, claimed that the larger number of Soviet missiles could wipe out the entire one thousand U.S. Minuteman missile force and fifty-four Titan missiles. But the SS-18s may have been less accurate than the United States thought. For example, NIE 11-3/8-78 estimated that had the Soviet Union initiated an attack on American missile silos in 1978, only about six hundred U.S. silo-based missiles would survive a one-on-one Soviet missile attack, and no more than about four hundred would survive a two-on-one strike. However, using flight test data from Katayev, Pavel Podvig estimated that 890 of the 1,054 U.S. silo-based missiles would have survived a one-on-one attack and 800 would have survived an attack in which each silo is targeted by two Soviet warheads. Podvig, "The Window of Vulnerability that Wasn't: Soviet Military Buildup in the 1970s," *International Security,* Vol. 3, No. 1, Summer, 2008. Bush, then CIA director, later told Congress the two teams reached the following conclusions: "1. Team A's conclusions lead to estimates of ICBM accuracy which do not imply a severe threat to Minuteman until about 1980. 2. The Team B estimates of accuracy imply that such a threat could materialize much sooner." See "DCI Congressional Briefing," January 1977, Anne Cahn collection, TNSA. After the exercise was over, Team A pointed out that the Soviets lagged way behind the United States in theory, laboratory instrument quality and mass production of precision instruments such as guidance equipment needed for missile accuracy. See "Summary of Intelligence Community ('A Team') Briefing to PFIAB on Soviet ICBM Accuracy," Cahn collection, TNSA. The document is undated but the briefing was in December 1976. Hines noted U.S. and Soviet experts used different assumptions about nuclear blast to judge whether missile silos were vulnerable. Hines, p. 70. Missile accuracy is measured by "circular error probability," or CEP—the radius of a circle in which half the warheads fall. When the Soviets began deploying the first missiles with MIRVs in 1974, the U.S. intelligence consensus was they did not have a CEP better than 470 meters. These estimates were challenged by Team B, which suggested that Soviet missiles could become even more accurate (a smaller CEP). But according to Soviet flight test data, the CEP of the first-generation SS-18 was 700 meters; the SS-17 was 700 meters, and the SS-19 was 650 meters. The next generation of missiles, coming on line in the 1980s, were improved. The author is indebted to Pavel Podvig for these conclusions, based on Katayev, Hoover.

20 Soviet Forces for Strategic Nuclear Conflict Through the Mid-1980s, NIE 11-3/8-76, Dec. 21, 1976, Vol. 1, Key Judgments and Summary, p. 3.

21 Eugene V. Rostow, the Yale law professor, was committee chairman. Dozens of members eventually held appointments in the Reagan administration, including

Nitze and Pipes. Charles Tyroller II, ed., *Alerting America: The Papers of the Committee on the Present Danger* (Washington: Pergamon-Brassey's, 1984).

22 Brzezinski became concerned about weaknesses in the command and control system when an exercise to simulate evacuating the president on Jan. 28, 1977, went awry. Brzezinski, *Power and Principle: Memoirs of the National Security Advisor, 1977–1981* (New York: Farrar, Straus, & Giroux, 1983), pp. 14–15. Brzezinski asked William E. Odom, then a colonel general on the White House National Security Council staff, to study the chain of command and control of nuclear weapons. The study revealed weaknesses in the system. The two presidential directives were an outgrowth of the study. Odom interview, Feb. 3, 2006; Odom, "The Origins and Design of Presidential Decision-59: A Memoir," in Henry D. Sokolski, ed., *Getting Mad: Nuclear Mutual Assured Destruction, Its Origins and Practice* (Carlisle, Pa.: U.S. Army War College, 2004). On targeting the Soviet leadership, see Hines, vol. 2, p. 118. Andrew W. Marshall, the director of the Office of Net Assessment in the Office of the Secretary of Defense, told Hines that "PD-59 was developed to reinforce deterrence by making it clear to the Soviet leadership that they would not escape destruction in any exchange. The objective was to clarify and personalize somewhat the danger of warfare and nuclear use to Soviet decision-makers."

CHAPTER 1: AT THE PRECIPICE

1 See *www.cheyennemountain.af.mil.*

2 Morrow later promoted NASA programs. See Kiron K. Skinner, Annelise Anderson and Martin Anderson, eds., *Reagan: A Life in Letters* (New York: Free Press, 2003), p. 107.

3 Martin Anderson, *Revolution: The Reagan Legacy* (New York: Harcourt Brace Jovanovich, 1988), pp. 80–83.

4 Reagan radio address, May 29, 1979, "Miscellaneous 1," reproduced in *Reagan in His Own Hand: The Writings of Ronald Reagan That Reveal His Revolutionary Vision for America,* Kiron K. Skinner, Annelise Anderson, Martin Anderson, eds. (New York: Free Press, 2001), p. 104. The treaty was signed by Carter and Brezhnev in Vienna on June 18.

5 Draft copy, "Policy Memorandum No. 3," August 1979, author's possession. Anderson knew Reagan had in earlier years disagreed with President Nixon's decision to limit missile defenses in the 1972 ABM treaty. "We bargained that away in exchange for nothing," Reagan had said. See "Defense IV," Sept. 11, 1979, *Reagan in His Own Hand.* Anderson interview, Sept. 10, 2008.

6 In his memoir, Reagan wrote: "Nothing was more important to mankind than assuring its survival and the survival of our planet. Yet for forty years nuclear weapons had kept the world under a shadow of terror. Our dealings with the Soviets—and theirs with us—had been based on a policy known as 'mutual assured destruction'—the 'MAD' policy, and madness it was. It was the craziest thing I had ever heard of: Simply put, it called for each side to keep enough nuclear weapons at the ready to obliterate each other, so that if one attacked, the second had enough bombs left to annihilate its adversary in a matter of minutes. We were a button push away from oblivion." Ronald Reagan, *An American Life* (New York: Simon & Schuster, 1990), p. 13.

7 Ronald Reagan, *The Reagan Diaries* (New York: HarperCollins, 2007), June 7, 1981.

8 Martin Anderson, presentation, Oct. 11, 2006, Hoover Institution, Stanford University, "Implications of the Reykjavik Summit on Its Twentieth Anniversary." Also, communication with author, Sept. 10, 2008.

9 Tony Thomas, *The Films of Ronald Reagan* (Secaucus, N.J.: Citadel Press, 1980), pp. 98–99.

10 Laurence W. Beilenson, *The Treaty Trap: A History of the Performance of Political Treaties by the United States and European Nations* (Washington, D.C.: Public Affairs Press, 1969), pp. 212, 219–221.

11 The author covered the Reagan campaign as a reporter for Knight-Ridder newspapers, and never picked up on Reagan's nuclear abolitionist views. Yet his thinking was expressed in earlier years. See Reagan's 1963 speech text, "Are Liberals Really Liberal?" in *Reagan in His Own Hand*, and Reagan's address to the 1976 Republican National Convention, Anderson, pp. 69–71.

12 Reagan, "Peace: Restoring the Margin of Safety," address to the Veterans of Foreign Wars Convention, Chicago, August 18, 1980.

13 David Hoffman, "Reagan's Lure Is His Optimism," *Detroit Free Press,* Summer 1980.

14 Reagan, *An American Life,* p. 267.

15 Anatoly Dobrynin, *In Confidence: Moscow's Ambassador to America's Six Cold War Presidents* (New York: Times Books, 1995), p. 484.

16 Lou Cannon, *Ronald Reagan: The Role of a Lifetime* (New York: Simon & Schuster, 1991), pp. 299–301. Reagan's diary for April 23 includes one version of what he calls a "script" of a letter written by hand. This is a short letter. In *An American Life,* pp. 272–273, Reagan reprints a broader version of the handwritten letter, apparently reflecting revisions by the State Department and others.

17 James A. Baker III, *"Work Hard, Study . . . And Keep Out of Politics!"* (New York: G. P. Putnam's Sons, 2006), p. 163.

18 Reagan, *An American Life,* p. 273.

19 Thomas C. Reed, *At the Abyss: An Insider's History of the Cold War* (New York: Ballantine Books, 2004), pp. 266–270.

20 Gus Weiss, "The Farewell Dossier," *Studies in Intelligence*, Center for the Study of Intelligence, Central Intelligence Agency, vol. 39, no. 5, 1996.

21 Pelton volunteered information about the program as early as his first contact with the Soviets on Jan. 15, 1980, and received $20,000 from them in October. He received another $15,000 in 1983. Pelton was arrested in 1985 and convicted of spying in 1986. See *United States of America v. Ronald William Pelton,* Indictment, U.S. District Court for the District of Maryland, Dec. 20, 1985, case no. HM-850621.

22 Sherry Sontag and Christopher Drew, *Blind Man's Bluff: The Untold Story of American Submarine Espionage* (New York: PublicAffairs, 1998), p. 230.

23 Christopher Andrew and Oleg Gordievsky, *KGB: The Inside Story* (New York: HarperCollins, 1990), p. 583.

24 Thomas C. Reed communication with author, Nov. 21, 2006.

25 Richard Halloran, "Pentagon Draws Up First Strategy for Fighting a Long Nuclear War," *New York Times,* May 30, 1982, p. 1.

26 Charles Mohr, "Preserving U.S. Command After Nuclear Attack," *New York Times,* June 28, 1982, p. 18.

27 Thomas C. Reed, interview, Dec. 4, 2004.

28 John Lewis Gaddis, *Strategies of Containment: A Critical Appraisal of American National Security Policy During the Cold War,* rev. ed. (Oxford: Oxford University Press, 2005), p. 354.

29 Reed, p. 236.

30 Gaddis, p. 354.

31 Reagan diary, March 26, 1982.

32 NSDD 32 is dated May 20, 1982. But the next presidential directive, NSDD 33, is dated a week earlier, May 14. Reed said Clark put it into the system the day before he was to deliver a public speech, on May 21, describing the new approach.

33 Reagan admitted having trouble. "Some of the journalists who write so easily as to why we don't sit down and start talking with the Soviets should know just how complicated it is," he wrote. Reagan diary, April 21, 1982.

34 Reagan, *An American Life,* p. 553. See Dobrynin, pp. 502–503. In November 1981, Reagan had unveiled another arms control proposal, for intermediate-range nuclear forces in Europe. This was his "zero option," proposing that the United States would forgo deployment of the Pershing IIs and GLCMs if the Soviets dismantled their Pioneers. Although it seemed one-sided at the time, it later proved to be the template for the 1987 treaty eliminating this entire class of weapons.

35 Reagan diary, May 24, 1982.

36 Carl Bernstein, "The Holy Alliance," *Time* magazine, Feb. 24, 1992, pp. 28–35.

37 George Weigel, *Witness to Hope: The Biography of Pope John Paul II* (New York: HarperCollins, 1991), p. 441, and note 13, p. 905.

38 Steven R. Weisman, "Reagan, in Berlin, Bids Soviet Work for a Safe Europe," *New York Times,* June 12, 1982, p. 1; and Edmund Morris, *Dutch: A Memoir of Ronald Reagan* (New York: Random House, 1999), p. 461.

39 George Shultz, *Turmoil and Triumph: My Years as Secretary of State* (New York: Charles Scribner's Sons, 1993), p. 5.

40 This assessment was made in 1979 by Undersecretary of Defense for Research and Engineering William J. Perry before the House Armed Services Committee. Also see *Strategic Command, Control and Communications: Alternative Approaches for Modernization,* Congressional Budget Office, October 1981.

41 Reed communication with author, Nov. 21, 2006.

42 NSDD 55. *http://www.fas.org/irp/offdocs/nsdd/index.html.*

43 James Mann, *Rise of the Vulcans: The History of Bush's War Cabinet* (New York: Viking, 2004), Ch. 9.

44 Reagan diary, Nov. 13, 1982. Dobrynin, pp. 511–512.

45 "Report of the President's Commission on Strategic Forces," April 1983, p. 4.

46 In December, Congress voted to reduce funding until the basing could be resolved, but did not kill the missile altogether.

47 Donald R. Baucom, *The Origins of SDI: 1944–1983* (Lawrence, Kansas: University Press of Kansas), p. 184. Baucom was staff historian for the U.S. Strategic Defense Initiative Organization.

48 Bob Sims, interview, Feb. 26, 1985.

49 Skinner, pp. 430–432. The essay is dated May 7, 1931.

50 Anderson, Hoover presentation.

51 A handwritten annotation says the speech was "written around 1962," but archivists think it may have been 1963. See Skinner, pp. 438–442.

52 Among those who attended were Bendetsen and two members of the so-called kitchen cabinet, William A. Wilson, then U.S. ambassador to the Holy See, and Joseph Coors. "Daily Diary of President Ronald Reagan," Jan. 8, 1992, RRPL. Graham was excluded. See Baucom, Ch. 7. Soon after the White House meeting, in early 1982, the group began to splinter over tactics. Bendetsen wanted to work quietly, but Graham decided to go public and published *High Frontier: A New National Strategy,* a 175-page study on using space platforms and existing or near-term technology. In another split, Graham envisioned non-nuclear defense, while physicist Edward Teller was pushing nuclear-pumped lasers. According to Baucom, for the rest of the year, Bendetsen continued to seek White House action on his Jan. 8 memorandum. A White House science office committee was also studying the idea. Late in the year, Bendetsen went as far as to write a proposed insert for a Reagan State of the Union speech endorsing strategic defense and sent it to the White House. Baucom, pp. 169–170. Another account of this period is contained in William J. Broad, *Teller's War: The Top Secret Story Behind the Star Wars Deception* (New York: Simon & Schuster, 1992), pp. 114–115.

53 Broad, p. 118, quotes Ray Pollack, a White House official at the meeting.

54 Edward Teller with Judith Shoolery, *Memoirs: A Twentieth-Century Journey in Science and Politics* (Cambridge: Perseus Publishing, 2001), p. 530.

55 Reagan diary, Sept. 14, 1982. Teller described his idea as a laser "driven by a nuclear explosion." Later in the 1980s, Teller endorsed a non-nuclear approach. Teller, pp. 528, 535–536.

56 Anderson, p. 97, and interview, Nov. 10, 2008. Also, "The Schedule of President Ronald Reagan," Wednesday, Dec. 22, 1982, courtesy Annelise and Martin Anderson.

57 The commission, chaired by Brent Scowcroft, recommended April 6, 1983, that the United States put one hundred MX missiles in existing Minuteman silos and move to build a new generation of small, single-warhead missiles for the longer term. The commission said the "window of vulnerability" wasn't serious enough to warrant expensive schemes such as Dense Pack or setting up ABM for silos. See "Report of the President's Commission," p. 17. Congress eventually approved fifty MX missiles in May 1985.

58 In addition to Baucom's detailed account, see Cannon, pp. 327–333; Hedrick Smith, *The Power Game* (New York: Random House, 1988), pp. 596–616; Frances Fitzgerald, *Way Out There in the Blue: Reagan, Star Wars and the End of the Cold War* (New York: Simon & Schuster, 2000), Ch. 5; Morris, p. 471; Robert C. McFarlane, with Zofia Smardz, *Special Trust* (New York: Cadell & Davies, 1994), pp. 229–230; and Frederick H. Hartmann, *Naval Renaissance: The U.S. Navy in the 1980s* (Annapolis: Naval Institute Press, 1990), Ch. 14.

59 McFarlane, pp. 226–229.

60 Reagan diary, Feb. 11, 1983.

61 Reagan diary, Feb. 15, 1983.

62 Jack F. Matlock Jr., *Reagan and Gorbachev: How the Cold War Ended* (New York: Random House, 2004), p. 55. Shultz, p. 165.

63 Gordievsky, interview, Aug. 29, 2005; Oleg Gordievsky, *Next Stop Execution: The Autobiography of Oleg Gordievsky* (London: Macmillan, 1995).

64 Andrew and Gordievsky, p. 589.

65 Reagan, *An American Life,* p. 570.

66 Reagan, *An American Life,* p. 569.

67 McFarlane warned Reagan twice he should consult Congress and the allies, but Reagan rejected the advice, *Special Trust*, pp. 230–231.

68 "U.S. Relations with the USSR," NSDD 75, Jan. 17, 1983. Pipes, the Harvard professor who had led Team B, was on the White House National Security Council staff and drafted the directive. In his memoir, Pipes said that inducing change in the Soviet regime was the goal. Pipes, pp. 188–208. Raymond L. Garthoff said it was a compromise and the "main thrust of the directive . . . was pragmatic and geopolitical." Garthoff, *The Great Transition* (Washington, D.C.: Brookings Institution, 1994), p. 33.

69 In a letter Feb. 19, 2004, to Shultz, McFarlane recalled that Reagan had not made strategic defense a priority "through no less than four budget cycles" since taking office. Letter courtesy McFarlane.

70 Cannon, p. 331.

71 Shultz doubted the technology was ready, doubted the expertise of the joint chiefs and told Reagan the proposal was a "revolution in our strategic doctrine." Shultz, p. 250.

72 Reagan diary, March 22, 1983.

73 Address by the president to the nation, March 23, 1983.

CHAPTER 2: WAR GAMES

1 Dmitri Volkogonov, *Autopsy for an Empire: The Seven Leaders Who Built the Soviet Regime* (New York: Free Press, 1998), p. 361.

2 On July 16, 1982, Nitze, then negotiator for the United States, tried to work out a settlement in a "walk in the woods" with his Soviet counterpart, but the Soviets did not take up the ideas. Nitze, *From Hiroshima to Glasnost: At the Center of Decision, A Memoir* (New York: Grove Weidenfeld, 1989), pp. 376–389.

3 Aleksander Savelyev and Nikolay Detinov, *The Big Five: Arms Control Decision-making in the Soviet Union* (Westport, Conn.: Praeger, 1995), p. 57. Also see Oleg Golubev et al., *Rossiskaya Systema Protivoraketnoi Oboroniy* [Russian System of Anti-Missile Defense] (Moscow: Tekhnokonsalt, 1994), p. 67.

4 "Meeting of the Politburo of the Central Committee of the Communist Party of the Soviet Union," May 31, 1983, *Communist Party of the Soviet Union on Trial,* Fond 89, Opis 42, Delo 53. Hoover, 14 pp.

5 "The Problem of Discovering Preparation for a Nuclear Missile Attack on the USSR," reproduced in Christopher Andrew and Oleg Gordievsky, *Comrade Kryuchkov's Instructions: Top Secret Files on KGB Foreign Operations, 1975–1985* (Stanford: Stanford University Press, 1991), p. 76.

6 Gordievsky, interview, Aug. 29, 2005.

7 Markus Wolf, *Man Without a Face: The Autobiography of Communism's Greatest Spymaster* (New York: PublicAffairs, 1999), pp. 246–247; Ben B. Fischer, "A Cold War Conundrum: The 1983 Soviet War Scare," Center for the Study of Intelligence, CIA, September 1997, pp. 14–17. The underground bunker was sealed by the West German military in 1993, but later reopened as a national historic building and tours offered. See *http://www.bunker5001.com.*

8 Volkogonov, p. 361.

9 Yevgeny Chazov, *Health and Power* (Moscow: Novosti, 1992), pp. 181–184.

10 "The History of the USS Enterprise (CVN-65) in 1982," from Commanding officer, USS Enterprise, R. J. Kelly, to Chief of Naval Operations, March 28, 1983.

11 Pete Earley, *Family of Spies: Inside the John Walker Spy Ring* (New York: Bantam Books, 1988), p. 248.

12 John F. Lehman Jr., *Command of the Seas: Building the 600 Ship Navy* (New York: Charles Scribner's Sons, 1988), Ch. 4, and p. 137.

13 Confidential source.

14 "The History of USS Enterprise (CVN-65) in 1983," Memorandum from J. J. Dantone to Chief of Naval Operations, April 23, 1984, and "Command History for Calendar Year 1983," Memorandum from Commanding Officer, Carrier Airborne Early Warning Squadron 113, T. A. Chiprany, to Chief of Naval Operations, March 1, 1984. Watkins testimony is from Seymour M. Hersh, *The Target Is Destroyed: What Really Happened to Flight 007 and What America Knew About It* (New York: Random House, 1986), p. 24.

15 Hersh, pp. 25–26.

16 Andrei Illesh, "Secret of the Korean Boeing 747," *Izvestia,* January 24, 1991, p. 5. This was part of a lengthy series by the journalist.

17 Whitworth had received $60,000 from Walker just before he sailed on the *Enterprise* in late 1982. Over nearly ten years, Whitworth received $332,000 for leaking secrets to the Soviets.

18 Howard Blum, *I Pledge Allegiance . . . : The True Story of the Walkers: An American Spy Family* (New York: Simon & Schuster, 1987), p. 299.

19 Affidavit of Rear Admiral William O. Studeman, director of naval intelligence, in *United States of America, Plaintiff, vs. Jerry Alfred Whitworth, Defendant,* Criminal Case No. 85-0552 JPV, Aug. 25, 1986, reproduced as Appendix A in "Meeting the Espionage Challenge: A Review of United States Counterintelligence and Security Programs," Report of the Select Committee on Intelligence, United States Senate, 99th Congress, 2d Session, Report 99-522, Oct. 3, 1986.

20 Affidavit of Studeman in *United States of America, Plaintiff, vs. John Anthony Walker, Jr., Defendant,* Criminal No. H-85-0309, reproduced in Robert W. Hunter, *Spy Hunter: Inside the FBI Investigation of the Walker Espionage Case* (Annapolis: Naval Institute Press, 1999), Appendix C, pp. 222–234.

21 Christopher Andrew, *For the President's Eyes Only: Secret Intelligence and the American Presidency, from Washington to Bush* (New York: HarperCollins, 1995), p. 472.

22 Don Oberdorfer, *From the Cold War to a New Era* (Baltimore: Johns Hopkins University Press, 1998), pp. 37–38.

23 United Press International, Aug. 30, 1983, "Presidential Fence Is Finished."

24 Politburo minutes, Aug. 4, 1983. Archive of the President of the Russian Federation, Volkogonov Collection, Reel 17, Container 25, on file at the National Security Archive, READD Record 9965.

25 Andrew and Gordievsky, *Comrade,* p. 82.

26 Gordievsky, interview, Aug. 29, 2005.

CHAPTER 3: WAR SCARE

1 This account is based on reports by the International Civil Aviation Organization, Dec. 2, 1983, and May 28, 1993, and on the Osipovich interview by Illesh.

2 The 1993 report of the ICAO stated: "The proximity of the RC-135 and KE 007 resulted in 1983 in confusion and the plotting of the track of only one aircraft." Pp. 47–48.

3 Seymour M. Hersh, *The Target Is Destroyed: What Really Happened to Flight 007 and What America Knew About It* (New York: Random House, 1986), p. 78.

4 The plane rocking is mentioned in Osipovich interview, August 1997, for *The Cold War,* a 24-part television documentary produced by Jeremy Isaacs Productions for CNN and broadcast on BBC2, 1989–1999. Liddell Hart Center for Military Archives, Kings College, London, file no. 28/109.

5 Osipovich, *The Cold War* transcript.

6 Nancy Reagan with William Novak, *My Turn* (New York: Dell, 1989), p. 271.

7 Hersh, Ch. 8.

8 Cable "To All Diplomatic Posts," Sept. 5, 1983, carrying "text of the background statement delivered by Under Secretary [Lawrence] Eagleburger September 5 concerning the flight of the US RC-135." RRPL.

9 Douglas MacEachin, interview, July 25, 2005.

10 On Dec. 29, 1987, the State Department released an intelligence assessment showing the United States knew after the shoot down that it was due to Soviet ineptitude. Representative Lee Hamilton released the declassified assessment January 12, 1988. J. Edward Fox, assistant secretary of state for legislative affairs, said, "We had concluded by the second day (Sept. 2, 1983) that the Soviets thought they were pursuing a U.S. reconnaissance aircraft throughout most, if not all, of the overflight."

11 Robert M. Gates, *From the Shadows: The Ultimate Insider's Story of Five Presidents and How They Won the Cold War* (New York: Simon & Schuster, 1996), pp. 267–268. Also see George Shultz, *Turmoil and Triumph: My Years as Secretary of State* (New York: Charles Scribner's Sons, 1993), p. 364.

12 Dmitri Volkogonov, *Autopsy for an Empire: The Seven Leaders Who Built the Soviet Regime* (New York: Free Press, 1998), p. 363.

13 Anatoly Dobrynin, *In Confidence: Moscow's Ambassador to America's Six Cold War Presidents* (New York: Times Books, 1995), p. 537.

14 TASS, Sept. 1, 1983, 17:17 in English, "Soviet Air Space Violated," FBIS, USSR International Affairs, Northeast Asia, Sept. 1, 1983, p. C2.

15 Meeting of the Politburo of the Central Committee of the Soviet Union, Sept. 2, 1983, courtesy Svetlana Savranskaya, TNSA.

16 Volkogonov, pp. 365–366.

17 "Provocateurs Cover Traces," TASS report in *Pravda*, Sept. 5, 1983, p. 5, FBIS, Sept. 6, 1983, USSR International Affairs, Northeast Asia, p. C 2-4.

18 On Sept. 5, Reagan signed NSDD 102, which punished Aeroflot, the Soviet national airline, and caused it to close offices in Washington and New York; seeking to force the Soviets to accept responsibility through public statements and compensation for families of the victims. Reagan reaffirmed existing sanctions on Aeroflot, and nonrenewal of a transportation treaty.

19 Gates, p. 290.

20 Volkogonov, p. 375.

21 Yevgeny Chazov, *Health and Power* (Moscow: Novosti, 1992), p. 184.

22 Christopher Andrew and Oleg Gordievsky, *Comrade Kryuchkov's Instructions: Top Secret Files on KGB Foreign Operations, 1975–1985* (Stanford: Stanford University Press, 1991), pp. 594–595.

23 Oleg Gordievsky, *Next Stop Execution: The Autobiography of Oleg Gordievsky* (London: Macmillan, 1995), p. 272.

24 Andrew and Gordievsky, p. 594.

25 Dobrynin, pp. 537–538.

26 Geoffrey Howe, *Conflict of Loyalty* (New York: St. Martin's Press, 1994), pp. 349–350.

27 Margaret Thatcher, *The Downing Street Years* (New York: HarperCollins, 1993), p. 324.

28 Thatcher, p. 451.

29 Archie Brown, *The Gorbachev Factor* (Oxford: Oxford University Press, 1996), pp. 77–78.

30 Elizabeth Teague, "War Scare in the USSR," in *Soviet/East European Survey: Selected Research and Analysis from Radio Free Europe/Radio Liberty,* Vojtech Mastny, ed. (Durham: Duke University Press, 1985), pp. 71–76.

31 Dusko Doder, "Soviets Prepare People for Crisis in U.S. Ties," *Washington Post,* Oct. 30, 1983, p. A34.

32 Savranskaya, interview, May 13, 2005.

33 Reagan diary, Oct. 10, 1983.

34 Edmund Morris, *Dutch: A Memoir of Ronald Reagan* (New York: Random House, 1999), pp. 498–499.

35 "Memorandum of conversation," Oct. 11, 1983, RRPL. Also see Jack F. Matlock Jr., *Autopsy on an Empire: The American Ambassador's Account of the Collapse of the Soviet Union* (New York: Random House, 1995), p. 83.

36 Desmond Ball, "Development of the SIOP, 1960–1983," in *Strategic Nuclear Targeting,* pp. 79–83.

37 Reagan diary, Nov. 18, 1983.

38 Reagan, *An American Life,* p. 586.

39 Report of the DOD Commission on Beirut International Airport Terrorist Act, Oct. 23, 1983, issued Dec. 20, 1983.

40 The invasion was dubbed "Operation Urgent Fury" by the U.S. military, and it brought a public relations boost to the White House, but it was a small operation against weak foes. Eighteen U.S. troops were killed and 86 wounded.

41 Gates recalled that Casey briefed Reagan on the Soviet fears of nuclear war on

December 22 based on separate information from Soviet military intelligence sources. Gates, p. 272.

42 McFarlane, interview, April 25, 2005. Gates concluded, "A genuine belief had taken root within the leadership of the [Warsaw] Pact that a NATO preemptive strike was possible." Gates, p. 272.

43 Matlock, "Memorandum for Robert C. McFarlane," Oct. 28, 1983, RRPL, Matlock Files, Box 90888.

44 Andrew and Gordievsky, p. 600.

45 McFarlane, interview, April 25, 2005.

46 Andrew and Gordievsky, *Comrade Kryuchkov's Instructions,* p. 85.

47 Andrew and Gordievsky, p. 600.

48 Shultz, p. 376.

49 Draft Presidential Letter to Andropov, Dec. 19, 1983, RRPL, National Security Council files, Head of State, USSR, Andropov, Box 38.

50 Michael Getler, "Speech Is Less Combative; Positive Tone May Be Change of Tune," *Washington Post*, p. 1, Jan. 17, 1984.

51 Fritz W. Ermarth, "Observations on the 'War Scare' of 1983 from an Intelligence Perch," Parallel History Project on NATO and the Warsaw Pact, November 6, 2003. See *www.php.isn.ethz.ch*.

52 "Implications of Recent Soviet Military-Political Activities," Special National Intelligence Estimate SNIE 11-10-84/JX, May 18, 1984.

53 Ermarth later said that what animated Soviet behavior "was not fear of an imminent military confrontation but worry that Soviet economic and technological weaknesses and Reagan policies were turning the 'correlation of forces' against them on a historic scale." See "Observations."

54 Ermarth acknowledged gaps in his knowledge about U.S. naval activity. "We had an abundance of intelligence on the Red side, but our ability to assess it was hampered by lack of knowledge about potentially threatening Blue activities we knew or suspected were going on. This is a classic difficulty and danger for intelligence, particularly at the national level. Our leaders in intelligence and defense must strive to overcome it, particularly in confrontational situations." Ermarth, "Observations."

55 Ermarth, interview, Feb. 20, 2006.

56 Gates, p. 273.

57 The review was conducted by the President's Foreign Intelligence Advisory Board under President George H. W. Bush. According to Ermarth, who was allowed to review the document, it concluded that the 1984 SNIE did not take seriously enough the Soviet fears of nuclear war. Also see Don Oberdorfer, *From the Cold War to a New Era* (Baltimore: Johns Hopkins University Press, 1998), p. 67.

CHAPTER 4: THE GERM NIGHTMARE

1 Ken Alibek with Stephen Handelman, *Biohazard: The Chilling True Story of the Largest Covert Biological Weapons Program in the World—Told from Inside by the Man Who Ran It* (New York: Random House, 1999), p. 20.

2 Igor V. Domaradsky and Wendy Orent, *Biowarrior: Inside the Soviet/Russian Biological Warfare Machine* (New York: Prometheus Books, 2003), p. 157.

Domaradsky published his memoir in Russian in 1995 as *Perevertish, Rasskaz 'Neudobnogo' Cheloveka,* Moscow, 1995, or approximately, *Turncoat, Story of an "Inconvenient" Man.* The Domaradsky-Orent translation includes additional elaboration.

3 Popov interviews, Jan. 21, 2005, March 31, 2005, May 16, 2005 (with Taissia Popova), and Feb. 22, 2007, as well as correspondence.

4 According to Michael Gait, who sponsored Popov at the laboratory, in 1980 the task was how to make short sections of DNA "using our new chemical methods of solid phase, machine-aided synthesis that I and a few others in the world had developed. These short sections were being used in several applications in molecular biology including whole gene synthesis. They indeed wanted this technology in Russia and Sergei was sent to learn it." Gait, communication with author, July 8, 2008.

5 The other organization was the M. M. Shemyakin Institute of Bioorganic Chemistry of the Russian Academy of Sciences, named for its founder. At the time of the interferon work, it was under the direction of Shemyakin's successor, Yuri Ovchinnikov, who became a founder and architect of the secret biological weapons program. In 1992, the institute was renamed the M. M. Shemyakin and Yu. A. Ovchinnikov Institute of Bioorganic Chemistry.

6 Center for Disease Control and Prevention, Department of Health and Human Services, "Smallpox Overview," Aug. 9, 2004.

7 Jonathan B. Tucker, *Scourge: The Once and Future Threat of Smallpox* (New York: Atlantic Monthly Press), 2001, pp. 2–3.

8 This account is based on Domaradsky's memoir as well as interviews with him, August 1999 and Sept. 6, 2004.

9 Based on a tour, May 24, 2000, and information from employees.

10 Secret military institutes and bureaus in Soviet times were usually identified by a post office box number.

11 Centers for Disease Control and Prevention, Department of Health and Human Services, "Consensus Statement: Tularemia as a Biological Weapon: Medical and Public Health Management," July 1, 2005, drawn from D. T. Dennis, T.V. Inglesby, D.A. Henderson et al., *Journal of the American Medical Association,* June 6, 2001, vol. 285, no. 21: 2763–2773.

12 Lisa Melton, "Drugs in Peril: How Do Antibiotics Work?" and "Bacteria Bite Back: How Do Bacteria Become Resistant to Antibiotics?"; and Robert Bud, "The Medicine Chest: The History of Antibiotics," The Wellcome Trust, *http://www.wellcome.ac.uk.*

13 Alibek, p. 161.

14 The term was taken from five health problem commissions set up in the 1950s and 1960s. According to Raymond A. Zilinskas, "Problem No. 5" was responsible for defense of the population against bacteria, including biological weapons. The commission operated out of the N. F. Gamaleya Scientific Research Institute of Epidemiology and Microbiology of the Soviet Academy of Medical Sciences, in Moscow, and all research was top secret. See Zilinskas, "The Anti-Plague System and the Soviet Biological Warfare Program," *Critical Reviews in Microbiology,* vol. 32, pp. 47–64, 2006.

15 On Lysenko, see Valery N. Soyfer, *Lysenko and the Tragedy of Soviet Science* (New Brunswick, N.J.: Rutgers University Press, 1994), Leo and Rebecca Gruliow, trans.; Zhores Medvedev, *The Rise and Fall of T. D. Lysenko* (New York: Columbia University Press, 1969), I. Michael Lerner, trans.; Medvedev, *Soviet Science* (New York: W. W. Norton, 1978); and David Joravsky, *The Lysenko Affair* (Cambridge: Harvard University Press, 1970). On Vavilov, see Peter Pringle, *The Murder of Nikolai Vavilov* (New York: Simon & Schuster, 2008).

16 George W. Christopher, Theodore J. Cieslak, Julie A. Pavlin, and Edward M. Eitzen, Jr., "Biological Warfare: A Historical Perspective," in *Biological Weapons: Limiting the Threat,* Joshua Lederberg, ed., Belfer Center for Science and International Affairs (Cambridge, Mass: MIT Press, 1999), p. 18. For additional details, see *The Problem of Chemical and Biological Warfare,* Stockholm International Peace Research Institute, Vol. 1, "The Rise of CBW Weapons," Chapter 2, and "Biological and Toxin Weapons: Research, Development and Use from the Middle Ages to 1945," SIPRI Chemical and Biological Warfare Studies, No. 18, Stockholm International Peace Research Institute, Erhard Geissler, John Ellis, Courtland Moon, eds. (Oxford: Oxford University Press, 1999).

17 SIPRI, *The Problem of Chemical and Biological Warfare,* Ch. 2, p. 128.

18 The U.S. Senate Foreign Relations Committee favorably reported the protocol in 1926, but there was strong lobbying against it, and it was withdrawn from Senate consideration because it lacked the necessary two-thirds vote. The protocol entered into force on Feb. 8, 1928, without the United States. The protocol was ratified by the United States in 1975. George Bunn, *Gas and Germ Warfare: International History and Present Status,* Proceedings of the National Academy of Sciences of the United States of America, January 1970, vol. 65, no. 1, pp. 253–260; and U.S. Department of State, *http://www.state.gov/t/ac/trt/4784.htm.*

19 "There is no evidence that the enemy ever resorted to this means of warfare," said a U.S. report, "Biological Warfare, Report to the Secretary of War by Mr. George W. Merck, Special Consultant for Biological Warfare," Jan. 3, 1946. But the history of this period shows the Japanese program was intense and deadly. See Sheldon Harris, *Factories of Death: Japanese Biological Warfare, 1932–1945, and the American Cover-up* (New York: Routledge, 2002); Peter Williams and David Wallace, *Unit 731: Japan's Secret Biological Warfare in World War II* (New York: Free Press, 1989); Daniel Barenblatt, *A Plague upon Humanity: The Secret Genocide of Axis Japan's Germ Warfare Operation* (New York: HarperCollins, 2004); and Hal Gold, *Unit 731 Testimony* (North Clarendon, Vt.: Tuttle Publishing, 1996).

20 On the civil war, see Alibek, p. 32. The army in 1926 set up the Vaccine-Serum Laboratory, responsible for developing vaccines and sera against common infectious diseases, at Vlasikha, outside of Moscow. This laboratory undertook secret research on offensive germ warfare, according to Jonathan B. Tucker and Raymond A. Zilinskas, *The 1971 Smallpox Epidemic in Aralsk, Kazakhstan, and the Soviet Biological Warfare Program,* Occasional Paper No. 9, James Martin Center (Formerly the Center for Nonproliferation Studies), 2002, p. 5. The system was renamed the Biotechnical Institute in 1934, and in 1937 moved to Gorodomlya Island, in the Tver oblast. Zilinskas, communication with author. Documents in the Russian military archives indicate that in 1937 the laboratory was engaged in

offensive biowarfare work, including gravity bombs and anthrax. Russian State Military Archive, Fond 4, Opis 14, Delo 1856. The author is indebted to Mikhail Tsypkin for these documents.

21 "Soviet Russia, Bacteriological Warfare," January 17, 1927, CX 9767, a report from the British S.I.S., file WO 188/784, British National Archives. The report said tests were planned with anthrax, plague and encephalitis.

22 Alibek, pp. 33–37.

23 The Hirsch report contained detailed information on Soviet activities from 1939 to 1945, based on his interrogation of Soviet prisoners of war and material taken from German intelligence files. It identified the island as a BW proving ground. Wilson E. Lexow and Julian Hoptman, "The Enigma of Soviet BW," *Studies in Intelligence,* vol. 9, Spring 1965. Also, Special National Intelligence Estimate, "Implications of Soviet Use of Chemical and Toxin Weapons for US Security Interests," SNIE 11-17-83, September 15, 1983, Annex B.

24 "Soviet Capabilities and Probable Courses of Action Through Mid-1959," NIE 11-4-54, Sept. 14, 1954, p. 24.

25 Lexow and Hoptman, "The Enigma."

26 "U.S. Army Activity in the U.S. Biological Warfare Programs," Feb. 24, 1977, Vol. 1. This is the official history. Vol. 2, Annex A, is the Merck report to the secretary of war, recapitulating the events of the biological weapons program during the war, Jan. 3, 1946. Also see Theodore Rosebury, *Peace or Pestilence* (New York: McGraw-Hill, 1949), pp. 6–7.

27 Milton Leitenberg, *The Problem of Biological Weapons* (Stockholm: National Defence College, 2004), pp. 49–94.

28 The United Kingdom, the United States and Canada began a joint program for an anthrax cluster bomb. The United States was to provide agent production, and Canada provide safe facilities for trials. It was called the "N-bomb" project. By war's end, field trials had shown the feasibility of tactical use of biological weapons agents in cluster bombs, but the U.S. plant had not begun production, nor approved the use of biological warfare. Separately, at Porton Down, the United Kingdom created an unsophisticated anti-livestock weapon, a squat, cylindrical cattle cake of linseed meal laced with anthrax spores. The production lines made 5 million cattle cakes between late 1942 and April 1943. The plan was to spread the cattle cakes into German fields, dropping them from bombers, to cripple German animal production—only in retaliation if the Germans used such weapons first. The Germans did not; the cattle cakes remained unused and were destroyed after the war. Confidential source; also see *Deadly Cultures,* eds. Mark Wheelis, Lajos Rózsa and Malcolm Dando (Cambridge, Mass.: Harvard University Press, 2006), p. 4; and Brian Balmer, *Britain and Biological Warfare: Expert Advice and Science Policy, 1930–1965* (Hampshire and New York: Palgrave, 2001).

29 Ed Regis, *The Biology of Doom: The History of America's Secret Germ Warfare Project* (New York: Henry Holt & Co., 1999), pp. 71–74.

30 U.S. Army history, p. 38. Also, see Conrad C. Crane, "No Practical Capabilities: American Biological and Chemical Warfare Programs During the Korean War," *Perspectives in Biology and Medicine,* vol. 45, no. 2 (Spring 2002): 241–249. Crane concluded: "When the war ended, American chemical and biological weapons

stocks were not much more than when it began." The available biological weapons stocks included only anti-crop rust.

31 Tularemia strains were used, for which there were effective antibiotics.

32 The tests are listed in the U.S. Army study, Vol. II, Appendix IV, to Annex E, tables 1–6.

33 Matthew Meselson, "Averting the Hostile Exploitation of Biotechnology," *CBW Conventions Bulletin,* June 2000, pp. 16–19. Also see Jeanne Guillemin, *Biological Weapons: From the Invention of State-sponsored Programs to Contemporary Bioterrorism* (New York: Columbia University Press, 2005), pp. 103–105. The British carried out five series of sea trials between 1948 and 1955 with some American support. Balmer, *Britain and Biological Warfare.* Also see *www.fas.org/bwc.*

34 Regis, p. 206, quotes from the final report of this test that a single weapon was calculated to have covered 2,400 square kilometers, or 926.5 square miles. British research had also shown that off-target releases by ship, plane or vehicle had considerable advantages over bursting munitions such as those envisioned during World War II.

35 Confidential source familiar with the British trial results.

36 Meselson was assisted by a researcher, Milton Leitenberg, who said in a communication with the author that the petition had origins in opposition to the use of the agents in the Vietnam War. Donald F. Hornig, "Memorandum for the President," Dec. 8, 1966, LBJ Library, courtesy Meselson archive. On the military's opposition, see *Foreign Relations of the United States, 1964–1968,* Volume X: National Security Policy, Documents No. 173 and 178.

37 Richard D. McCarthy, *The Ultimate Folly: War by Pestilence, Asphyxiation and Defoliation* (New York: Knopf, 1970), p. 109.

38 NBC's *First Tuesday,* on Feb. 4, 1969.

39 Robert A. Wampler, ed., "Biowar: The Nixon Administration's Decision to End U.S. Biological Warfare Programs," TNSA EBB 58, doc. 1. Also, *Foreign Relations of the United States, 1969–1976, Vol. E-2,* Documents on Arms Control, 1969–1972, Part 3: Chemical and Biological Warfare; Geneva Protocol; Biological Weapons Convention.

40 *Chemical and Bacteriological (Biological) Weapons and the Effects of Their Possible Use,* Report of the Secretary-General, the United Nations, Department of Political and Security Council Affairs, New York, 1969.

41 "Health Aspects of Chemical and Biological Weapons," Report of a WHO Group of Consultants, World Health Organization, Geneva, 1970; submitted to the Secretary-General of the United Nations, Nov. 28, 1969, p. 19.

42 Jonathan B. Tucker, "A Farewell to Germs: The U.S. Renunciation of Biological and Toxin Warfare, 1969–1970," *International Security,* vol. 27, no. 1, Summer 2002, pp. 107–148. Also see *Foreign Relations of the United States, 1969–1976.*

43 Kissinger Telephone Conversations, DNSA, Nov. 25, 1969, 12:30 P.M., and 6:30 P.M. National Archives, Richard Nixon Presidential Library and Museum, Henry A. Kissinger Telephone Conversation Transcripts (Telcons). Chronological File. Box 3. November 18–28, 1969.

44 H. R. Haldeman, *The Haldeman Diaries* (New York: G. P. Putnam's Sons, 1994), p. 111.

45 William Safire, "On Language: Weapons of Mass Destruction," *The New York Times Magazine,* April 19, 1998, p. 22.

46 Matthew Meselson, "The United States and the Geneva Protocol of 1925," September 1969, Meselson personal archive. Jeanne Guillemin, *Biological Weapons: From the Invention of State-sponsored Programs to Contemporary Bioterrorism* (New York: Columbia University Press, 2005), p. 123. Also see *BioEssays* 25:12, pp. 1236–1246, 2003.

47 White House science adviser Lee A. DuBridge said the President's Science Advisory Committee recommended that the U.S. "renounce all offensive BW; stop completely the procurement of material for offensive BW; destroy existing stockpiles of BW agents and maintain no stockpiles in the future." TNSA EBB 58, doc. 5. Also see "Averting the Hostile Exploitation of Biotechnology," *CBW Conventions Bulletin,* Quarterly Journal of the Harvard Sussex Program on CBW Armament and Arms Limitation, issue no. 48, June 2000, pp. 16–19.

48 "HAK Talking Points, Briefing for Congressional Leadership and Press," TNSA EBB 58, doc. 11.

49 Public Papers of the Presidents, 1969, pp. 968–1970.

50 Memorandum for the President, July 6, 1970, from Melvin Laird, Tab A, "Material to be destroyed (biological and toxin)," TNSA EBB 58, doc. 22.

51 Report to the National Security Council, U.S. Policy on Chemical and Biological Warfare and Agents, TNSA EBB 58, docs. 6a and 6.

52 *Foreign Relations, 1969–1972, Vol. E-2,* "Minutes of NSC Meeting on Chemical Warfare and Biological Warfare, Nov. 18, 1969."

53 Raymond L. Garthoff has offered a suggestion, which remains unproven, that U.S. disinformation persuaded the Soviets that the United States was continuing work on biological weapons after the Nixon decision. According to Garthoff, the FBI fed disinformation to the Soviets that the United States was undertaking a clandestine BW program. See Garthoff, "Polyakov's Run," *Bulletin of the Atomic Scientists,* vol. 56, no. 5, September/October 2000, p. 37. It is known there was a disinformation campaign for chemical weapons, which is described by David Wise in *Cassidy's Run: The Secret Spy War over Nerve Gas* (New York: Random House, 2000). Details of a disinformation campaign on BW are not known.

CHAPTER 5: THE ANTHRAX FACTORY

1 Jonathan B. Tucker and Raymond A. Zilinskas, "The 1971 Smallpox Epidemic in Aralsk, Kazakhstan, and the Biological Warfare Program." The paper includes "An Epidemiological Analysis of the 1971 Smallpox Outbreak in Aralsk, Kazakhstan," by Alan P. Zelicoff, Sandia National Laboratories, pp. 12–21.

2 Burgasov later gave bogus explanations for the Sverdlovsk anthrax epidemic, saying it was caused by contaminated meat. However, his comments in this case seem worth examining; he would have known the truth at the time.

3 Yevgenia Kvitko, "Smallpox, Another Useful Weapon," an interview with Pyotr Burgasov, *Moscow News,* no. 47, Nov. 21, 2001. Burgasov made several errors in the statement. He was wrong that there were no survivors. Also, the smallpox formula was not "developed" at the island, which was a testing site.

4 The British closed down their bioweapons program in the 1950s. For the British

declaration of Aug. 6, 1968, see "The Problem of Chemical and Biological Warfare," SIPRI, Vol. 4, *CB Disarmament Negotiations, 1920–1970*, p. 255. For additional insights on the thinking, see "Cabinet, The Queen's Speech on the Opening of Parliament," Oct. 16, 1969, British National Archives, file FCO 66/297.

5 *Foreign Relations of the United States, 1969–1972:* Vol. E-2, *Documents on Arms Control.* The State Department transcribed portions of the following: National Archives, Nixon Presidential Materials, White House Tapes, with Kissinger, April 10, 1972, 12:44–1:06 P.M., Conversation No. 705–13, and with Connally, April 11, 1972, 3:06–5:05 P.M., Conversation No. 706–5. See *http://www.state.gov/r/pa/ho/frus/nixon/e2/83722.htm.*

6 Domaradsky, *Biowarrior: Inside the Soviet/Russian Biological Warfare Machine* (New York: Prometheus Books, 2003), p. 120.

7 James D. Watson, with Andrew Berry, *DNA: The Secret of Life* (New York: Knopf, 2003), Ch. 4.

8 Ken Alibek, with Stephen Handelman, *Biohazard: The Chilling True Story of the Largest Covert Weapons Program in the World—Told from Inside by the Man Who Ran It* (New York: Random House, 1999), p. 41.

9 Joshua Lederberg, ed., *Biological Weapons: Limiting the Threat* (Cambridge, Mass.: Belfer Center for Science and International Affairs, 1999), "Germs as Arms: Basic Issues," Table 1.1, p. 4.

10 The formal title was the Interdepartmental Scientific-Technical Council for Molecular Biology and Genetics. Domaradsky said orders to begin this work were first given in 1971, the year before he came to Moscow. However, other evidence, including dates given by Alibek, suggests the decisions came later, in 1973–1974. Estimates vary on the precise size of the program. A document in Katayev estimates the main organization, Biopreparat, had thirty facilities and twenty-five thousand employees, but some of these may have been working on legitimate civilian projects. "Khim-Prom," Katayev, Hoover, no date. Alibek, p. 43, says there were thirty thousand employees in Biopreparat, with sixty thousand in the biological weapons effort overall at the peak.

11 Domaradsky, p. 151. The open decree was April 19, 1974. A separate secret decree May 21, 1974, established the microbiology institute at Obolensk, and the founding decree for the institute at Koltsovo came Aug. 2, 1974.

12 Alibek, p. 41.

13 "Iz vystupleniya predstavitelya SSSR v Komitete po razoruzhenniu A. A. Roshchina 12 iyunia 1975g" [From the appearance of the representative of the USSR at the Conference on Disarmament], Katayev, Hoover.

14 William Beecher, "Soviets Feared Violating Germ Weapons Ban," *Boston Globe,* Sept. 28, 1975, p. 1. Beecher identified facilities in Sverdlovsk, Zagorsk and Omutninsk. These were part of the older military system, not the concealed Biopreparat facilities.

15 Robert A. Wampler and Thomas S. Blanton, eds., "U.S. Intelligence on the Deadliest Modern Outbreak," TNSA, EBB No. 61, doc. 1. *Posev,* a Russian émigré journal, published an article in October 1979 about a germ warfare accident, but identified the wrong city, saying it was in Novosibirsk.

16 Associated Press, March 21, 1980.

17 David K. Willis, "Soviets: U.S. Double-crossed Us on Germ Warfare Charges," *Christian Science Monitor,* March 28, 1980, p. 10. When the public statement was made, Willis reported, "The Soviets were furious. First they had been approached in private, and now it was around the world."

18 TNSA EBB No. 61, doc. 10. Willis reported the Soviets issued three separate public statements March 19–20.

19 Jeanne Guillemin, *Anthrax: The Investigation of a Deadly Outbreak* (Berkeley: University of California Press, 1999), p. 8. Israelyan admitted it was a fabrication. Victor Israelyan, *On the Battlefields of the Cold War: A Soviet Ambassador's Confession* (University Park, Pa.: Pennsylvania State University Press, 2003), p. 315.

20 Final Declaration of the First Review Conference, March 21, 1980.

21 TNSA EBB No. 61, doc. 10. The message may have been written imprecisely. An outbreak of inhalation anthrax might be expected to have fast impact, while contaminated meat could be prolonged because of transport and storage. But the larger point was that the United States believed it had been inhalation anthrax.

22 Meselson, "Memorandum to files regarding Sverdlovsk," 1980, 7 pages, courtesy Meselson archive. Meselson, interview, Sept. 18, 2008. Meselson worked alone with Hoptman, but his analysis was fed into a government working group. After several months of examining the intelligence, the group concluded there had been an accidental release at the Sverdlovsk facility that caused an emission of anthrax spores and resulted in the first wave of deaths, possibly followed by a second wave caused by contaminated meat that was purchased on the black market. Leslie H. Gelb, "Keeping an Eye on Russia," *The New York Times Magazine,* Nov. 29, 1981. Also see Guillemin, p. 9.

23 Alibek, Ch. 5 and 8.

24 He was known then as Kanatjan Alibekov. He changed his name to Ken Alibek years later upon arrival in the United States.

25 Alibek, p. 53.

26 Alibek said 836 was a code number for a natural strain of anthrax that the Soviets had found in Kirov in the 1950s. Alibek, interview, June 18, 2007.

27 Roger Roffey, Kristina S. Westerdahl, *Conversion of Former Biological Weapons Facilities in Kazakhstan, A Visit to Stepnogorsk, July 2000,* Swedish Defense Research Agency, May 2001. Report No. FOI-R-0082-SE, based on a conference held in Stepnogorsk, July 24–26, 2000. Also, Gulbarshyn Bozheyeva, Yerlan Kunakbayev and Dastan Yeleukenov, *Former Soviet Biological Weapons Facilities in Kazakhstan: Past, Present, and Future,* Occasional Paper No. 1, Center for Nonproliferation Studies, Monterey Institute of International Studies, June 1999.

28 Alibek says overall the Soviet capacity was five thousand tons a year, but the actual military mobilization plans were less. A plant in Kurgan was to make one thousand tons, Penza five hundred tons and Stepnogorsk three hundred tons, for a total of eighteen hundred a year.

CHAPTER 6: THE DEAD HAND

1 Mikhail Gorbachev, *Memoirs* (New York: Doubleday, 1996), p. 152.

2 Angus Roxburgh, *The Second Russian Revolution* (London: BBC Books, 1991), p. 17; and Archie Brown, *The Gorbachev Factor* (Oxford: Oxford University Press, 1996),

pp. 67–68. By Volsky's account, Andropov flew into a rage at the deletion, and Gorbachev was sent to calm him down. Gorbachev claimed in his memoirs that neither Chernenko, Andropov nor Volsky ever talked to him about it.

3 Margaret Thatcher, *The Downing Street Years* (New York: HarperCollins, 1993), p. 458.

4 Don Oberdorfer, *From the Cold War to a New Era* (Baltimore: Johns Hopkins University Press, 1998), p. 80.

5 Gorbachev, p. 155.

6 Anatoly Chernyaev, *My Six Years with Gorbachev* (University Park, Pa.: University of Pennsylvania Press, 2000), p. 8.

7 Valery E. Yarynich, *C³: Nuclear Command, Control Cooperation* (Washington: Center for Defense Information, 2003), pp. 140–141; and Yarynich interviews and correspondence, 1998–2009.

8 Yarynich, pp. 142–145.

9 Yarynich, p. 146.

10 TV Center, Moscow, revealed the "Grot" code name, long a secret, in a broadcast Oct. 10, 2008. Also see GlobalSecurity.org. Bruce Blair, president of the Center for Defense Information, wrote in the *Washington Post* on May 25, 2003, that at Kosvinsky, Russian commanders can communicate to strategic forces using very-low-frequency (VLF) radio signals. He added, "The facility is the critical link to Russia's 'dead hand' communications network, designed to ensure semi-automatic retaliation to a decapitating strike."

11 The decision was dated August 30, 1974, according to a history of Yuzhnoye, S. N. Konyukhov, ed., "Prizvany vremenem: Rakety i kosmicheskiye apparaty konstruktorskogo buro 'Yuzhnoye'" [Called up for service by the time: Missiles and spacecraft of the "Yuzhnoye" Design Bureau] (Dnepropetrovsk, Ukraine: ART-PRESS, 2004).

12 A document from the Katayev archive dated February 1982 confirms that the system was under construction then but not yet tested. The Katayev records also show six SS-17 missiles brought on duty in 1984 as Perimeter. See Podvig, "The Window of Vulnerability That Wasn't," *International Security,* vol. 3, no. 1, Summer 2008.

13 Further confirmation of plans for a fully automatic retaliatory system is contained in an internal Soviet defense document in Katayev, Hoover. Oleg Belyakov, who worked in Katayev's department, complained in a 1985 memo that not enough attention had been paid "to a proposal, extremely important from the military and political point of view, to create a fully-automated retaliatory strike system that would be activated from the top command levels in a moment of crisis (with a notification to the adversary)." The comment about a "super-project" is from Katayev, *Some Facts.* Hines quotes Viktor M. Surikov, who had spent thirty years in building, designing and testing missiles, as saying the Dead Hand was designed by his team and approved by the Central Committee, but a fully automatic system was later rejected by Marshal Sergei Akhromeyev, chief of the General Staff. Hines et al., *Soviet Intentions 1965–1985,* BDM Federal Inc., vol. 2, pp. 134–135.

14 This description is from Yarynich interviews with the author, as well as *C³*, p. 156; Korobushin interview, Hines, vol. 2, p. 107; Bruce Blair, *Global Zero Alert for*

Nuclear Forces, Brookings Occasional Papers (Washington: Brookings Institution, 1995), pp. 43–56.

15 The United States was the chief adversary, but Western European or other targets might also have been included. China had a relatively small nuclear force.

16 Yarynich details the test on p. 170 in *C³*. The delay was described in an interview with the author.

CHAPTER 7: MORNING AGAIN IN AMERICA

1 Reagan, *An American Life,* p. 589.

2 Massie first met with Reagan January 17, 1984, before the trip. She reports meeting him twenty-two times in his second term, and taught him the Russian proverb *Doveryai no proveryai,* or "Trust, but Verify." See *http://www.suzannemassie.com.* Also see Deborah Hart Strober and Gerald S. Strober, *The Reagan Presidency: An Oral History of the Era* (Washington, D.C.: Brassey's, 2003), pp. 222–228. Reagan's diary, March 1, 1984.

3 Jack F. Matlock Jr., *Reagan and Gorbachev: How the Cold War Ended* (New York: Random House, 2004), p. 88.

4 Reagan diary, March 2, 1984.

5 Reagan, *An American Life,* pp. 594–597.

6 Christopher Andrew and Oleg Gordievsky, *KGB: The Inside Story* (New York: HarperCollins, 1990), p. 602.

7 Andrew and Gordievsky, pp. 603–604.

8 NSDD 119, Jan. 6, 1984. Christopher Simpson, *National Security Directives of the Reagan and Bush Administrations: The Declassified History of U.S. Political and Military Policy, 1981–1991* (Boulder: Westview Press, 1995), pp. 374–378.

9 Peter Grier, "The Short Happy Life of the Glick-Em," *Air Force* magazine, Journal of the Air Force Association, vol. 85, no. 7, July 2002.

10 Anatoly Chernyaev, *My Six Years with Gorbachev* (University Park, Pa.: University of Pennsylvania Press, 2000), p. 9.

11 Herbert E. Meyer, vice chairman, National Intelligence Council, "What Should We Do About the Russians?" June 28, 1984, NIC 03770-84.

12 Matlock, p. 95.

13 Reagan diary, April 9, 1984.

14 David Hoffman, "Chernenko 'Disappointed' White House," *Washington Post,* April 10, 1984, p. 9.

15 Reagan, *An American Life,* p. 602. Also see SNIE 11-9-84, *Soviet Policy Toward the United States in 1984,* Aug. 9, 1984.

16 Seweryn Bialer, *The Soviet Paradox: External Expansion, Internal Decline* (New York: Knopf, 1986), see Ch. 6.

17 George Shultz, *Turmoil and Triumph: My Years as Secretary of State* (New York: Charles Scribner's Sons, 1993), p. 480.

18 Shultz, p. 484. Gromyko recounted the moment to Dobrynin as if it had been more an exchange of slogans. Anatoly Dobrynin, *In Confidence: Moscow's Ambassador to America's Six Cold War Presidents* (New York: Times Books, 1995), p. 556.

19 Shultz, p. 484; Andrei Gromyko, Harold Shukman, trans., *Memories* (London: Hutchison, 1989), p. 307.

20 Don Oberdorfer, *From the Cold War to a New Era* (Baltimore: Johns Hopkins University Press, 1998), p. 93.

21 Steve Coll, *Ghost Wars* (New York: Penguin Books, 2004), p. 102.

22 Andrew and Gordievsky, p. 604.

23 Shultz, p. 477. Andropov had proposed a unilateral moratorium on space weapons the previous year, just before the KAL shoot-down.

24 Nigel Hey, *The Star Wars Enigma: Behind the Scenes of the Cold War Race for Missile Defense* (Dulles, Va.: Potomac Books, 2006), p. 136.

25 The *New York Times* raised questions Aug. 18, 1993, about whether the test was rigged. The General Accounting Office found no evidence that it was, though the playing field was slightly tilted by heating the target so it would be easier for the interceptor to discover and turning the target sideways. The investigation revealed that the United States had also devised a deception program that would have exploded the target regardless to spook the Soviets. However, the deception program was not used in the June 1984 test. It had been readied in the first two experiments, but the interceptor and rocket missed by such a wide margin that the deception explosion was not used. "Ballistic Missile Defense: Records Indicate Deception Program Did Not Affect 1984 Test Results," United States General Accounting Office, GAO/NSIAD-94-219, July 1994.

26 George Raine, "Creating Reagan's Image; S.F. Ad Man Riney Helped Secure Him a Second Term," *San Francisco Chronicle,* June 9, 2004, p. C1.

27 Shultz, p. 478.

CHAPTER 8: "WE CAN'T GO ON LIVING LIKE THIS"

1 Except where otherwise noted, Margaret Thatcher's recollections are from her memoir, *The Downing Street Years* (New York: HarperCollins, 1993), pp. 452–453, and 459–463. Mikhail Gorbachev's recollections are chiefly from his *Memoirs* in English and in Russian, *Zhizn' i reformi,* two vols. (Moscow: Novosti, 1995). In some cases, as noted, Gorbachev's comments are from the author's interview in 2006; and *Conversations with Gorbachev,* transcribed interviews with himself and Zdeněk Mlynář (New York: Columbia University Press, 2002). Raisa Gorbachev mentioned the Chernenko permission in her memoir *I Hope: Reminiscences and Reflections* (New York: HarperCollins, 1991), p. 125.

2 Geoffrey Howe, interview with BBC's "The Westminster Hour," May 2005.

3 Archie Brown, *The Gorbachev Factor* (Oxford: Oxford University Press, 1996), p. 77.

4 Gordievsky, interview, August 29, 2005; and *Next Stop,* pp. 305–313.

5 Gorbachev told a British official during the visit that the first modern English novel he read was Snow's *Corridors of Power.* Archie Brown, *Seven Years That Changed the World: Perestroika in Perspective* (Oxford: Oxford University Press, 2007), p. 46. Also, *The Observer,* London, Dec. 23, 1984, p. 4; "The Westminster Hour," BBC series *Power Eating,* by Anne Perkins, May 2005.

6 Geoffrey Howe, *Conflict of Loyalty* (New York: St. Martin's, 1994), pp. 358–360.

7 The ad appeared Feb. 22, 1984. On the first page, which Gorbachev used for his prop, were the boxes and dots. On the second page, in bold headline, the advertisement asked "COULD THIS BE EARTH'S LAST CHART?" It was sponsored by a businessman, Harold Willens, who had spelled out his hopes to stop the arms race

in a book, *The Trimtab Factor: How Business Executives Can Help Solve the Nuclear Weapons Crisis* (New York: William Morrow and Co., Inc., 1984). Willens, chairman of the California bilateral nuclear freeze initiative campaign of 1982, attributed his antinuclear views to his experiences in the Pacific as a marine. He visited Hiroshima and Nagasaki weeks after the World War II bombing and was horrified at what he saw. Willens had fled the Soviet Union with his parents when he was eight years old and settled in Los Angeles, where he became a successful businessman.

8 See "Memorandum of Conversation," meeting with British Prime Minister Margaret Thatcher, Dec. 22, 1984, Camp David. *http://www.margaretthatcher.org*.

9 Gorbachev, interview, June 30, 2006.

10 In the Dec. 23, 1983, issue of *Science,* two articles by teams of scientists argued that a nuclear war would have devastating environmental and ecological effects on the globe. In January 1984, a Vatican working group issued a report describing nuclear winter. "Nuclear Winter: A Warning," Pontificiae Academiae Scientiarvm Docvmenta, 11, Jan. 23–25, 1984. Among the scientists who participated was Yevgeny Velikhov, who became a key adviser to Gorbachev.

11 Thatcher interview with John Cole, BBC, Dec. 17, 1984.

12 See *www.margaretthatcher.org*.

13 Memorandum of conversation, Dec. 22, 1984.

14 Gorbachev's maternal grandfather had become a supporter of the Bolsheviks because the family was given the land they worked on after the revolution. "In the oral history of our family, it was constantly repeated: the revolution gave our family land," he said. *Conversations,* p. 14.

15 David Remnick, "Young Gorbachev," *Washington Post,* p. B1, Dec. 1, 1989.

16 The Soviet Union was not a rule-of-law state in the Western sense. But the law faculties were often used to groom future recruits for service in diplomacy, security services and party work.

17 Gorbachev and Mlynář, *Conversations,* p. 18.

18 The full title was *History of the Communist Party of the Soviet Union (Bolsheviks), Short Course,* 1939.

19 Brown, p. 39.

20 In the Soviet system, the procuracy was more than just a prosecutor. The office also had an accountant's auditing function and served as a watchdog for the party.

21 Ever since the Bolshevik revolution, the Communist Party leadership strove to keep the restiveness of youth in check through Komsomol. See Steven L. Solnick, *Stealing the State: Control and Collapse in Soviet Institutions* (Cambridge: Harvard University Press, 1999).

22 Raisa Gorbachev, pp. 93–99.

23 Gorbachev, *Conversations,* p. 38.

24 Robert G. Kaiser, *Why Gorbachev Happened: His Triumphs and His Failure* (New York: Simon & Schuster, 1991), p. 41.

25 *Time* magazine editors, *Mikhail S. Gorbachev: An Intimate Biography* (New York: Time Inc., 1998), p. 98.

26 Brown, p. 45.

27 Gorbachev, *Conversations,* p. 47.

28 Gorbachev, *Conversations,* pp. 42–43.

29 Gorbachev succeeded Fedor Kulakov, who died July 17, 1978. Kulakov, who was previously first secretary in Stavropol, had been a mentor. Gorbachev delivered a eulogy for him in Red Square. However, the delay between his death in July and Gorbachev's elevation in November may have meant internal wrangling over the appointment.

30 Volkogonov, p. 446, notes that Gorbachev's assignment was doomed; decrees were never going to solve agricultural problems that dated back to Stalin's disastrous campaign against the peasants.

31 The most significant source of unorthodox thinking was in Novosibirsk, Siberia, where an outspoken reform economist, Abel Aganbegyan, had come up with a candid and devastating critique of the Soviet economy. A colleague, Tatyana Zaslavskaya, a sociologist, prepared a landmark internal paper challenging the entire structure of the Soviet economy, which was debated at a 1983 conference in Novosibirsk. See Tatyana Zaslavskaya, *The Second Socialist Revolution: An Alternative Soviet Strategy* (Bloomington: Indiana University Press, 1990).

32 Robert D. English, *Russia and the Idea of the West: Gorbachev, Intellectuals and the End of the Cold War* (New York: Columbia University Press, 2000), pp. 172–173.

33 *Narodnoye Khozyaistvo SSSR v 1983 g.* [Agriculture in the USSR in 1983] (Moscow: Finances and Statistics, 1984), p. 269.

34 Henry Kreisler, "Conversation with Alexander Yakovlev," Nov. 21, 1996, Conversations with History, Institute of International Studies, University of California, Berkeley. Also, English, p. 184.

35 English, p. 190.

36 Eduard Shevardnadze, *The Future Belongs to Freedom* (New York: Free Press, 1991), pp. 23, 37.

37 Yegor Ligachev, *Inside Gorbachev's Kremlin* (New York: Pantheon Books, 1993), p. 58.

38 Chernyaev diary, Feb. 26 and March 2, 1985.

39 Alexander Yakovlev, *Sumerki* (Moscow: Materik, 2003), pp. 459–461.

40 Brown, *Seven Years That Changed the World,* p. 32.

41 March 11 comments from minutes of the Politburo meeting, the Library of Congress, Washington, D.C., Volkogonov Collection, Reel 17, Container 25.

42 Georgi Shakhnazarov, *Tsena Svobody: Reformatsiya Gorbacheva Glazami yevo Pomoshnika* (Moscow: Rossika-Zevs, 1993), pp. 35–36.

CHAPTER 9: YEAR OF THE SPY

1 Robert M. Gates, *From the Shadows: The Ultimate Insider's Story of Five Presidents and How They Won the Cold War* (New York: Simon & Schuster, 1996), p. 329.

2 Reagan diary, April 19, 1985. Reagan acknowledged in his memoir, "I can't claim that I believed from the start that Mikhail Gorbachev was going to be a different sort of Soviet leader." Reagan, *An American Life* (New York: Simon & Schuster, 1990), p. 614.

3 Reagan, *An American Life,* pp. 615–616.

4 Reagan diary, March 20, 1985. In his memoir, Reagan said he told aides "we'd have to be as tough as ever in dealing with the Soviets" but "we should work hard to establish channels directly" between himself and Gorbachev, p. 615.

5 According to Matlock, Nicholson had strayed into a restricted area. The United
States "was given a version that mixed fact with fiction to place the responsibility
on Nicholson, not on the Soviet sentry. The official Soviet explanation was that
Nicholson had entered a clearly marked prohibited area, was illegally
photographing a Soviet military installation, and when spotted refused the sentry's
order to halt. Instead, he tried to escape and was therefore shot. It was this
inaccurate version that convinced Weinberger and Reagan that the shooting had
been deliberate." Matlock, *Reagan and Gorbachev,* pp. 112–113.

6 George Shultz *Turmoil and Triumph: My Years as Secretary of State* (New York:
Charles Scribner's Sons, 1993), p. 537.

7 Reagan, *An American Life,* p. 617.

8 In a letter to Gorbachev April 30, 1985, Reagan said the Nicholson incident was
clouding efforts to improve relations. Shultz, p. 537.

9 Gates, address to Boston Committee on Foreign Relations, Nov. 28, 1984.

10 Shultz, p. 507.

11 "Gorbachev, the New Broom," Office of Soviet Analysis, Directorate of
Intelligence, Central Intelligence Agency, 13 pp., June 1985, released to author
under FOIA, partially redacted.

12 Gates, pp. 331–332. Gates said in his memoir that Casey's cover note went too far,
and was "transparent advocacy" added on top of intelligence analysis. Casey "did
not offer any balance or pretense of objectivity," Gates said. But Gates also said that
"many of us in CIA" agreed with Casey's appraisal of Soviet motives and strategy.

13 Anatoly Chernyaev, *My Six Years with Gorbachev* (University Park, Pa.: University
of Pennsylvania Press, 2000), p. 25.

14 Alexander Yakovlev, "On Reagan," State Archive of the Russian Federation,
Moscow. Yakovlev Collection. Fond 10063, Opis 1, Delo 379. Translated by
Svetlana Savranskaya.

15 Gorbachev, *Ponyat' Perestroiku* (Moscow: Alpina Bizness Books, 2006), p. 33.

16 Gates speech, Texas A&M University, Nov. 19, 1999.

17 Except where noted separately, this account of the Ames case is based on "An
Assessment of the Aldrich H. Ames Espionage Case and Its Implications for U.S.
Intelligence," Senate Select Committee on Intelligence, Nov. 1, 1994, parts 1
and 2.

18 Victor Cherkashin, who was deputy resident then, said the Ames letter offered
information on CIA operations and included "a small sheaf" of documents that
seemed unremarkable, mostly about U.S. intelligence on Soviet naval forces in the
Middle East. Victor Cherkashin with Gregory Feifer, *Spy Handler: Memoir of a
KGB Officer* (New York: Basic Books, 2005), p. 16.

19 Except where noted separately, this account of Gordievsky's actions is based on
Next Stop and author's interview.

20 Barry G. Royden, "Tolkachev, a Worthy Successor to Penkovsky," Center for the
Study of Intelligence, CIA, Studies in Intelligence, vol. 47, no. 3. Also, James L.
Pavitt, deputy CIA director for operations, remarks to Foreign Policy Association,
June 21, 2004.

21 Milt Bearden and James Risen, *The Main Enemy: The Inside Story of the CIA's Final
Showdown with the KGB* (New York: Random House, 2003), p. 37.

22 Bearden and Risen, p. 12.

23 Gordievsky describes the escape in *Next Stop.* David Wise, in *Nightmover: How Aldrich Ames Sold the CIA to the KGB for $4.6 Million* (New York: HarperCollins, 1995), offers a different story of the escape, quoting CIA officials as saying that Gordievsky was secreted inside a specially built Land Rover and driven right out of the British embassy in Moscow all the way to Finland. Gordievsky claims this was a story the KGB leaked to the Western press.

24 Wise, p. 135, raises the possibility that Yurchenko did not know about Ames.

25 Hired by the CIA in 1981, at age twenty-eight, Howard went through training to be a clandestine agent in the Soviet Union and knew much top-secret information. But in the months before his scheduled departure for Moscow, Howard failed a series of CIA polygraph examinations and was fired from the CIA in May 1983. Bitter and furious, he walked out of headquarters with all the agency's Soviet secrets. In late 1984 and early 1985, apparently out of revenge, Howard began selling his knowledge to the KGB at the meetings in Vienna. He may have told them about a British double agent. He is believed to have told them about other spies, and some of the CIA's most sophisticated technical means for spying.

26 On Casey, see Gates, p. 363. Howard slipped the FBI and fled the country. See David Wise, *The Spy Who Got Away* (New York: Random House, 1988), chs. 24–26.

27 Within a KGB residency, Line X referred to scientific and technical intelligence and Line PR to political, economic and military strategic intelligence and active measures. See Appendix E, "The Organization of a KGB Residency," in Christopher Andrew and Vasili Mitrokhin, *The Mitrokhin Archive: The KGB in Europe and the West* (London: Allan Lane/The Penguin Press, 1999), p. 743.

28 "Affidavit in support of criminal complaint, arrest warrant, and search warrants," *United States of America vs. Robert Philip Hanssen,* United States District Court for the Eastern District of Virginia, pp. 20–21. Martynov, a KGB Line X officer assigned to the Soviet embassy in Washington from October 1980 to November 1985 was compromised by Ames and later executed. Sergei Motorin, a KGB line PR officer assigned to the embassy in Washington from June 1980 to January 1985, was also compromised by Ames and executed. Boris Yuzhin was a KGB Line PR officer working undercover as a TASS correspondent in San Francisco. He was compromised by both Ames and Hanssen. In December 1986, he was arrested, and later sentenced to fifteen years in prison. In 1992 he was released under a general amnesty grant and subsequently emigrated to the United States.

29 The woman lived in Montreal, married to a Soviet diplomat. The CIA took Yurchenko there, but she rejected him when he knocked on her door. Bearden recalled she abruptly told Yurchenko she had loved a KGB colonel, not a traitor, and shut the door in his face.

CHAPTER 10: OF SWORDS AND SHIELDS

1 Vladimir Medvedev, *Chelovek za Spinoi* (Moscow: RUSSLIT, 1994), p. 208.

2 An invaluable window on these early developments is the Chernyaev diary. Chernyaev worked in 1985 as deputy director in the Central Committee's International Department, and became an assistant to Gorbachev in 1986. Some of

the diary entries, edited, appear in the English edition of Chernyaev's memoir, *My Six Years with Gorbachev*. English translations of the diary for 1985–1988 have been published by TNSA. Date citations are from the full diary, and page numbers refer to the book. The author is grateful to Svetlana Savranskaya for assistance with the Chernyaev diary.

3 The trip to Leningrad began May 15 and the Smolny speech was two days later. Serge Schmemann, "First 100 Days of Gorbachev: A New Start," *New York Times*, June 17, 1985, p. 1.

4 Mikhail Gorbachev, *Memoirs* (Moscow: Novosti, 1995), p. 201.

5 Chernyaev, p. 33, and diary May 22, 1985.

6 Chernyaev, p. 29, and diary April 11, 1985.

7 The campaign was inspired by Andropov's similar but ill-fated attempts to impose more discipline on society. Gorbachev's early economic reforms were relatively meek and ill-fated attempts at "acceleration" of the existing system, compared to the more radical approaches he would attempt later.

8 Chernyaev diary, July 6, 1985.

9 Sergei Akhromeyev and Georgi M. Kornienko, *Glazami Marshala i Diplomata* [In the Eyes of a Marshal and a Diplomat] (Moscow: International Relations, 1992), in Russian, p. 64.

10 Clifford Gaddy, *The Price of the Past* (Washington, D.C.: Brookings Institution, 1996), p. 49.

11 Akhromeyev, pp. 34–35. See Thomas M. Nichols, *The Sacred Cause* (Ithaca: Cornell University Press, 1993), p. 134.

12 Gorbachev, pp. 203–205.

13 Gorbachev, *Zhizn i Reformi*, vol. 1, p. 207 (Moscow: Novosti, 1995). His use of Moloch is a literary allusion to a symbol of cruel and unusual force demanding human sacrifice.

14 Ksenia Kostrova, interview, August 2007. Ksenia is Katayev's granddaughter.

15 This account is based on Katayev, Hoover, and materials in author's possession.

16 A CIA estimate, made in 1986, was 15–17 percent. (This estimate was a revision from 13–14 percent earlier. The reason for the revision was a recalculation of prices made by the Soviets in 1982.)

17 Katayev, "Chto Takoe VPK" [What Was the VPK], undated, author's possession. This paper is similar to a chapter Katayev contributed to *The Anatomy of Russia Defense Conversion*, edited by Vlad E. Genin (Walnut Creek, Calif.: Vega Press, 2001), p. 52.

18 Andrei Grachev, *Gorbachev* (Moscow: Vagrius, 2001), p. 178. Gorbachev nursed a hope to use the defense sector to somehow boost the flagging Soviet economy. Gaddy, pp. 55–56.

19 Robert D. English, *Russia and the Idea of the West: Gorbachev, Intellectuals and the End of the Cold War* (New York: Columbia University Press, 2000), pp. 193–228.

20 See Stephen F. Cohen and Katrina vanden Heuvel, *Voices of Glasnost: Interviews with Gorbachev's Reformers* (New York: W. W. Norton & Co., 1989), pp. 157–173.

21 Letter to Politburo of November 26, 1985, "On distortion of facts in reports and information coming to the CPSU Central Committee," State Archive of the

Russian Federation, Fond 3, Opis 111, Delo 144, pp. 39–41, courtesy Svetlana Savranskaya.

22 Georgi Shakhnazarov, *Tsena Svobody: Reformatsiya Gorbacheva Glazami yevo Pomoshnika* (Moscow: Rossika-Zevs, 1993), p. 88.

23 Steve Coll, *Ghost Wars* (New York: Penguin Books, 2004), p. 127.

24 Chernyaev diary, June 20, 1985.

25 Matlock recalls the Soviets already had in place 414 Pioneers, each with three warheads, while NATO at that point had deployed only 143 warheads on intermediate-range missiles in Europe, made up of 63 Pershing IIs and 80 ground-launched cruise missiles. Matlock, *Reagan and Gorbachev*, p. 116.

26 Reagan letter to Gorbachev, April 30, 1985, RRPL.

27 Chernyaev diary, April 16, 1985.

28 A contentious issue this year was whether Reagan's proposed Strategic Defense Initiative would remain within a narrow interpretation of the 1972 treaty on missile defense, or whether the administration was seeking to use a broader interpretation of the treaty to allow research to move ahead. McFarlane suggested October 6 the treaty permitted research, testing and development of new systems— appearing to put the administration on record for using a broader interpretation of the treaty. The Soviets were alarmed at this, as were U.S. allies. George Shultz, *Turmoil and Triumph: My Years as Secretary of State* (New York: Charles Scribner's Sons, 1993), pp. 579–582. An account critical of Shultz appears in Frances Fitzgerald, *Way Out There in the Blue* (New York: Simon & Schuster, 2000), pp. 290–300.

29 Shultz, pp. 570–571.

30 Anatoly Dobrynin, *In Confidence: Moscow's Ambassador to America's Six Cold War Presidents* (New York: Times Books, 1995), p. 573.

31 Chernyaev diary, July 1, 1985.

32 English, p. 202.

33 Minutes of the Politburo, June 29, 1985. Volkogonov Collection, Library of Congress, Reel 18. TNSA.

34 Chernyaev diary, June 15, 1985.

35 Andrew and Gordievsky, *Comrade Kryuchkov's Instructions: Top Secret Files on KGB Foreign Operations, 1975–1985* (Stanford: Stanford University Press, 1991), pp. 107–115.

36 Unless otherwise specified, this and other comments by Katayev on missile defense are from an undated monograph, "Kakoi byla reaktzia v SSSR na zayavlenia R. Reagana o razvertyvanii rabot v CShA po SOI," or "What was the reaction of the Soviet Union to the announcement of R. Reagan on the deployment of works in the United States on the SDI," twelve pages, Katayev, Hoover.

37 Katayev. The author is indebted to Pavel Podvig for identifying and explaining this.

38 Konstantin Lantratov, "The Star Wars Which Never Was," January 1995. See *www.buran.ru/htm/str163.htm.*

39 Roald Z. Sagdeev, *The Making of a Soviet Scientist* (New York: John Wiley & Sons, 1994), p. 273.

40 Velikhov, interviews by author.

41 Called "IS," this system was developed in the 1960s and tested in the 1970s and

early 1980s, but Andropov's 1983 moratorium seems to have marked the end of active use. See *www.russianspaceweb.com/is.html.*

42 A ruby laser emits energy in the visible (red) region.

43 P. V. Zarubin, "Academician Basov, high-powered lasers and the anti-missile defence problem," *Quantum Electronics*, No. 32, 2002, pp. 1048–1064.

44 Velikhov described a similar project, known as Gamma, which he said never got off the ground.

45 The declaration was Sept. 24, 1982. Velikhov was also editor of *The Night After . . . Climatic and Biological Consequences of a Nuclear War* (Moscow: Mir Publishers, 1985).

46 The group was the Soviet Scientists' Committee for the Defense of Peace Against the Nuclear Threat.

47 Velikhov said the 1983 report remains secret. But some parts are evident in: Yevgeny Velikhov, Roald Sagdeev, Andrei Kokoshin, eds., *Weaponry in Space: The Dilemma of Security* (Moscow: Mir, 1986).

48 The chart showing thirty-eight warheads is from Katayev, Hoover. Other data on the SS-18 is from Podvig, *Russian Strategic Nuclear Forces* (Cambridge: MIT Press, 2001), pp. 218–219. See "Multiple (as in 'up top 38') warheads," *http://russian forces.org*. For the U.S. expectations of asymmetric response, see "Possible Soviet Responses to the US Strategic Defense Initiative," NIC M 83-10017, Sept. 12, 1983, Director of Central Intelligence.

49 Gorbachev interview, June 30, 2006.

50 Nichols, p. 133.

51 Chernyaev diary, Sept. 1, 1985.

52 Reagan diary, Sept. 10, 1985.

53 Reagan diary, Oct. 22, 1985. Shultz said the Soviet offer September 27 was heavily weighted against the United States in the way it was structured. Shultz, pp. 576–577.

54 *Soviet Military Power*, April 1985, p. 55.

55 Robert C. McFarlane, with Zofia Smardz, *Special Trust* (New York: Cadell & Davis, 1994), pp. 307–308. Matlock, p. 133.

56 Reagan diary, Sept. 26, 1985.

57 Robert M. Gates, *From the Shadows: The Ultimate Insider's Story of Five Presidents and How They Won the Cold War* (New York: Simon & Schuster, 1996), p. 342.

58 Shultz disagreed with this view. Shultz, p. 586.

59 Gates, p. 343. The Soviet outlook wasn't very ambitious either. Moscow "did not pin great hopes on the summit," Dobrynin said, p. 586. Chernyaev recalls the thrust was not to deviate from existing positions on arms control, "not to get worked up" over regional conflicts, and "in a word, not to provoke Reagan in order not to intensify the threat, not to play up to the hawks." Chernyaev diary, Nov. 12, 1985. Gorbachev had leeway to go beyond these guidelines, and he did.

60 Gates, p. 343. NIE 11-18-85, Nov. 1, 1985.

61 Reagan diary, Nov. 13, 1985.

62 Suzanne Massie, interview for the television documentary *The Cold War*, Sept. 2, 1997, Liddell Hart Center for Military Archives, Kings College, London.

63 Matlock, pp. 150–154 and Jack F. Matlock, Jr., *Superpower Illusions* (New Haven: Yale University Press, 2010) p. 317, note 11.

64 Yegor Gaidar, "The Soviet Collapse: Grain and Oil," American Enterprise Institute for Public Policy Research, April 2007. Also see Gaidar's *Collapse of an Empire: Lessons for Modern Russia* (Washington, D.C.: Brookings Institution Press, 2007).

65 Shultz, pp. 589–596. McFarlane, pp. 314–316. Oberdorfer, who covered the trip for the *Washington Post*, reports that Gorbachev said he would be willing to reduce existing nuclear weapons to zero on condition the two sides stopped the "militarization of space," Don Oberdorfer, *From the Cold War to a New Era* (Baltimore: Johns Hopkins University Press, 1998), p. 137.

66 Reagan diary, Nov. 5, 1985.

67 Reagan diary, Nov. 6, 1985.

68 Reagan, *An American Life*, p. 632.

69 Sagdeev, pp. 268–269.

70 Gates, p. 358.

71 Matlock, pp. 134–135, 158.

72 Oberdorfer, p. 143.

73 Reagan, *An American Life*, p. 635.

74 This account of the summit meetings is based on the official U.S. minutes, unless otherwise specified.

75 Gorbachev, p. 406.

76 Reagan diary, Nov. 19, 1985.

77 Reagan, *An American Life*, p. 636.

78 Gorbachev, p. 408.

79 Dobrynin recalls that this agreement for reciprocal visits was precooked quietly by him, p. 589. Reagan had also envisioned meeting again. Matlock, p. 153.

80 Lou Cannon, *Ronald Reagan: The Role of a Lifetime* (New York: Simon & Schuster, 1991), p. 754. In his memoir, Larry Speakes, the White House spokesman then, rendered the quotation slightly differently. In *Speaking Out: Inside the Reagan White House* (New York: Charles Scribner's Sons, 1988), p. 138. Speakes quoted Reagan: "I bet the hardliners in both our countries are squirming."

81 Reagan said it before the Japanese Diet, Nov. 11, 1983, and in his annual address to the United Nations General Assembly in 1984. In an exchange of letters before Geneva, Reagan and Gorbachev had also discussed including this language in their concluding summit statement.

82 "Exchange of Televised Addresses by President Reagan and Soviet General Secretary Gorbachev," Public Papers of the Presidents, 1985 Pub. Papers 4, Jan. 1, 1986.

CHAPTER 11: THE ROAD TO REYKJAVIK

1 Nikolai Chervov, *Yaderny Krugovorot* [Nuclear Continuum] (Moscow: Olma-Press, 2001).

2 Valery Boldin, *Ten Years That Shook the World: The Gorbachev Era as Witnessed by His Chief of Staff* (New York: Basic Books, 1994), p. 115.

3 Akhromeyev's views are from his memoir with Georgi M. Kornienko. Akhromeyev kept the proposal outside normal interagency channels for arms control proposals, where it most certainly would have been stopped. The proposal definitely had a strong propaganda value, and Gorbachev acknowledges in *Memoirs* that he

announced it before the forthcoming Party Congress for maximum impact. But the author believes that Akhromeyev and Gorbachev also believed in the goals of the proposal, and felt the nuclear danger was real. So, from their perspective, it was not just an artificial statement without meaning, as in the past.

4 There are differing accounts about the origins of the initiative, although most credit Akhromeyev. Gorbachev has said he and Shevardnadze had talked about it soon after Shevardnadze's appointment. Savelyev and Detinov also say it came from the General Staff and defense ministry. Akhromeyev says he shared the military's draft with Kornienko at the Foreign Ministry. In the author's possession is a copy of the color chart used to explain the plan at a press conference in Moscow on Jan. 18, 1986. On the back is written, in hand, that the plan was brought into being and edited by Akhromeyev. Katayev, Hoover.

5 Gorbachev had already imposed a unilateral moratorium on Soviet nuclear tests, and used the January 15 announcement to extend it.

6 "Statement by M. S. Gorbachev, General Secretary of the CPSU Central Committee," *Izvestia,* Jan. 16, 1986, BBC Summary of World Broadcasts, Jan. 17, 1986. *Time* magazine reported on the Vremya broadcast, Jan. 27, 1986.

7 Anatoly Chernyaev, *My Six Years with Gorbachev* (University Park, Pa.: University of Pennsylvania Press, 2000), pp. 45–46, and diary, Jan. 18, 1986.

8 George Shultz, *Turmoil and Triumph: My Years as Secretary of State* (New York: Charles Scribner's Sons, 1993), pp. 699–714; and Don Oberdorfer, *From the Cold War to a New Era* (Baltimore: Johns Hopkins University Press, 1998), pp. 156–168.

9 Jack F. Matlock Jr., *Reagan and Gorbachev,* p. 178. David Hoffman and Walter Pincus, "President 'Grateful,' Aides Cautious on Soviet Arms Control Proposal," *Washington Post,* Jan. 17, 1986, p. A1. David Pace, AP, Jan. 28, 1986, "Sen. Nunn Wary of Gorbachev Arms Proposal."

10 Reagan diary, Jan. 15, 1986.

11 Robert M. Gates, *From the Shadows: The Ultimate Insider's Story of Five Presidents and How They Won the Cold War* (New York: Simon & Schuster, 1996), p. 377.

12 Reagan diary, Feb. 3, 1986.

13 The call came on Jan. 31, 1986. Chernyaev diary, Jan. 18 and Feb. 1, 1986.

14 Robert D. English sums up Chernyaev's life and times in his introduction to *My Six Years.* The author is also indebted to Svetlana Savranskaya for additional information.

15 An edited compilation of their notes was published in 2006, *V Politburo TsK KPSS: Po Zapisyam Anatolia Chernyaeva, Vadima Medvedeva, Georgiya Shakhnazarova, 1985–1991* (Moscow: Alpine Business Books, 2006).

16 See *Mikhail Gorbachev: Selected Speeches and Articles* (Moscow: Progress, 1987), p. 341.

17 National Security Decision Directive 196, Nov. 1, 1985.

18 *V Politburo,* p. 32.

19 *United States Nuclear Tests: July 1945 through September 1992,* Department of Energy, Washington, D.C., DOE/NV-209 (Rev. 14), Dec. 1994.

20 Chernyaev, pp. 55–57. Some additional quotations from Chernyaev's notes, not contained in the book, were provided by Svetlana Savranskaya.

21 Grigori Medvedev, *The Truth About Chernobyl* (Basic Books, 1991), Evelyn Rossiter,

trans.; Piers Paul Read, *Ablaze: The Story of the Heroes and Victims of Chernobyl* (New York: Random House, 1993); and Zhores Medvedev, *The Legacy of Chernobyl* (New York: W. W. Norton & Co., 1990). Also see the extensive work of the United Nations Chernobyl Forum Experts Group, including "Environmental Consequences of the Chernobyl Accident and Their Remediation: Twenty Years of Experience," available at *http://www.iaea.org/NewsCenter/Focus/Chernobyl/*. For a technical account of the reasons for the accident, see "INSAG-7: The Chernobyl Accident, Updating of INSAG-1," Safety Series No. 75-INSAG-7, IAEA Safety Series, International Atomic Energy Agency, Vienna, 1992.

22 Zhores Medvedev, p. 24. Valery Legasov, an academician and deputy director of the Kurchatov Institute in Moscow, who served on an early response team, later listened to tape recordings of the operators' telephone conversations. This exchange was recorded on the tapes. Two years after the disaster, Legasov committed suicide. The tape transcripts were found in his safe.

23 Grigori Medvedev, p. 74.

24 "Urgent Report," A. N. Makukhin, First Deputy Director, Ministry of Energy and Electrification, April 26, 1986, No. 1789-2c, Volkogonov Collection, Library of Congress, from Archive of the President of the Russian Federation, Reel 18, Container 27.

25 These comments were made on the twentieth anniversary of the accident. See BBC News, April 24, 2006, at *http://news.bbc.co.uk/go/pr/fr/-/2/hi/europe/4918940.stm*.

26 Chernyaev, p. 65.

27 *V Politburo,* p. 41.

28 Dmitri Volkogonov, *Autopsy for an Empire: The Seven Leaders Who Built the Soviet Regime* (New York: Free Press, 1998), p. 478. Read reports Ligachev argued "for saying as little as possible," and that a vote was taken in which Ligachev prevailed.

29 "Information about the accident at Chernobyl nuclear power station April 26, 1986," Fond 89, Hoover. An essential guide to these documents is Larissa Soroka, *Guide to the Microfilm Collection in the Hoover Institution Archives; Fond 89: Communist Party of the Soviet Union on Trial* (Stanford: Hoover Institution Press, 2001). An hour later, a second TASS statement said the accident was the first ever in the Soviet Union, and noted other accidents in other countries. Read, p. 175.

30 Volkogonov, pp. 478–479.

31 "Ot Sovieta Ministrov SSSR" [From the Council of Ministers USSR], Fond 89, Perechen 53, Delo 2, Hoover Institution.

32 A subsequent account claims the red glow was not the burning core, but a piece that had been blasted loose during the explosion. Alexander R. Sich, "Truth Was an Early Casualty," *Bulletin of the Atomic Scientists*, May/June 1996, pp. 32–42.

33 Michael Dobbs, *Down with Big Brother: The Fall of the Soviet Empire* (New York: Knopf, 1997), p. 160.

34 Fond 89, Perechen 51, Delo 19, Hoover.

35 Reagan diary, April 30, 1986.

36 Fond 89, Perechen 53, Delo 6, Hoover. The memo carries a stamp by the Central Committee indicating it was circulated on May 16, two days after Gorbachev's televised speech. In an interview in 2008 with Irina Makarova, Gubarev said Gorbachev seemed "absolutely in the dark about what was happening." Gubarev

later wrote a play, *Sarcophagus,* which suggested that the accident was due to operator and human error, not the design of the reactor.

37 Chernyaev, p. 66. Also see *V Politburo,* pp. 61–66.

38 Tarasenko, interview, Feb. 3, 2005.

39 Eduard Shevardnadze, *The Future Belongs to Freedom* (New York: Free Press, 1991), pp. 175–176.

40 Sergei Akhromeyev and Georgi M. Kornienko, *Glazami Marshala i Diplomata* (Moscow: International Relations, 1992), pp. 98–99.

41 Mikhail S. Gorbachev, *Gody Trudnykh Reshenii* [Years of Difficult Decisions] (Moscow: Alfa-print, 1993), pp. 46–55.

42 "Chernobyl's Legacy: Health, Environmental and Socio-economic Impacts," the Chernobyl Forum, 2003–2005. In another estimate, at least six thousand more died from radiation exposure, and perhaps many more. David R. Marples, "The Decade of Despair," *Bulletin of the Atomic Scientists,* May–June 1996, pp. 22–31.

43 Shultz, p. 724.

44 Reagan diary, May 20, 1986.

45 Shultz, pp. 716–717.

46 Chernyaev, p. 83. This was a reference to the nuclear-pumped X-ray laser that was being advocated by Teller, although Reagan did not envision a nuclear program.

47 Reagan, *An American Life,* p. 661. The Soviets were eager to do parallel experiments.

48 See *USSR Nuclear Weapons Tests and Peaceful Nuclear Explosions: 1949 through 1990, Ministry of the Russian Federation for Atomic Energy, Ministry of Defense of the Russian Federation,* Russian Federal Nuclear Center VNIIEF, 1996. The U.S. data is from *United States Nuclear Tests.*

49 Frank von Hippel, *Citizen Scientist: From the Environment to Dissent, a Leading Scientist Talks About the Future of the Planet* (New York: Touchstone, 1991). An example of their brainstorming came in the first days after the Chernobyl accident. Von Hippel urged Velikhov to distribute potassium iodide tablets to the population, to forestall the uptake of radioactive iodine into the thyroid of people exposed. Velikhov rushed the idea to the Kremlin. On May 1, the Ministry of Foreign Trade was ordered to "urgently sign contracts to purchase from abroad the necessary amount of medications" and the Health Ministry to "examine the received offers." Protocol No. 3, May 1, 1986, Fond 89, Perechen 51, Delo 19, Hoover. In the end, the advice was not taken out of fear of causing mass panic. Velikhov interview, 2004. According to a later report by the United Nations, radiation doses to the thyroid "were particularly high in those who were children at the time and drank milk with high levels of radioactive iodine. By 2002, more than 4000 thyroid cancer cases had been diagnosed in this group, and it is most likely that a large fraction of these thyroid cancers is attributable to radioiodine intake." See "Chernobyl's Legacy," p. 7.

50 Frank von Hippel, "Contributions of Arms Control Physicists to the End of the Cold War," *Physics and Society,* vol. 25, no. 2, April 1996, pp. 1, 9–10. The conference was part of the Niels Bohr Centennial celebration, Sept. 27–29, 1985.

51 Of three proposals considered, Cochran said NRDC's was accepted because the group could move quickly. The agreement was signed May 28 between Velikhov

and Adrian DeWind, chairman of the NRDC. Cochran, communication with author, July 9, 2008; von Hippel, *Citizen Scientist,* pp. 91–92.

52 Cochran had asked Charles Archambeau, a theoretical seismologist at the University of Colorado, to help organize the seismologists and equipment. Archambeau recruited John Berger, Institute of Geophysics and Planetary Physics, Scripps Institution of Oceanography, University of California, San Diego, La Jolla, California, to organize the team to man the Soviet and U.S. installations and identify and order the needed equipment. Archambeau and Berger recruited James N. Brune from the University of Nevada and several others.

53 Natural Resources Defense Council, "Nuclear Test Ban Verification Project," Status Report, November 1986; and Thomas B. Cochran, *The NRDC/Soviet Academy of Sciences Joint Nuclear Test Ban Verification Project,* Physics and Global Security, vol. 16, no. 3, July 1987, pp. 5–8.

54 Cochran, communication with author, July 8, 2008. The Soviet documents are at Katayev, Hoover.

55 The Central Committee approval was July 9 as Cochran and his team were just arriving on the site. Katayev, Hoover.

56 Chernyaev, pp. 77–78.

57 Gorbachev letter to Reagan, Sept. 15, 1986, RRPL.

58 Reagan diary, Sept. 19, 1986.

59 Chernyaev notes from the Politburo session, Sept. 22, 1986. See *The Reykjavik File: Previously Secret Documents from U.S. and Soviet Archives on the 1986 Reagan-Gorbachev Summit,* TNSA EBB 203, doc. 3.

60 Chernyaev, pp. 79–84. Also see David Holloway, "The Soviet Preparation for Reykjavik: Four Documents," in the conference report *Implications of the Reykjavik Summit on Its Twentieth Anniversary* (Stanford: Hoover Institution Press, 2007), pp. 45–95.

61 Chernyaev, p. 81.

62 "Talking Points," three pp., John Poindexter to the President, no date, RRPL, document no. 9155, Box 90907, European and Soviet Affairs Directorate, NSC.

63 Two sets of notes of the Reykjavik discussions were used for this account. While there are some differences, they largely agree on the substance of what was said. The United States notes are summaries and have been declassified by the State Department; see TNSA, EBB No. 203. The Soviet notes are more detailed, in the form of transcribed speech, and were published in four installments in 1993 by the journal *Mirovaya Ekonomika I Mezhdurnarodnyye Otnosheniya* and translated by FBIS.

64 The U.S. team was led by Nitze, and the Soviet team by Akhromeyev. See Strobe Talbott, *The Master of the Game: Paul Nitze and the Nuclear Peace* (New York: Knopf, 1988), pp. 317–322.

65 Shultz, p. 763.

66 Reagan, *An American Life,* p. 677.

67 This account of the final dialogue is from Shultz, and Reagan gives a similar account. However, Gorbachev said Reagan reproached him, "You planned from the start to come here and put me in this situation!" Gorbachev recalls he replied he was prepared to go back inside and sign a comprehensive arms control

document "if you drop your plans to militarize space." He quotes Reagan as responding, "I am really sorry." Gorbachev, *Memoirs,* p. 419.

68 Reagan diary, Oct. 12, 1986.

69 Gorbachev press conference, Oct. 14, 1986, BBC Summary of World Broadcasts, SU/8389/A1/1.

CHAPTER 12: FAREWELL TO ARMS

1 Svetlana Savranskaya and Thomas Blanton, eds., "The Reykjavik File," TNSA EBB 203, doc. 19.

2 TNSA EBB 203, doc. 21.

3 Anatoly Chernyaev, *My Six Years with Gorbachev* (University Park, Pa.: University of Pennsylvania Press, 2000), p. 87.

4 Gorbachev needed to raise prices that had long been set artificially low, but he could not bring himself to do it. Stable prices were part of the social compact with the population that went back to the late 1950s and early 1960s. Yegor Gaidar, *Collapse of an Empire: Lessons for Modern Russia* (Washington, D.C.: Brookings Institution, 2007), pp. 122–139.

5 Politburo instruction No. P34/I to the Ministry of Defense, Oct. 14, 1986, as referenced in an excerpt from Protocol No. 66 of the Politburo meeting, May 19, 1987. Katayev, Hoover.

6 Sergei Akhromeyev and Georgi M. Kornienko, *Glazami Marshala i Diplomata* (Moscow: International Relations, 1992), pp. 124–126.

7 Gorbachev broadcast on Soviet television, Oct. 22, 1982, BBC Summary of World Broadcasts, SU/8398/A1/1.

8 In his televised address from the Oval Office October 14, Reagan said, "We offered the complete elimination of all ballistic missiles—Soviet and American—from the face of the Earth by 1996." He also described a 50 percent cut in other weapons along with elimination of the missiles.

9 Don Oberdorfer, *From the Cold War to a New Era* (Baltimore: Johns Hopkins University Press, 1998), p. 208. Crowe said in his memoir that he told Reagan the plan was "ill-advised," but he does not quote directly from his presentation. William J. Crowe Jr., *The Line of Fire: From Washington to the Gulf, the Politics and Battles of the New Military* (New York: Simon & Schuster, 1993), pp. 266–269.

10 Reagan diary, Oct. 27, 1986.

11 TNSA EBB 203, doc. 23.

12 The arrival of Stinger shoulder-fired antiaircraft weapons to the U.S.-backed Afghan resistance in September marked a turning point in the six-year-old war. Congress pumped $470 million in secret aid to the fighters in fiscal year 1986 and increased that to $630 million the next year. Steve Coll, *Ghost Wars* (New York: Penguin Books, 2004), pp. 149, 151.

13 Chernyaev, p. 95.

14 Reagan, who earlier adhered to the SALT II limits, decided that the United States would no longer do so, and the United States broke through in late November 1986.

15 This was a reference to Marshal Nikolai Ogarkov, who was removed as chief of the General Staff in September 1984 but at the time remained in the defense ministry

and continued to be outspoken about the need to provide advanced technology to the military.

16 The radar issue was first raised by the United States in 1983; Gates was repeating the charge.

17 William M. Welch, "Soviets Have Far Outspent U.S. on Nuclear Defense, CIA Says," AP, Nov. 25, 1985. The *spravka* is in Katayev, Hoover.

18 Sakharov said February 15, "A significant cut in ICBMs and medium-range and battlefield missiles, and other agreements on disarmament, should be negotiated as soon as possible, independently of SDI . . . I believe that a compromise on SDI can be reached later." Sakharov, *Moscow and Beyond* (New York: Knopf, 1991), p. 21.

19 See "The INF Treaty and the Washington Summit: 20 Years Later," TNSA EBB No. 238.

20 Podvig, *Russian Strategic Nuclear Forces* (Cambridge: MIT Press, 2001), pp. 224–226. Gorbachev, *Memoirs,* pp. 443–444.

21 Katayev's account is drawn from his memoir; a lengthy monograph, "Structure, Preparation and Application of Decisions in Political-Military Problems in the Soviet Union"; and a monograph on civil-military relations.

22 Chernyaev, p. 103, n 4.

23 Margaret Thatcher, *The Downing Street Years* (New York: HarperCollins, 1993), pp. 481–482.

24 Gorbachev, *Zhizn' i reformi,* vol. 2, pp. 36–37. George Shultz, *Turmoil and Triumph: My Years as Secretary of State* (New York: Charles Scribner's Sons, 1993), p. 890.

25 An upgrade was planned to give the Oka a range of 372 miles, but it was never carried out. Katayev.

26 TNSA, EBB 238.

27 Gorbachev approved May 19. Katayev.

28 Yarynich, interviews with author.

29 This account is based on K. Lantratov, "Zvezdnie Voini, Kotorikh ne bylo" [Star Wars That Never Was], at *www.buran.ru/htm/str163.htm.* Two days after the crash, on May 17, Defense Minister Sokolov sent a message to the Central Committee, saying new programs would be readied for anti-satellite combat as well as the SK-1000 list that had been put on Gorbachev's desk in 1985. The Politburo referred Sokolov's message for further study by a four-man committee on May 19. However, most of the projects were never built. "On questions of perfecting the structure of the strategic nuclear forces of the USSR and counteracting the American program to create a multi-echelon system of anti-missile defense," a memo. Katayev, Hoover.

30 "On completed investigation of the criminal case against Rust," Central Committee memorandum, July 31, 1987, Hoover, Fond 89, Perechen 18, Delo 117; a documentary by Danish radio, DR, at *http://www.dr.dk/Tema/rust/english /index.html;* Peter Finn, the *Washington Post,* May 27, 2007, p. A20; *The Observer,* Sunday, Oct. 27, 2002, interview by Carl Wilkinson.

31 *Pravda,* May 28, 1992; see Michael Dobbs, *Down with Big Brother: The Fall of the Soviet Empire* (New York: Knopf, 1997), pp. 180–181.

32 Gorbachev, *Memoirs,* p. 232.

33 Chernyaev, p. 119.

34 Chernyaev, p. 119. Also, "On Violation of Soviet Airspace and Measures to Strengthen Leadership of USSR Armed Forces," Volkogonov Collection, Archive of the President of the Russian Federation, Reel 17, Container 25.

35 Chernyaev diary, June 15, 1987.

36 Katayev, Hoover.

37 Cochran told the author that by measuring the spacing between the centers of the radio transmitter housings, one could calculate the signal half-wavelength and therefore the frequency of the transmitter. This was evidence that the frequency was too low (the wavelength too long) to be a battle management radar.

38 Cochran, interviews, Aug. 19, 2004, and Feb. 25, 2008. Also, courtesy Cochran, "Preliminary Report to the Speaker of the House on Fact-Finding Trip to the Soviet Union"; "Memorandum," to Senator Edward M. Kennedy from Christopher E. Paine, Sept. 9, 1987; "Chronology of Trip from Moscow to Krasnoyarsk Radar Site," Sept. 5, 1987. TASS reported the Gorbachev offer. On the Soviet leadership, Katayev, including, "Consideration of the question connected with problems of 'violations' of the ABM agreement," Nov. 21, 1987, signed by Shevardnadze, Zaikov, Chebrikov, Yazov, Dobrynin and Maslyukov, and a Central Committee staff report on the same date; also see William J. Broad, "Inside a Key Russian Radar Site: Tour Raises Questions on Treaty," *New York Times,* Sept. 7, 1987, p. A1.

39 George Shultz, p. 1001.

40 Leon Aron, *Yeltsin: A Revolutionary Life* (New York: St. Martin's Press, 2000), pp. 200–206. Also see Archie Brown, *The Gorbachev Factor* (Oxford: Oxford University Press, 1996), p. 168.

41 "Gorbachev: Soviet Economic Modernization and the Military," Defense Intelligence Agency, Defense Research Comment DRC-82-87, November 1987. The paper was presented to the Joint Economic Committee on Sept. 14, 1987.

42 "Whither Gorbachev: Soviet Policy and Politics in the 1990s," NIE 11-18-87, November 1987, carried many of the same points that Gates had made in the memo. The assessment failed to catch the dynamic of radical change. TNSA EBB 238. Shultz said, "I felt a profound, historic shift was underway: the Soviet Union was, willingly or unwillingly, consciously or not, turning a corner; they were not just resting for round two of the cold war." Shultz, p. 1003.

CHAPTER 13: GERMS, GAS AND SECRETS

1 Domaradsky and Wendy Orent, *Biowarrior* (New York: Prometheus Books, 2003), pp. 233–250.

2 Popov, interviews by author.

3 Ken Alibek, with Stephen Handelman, *Biohazard: The Chilling True Story of the Largest Covert Biological Weapons Program in the World—Told from Inside by the Man Who Ran It* (New York: Random House, 1999), pp. 87–106.

4 Alibek, p. 118. If Alibek's account is correct, Gorbachev signed this only a month after his January 1986 speech calling for abolition of all nuclear and chemical weapons. The document has never been made public.

5 Chernyaev interview, Feb. 4, 2005. Chernyaev said, "Gorbachev was in favor of ending it. But he was being deceived. I don't remember when, but he was given a

report they were already closing down the military part of this program . . . Shevardnadze told him several times, 'They lie to us, Mikhail Sergeyevich,' on the subject of this program." When I asked Chernyaev who was deceiving Gorbachev, he replied, "The manufacturers of this weapon who dealt with this system. The military and the scientists who were involved."

6 "Visit to Moscow of Professor Matthew Meselson," Moscow 14971, State Department cable to Washington, Aug. 29, 1986, courtesy Meselson archive. Also see Jeanne Guillemin, *Anthrax: The Investigation of a Deadly Outbreak* (Berkeley: University of California Press, 1999), p. 18. While still in Moscow, Meselson asked U.S. officials if they had any questions to pose to his Soviet hosts, according to the cable. Meselson told the author the officials did not respond. After his trip, on September 12 in Washington, Meselson briefed officials from the CIA, Departments of State and Defense, and the Arms Control and Disarmament Agency. Meselson repeated that the Soviet explanation about bad meat "seemed to hang together." The U.S. officials did not believe him and thought he had not asked tough questions. TNSA EBB 61, doc. 27.

7 The papers are attached to a letter to Gorbachev from the Big Five, dated approximately August 1, 1986. Katayev. The review conference was held in Geneva, September 8–26, 1986. Israelyan, "Fighting Anthrax: A Cold Warrior's Confession," *Washington Quarterly* (Washington, D.C.: Center for Strategic and International Studies and Massachusetts Institute of Technology, 2002), Spring 2002, pp. 17–29. Also see remarks by Soviet Ambassador Israelyan, Summary Record of the 5th Meeting, BWC/CON./11/SR.5, Sept. 19, 1986; R. Jeffery Smith, "Soviets Offer Account of '79 Anthrax Outbreak," *Washington Post*, Oct. 9, 1986; and *Science,* Oct. 19, 1986.

8 "Anthrax Epidemic in Sverdlovsk 1979 and Soviet Compliance with the BW Disarmament Convention, CISAC-Moscow October 8, 1986," Joshua Lederberg papers, Box 116, Folder 1. Lederberg and Meselson met in September and Lederberg wrote a note Sept. 12, 1986, "Memorandum from Joshua Lederberg," Box 116, Folder 3. In the note, Lederberg said Meselson was told the anthrax was spread by contaminated bonemeal sold in Sverdlovsk, and also by an infected cattle carcass sold at the ceramics factory. Lederberg noted, ". . . there was no military involvement." Sometime after this note, Lederberg called CIA director William Casey and told him that he should take Meselson's account "seriously." Handwritten note to Meselson from Lederberg, Sept. 25, 1986. Box 115, Folder 13. Separately the Defense Intelligence Agency issued a report in 1986 warning "the Soviets are rapidly incorporating biotechnical developments into their offensive BW program to improve agent utility on the battlefield." See "Soviet Biological Warfare Threat," Defense Intelligence Agency, 1986, report DST-1610F-057-86.

9 "On improvement of organization of works on special problems," no date, an information memo in Katayev's files listing the turning points and decisions on biological weapons from 1986 onward. Katayev, Hoover.

10 BBC Summary of World Broadcasts, Aug. 10, 1987, SU/8642/A1/1. Smidovich interview, April 23, 2008. Vice President George Bush had proposed inspections on demand in 1984, and the Soviets refused at the time.

11 The order accelerated by three years the deadline for having "biological sites" prepared "for international verification for presence of chemical weapons." The new deadline was January 1, 1989. The *spravka* is undated. Katayev, Hoover.

12 Matthew S. Meselson, "The Biological Weapons Convention and the Sverdlovsk Anthrax Outbreak of 1979," *Public Interest Report, Journal of the Federation of American Scientists,* vol. 41, no. 7, Sept. 1988, pp. 1–6. This article is Meselson's account of the Soviet visit to the United States in 1988 as well as his 1986 visit to Moscow. He reported the Soviets had identified one source of contaminated bonemeal used as a cattle feed supplement from a "meat processing plant at Aramil, a town 15 km southeast of Sverdlovsk." The story was that the Aramil plant had not followed sterilization and autoclave procedures in making the bonemeal, therefore allowing the anthrax bacteria to spread to cattle and, when the cattle were slaughtered, to consumers. In 1991, Peter Gumbel, Moscow bureau chief of the *Wall Street Journal,* investigated the Sverdlovsk outbreak by going to the city three times, including to Aramil. "In fact, there is no meat processing plant in Aramil," he reported. He found a small flour mill there instead, and quoted the director as saying he never produced bonemeal. Gumbel said in his article that "sloppy note-taking" by Meselson "could possibly account for this discrepancy," but Gumbel suggested a Soviet cover-up. He wrote that "the official Soviet version is riddled with inconsistencies, half-truths and plain falsehoods." Peter Gumbel, "Sverdlovsk—What Really Happened?—The Scientific Evidence: The Anthrax Mystery," *Wall Street Journal,* Oct. 21, 1991, p. A18. Meselson told the author the Aramil discrepancy was a note-taking mix-up on his part. On Burgasov, see R. Jeffrey Smith, Philip J. Hilts, "Soviets Deny Lab Caused Anthrax Cases," *Washington Post*, April 13, 1988. The CIA was unconvinced by the Soviet visitors in 1988. On May 12, the Directorate of Intelligence issued a top-secret report. Although most is redacted, the title was "Soviet Explanation of Anthrax Incident at Sverdlovsk: The Deception Continues."

13 Alibek, p. 148.

14 "Biological Weapons Proliferation Prevention Project Integration: 100% Final Submittal—Phase 0 Feasibility Study for Threat Reduction Activities at Vozrozhdeniya Island, Uzbekistan," Bechtel National Inc., August 31, 2001, released to author under FOIA, Defense Threat Reduction Agency; "Vozrozhdeniya Island (VI) Pathogenic Destruction Operations (VIPDO) Final Report," June 6, 2002, released to author under FOIA.

15 The reader is reminded that while biological weapons were made from living organisms, such as pathogens, chemical weapons are made from inert substances that cause damage and death to living organisms.

16 Tucker, p. 158.

17 Most of the weapons were quite old, according to documents in the Katayev files.

18 John-Thor Dahlburg, "Soviets Lift Secrecy on Chemical Weapons Program," Associated Press, Oct. 4, 1987; Celestine Bohlen, "Soviets Allow Experts to Tour Chemical Weapons Facility," *Washington Post*, Oct. 5, 1987. On the weapons, Katayev, Hoover.

19 Reagan diary, Dec. 18, 1987. This entry has been partly redacted.

20 Mirzayanov, interview with author; Oleg Vishnyakov, " 'I Was Making Binary Bombs,' This Man Is Talking After Five Years of Silence. He Was Poisoned by Chemical Weapons Made by His Own Hands," *Novoye Vremya,* no. 50, Dec. 1992, pp. 46–48, 49. An account is also given in David Wise, *Cassidy's Run* (New York: Random House, 2000), Ch. 20.

CHAPTER 14: THE LOST YEAR

1 Gorbachev had hoped for a treaty to cut strategic weapons in half at the Moscow summit, but the United States was not ready. "Reagan, Gorbachev and Bush at Governor's Island," TNSA EBB No. 261.

2 Brent Scowcroft, who became Bush's national security adviser in the White House, was deeply cautious about Gorbachev. George Bush and Brent Scowcroft, *A World Transformed* (New York: Knopf, 1998), pp. 12–13.

3 "Session of the CPSU Politburo," June 20, 1988. *Masterpieces of History: Soviet Peaceful Withdrawal from Eastern Europe,* Svetlana Savranskaya, Thomas Blanton and Vlad Zubok, eds. (Budapest: Central European University Press, 2009), Doc. 26.

4 See TNSA EBB 261. To bypass possible military opposition, Gorbachev took the paperwork to the Defense Ministry for approval on a Sunday when Minister Dmitri Yazov was not present, Shevardnadze said at a Politburo meeting on December 27. "Comrades were not in place" then, he said. News reports at the time said that Akhromeyev decided to retire in protest of the troop cuts. In his memoir, Gorbachev said this was "sheer nonsense." Gorbachev, *Memoirs,* p. 459. Akhromeyev said the decision to retire came in September 1988, before the speech, but he was disenchanted. He remained an adviser to Gorbachev. Sergei Akhromeyev and Georgi M. Kornienko, *Glazami Marshala i Diplomata* (Moscow: International Relations, 1992), pp. 213–215.

5 Reagan diary, Dec. 7, 1988.

6 Any evaluation of Reagan's legacy must deal with not only his avowed dream of nuclear abolition, but the fact that he did not consummate a strategic arms treaty by the end of his presidency. Some have argued that if he had been more interested in negotiating arms reductions in his first term, he might have had more to show at the end of his second. However, the author believes that Reagan's first-term military buildup and challenge to the Soviets were set by his own internal compass—his campaign pledges, his desire to stand up to Moscow and his negotiator's sense of timing and tactics. He could not have done it otherwise.

7 Bush said, "Wanting to avoid specifics, I pledged general continuity with Reagan's policies toward the Soviet Union. I told Gorbachev I would be putting together a new team. I had no intention of stalling things, but I naturally wanted to form my own national security policies." Bush and Scowcroft, p. 7.

8 *Masterpieces,* Gorbachev at Politburo, Dec. 27–28, 1988, doc. 34.

9 *This Week with David Brinkley,* ABC News, Jan. 22, 1989.

10 James A. Baker III, *The Politics of Diplomacy: Revolution, War and Peace, 1989–1992* (New York: G. P. Putnam's Sons, 1995), p. 68.

11 Bush letter to Sadruddin Aga Khan, March 13, 1989, in Bush, *All the Best, George Bush,* p. 416.

12 Dennis Ross, director of policy planning at the State Department, said "testing" was his idea. "For those who said Gorbachev was not for real, I said, let's test the proposition. If he's for real, then he's going to respond." Ross, interview, June 2, 2008. In a speech at Texas A&M University in May 1989, Bush unveiled the results of the policy reviews, an approach that he called going "beyond containment." He did not offer major new initiatives, but set the tone for the "testing" approach, which was also codified in NSD 23, written in March and signed in September 1989. The directive said, "the United States will challenge the Soviet Union step by step, issue by issue, institution by institution, to behave . . ."

13 Cheney made the comment on CNN. When Baker went to Moscow a few weeks later, the first thing he told Shevardnadze was, "We have no interest in seeing perestroika fail." Baker, p. 73.

14 William C. Wohlforth, ed., *Cold War Endgame: Oral History, Analysis, Debates* (University Park, Pa.: Pennsylvania State University Press, 2003), p. 26. An analysis of the pause in 1989 is contained in an essay in the same volume, "Once Burned, Twice Shy? The Pause of 1989," Darek H. Chollet and James M. Goldgeier, pp. 141–173. By contrast, in three long and illuminating cables from Moscow in February, Matlock laid out the extent of change. "In sum," Matlock said, "the Soviet Union has, in effect, declared the bankruptcy of its system, and just as with a corporation which has sought the protection of Chapter XI, there is no turning back." Matlock included a section on "The Military Burden," which accurately captured Gorbachev's desire to restrain the military to save the domestic economy. "The Soviet Union over the Next Four Years," Feb. 3, 1989. The subsequent cables covered Soviet foreign policy and U.S.-Soviet relations. *Masterpieces,* docs. 42, 44, 46.

15 On the Shevardnadze warning, a confidential source. Baker, *Politics of Diplomacy*, pp. 82–83. The Gorbachev offer was certainly a gambit to influence Europe, but also a genuine proposal. The United States was pushing allies to modernize the eighty-eight short-range Lance nuclear-tipped missiles in Europe. After implementation of the 1987 INF treaty, these shorter-range missiles would be among the remaining battlefield nuclear weapons available to NATO against a possible Soviet conventional attack. (There were also thousands of other weapons on bombers.) West Germany was balking at modernization, since use of the Lance missiles in war would quite probably be on its soil. Baker thought Gorbachev was undercutting support for Lance modernization. Wohlforth, *Cold War Endgame*, p. 32; and Michael R. Beschloss and Strobe Talbott, *At the Highest Levels: The Inside Story of the End of the Cold War* (Boston: Little, Brown, 1993), p. 67. Baker said of Gorbachev, in an interview with the author, "the way he went about it was the gimmicky part. He did it in order to divide us from our European allies." When I asked Baker if he thought he could have responded differently, he said no. "It was a unilateral move. It wasn't a question of our having to accept it." Baker, interview, Sept. 4, 2008. While Katayev's files show the Kremlin was well aware of the politics in Europe, they also suggest that Gorbachev was serious about tactical nuclear reductions. The issue was included on a Kremlin work plan for arms control in 1989. A memo in the files argues that these weapons in Europe were dangerous and militarily useless. The undated memo said a group of specialists for

the Big Five—whom Katayev described as the "non-military" experts in the working group—"believe that short-range land-based nuclear weapons are the most inconvenient and dangerous for all countries in the deterrence arsenal." Katayev.

16 Fitzwater quickly regretted the words. Marlin Fitzwater, *Call the Briefing: Reagan and Bush, Sam and Helen: A Decade with Presidents and the Press* (New York: Times Books, 1995), Ch. 10.

17 *Masterpieces,* July 20, 1989, doc. 73.

18 "Work Plan," a list of decisions and deadlines for 1989, Katayev.

19 "On reduction of the Armed Forces and spending of the Soviet Union on defense," January 1989, Katayev.

20 "Growth of Military Spending USSR and USA in 1980–1991," a chart, Katayev. In January, Gorbachev ordered a reduction of 14.2 percent in military spending, compared to 1987, and a cut in arms manufacture by 19.2 percent, over a two-year period. Military spending in the Soviet Union was 69.5 billion rubles in 1987, 73 billion in 1988, 77.3 billion in 1989, 71 billion in 1990 and 66.5 billion in 1991, the chart says.

21 Akhromeyev, pp. 204–205.

22 Bush and Scowcroft, p. 130. Bush gave a letter suggesting a summit meeting to Akhromeyev during his visit to the United States, to courier back to Gorbachev, bypassing Shevardnadze, who was furious when he found out.

23 Anatoly Chernyaev, *My Six Years with Gorbachev* (University Park, Pa.: University of Pennsylvania Press, 2000), pp. 225–226.

24 Baker, interview with author, Sept. 4, 2008. See Baker, *Politics of Diplomacy,* pp. 144–152. The Bush administration remained deeply divided over Gorbachev. On October 16, Baker gave a policy speech to the Foreign Policy Association in New York, saying the United States and Soviet Union should find "points of mutual advantage." The next day, Vice President Dan Quayle rejected the idea of helping Soviet reform and said "let them reform themselves." Baker then squelched a pessimistic speech that Gates, then deputy national security adviser, intended to give. Baker, pp. 156–157; Robert M. Gates, *From the Shadows: The Ultimate Insider's Story of Five Presidents and How They Won the Cold War* (New York: Simon & Schuster, 1996), p. 480.

25 The origin of this trip was the work that Velikhov had done with Cochran of the NRDC on seismic monitoring. The other scientists were Steve Fetter, University of Maryland; Lee Grodzins, Massachusetts Institute of Technology; Harvey Lynch, Stanford Linear Accelerator; and Martin Zucker, Brookhaven National Laboratory. "Fact Sheet: The Black Sea Experiment," Natural Resources Defense Council, Washington, D.C. Frank von Hippel came as an observer. Others who also participated included George Lewis of the Center for International Security and Arms Control at Stanford University; Valerie Thomas, Princeton University; William Arkin, the Institute of Policy Studies; Barry Blechman, of Defense Forecast; John Adams, executive director of the NRDC; S. Jacob Scherr and Robert S. (Stan) Norris of the NRDC; and Christopher E. Paine of Senator Edward Kennedy's staff.

26 Sergei Kortunov, a Foreign Ministry official, said the KGB was unhappy about

showing the warhead to foreigners, and tried to block him from participating in preparatory meetings. Kortunov interview, Aug. 30, 2004.

27 Three groups of experiments were conducted. See Steve Fetter et al., "Gamma-Ray Measurements of a Soviet Cruise-Missile Warhead," *Science,* vol. 248, May 18, 1990, pp. 828–834; Thomas B. Cochran, "Black Sea Experiment Only a Start," *Bulletin of the Atomic Scientists* (November 1989), pp. 13–16. Robert S. (Stan) Norris of the NRDC distributed copies of *Soviet Nuclear Weapons,* a groundbreaking 433-page book that had more open information about Soviet weapons systems than was available inside the country at the time. Norris, communication with author, June 19, 2008.

28 Velikhov, interview, Sept. 2, 2004.

29 Von Hippel, interview, Jan. 24 and June 1, 2004. Also, Cochran interview, Aug. 19, 2004.

30 Shevardnadze was among the "Big Five" officials who signed the Nov. 21, 1987, document. The speech was Oct. 23, 1989. Later, Akhromeyev wrote in his memoir that he had told Shevardnadze the truth in 1985. Akhromeyev claimed that the military had not misled the political leadership—in fact, it was the political leaders who ordered the station built in the wrong location in order to save money. Akhromeyev, p. 255.

31 Katayev, Hoover.

32 The decision of Oct. 6, 1989, is recorded in Katayev's *spravka* titled "On Improvement of Organization of Works on Special Problems," no date, Hoover. The reference to "parity" really means to preserve what the Soviet system had built; the United States had none.

33 Davis, interview, May 19 and August 11, 2005.

34 MacEachin, interview, July 25, 2005.

35 Ken Alibek with Stephen Handelman, *Biohazard: The Chilling True Story of the Largest Covert Biological Weapons Program in the World—Told from Inside by the Man Who Ran It* (New York: Random House, 1999), pp. 153–164. He said the vehicle was *Yersinia pseudotuberculosis,* but Popov said it was *Legionella.*

36 Popov, interview, March 31, 2005.

CHAPTER 15: THE GREATEST BREAKTHROUGH

1 Pasechnik had specialized in the separation and concentration of radiochemicals in this period. I have drawn on confidential sources for this chapter. For published accounts, see James Adams, *The New Spies: Exploring the Frontiers of Espionage* (London: Hutchinson, 1994), Ch. 20, "The Weapon of Special Designation." Adams interviewed Pasechnik in September 1993. Also, Simon Cooper, "Life in the Pursuit of Death," *Seed,* issue 4, January–February 2003, p. 68. Pasechnik died Nov. 21, 2001, in Salisbury, England, after a stroke.

2 The Soviet system created larger industrial enterprises and nestled the BW institutes inside them. In this case, the industrial organization was NPO Farmpribor, of which Pasechnik was general director.

3 Davis, the chief biological weapons specialist on the U.K. Defense Intelligence Staff, offered a detailed description of Biopreparat's scope in an article in 1999, "Nuclear Blindness: An Overview of the Biological Weapons Programs of the Former Soviet

Union and Iraq," *Emerging Infectious Diseases,* vol. 5, no. 4, July–August 1999, pp. 509–512.

4 U.S. Congress, Office of Technology Assessment, *Technologies Underlying Weapons of Mass Destruction* OTA-BP-ISC-115 (Washington, D.C.: U.S. Government Printing Office, December 1993), p. 96. See W. Seth Carus, *Bioterrorism and Biocrimes: The Illicit Use of Biological Agents Since 1900* (Amsterdam: Fredonia Books, 2002), pp. 17 and 23.

5 Ken Alibek with Stephen Handelman, *Biohazard: The Chilling True Story of the Largest Covert Biological Weapons Program in the World—Told from Inside by the Man Who Ran It* (New York: Random House, 1999), pp. 139–140.

6 Cooper, p. 105; and Adams, Ch. 20, pp. 270–283.

7 Davis, interviews.

8 Alibek, interview, June 18, 2007, and Alibek, pp. 137, 143.

9 Jones interview by Glenn Frankel of the *Washington Post* in London, August 10, 2004.

10 Alibek confirmed this. "Plague and smallpox were considered strategic weapons" by the Soviet Union, he told the author. In 1992, Davis was honored by Queen Elizabeth, who recognized his contribution to proving that the Soviet Union had a massive strategic biological weapons program.

11 Pasechnik described Soviet research into three key areas: characteristics of each pathogen, susceptibility of targets and vulnerability of users. They tried to improve the production rates and the yield of viable, live microorganisms; increase virulence; boost resistance to antibiotics; maximize viability of the germs during and after dissemination; degrade defenses of the human target; protect the person who launched the pathogens by vaccination; and come up with better detection systems to warn the user.

12 Gorbachev, *Memoirs,* p. 524.

13 The press conference by Guenter Schabowski at the GDR International Press Center took place just before 7 P.M. Cold War International History Project, translated by Howard Sargent.

14 25 Weekly Comp. Pres. Docs. 1712, Nov. 9, 1989. Bush said Gorbachev sent him a message that day asking the United States not to overreact. George Bush and Brent Scowcroft, *A World Transformed* (New York: Knopf, 1998), pp. 148–151.

15 *Masterpieces,* p. 242.

16 A U.S. participant told the author BW issues were not included in the staff papers for the summit, nor mentioned by Bush to Gorbachev.

17 "On Improvement of Organization of Works on Special Problems," Katayev, Hoover.

18 Alibek, p. 150.

19 This account is based on documents from Katayev, Hoover, including Yazov's protest, "On the draft resolution of the Tsk KPSS 'On directives to the USSR delegation at the Soviet-American consultations on issues of banning bacteriological and toxin weapons,'" signed by Yazov January 10, 1990; Karpov's response, January 11, 1990, in a letter to Lazarev, V. F.; and a separate *spravka* signed by N. Shakhov, deputy head of Katayev's department, outlining the official position on the Sverdlovsk accident.

20 MacEachin's job was to synthesize the intelligence from several agencies for the ungroup, as well as describing how the agencies differed, and to seek data from the agencies when the ungroup needed it.

21 MacEachin, interview, July 25, 2005.

22 Ross, interview, June 2, 2008.

23 Anatoly Chernyaev, *My Six Years with Gorbachev* (University Park, Pa.: University of Pennsylvania Press, 2000), p. 244.

24 James A. Baker III, *The Politics of Diplomacy: Revolution, War and Peace, 1989–1992* (New York: G. P. Putnam's Sons, 1995), p. 240. Akhromeyev said Shevardnadze's February concession was "just his mistake." Sergei Akhromeyev and Georgi M. Kornienko, *Glazami Marshala i Diplomata* (Moscow: International Relations, 1992), p. 273.

25 A similar thought was expressed by Akhromeyev at a meeting in Zaikov's office to discuss biological weapons. Katayev took notes, although the date is not clear. The subject was preparing the biological weapons facilities for possible inspection. Katayev noted that Akhromeyev said, "from 6 to 12 months is required to resume the production." Katayev, Hoover.

26 Alibek, pp. 177–178.

27 The instructions sidestepped past violations. "Additional directives for the USSR delegation to the Soviet American consultations on question of prohibition of bacteriological and toxin weapons," Central Committee, no date. A cover sheet indicates Politburo approval April 25, 1990, and that they were an expansion of April 2 directives along similar lines. Courtesy Svetlana Savranskaya.

28 Alibek, pp. 189–191.

29 Matlock, communication with author, May 27, 2008.

30 "Memorandum of conversation between the U.S. ambassador to the USSR, J. Matlock, and the British ambassador, R. Braithwaite," May 14, 1990, Katayev, Hoover. Braithwaite provided a diary extract for the May 14 meeting.

31 "To the President of the Union of Soviet Socialist Republics, Comrade M. S. Gorbachev," May 15, 1990, Katayev, Hoover. This document is strong evidence that, by this point, Gorbachev and Shevardnadze did know of the offensive biological weapons program, as Pasechnik had said.

32 The term *recipe* in this context generally meant a biological weapons preparation.

33 It is not known how much of this was true. Some of it is confirmed by the fragmentary Katayev handwritten notes from the meetings in 1989, in which dismantlement was discussed, but at the time, they were still debating whether to preserve the equipment. Other evidence, including Pasechnik's debriefings, indicated that pathogens were still being tested, manufactured and weaponized in 1989.

34 The two earlier decisions were taken Dec. 6, 1989, and March 16, 1990, after the Pasechnik defection.

35 Two of the sites he identified had been used in the pre-1969 biological weapons program: the Dugway Proving Ground in Utah and the Pine Bluff, Arkansas, storage facility. A third site he mentioned was described as a private company, Cetus Corporation, of Amityville, California, which has never been found.

36 Interviews with Baker on Sept. 4, 2008; MacEachin, July 25, 2005; Ross, June 2,

2008. Shevardnadze's formal instructions for the ministerial meeting with Baker were to repeat that the Soviet side wanted to strengthen trust and broaden openness on the topic. See Fond 89, perechen 10, Delo 61, Hoover. Baker described the visit to Zagorsk in his memoir, *The Politics of Diplomacy,* p. 248, but did not mention the BW paper. Baker also described the ride to Zagorsk in an interview for the PBS *Frontline* documentary *Plague War,* aired Oct. 13, 1998. See *www.pbs.org/wgbh/pages/frontline/shows/plague/interviews/baker.html.*

37 Rodric Braithwaite, *Across the Moscow River* (New Haven: Yale, 2002), pp. 141–143.

38 Baker, p. 247.

39 See Raymond L. Garthoff, *The Great Transition* (Washington, D.C.: Brookings Institution, 1994), pp. 425–428; Beschloss and Talbott, pp. 219–228; Don Oberdorfer, *From the Cold War to a New Era* (Johns Hopkins University Press, 1998), pp. 410–430; Baker, p. 253; Bush and Scowcroft, p. 283.

40 Matlock said that at first "the bureaucracy in Washington was not happy with the idea of reciprocal visits. They said, in effect, they are violating, we are not. Why should we show them what we are doing? I argued that we should accept reciprocal visits: What did we have to lose?" Matlock, communication with author May 27, 2008.

41 Gorbachev, interview, June 10, 2004.

42 Thatcher also said to Gorbachev, of the biological weapons program, "It is possible that this is done as a counterweight to SDI." Archive of the Gorbachev Foundation, Fond 1, Opis 1, courtesy Pavel Stroilov. Braithwaite recalled, "Gorbachev claimed to know nothing but promised to investigate. Intelligence analysts in London and Washington, many of whom still thought there was little to choose between Gorbachev and his predecessors, believed that he knew perfectly well what was going on, and was party to his generals' deliberate deception." pp. 141–143.

43 Baker and Shevardnadze met in Paris, July 16–18. The document, prepared jointly by the United States and Britain, painted a picture of a large-scale Soviet germ warfare program that violated the Biological Weapons Convention. Katayev.

44 "Biological weapons," the Shevardnadze talking points, in draft and final form; also, agendas for the meetings of July 27 and 30, 1990. Katayev.

45 Eduard Shevardnadze, *The Future Belongs to Freedom* (New York: Free Press, 1991), p. 72. Nikita Smidovich, his aide for chemical and biological weapons policy, said this refers to what he told Baker about biological weapons.

46 MacEachin, interviews, Feb. 7 and 13, 2006.

47 The negotiations resulted in an agreement the first visits would be January 7–20, 1991.

48 Baker, p. 312.

49 Chernyaev, p. 291.

50 Shevardnadze, pp. 197, 212.

51 Michael Dobbs, *Down with Big Brother: The Fall of the Soviet Empire* (New York: Knopf, 1997), p. 325.

52 Confidential source.

53 This account of the visits is based in part on confidential sources. Also, Davis

interview, Aug. 11, 2005; Alibek interview, June 18, 2007; Alibek's *Biohazard,* pp. 193–206; Davis interview by *Frontline,* "Plague War"; and David C. Kelly, "The Trilateral Agreement: Lessons for Biological Weapons Verification," Chapter 6 in *Verification Yearbook, 2002* (London: The Verification Research, Training and Information Center, 2002), pp. 75–92.

54 Davis said they could see enough, and did not want to risk ruining the whole mission on this point. Davis, communication with author, Nov. 4, 2008.

55 Popov said the man who tried to stop Davis later received a monetary bonus for his effort.

CHAPTER 16: THE YEAR OF LIVING DANGEROUSLY

1 See Yegor Gaidar, *Collapse of an Empire,* pp. 201–219.

2 Anatoly Chernyaev, *My Six Years with Gorbachev* (University Park, Pa.: University of Pennsylvania Press, 2000), p. 343.

3 Chernyaev, *1991 g.: Dnyevnik Pomoshchnika Prezidenta SSSR* [1991: Diary of an Assistant to the President of the USSR] (Moscow: Terra, 1997), p. 126.

4 Valentin Stepankov and Yevgeny Lisov, *Kremlyovskii Zagovor* (Perm: Ural-Press, Ltd., 1993), p. 271. Also see Michael Dobbs, *Down with Big Brother: The Fall of the Soviet Empire* (New York: Knopf, 1997), pp. 336–344; and Anatol Lieven, *The Baltic Revolution* (New Haven: Yale University Press, 1993).

5 Gorbachev said he had not planned the Vilnius violence, *Memoirs,* p. 651.

6 Chernyaev, pp. 320–323.

7 Archive of the Gorbachev Foundation, Fond 1, Opis 1, courtesy Pavel Stroilov. The meetings and correspondence are also referenced in a letter which Major sent to Gorbachev on April 5. Katayev, Hoover.

8 Katayev, Hoover.

9 Jack F. Matlock Jr., *Autopsy on an Empire: The American Ambassador's Account of the Collapse of the Soviet Union* (New York: Random House, 1995), pp. 537–539.

10 Matlock, *Autopsy,* pp. 539–541.

11 Chernyaev, p. 352. Matlock also details the misunderstandings in his foreword to *My Six Years.*

12 Chernyaev, p. 352.

13 Beschloss and Talbott, *At the Highest Levels,* p. 400.

14 Chernyaev said he, too, had told Gorbachev of rumors about suspicious military movements around Moscow. Gorbachev was "offended" by these signals, he recalled. Chernyaev said the Supreme Soviet speeches of Kryuchkov, Yazov and Pugo had infuriated Gorbachev. Chernyaev, p. 354.

15 This account is based on Matlock, pp. 539–546; and Chernyaev, pp. 352–353.

16 Blair, interview, Feb. 20, 2004; Yarynich interview, April 20, 2003.

17 "On reply to the U.S. President on the question of biological weapons," July 4, 1991, Katayev, Hoover.

18 At the time, the idea of a "grand bargain" was being floated—massive aid in exchange for true market reform and democracy. But Bush never approved large-scale aid and Gorbachev never got to true market reform. Despite a dramatic

appeal for aid to the larger group of Western leaders, Gorbachev failed to secure a major economic package at the summit.

19 Chernyaev, pp. 358–359.

20 "White House Fact Sheet on the Strategic Arms Reduction Treaty," Presidential Documents, vol. 27, p. 1086.

21 Chernyaev, p. 369.

22 Why this moment? The new union treaty was clearly a factor. However, Gorbachev has also said the hard-liners may have overheard the discussion with Yeltsin about replacing them, which took place at the end of July, in a room at the presidential compound, Novo-Ogaryovo, outside of Moscow. The room was bugged. Gorbachev, *Memoirs,* p. 643.

23 Gorbachev, *The August Coup: The Truth and the Lessons* (New York: HarperCollins, 1991), p. 19.

24 Chernyaev, *Diary of an Assistant,* p. 190.

25 By some accounts, the codes on the suitcase were erased and they were not usable. However, the exact condition is not known.

26 Dobbs, pp. 387–389.

27 Yevgeny Shaposhnikov, *Vybor* (Moscow: Nezavisimoye Izdatelstvo, 1995), pp. 44–45.

28 Yarynich, communication with author, August 2004.

29 Gorbachev has recalled that on August 27 he came home to find that Raisa was in tears. She had burned all the letters he had written to her over the years. She said she could not imagine someone else reading them if another coup were to happen. Andrei S. Grachev, *Final Days* (Boulder: Westview Press, 1995), p. 171.

30 Dobbs, pp. 418–420.

CHAPTER 17: A GREAT UNRAVELING

1 Nunn, interview, March 10, 2005.

2 Vinson of Georgia, for decades the chairman of the House Armed Services Committee, was Nunn's great-uncle. Senator Stennis of Mississippi was then chairman of Armed Services. Another person who influenced Nunn was Senator Richard Russell of Georgia, who had also been chairman of the Armed Services committee. Russell died in 1971 and Nunn was elected to his seat.

3 Kenneth W. Thompson, ed., *Sam Nunn on Arms Control* (Lanham, Md.: University Press of America, 1987), p. 19.

4 The visit was February 4–17, 1974. Nunn was accompanied by Frank Sullivan of the Senate Armed Services Committee. Nunn, interview, March 10, 2005. Frank Sullivan, interview, Jan. 31, 2006. Also see Nunn, "Changing Threats in the Post-Cold War World," speech, Monterey Institute of International Studies, Monterey, Calif., Aug. 20, 1995; and U.S. Senate, 93d Congress, 2d Session, April 2, 1974, "Policy, Troops and the NATO Alliance, Report of Senator Sam Nunn to the Committee on Armed Services, United States Senate." Courtesy of Manuscript, Archives and Rare Book Library, Robert W. Woodruff Library, Emory University, Atlanta, Ga.

5 David Miller, *The Cold War: A Military History* (New York: Thomas Dunne Books, St. Martin's Press, 1998), p. 360.

6 Nunn told me the psychology of defeat and its effect on the American military after Vietnam led him to conclude that the Russian military would be demoralized after losing their empire. Nunn, communication with author, Aug. 26, 2008. See Nunn, "Vietnam Aid—The Painful Options," Report to the Senate Armed Services Committee, Feb. 12, 1975, 94th Congress, 1st Session.

7 In the mid-1980s, Nunn and Senator John Warner (R-Va.) proposed creating risk reduction centers in the United States and Soviet Union to share information in a crisis. The first-phase ideas were accepted by Reagan and Gorbachev at Geneva in 1985, and on Sept. 15, 1987, the United States and the Soviet Union signed an agreement establishing Nuclear Risk Reduction Centers in Washington and Moscow. Nunn and Warner had also suggested a more ambitious effort, which was not adopted. "Outline of nuclear risk reduction proposal," fact sheet, undated, and "Nuclear Risk Reduction Center," Cathy Gwin, communication with author, July 28, 2008.

8 George Bush and Brent Scowcroft, *A World Transformed* (New York: Knopf, 1998), pp. 539, 545–547.

9 "Address to the Nation on Reducing United States and Soviet Nuclear Weapons," Presidential Documents, vol. 27, p. 1348.

10 "Soviet Tactical Nuclear Forces and Gorbachev's Nuclear Pledges: Impact, Motivations, and Next Steps," Interagency Intelligence Memorandum, Director of Central Intelligence, November 1991.

11 Cochran of the NRDC tried to persuade Soviet officials to take actions to verify the pullbacks, but at the time they were not interested. See "Report on the Third International Workshop on Verified Storage and Destruction of Nuclear Warheads," NRDC, Dec. 16–20, 1991.

12 George Bush, *All the Best, George Bush: My Life in Letters and Other Writings* (New York: Touchstone, 1999), p. 539. The State Department memo was written four days later. Baker, *The Politics of Diplomacy* (New York: G.P. Putnam's Sons, 1995), p. 558.

13 Gates, prepared statement to the House Armed Services Committee, Defense Policy Panel, December 10, 1991, in *Preventing Chaos in the Former Soviet Union: The Debate on Providing Aid,* Report of the Committee on Armed Services, 102nd Congress, Second Session, Jan. 17, 1992, pp. 166–188.

14 An American diplomat in Moscow cabled back to Washington a conversation with a Russian official who said the country "has virtually no adequate storage sites for the huge quantities of weapons-grade material that will result from destruction of substantial numbers of warheads." "Russian views on destruction/storage of dismantled nuclear warheads," Moscow cable to the State Department, Jan. 14, 1992, declassified to author under FOIA. The remark about plutonium pits was made by Viktor Mikhailov, who was then deputy minister of atomic energy, to Frank von Hippel in October 1991, while on a visit to Washington. Von Hippel, interview, June 1, 2004. The need for safe storage was raised at two unofficial workshops sponsored by the NRDC and the Federation of American Scientists in Washington, Oct. 18–19, 1991, and in Kiev, Dec. 16–20, 1991, both with Soviet participation. During the Kiev conference, Mikhailov mentioned the rail cars to a conference participant.

15 Blair, testimony to the House Committee on Armed Services, July 31, 1991. In September, Blair arranged a trip to Washington for Gennady Pavlov, a retired colonel in the Strategic Rocket Forces who taught at the forces' academy. Blair and Pavlov testified jointly before a Senate panel September 24 and provided a good description of who held the nuclear suitcases, what had happened to Gorbachev's during the coup and the order of Soviet nuclear launch procedures. U.S. Senate, 102nd Congress, 1st Session, Sept. 24, 1991, "Command and Control of Soviet Nuclear Weapons: Dangers and Opportunities Arising from the August Revolution," Hearing before the Subcommittee on European Affairs, Committee on Foreign Relations.

16 See Carter, John D. Steinbruner and Charles A. Zraket, *Managing Nuclear Operations* (Washington, D.C.: Brookings Institution, 1987).

17 Dick Combs, who was on Senator Nunn's staff and present at the meeting with Aspin, interview, Nov. 28, 2004.

18 In a legislative maneuver, they had tried to spring the proposal on a House-Senate conference without having been approved on the floor of each chamber.

19 Don Oberdorfer, "First Aid for Moscow: The Senate's Foreign Policy Rescue," *Washington Post,* Dec. 1, 1991, p. C2.

20 In Washington, Oct. 17–24, 1991, Mikhailov participated in an NRDC workshop on verification issues, and briefed members of Congress. NRDC, "Report on the Third International Workshop," p. 3. Christopher Paine interview, July 31, 2008.

21 Nunn, "Soviet Defense Conversion and Demilitarization," *Congressional Record, Senate,* vol. 137, no. 167, 102nd Cong. 1st Sess., Nov. 13, 1991.

22 Lugar daily calendar, courtesy office of Senator Lugar.

23 Carter, interview, Dec. 14, 2005.

24 Bush and Scowcroft, pp. 543–544.

25 Baker, interview, Sept. 4, 2008.

26 Baker, *The Politics of Diplomacy,* pp. 562–563. "America and the Collapse of the Soviet Empire: What Has to Be Done," Secretary Baker, Princeton, Dec. 12, 1991, U.S. Department of State Dispatch, vol. 2, no. 50, pp. 887–893.

27 Chetek caused controversy at a symposium of Canadian environmentalists in April 1991. Mikhailov attended, along with Alexander Tchernyshev. John J. Fialka, "Soviet Concern Has Explosive Solution for Toxic Waste—Firm Pushes Nuclear Blasts as Cheap Way for Nations to Destroy the Materials," *Wall Street Journal,* Oct. 25, 1991. Also see William E. Burrows and Robert Windrem, *Critical Mass* (New York: Simon & Schuster, 1994). Arzamas-16 was among the shareholders of Chetek. Dmitri Bogdanovich, Vlast, No. 102, Jan. 13, 1992.

28 The United States carried out 27 such explosions between 1961 and 1973. The Soviet Union carried out 124 between 1965 and 1988.

29 "Press Release, Ministry of Atomic Power and Industry, USSR, and International Joint Stock Company 'CHETEK,'" Dec. 11, 1991, in NRDC, "Report of the Third International Workshop," appendix F.

30 Mark Hibbs, "Soviet Firm to Offer Nuclear Explosives to Destroy Wastes," *Nucleonics Week,* Oct. 24, 1991, vol. 32, no. 43, p. 1. Fred Hiatt, "Russian Nuclear Scientists Seek Business, Food," *Washington Post,* Jan. 18, 1992, p. A1.

31 In a study of the impact of hypermilitarization on the Russian economy, Clifford G.

Gaddy noted, "The lowly saucepan became the symbol of resistance to conversion by the defense-industrial complex. In effect, the message they sent was: 'If we are going to convert, it has to be on our terms, in a way commensurate with our status. Otherwise, we won't convert at all!' " Gaddy, *The Price of the Past: Russia's Struggle with the Legacy of a Militarized Economy* (Washington, D.C.: Brookings Institution Press, 1996), p. 65.

32 "Soviet Defense Industry: Confronting Ruin," SOV 91-10042, October 1991.

33 Burns served in the army thirty-four years, and worked on the INF treaty negotiations as senior military member of the Joint Chiefs of Staff delegation. He was ACDA director 1988–1989.

34 Burns, interview, Aug. 12, 2004.

35 Sergei Popov and Taissia Popova, interview, May 16, 2005. Gait, communication with author, July 7, 2008.

36 Ken Alibek, *Biohazard: The Chilling True Story of the Largest Covert Weapons Program in the World—Told from the Inside by the Man Who Ran It* (New York: Random House, 1999), pp. 226–240. Alibek, interview, June 18, 2007.

37 David Hoffman, "Baker Witnesses an End, a Beginning; Visit Marked by Gorbachev's Humiliation, Ex-Republics' Rise," *Washington Post,* Dec. 21, 1991, p. A1.

38 William C. Wohlforth, ed., *Cold War Endgame: Oral History, Analysis, Debates* (University Park, Pa.: Pennsylvania State University Press, 2003), p. 126.

39 James A. Baker III, *The Politics of Diplomacy: Revolution, War and Peace, 1989–1992* (New York: G. P. Putnam's Sons, 1995), pp. 572, 575. Also, "JAB notes from 1-on-1 mtg. w/B. Yeltsin during which command & control of nuclear weapons was discussed, 12/16/1993," courtesy Baker. Under the Soviet system, there were three *Cheget* suitcases, with the president, defense minister and chief of the general staff each having one. But according to Baker's notes, it seems that at this moment, the three were distributed among Yeltsin, Shaposhnikov and Gorbachev.

40 Gorbachev, *Memoirs,* p. 670.

41 Andrei S. Grachev, *Final Days: The Inside Story of the Collapse of the Soviet Union* (Boulder: Westview Press, 1995), pp. 189–190.

42 Katayev, a chart, March 1991.

CHAPTER 18: THE SCIENTISTS

1 Yeltsin's Address to the Nation, Central Television, Dec. 29, 1991, BBC Summary of World Broadcasts.

2 Leon Aron, *Yeltsin: A Revolutionary Life* (New York: St. Martin's Press, 2000), p. 483.

3 Vladimir Gubarev, *Chelyabinsk-70* (Moscow: Izdat, 1993); and *Lev i Atom: Akademik L. P. Feoktistov: Aftoportpet ha fone vospominaniye* [Academician Lev P. Feoktistov: A Self-Portrait and Reminiscences] (Moscow: Voskresenye Press, 2003).

4 Avrorin, the Chelyabinsk director, sent his first e-mail in April. Cochran correspondence files, 1991–1992.

5 James A. Baker III, *The Politics of Diplomacy: Revolution, War and Peace, 1989–1992* (New York: G. P. Putnam's Sons, 1995), pp. 614–616. This account is based on my notes and account in the *Washington Post*, "Atom Scientists at Ex-Soviet Lab Seek Help; Baker Hears Appeals on Tour of Arms Complex," Feb. 15, 1992, p. A1;

Thomas L. Friedman, "Ex-Soviet Atom Scientists Ask Baker for West's Help," *New York Times*, Feb. 15, 1992, p. 1.

6 "Moscow Science Counselors Meeting," State Department cable, Jan. 31, 1992.

7 "Comprehensive Report of the Special Advisor to the DCI on Iraq's WMD," CIA, Sept. 30, 2004.

8 Glenn E. Schweitzer, who became the first executive director of the science center, said these were his best estimates. *Moscow DMZ* (Armonk, N.Y.: M. E. Sharpe, 1996), pp. 103–104.

9 This was a tiny amount compared to the $295 billion annual American defense budget that year.

10 The institute developed diagnostic and measuring equipment for underground nuclear tests.

11 Anne M. Harrington, interviews, July 30 and August 11, 2004.

12 In 1996, after about two and a half years of operation, the ISTC estimated that nuclear weapons scientists and engineers received 63 percent of its grants and missile specialists 16 percent. ISTC brochure.

13 Victor Vyshinsky, interview, Oct. 13, 1998.

14 See "Statement of the Director of Central Intelligence Before the Senate Armed Services Committee," Jan. 22, 1992.

15 Andrei Kolesnikov, "Russian Scientists Accused of Wanting to Help North Korea Become a Nuclear Power," *Moscow News,* April 2, 1993. Evegni Tkachenko, TASS, Feb. 10, 1993, cited the local newspaper *Chelyabinski Rabochi,* which quoted local officials as saying the recruitment was engineered by North Korea to modernize their missile forces. On February 24, Tkachenko quoted Bessarabov as saying there was no work at the institute, where his ruble salary was equivalent to $6 a month. Interview with retired federal security official, Sept. 1, 2004.

16 Michael Dobbs, "Collapse of Soviet Union Proved Boon to Iranian Missile Program," TWP, Jan. 13, 2002, p. A19; notes, Dobbs interview with Vadim Vorobei, Moscow 2001. A fascinating account of a second Russian missile expert's sojourn in Tehran is in Yevgenia Albats, "Our Man in Tehran," *Novaya Gazeta,* No. 10, pp. 4–5, March 1998. The missile expert was identified only by a pseudonym, but the experience he described is parallel to Vorobei's.

17 Gharbiyeh set out to obtain advanced missile guidance systems. In November 1994, he appeared at Energomash, a giant Soviet-era rocket engine manufacturer, with a delegation of Iraqis who were disguised as "Jordanian" businessmen. Energomash had built about sixty types of engines over a half century, but in the years after the Soviet collapse, work was scarce, and Energomash was desperate for orders from abroad. Gharbiyeh presented a business card from the "Gharbiyeh Company." No one at Energomash checked the passports or identity of the businessmen. The visitors outlined technical specifications of the rocket engines they wanted to buy, and on November 18, signed a letter of intent with three Energomash officials to procure them. Victor Sigaev, deputy general director for external economic affairs, and Felix Evmenenko, chief of security for the department for information and international cooperation, NPO Energomash interview, December 1998. They said the deals never went through, the engines were not built and they only learned later that the visitors were from Iraq. Evmenenko said they were given approval in

advance from the Russian government to have the initial meeting. The visitors were told that any deal would have to be formally approved by the government, and they never returned, he added.

18 Gharbiyeh purchased the gyroscopes from the Scientific Research Institute of Chemical and Building Machinery in Sergiev Posad, north of Moscow. Using a front company he created, Gharbiyeh negotiated to buy the gyros and other equipment with three deputy directors and the chief accountant at the institute. He had the gyros tested at a Moscow-based company, Mars Rotor. Vladimir Orlov and William C. Potter, "The Mystery of the Sunken Gyros," *Bulletin of the Atomic Scientists,* November/December 1998, vol. 54, no. 6. Also, "Ob ugolovnom dele nomer 43" [Re: Criminal Case No. 43], a summary from the Federal Security Service of Russia, 1997, in Russian, author's possession.

19 "To the Chairman of the Government of the Russian Federation, V. S. Chernomyrdin," letter from Nechai as well as union and city leaders, Sept. 6, 1996. This account is also drawn from Boris Murashkin, interview, Dec. 3, 1996, Chelyabinsk; "Pominki v Snezhinske" [Wake in Snezhinsk], Grigory Yavlinsky, *Obshchaya Gazeta,* Nov. 6–13, 1996; "Minatom Poobeshali Prioritetnoye Finansirovaniye" [Minatom Promised Priority Financing], Atompressa, no. 35, vol. 227, October 1996, p. 3; "Proshu Pokhronit Menya V Pyatnitzu" [Please Bury Me on Friday], Vladislav Pisanov, *Trud,* Nov. 6–14, 1996; and "Russian Turmoil Reaches Nuclear Sanctum; Suicide of Lab Director in 'Closed City' Underscores Angst," David Hoffman, *Washington Post,* Dec. 22, 1996, p. A29.

CHAPTER 19: REVELATIONS

1 Hecker's father, an Austrian who had been drafted into the German army, was lost at the Russian front four months after he was born. He never saw him again. As a young boy in Austria, Hecker had grown up with only dark impressions of Russia, reinforced by his teachers, who returned from the front with grim war stories. At thirteen years old, he emigrated to the United States, and later earned a doctorate in metallurgy and materials from the Case Institute of Technology before going to work at Los Alamos. He rose to become director of the laboratory in 1986. Almost immediately, he was drawn into the arms control debates. In 1988, Hecker and other U.S. scientists carried out a joint nuclear weapons verification experiment with Soviet scientists. The experiments brought the Americans into contact for the first time with Victor Mikhailov, the leading Soviet expert on nuclear testing diagnostics. Hecker, interview, Dec. 9, 2008.

2 See "Russian-American Collaborations to Reduce the Nuclear Danger," *Los Alamos Science,* Los Alamos National Laboratory, no. 24, 1996, pp. 1–93; and Steve Coll and David B. Ottaway, "Secret Visits Helped Define 3 Powers' Ties," *Washington Post,* April 11, 1995, p. A1.

3 The International Convention on the Prevention of Marine Pollution by Dumping of Wastes and Other Matter, Dec. 29, 1972, entered into force for the Soviet Union in 1976.

4 At first, he disclosed waste dumping, and later the reactors were revealed in February 1992 in the newspaper *Sobesednik,* by Alexander Yemelyanenkov, who represented Arkhangelsk in parliament. Josh Handler, interview, Dec. 19, 2003.

Andrei Zolotkov, "On the Dumping of Radioactive Waste at Sea Near Novaya Zemlya," Greenpeace Nuclear Seas Campaign and Russian Information Agency, Monday, Sept. 23, 1991, Moscow. The author also received recollections from Zolotkov, Oct. 13, 2008; Floriana Fossato, Aug. 6, 2008; John Sprange, Aug. 10, 2008; and Dima Litvinov, Aug. 6, 2008.

5 See "Facts and Problems Related to Radioactive Waste Disposal in Seas Adjacent to the Territory of the Russian Federation," Office of the President of the Russian Federation, Moscow, 1993.

6 Yablokov, interview, June 25, 1998. Yeltsin formed the commission Oct. 24, 1992.

7 After the Bush-Gorbachev unilateral withdrawals in September and October 1991, talks with Moscow made little progress, Undersecretary of State Reginald Bartholomew told Congress. "Trip Report: A Visit to the Commonwealth of Independent States," Senate Armed Services Committee, 102nd Congress, 2nd Session, S Prt. 102-85, March 10, 1985.

8 "Next Steps on Safety, Security, and Dismantlement," Jan. 24, 1992, cable to the State Department and the White House from Moscow. Declassified in part to author Sept. 22, 2006, under FOIA.

9 Burns, interview, Aug. 12, 2004.

10 "Delegation on Nuclear Safety, Security and Dismantlement (SSD): Summary Report of Technical Exchanges in Albuquerque, April 28–May 1, 1992," State Department cable.

11 Note made by a participant who asked to remain anonymous, undated.

12 Keith Almquist, communications with author, Dec. 14, 2008, and Jan. 24, 2009. Later, Sandia procured materials for another ninety-nine upgrades and sent these in standard shipping containers to a Russian rail car factory in Tver, Russia, and then contracted with the factory to do the conversions. The upgrades involved changing the insulation and locking down the movable platform. Sandi also provided alarm-monitoring equipment. Some older Russian rail cars were made of wood. The United States also provided armored blankets and "supercontainers" to protect warheads from gunfire.

13 "President Boris Yeltsin's Statement on Arms Control," TASS, Jan. 29, 1992.

14 This account is based on Mirzayanov interview, July 26, 2008; Mirzayanov, *Vyzov* (Kazan: Dom Pechati, 2002), published in English as *State Secrets: An Insider's Chronicle of the Russian Chemical Weapons Program* (Denver: Outskirts Press, 2009); and Mirzayanov, "Dismantling the Soviet/Russian Chemical Weapons Complex: An Insiders View," in Amy Smithson, ed., *Chemical Weapons Disarmament in Russia: Problems and Prospects* (Washington, D.C.: Stimson Center, October 1995), pp. 21–34.

15 On the Lenin Prizes, Mirzayanov originally believed they were for the binary *novichok* agents, but later learned that they had received the prize for creating another binary.

16 The article was signed by Mirzayanov and Lev Fedorov, a chemist who, in the 1990s, founded and headed the Association for Chemical Security, a group concerned about storage and destruction of chemical weapons arsenals.

17 His coauthor, Fedorov, was interrogated, as were some journalists, but not charged.

18 The Convention on the Prohibition of the Development, Production, Stockpiling

and Use of Chemical Weapons and on Their Destruction was adopted in Geneva on Sept. 3, 1992, by the Conference on Disarmament. It was opened for signature in Paris from Jan. 13 to 15, 1993, and entered into force on April 29, 1997. Both Russia and the United States ratified the treaty.

19 Mirzayanov drew support from around the world. Scientists, politicians and human rights activists wrote letters on his behalf to the authorities in Moscow. Mirzayanov and Colby later married. Mirzayanov now lives in the United States.

20 On March 11, 1994, the attorney general closed the case. During the proceedings, another disenchanted veteran of the chemical weapons program, Vladimir Uglev, had corroborated what Mirzayanov said. Uglev later threatened to release the formulas of the *novichok* agents unless the case was dropped. Oleg Vishnyakov, "Interview with a Noose Around the Neck," *Novoye Vremya,* Moscow, no. 6, Feb. 1993, pp. 40–41, as translated in JPRS-UMA-92-022, June 29, 1993. Vladimir Uglev, interview, June 10, 1998. Uglev said his threat to reveal the formulas was a bluff. "I don't know if I could have done that," he said.

21 This account is based on interviews with Blair, Feb. 20 and March 9, 2004; *The Logic of Accidental Nuclear War* (Washington, D.C.: Brookings Institution Press, 1993); "The Russian C³I," a paper by Valery E. Yarynich, Feb. 24, 1993, and a copy of Yarynich's review, May 31, 1993, both courtesy of Blair; and interviews with Yarynich.

22 Yarynich had already made two authorized presentations overseas on nuclear command and control. On April 23–25, 1992, Yarynich was delegated by the General Staff to participate in a conference in Estonia, and he made another presentation Nov. 19–21, 1992, in Stockholm.

23 After Blair's op-ed appeared, Yarynich wrote his own article, emphasizing the role of Perimeter as a "safety catch" against a mistaken launch. He also called for more openness about nuclear command and control systems. "The Doomsday Machine's Safety Catch," *New York Times,* Feb. 1, 1994, p. A17. Other articles began to appear by Russian experts on Perimeter, and Yarynich published a more detailed description in his book, *C³: Nuclear Command, Control, Cooperation* (Washington, D.C.: Center for Defense Information, 2003), pp. 156–159.

CHAPTER 20: YELTSIN'S PROMISE

1 Braithwaite, *Across the Moscow River* (New Haven: Yale, 2002), pp. 142–143. Also, Braithwaite diary entries and communication with author, May 19, 2008. A confidential source told the author Yeltsin also called the biological weapons scientists "misguided geniuses."

2 James A. Baker III, *The Politics of Diplomacy: Revolution, War and Peace, 1989–1992* (New York: G.P. Putnam's Sons, 1995), p. 620. On the same day he met with Baker, Yeltsin issued a lengthy statement on arms control in which he declared that Russia "is for strict implementation of the 1972 Biological Weapons Convention." "President Boris Yeltsin's Statement on Arms Control," TASS, Jan. 29, 1992. Also, Ann Devroy, R. Jeffrey Smith, "U.S., Russia Pledge New Partnership; Summits Planned in Washington, Moscow," *Washington Post,* p. A1, Feb. 2, 1992.

3 Popov, interview, May 16, 2005; Gait, communication with author, July 7–8, 2008.

4 Ken Alibek with Stephen Handelman, *Biohazard: The Chilling True Story of the*

Largest Covert Weapons Program in the World—Told from the Inside by the Man Who Ran It (New York: Random House, 1999), pp. 242–244.

5 Braithwaite, journal entry.

6 At the Third Review Conference of the BWC, held in Geneva Sept. 9–27, 1991, the parties, which included the Soviet Union, agreed to a series of confidence-building measures, including "declaration of past activities in offensive and/or defensive biological research and development programmes" and agreed that exchange of data should be sent annually to the U.N. no later than April 15, covering the previous calendar year.

7 "Decree of the President of the Russian Federation from April 11, 1992, No. 390, On Providing Fulfillment of International Obligations in the Field of Biological Weapons."

8 In his diary Braithwaite wrote of his reaction, "I say that the right response is to take it at face value, and that the Prime Minister should ram the thought home by sending Yeltsin a personal message congratulating him on his courageous and decisive action. That will make it harder for the Russians to backslide or weave about." Braithwaite, diary entry, April 23, 1992.

9 "Declaration of Past Activity Within the Framework of the Offensive and Defensive Programs of Biological Research and Development," also known as "Form F." Yeltsin admitted to the newspaper *Izvestia* the military was trying to hide the biological weapons program from him. He recalled his conversation with Bush at Camp David this way: "I said I could not give him firm assurances of cooperation. Certainly, this is not acceptable among politicians, but I said this: 'We are still deceiving you, Mr. Bush. We promised to eliminate bacteriological weapons. But some of our experts did everything possible to prevent me from learning the truth. It was not easy but I outfoxed them. I caught them red-handed.' " Yeltsin offered few details but said he had discovered two test sites where experts were experimenting with anthrax on animals. *Izvestia,* April 22, 1992.

10 Braithwaite journal entries for these dates.

11 *Komsomolskaya Pravda*, May 27, 1992, p. 2.

12 "Text of President Yeltsin's Address to US Congress," TASS, June 17, 1992.

13 The drafts were discussed June 4, June 15 and July 28, primarily with officials in the U.S. Arms Control and Disarmament Agency, according to records made available to the author. Also, R. Jeffrey Smith, "Russia Fails to Deter Germ Arms; U.S. and Britain Fear Program Continues in Violation of Treaty," *Washington Post*, Aug. 31, 1992, p. 1.

14 Frank Wisner, interview, Aug. 12, 2008. See TNSA EBB 61, doc. 32, for Wisner's talking points. For this account I have also relied on an authoritative confidential source.

15 "A Deputy's Request," Larissa Mishustina, undated. Alexei Yablokov, letter to Yeltsin, Dec. 3, 1991. *Spravka,* signed by Yablokov, Dec. 6, 1991. All three documents courtesy Meselson archive. Yablokov says in both the *spravka* and the letter to Yeltsin that documents on the Sverdlovsk case were destroyed by instructions from the Council of Ministers of the Soviet Union on Dec. 4, 1990, No. 1244-167, "On Works of Special Problems."

16 Guillemin was at the time a professor at Boston College and has since become a

senior fellow at the Security Studies Program at MIT in the Center for International Studies. The story of the expedition is told in greater detail in her book. She and Meselson are married.

17 Meselson conveyed this paper to the Proceedings of the National Academy of Sciences, where it was published. Faina A. Abramova, Lev M. Grinberg, Olga V. Yampolskaya and David H. Walker, "Pathology of Inhalational Anthrax in 42 Cases from the Sverdlovsk Outbreak of 1979," PNAS, Vol. 90, pp. 2291–2294, March 1993.

18 Meselson et al., *Science,* vol. 266, no. 5188, November 18, 1994.

19 Alibek, pp. 244–256.

20 Confidential source, and David Kelly, "The Trilateral Agreement: Lessons for Biological Weapons Verification," Chapter 6 in *Verification Yearbook 2002* (London: Verification Research, Training and Information Center, December 2002).

21 Kelly interview with Joby Warrick of the *Washington Post,* June 17, 2002. Warrick notes. In fact, the Pokrov plant was a standby factory for producing smallpox and anti-livestock diseases in the event of war mobilization. According to a confidential source, the plant was capable of producing ten tons a year of smallpox agent. Joby Warrick, "Russia's Poorly Guarded Past; Security Lacking at Facilities Used for Soviet Bioweapons Research," *Washington Post,* June 17, 2002, p. A1.

22 Letter from President Clinton to Congress, Nov. 12, 1996. State Department press guidance for worldwide embassies on July 7, 1998, said, "In November, 1995, the United States imposed sanctions on a Russian citizen named Anatoly Kuntsevich for knowingly and materially assisting the Syrian CW program." State Department cable 122387, released under FOIA to author.

CHAPTER 21: PROJECT SAPPHIRE

1 Gerald F. Seib, "Kazakhstan Is Made for Diplomats Who Find Paris a Bore—At Remote New Embassy, They Dodge Gunmen, Lecture on Economics," *Wall Street Journal Europe,* April 22, 1992, p. 1. This account of Project Sapphire is based on interviews with Weber; Jeff Starr; a personal communication from Elwood H. Gift, Oct. 22, 2008; and "Project Sapphire After Action Report," Defense Threat Reduction Agency, U.S. Department of Defense, declassified to author under FOIA, Sept. 21, 2006. Several other useful published sources were William C. Potter, "Project Sapphire: U.S.-Kazakhstani Cooperation for Nonproliferation," in John M. Shields and William C. Potter, eds., *Dismantling the Cold War: U.S. and NIS Perspectives on the Nunn-Lugar Cooperative Threat Reduction Program,* CSIA Studies in International Security (Cambridge: MIT Press, 1997); and John A. Tirpak, "Project Sapphire," *Air Force* magazine, Journal of the Air Force, vol. 78, no. 8, August 1995; and Philipp C. Bleek, "Global Cleanout: An emerging approach to the civil nuclear material threat," Belfer Center for Science and International Affairs, John F. Kennedy School of Government, Harvard University, September 2004, available at *www.nti.org.*

2 Embassy of Kazakhstan and Nuclear Threat Initiative, Washington, D.C., *Kazakhstan's Nuclear Disarmament,* 2007, see illustration after p. 80.

3 Martha Brill Olcott, *Kazakhstan: Unfulfilled Promise* (Washington, D.C.: Carnegie Endowment for International Peace, 2002), p. 204.

4 Gulbarshyn Bozheyeva, "The Pavlodar Chemical Weapons Plant in Kazakhstan: History and Legacy," *Nonproliferation Review,* James Martin Center for Nonproliferation Studies, Monterey Institute of International Studies, Monterey, California, Summer 2000, pp. 136–145.

5 Embassy of Kazakhstan, p. 94.

6 Olcott, Ch. 1, "Introducing Kazakhstan."

7 After some initial hesitation, Nazarbayev agreed to removal of all the strategic weapons back to Russia, and Kazakhstan ratified the Start 1 treaty and the Nuclear Non-Proliferation Treaty.

8 Mikhailov interview with *Nukem Market Report,* a monthly published by Nukem, Inc., based in Stamford, Connecticut, and one of the world's leading suppliers of nuclear fuel. Earlier estimates were about six hundred tons, but there was a high degree of uncertainty. Oleg Bukharin estimated independently in 1995 that Russia had thirteen hundred metric tons of HEU. Bukharin, "Analysis of the Size and Quality of Uranium Inventories in Russia," *Science and Global Security,* vol. 6, 1996, pp. 59–77.

9 Jeff Starr, interview, Aug. 26, 2008.

10 "The President's News Conference with President Nursultan Nazarbayev," Public Papers of the Presidents, 30 Weekly Comp. Pres. Doc. 289.

11 Norman Polmar and K. J. Moore, *Cold War Submarines: The Design and Construction of U.S. and Soviet Submarines* (Dulles, Va.: Brassey's, 2004), pp. 140–146. Gerhardt Thamm, "The ALFA SSN: Challenging Paradigms, Finding New Truths, 1969–79," *Studies in Intelligence*, vol. 52, no. 3, Central Intelligence Agency, Sept. 2008.

12 "Analysis of HEU Samples from the Ulba Metallurgical Plant," E. H. Gift, National Security Programs Office, Martin Marietta Energy Systems Inc., Oak Ridge, Tennessee, initially issued July 1994, revised May 1995.

13 Gift and others said they saw the crates labeled "Tehran, Iran," and were told it was beryllium, but none was actually shipped.

14 See Ashton B. Carter and William J. Perry, *Preventive Defense* (Washington, D.C.: Brookings Institution Press, 1999), p. 73.

15 Fairfax said these nuclear materials were often much harder to track than warheads. Fairfax, interview, Sept. 3, 2008, and communication with author, Sept. 9, 2008. Nearly all the seizures of stolen HEU or plutonium to date have been such bulk material. Matthew Bunn, communication with author, Oct. 11, 2008.

16 The remark was made by Nikolai Ponomarev-Stepnoi, an academician and vice chairman of the Kurchatov Institute in Moscow, in a meeting with a delegation headed by Ambassador James Goodby, March 24, 1994. State Department cable Moscow 08594, declassified for author under FOIA.

17 On the glove episode, "Status of U.S. Efforts to Improve Nuclear Material Controls in Newly Independent States," U.S. General Accounting Office, March 1996, report GAO/NSIAD/RCED-96-89, p. 25. On the navy case, Mikhail Kulik, "Guba Andreeva: Another Nuclear Theft Has Been Detected," *Yaderny Kontrol,* no. 1, Spring 1996, Center for Policy Studies in Russia, pp. 16–21.

18 For his cables on the fissile materials crisis, Fairfax received the State Department's 1994 award for excellence in reporting on environment, science and technology issues by the Bureau of Oceans, Environment and Science. Also, "Diversion of

Nuclear Materials: Conflicting Russian Perspectives and Sensitivities," State Department cable, Moscow 19996, July 14, 1994.

19 *Management and Disposition of Excess Weapons Plutonium,* Committee on International Security and Arms Control, National Academy of Sciences, (Washington, D.C.: National Academy Press, 1994).

20 Matthew Bunn, interview, Oct. 4, 2004, and communications Aug. 24, 2008, and Oct. 11, 2008. Both Fairfax and Bunn found that one way to ease the mistrust was to arrange visits by the Russians to facilities in the United States.

21 Rensslaer W. Lee III, *Smuggling Armageddon: The Nuclear Black Market in the Former Soviet Union and Europe* (New York: St. Martin's Griffin, 1998), pp. 89–103.

22 State Department cable Moscow 024061, Aug. 23, 1994, released in part to author under FOIA.

23 Von Hippel, interview, June 1, 2004. "My Draft Recommendations and Notes from Mayak Workshop," von Hippel files, Oct. 23, 1994. Von Hippel, "Next Steps in Material Protection, Control, and Accounting Cooperation," Nov. 15, 1994.

24 They were uranium metal, uranium oxides, uranium-beryllium alloy rods, uranium oxide-beryllium-oxide rods, uranium-beryllium alloy, uranium-contaminated graphite and laboratory salvage. Memorandum, Defense Nuclear Facilities Safety Board, Dec. 21, 1995. Beryllium is an ingredient in making nuclear warheads.

25 "DoD News Briefing," Wednesday, Nov. 23, 1994. Office of the Assistant Secretary of Defense (Public Affairs), *www.defenselink.mil.*

26 The United States paid Kazakhstan about $27 million for the material. About $3 million was paid to the Ulba plant, and Weber had the privilege of presenting the check to Mette.

27 Bunn, interview by author. Holdren later provided a summary of the PCAST study in an open paper, "Reducing the Threat of Nuclear Theft in the Former Soviet Union: Outline of a Comprehensive Plan," John P. Holdren, November 1995. The title of the PCAST study was "Cooperative U.S./Former Soviet Union Programs on Nuclear Materials Protection, Control and Accounting," classified S/Noforn, Office of Science and Technology Policy, Executive Office of the President, March 1995.

28 Bunn, communication with author, August 25, 2008. Also see Andrew and Leslie Cockburn, *One Point Safe: A True Story* (New York: Anchor, 1997), Ch. 11. On Sept. 28, 1995, nearly four months after the briefing, Clinton signed a presidential order, PDD-41, "Further Reducing the Nuclear Threat." The order gave the Energy Department primary responsibility for nuclear materials protection in the former Soviet Union, a shift from the Defense Department. Bunn helped draft the presidential order, but he told me the lack of high-level support after it was signed meant it had less impact than he had hoped.

29 Engling, interviews, Sept. 29 and Oct. 13, 2003.

30 The highly-enriched uranium was kept at the institute's facility in the suburb of Pyatikhatki. Nuclear Threat Initiative, *www.nit.org.*

CHAPTER 22: FACE TO FACE WITH EVIL

1 Acting CIA director William Studeman said the U.S. intelligence community believed the Russian Defense Ministry wanted to continue supporting research into

dangerous pathogens and maintain facilities for war mobilization of biological weapons. See "Accuracy of Russia's Report on Chemical Weapons," FOIA, *www.cia.gov.* The document appears to have been written in 1995.

2 See Ken Alibek with Stephen Handelman, *Biohazard: The Chilling True Story of the Largest Covert Biological Weapons Program in the World—Told from Inside by the Man Who Ran It* (New York: Random House, 1999), Ch. 19, pp. 257–269.

3 Gennady Lepyoshkin, interview, March 28, 2005.

4 In addition to Weber and Lepyoshkin interviews, this account is based on photographs, forty-nine documents and nine videotapes describing Stepnogorsk before and after dismantlement obtained by the author under the FOIA from the U.S. Defense Threat Reduction Agency, 2005–2007. Other sources included Roger Roffey, Kristina S. Westerdahl, "Conversion of Former Biological Weapons Facilities in Kazakhstan, A Visit to Stepnogorsk," Swedish Defense Research Agency, FOI-R-0082-SE, May 2001; and Judith Miller, Stephen Engelberg and William Broad, *Germs: Biological Weapons and America's Secret War* (New York: Simon & Schuster, 2001), pp. 171–176.

5 Anne M. Harrington, "Redirecting Biological Weapons Expertise: Realities and Opportunities in the Former Soviet Union," *Chemical Weapons Convention Bulletin,* no. 29, Sept. 1995, pp. 2–5. This account is also based on an interview with Harrington.

6 Weber recalled, "To me what was so interesting was the planning. They were going to hit us with nuclear weapons, then hit us with biological weapons to kill those that nuclear weapons missed. Then, wipe out our crops and our livestock to deny the ability of those who survived to live, to feed themselves. And they were going to grow crops and raise livestock in that post–nuclear exchange environment."

7 Nikolai Urakov, speech text and author's notes, May 24, 2000.

EPILOGUE

1 They published their appeal in the *Wall Street Journal,* Jan. 4, 2007, p. A15. Also see *Reykjavik Revisited: Steps Toward a World Free of Nuclear Weapons,* Shultz et al., eds. (Stanford: Hoover Institution Press, 2007). The four authors established the Nuclear Security Project. See *www.nuclearsecurity.org.* Also see Hans M. Kristensen, Robert S. Norris and Ivan Oelrich, *From Counterforce to Mutual Deterrence: A New Nuclear Policy on the Path Toward Eliminating Nuclear Weapons.* Occasional Paper No. 7, FAS and NRDC, April 2009.

2 Warhead data are from the authoritative Nuclear Notebook, by Robert S. Norris and Hans M. Kristensen, *Bulletin of the Atomic Scientists,* vol. 64, no. 1, pp. 50–53, 58, March/April 2008, and vol. 64, no. 2, pp. 54–57, 62, May/June 2008.

3 Bruce G. Blair, "De-alerting Strategic Forces," Ch. 2 in *Reykjavik Revisited.* Blair estimates that 1,382 U.S. and 1,272 Russian missiles are maintained on high alert, p. 57.

4 "The Nunn-Lugar Scorecard," Sen. Richard Lugar, R-Ind., accessed at *www.lugar.senate.gov.*

5 Matthew Bunn, *Securing the Bomb,* Project on Managing the Atom, Belfer Center for Science and International Affairs, John F. Kennedy School of Government, Harvard University, commissioned by the Nuclear Threat Initiative, 2008, pp. 90–93.

6 Bunn, p. 51.

7 Stephen Bourne, ISTC, communication with author, Dec. 8, 2008. The total project funding as of December 2008 was $804.45 million. Not all the scientists were receiving these grants all the time, but the author found many examples in which the grants were a lifeline for the weapons scientists and engineers.

8 "Vozrozhdeniya Island Pathogenic Destruction Operations (VIPDO) Final Report," Cooperative Threat Reduction Program, June 6, 2002, obtained by author under FOIA from Defense Threat Reduction Agency. The anthrax was doused in calcium hypochlorite.

9 One of the biggest mistakes was a facility which the United States built, at a cost of $95.5 million, to convert toxic liquid rocket fuel and oxidizer to commercial products. After the money was spent, the Russians informed the United States that they had used the fuel for space launches. Cooperative Threat Reduction Program Liquid Propellant Disposition Project (D-2002-154), Office of the Inspector General, Department of Defense, Sept. 30, 2002. Another puzzle has been the Russian handling of the Fissile Material Storage Facility. Although it was built to handle one hundred metric tons of plutonium or four hundred tons of highly-enriched uranium, the Russians have loaded only about one-sixth of it, and with plutonium only. It is not clear why such an expensive and modern facility remains so empty. The United States and Russia have been in conflict over congressional demands for a degree of transparency about what is stored there. Nunn and Lugar, interviews with author after visit to the facility, Aug. 31, 2007.

10 The Cooperative Threat Reduction programs were a mere .07 percent of the Defense Department's overall budget request for fiscal year 2009, 3.86 percent of the Energy Department's request and .8 percent of the State Department's request. See Bunn, p. 116.

11 Valentin Yevstigneev, interview, Feb. 10, 2005. Yevstigneev's comment repeated the claim made in an article published May 23, 2001, in the Russian newspaper *Nezavisamaya Gazeta*. Stanislav Petrov, the general in charge of chemical weapons, was a coauthor. The piece claimed the Sverdlovsk anthrax outbreak was the result of "subversive activity" against the Soviet Union. Stanislav Petrov et al., "Biologicheskaya Diversia Na Urale" [Biological Sabotage in the Urals], NG, May 23, 1001.

12 The closed military facilities are: the Scientific-Research Institute of Microbiology of the Ministry of Defense of the Russian Federation, Kirov, which is the main biological weapons facility of the military; the Virology Center of the Scientific-Research Institute of Microbiology of the Ministry of Defense, Sergiev Posad; and the Department of Military Epidemiology of the Scientific Research Institute of Microbiology of the Ministry of Defense, Yekaterinburg.

13 When the United States and Russia signed the Chemical Weapons Convention in 1997 they promised to destroy stocks of chemical weapons by 2012. The sarin and other chemical weapons mentioned here are to be eliminated by the plant now under construction with U.S. assistance, near Shchuchye.

14 Alan Cullison and Andrew Higgins, "Files Found: A Computer in Kabul Yields a Chilling Array of al Qaeda Memos," *Wall Street Journal,* Dec. 31, 2001, p. 1.

15 George Tenet, *At the Center of the Storm: My Years at the CIA* (New York:

HarperCollins, 2007), pp. 278–279. Also, 9/11 Commission report, chapter 5, p. 151. Sufaat received a degree in biological sciences with a minor in chemistry from California State University, in 1987. 9/11 Commission, note 23, p. 490.

16 Tenet, p. 279.

17 *World at Risk: The Report of the Commission on the Prevention of Weapons of Mass Destruction Proliferation and Terrorism,* Bob Graham, chairman (New York: Vintage, 2008), p. 11.

INDEX

Ksenia Kostrova and the Hoover Institution Archives: Insert page 3, bottom right
Ronald Reagan Library: Insert page 4, top
Ray Lustig / *Washington Post:* Insert page 4, bottom
Reuters: Insert page 5, top
RIA Novosti: Insert page 5, bottom left
Ksenia Kostrova and the Hoover Institution Archives: Insert page 5, bottom right
Ronald Reagan Library: Insert page 6, top and bottom
RIA Novosti: Insert page 7, top
Thomas B. Cochran: Insert page 7, bottom right and left
Dr. Svetlana Savranskaya and the National Security Archive: Insert page 8, top
Valery Yarynich: Insert page 8, bottom
TASS via Agence France-Presse: Insert page 9, top
AP Photo / Liu Heung Shing: Insert page 9, bottom left and right
Raymond Zilinskas at the Monterey Institute: Insert page 10, top left
Ksenia Kostrova and the Hoover Institution Archives: Insert page 10, bottom
Ray Lustig / *Washington Post:* Insert page 11, top
Andy Weber: Insert page 11, bottom left and right
Christopher Davis: Insert page 12, top
George Bush Presidential Library and Museum: Insert page 12, bottom
James A. Parcell / *Washington Post*: Insert page 13, top
Andy Weber: Insert page 13, middle and bottom
Andy Weber: Insert page 14, top and bottom
Andy Weber: Insert page 15, top and bottom